CLARENCE BYRD
Athabasca University

IDA CHEN
Clarence Byrd Inc.

Byrd & Chen's
Canadian
Tax
Principles

2012–2013 EDITION

Volume I

PEARSON

Toronto

ISBN 978-0-13-299068-4

Vice-President, Editorial Director: Gary Bennett
Editor-in-Chief: Nicole Lukach
Marketing Manager: Jenna Wulff
Supervising Developmental Editor: Suzanne Schaan
Developmental Editor: Suzanne Simpson Millar
Lead Project Manager: Avinash Chandra
Manufacturing Manager: Jane Schell
Production Editor: Lila Campbell
Cover Designer: Anthony Leung

10 9 8 7 6 5 4 3 2 1 [EBM]

PREFACE

Objectives

The Text

Subject Coverage

The objective of this text is to provide coverage of all of the subjects that are taught in Canadian college and university tax courses. In so doing, it also provides comprehensive coverage of all the tax issues that are required in the educational programs of Canada's three professional accounting organizations.

This material is designed to be used in a two semester university or college course and is far too extensive to be completely covered in a single one semester course. The traditional split in the material would be to cover Chapters 1 through 11 in a first course dealing with the determination of Net Income For Tax Purposes for all taxpayers, as well as the calculation of Taxable Income and Tax Payable for individuals. This could be followed by a second course where the focus is on the taxation of corporations. The relevant material on corporations is found in Chapters 12 through 17. The remaining Chapters 18 through 21 deal with partnerships, trusts, international taxation, and GST/HST.

Level Of Coverage

In terms of style, we have attempted to strike a balance between the kind of complete documentation that can render the material incomprehensible to anyone other than a tax professional, and the total elimination of references that would make it impossible for readers to expand their understanding of particular points. In those situations where we feel the issue is sufficiently complex that further investigation may be required, we have provided a list of references to the relevant Sections of the *Income Tax Act* or other related materials. In contrast, no direction has been provided when the material is either very straightforward, or where the relevant parts of the *Act* would be obvious.

This book can be used with or without additional source material. Some instructors require students to acquire a copy of the *Income Tax Act* and permit its use as a reference during examinations. For instructors wishing to take this approach, frequent references to the *Act* have been included. In addition, there is an electronic version of the *Income Tax Act* on the accompanying Student CD-ROM.

For instructors not wishing to require the use of the *Income Tax Act*, we have designed the problem material so that students should be able to solve all of the included problems relying solely on the text as a reference.

The Need For Two Volumes

In the 29 years that we have been writing this text, we have seen the content grow from about 400 pages to almost 1,500 pages. We initially dealt with this increase in size by providing a separate Study Guide. However, the text alone has grown to over 1,000 pages and, while accommodating this in a single volume is feasible, the result would be far less useful to students than dividing the material into two reasonably sized volumes.

If there was any consensus among our users as to which subjects should be dealt with in each volume, they could be made available separately. However, virtually all of our users omit material from Volume I and include material from Volume II. Further, there is no consistent pattern as to which material is omitted and which material is included. Given this, it would not be possible to produce separate volumes that meet the needs of all of our users.

The Study Guide

The major objective of the Study Guide is to provide students with convenient access to the solutions for the Exercises and Self Study Problems that are in the two volumes of the text. Having these solutions in a separate volume makes it much easier for students to simultaneously view the problem while solving it and then consult its complete and detailed solution.

The Study Guide also provides a number of additional features to enhance the learning experience. These can be described as follows:

- Detailed instructions on "How To Work Through" each Chapter in the text. This includes advice on when to attempt Exercises and Self Study Problems as the student reads through the text.

- A detailed list of "Learning Objectives" for each Chapter. This allows the student to ensure that he/she has understood all of the relevant subjects covered in the Chapter.

- Sample completed tax returns for both individuals and corporations. These are useful practice for students using the ProFile tax software that is available with this text.

- At the end of each Chapter in the text, there is a list of key terms that were used in that Chapter. All of these terms are alphabetically listed in a Glossary that is at the back of the Study Guide. This provides an easy way to find the meaning of a term that was introduced in one Chapter, but is being referred to again in a subsequent Chapter.

Study Tools And Resources For Students

The inner front cover of Volume 1 has a complete description of the abundant study tools, resources and software that are available. This includes what's on the textbook website at:

www.pearsoncanada.ca/byrdchen/ctp2013

Problem Material

For Students

Canadian Tax Principles contains a large number of problems that have complete and detailed solutions available to students. The various types of problems are as follows:

Exercises   These are short problems that are focused on a single issue. Each Exercise is presented in the *Canadian Tax Principles* text, directly following the material that is relevant to its solution. Solutions to these Exercises can be found in the Study Guide.

Self Study Problems   These problems are more complex than the Exercises and often deal with more than one subject. They are found in each Chapter of *Canadian Tax Principles*, immediately following the text. Solutions to the Self Study Problems are included in the Study Guide.

Self Study Tax Software Problems   These problems are designed to be solved using the ProFile software that is available with *Canadian Tax Principles*. These problems, along with their solutions, are found in the Study Guide. The completed tax returns are available on the Student CD-ROM included with the text.

Practice Examinations   A 90 minute practice examination, along with a solution and suggested marking guide, is available on the Student CD-ROM for each of the first 11 chapters. These examinations contain various types of problems, including multiple choice, true/false and essay questions, as well as longer problems.

Glossary Flash Cards and Key Terms Self-Tests   These self-test resources, which require an understanding of the key terms that are in the Glossary, can be found on the Student CD-ROM and the text website.

Problem Material For Instructors

Canadian Tax Principles contains several types of problems designed for instructors:

Assignment Problems   These problems vary in difficulty and include the most difficult non-comprehensive problems in the text. They are found in each chapter of *Canadian Tax Principles*, immediately following the text. They are sometimes adapted from professional examinations and may involve a number of different issues. Solutions to these problems are available in a separate solutions manual provided only to instructors. This solutions manual is not available to students.

Assignment Problems (Comprehensive)   These comprehensive problems are the most challenging type of problem material in the text. They are cumulative in that they incorporate issues from previous chapters. There are two comprehensive assignment problems per chapter in Chapters 6 through 11 and they are found at the end of the Assignment Problems for the chapter. Solutions to these problems are in a separate solutions manual provided only to instructors.

Assignment Tax Software Problems   Assignment Tax Software Problems dealing with personal tax returns are found at the end of Chapters 4 through 11. An additional Assignment Tax Software Problem, involving a corporate tax return, is located at the end of Chapter 14. Solutions to Assignment Tax Software Problems are available in a separate solutions manual provided only to instructors.

Examination Problems   For instructors adopting *Canadian Tax Principles*, a large and comprehensive selection of problems and solutions for use on examinations is available. These include multiple choice questions (over 600), true/false questions (over 200), essay questions (over 400), exercises (over 400), as well as more comprehensive types of problem ranging in difficulty from easy to very difficult (over 150).

Student CD-ROM

The Student CD-ROM can be found beside the inner back cover of Volume I of the text. It contains the following resources:

- **The CICA's Federal Income Tax Collection (FITAC)**   This comprehensive electronic tax research library contains the *Income Tax Act*, the *Income Tax Regulations*, the CRA's Interpretation Bulletins, as well as many other tax resources.

- **Electronic Copy Of *Canadian Tax Principles***   FITAC contains an electronic copy of Chapters 1 through 18 of the *Canadian Tax Principles* text. It is electronically linked with other resources, such as the *Income Tax Act*, that are included in the FITAC database.

- **Practice Examinations**   There is a practice examination for each of the first 11 chapters of the text. A detailed marking guide is also provided for each examination.

- **2012 Tax Rates**   A complete list of 2012 tax rates and credits is available on the Student CD-ROM as a .PDF file. The list is also available at the front of both Volumes 1 and 2.

- **Power Point Presentations**   There is a PowerPoint presentation for each of the 21 chapters. These provide the basis for a quick review of the material covered in the chapter.

- **Key Term Flash Cards And Quizzes**   There are flash cards for key terms as well as quizzes involving the matching of key terms.

- **Supplementary Readings**   There are several tax subjects that are of interest to some of our users, but not of sufficient general interest to warrant their inclusion in the text (e.g., transfer pricing for international transactions). We have included this material on the Student CD-ROM for those users who are interested in these subjects.

ProFile Tax Preparation Software

For Students

For users of *Canadian Tax Principles*, we provide access to Intuit's professional tax preparation software, ProFile, which includes tax return preparation capabilities for individuals, corporations and trusts.

Instructions on how to access this software are available on the inner back cover of Volume I. The Study Guide contains Self Study tax software problems, along with their solutions. The completed tax returns are available on the Student CD-ROM.

For Instructors

In addition to the use of ProFile personally, instructors will also be able to access a free academic site license of the complete ProFile Professional Tax Software Suite, as well as product support. Instructions on how to access this software are available on the inner back cover of Volume I.

There are assignment problems requiring the use of ProFile for individual returns at the end of Chapters 4 through 11. In addition, there is an assignment problem involving the use of ProFile for corporations at the end of Chapter 14. Solutions to these problems are available in a separate solutions manual which is available only to instructors.

The Federal Budget

The Process

One of the great difficulties in preparing material on Canadian taxation is the fact that changes in the relevant legislation are made each year. This is complicated by the fact that the arrival date for each year's budget is no longer entirely predictable. Between 2002 and 2012, the arrival date ranged from December 10th of the preceding year (the 2002 budget) to May 2nd of the budget year (the 2006 budget). The 2012 budget was presented on March 29, 2012.

This text reflects the March 29, 2012 budget proposals that are effective for calendar 2012.

Proposed Changes In The March 29, 2012 Budget

The March, 2012 budget did not contain a large number of proposals. In particular, there were no significant changes related to the taxation of businesses. A brief summary of the more important proposals included in the March 29, 2012 budget is as follows:

Personal Income Tax Measures

- There are several proposed changes to the Registered Disability Savings Plans (RDSPs), including a proportional repayment rule for withdrawals, an increase in the maximum and minimum withdrawals, a new tax-free rollover from an RESP to a RDSP, and an extension of the period for which an RDSP may remain open when a beneficiary is not longer eligible for the disability tax credit.
- New designation rules which will allow a corporation to split a single dividend into eligible and non-eligible components.
- The inclusion of employer's contributions to disability insurance plans in the employee's income when the contributions are not in respect of a periodic wage loss replacement plan.
- New rules for Retirement Compensation Plans (RCAs) that prevent these plans from engaging in non-arm's length transactions.
- A special tax on excess contributions to an Employee Profit Sharing Plan (EPSPs).
- Eligibility for Old Age Security (OAS) and Guaranteed Income Supplement (GIS) will shift from age 65 to age 67. This does not start until 2013.

Business Tax Measures

- Several changes related to the accelerated capital cost allowance that is available for clean energy generation equipment.
- A phase out of the Atlantic Investment Tax Credit for oil, gas, and mining activities.
- Several changes in the rules for Scientific Research And Experimental Development, including a reduction in the rate applicable to pool balances from 20 percent to 15 percent, the exclusion of capital expenditures from amounts eligible for SR&ED deductions and credits, and a reduction in the rate at which the prescribed proxy is calculated. None of these changes are effective until after 2012.
- New rules to prevent tax avoidance through the use of partnerships.

International

- A change in the debt to equity ratio that is used in the thin capitalization rules from 2-to-1, to 1.5-to-1.
- A phase out of the Overseas Employment Tax Credit (OETC).
- New rules related to foreign affiliate dumping.

GST/HST

- A doubling of the quick method threshold from $200,000 to $400,000, as well as a doubling of the simplified input tax credit method threshold from $500,000 to $1,000,000 in taxable sales, and from $2,000,000 to $4,000,000 for taxable purchases. These changes are effective for fiscal years beginning after 2012.

In addition to the changes in the preceding lists, there were several additional changes designed to strengthen the charitable sector.

Acknowledgments

We would like to thank the many students who have used this book, the instructors who have adopted it at colleges and universities throughout Canada, as well as the assistants and tutors who have been involved in these courses.

In terms of the content of the book, we would like to give special thanks to:

Gary Donell, senior advanced tax trainer with CRA, who did a technical review of significant portions of the text and problems. He made many valuable suggestions that have contributed greatly to the accuracy and clarity of the material. In addition, he was responsible for writing much of the Chapter 18 material on partnerships and the Chapter 20 material on international taxation. Mr. Donell has undertaken this work independently of his employment with the CRA. The views that are contained in this publication do not, in any way, reflect the policies of that organization.

Victor Waese, an instructor at the British Columbia Institute Of Technology. For many years, Victor has kept us honest by pointing out where our material was not accurate or was lacking in clarity. He has made a significant contribution to the accuracy and usefulness of this text.

Over the years, the following individuals have provided valuable feedback on our material. In this edition, they have also contributed questions and cases to the Test Items File (a.k.a., exam bank). These individuals are:

- **Ann Bigelow** - Western University (London)
- **Heather Plume** - Capilano University (North Vancouver)
- **Larry Goldsman** - McGill University (Montreal)

Also of great help in improving this text were the comments and corrections provided by the following instructors:

- **Joseph Armanious** - McGill University (Montreal)
- **Lowell Auger** - Fanshawe College (London)
- **Ivan Desjardins** - Thompson Rivers University (Kamloops)
- **David Hiscock** - University of Guelph (Guelph)
- **Wayne Hughes** - Humber College (Toronto)
- **Susan Hurley** - Northern Alberta Institute of Technology (Edmonton)
- **Jane Kaake** - Durham College (Oshawa)
- **Kayla Levesque** - Cambrian College (Sudbury)
- **Judith Marriott** - North Island College (Courtenay, B.C.)
- **Kathryn Pedwell** - University of Ottawa (Ottawa)
- **Jay Perry** - Niagara College (Niagara-On-The-Lake)
- **Lianne Smith-Stowe** - Georgian College (Barrie)
- **Mumsy Ullattikulam** - Langara College (Vancouver)

It's Our Fault

As always, we have made every effort to accurately reflect appropriate tax rules. Every word in the text, problems, and solutions has been read by at least two and, in most cases three, individuals. However, it is virtually certain that errors remain. These errors are solely the responsibility of the authors and we apologize for any confusion that they may cause you.

We welcome any corrections or suggestions for additions or improvements. These can be sent to us at:

byrdinc@sympatico.ca

Clarence Byrd, Athabasca University

Ida Chen, Clarence Byrd Inc.

July, 2012

2012 Rates And Other Data (Including Web Sites)

> Note that for your convenience, this information is also available on the **Student CD-ROM** as a .PDF file.

Information Applicable To Individuals

Federal Tax Rates For Individuals

Taxable Income In Excess Of	Federal Tax	Marginal Rate On Excess
$ -0-	$ -0-	15%
42,707	6,406	22%
85,414	15,802	26%
132,406	28,020	29%

Federal Tax Credits For Individuals

Personal Credits [ITA 118]

Single Persons This basic personal credit is equal to 15% of $10,822 ($1,623).

Married Persons This basic personal credit is equal to 15% of $10,822 ($1,623).

Family Caregiver Amount (FCA) Included in the relevant credits below.

Spousal The spousal credit is equal to 15% of $10,822 ($1,623), less 15% of the spouse's Net Income For Tax Purposes. This amount is increased by $2,000 (to $12,822) if the spouse qualifies for the FCA. Not available when the spouse's income is more than $10,822 (or $12,822).

Eligible Dependant This credit is the same as the one that is available for a spouse. This amount is also increased by $2,000 if the eligible dependant qualifies for the FCA, provided the child amount has not been claimed for this dependant.

Child 15% of $2,191 ($329) for each child who is under the age of 18 years at the end of the year. This amount is increased by $2,000 (to $4,191) if the child qualifies for the FCA.

Caregiver 15% of $4,402 ($660), less 15% of the dependant's Net Income in excess of $15,033. This amount is increased by $2,000 (to $6,402) if the related adult qualifies for the FCA.

Infirm Dependants Over 17 15% of $6,402 ($960), less 15% of the dependant's Net Income in excess of $6,420. This amount always includes the extra $2,000 for the FCA. Not available when the dependant's income is more than $12,822.

Age 15% of $6,720 ($1,008). The base for this credit is reduced by the lesser of $6,720 and 15% of the individual's net income in excess of $33,884. Not available when income is more than $78,684. If the individual cannot use this credit, it can be transferred to a spouse or common-law partner.

Pension 15% of the first $2,000 of eligible pension income. This produces a maximum credit of $300 [(15%)($2,000)]. If the individual cannot use the credit, it can be transferred to a spouse or common-law partner.

Canada Employment Credit 15% of $1,095. This produces a maximum credit of $164.

Other Credits (Various ITA)

Adoption Expenses 15% of eligible expenses, up to a maximum of $1,716 [(15%)($11,440)]. The eligible amount is reduced by reimbursements.

Public Transit Passes Credit 15% of the cost of monthly or longer transit passes.

Child Fitness Credit A maximum of 15% of $500 ($75) per year for eligible fees paid for each child who is under 16 (under 18 if the child qualifies for the disability tax credit). An additional credit, based on a maximum of $500 in fees, is available for children who qualify for the disability tax credit.

Children's Arts Credit A maximum of 15% of $500 ($75) per year for eligible fees paid for each child under 16 (under 18 if the child qualifies for the disability tax credit). An additional credit, based on a maximum of $500 in fees, is available for children who qualify for the disability tax credit.

First Time Home Buyer's Tax Credit 15% of the first $5,000 ($750) of the cost of an eligible home.

Volunteer Firefighter Credit 15% of $3,000 ($450) for volunteer firefighters who perform at least 200 hours of volunteer firefighting services during a taxation year.

Charitable Donations The general limit on amounts for this credit is 75% of Net Income. There is an addition to this general limit equal to 25% of any taxable capital gains and 25% of any recapture of CCA resulting from a gift of capital property. In addition, the income inclusion on capital gains arising from a gift of some publicly traded shares is reduced from one-half to nil. For individuals, the credit is 15% of the first $200 and 29% of the remainder. For corporations, charitable donations are a deduction from Net Income.

Medical Expenses The medical expense tax credit is determined by the following formula:

$$[15\%]\ [(B - C) + D], \text{ where:}$$

B is the total of an individual's medical expenses for himself, his spouse or common-law partner, and any of his children who have not reached 18 years of age at the end of the year.

C is the lesser of 3% of the individual's Net Income For Tax Purposes and $2,109 (2012 figure).

D is the total of all amounts each of which is, in respect of a dependant of the individual (other than a child of the individual who has not attained the age of 18 years before the end of the taxation year), an amount determined by the formula:

$$E - F, \text{ where:}$$

E is the total of the dependant's medical expenses

F is the lesser of 3% of the dependant's Net Income For Tax Purposes and $2,109 (2012 figure).

Refundable Medical Expense Supplement The individual claiming this amount must be over 17 and have earned income of at least $3,268. The amount is equal to the lesser of $1,119 and 25/15 of the medical expense tax credit (25% of allowable medical expenses). The refundable amount is then reduced by 5% of family Net Income in excess of $24,783. Not available when family income is more than $47,163.

Disability - All Ages 15% of $7,546 ($1,132). If not used by the disabled individual, it can be transferred to a person claiming that individual as a dependant.

Disability Supplement - Under 18 And Qualifies For The Disability Tax Credit   15% of $4,402 ($660), reduced by child care and attendant care expenses in excess of $2,578.

Tuition Fees Which Includes Examination And Ancillary Fees

- 15% of qualifying tuition fees
- 15% of examination fees for both post-secondary examinations and examinations required in a professional program
- 15% of ancillary fees that are imposed by a post-secondary educational institution on all of their full or part-time students. Up to $250 in such ancillary fees can be claimed even if not required of all students.

Education   15% of $400 ($60) per month of full time attendance. 15% of $120 ($18) per month of part time attendance.

Textbook   15% of $65 ($10) per month of full time attendance. 15% of $20 ($3) per month of part time attendance.

Interest On Student Loans   15% of interest paid on qualifying student loans.

Transfer Of Tuition, Education, And Textbook   If the individual cannot use these credits, is not claimed as a dependant by his spouse, and does not transfer the unused credits to a spouse, then a parent or grandparent of the individual can claim up to $750 [(15%)($5,000)] of any unused tuition, education, or textbook credits. The amount that can be transferred is reduced by any amounts of these credits claimed by the student for the year.

Employment Insurance   15% of amounts paid by employees up to the maximum Employment Insurance premium of $840 (1.83% of $45,900). This produces a maximum tax credit of $126 [(15%)($840)].

Canada Pension Plan   15% of amounts paid by employees up to the maximum Canada Pension Plan contribution of $2,307 [4.95% of ($50,100 less $3,500)]. This produces a maximum tax credit of $346 [(15%)($2,307)]. For self-employed individuals the maximum payment is $4,613.

Political Donations   Three-quarters of the first $400, one-half of the next $350, one-third of the next $525, to a maximum credit of $650.

Dividend Tax Credit

- **Eligible Dividends** are grossed up by 38%. The federal dividend tax credit is equal to 6/11 of the gross up. The credit can also be calculated as 15.02% of the grossed up dividends, or 20.7272% of the actual dividends received.

- **Non-Eligible Dividends** are grossed up by 25%. The federal dividend tax credit is equal to 2/3 of the gross up. The credit can also be calculated as 13-1/3% of the grossed up dividends, or 16-2/3% of the actual dividends received.

Investment Tax Credits   Credits based on various rates for making certain types of qualifying expenditures.

Other Data For Individuals

Dividend Gross Up

Eligible Dividends   the gross up is 38% of dividends received.

Non-Eligible Dividends   the gross up is 25% of dividends received.

RRSP Deduction Room   For 2012, the addition to RRSP deduction room is equal to the lesser of $22,970 and 18% of 2011 Earned Income, reduced by the 2011 Pension Adjustment and the 2012 Past Service Pension Adjustment, and increased by the 2012 Pension Adjustment Reversal.

Clawback (OAS and EI) Limits   The tax (clawback) on Old Age Security (OAS) benefits is based on the lesser of 100% of such benefits and 15% of the amount of the 2012 "threshold income" in excess of $69,562. For this purpose, "threshold income" is equal to Net Income For Tax Purposes, calculated without the ITA 60(w) deduction for the tax on OAS benefits.

Under the *Employment Insurance Act*, there is a similar clawback requirement with respect to Employment Insurance (EI) benefits. In this case, EI benefits must be repaid to the extent of the lesser of 30% of the EI benefits received, and 30% of the amount by which "threshold income" exceeds $57,375 (this amount is 1.25 times the maximum insurable earnings for EI purposes). For this purpose, "threshold income" is defined as Net Income For Tax Purposes, calculated without the deduction for either the ITA 60(w) deduction for tax paid on OAS benefits or the ITA 60(v.1) deduction for repayment of EI benefits received.

Capital Gain Inclusion Rates

Period	Inclusion Rate
1972 through 1987	1/2
1988 and 1989 and February 28, 2000 through October 17, 2000	2/3
1990 through February 27, 2000	3/4
October 18, 2000 to present	1/2

Provincial Tax Rates And Provincial Credits For Individuals   Provincial taxes are based on Taxable Income, with most provinces adopting multiple rates. The number of brackets range from three (e.g., Ontario uses 5.05%, 9.15%, and 11.16%) to five (e.g., British Columbia uses 5.06%, 7.7%, 10.5%, 12.3%, and 14.7%). The exception to this is Alberta, which uses a single flat rate of 10% on all Taxable Income. Provincial tax credits are generally based on the minimum provincial rate applied to a credit base that is similar to that used for federal credits. In addition to regular rates, several provinces use surtaxes.

Information Applicable To Individuals And Corporations

Prescribed Rate (ITR 4301)   The following figures show the base rate that would be used in calculations such as imputed interest on loans. It also shows the rates applicable on amounts owing to and from the CRA. For recent quarters, the interest rates were as follows:

Year	Quarter	Base Rate	Owing From*	Owing To
2011	All Four Quarters	1%	3%	5%
2012	**First**	**1%**	**3%**	**5%**
2012	Second	1%	3%	5%

*The rate on refunds to corporations is limited to the regular prescribed rate, without the additional 2%, i.e., the base rate.

Automobile Deduction Limits

- CCA is limited to the first $30,000 of the automobiles cost, plus applicable GST/HST/PST (not including amounts that will be refunded through input tax credits).

- Interest on financing of automobiles is limited to $10 per day.

- Deductible leasing costs are limited to $800 per month (other constraints apply).

CCA Rates   See Appendix to Chapter 5

Quick Method Rates (GST Only)

	Percentage On GST Included Sales	
	First $30,000	On Excess
Retailers And Wholesalers	0.8%	1.8%
Service Providers And Manufacturers	2.6%	3.6%

Note that different rates are applicable in the provinces that have adopted an HST system.

Information Applicable To Corporations

Corporate Tax Rates   The federal corporate tax rates for 2012 are as follows (federal tax abatement removed):

General Business (Before General Rate Reduction)	28%
General Business (After General Rate Reduction Of 13%)	15%
Income Eligible For M&P Deduction	15%
Income Eligible For Small Business Deduction	11%
Part IV Refundable Tax	33-1/3%
Part I Refundable Tax On Investment Income Of CCPC (ART)	6-2/3%

Provincial tax rates on corporations vary from a low of nil on amounts eligible for the small business deduction in Manitoba, to a high of 16% on general corporate income in Nova Scotia and Prince Edward Island.

Small Business Deduction Formula   For 2012, the small business deduction is equal to 17% of the lesser of:

A.   Net Canadian active business income.

B.   Taxable Income, less:

    1.   100/28 times the ITA 126(1) credit for taxes paid on foreign non-business income, calculated without consideration of the additional refundable tax under ITA 123.3 or the general rate reduction under ITA 123.4; and

    2.   4 times the ITA 126(2) credit for taxes paid on foreign business income, calculated without consideration of the general rate reduction under ITA 123.4.

C.   The annual business limit of $500,000, less any portion allocated to associated corporations, less the reduction for large corporations.

Manufacturing And Processing Deduction Formula   For 2012, the Manufacturing And Processing Deduction is equal to 13% of the lesser of:

A.   Manufacturing and processing profits, less amounts eligible for the small business deduction; and

B.   Taxable Income, less the sum of:

    1.   the amount eligible for the small business deduction;

    2.   4 times the foreign tax credit for business income calculated without consideration of the ITA 123.4 general rate reduction; and

    3.   where the corporation is a Canadian controlled private corporation throughout the year, aggregate investment income as defined in ITA 129(4).

Foreign Tax Credits For Corporations   The Foreign Non-Business Income Tax Credit is the lesser of:

- The tax paid to the foreign government (for corporations, there is no 15% limit on the foreign non-business taxes paid); and

- An amount determined by the following formula:

$$\left[\frac{\text{Foreign Non} - \text{Business Income}}{\text{Adjusted Division B Income}}\right] [\text{Tax Otherwise Payable}]$$

The Foreign Business Income Tax Credit is equal to the least of:

- The tax paid to the foreign government;

- An amount determined by the following formula:

$$\left[\frac{\text{Foreign Business Income}}{\text{Adjusted Division B Income}}\right] [\text{Tax Otherwise Payable}] ; \text{ and}$$

- Tax Otherwise Payable for the year, less any foreign tax credit taken on non-business income under ITA 126(1).

Aggregate Investment Income   Aggregate Investment Income is defined in ITA 129(4) as the sum of:

- net taxable capital gains for the year, reduced by any net capital loss carry overs deducted during the year; and

- income from property including interest, rents, and royalties, but excluding dividends that are deductible in computing Taxable Income. Since foreign dividends are generally not deductible, they would be included in aggregate investment income.

Additional Refundable Tax On Investment Income (ART)   ART is equal to 6-2/3% of the lesser of:

- the corporation's "aggregate investment income" for the year [as defined in ITA 129(4)]; and

- the amount, if any, by which the corporation's Taxable Income for the year exceeds the amount that is eligible for the small business deduction.

Refundable Portion Of Part I Tax Payable   For 2012, the Refundable Portion Of Part I Tax Payable is defined as the least of three items:

Item 1   the amount determined by the formula

A - B, where

A   is 26-2/3% of the corporation's aggregate investment income for the year, and

B   is the amount, if any, by which the foreign non-business income tax credit exceeds 9-1/3% of its foreign investment income for the year.

Item 2   26-2/3% of the amount, if any, by which the corporation's taxable income for the year exceeds the total of:

- the amount eligible for the small business deduction;
- 100/35 of the tax credit for foreign non-business income; and
- 4 times the tax credit for foreign business income.

Item 3   the corporation's tax for the year payable under Part I.

Part IV Tax   Part IV tax is assessed at a rate of 33-1/3% of portfolio dividends, plus dividends received from a connected company that gave rise to a dividend refund for the connected company as a result of the payment.

Refundable Dividend Tax On Hand (RDTOH)   The RDTOH is defined in ITA 129(3) as:

- The Refundable Portion Of Part I tax for the year; plus
- The total of the taxes under Part IV for the year; plus
- The corporation's RDTOH at the end of the preceding year; less
- The corporation's dividend refund for its preceding taxation year.

General Rate Income Pool   A CCPC's General Rate Income Pool (GRIP) is defined as follows:

- The GRIP balance at the end of the preceding year; plus
- 72% of the CCPC's Taxable Income after it has been reduced by amounts eligible for the small business deduction and aggregate investment income; plus
- eligible dividends received during the year; plus
- adjustments related to amalgamations and wind-ups; less
- eligible dividends paid during the preceding year.

Low Rate Income Pool   A non-CCPC's Low Rate Income Pool (LRIP) is defined as follows:

- The LRIP balance at the end of the preceding year; plus
- non-eligible dividends received during the year; plus
- adjustments for reorganizations; plus
- adjustments for non-CCPCs that were a CCPC, a credit union, or an investment company, in a previous year; less
- non-eligible dividends paid during the year; less
- any Excessive Eligible Dividend Designations during the year.

Tax Related Web Sites

GOVERNMENT

Canada Revenue Agency   www.cra.gc.ca
Department of Finance Canada   www.fin.gc.ca

CHARTERED ACCOUNTING FIRMS

BDO   www.bdo.ca/library/publications/tax/index.cfm
Ernst & Young   www.ey.com/CA/en/Services/Tax
KPMG   www.kpmg.com/Ca/en/WhatWeDo/Tax/Pages/default.aspx
PricewaterhouseCoopers   www.ca.taxnews.com

OTHER

Canadian Institute of Chartered Accountants   www.cica.ca
Certified General Accountants Association Of Canada   www.cga-canada.org
Canadian Tax Foundation   www.ctf.ca
ProFile Tax Suite   www.profile.intuit.ca/professional-tax-software

CONTENTS

The textbook is published in two Volumes:	Volume I = Chapters 1 to 10 Volume II = Chapters 11 to 21

Detailed contents of Volume I, Chapters 1 to 10 follows.

CHAPTER 3

Income Or Loss From
An Office Or Employment

(continued)

CHAPTER 3, continued

CHAPTER 4

Taxable Income And Tax Payable
For Individuals

(continued)

CHAPTER 8

Capital Gains And Capital Losses

CHAPTER 9

Other Income, Other Deductions, And Other Issues

CHAPTER 10

Retirement Savings And Other Special Income Arrangements

Glossary

The Glossary can be found:

- at the back of the separate paper Study Guide, and

- on the Student CD-ROM within the FITAC version of *Canadian Tax Principles*.

Supplementary Readings

The Supplementary Readings can be found on the Student CD-ROM.

No. 1 - Application Of The Median Rule

No. 2 - Stock Option Shares Deemed
      Not Identical Property

No. 3 - Election For Pre-1982 Residences

No. 4 - Determining M&P Profits

No. 5 - SR & ED Expenditures

No. 6 - Final Returns For Deceased Taxpayers

No. 7 - Business Valuations

No. 8 - Tax Shelters

No. 9 - Transfer Pricing

CHAPTER 1

Introduction To Federal Taxation In Canada

The Canadian Tax System

Alternative Tax Bases

1-1.   There are a variety of ways in which taxes can be classified. One possible basis of classification would be the economic feature or event that is to be taxed. Such features or events are referred to as the base for taxation and a large number of different bases are used in different tax systems throughout the world. Some of the more common tax bases are as follows:

Income Tax   A tax on the income of certain defined entities.

Property Tax   A tax on the ownership of some particular set of goods.

Consumption Tax   A tax levied on the consumption or use of a good or service. Also referred to as sales tax or commodity tax.

Value Added Tax   A tax levied on the increase in value of a good or service that has been created by the taxpayer's stage of the production or distribution cycle.

Tariffs or Customs Duties   A tax imposed on the importation or exportation of certain goods or services.

Transfer Tax   A tax on the transfer of property from one owner to another.

User Tax   A tax levied on the user of some facility such as a road or airport.

Capital Tax   A tax on the invested capital of a corporation.

Head Tax   A tax on the very existence of some classified group of individuals.

1-2.   At one time or another, some level of Canadian government has used, or is still using, all of these bases for taxation. For example, the Canadian federal government currently has, in addition to income taxes on corporations, individuals, and trusts, such taxes as the Goods and Services Tax (GST), an alcoholic beverages tax, special transaction taxes, a gasoline tax, as well as others. However, the dominant form of Canadian taxation at the federal level is the income taxes levied on both corporations and individuals. This fact is reflected in Figure 1-1 (following page) which provides a percentage distribution of the $254.2 billion in tax revenues that the federal government expects to collect during fiscal 2012-2013.

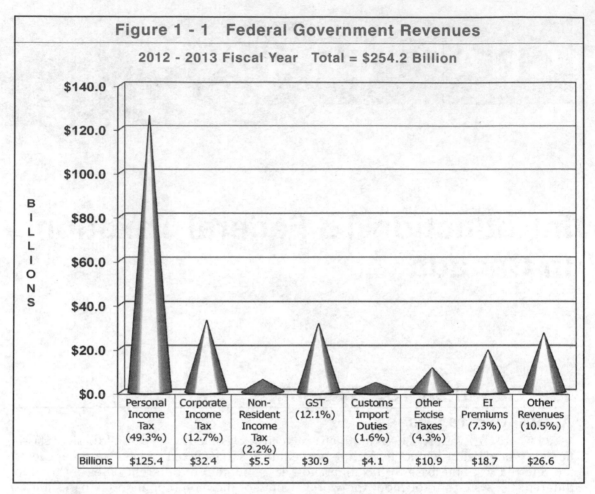

Figure 1 - 1   Federal Government Revenues

2012 - 2013 Fiscal Year   Total = $254.2 Billion

	Personal Income Tax (49.3%)	Corporate Income Tax (12.7%)	Non-Resident Income Tax (2.2%)	GST (12.1%)	Customs Import Duties (1.6%)	Other Excise Taxes (4.3%)	EI Premiums (7.3%)	Other Revenues (10.5%)
Billions	$125.4	$32.4	$5.5	$30.9	$4.1	$10.9	$18.7	$26.6

1-3.   The statistics in Figure 1-1 were obtained from the March 29, 2012 Federal Budget papers. They are available in the "Outlook For Budgetary Revenues" and include the estimated effects of the 2012 Budget measures.

1-4.   Figure 1-1 makes it clear that personal income taxes constitute, by far, the most important source of federal government revenues. The share of federal government revenues provided by personal income taxes is expected to be 49.3 percent of the total in 2012-2013, up from the 48.2 percent that was applicable to 2011-2012.

1-5.   Corporate income taxes are forecast at 12.7 percent of 2012-2013 federal revenues. Reflecting the corporate tax cuts that have been implemented in recent years, this is lower than the 16.8 percent of federal government revenues that these taxes produced in 2007-2008. This percentage is not expected to vary much in the near future, with the 2016-2017 fraction estimated to be 12.8 percent.

1-6.   Although the GST is still an important source of federal government revenues, the drop in the basic rate from 7 percent to 6 percent in 2006, followed by a further decrease to 5 percent in 2008, has resulted in this tax producing a smaller percentage of federal revenues. It has gone from 14.0 percent of the total in 2004-2005 to an estimated 12.1 percent of the total in 2012-2013. In 2016-2017, it is expected to be 11.9 percent.

Taxable Entities In Canada

Federal Income Tax

1-7.   Three types of entities are subject to federal income taxation. These are:

- Individuals (human beings)
- Corporations
- Trusts

1-8.   You should note that the *Income Tax Act* uses the term "person" to refer to all three types of taxable entities. This can be a bit confusing in that the dictionary defines person as "a human being, whether man, woman, or child". Despite this conventional usage of the term person, the *Income Tax Act* applies it to both corporations and trusts. When the *Act* wishes to refer to a human taxpayer, it uses the term "individual".

1-9.   For income tax purposes, unincorporated businesses such as partnerships and proprietorships are not viewed as taxable entities. Rather, income earned by an unincorporated business organization is taxed in the hands of the proprietor (who would be an individual) or the partner. Note that members of a partnership may be individuals, trusts, or corporations.

1-10.   As discussed in Chapter 2, "Procedures And Administration", all three types of taxable entities are required to file income tax returns. The return for an individual is referred to as a T1, for a corporation, a T2, and for a trust, a T3. Proprietorships and partnerships are not required to file income tax returns.

GST/HST

1-11.   The requirement to register to collect and remit GST/HST generally extends to any person engaged in commercial activity in Canada. You should note that the definition of a person for GST/HST purposes is different than that used in the *Income Tax Act*. For income tax purposes, a "person" is restricted to an individual, a corporation, or a trust. Unincorporated businesses do not file separate income tax returns.

1-12.   Under GST/HST legislation, the concept of a person is much broader, including individuals, partnerships, corporations, estates of deceased individuals, trusts, charities, societies, unions, clubs, associations, commissions, and other organizations. Chapter 21, "Goods And Services Tax", includes detailed coverage of the GST/HST.

Exercise One - 1

Subject: Taxable Entities For Income Tax Purposes

Which of the following entities could be required to file an income tax return?

- Max Jordan (an individual)
- Jordan's Hardware Store (an unincorporated business)
- Jordan & Jordan (a partnership)
- The Jordan family trust (a trust)
- Jordan Enterprises Ltd. (a corporation)
- The Jordan Foundation (an unincorporated charity)

Exercise One - 2

Subject: Taxable Entities For GST Purposes

Which of the following entities could be required to file a GST return?

- Max Jordan (an individual)
- Jordan's Hardware Store (an unincorporated business)
- Jordan & Jordan (a partnership)
- The Jordan family trust (a trust)
- Jordan Enterprises Ltd. (a corporation)
- The Jordan Foundation (an unincorporated charity)

End of Exercises. Solutions available in Study Guide.

Federal Taxation And The Provinces
Personal Income Taxes
1-13.   Under the Constitution Act, the federal, provincial, and territorial governments have the power to impose taxes. The provinces and territories are limited to direct taxation as delegated in the Act, a constraint that leaves all residual taxation powers to the federal government. The provinces are further limited to the taxation of income earned in the particular province and the income of persons resident in that province. Within these limitations, all of the provinces and territories impose both personal and corporate income taxes.

1-14.   Under the federal/provincial tax collection agreement, provincial taxes are calculated by applying a provincial tax rate to a Taxable Income figure. With the exception of Quebec, all of the provinces use the same Taxable Income figure that is used at the federal level.

1-15.   Despite the use of the federal Taxable Income figure, the provinces have retained considerable flexibility in their individual tax systems. This flexibility is achieved in two ways:

   • Each province can apply different rates and surtaxes to as many tax brackets as it wishes.

   • More importantly, each province is able to set different provincial credits to apply against provincial Tax Payable. While most provinces have provincial credits that are similar to credits that are established at the federal level, the value of these credits varies considerably at the provincial level and many provinces have additional types of credits.

1-16.   The provincial differences complicate the preparation of tax returns. The level of complication varies from province to province, depending on the degree to which provincial tax brackets and provincial tax credits resemble those applicable at the federal level.

1-17.   Because of these complications, the problem material in this text will, in general, not require the calculation of provincial taxes for individuals. However, because the combined federal/provincial rate is important in many tax-based decisions (e.g., selecting between alternative investments), we will continue to refer to overall combined rates, despite the fact that such figures are very specific to the province in which the income is taxed, as well as the characteristics associated with the individual filing the return.

Exercise One - 3

Subject: Federal And Provincial Taxes Payable

John Forsyth has Taxable Income of $27,000. For the current year, his federal tax rate is 15 percent, while the corresponding provincial rate is 7.5 percent. Determine Mr. Forsyth's combined federal and provincial tax payable, before consideration of any available credits against Tax Payable.

End of Exercise.   Solution available in Study Guide.

Corporate Income Taxes
1-18.   The system used to calculate provincial corporate income tax payable is similar to the system that is applicable to individuals. Provincial corporate income tax is levied on Taxable Income. All of the provinces, with the exception of Alberta and Quebec, use the federal *Income Tax Act* to compute Taxable Income. Even in Alberta and Quebec, the respective provincial Tax Acts have many of the same features as the federal *Act*.

1-19.   With respect to the collection of corporate income taxes, only Alberta and Quebec collect their own corporate income taxes. In all other provinces and territories, corporate income taxes are collected by the federal government on behalf of the provinces.

GST, HST And PST

1-20. In making its 1987 proposals for sales tax reform, the federal government suggested a joint federal/provincial sales tax. Lack of interest by provincial governments meant the proposal was not implemented at that time. Instead, the GST was introduced at the federal level and provincial sales taxes were left in place without significant alteration. With the exception of Alberta, where no provincial sales tax has ever been levied, there were two different sales taxes collected, accounted for, and remitted.

1-21. This situation was very costly and time consuming for businesses. Not only were they faced with the costs of filing sales tax returns in multiple jurisdictions, but each jurisdiction had its own rules for the goods or services on which the tax was applicable. This was clearly an inefficient approach to generating tax revenues and, not surprisingly, considerable pressure developed for the harmonization of the separate federal and provincial sales taxes.

1-22. Despite the obvious efficiencies that would result from harmonization, progress has been slow. In 1992, Quebec began to operate under a somewhat harmonized system. Unlike the harmonized systems that later developed in other provinces, Quebec chose to administer its own sales tax (QST). While its coverage is similar to the federal GST, the goods and services to which the QST applies differ from those subject to GST.

1-23. In several provinces there is a harmonized sales tax (HST) which is, in effect, a combined federal/provincial sales tax. These provinces are New Brunswick, Nova Scotia, Newfoundland, and Ontario. While British Columbia was part of this group, a referendum has forced the government in that province to drop out of this system.

1-24. These systems differ from the Quebec model in that the HST is a single tax administered by the federal government. Note, however, individual provinces have chosen to exempt certain goods and services that are taxed under the GST regime. For example, the provincial portion of the HST is not charged on print newspapers, diapers, and books.

1-25. These changes have left Canada with a somewhat fragmented system:

- New Brunswick, Newfoundland, Nova Scotia, and Ontario have a harmonized system.
- Quebec has GST, plus a separate QST regime.
- British Columbia, Manitoba, Saskatchewan, and Prince Edward Island have GST, plus a provincial sales tax.
- Alberta has GST and no provincial sales tax.

Tax Policy Concepts

Taxation And Economic Policy

1-26. The traditional goal of tax legislation has been to generate revenues for the relevant taxing authority. However, it is clear that today's approach to tax legislation is multi-faceted. We use tax legislation as a tool to facilitate a number of economic policy objectives:

Resource Allocation Tax revenues are used to provide public goods and services. Pure public goods such as the cost of our national defense system are thought to benefit all taxpayers. As it is not possible to allocate costs to individuals on the basis of benefits received, such costs must be supported with general tax revenues. Similar allocations occur with such widely used public goods as education, health care, and pollution control. In some cases, the tax system also has an influence on the allocation of private goods. For example, excise taxes are used to discourage the consumption of alcohol and tobacco products.

Distribution Effects Our tax system is used to redistribute income and wealth among taxpayers. Such provisions as the federal GST tax credit and provincial sales tax exemptions on food and low priced clothing have the effect of taking taxes paid by higher income taxpayers and distributing them to lower income wage earners or taxpayers with higher basic living costs in proportion to their income.

Stabilization Effects   Taxes may also be used to achieve macroeconomic objectives.   At various times, tax policy has been used to encourage economic expansion, increase employment, and to assist in holding inflation in check.   An example of this is the emphasis on stimulating the economy that is found in the last two budgets.

Fiscal Federalism   This term refers to the various procedures that are used to allocate resources among different levels of government. For 2012-2013, it is estimated that transfers to other levels of government will amount to $58.4 billion, as compared to transfers to persons of $72.2 billion, and direct program spending of $114.7 billion. In the next step in the chain, a portion of provincial tax revenue is transferred to municipal governments.

Taxation And Income Levels
General Approaches
1-27.   Policy makers are concerned about the relationship between income levels and rates of taxation. Taxes can be proportional, in that a constant rate is applied at all levels of income. In theory, this is our approach to taxing the income of corporations. For public companies, the system is based on a flat rate that is applicable to all income earned by the company. However, a wide variety of provisions act to modify the application of this rate, resulting in a situation where many Canadian companies are not subject to this notional flat rate.

1-28.   As an alternative, taxation can be regressive, resulting in lower effective rates of taxation as higher income levels are reached. Sales taxes generally fall into this regressive category as lower income individuals spend a larger portion of their total income and, as a consequence, pay a greater portion of their total income as sales taxes levied on their expenditures.

Example Consider the Werner sisters:

Gertrude Werner has income of $200,000 and spends $40,000 of this amount. She lives in a province with a 13 percent harmonized sales tax (HST) on expenditures, resulting in the payment of $5,200 in HST. This represents a 2.6 percent effective tax rate on her $200,000 income.

Ingrid Werner has income of $40,000 and spends all of this amount. She lives in the same province as her sister, resulting in the payment of $5,200 in HST. This represents a 13 percent effective tax rate on her $40,000 income.

Exercise One - 4

Subject: Regressive Taxes

Margie Jones has Taxable Income for the current year of $895,000, of which $172,000 is spent on goods and services that are subject to Harmonized Sales Tax (HST) at a rate of 13 percent. Her sister, Jane Jones, is a part-time student living in the same province and has Taxable Income of $18,000. During the current year, as a result of using some of her savings, she spends $27,500 on goods and services that are all subject to HST. Determine the effective sales tax rate as a percentage of the income of the two sisters.

End of Exercise. Solution available in Study Guide.

1-29.   In contrast to the regressive nature of sales taxes, the present system of personal income taxation is designed to be progressive, since higher rates are applied to higher levels of income. For 2012, the federal rates range from a low of 15 percent on the first $42,707 of Taxable Income to a high of 29 percent on Taxable Income in excess of $132,406.

Progressive Vs. Regressive
1-30.   As noted in the preceding paragraph, the federal income tax system taxes individuals

using a progressive system. The major arguments in favour of this approach can be described as follows:

Equity Higher income individuals have a greater ability to pay taxes. As their income is above their basic consumption needs, the relative cost to the individual of having a portion of this income taxed away is less than the relative cost to lower income individuals, where additional taxation removes funds required for such essentials as food and housing.

Stability Progressive tax rates help maintain after-tax income stability by shifting people to lower tax brackets in times of economic downturn and to higher brackets when there is economic expansion. The resulting decreases or increases in income taxes serve to cushion the economic swings.

1-31. There are, however, a number of problems that can be associated with progressive rates. These can be briefly described as follows:

Complexity With progressive rates in place, efforts will be made to divide income among as many individuals (usually family members) as possible. These efforts to make maximum use of the lower tax brackets necessitate the use of complex anti-avoidance rules by taxation authorities.

Income Fluctuations In the absence of relieving provisions, progressive rates discriminate against individuals with highly variable income streams. That is, under a progressive system, an individual with $1,000,000 in income in one year and no income for the next three years will pay substantially more in taxes than an individual with the same $1,000,000 total earned over four years at a rate of $250,000 per year.

Family Unit Problems Progressive tax rates discriminate against single income family units. A family unit in which one spouse makes $200,000 and the other has no Taxable Income would pay significantly more in taxes than would be the case if each spouse earned $100,000.

Economic Growth It is clear that the high tax brackets that can be associated with a progressive system can discourage both employment and investment efforts. This could serve to limit economic growth.

Tax Concessions The high brackets associated with progressive systems lead to pressure for various types of tax concessions to be made available. Because high income individuals have a greater ability to effectively take advantage of favourable provisions in the income tax legislation, they may actually wind up paying taxes at lower effective rates. In response to the possibility that, in extreme cases, some high income individuals pay no income taxes at all, there is an alternative minimum income tax that is imposed on certain taxpayers.

Tax Evasion Progressive rates discourage income reporting and encourage the creation of various devices to evade taxation. Evasion strategies range from simple bartering, to cash only transactions, and finally to organized crime activities.

Reduced Tax Revenues There is evidence that, if marginal tax rates are too high, the result may be reduced aggregate tax revenues. Some authorities believe that this begins to occur at rates between 40 and 50 percent. We would note that when the federal rates are combined with the various provincial rates, the resulting rates are in this range.

Flat Tax Systems

1-32. While progressive tax systems continue to be pervasive, there has been a worldwide trend towards flattening rate schedules. One of the reasons for this trend is the fact that effective tax rates are not as progressive as the rate schedules indicate. As mentioned in the preceding paragraph, high bracket taxpayers tend to have better access to various types of tax concessions which can significantly reduce the effective rates for these individuals.

1-33.   Given this situation, it has been suggested that we could achieve results similar to those which, in fact, prevail under the current system by applying a single or flat rate of tax to a broadened taxation base. In this context, the term base broadening refers to the elimination of tax concessions, resulting in tax rates that are applied to a larger income figure.

1-34.   Starting in 2001, Canada's first and, to date, only flat tax system for individuals was implemented. Not surprisingly, it is in place in Alberta. Under this system, the provincial tax rate on all of the income of individuals is a flat rate of 10 percent.

Tax Incidence

1-35.   Tax incidence refers to the issue of who really pays a particular tax. While statutory incidence refers to the initial legal liability for tax payment, the actual economic burden may be passed on to a different group. For example, certain taxes on production might be the legal liability of the producer. However, they may be partly or entirely shifted to consumers through price increases on the goods produced.

1-36.   Policy makers must be concerned with this to ensure that the system is working as intended. It is generally assumed that the incidence of personal income tax falls on individuals. In addition, in their role as consumers, individuals also assume the responsibility for a large portion of the various sales taxes that are levied in Canada. The incidence of corporate taxes is more open to speculation. Shareholders may bear the burden of corporate taxes in the short run. However, most authorities believe that, in the long run, this burden is shared by employees and consumers.

Tax Expenditures

1-37.   In contrast to government funding programs that provide payments to various entities in the economy, tax expenditures reflect revenues that have been given up by the government through the use of tax preferences, concessions, and other tax breaks. These expenditures may favour selected individuals or groups (senior citizens), certain kinds of income (capital gains), or certain characteristics of some taxpayers (the disabled).

1-38.   In an effort to quantify the importance of these expenditures, the Department of Finance produces the publication, "Tax Expenditures And Evaluations" each year. The 2011 edition contains estimates for 2006 to 2008 and projections for 2009 to 2011, of the costs of various income tax and GST expenditures. Examples of the 2006 estimates and 2011 projections of the cost of some of these expenditures include:

- Charitable donations tax credit - $2.3 billion in 2006, $2.3 billion in 2011.

- Tax credit for spouse - $1.2 billion in 2006 - $1.4 billion in 2011.

- The favourable treatment of capital gains - $5.1 billion in 2006, $3.6 billion in 2011.

- The deduction of RRSP contributions - $7.3 billion in 2006, $7.4 billion in 2011.

- Tax free gains on principal residences - $4.3 billion in 2006, $4.2 billion in 2011.

1-39.   It is clear that such tax expenditures are of considerable significance in the management of federal finances. It is equally clear that the provision of this type of government benefit has become entrenched in our tax system. This situation can be explained by a number of factors:

- It is less costly to administer tax expenditures than it is to administer government funding programs.

- More decisions are left to the private sector so that funds may be allocated more efficiently.

- Tax expenditures reduce the visibility of certain government actions. This is particularly beneficial if some social stigma is attached to the programs. For example, a child tax benefit system is more acceptable than increasing social assistance payments.

• Tax expenditures reduce the progressivity of the tax system. As many of the tax expenditures, such as tax shelters, are more available to higher income taxpayers, they serve to reduce effective tax rates in the higher rate brackets.

1-40.   Tax expenditures are not only very substantial, they are also difficult to control. This was noted by Auditor General Kenneth Dye in his 1985 Annual Report as follows:

A cost conscious Parliament is in the position of a team of engineers trying to design a more fuel efficient automobile. They think they have succeeded, but the engine seems to go on consuming as much gas as it did before. They cannot understand the problem until they notice that, hidden from view, a myriad of small holes have been punched through the bottom of the gas tank. This is too often the way of tax expenditures. Revenue leaks away, and MPs do not know about it until it is too late.

Qualitative Characteristics Of Tax Systems

General Concepts

1-41.   Accounting standard setting bodies have established such concepts as relevance and reliability as being desirable qualitative characteristics of accounting information. While not established with the same degree of formality, it is clear that there are similar concepts that can be used to evaluate tax systems. Some of these desirable qualitative characteristics can be described as follows:

Equity Or Fairness   Horizontal equity entails assessing similar levels of taxation for people in similar economic circumstances. If two individuals each have Taxable Income of $50,000, horizontal equity would require that they each pay the same amount of taxes.

In contrast, vertical equity means dissimilar tax treatment of people in different circumstances. If an individual has Taxable Income of $100,000, he should pay more taxes than an individual with Taxable Income of $50,000.

Neutrality   The concept of neutrality calls for a tax system that interferes as little as possible with decision making. An overriding economic assumption is that decisions are always made to maximize the use of resources. This may not be achieved when tax factors affect how taxpayers save, invest, or consume. Taxes, by influencing economic decisions, may cause a less than optimal allocation of resources.

Adequacy   A good tax system should meet the funding requirements of the taxing authority. It is also desirable that these revenues be produced in a fashion that is dependable and relatively predictable from year to year.

Elasticity   Tax revenues should be capable of being adjusted to meet changes in economic conditions, without necessitating tax rate changes.

Flexibility   This refers to the ease with which the tax system can be adjusted to meet changing economic or social conditions.

Simplicity And Ease Of Compliance   A good tax system is easy to comply with and does not present significant administrative problems for the people enforcing the system.

Certainty   Individual taxpayers should know how much tax they have to pay, the basis for payments, and the due date. Such certainty also helps taxing authorities estimate tax revenues and facilitates forecasting of budgetary expenditures.

Balance Between Sectors   A good tax system should not be overly reliant on either corporate or individual taxation. Attention should also be given to balance within these sectors, insuring that no type of business or type of individual is asked to assume a disproportionate share of the tax burden.

International Competitiveness   If a country's tax system has rates that are out of line with those in comparable countries, the result will be an outflow of both business and skilled individuals to those countries that have more favourable tax rates.

Conflicts Among Characteristics

1-42.   In designing a tax system, many compromises are required. Examples include the fact that flexibility is often in conflict with certainty, equity requires trade-offs in simplicity and neutrality, and some taxes with very positive objectives are very non-neutral in nature. An example of this last conflict is that the rates available to small businesses are very favourable because the government believes that this attracts investment to this sector, thereby encouraging employment and the development of active business efforts. However, this may not result in the optimal allocation of resources to the business sector as a whole.

Evaluation Of The Canadian System

1-43.   Canadian policy makers often refer to the preceding qualitative characteristics in discussions involving taxation policies. This would make it appropriate to consider how the current system of federal taxation stacks up against these criteria. While any comprehensive evaluation of this question goes well beyond the objectives of this text, we offer the following brief comments:

- With respect to equity, Canada continues to have situations in which high income individuals pay little or no tax and relatively low income individuals are subjected to fairly high effective rates. While the alternative minimum tax was instituted to correct this problem, inequity is unlikely to be eliminated in a tax system that attempts to accomplish as many diverse objectives as does the current Canadian system.

- As noted previously, the Canadian system has a very heavy reliance on the taxation of personal income and receives a very low portion of its revenues from the corporate sector.

- The Canadian system has had problems with stability and dependability of revenues.

- The Canadian tax system is very complex, making compliance difficult for many taxpayers. In addition, administration of the legislation is made more difficult by the large number of provisions and the lack of clarity in their content.

   The inability to achieve a harmonized GST/HST system has made this situation much worse. As we have noted, different provinces have adopted different systems, thereby complicating inter-provincial transactions. Further, in a given province, there are significant variations in the types of goods and services that are subject to taxation within a given system.

- While international competitiveness is often cited as a problem for Canada, particularly with respect to comparisons with the U.S., the situation has improved significantly in recent years. Of particular importance in this area is the fact that tax rates on Canadian corporations have been reduced. These reductions in corporate taxes leave Canada with rates that compare very favorably with most foreign jurisdictions.

Income Tax Reference Materials

Introduction

1-44.   To this point in our discussion of the Canadian tax system and related tax policy concepts, we have considered a variety of taxation bases as they apply at both the federal and provincial level. However, with the exception of Chapter 21 which deals with the goods and services tax, the focus of this book is on the federal taxes that are assessed on the income of individuals, corporations, and trusts.

1-45.   Reference materials related to the federal income tax are very extensive. In addition to the *Income Tax Act* there are many other sources of information. These include other legislative materials, other publications of the Canada Revenue Agency (CRA), documents related to court decisions, as well as interpretive materials from a wide variety of sources.

1-46.   If presented in paper format, a complete library of these materials would run to thousands of pages and would have to be included in a large number of separate volumes. Given this, most tax practitioners work with an electronic database that provides for easy access through key word searches.

1-47.   These electronic databases are published by several Canadian organizations, including CCH, Carswell, and the CICA. Through our affiliation with the CICA, we are able to provide you with a copy of their Federal Income Tax Collection (FITAC). This electronic database can be found on the Student CD-ROM which accompanies this text. It includes:

- The *Income Tax Act* and *Income Tax Regulations*.
- Most CRA publications including Interpretation Bulletins, Information Circulars, Guides, and forms.
- An electronic copy of this text that is searchable and has electronic links to other reference materials in the database.

1-48.   A general description of all of these materials will be found in the sections which follow.

The Income Tax Act
Importance
1-49.   This is the most important source of information for dealing with matters related to the federal income tax. Interpretation and guidance can be found in many other sources. However, at the end of the day, this document provides the basis for any final decision related to the amount of income tax that will have to be paid by an individual, corporation, or trust.

1-50.   It is a very long document, running about 2,000 pages in paper format. It is also written in a very legalistic style which, in our opinion, cannot be readily understood by most individuals. Given this, the design of our text is such that it does not require the use of the *Income Tax Act* in order to understand its content or complete the related problem material.

1-51.   While the design of this text does not require the use of the *Income Tax Act* as a reference, it is still important to have some understanding of the structure of this document. One reason for this is that the organization of this book generally follows the structure of the *Income Tax Act*. In addition, you will find many references to the *Act* embedded as part of the text. There are two reasons for this:

- The most important reason for these references is to allow interested individuals to explore a particular issue to a depth that goes beyond the scope of this text. The presence of *Income Tax Act* references greatly facilitates this process.

- The use of references can also be convenient. In dealing with a particular subject, it is often more efficient to refer to a subject with a reference to the *Act* than to repeatedly use the full description of the subject.

1-52.   Given this situation, we will provide a description of the basic structure and content of this important legislation.

Structure Of The Federal Income Tax Act
1-53.   Figure 1-2 diagrams the basic structure of the *Act*. As can be seen in this diagram, the major divisions of the *Income Tax Act* are referred to as Parts. Some, but not all of these Parts,

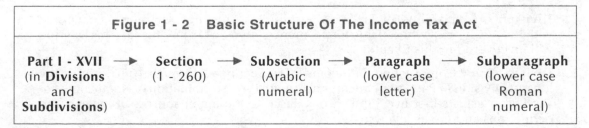

Figure 1 - 2   Basic Structure Of The Income Tax Act

Part I - XVII (in **Divisions** and **Subdivisions**) →	**Section** (1 - 260) →	**Subsection** (Arabic numeral) →	**Paragraph** (lower case letter) →	**Subparagraph** (lower case Roman numeral)

contain two or more Divisions (e.g., Part I of the *Act* contains Divisions A through J). Some Divisions, but again not all of them, contain Subdivisions. For example, Division B of Part I contains Subdivisions a through k.

1-54.   All of the Parts contain at least one Section. However, there is considerable variance in the size of the Parts. Part I.2, "Tax On Old Age Security Benefits", contains only one Section. In contrast, Part I, the largest and most important Part of the *Act*, contains Sections 2 to 180.2.

1-55.   While the Sections of the *Act* are numbered 1 through 260, there are actually more than 260 Sections. This reflects the fact that when a new Section is added, it has been more convenient to attach a decimal designation to the new Section, as opposed to renumbering all of the Sections that follow the new Section. For example, over several years, the Department of Finance has added five new Sections after Section 12. They have been numbered Section 12.1 through Section 12.5. If they had used whole numbers for these new Sections, it would have been necessary to renumber all of the remaining Sections in the *Act*.

1-56.   Sections may be further subdivided into Subsections [designated with Arabic numerals as in Subsection 84(1)]. This is followed by Paragraphs [designated with lower case letters as in Paragraph 84(1)(b)], and by Subparagraphs [designated with lower case Roman numerals as in Subparagraph 84(1)(b)(i)]. In some cases, the outlining process goes even further with Clauses (designated with upper case letters) and Subclauses (designated with upper case Roman numerals). Putting all of this together means that the reference:

ITA 115(1)(a)(i)(A)(I)

would be read as *Income Tax Act* Section 115, Subsection (1), Paragraph (a), Subparagraph (i), Clause A, Subclause I. Normally the relevant Part of the *Act* (Part I in this case) is not indicated in such references.

Parts Of The Act

1-57.   The Parts of the *Income Tax Act* are numbered I through XVII. As was the case with Sections of the *Act*, there are more than 17 Parts because of the use of designations within a single Roman numeral. The most extreme example of this would be the existence of Parts XII.1, XII.2, XII.3, XII.4, XII.5, and XII.6.

1-58.   About 70 percent of the Sections of the *Income Tax Act* are found in Part I, which is titled "Income Tax". This Part contains Sections 2 through 180 of the *Act* and, because of its importance, we will provide a more detailed description of this Part in the following material.

1-59.   Parts I.1 through XVII cover a variety of special taxes as well as rules related to matters of administration, enforcement, and interpretation. For example, Part V is titled "Tax In And Penalties In Respect Of Registered Charities" and Part XII.3 is titled "Tax On Investment Income Of Life Insurers". As the great bulk of our attention in this text will be focused on Part I of the *Act*, there is little point in providing a list of these Parts for you to read. However, if you have further interest in their content, we would refer you to the complete copy of the *Income Tax Act* that is included on the Student CD-ROM that accompanies this text.

Part I Of The Act

1-60.   Part I, the largest and most important Part of the *Income Tax Act*, is divided into eleven Divisions. Some of these Divisions are further divided into Subdivisions. The Divisions and their more significant Subdivisions are described in the following paragraphs:

Division A: "Liability For Tax" (ITA Section 2)   This short Division is concerned with the question of who is liable for payment of income tax in Canada. This Division will be covered in this Chapter 1.

Division B: "Computation Of Income" (ITA Sections 3 through 108)   This is the longest Division in Part I and concerns itself with the determination of Net Income For Tax Purposes. Its first five Subdivisions describe the major sources of income and deductions and are as follows:

- **Subdivision a** - "Income Or Loss From An Office Or Employment"   This Subdivision deals with the ordinary wages and salaries that are earned by individuals while an employee of a business entity. The material in this Subdivision provides the basis for Chapter 3.

- **Subdivision b** - "Income Or Loss From A Business Or Property"   This Subdivision deals with business income earned by corporations, trusts, and by individuals through proprietorship or partnership arrangements. Also covered in this Subdivision is property income which includes rents, interest, dividends, and royalties. The material in this Subdivision provides the basis for Chapters 5, 6, and 7.

- **Subdivision c** - "Taxable Capital Gains And Allowable Capital Losses"   This Subdivision deals with gains and losses resulting from the disposal of capital property. The material in this Subdivision is dealt with in Chapter 8.

- **Subdivision d** - "Other Sources Of Income"   Covered here are miscellaneous income sources, such as spousal support received and various types of pension income, that do not fit into any of the major categories dealt with in Subdivisions a, b, and c. This material is covered in Chapter 9.

- **Subdivision e** - "Deductions In Computing Income"   Covered here are miscellaneous deductions such as moving expenses, child care costs, and spousal support paid. These are deductions that do not fit into any of the categories in Subdivisions a, b, and c. This material is also covered in Chapter 9.

Subdivisions a, b, and c each provide for both inclusions and deductions and, as a consequence, require the calculation of a net income figure. The deductions that are specified in Subdivisions a, b and c can only be deducted from inclusions in that same Subdivision. That is, deductions related to business income (Subdivision b) cannot be deducted from the inclusions for employment income (Subdivision a). This becomes a very important point when the inclusions in a particular Subdivision are not sufficient to support all of the available deductions in that Subdivision.

The remaining six Subdivisions of Division B do not provide new sources of income but, rather, provide additional rules related to the determination of Net Income. These remaining Subdivisions are as follows:

- **Subdivision f** - "Rules Relating To Computation Of Income"   This Subdivision contains a variety of rules related to the deductibility of expenses, income attribution, and the death of a taxpayer. These rules are covered in Chapters 6 and 9.

- **Subdivision g** - "Amounts Not Included In Computing Income"   This is a very specialized Subdivision, dealing with certain types of exempt income. It is not given significant coverage in this text.

- **Subdivision h** - "Corporations Resident In Canada And Their Shareholders"   This Subdivision presents a number of rules related to the taxation of Canadian resident corporations. This material is covered in Chapters 12, 13, and 14.

- **Subdivision i** - "Shareholders Of Corporations Not Resident In Canada"   This is a specialized Subdivision. Limited coverage is available in Chapter 20.

- **Subdivision j** - "Partnerships And Their Members"   This Subdivision, dealing with rules related to partnerships, is given detailed coverage in Chapter 18.

- **Subdivision k** - "Trusts And Their Beneficiaries"   This Subdivision, dealing with the taxation of trusts, is given detailed consideration in Chapter 19.

Division C: "Computation Of Taxable Income" (ITA Sections 109 through 114.2) This Division covers the conversion of Division B income (commonly referred to as Net Income For Tax Purposes, or simply Net Income) into Taxable Income for residents. For individuals, it is given initial coverage in Chapter 4, followed by more detailed coverage in Chapter 11. For corporations, the coverage is in Chapter 12.

Division D: "Taxable Income Earned In Canada By Non-Residents" (ITA Sections 115 through 116)   Coverage of this material can be found in Chapter 20.

Division E: "Computation Of Tax" (Sections 117 through 127.41)   This Division is concerned with determining the taxes that are payable on the Taxable Income determined in Divisions C and D. It has five Subdivisions as follows:

- Subdivision a   - Rules applicable to individuals
- Subdivision a.1 - Child tax benefit
- Subdivision a.2 - Working Income Tax Benefit
- Subdivision b   - Rules applicable to corporations
- Subdivision c   - Rules applicable to all taxpayers

The computation of tax for individuals is largely covered in Chapter 4, with some additional coverage in Chapter 11. The corresponding material for corporations is found in Chapters 12 and 13.

Division E.1:   "Minimum Tax" (Sections 127.5 through 127.55)   This Division is concerned with the obligation of individuals to pay a minimum amount of tax, as well as the computation of this alternative minimum tax. This material is covered in Chapter 11.

Division F: "Special Rules Applicable In Certain Circumstances" (Sections 128 through 143.3)   Much of this Division is devoted to very specialized situations (bankruptcies) or organizations (cooperative corporations). While these situations are not given coverage in this text, the Division covers two subjects that are of more general importance. These are immigration to, and emigration from, Canada which are covered in Chapter 20, and refundable dividends for private corporations which is covered in Chapter 13.

Division G: "Deferred And Other Special Income Arrangements" (Sections 144 through 148.1)   This important Division covers the rules related to Registered Retirement Savings Plans, Registered Pension Plans, Deferred Profit Sharing Plans, as well as other deferred income arrangements. Detailed attention is given to this material in Chapter 10.

Division H: "Exemptions" (Sections 149, 149.1, and 149.2)   Covered here are exemptions for individuals and organizations such as certain employees of foreign countries, pension trusts, and charitable organizations. These topics are not given coverage in this text.

Divisions I And J: "Returns, Assessments, Payments And Appeals" and "Appeals To The Tax Court Of Canada And The Federal Court" (Sections 150 through 180)   These Divisions deal with the resolution of disputes between taxpayers and the Canada Revenue Agency (CRA). Coverage of this material is found in Chapter 2.

Other Income Tax Legislation

1-61.   While the *Income Tax Act* constitutes the major source of legislation relevant to the study of the federal income tax, there are four other sources of legislative materials that are relevant. These are draft legislation, the Income Tax Regulations, the Income Tax Application Rules, 1971, and a group of International Tax Treaties between Canada and other countries. A general description of these legislative materials follows.

Draft Legislation

1-62.   It is traditional for the federal government to issue a budget in the first half of each year. Budgets are presented as a Notice Of Ways And Means Motion. As such, its content is of a general nature and does not contain the actual legislative provisions that are required to implement the proposals that are being put forward. The preparation of this legislation takes a considerable period of time and, when it is completed, it is presented as draft legislation. Additional time will pass before this draft legislation is passed by parliament.

1-63.   These time lags sometimes create a somewhat awkward situation in which returns for a particular taxation year must sometimes be filed prior to the actual passage of the legislation relevant to that year.   Tax planning can be further complicated by an election call by the governing party. If the election is scheduled after a budget statement, but prior to the passage of the relevant legislation, there will be uncertainty as to whether the budget proposals will, in fact, be implemented.

Income Tax Regulations

1-64.   Section 221 of the *Income Tax Act* allows the Governor In Council to make Regulations concerning the administration and enforcement of the *Income Tax Act*. Some of the items listed in this Section include:

- prescribing the evidence required to establish facts relevant to assessments under this *Act*;

- requiring any class of persons to make information returns respecting any class of information required in connection with assessments under this *Act*;

- prescribing anything that, by this *Act*, is to be prescribed or is to be determined or regulated by regulation; and

- defining the classes of persons who may be regarded as dependent for the purposes of this *Act*.

1-65.   While these Regulations cannot extend the limits of the law, they can serve to fill in details and, to some extent, modify the statutes. For example, most of the rules for determining the amount of Capital Cost Allowance that can be deducted are established in the Regulations. Such Regulations provide an essential element of flexibility in the administration of the *Act* in that they can be issued without going through a more formal legislative process.

1-66.   You should also note that references to material in the Regulations are often referred to in the *Income Tax Act* as "prescribed". For example, the rate the CRA charges on late tax payments, a "prescribed" rate of interest, is determined by a procedure that is described in Regulation 4301.

International Tax Treaties

1-67.   Canada currently has tax treaties (also known as tax conventions) with over 90 countries. The most important of these are the Tax Conventions with the United States and the United Kingdom. While there is considerable variation in the agreements, most of them are based on the model convention developed by the Organization For Economic Co-operation And Development (OECD).

1-68.   The purpose of these treaties is twofold. First, they attempt to avoid double taxation of taxpayers who may have reason to pay taxes in more than one jurisdiction and, second, they try to prevent international evasion of taxes. In situations where there is a conflict between the Canadian *Income Tax Act* and an international tax treaty, the terms of the international tax treaty prevail.

1-69.   Chapter 20 will provide additional discussion of Canada's tax treaties. Particular attention will be given to the treaty between the U.S. and Canada.

Income Tax Application Rules, 1971

1-70.   When capital gains taxation was introduced in Canada in 1972, a large number of transitional rules were required, primarily to ensure that the effects of the new legislation were not retroactive. These transitional rules are called the Income Tax Application Rules, 1971, and they continue to be of some significance in a limited number of situations. However, because of their declining general importance, they are given attention only in Supplementary Reading No. 1, "Median Rule", which is included on the Student CD-ROM which is provided with this text.

Other Sources Of Income Tax Information

Electronic Library Resources

1-71.   As noted in Paragraph 1-46, most tax practitioners rely on an electronic library for their tax reference materials. Also as noted, the Student CD-ROM which is provided with this text contains one of these libraries — the CICA's Federal Income Tax Collection (FITAC).

CRA Web Site

1-72.   The CRA has an extensive web site at **www.cra-arc.gc.ca**. Almost all of the forms, Guides, Interpretation Bulletins and other documents provided by the CRA that are described in Paragraph 1-73 are available on the web site. The forms and publications can be viewed and printed online or downloaded to a computer in one or more formats. There is also an online request service available to have printed forms or publications mailed out.   The web site is constantly being expanded to provide more forms and publications and more information on electronic services such as EFILE, NETFILE, and TELEFILE.

CRA Publications

1-73.   The CRA provides several publications to the public which, while they do not have the force of law, can be extremely helpful and influential in making decisions related to income taxes. These can be described as follows:

Interpretation Bulletins   To date, over 500 Interpretation Bulletins have been issued by the CRA. Note, however, that many of these are no longer in force. The objective of these Bulletins is to give the CRA's interpretation of particular sections of the law that it administers and to announce significant changes in departmental interpretation along with the effective dates of any such changes. Examples of important Interpretation Bulletins include IT-63R5 dealing with an employee's personal use of an automobile supplied by an employer, and IT-221R3 which provides guidance on the determination of an individual's residence status. Note that the R5 and R3 in these Bulletin numbers refer to fifth and third revisions, respectively, of the Bulletins.

Information Circulars   While over 300 of these circulars have been issued, less than 100 are currently in effect. The objective of these publications is to provide information regarding procedural matters that relate to both the *Income Tax Act* and the provisions of the Canada Pension Plan, and to announce changes in organization, personnel, operating programs, and other administrative developments.

Income Tax Technical News   The Income Tax Rulings Directorate of the CRA periodically issues a newsletter titled *Income Tax Technical News*. This newsletter provides up-to-date information on current tax issues and is considered by the CRA to have the same weight as Interpretation Bulletins.

CRA News Releases, Tax Tips, And Fact Sheets   The CRA publishes News Releases on a variety of subjects, such as prescribed interest rates, corporate EFILE, deferral of taxation on employee stock options, and maximum pensionable earnings. They also provide information on when monthly payments will be released under the Child Tax Benefit System and when quarterly payments will be released under the GST tax credit program. Some of the News Releases take the form of questions and answers, while others deal with the subject in some depth. They are usually issued in advance of the relevant legislation or coverage in an Interpretation Bulletin or Information Circular.

Guides And Pamphlets   The CRA publishes a large number of non-technical Pamphlets and Guides that provide information on particular topics of interest to taxpayers. Examples of Pamphlets are "Canadian Residents Going Down South" (P151) and "Tax Information For People With Disabilities" (P149). Examples of Guides are "Business And Professional Income" (T4002), "Preparing Returns For Deceased Persons" (T4011), and "RRSPs And Other Registered Plans For Retirement" (T4040).

Advance Income Tax Rulings And Technical Interpretations   In recognition of the considerable complexity involved in the interpretation of many portions of the *Income Tax*

Act, the Income Tax Rulings Directorate of the CRA will, for a fee, provide an Advance Income Tax Ruling on how it will tax a proposed transaction, subject to certain limitations and qualifications. Advance Income Tax Rulings are available to the public, but only in severed format with much of the relevant information that may permit identification of the parties deleted. The result is that such publications are of questionable value.

The Income Tax Rulings Directorate of the CRA also provides both written and telephone Technical Interpretations to the public (other than for proposed transactions where an Advance Income Tax Ruling is required) free of charge. Such interpretations however are not considered binding on the CRA.

Court Decisions

1-74.   Despite the huge volume of information available for dealing with income tax matters, disputes between taxpayers and the CRA regularly find their way into the Canadian court system. Of the hundreds of tax cases that are reported each year, the great majority do not involve tax evasion or other criminal offences. Rather, they involve an honest difference of opinion between the taxpayer and the CRA. Common areas of litigation include:

- the deductibility of both business and employment related expenses;
- whether an individual is working as an employee or an independent contractor;
- establishing a property's fair market value;
- the question of whether a transaction took place at arm's length;
- the deductibility of support payments;
- distinguishing between profits that are capital in nature and those that are ordinary business income; and
- the deductibility of farm losses against other sources of income.

1-75.   With the large number of court cases and the fact that they cover the great majority of issues that might arise in the application of income tax legislation, attention must be given to the precedents that have been established in the court decisions. While court decisions cannot be used to change the actual tax law, court decisions may call into question the reasonableness of interpretations of the ITA made by either the CRA or tax practitioners. Given the volume and complexity of court cases on income tax, we will cite only very important cases in our coverage of the various subjects in this text. However, a careful review of all relevant case material would be essential in researching any complex tax issue.

Internal Documents

1-76.   As we have seen, the formal income tax legislation includes the *Income Tax Act*, Income Tax Regulations, international tax treaties, Income Tax Application Rules, 1971, as well as draft legislation. In addition, the Canada Revenue Agency (CRA) issues directives to its tax services offices in which interpretations and suggested procedures are set forth. However, these directives are not available to the public and their nature can only be determined by inference and experiences with assessments and court cases.

Liability For Income Tax

Charging Provision For Canadian Residents

1-77.   The portion of any tax legislation that specifies who is liable to pay tax is called a charging provision. Section 2 of the *Income Tax Act* contains two Subsections dealing with this subject. ITA 2(1), the more important of these Subsections, establishes that, in general, Canadian income taxation is based on residence. This Subsection states the following:

> **ITA 2(1)**   An income tax shall be paid, as required by this *Act*, on the taxable income for each taxation year of every person resident in Canada at any time in the year.

1-78.   There are several terms used in this charging provision that require further explanation:

Person   The charging provision makes it clear that responsibility for paying the federal income tax lies with "persons". In contrast to its usual dictionary meaning (i.e., human being), the *Income Tax Act* uses this term to refer to individuals, corporations, and trusts. When a provision of the *Act* is directed at human taxpayers, the term "individual" is generally used.

This reference establishes the fact that there are three entities which must file income tax returns — individuals, corporations, and trusts.

Resident   ITA 2(1) also establishes that Canadian residents are liable for Canadian income tax, without regard to their citizenship. This is in contrast to the situation in the United States where U.S. citizens are liable for U.S. income taxes, without regard to where they reside.

While the *Income Tax Act* does not provide a definition of resident, in many cases the application of this concept is self-evident. For an individual who has lived and worked in Red Deer, Alberta for his entire life, never leaving Canada even for short vacations, it is not difficult to establish Canadian residency.

However, for corporations and trusts, as well as for individuals in certain types of circumstances, determining residency can become a fairly complex process. It is also, because of the large differences in tax rates in alternative jurisdictions, a matter of some importance. Detailed consideration of the issues related to residency can be found in Chapter 20, International Issues In Taxation.

Taxation Year - Corporations   ITA 249(1)(a) indicates that for a corporation, the taxation year is a "fiscal period". ITA 249.1 defines the fiscal period of a corporation as a period for which accounts are made up that does not exceed 53 weeks. These definitions establish the fact that corporations are not required to use the calendar year as their taxation year.

Taxation Year - Individuals And Trusts   For most tax purposes, trusts are treated as individuals. In this context, ITA 249(1)(b) indicates that, for individuals other than a testamentary trust (a trust that arises as the result of the death of an individual), the taxation year is the calendar year. This means that an inter vivos trust (a trust other than a testamentary trust) must use a calendar year as its taxation year. In contrast, ITA 249(1)(c) allows a testamentary trust to use a taxation year other than a calendar year.

Taxable Income   Taxable income is defined in Section 2 of the *Act* as follows:

>   **ITA 2(2)**   The taxable income of a taxpayer for a taxation year is the taxpayer's income for the year plus the additions and minus the deductions permitted by Division C.

The process of converting Net Income For Tax Purposes into Taxable Income will be given some attention at a later point in this Chapter. However, detailed coverage will be found in Chapters 4 and 11.

Charging Provision For Non-Residents
General Charging Provision
1-79.   The second charging provision in the *Income Tax Act* deals with the taxation of non-residents. It is as follows:

>   **ITA 2(3)**   Where a person who is not taxable under subsection (1) for a taxation year
>
>   (a)   was **employed** in Canada,
>   (b)   carried on a **business** in Canada, or
>   (c)   disposed of a **taxable Canadian property**,
>
>   at any time in the year or a previous year, an income tax shall be paid, as required by this *Act*, on the person's taxable income earned in Canada for the year determined in accordance with Division D.

1-80. We will give a limited amount of attention to the taxation of non-residents in this Chapter. However, detailed consideration of the issues associated with the taxation of non-residents will be found in Chapter 20, International Issues In Taxation.

Employment Income Earned By Non-Residents

1-81. As the term is used in ITA 2(3)(a), Canadian employment income refers to income earned by a non-resident while working as an employee in Canada, generally without regard to the location of the employer. An example of this would be a U.S. citizen who is a resident of Detroit, Michigan, but is employed at an automobile plant in Windsor, Ontario. Such an individual would be subject to Canadian taxes on his employment income. However, as the individual is a non-resident, his other sources of income would not be taxed in Canada.

Business Income Earned By Non-Residents

1-82. The second situation in which non-residents are subject to Canadian taxes is specified in ITA 2(3)(b). This paragraph indicates that persons who carried on business in Canada during a taxation year are subject to Canadian taxes on that income. Many of the difficulties associated with implementing this provision are related to determining what constitutes "carrying on business in Canada". This clearly includes producing or manufacturing products in Canada. In addition, ITA 253 indicates that it includes situations where a business is offering things for sale in Canada through an employee.

1-83. This broad interpretation is, however, mitigated in those circumstances where the non-resident is a resident of a country with which Canada has a tax treaty. For example, if a U.S. corporation had sales staff selling products in Canada, ITA 253 would suggest that it should be taxed as a non-resident carrying on business in Canada. However, the Canada-U.S. tax treaty overrides ITA 253 in that this agreement exempts a U.S. enterprise from Canadian taxation unless it is carrying on business through permanent establishments in Canada.

1-84. It is also important to distinguish between those situations in which a non-resident is offering something for sale in Canada through an employee and those situations in which a non-resident is selling to an independent contractor who resells the item in Canada. In the former case, the non-resident person is carrying on business in Canada, while in the latter case the non-resident is not.

Dispositions Of Taxable Canadian Property By Non-Residents

1-85. ITA 2(3)(c) specifies the third situation in which non-residents are subject to Canadian taxation. This provision indicates that non-residents are subject to Canadian taxation on gains resulting from the disposition of "taxable Canadian property".

1-86. The concept of taxable Canadian property is discussed more completely in Chapter 20. However, you should note at this point that the major items included in taxable Canadian property are:

- real estate situated in Canada;
- capital property used to carry on a business in Canada;
- shares of Canadian private companies; and
- partnership interests in situations where more than 50 percent of the partnership's property is made up of taxable Canadian property.

1-87. This provision means that, if a resident of the state of Washington disposes of a vacation property that he owns in Whistler, British Columbia, any gain on that sale will be subject to Canadian taxation.

1-88. A problem here is that, because of the difficulties associated with collecting taxes from non-residents, ITA 116(5) indicates that, if there is a gain from the sale of taxable Canadian property by a non-resident, the person purchasing the property is responsible for the required taxes (see Chapter 20 for a discussion of the relevant 25 percent withholding). Exceptions to this occur if:

- the purchaser had no reason to believe that the seller of the property was a non-resident;

- the minister has issued a clearance certificate indicating that the non-resident has made arrangements for paying the taxes.

Property Income Earned By Non-Residents

1-89.   The charging provisions in ITA 2 do not cover Canadian source property income of non-residents (e. g., rents, interest, or royalties). However, this type of income is covered in Part XIII of the *Act*. While the tax rate is usually reduced for payments to non-residents in countries where Canada has a tax treaty, the general provision in Part XIII requires a flat 25 percent tax on Canadian property income paid to non-residents.

1-90.   This tax is withheld at the source of income, is based on the gross amount of such income, and no provision is made for any expenses related to acquiring the income. Since this inability to deduct expenses could result in serious inequities, there are provisions that allow a non-resident to elect to file a Canadian tax return for certain types of property income under Part I of the *Act*. These Part XIII tax provisions are discussed more thoroughly in Chapter 20 which deals with international taxation.

Exercise One - 5

Subject: Non-Resident Liability For Tax

Ms. Laurie Lacombe, a U.S. citizen, has Canadian employment income of $22,000. She lives in Blaine, Washington and is a resident of the United States for the entire year. Ms. Lacombe does not believe that she is subject to taxation in Canada. Is she correct? Explain your conclusion.

End of Exercise. Solution available in Study Guide.

Alternative Concepts Of Income

The Economist's View

1-91.   In the past, economists have viewed income as being limited to rents, profits, and wages. In general, capital gains, gratuitous receipts, and other such increases in net worth were not included. In this context, most economists perceived income to be a net concept. That is, income is equal to revenues, less any related expenses.

1-92.   In more recent times, the economist's concept of income has moved in the direction of including measures of net worth or capital maintenance. The oft cited quotation "Income is the amount that can be spent during the period and still be as well off at the end of the period as at the beginning." is perhaps as good a description of the current concept as any available.

1-93.   This broader concept of income is based on the idea that income should include all increases in net economic power that occur during the relevant measurement period.

The Accountant's View

1-94.   What we currently view as Net Income from an accounting point of view is the result of applying a fairly flexible group of rules that are referred to as generally accepted accounting principles (GAAP). In general, Net Income is determined by establishing the amount of revenue on the basis of point of sale revenue recognition. Then, by using a variety of cash flows, accruals, and allocations, the cost of assets used up in producing these revenues is matched against these revenues, with this total deducted to produce the accounting Net Income for the period.

1-95.   If this same process is viewed from the perspective of the Balance Sheet, Net Income is measured as the increase in net assets for the period under consideration, plus any distributions that were made to the owners of the business during that period.

1-96.   The current accounting model generally values assets at historical cost and records changes in value only when supported by an arm's length transaction. This means that many of the increases in wealth that would be included in the economist's concept of income would not be included in accounting Net Income.

1-97.   However, the gap between the two approaches is gradually being narrowed as accounting standard setters show an increased willingness to incorporate fair value measurement into their pronouncements, both with respect to Balance Sheet values and with respect to inclusions in Net Income.

The Income Tax Act View

1-98.   As was the case with the determination of accounting income, the *Income Tax Act* uses a complex set of rules to arrive at a figure that we will refer to as Net Income For Tax Purposes. While tax references often refer to this figure simply as Net Income, we will use the lengthier designation in order to distinguish this figure from accounting Net Income.

1-99.   Net Income For Tax Purposes is made up of several different types of income and, in addition, these different types of income must be combined using what tax practitioners refer to as an ordering rule. While the detailed computation of Net Income For Tax Purposes will occupy us through most of the first half of this text, we will provide a general discussion of its various components, as well as the ordering rule for combining these components, in the next section of this Chapter.

Net Income For Tax Purposes

Structure

1-100.   The procedures for determining Net Income For Tax Purposes are specified in Division B of the *Income Tax Act*. In fact, this figure is sometimes referred to in tax literature as Division B Income. Once Net Income For Tax Purposes has been established, the items specified in Division C of the *Income Tax Act* are subtracted to determine Taxable Income. This Taxable Income figure provides the basis for calculating the federal income tax that is payable by individuals, corporations, and trusts that are resident in Canada.

1-101.   Net Income For Tax Purposes is made up of four types of income, each of which requires a net separate calculation. Each net calculation is based on a group of inclusions and deductions that are specific to that type of income. For example, net employment income is made up of inclusions for items such as wages or salaries received, along with deductions for items such as union dues and the costs of required travel. Note that if an individual had business income deductions in excess of business income inclusions, this excess could not be applied in the calculation of net employment income.

1-102.   In addition to the net calculations required for the four types of income, Net Income For Tax Purposes includes a group of other inclusions that do not fit in the four basic income categories, as well as a group of other deductions that are not related to the major categories of income.

Components

1-103.   The four types of income that are included as components of Net Income For Tax Purposes can be described as follows:

> **Net Employment Income (Loss)**   Net employment income is made up of inclusions related to the activities of individuals who are serving as employees, less deductions related to that activity. These inclusions and deductions are specified in Division B, subdivision a, of the *Income Tax Act*. While it is possible to have a negative amount (employment loss), this would be fairly unusual. Note that, unlike the situation with other types of income, only individuals can earn employment income.

Net Business Income (Loss)   Net business income is made up of inclusions related to carrying on a business, less deductions related to that activity. These inclusions and deductions are specified in Division B, subdivision b, of the *Income Tax Act*. Business income can be earned by individuals, corporations, and trusts.

Net Property Income (Loss)   Net property income is made up of inclusions related to the holding of property, less deductions related to holding such property. Examples of property income would include interest received on debt securities, dividends received on equity securities, and lease payments received on rental property. As was the case with net business income, inclusions and deductions related to property income are covered in Division B, subdivision b, of the *Income Tax Act*. While there are some differences in the rules for determining property income and those for determining business income, the calculations are sufficiently similar that they are included in a single subdivision. As was the case with business income, property income can be earned by individuals, corporations, and trusts.

Capital Gains and Capital Losses   Capital gains and losses arise when an asset that has been used to produce business or property income is sold. The inclusions and deductions related to this type of income are specified in Division B, subdivision c, of the *Income Tax Act*. As was the case with business and property income, capital gains and losses can arise on dispositions by individuals, corporations, and trusts.

As you are probably aware, in Canada only one-half of capital gains are taxed and only one-half of capital losses are deductible. This has created the need for the use of special terminology. More specifically:

- When referring to the taxable one-half of a capital gain, the term **Taxable Capital Gain** will be used. When the term capital gain is used, it is a reference to 100 percent of the gain.

- When referring to the deductible one-half of a capital loss, the term **Allowable Capital Loss** will be used. When the term capital loss is used, it is a reference to 100 percent of the loss.

Unlike employment, business, and property losses, a net allowable capital loss (allowable capital losses in excess of taxable capital gains) cannot be deducted against any other type of income. This will be explained in more detail in the next section.

1-104.   The remaining two components of Net Income For Tax Purposes can be described as follows:

Other Sources Of Income   There are some additional sources of income that do not fit into any of the basic categories of income. These inclusions, which are largely applicable to individual taxpayers, are specified in Division B, subdivision d, of the *Income Tax Act*. Examples of these subdivision d inclusions would be pension income received, spousal support received, and social assistance payments received.

Other Deductions From Income   Similar to the situation with inclusions, there are some deductions that do not relate to any of the basic income categories. These deductions, which are again largely related to individuals, are specified in Division B, subdivision e of the *Income Tax Act*. Examples of these subdivision e deductions include spousal support paid, moving expenses, and RRSP contributions.

1-105.   As a final point here, we would note that, if an amount received does not fall into one of these categories, it is not part of Net Income For Tax Purposes and, in general, it would not be subject to federal income tax. Examples of this would include lottery winnings, amounts inherited, and gambling profits. An "exception" to gambling profits being non-taxable could arise if the CRA concluded that an individual's gambling activities were so extensive that the individual was carrying on a gambling business.

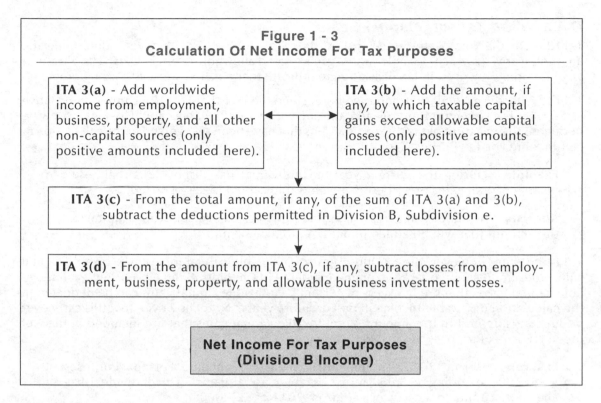

Figure 1 - 3
Calculation Of Net Income For Tax Purposes

> **ITA 3(a)** - Add worldwide income from employment, business, property, and all other non-capital sources (only positive amounts included here).

> **ITA 3(b)** - Add the amount, if any, by which taxable capital gains exceed allowable capital losses (only positive amounts included here).

> **ITA 3(c)** - From the total amount, if any, of the sum of ITA 3(a) and 3(b), subtract the deductions permitted in Division B, Subdivision e.

> **ITA 3(d)** - From the amount from ITA 3(c), if any, subtract losses from employment, business, property, and allowable business investment losses.

> **Net Income For Tax Purposes**
> **(Division B Income)**

Combining The Components - ITA Section 3

Ordering Rules

1-106.   In the previous section we noted that four types of income are included in Net Income For Tax Purposes, along with two other components which deal with miscellaneous inclusions and miscellaneous deductions. While it would be possible to simply add up these figures, this is not the approach that is required by the *Income Tax Act*. Section 3 of the *Income Tax Act* requires that these various components be combined in a very specific manner.

1-107.   This type of Section is referred to in tax work as an ordering rule and, while we will encounter several other such rules in the course of this text, we are concerned here with Section 3 which is the ordering rule for combining the various components of Net Income For Tax Purposes.

1-108.   While some of the ideas involved in applying this formula will not be fully explained until later in the text, it is useful at this stage to provide the basic structure of this formula in order to enhance your understanding of how the material on the individual components of Net Income For Tax Purposes is organized.

1-109.   The Section 3 rules are made up of four basic paragraphs, ITA 3(a), 3(b), 3(c), and 3(d). A discussion of each of these paragraphs follows. In addition, the ITA 3 rules are presented graphically in Figure 1-3.

ITA 3(a) Sources Of Income

1-110.   The ordering process begins in ITA 3(a) with the addition of all **positive** sources of income other than taxable capital gains. This includes positive amounts of employment income, business income, property income, and other miscellaneous inclusions from Subdivision d of Division B.

1-111.   Note that, while the individual components of this total are net amounts (e.g., employment income is made up of inclusions, net of deductions), the total is not a net calculation. For example, a business loss would not be deducted against a positive employment income under ITA 3(a). Rather, such losses would be deducted at a later point in the calculation of Net Income For Tax Purposes.

ITA 3(b) Net Taxable Capital Gains

1-112.   To the total determined in ITA 3(a), ITA 3(b) requires that you "determine the amount, if any, by which" taxable capital gains exceed allowable capital losses. The phrase "if any" is commonly used in tax legislation to indicate that negative amounts are ignored.

1-113.   It is of particular importance here, since the fact that ITA 3(b) cannot be negative establishes the very important rule that the current year's allowable capital losses can only be deducted to the extent of taxable capital gains that have been recognized in the calculation of Net Income For Tax Purposes for the current year.

> **Example**   During the current year, an individual has dispositions that result in taxable capital gains of $12,000 and allowable capital losses of $15,000.

> **Analysis**   As there is no excess of taxable capital gains over allowable capital losses, the amount that will be added under ITA 3(b) will be nil.

1-114.   Note, however, the $3,000 excess of allowable capital losses over taxable capital gains does not disappear. As is explained in detail in Chapters 4 and 11, current year allowable capital losses that are in excess of current year taxable capital gains can be deducted in the calculation of Taxable Income in past or future years. Note, however, that this carry over deduction is limited to the amount of net taxable capital gains that are included in the Net Income For Tax Purposes of the carry over year.

> **Example**   During 2012, an individual has a Net Income For Tax Purposes of $100,000, including $15,000 in net taxable capital gains. This individual has an allowable capital loss carry forward from 2011 of $25,000.

> **Analysis**   While the $100,000 Net Income For Tax Purposes is much larger than the available loss carry forward, the deduction in the determination of Taxable Income is limited to $15,000, the amount of the 2012 net taxable capital gains. The resulting Taxable Income will be $85,000 ($100,000 - $15,000).

1-115.   Unused allowable capital losses can be carried back to any of the preceding three taxation years. This will result in an amended Tax Payable for that year and a claim for a refund. If there are not sufficient taxable capital gains in the three preceding years to absorb the unused losses, they can then be carried forward to any subsequent taxation year. In a subsequent year, they will be deducted in the calculation of that year's taxable income, which will reduce the taxes that will have to be paid in that year.

ITA 3(c) Subdivision e Deductions

1-116.   The ITA 3(c) component of the calculation starts with the amount, if any, of the total from ITA 3(a) and ITA 3(b). Here again, the phrase "if any" indicates that only positive amounts will be used. If the total from ITA 3(a) and ITA 3(b) is nil, Net Income For Tax Purposes is nil and the calculation is complete.

1-117.   Alternatively, if the total is positive, it is reduced by any Division B, Subdivision e deductions that are available. These deductions will be covered in detail in Chapters 9 and 10. Common examples of such deductions include spousal support paid, moving expenses, child care costs, and RRSP contributions.

1-118.   Note the importance of order here. ITA 3(c) requires that subdivision e amounts be deducted prior to business and property losses. This is important because subdivision e deductions are, in many cases, only deductible in the year to which they relate (e.g., if you cannot deduct spousal support in the current year, you cannot deduct it in a past or future year). In contrast, if you cannot use a business or property loss in the current year, it can be carried over to a past year or a future year.

ITA 3(d) Losses

1-119.   The ITA 3(d) component of the calculation begins with the amount, if any, carried forward from ITA 3(c). As we have noted, if this amount is nil, Net Income For Tax Purposes is nil and the calculation is complete.

1-120.   If the ITA 3(c) amount is positive, the taxpayer can deduct any current year losses other than allowable capital losses. This would include the deduction of any current year business losses, property losses, employment losses, and allowable business investment losses (allowable business investment losses are a special type of allowable capital loss that can be deducted against any type of income). Current period farm losses are also deductible here, subject to certain restrictions that are described in Chapter 6 (see the section on Income For Farmers).

Loss Carry Overs

1-121.   As we have noted, allowable capital losses that arise in the current year can only be deducted to the extent of taxable capital gains. Also as noted, other types of losses that arise in the current year can only be deducted to the extent that there is a positive total of other types of income and deductions after ITA 3(c). We have also mentioned the fact that these losses do not disappear — they can be carried back to claim a refund of taxes paid or forward to reduce future taxes payable.

1-122.   Regardless of the type of loss, the carry back period is limited to the preceding 3 years. For example, a 2012 business loss can be deducted against amounts of Taxable Income that were recorded in 2009, 2010, or 2011.

1-123.   In contrast, the limit on the carry forward period varies with the type of loss. In somewhat simplified form the rules are as follows:

Carry Forward Of Allowable Capital Losses   Unused allowable capital losses can be carried forward and applied in the determination of Taxable Income in any future taxation year, but may only be deducted to the extent of the net taxable capital gains in those other years.

Carry Forward Of Other Types Of Losses   Employment, business, and property losses that cannot be used in the year in which they arise, can be carried forward and deducted in the determination of Taxable Income in any of the next 20 years. With the exception of certain types of farm losses (a type of business loss), the carry forward amounts can be applied against any type of income.

1-124.   The detailed rules for this carry forward process are fairly complex, involving a number of rules that are not described in this brief summary. These rules are given detailed consideration in Chapter 11.

Net Income For Tax Purposes - Example

1-125.   The following example provides an illustration of how the ITA 3 rules are applied.

Example Jonathan Morley has the following income and loss components for the year:

Employment Income	$17,000
Business Loss (From Restaurant)	(21,000)
Property Income	9,000
Taxable Capital Gains	14,000
Allowable Capital Losses	(19,000)
Subdivision e Deductions (Spousal Support Paid)	(9,000)

Analysis Mr. Morley's Net Income For Tax Purposes would be calculated as follows:

Income Under ITA 3(a):		
Employment Income	$17,000	
Business Loss (See ITA 3(d) below)	Nil	
Property Income	9,000	$26,000
Income Under ITA 3(b):		
Taxable Capital Gains	$14,000	
Allowable Capital Losses	(19,000)	Nil
Balance From ITA 3(a) And (b)		$26,000
Subdivision e Deductions		(9,000)
Balance Under ITA 3(c)		$17,000
Deduction Under ITA 3(d):		
Business Loss		(21,000)
Net Income For Tax Purposes (Division B Income)		**Nil**

1-126.   Mr. Morley's Business Loss exceeds the amount calculated under ITA 3(c), resulting in a Net Income For Tax Purposes of nil. However, there would be a carry over of the unused business loss equal to $4,000 ($21,000 - $17,000), and of the unused allowable capital loss in the amount of $5,000 ($14,000 - $19,000).

Exercise One - 6

Subject: Net Income For Tax Purposes

For the current year, Mr. Norris Blanton has net employment income of $42,000, a business loss of $15,000, taxable capital gains of $24,000, and Subdivision e deductions of $13,000. What is the amount of Mr. Blanton's Net Income For Tax Purposes for the current year?

Exercise One - 7

Subject: Net Income For Tax Purposes

For the current year, Ms. Cheryl Stodard has interest income of $33,240, taxable capital gains of $24,750, allowable capital losses of $19,500, and a net rental loss of $48,970. What is the amount of Ms. Stodard's Net Income For Tax Purposes for the current year? Indicate the amount and type of any loss carry overs that would be available at the end of the current year.

Exercise One - 8

Subject: Net Income For Tax Purposes

For the current year, Mrs. Marie Bergeron has net employment income of $42,680, taxable capital gains of $27,400, allowable capital losses of $33,280, Subdivision e deductions of $8,460, and a business loss of $26,326. What is the amount of Mrs. Bergeron's Net Income For Tax Purposes for the current year? Indicate the amount and type of any loss carry overs that would be available at the end of the current year.

End of Exercises. Solutions available in Study Guide.

Net Income To Taxable Income

1-127.   Once we have determined the amount of Net Income For Tax Purposes, it must then be converted into Taxable Income by deducting the items specified in Division C of the *Income Tax Act*. This is, in fact, a fairly complex process that will be covered in detail in Chapters 4 and 11.

1-128.   While we are deferring detailed coverage of this subject, it is useful as part of this overview for you to be aware of the major items that will be involved in the conversion of Net Income For Tax Purposes to Taxable Income. They are as follows:

- Losses carried over from other years.
- Social assistance and worker's compensation payments that have been included in Net Income For Tax Purposes.
- A deduction related to amounts of employment income resulting from the exercise or sale of stock options.
- A deduction related to the employment income benefit that can result from an employer-provided home relocation loan.
- A deduction related to capital gains on qualified property (the lifetime capital gains deduction).
- A deduction related to the costs of living in certain areas of the Canadian north.

Principles Of Tax Planning

Introduction

1-129.   Throughout this text, there will be a great deal of emphasis on tax planning and, while many of the specific techniques that are involved can only be fully explained after the more detailed provisions of tax legislation have been covered, there are some basic tax planning principles that can be described at this point.

1-130.   Our objective here is simply to provide a general understanding of the results that can be achieved through tax planning so that you will be able to recognize the goal of more specific tax planning techniques when they are examined. In addition, this general understanding should enable you to identify other opportunities for tax planning as you become more familiar with this material.

1-131.   The basic goals of tax planning can be summarized as follows:

- Tax avoidance or reduction.
- Tax deferral.
- Income splitting.

1-132.   While these classifications can be used to describe the goals of all tax planning arrangements, such arrangements seldom involve a clear cut attempt to achieve only one of these goals. For example, the principal reason for making contributions to a Registered Retirement Savings Plan is to defer taxes until later taxation years. However, such a deferral can result in the taxpayer avoiding some amount of taxes if he is taxed at a lower rate in those later years.

Tax Avoidance Or Reduction

1-133.   The most desirable result of tax planning is to permanently avoid the payment of some amount of tax. This very desirability is probably the most important explanation for the scarcity of such arrangements and, while the number of possibilities in this area is limited, they do exist.

1-134.   An outstanding example of tax avoidance is the capital gains deduction that is available on the disposition of qualified farming or fishing property, and qualified small business corporation shares. The first $750,000 of capital gains on such dispositions can be received by the taxpayer on a tax free basis. For individuals in a position to enjoy the benefits of this provision, it is one of the best tax avoidance mechanisms available (see Chapter 11 for a detailed discussion of this provision).

1-135.   Other forms of complete tax avoidance can be found in the employee benefits area, in that some types of benefits can be given to employees without being considered taxable. These would include an employer's contributions to disability and private health care insurance, and the provision of discounts to employees on products or services normally sold by the employer (see Chapter 3).

1-136.   Additional opportunities in this area require more complex arrangements. Such arrangements involve the use of trusts and private corporations and cannot be described in a meaningful manner at this stage of the material.

Tax Deferral

1-137.   The basic concept behind tax planning arrangements involving the deferral of tax payments is the very simple idea that it is better to pay taxes later rather than sooner. This is related to the time value of money and also involves the possibility that some permanent avoidance of taxes may result from the taxpayer being taxed at a lower marginal income tax rate at the time the deferred amounts are brought into taxable income.

1-138.   Such deferral arrangements may involve either the delayed recognition of certain types of income or, alternatively, accelerated recognition of deductions. As an example of delayed recognition of income, an employer can provide a benefit to an employee in the form of contributions to a registered pension plan. Such benefits will not be taxed in the year in which they are earned. Rather, they will be taxed at a later point in time when the employee begins to receive benefits from the registered pension plan.

1-139.   As an example of expense acceleration, the ownership of a rental property may allow the owner to deduct its capital cost at a rate that is usually in excess of any decline in the physical condition or economic worth of the building. While this excess deduction will normally be added back to the taxpayer's income when the building is sold, the payment of taxes on some part of the rental income from the property has been deferred.

1-140.   Deferral arrangements are available in a number of different situations and currently represent one of the more prevalent forms of tax planning.

Income Splitting

General Idea

1-141.   Progressive rates are built into Canadian federal income tax legislation. This means that the taxes payable on a given amount of taxable income will be greater if that amount accrues to one taxpayer, than would be the case if that same total amount of taxable income is split between two or more people. While not technically a form of income splitting, the same effect can be achieved by having a given sum of income allocated from an individual in a high tax bracket to an individual in a low tax bracket.

1-142.   This does not mean that it would be advantageous to give part of your income away to perfect strangers. What it does mean is that, within a family or other related group, it is desirable to have the group's aggregate taxable income allocated as evenly as possible among the members of the group.

Example

1-143.   The tax savings that can be achieved through income splitting are among the most dramatic examples of the effectiveness of tax planning. For example, if Mr. Jordan had taxable income of $529,624 (this is four times $132,406, the bottom threshold of the highest federal tax bracket in 2012 of 29 percent), his basic federal tax payable in 2012 would be $143,213 (this simplified calculation does not take into consideration the various tax credits that would be available to Mr. Jordan).

1-144.   Alternatively, if Mr. Jordan was married and the $529,624 could be split on the basis of $264,812 to him and $264,812 to his wife, the federal taxes payable would total $132,836 [(2)($66,418)], a savings of $10,377 ($143,213 - $132,836).

1-145.　If we carry this one step further and assume that Mr. Jordan is married and has two children, and that the $529,624 in taxable income can be allocated on the basis of $132,406 to each individual, the total federal taxes payable will be reduced to $112,080 [(4)($28,020)]. This represents a savings at the federal level of $31,133 ($143,213 - $112,080) when compared to the amount of taxes that would have been paid if Mr. Jordan had been taxed on the entire $529,624.

1-146.　When we add provincial effects, the potential savings could be in excess of $50,000, a substantial reduction on income of $529,624. Making this savings even more impressive is the fact that it is not a one shot phenomena but, rather, a savings that could occur in each year that the income splitting plan is in effect.

Problems With Income Splitting

1-147.　While income splitting can be one of the most powerful planning tools available to taxpayers, there are several problems associated with implementing such schemes:

- There are only a limited number of simple approaches to implementation. Most of the really effective income splitting arrangements are complex and expensive to implement, limiting their use largely to wealthy individuals.

- Splitting income with children often involves losing control over assets, a process that is emotionally difficult for some individuals.

- Splitting income involves decisions as to which individual family members are the most worthy of receiving benefits.

- The effect of the "kiddie tax", a high rate tax assessed on certain types of income received by minors, has made income splitting much more difficult. This tax is described in detail in Chapter 11.

1-148.　We would note, however, that the introduction of pension income splitting (see Chapter 9) has made income splitting available to a much broader group of Canadians.

Exercise One - 9

Subject:　Tax Planning

Mr. Stephen Chung, a successful flamenco dancer, has decided to make contributions to an RRSP in the name of his spouse, the mother of his twelve children, rather than making contributions to his own plan. What type of tax planning is involved in this decision? Explain your conclusion.

Exercise One - 10

Subject:　Tax Planning

Mr. Green's employer pays all of the premiums on a private dental plan that covers Mr. Green and his family. What type of tax planning is illustrated by this employee benefit? Explain your conclusion.

End of Exercises.　Solutions available in Study Guide.

Abbreviations To Be Used

1-149.　In our writing, we try to avoid using abbreviations because we believe that there is a tendency in accounting and tax writing to use so many of them that the material can become unreadable. However, in the tax area, some sources are so commonly cited that it is clearly inefficient to continue using their full description. As a result, in the remainder of this text, we will use the following abbreviations on a regular basis:

- **CRA** - Canada Revenue Agency
- **ITA** - Federal *Income Tax Act*
- **IT** - Interpretation Bulletins
- **GST** - Goods and Services Tax
- **HST** - Harmonized Sales Tax
- **GAAP** - Generally Accepted Accounting Principles
- **CCA** - Capital Cost Allowance (see Chapter 5)
- **UCC** - Undepreciated Capital Cost (see Chapter 5)

Key Terms Used In This Chapter

1-150.   The following is a list of the key terms used in this Chapter. These terms, and their meanings, are compiled in the Glossary Of Key Terms located at the back of the separate paper Study Guide.

Advance Tax Ruling	Interpretation Bulletins
Allowable Capital Loss	Net Income For Tax Purposes
Business Income	Ordering Rule
Capital Asset	Person
Capital Gain/Loss	Progressive Tax System
Capital Tax	Property Income
Consumption Tax	Property Tax
Customs Duties	Qualitative Characteristics
Division B Income	Regressive Tax System
Employment Income	Resident
Fiscal Period	Tariffs
Flat Tax System	Tax Base
Goods And Services Tax	Tax Deferral
GST	Tax Expenditure
Harmonized Sales Tax	Tax Incidence
Head Tax	Tax Planning
Income	Taxable Canadian Property
Income Splitting	Taxable Capital Gain
Income Tax	Taxable Entity
Income Tax Application Rules	Taxable Income
Income Tax Regulations	Taxation Year
Income Tax Technical News	Transfer Tax
Information Circulars	Value Added Tax

References

1-151.   For more detailed study of the material in this Chapter, we would refer you to the following:

ITA 2(1)	Tax Payable By Persons Resident In Canada
ITA 3	Income For Taxation Year
ITA 248(1)	Definitions (Taxable Canadian Property)
ITA 249	Definition Of "Taxation Year"

Problems For Self Study

(The solutions for these problems can be found in the separate Study Guide.)

Self Study Problem One - 1 (Regressive Taxation)

A regressive tax can be described as one which is assessed at a lower rate as income levels increase. Despite the fact that the Harmonized Sales Tax (HST) is based on a single rate, it is referred to as a regressive form of taxation.

Required: Explain how a tax system with a single rate can be viewed as regressive.

Self Study Problem One - 2 (Flat Rate Tax)

At a recent cocktail party, Mr. Right was heard complaining vehemently about the lack of progress towards tax simplification. He was tired of spending half of his time filling out various CRA forms and, if the matter were left to him, he could solve the problem in 10 minutes. "It is simply a matter of having one tax rate and applying that rate to 100 percent of income."

Required: Discuss Mr. Right's proposed flat rate tax system.

Self Study Problem One - 3 (Qualitative Characteristics)

With the growing importance of free trade and e-commerce, Canada is contemplating increased harmonization of the Canadian tax system with other major tax regimes in the world. Harmonization with the United States is the first priority, with harmonization with other major economic groups being secondary. Assume the following changes are proposed:

A. Taxing all e-commerce transactions based on where the goods and services are delivered.

B. Full deduction of mortgage interest related to principal residences, combined with taxation of capital gains arising on dispositions of these residences. Currently in Canada, the capital gains on the disposition of principal residences are not taxed and mortgage interest related to principal residences is not deductible.

C. Requiring corporations that are under common control to file a single consolidated tax return for all of the corporations in the group.

D. Conversion of the GST system into a national sales tax to be applied to the sale of goods and services at the retail level.

Required: Indicate a significant tax advantage, other than the benefits associated with international harmonization, that would result from introducing each of the proposed changes. In addition, analyze each proposed change using two of the qualitative characteristics of tax systems that are listed in your text.

Self Study Problem One - 4 (Sources Of Tax Information)

The principal source of Canadian income tax information is the *Income Tax Act*. There are, however, other sources that are of considerable significance in the application of these rules.

Required: List and briefly describe these other sources of information on Canadian income tax matters.

Self Study Problem One - 5 (Net Income For Tax Purposes)

The following two Cases make different assumptions with respect to the amounts of income and deductions of Miss Nora Bain for the current taxation year:

	Case A	Case B
Employment Income	$34,000	$18,500
Income (Loss) From Business	(36,000)	(28,200)
Income From Property	21,000	12,000
Taxable Capital Gains	42,000	9,000
Allowable Capital Losses	(57,000)	(12,000)
Subdivision e Deductions (Spousal Support)	(5,500)	(10,500)

Required   For both Cases, calculate Miss Bain's Net Income For Tax Purposes (Division B income). Indicate the amount and type of any loss carry overs that would be available at the end of the current year.

Self Study Problem One - 6 (Net Income For Tax Purposes)

The following four Cases make different assumptions with respect to the amounts of income and deductions of Mr. Knowlton Haynes for the current year:

	Case A	Case B	Case C	Case D
Employment Income	$45,000	17,000	$24,000	$18,000
Income (Loss) From Business	(20,000)	(42,000)	(48,000)	(20,000)
Income From Property	15,000	12,000	47,000	7,000
Taxable Capital Gains	25,000	22,000	22,000	13,000
Allowable Capital Losses	(10,000)	(8,000)	(73,000)	(18,000)
Subdivision e Deductions	(5,000)	(6,000)	(4,000)	(12,000)

Required   For each Case, calculate Mr. Haynes' Net Income For Tax Purposes (Division B income). Indicate the amount and type of any loss carry overs that would be available at the end of the current year.

Self Study Problem One - 7 (Net Income For Tax Purposes - Two Cases)

The following two Cases make different assumptions with respect to the amounts of income and deductions for the current year for Christophe Szabo, a Canadian resident.

Case A   Christophe has employment income of $46,700, interest income of $3,500, a net rental loss of $22,250, and a net business loss of $37,260. Dispositions of capital property during the current year had the following results:

Taxable Capital Gains	$13,470
Allowable Capital Losses	10,540

Christophe paid deductible spousal support of $500 per month. His cash position was significantly improved when he won a provincial lottery prize of $450,000 during the year.

Case B   Christophe had employment income of $75,400, interest income of $4,560, and a net rental loss of $12,200.

Dispositions of capital property during the current year had the following results:

Taxable Capital Gains	$8,725
Allowable Capital Losses	9,460

Subdivision e deductions for the current year were child care costs of $4,520, RRSP contributions of $6,570, and spousal support payments of $3,600.

Required: For both Cases, calculate Christophe's Net Income For Tax Purposes (Division B income). Indicate the amount and type of any loss carry overs that would be available at the end of the current year.

Assignment Problems

(The solutions to these problems are only available in
the solutions manual that has been provided to your instructor.)

Assignment Problem One - 1 (Application Of General Tax Principles)

Many of the provisions of the *Income Tax Act* are written in very general terms. For example, ITA 18 lists a number of general characteristics that must apply before a particular expense can be deducted in the computation of business income.

Required: Indicate the situations in which such generally worded provisions of the *Income Tax Act* will be overridden.

Assignment Problem One - 2 (Conflicting Objectives)

The tax systems of various countries are designed to meet a variety of objectives. In addition to raising revenues, we call on our tax systems to provide fairness, to have the characteristic of simplicity, to meet social or economic goals, to balance regional disparities, and to be competitive on an international basis. While it would be a fairly simple matter to design a system that would meet any single one of these objectives, we frequently encounter conflicts when we attempt to create a system that meets several of these objectives.

Required: Discuss the possible conflicts that can arise when a tax system is designed to meet more than a single objective.

Assignment Problem One - 3 (Qualitative Characteristics Of Tax Systems)

Discuss whether the following situations meet the objectives and match the characteristics of a good tax system. Identify any conflicts that exist and the probable economic incidence of the tax or tax expenditure.

A. Diamonds are South Africa's major export. Assume that a tax is levied on diamond production of Par Excellence Inc., which has a monopoly in the country. Movements of diamonds are closely monitored and accounted for.

B. Chimeree Inc. owns the largest diamond mine in Sierra Leone. A tax is levied on diamond production. Movements of diamonds are not closely controlled, and helicopters pick up shipments under the cover of darkness.

C. Gains on dispositions of principal residences are exempt from income tax in Canada.

D. A rule stipulates that only 50 percent of the cost of business meals can be deducted in calculating Canadian business income for personal and corporate Taxable Income.

E. A newly created country levies a head tax which requires every resident adult to pay an annual tax.

Assignment Problem One - 4 (Introduction Of Head Tax)

Concerned with her inability to control the deficit, the Minister of Finance has indicated that she is considering the introduction of a head tax. This would be a tax of $200 per year, assessed on every living Canadian resident who, on December 31 of each year, has a head. In order to enforce the tax, all Canadian residents would be required to have a Head Administration Tax identification number (HAT, for short) tattooed in an inconspicuous location on their scalp. A newly formed special division of the RCMP, the Head Enforcement Administration Division (HEAD, for short), would run spot checks throughout the country in order to ensure that everyone has registered and received their HAT.

The Minister is very enthusiastic about the plan, anticipating that it will produce additional revenues of $5 billion per year. It is also expected to spur economic growth through increased sales of Canadian made toques.

As the Minister's senior policy advisor, you have been asked to prepare a memorandum evaluating this proposed new head tax.

Required: Prepare the memorandum.

Assignment Problem One - 5 (Net Income And Taxable Income)

Explain the terms Net Income For Tax Purposes and Taxable Income.

Assignment Problem One - 6 (Alternative Views Of Income)

Distinguish between the accountant's, the economist's, and the *Income Tax Act* views of income.

Assignment Problem One - 7 (Net Income For Tax Purposes - Two Cases)

The following two Cases make different assumptions with respect to the amounts of income and deductions for the current year for Christina Szabo, a Canadian resident.

Case A   Christina had employment income of $46,200, as well as income from an unincorporated business of $13,500. A rental property owned by Christina experienced a net loss of $2,350. Dispositions of capital property during the current year had the following results:

Taxable Capital Gains	$14,320
Allowable Capital Losses	23,460

Christina paid deductible spousal support of $4,800 during the current year. While gambling was an unusual pastime for Christina, a recent trip to Las Vega resulted in roulette winnings of $123,000. The expenses of the trip were $8,450.

Case B   Christina had employment income of $64,000, interest income of $2,600, and net rental income of $4,560. Christina had a 50 percent interest in a partnership. During the current year the partnership had a business loss of $144,940. Dispositions of capital property during the current year had the following results:

Taxable Capital Gains	$32,420
Allowable Capital Losses	29,375

Deductible contributions of $12,480 were made to Christina's RRSP.

Required: For both Cases, calculate Christina's Net Income For Tax Purposes (Division B income). Indicate the amount and type of any loss carry overs that would be available at the end of the current year.

Assignment Problem One - 8 (Net Income For Tax Purposes)

The following four Cases make different assumptions with respect to the amounts of income and deductions of Farah DeBoo for the current year:

	Case A	Case B	Case C	Case D
Employment Income	$78,400	$23,600	$33,400	$46,200
Income (Loss) From Business	(12,300)	(4,500)	(42,300)	(22,300)
Rental Income (Loss)	8,400	16,000	3,400	(32,400)
Taxable Capital Gains	42,500	12,500	21,400	41,200
Allowable Capital Losses	(16,300)	(18,600)	(20,700)	(43,400)
Subdivision e Deductions	(8,100)	(3,200)	(12,400)	(9,300)

Required For each Case, calculate Ms. DeBoo's Net Income For Tax Purposes (Division B income). Indicate the amount and type of any loss carry overs that would be available at the end of the current year.

CHAPTER 2

Procedures And Administration

Introduction

2-1. This Chapter begins with a brief overview of the administration of the Canada Revenue Agency (CRA). This is followed by a description of filing and tax payment procedures applicable to individuals, corporations, and trusts.

2-2. This material on filing and tax payment procedures will be followed by a description of the assessment and reassessment process, including the various avenues that can be followed in appealing unfavourable assessments. Attention will also be given to issues related to tax avoidance and tax evasion, collection and enforcement procedures, and taxpayer relief provisions.

Administration Of The Department

2-3. The CRA has the responsibility for carrying out the tax policies that are enacted by Parliament. In carrying out these policies, the chief executive officer of the CRA is the Commissioner Of Revenue. The duties of the Minister of National Revenue, as well as those of the Commissioner of Revenue, are described in the *Act* as follows:

ITA 220(1) The Minister shall administer and enforce this Act and the Commissioner of Revenue may exercise all the powers and perform the duties of the Minister under this Act.

2-4. The Minister of National Revenue is responsible for the CRA and is accountable to Parliament for all of its activities, including the administration and enforcement of program legislation such as the *Income Tax Act* and the *Excise Tax Act*. The Minister has the authority to ensure that the CRA operates within the overall government framework and treats its clients with fairness, integrity, and consistency.

2-5. The CRA has a Board of Management consisting of 15 members appointed by the Governor in Council, 11 of whom have been nominated by the provinces and territories. The Board has the responsibility of overseeing the management of the CRA, including the development of the Corporate Business Plan, and the management of policies related to resources, services, property, personnel, and contracts. The Commissioner of the CRA, who is a member of the CRA Board, is responsible for the CRA's day-to-day operations.

2-6. Unlike the boards of Crown corporations, the CRA Board is not involved in all the activities of the CRA. In particular, the CRA Board has no authority in the administration and enforcement of legislation, which includes the *Income Tax Act* and the *Excise Tax Act*, for which the CRA remains fully accountable to the Minister of National Revenue. In addition, the CRA Board is denied access to confidential client information.

2-7.   Following the ministerial mandate found in ITA 220(1), ITA 221(1) provides that the Governor in Council has the power to make Income Tax Regulations for various specific purposes or for the purpose of carrying out other provisions of the *Income Tax Act*. Unlike the provisions of the *Income Tax Act*, these Regulations may be passed by Order-In-Council without ratification by Parliament. They generally become effective when they are published in the Canada Gazette.

Returns And Payments - Individuals

Requirement To File - ITA 150

2-8.   ITA 150(1) is a general rule that requires all persons (individuals, corporations, and trusts) to file a tax return. However, ITA 150(1.1)(b) exempts individuals from filing tax returns except when certain conditions are met. In a somewhat indirect manner, the combination of these two provisions means that an individual, who is a resident, must file a T1 tax return if:

- they owe taxes for the year;
- they have a taxable capital gain for the year;
- they have disposed of a capital property during the year; or
- they have an outstanding balance under the home buyers plan or lifelong learning plan legislation (see Chapter 10 for an explanation of these RRSP related balances).

2-9.   Other more specific reasons for filing a return can be found in the *Income Tax Act*. For example, spouses who choose to split pension income must file tax returns in order to implement this decision. Even when there is no requirement to file, if an individual is entitled to a refund, it will only be available if a return is filed. Further, it is beneficial for others to file, especially low income taxpayers, in order to be eligible for income-based benefits such as the child tax benefit, the GST credit and the Guaranteed Income Supplement. If they fail to file, they will not receive these amounts, even if they qualify.

2-10.   Individuals can either file a paper form or, alternatively, use an electronic filing method. The advantage of electronic filing for the taxpayer, particularly if he is entitled to a refund, is that the return will be processed more quickly. For the CRA, electronic filing eliminates the possibility of errors in the process of transferring information from paper forms to their computerized records. While supporting documents (e.g., a receipt for a charitable donation) cannot be included with an electronic filing, the CRA retains the right to request that such receipts be provided.

2-11.   Taxpayers have three alternatives for electronic filing. They can be described as follows:

EFILE   EFILE On-Line For Tax Professionals allows registered EFILE service providers to transmit returns to the CRA using the Internet. The system can be used by virtually all taxpayers, but returns must be transmitted through an electronic filer registered with the CRA.

NETFILE   This transmission service allows taxpayers to file their own personal income tax returns directly to the CRA using an approved software program and the Internet. This system can be used by almost all individuals, including those with complex returns. The only requirement is that the individual have an access code. This code is included in an individual's tax return package, or can be obtained on-line or through a request to the CRA.

TELEFILE   Under the TELEFILE system, returns are filed via a touch tone telephone. This system has information constraints that make it useful only for individuals with relatively simple returns. To use the system, an access code is required. This code is available in an individual's tax return package, or can be requested from the CRA.

2-12.   For 2011, 24,512,273 individual tax returns were filed, up from 24,365,078 in 2010. Statistics on the type of filing methods used are as follows:

Method Of Filing	2010	2011
Paper	9,132,581	8,569,627
EFILE	10,103,782	10,563,392
NETFILE	4,741,021	5,025,772
TELEFILE	387,694	353,482
Total Filings	24,365,078	24,512,273

2-13.   Continuing a long-term trend, the number of paper filings declined in 2011. While EFILE and NETFILE continue to grow, TELEFILE experienced a small decline.

Due Date For Individual Returns

General Rule

2-14.   As noted in Chapter 1, individuals must use the calendar year as their taxation year. This means that for every individual, the taxation year ends on December 31. Given this, ITA 150(1)(d)(i) indicates that, in general, individuals must file their tax return for a particular year on or before April 30 of the following year. Although the filing due date is extended to the next business day if the due date falls on a weekend, we will use April 30 (or June 15 if applicable as explained in the following material) as the due date in our examples and problems.

Individuals Who Are Partners Or Proprietors

2-15.   Recognizing that individuals who are involved in an unincorporated business may need more time to determine their income for a taxation year, the *Income Tax Act* provides a deferral of the filing deadline. If an individual, or his cohabiting spouse or common-law partner, carried on a business during the year, ITA 150(1)(d)(ii) extends the due date for filing to June 15 of the calendar year following the relevant taxation year.

2-16.   An interesting feature of this provision is that, while the return does not have to be filed until June 15, payment of all taxes owing is required by the usual date of April 30. Any amounts that are not paid by April 30 will be assessed interest at the prescribed rate until such time as the outstanding balance is paid.

Exercise Two - 1

Subject: Individual Tax Payment Date

Brandon Katarski's 2012 Net Income includes business income. When is his 2012 tax return due? By what date must his 2012 tax liability be paid in order to avoid the assessment of interest on amounts due?

End of Exercise. Solution available in Study Guide.

Deceased Taxpayers

2-17.   As discussed in Supplementary Reading No. 6, Final Returns For Deceased Taxpayers on the Student CD-ROM, there are many tax related complications that arise when an individual dies. In order to provide the deceased individual's representatives with sufficient time to deal with these complications, the *Act* indicates the following:

ITA 150(1)(b)   In the case of an individual who dies after October of the year and before the day that would be the individual's filing due date for the year if the individual had not died, (a return must be filed) by the individual's legal representatives on or before the day that is the later of the day on or before which the return would otherwise be required to be filed and the day that is 6 months after the day of death.

2-18.   For an individual whose filing due date is April 30, this provision means that if death occurs between November 1 of the previous year and April 30 of the current year, the return for the previous year does not have to be filed until six months after the date of death.

Example   A single individual who is not involved in an unincorporated business dies on March 1, 2013 without having filed a 2012 return.

Analysis   The due date for the 2012 return is September 1, 2013, six months after the individual's death.   The due date for the 2013 final return is April 30, 2014.

2-19.   The provision works somewhat differently for an individual who has a June 15 filing due date due to business income. If such an individual dies between November 1 and December 15 of a taxation year, the later of six months after the date of death and the normal filing due date, will be the normal filing date of June 15. This means that for decedents who would normally have a June 15 filing due date, the six month extension is available if they die between December 16 of a taxation year and June 15 of the following year.

Example   An individual whose wife owns an unincorporated business dies on May 2, 2013 without having filed a 2012 tax return.

Analysis   The due date for the 2012 return is November 2, 2013, six months after the individual's death. The due date for the 2013 final return is June 15, 2014.

Exercise Two - 2

Subject: Deceased Taxpayer Filing Date

Sally Cheung dies on February 15, 2013. Sally's only income for 2012 and 2013 was from investments. Her husband's Net Income for these years included income from an unincorporated business. Her representatives must file her 2012 and 2013 tax returns by what dates?   Explain your answer.

End of Exercise. Solution available in Study Guide.

Withholdings - ITA 153
Salaries And Wages
2-20.   A large portion of the income taxes paid by individuals employed in Canada is collected through source deductions. Under ITA 153, any individual who earns employment income will have the estimated taxes on this income withheld from gross pay through payroll deductions made by their employer. The tax withheld is related to the amount of the individual's income, with the required withholdings intended to cover the tax payable on this income. However, it would be unusual for such withholding to be exactly equal to the taxes payable for the year. As a consequence, most individuals will either owe taxes and be required to file a tax return or, alternatively, be entitled to a refund that can only be obtained by filing a tax return.

2-21.   The amount withheld by an employer is based on a form that is filled out by each employee, Form TD1, "Personal Tax Credits Return". This form lists personal and other credits that are available to an individual and asks the employee to indicate which of these he will be claiming.

2-22.   Also on Form TD1, an individual can ask to have the amount withheld increased beyond the required amount. An individual might choose to do this if his employment income withholding is based on rates in a low tax rate province, but his residence is in a high tax rate province (e.g., an individual who works in Alberta, but lives in Saskatchewan). Another example where additional withholding might be useful could be an individual with large amounts of investment income that are not subject to withholding. In either of these cases, requesting additional withholding would allow the individual to avoid a large tax liability when his tax return is filed, or being required to pay instalments.

2-23.   A different type of problem can arise when an employed individual who is subject to source deductions has significant losses or other deductions that can be used to offset employment income.

> **Example** Monica Kinney has 2012 employment income of $85,414. She lives in Alberta where a 10 percent provincial tax rate is applied to all taxable income. Her employer would normally withhold based on the assumption that she will owe income taxes totalling $24,343 ($15,802 federal, plus $8,541 provincial, ignoring all tax credits). However, if Ms. Kinney has annual deductible spousal support payments of $20,000, her income will be reduced to $65,414 and her actual 2012 federal and provincial taxes payable will only be $17,943 ($11,402 + $6,541). As will be explained later, the government will not pay interest on the extra $6,400 in taxes withheld.

2-24.   Under ITA 153(1.1), Monica can request a reduction in the amount of source deductions withheld by her employer. As long as the losses or deductions can be documented in a reasonable fashion and they are expected to recur, the CRA will normally authorize the employer to reduce the amounts withheld from the employee's remuneration. Form T1213, "Request To Reduce Tax Deductions At Source" is used to make this request.

Other Payers

2-25.   In addition to requiring employers to withhold specified amounts from the salaries and wages of employees, ITA 153 contains a fairly long list of other types of payments from which the payer must withhold prescribed amounts. These include:

- retiring allowances
- death benefits
- payments from Registered Retirement Savings Plans
- payments from Registered Education Savings Plans
- distributions under retirement compensation arrangements

2-26.   In addition to payments listed in ITA 153, withholding is required on certain payments to non-residents. While the general rate of tax on the Canadian source income of non-residents is established in ITA 212 as 25 percent, the amount that will actually be withheld is usually modified by international tax treaties. For a more complete discussion of this type of withholding, see Chapter 20, International Issues In Taxation.

Instalment Payments For Individuals - ITA 156

Basis For Requiring Instalments

2-27.   As discussed in the previous section, amounts to be applied to future tax liabilities must be withheld by the payer from certain types of income. Such income includes employment income, as well as other less common sources.

2-28.   For many individuals, particularly those earning employment income, the withholding of taxes constitutes the major form of tax payment in any taxation year. However, in situations where an individual has large amounts of income that are not subject to withholding (e.g., self-employment income or investment income), quarterly instalment payments may have to be made towards the current year's tax liability.

2-29.   In the *Income Tax Act*, the requirement for paying instalments is stated in terms of when instalments are not required. Specifically, no instalments are required if:

> **ITA 156.1(2)(b)** The individual's net tax owing for the particular year, or for each of the 2 preceding taxation years, does not exceed the individual's instalment threshold for that year.

2-30.   In provinces other than Quebec, "net tax owing" is the amount, if any, by which the total federal and provincial tax owing for a particular year, exceeds all tax withheld for that year. An "individual's instalment threshold" is defined in ITA 156.1(1) as $3,000. In Quebec, net tax owing only includes federal taxes and the instalment threshold is $1,800.

2-31.   While the legislation is based on when instalments are not required, it is usually more useful to give guidance in terms of when instalments are required. As stated on the CRA web site:

> You have to pay your income tax by instalments for 2012 if your **net tax owing** is more than $3,000:
>
> * in 2012; and
> * in **either** 2011 **or** 2010.

Due Dates For Individuals

2-32.   For individuals required to pay instalments, the quarterly payments are due on March 15, June 15, September 15, and December 15.

Determining Amounts Of Instalments

2-33.   In simple terms, the required instalments will be based on the net tax owing for the current year, the preceding year, or a combination of the first and second preceding years. The *Canada Pension Plan Act* and the *Employment Insurance Act* provide for instalments identical to that of the *Income Tax Act*.   Since the CRA administers the Canada Pension Plan (CPP) and Employment Insurance (EI), where an individual has CPP contributions and/or EI premiums payable on self-employed income (see Chapter 3), the instalments are based on the total of net tax owing and any CPP contributions and EI premiums payable.

2-34.   In determining the amount to be paid as instalments, individuals have a choice of three alternatives for calculating the required quarterly instalments. These alternatives are as follows:

> **Alternative 1**   One-quarter of the estimated net tax owing (note this is not the equivalent of Tax Payable) for the current taxation year [ITA 156(1)(a)(i)].
>
> **Alternative 2**   One-quarter of the net tax owing for the immediately preceding taxation year [ITA 156(1)(a)(ii)].
>
> **Alternative 3**   The first two instalments (March 15 and June 15) based on one-quarter of the net tax owing for the second preceding taxation year.   The remaining two instalments (September 15 and December 15) equal the excess of the net tax owing for the preceding year over one-half of the net tax owing for the second preceding year [ITA 156(1)(b)], divided by two. Note that one-half of the net tax owing for the second preceding year is the amount that should have been paid in the first two instalments under this approach.
>
> In effect, in almost all situations, Alternative 3 requires the same total instalments as Alternative 2. However, if the net tax owing in the second preceding year is less than the net tax owing in the preceding year, there is some amount of tax deferral.

2-35.   The individual taxpayer can select the most advantageous of these alternatives. The basic rules for this selection are as follows:

* If the net tax owing is lowest in the current year, Alternative 1 will be selected.
* If the net tax owing is lowest in the preceding year, Alternative 2 will be selected.
* If the net tax owing is lowest in the second preceding year, Alternative 3 will be selected. While the total amount of the instalments will be the same as in Alternative 2, their present value will be less because of the reduced amount for the first two payments.

CRA's Instalment Reminder

2-36.   It is likely that the majority of individual taxpayers are not capable of calculating their required instalments. To assist such individuals, the CRA sends out quarterly Instalment Reminders. Taxpayers are assured that, if they pay the amounts specified in these reminders on the required dates, no interest will be assessed for late instalments.

2-37.   The amounts specified in these Instalment Reminders are based on Alternative 3. The reason that the CRA has adopted this approach is based on information availability:

Alternative 1   The CRA would not know the current year's Tax Payable until April 30 or June 15 of the following year. This would be too late for advising a taxpayer as to any of the current year's instalments under this approach.

Alternative 2   The CRA would not know the previous year's Tax Payable until April 30 or June 15 of the current year. This would too late for advising a taxpayer as to the first required instalment for the current year and, in the case of June 15 filers, too late to provide information on the second required instalment for the current year.

2-38.   Given this situation, Alternative 3 is the only approach that could be used by the CRA to provide taxpayers with instalment information that would unequivocally avoid any assessment of interest.

2-39.   While using the amounts specified in the Instalment Reminder is a risk free solution to remitting instalments, it may not be the best answer for an individual taxpayer.

Example   Ali Kern, a self-employed entrepreneur, had Taxable Income in both 2010 and 2011 that was in excess of $200,000. Unfortunately, in 2012 his business experienced significant losses, resulting in a Taxable Income of nil.

Analysis   The CRA's instalment reminder would base its calculations on the high levels of income that accrued during 2010 and 2011. Paying these amounts would be a very poor choice as it would, in essence, constitute an interest free loan to the government. Ali's best solution would be to make no instalments based on his current year net tax owing of nil.

2-40.   However, if an individual does not follow the advice given in the CRA's instalment reminder, the taxpayer is basing some or all of his payments on estimates. If his estimates are too low, he will be assessed interest.

Example Of Instalments For Individuals

2-41.   A simple example will serve to illustrate the alternative approaches to calculating instalments.

Example Mr. Hruba is not subject to any withholding and has the following amounts of net tax owing:

2010	$20,000
2011	32,000
2012 (Estimated)	24,000

Analysis The use of alternative 1 based on the 2012 estimate of $24,000 would result in quarterly instalments of $6,000 ($24,000 ÷ 4). The total instalments would be $24,000.

Alternative 2, based on the 2011 figure of $32,000 is the worst alternative. The quarterly instalments would be $8,000 ($32,000 ÷ 4), totaling $32,000 for the year.

Under alternative 3 (used in the CRA's Instalment Reminders), instalments 1 and 2 would each be $5,000 ($20,000 ÷ 4). However, instalments 3 and 4 would each be $11,000 [($32,000 - $10,000) ÷ 2], resulting in a total of $32,000.

This analysis would suggest that alternative 1 provides the best solution. While the first two payments under alternative 3 are somewhat lower ($5,000 vs. $6,000), the total amount under alternative 1 is significantly lower ($24,000 vs. $32,000).

2-42.   The CRA will calculate interest based on each instalment that should have been paid using the payment option that requires the least amount of interest to a specific date. The CRA will then calculate interest based on the instalments that were paid. If the former amount exceeds the latter, the individual will be assessed interest on the difference, provided the amount involved exceeds $25. Note that contra interest as explained in Paragraph 2-45 could also be relevant in calculating the applicable interest.

Exercise Two - 3

Subject: Individual Instalments

Marlene Carter, a resident of Ontario, had net tax owing for 2010 of $3,500, net tax owing for 2011 of $4,000, and expects to have net tax owing for 2012 of $1,500. Is she required to make instalment payments for 2012? If so, what would be the minimum quarterly payment?

Exercise Two - 4

Subject: Individual Instalments

John Lee, a resident of Newfoundland, had net tax owing for 2010 of $3,500, net tax owing for 2011 of $1,500, and expects to have net tax owing for 2012 of $4,500. Is he required to make instalment payments for 2012? If so, what would be the minimum quarterly payment?

Exercise Two - 5

Subject: Individual Instalments

Nigel Farnsworth had net tax owing for 2010 of $25,000, net tax owing for 2011 of $37,000, and expects to have net tax owing for 2012 of $32,000. What would be his minimum instalments for 2012 and when would they be due?

End of Exercises. Solutions available in Study Guide.

Interest

When Interest Is Charged

2-43.   Interest is assessed on any amounts that are not paid when they are due. This would include:

- Any balance owing for a taxation year on April 30th of the following year. We would remind you that the amount owing is due on April 30th, without regard to whether the taxpayer's filing due date is April 30 or June 15.

- Any portion of a required instalment payment that is not remitted on the required due date. The interest on deficient instalments is charged until the balance due date at which time interest begins to be charged on the balance due.

- On some penalties. For example, interest is charged under ITA 161(11) on penalties for late filing (see following discussion of this penalty).

2-44.   Interest is calculated on a daily basis on these amounts. In the case of amounts owing on April 30th, the start date for interest is May 1, with the accrual continuing until the amounts are paid. For deficient instalment amounts, the interest clock starts ticking on the date the instalment is due. This accrual would continue until an offset occurs (see next paragraph) or the due date for the balance owing. At this latter date, further interest would be based on the amount owing at that date.

2-45.   A further important point here is that interest accrued on late or deficient instalments can be offset by making instalment payments prior to their due date, or by paying an amount in excess of the amount required (creating contra interest). Note, however, if early or excess payments are made when there is no accrual of interest owed on late or deficient instalments, the government will not pay interest to the taxpayer on the excess.

Prescribed Rate Of Interest

2-46. There are a number of provisions in the *Income Tax Act* which require the use of an assumed rate of interest. In order to implement these provisions, ITR 4301 specifies a prescribed rate of interest. As defined in this Regulation, the regular prescribed rate is an annual rate that is revised each quarter, based on the effective yield on three month Government of Canada treasury bills during the first month of the preceding quarter.

2-47. At an earlier point in time, there was a single prescribed rate. However, the government found that this rate was sufficiently low that it was commonly advantageous for taxpayers not to make required tax payments. To solve this problem, they added 4 percent to the basic rate as described in the preceding paragraph. At the same time, they established a third rate to be used when amounts were owed to taxpayers. As a result, there are, in effect, three prescribed rates:

Regular Rate This rate, described in Paragraph 2-46, is applicable for all purposes except amounts owing to and from the CRA (e.g., the determination of the taxable benefit for an employee who receives an interest free loan from an employer). For the second quarter of 2012, this rate was 1 percent.

Regular Rate Plus 2 Percent This rate is applicable when calculating interest on refunds to individuals and trusts, but not corporations. For the second quarter of 2012, this rate was 3 percent.

In recent years, interest rates on short term investments have been lower than the prescribed rate plus 2 percent. To prevent corporations from overpaying instalments to take advantage of the higher interest rates available, the rate on amounts owed to corporations is only the regular rate and does not include the extra 2 percent.

Regular Rate Plus 4 Percent This rate is applicable when calculating interest on late or deficient instalments, unpaid source deductions, and other amounts owing to the CRA by all taxpayers. For the second quarter of 2012, this rate was 5 percent. Note that amounts paid to the CRA under this provision are not deductible for any taxpayer.

2-48. Recent rates applicable to amounts owing to the Minister, including the extra 4 percentage points, are as follows:

Quarter (Rates include extra 4 percent)	2010	2011	2012
First	5%	5%	5%
Second	5%	5%	5%
Third	5%	5%	N/A
Fourth	5%	5%	N/A

2-49. Many individuals are faced with the choice of either making their instalment payments or, alternatively, paying off other types of liabilities that they have accumulated. In many cases, the latter choice may be preferable.

Example Jasmine Ho has determined that her minimum tax instalments for 2011 total $30,000 ($7,500 each quarter). She also owes $30,000 on her Visa credit card for personal expenditures. She does not have the funds to eliminate the credit card debt and to pay her instalments.

Analysis The annual interest rate that will be charged on her Visa balance is likely to be around 20 percent. This compares to a current rate on late tax instalments of 5 percent. Without regard to financial planning issues, Jasmine would clearly reduce her interest costs by paying off the credit card debt, as opposed to making her instalment payments.

Penalties

Late Filing Penalty

2-50. If the deadline for filing an income tax return is not met, a penalty is assessed under ITA 162(1). For a first offence, this penalty amounts to 5 percent of the tax that was unpaid at the filing due date, plus 1 percent for each complete month (part months do not count) the unpaid tax is outstanding up to a maximum of 12 months. This penalty would be in addition to interest on the amounts due. If there are no taxes owed on the due date, or if the taxpayer is entitled to a refund, the late filing penalty would be nil.

2-51.   If the taxpayer has been charged a late filing penalty in any of the three preceding taxation years, ITA 162(2) can double the penalty on the second offence to 10 percent of the tax owing, plus 2 percent per month up to a maximum of 20 months.

2-52.   In terms of tax planning, the penalty for late filing is sufficiently severe that individuals should make every effort to file their income tax returns no later than the deadline (April 30 or June 15), even if all of the taxes owing cannot be paid at that time. This is of particular importance if they have filed late in one of the three preceding years.

2-53.   This point is sometimes forgotten when the previous offence resulted in a negligible penalty. The penalty for a second offence will double, even if the amount involved in the first penalty was very small.

Exercise Two - 6

Subject: Penalties And Interest For Individuals

Despite the fact that her net tax owing has been between $3,000 and $4,000 in the two previous years, and is expected to be a similar amount during 2012, Mary Carlos has made no instalment payments for 2012. While her normal filing date would be April 30, 2013, she does not file her 2012 return or pay the balance owing until July 20, 2013. What penalties and interest will be assessed for the 2012 taxation year?

End of Exercise. Solution available in Study Guide.

Late Or Deficient Instalments Penalty

2-54.   There is no penalty for late payment of income taxes or on moderate amounts of late or deficient instalments. However, there is a penalty when large amounts of late or deficient instalments are involved. This penalty is specified in ITA 163.1 and is equal to 50 percent of the amount by which the interest owing on the late or deficient instalments exceeds the greater of $1,000 and 25 percent of the interest that would be owing if no instalments were made. As this penalty does not kick in unless the amount of interest exceeds $1,000, it would only apply to fairly large amounts of late or deficient instalments.

Due Date For Balance Owing - Individuals

General Rule

2-55.   If the combination of amounts withheld and instalments paid falls short of the total taxes payable for the taxation year, there will be a balance owing. For living individuals, ITA 248(1) defines the "balance due date" as April 30, without regard to whether the taxpayer qualifies for the June 15 filing due date.

Deceased Taxpayer

2-56.   The due date for the amount owing for the year of death is generally April 30 of the year following death. However, if the taxpayer dies after October of that taxation year, and before May of the following year, the due date is defined as 6 months after the date of death. As with living individuals, the due date for the amount owing is not extended for deceased individuals with business income.

Example Before filing her 2012 tax return, Joanne Rivers dies on March 31, 2013. For 2012 and 2013, all of her income was from employment. While she was not required to make instalment payments in either year, it is likely that there will be a small net tax owing for both years. What are the due dates for these amounts?

Analysis Her 2012 return will be due on September 30, 2013, six months after her death. Any balance owing for 2012 will be due at that time. Her final return for 2013 will be due on April 30, 2014. Any balance owing for 2013 will be due at that time.

Final Returns For Deceased Taxpayers

2-57. Dealing with the death of an individual taxpayer is a very complex area of tax practice. In fact, for individuals with substantial estates, it is an area that requires the attention of a practitioner who specializes in the area. It is our view that complete coverage of this subject goes beyond the scope of this general text.

2-58. However, we will provide general coverage of some of the issues that arise when an individual dies. More specifically, in Chapter 8 we will discuss the deemed disposition of capital assets that occurs when an individual dies. In addition, in Chapter 11, we will consider the special rules related to the use of net capital loss carry overs in the year of death.

2-59. A further complication relates to the fact that, in the year of death, an individual may file multiple tax returns. We have decided not to include coverage of this subject in the main body of this text. However, for those of you with a specific interest in this subject, we have provided coverage of such filings in Supplementary Reading No. 6, Final Returns For Deceased Taxpayers.

Returns And Payments - Corporations

Due Date For Corporate Returns (ITA 150)

2-60. Unlike the case with individuals, the taxation year of a corporation can end on any day of the calendar year. This makes it impossible to have a uniform filing date and, as a consequence, the filing deadline for corporations is specified as six months after the fiscal year end of the company.

2-61. Under ITA 150(1)(a), corporations (other than corporations that are registered charities) that are resident in Canada at any time in the year, carry on business in Canada, have a taxable capital gain, dispose of Taxable Canadian Property, or would be subject to Canadian tax if not for an international tax treaty, are required to file Form T2 within this specified period. Information from the financial statements must accompany this form, along with other required schedules.

Filing Alternatives For Corporations

Electronic Filing

2-62. Until 2010, corporations had the option of filing a paper T2 or, alternatively, filing their return electronically. However, as of 2010, ITA 150.1(2.1) indicates that prescribed corporations no longer have the option of paper filing. For this purpose, prescribed corporations are those that have gross revenues in excess of $1 million.

Use Of Funotional Currency

2-63. If a Canadian enterprise has foreign operations, it is likely that some of their records will be maintained in a foreign currency. If these records are translated into Canadian dollars in order to file the required return, there may be a problem. The use of some translation methods can introduce what many analysts believe are distortions in the reported results.

2-64. To correct this situation, ITA 261 allows the determination of Canadian tax liabilities on the basis of financial statements prepared in the corporation's functional currency. For this purpose, functional currency is defined as follows:

"functional currency" of a taxpayer for a taxation year means the currency of a country other than Canada if that currency is, throughout the taxation year,

(a) a qualifying currency; and

(b) the primary currency in which the taxpayer maintains its records and books of account for financial reporting purposes.

2-65.   ITA 261 provides the following definition of qualifying currency:

"qualifying currency" at any time means each of
(a) the currency of the United States of America;
(b) the currency of the European Monetary Union;
(c) the currency of the United Kingdom;
(d) the currency of Australia; and
(e) a prescribed currency.   (**Note** At present there are no prescribed currencies.)

2-66.   You should also note that the term "functional currency" has a different meaning in the *Income Tax Act* than it does in Canadian and International Financial Reporting Standards. Financial reporting standards use this term to refer to the currency of the primary economic environment in which the corporation operates, without regard to the currency in which the corporation keeps its records.

Instalment Payments For Corporations
Instalment Threshold
2-67.   Corporations are generally required to make monthly instalment payments throughout their taxation year. However, this requirement is eliminated if either the estimated taxes payable for the current year or the taxes payable for the preceding taxation year do not exceed $3,000. In addition, special rules apply to some Canadian Controlled Private Corporations, or CCPCs (see Paragraph 2-71).

Calculating The Amount - General Rules (Excluding Small CCPCs)
2-68.   When instalments are required, they must be paid on or before the last day of each month, with the amount being calculated on the basis of one of three alternatives. As laid out in ITA 157(1)(a), these alternatives are as follows:

1. Twelve instalments, each based on 1/12 of the estimated tax payable for the current year.

2. Twelve instalments, each based on 1/12 of the tax that was payable in the immediately preceding year.

3. Two instalments, each based on 1/12 of the tax that was payable in the second preceding year, followed by 10 instalments based on 1/10 of the amount by which the taxes paid in the immediately preceding year exceeds the sum of the first two instalments.

2-69.   Choosing between these alternatives is usually a relatively simple matter. The instalment base that provides the minimum cash outflow and the greatest amount of deferral should be the one selected. For businesses that are experiencing year to year increases in their taxes payable, the third alternative will generally meet this objective.

Example The Marshall Company estimates that its 2012 taxes payable will be $153,000. In 2011, the Company paid taxes of $126,000. The corresponding figure for 2010 was $96,000.

Analysis Given the preceding information, the choices for instalment payments would be:

1. Twelve instalments of $12,750 each ($153,000 ÷ 12) totaling $153,000.
2. Twelve instalments of $10,500 each ($126,000 ÷ 12) totaling $126,000.
3. Two instalments of $8,000 each ($96,000 ÷ 12) and 10 instalments of $11,000 each [($126,000 - $16,000) ÷ 10] totaling $126,000.

While the cash outflows under alternative 3 total the same amount as those under alternative 2, alternative 3 would be selected because it provides a deferral from the first two payments to the last 10 payments.

2-70.   There is a technical point involving situations where the approach that has the lowest interest cost does not provide the lowest amount of payments. Consider the following:

Example   Nordell Ltd. estimates that its 2012 tax payable will be $99,000. In 2011, the Company paid taxes of $100,000. The corresponding figure for 2010 was nil.

Analysis   In terms of the time value of money, the best approach here would be to pay nothing for the first two instalments, followed by 10 payments of $10,000 ($100,000 ÷ 10). While the total payments would be slightly greater than the $99,000 that would be paid using the current year's base, this could still be attractive because of the large amount of deferral resulting from making no payments in the first two months. Unfortunately, in the case of corporations, ITA 161(4.1) indicates that, unless payments are based on the approach that produces minimum instalments for the year, interest could be assessed. As this approach would require the use of the current year as the instalment base, interest could be assessed with respect to the $8,250 ($99,000 ÷ 12) that should have been paid in each of the first two months of the taxation year.

Calculating The Amount - Small CCPCs

2-71.   "Small" CCPCs are allowed to pay instalments on a quarterly basis. ITA 157(1.2) defines a small CCPC as one for which:

* the Taxable Income of the corporation and its associated corporations does not exceed $500,000 during the current or the previous taxation year;

* the Taxable Capital Employed In Canada of the corporation and its associated corporations does not exceed $10 million for the current or previous year;

* an amount has been deducted under ITA 125 (the small business deduction) for the current or previous year; and

* a perfect compliance record has been maintained with respect to payments and filings (for GST, source deductions and income taxes) during the last 12 months.

2-72.   For CCPCs that meet this definition, ITA 157(1.1) provides three alternatives for calculating instalments:

1.   Four instalments, each based on 1/4 of the estimated tax payable for the current taxation year.

2.   Four instalments, each based on 1/4 of the tax that was payable in the immediately preceding taxation year.

3.   One instalment based on 1/4 of the tax that was payable in the second preceding taxation year, followed by 3 instalments based on 1/3 of the amount by which the taxes paid in the immediately preceding taxation year exceeds the first instalment.

2-73.   The payments are required on or before the last day of each of the fiscal quarters.

Exercise Two - 7

Subject: Corporate Instalments

Madco Ltd. is not a small CCPC. It has a December 31 year end. For 2010, its tax payable was $32,000, while for 2011, the amount was $59,000. For 2012, its estimated tax payable is $74,000. What would be the minimum instalments for 2012 and when would they be due? How would your answer differ if Madco Ltd. was a small CCPC?

End of Exercise. Solution available in Study Guide.

Exercise Two - 8

Subject: Corporate Instalments

Fadco Inc. is not a small CCPC. It has a November 30 year end. For the taxation year ending November 30, 2010, its tax payable was $102,000, while for the 2011 taxation year, the amount was $54,000. For the 2012 taxation year, its estimated tax payable is $17,000. What would be the minimum instalments for 2012 and when would they be due? How would your answer differ if Fadco Inc. was a small CCPC?

End of Exercise. Solution available in Study Guide.

Due Date For Balance Owing - Corporations

2-74. Regardless of the instalment base selected, any remaining taxes are due within two months of the corporation's fiscal year end. An exception is made in the case of companies that are Canadian controlled private corporations (CCPCs) throughout the year and have the ability to claim the small business deduction. For these corporations, the due date is three months after their fiscal year end, provided their Taxable Income did not exceed $500,000 for the previous year.

2-75. Note that the final due date for payment is earlier than the due date for filing returns. For example, a company with a March 31 year end that is not eligible for the small business deduction would not have to file its tax return until September 30. However, all of its taxes would be due on May 31. This means that this final payment will often have to be based on an estimate of the total amount of taxes payable.

Exercise Two - 9

Subject: Corporate Due Date

The taxation year end for Radco Inc. is January 31, 2012. Indicate the date on which the corporate tax return must be filed, as well as the date on which any final payment of taxes is due.

End of Exercise. Solution available in Study Guide.

Interest And Penalties For Corporations

2-76. The basic rules for interest on corporate balances owing or receivable are generally the same as those applicable to individuals. These were covered beginning in Paragraph 2-43. However, as described in Paragraph 2-47, interest on overpayments for corporations is calculated at the regular rate, not at the higher rate applicable to individuals and trusts.

2-77. Note that it is especially important that corporations avoid interest on late tax or instalment payments. Since corporations can usually deduct the interest expense that they incur, the payment of non-deductible interest on late tax payments represents an extremely high cost source of financing. For example, if a corporation is paying taxes at a rate of 35 percent, interest at a non-deductible rate of 5 percent is the equivalent of a deductible interest rate of 7.7 percent [5% ÷ (1 - .35)]. In general, corporations are able to access financing at rates that are lower than this.

2-78. The previously covered penalties applicable to individuals for late filing of returns and for large amounts of late instalments (see Paragraph 2-50 and 2-54) are equally applicable to corporations. In addition to the penalties applicable to individuals, ITA 235 contains a further penalty applicable to large corporations. It calls for a penalty equal to .0005 percent per month of a corporation's Taxable Capital Employed In Canada. This will be assessed for a maximum period of 40 months.

2-79.   This is a fairly harsh penalty in that, unlike the usual penalties that are based on any additional tax payable at the time the return should have been filed, this penalty is based on the capital of the enterprise, without regard to earnings or tax payable for the year. For example, CNR has Shareholders' Equity (roughly the equivalent of Taxable Capital Employed In Canada) of $4.857 billion. If the .0005 percent penalty was applied to this balance for 40 months, the total penalty would be $971,400.

Returns And Payments - Trusts

Testamentary Trusts

2-80.   ITA 108 defines a testamentary trust as one that arises on the death of an individual. Such trusts can have a fiscal year other than a calendar year and, as a consequence, their filing dates will vary. The basic rule is that the T3 return must be filed within 90 days of the end of the trust's taxation year.

2-81.   With respect to instalments, testamentary trusts are not required to make these payments. If the trust has a Tax Payable balance, this amount is due no later than 90 days after the end of the trust's taxation year. If a return is not filed by the filing due date, or if payment of any Tax Payable is not made at this time, testamentary trusts are subject to the same interest and penalty provisions that are applicable to individuals.

Inter Vivos Trusts

2-82.   As defined in ITA 108, an inter vivos trust is any trust other than a testamentary trust. In general, such trusts are those that are established by a living individual. This type of trust is required to use the calendar year as its taxation year and, as a consequence, all such trusts will have a common filing date. In this case, the date is 90 days after December 31, generally on March 31 of each calendar year.

2-83.   From a technical point of view, inter vivos trusts should make instalment payments. However, this requirement has been waived on an administrative basis. Unless instalments are made on a voluntary basis, the full amount of Tax Payable for an inter vivos trust is due no later than 90 days after the end of the trust's taxation year, generally March 31 of each calendar year. If the return is not filed by the filing due date, or if payment of any Tax Payable is not made at this time, inter vivos trusts are subject to the same interest and penalty provisions that are applicable to individuals.

Income Tax Information Returns

2-84.   ITA 221(1)(d) gives the CRA the right to require certain taxpayers to file information returns in addition to the returns in which they report their taxable income. These information returns are described in Part II of the Income Tax Regulations and must be filed using a prescribed form. Common examples of these returns and the related prescribed form would be as follows:

T3   This form is used by trustees (which includes trustees of some mutual funds) and executors to report the allocation of the trust's income.

T4   This form is used by employers to report remuneration and taxable benefits paid to employees and the various amounts withheld for source deductions.

T5   This form is used by organizations to report interest, dividend, and royalty payments.

T4RSP   This form is used by trustees to report payments out of Registered Retirement Savings Plans.

Refunds

2-85.   When tax has been withheld from income and/or instalments have been paid, the CRA's assessment may show that there has been an overpayment of income tax. In this situation, the taxpayer is entitled to a refund of any excess payments and, in the great majority of cases, such refunds are sent without any further action being taken. If, for some reason, the refund is not made, the taxpayer can apply for it in writing within the normal reassessment period (see later material in this Chapter). However, if there are other tax liabilities outstanding, such as amounts owing from prior years, the Minister has the right to apply the refund against these liabilities.

2-86.   A further point here is that refunds will not generally be made if the return is filed more than three years after the end of the relevant taxation year (e.g., a refund on a 2008 tax return that is filed in 2012 will not be paid).

2-87.   Interest is paid on overpayments of income tax at the rate prescribed in ITR 4301 (see Paragraph 2-47). For individuals, interest at the regular rate, plus two percentage points, begins to accrue on the later of two dates:

- 30 days after the balance due date (generally, April 30); or
- 30 days after the return is filed.

2-88.   For an individual with business or professional income, the normal filing date would be June 15. If such an individual was entitled to a refund and waited until this date to file, interest would not begin to accrue until July 15.

2-89.   For corporations, interest on refunds at the regular rate, without the additional two percentage points, begins to accrue at the later of two dates. These are:

- 120 days after the corporate year end; or
- 30 days after the corporation's tax return is filed (unless it is not filed prior to the due date, in which case the due date is applicable).

2-90.   Taxpayers can request that any refund due to them be transferred to their tax instalment account. The advantage of this is that the transfer would normally occur more quickly than the issuance of a refund cheque. This option is available on the corporate tax return, but is only available through a separate written request in the case of personal tax returns. This is one reason it is not commonly used by individuals.

Books And Records

2-91.   For income tax purposes, every person carrying on a business, as well as every person who is required to pay or collect taxes, must keep adequate books and records. This requirement is found in ITA 230. Such records must be maintained at the taxpayer's place of business or at the individual's residence in Canada.

2-92.   As specified in ITA 230(4), the general retention period is 6 years. However, ITR 5800 provides prescribed periods for certain specific types of situations (e.g., corporations that have been dissolved). Guidance on the application of these rules can be found in IC 78-10R5, "Books And Records Retention/Destruction".

Assessments

Initial Assessments

2-93.   ITA 152(1) requires that the Minister shall, with all due dispatch, examine each return of income and assess the tax as well as the interest and penalties payable. After examining the return, the Minister is required to send a notice of assessment to the person who filed the income tax return. In the case of individuals, this notice of assessment is usually received within one or two months of filing, especially if the return was filed electronically. A somewhat longer period is normally required for corporate income tax assessments.

Reassessments

2-94.   The first notice of assessment is based on a quick pass through the data in the return to check for completeness and arithmetic accuracy. If no obvious errors are found, it will simply indicate that the Minister accepts the information that was included in the taxpayer's return. It does not, however, free the taxpayer from additional scrutiny of the return.

2-95.   For individuals, most trusts, and Canadian controlled private corporations, the normal reassessment period is the period that ends three years after the day of mailing of an original assessment. This normal reassessment period is extended to four years for other corporations because of the greater complexity that may be involved in the review process.

2-96.   There are a number of exceptions to this normal reassessment period. These include:

- **ITA 152(4)(a)**   Reassessment can occur at any time if the taxpayer or person filing the return has made any misrepresentation that is attributable to neglect, carelessness or willful default, or has committed any fraud in filing the return or in supplying information under the *Income Tax Act*.

- **ITA 152(4)(c)**   Reassessment can occur at any time if the taxpayer has filed a waiver of the three year time limit. A taxpayer can revoke such a waiver at any time. The waiver remains in effect for six months after revocation.

- **ITA 152(4.2)**   Reassessment can occur outside the normal reassessment period if an individual or testamentary trust has requested a reduction in taxes, interest, or penalties. The ability to use this provision is limited to ten years after the particular year in question.

- **ITA 152(4.3)**   Reassessment can occur beyond the normal reassessment period when reassessment within the normal period affects a balance outside of this period.

- **ITA 152(6)**   Reassessment can occur outside the normal reassessment period in situations where the taxpayer is claiming certain specified deductions. An example of this type of situation could involve a loss being carried back in order to claim a refund of taxes paid.

Adjustments To Income Tax Returns

2-97.   There is no general provision in the *Income Tax Act* for filing a complete and detailed amended return and, in fact, such returns are generally not filed. However, this does not mean that amounts included in the returns of previous years cannot be altered. It simply means that, in most cases, the adjustment process takes place through the use of a letter, a prescribed form or through the CRA web site, rather than through the filing of a completely revised tax return for the year in question.

2-98.   Statutory authority for certain adjustments is found in ITA 152(6) which requires the Minister of National Revenue to reassess certain specific changes in the returns of previous years. For example, this provision requires reassessment for a previous year when a current year loss is applied to that earlier year.

2-99.   IC 75-7R3, "Reassessment of a Return of Income", provides an administrative solution to the problem of adjustments to returns. It permits such adjustments if the following conditions are met:

- the CRA is satisfied that the previous assessment was incorrect;
- the reassessment can be made within the normal reassessment period, the extended period available under ITA 152(6), or the taxpayer has filed a waiver;
- the requested decrease in taxable income does not solely depend on an increase in a permissive deduction such as capital cost allowance;
- the change is not based solely on a successful appeal to the courts by another taxpayer; and

- the taxpayer's return has been filed within three years of the end of the year to which it relates.

2-100.   For individuals, changes can be requested through the CRA web site by using the password protected My Account service, or by mailing Form T1-ADJ, "T1 Adjustment Request", or by sending a letter detailing the adjustment requested.   The calculations required to issue a reassessment are taken care of by the CRA. This informal procedure can be used any time within the normal reassessment period, provided the return has been filed within three years of the end of the year to which it relates.

2-101.   IC 84-1 describes administrative provisions for situations where a business wishes to alter a permissive deduction. This could happen, for example, when an enterprise has a loss that it cannot carry back in full. This results in a carry forward that can be lost if the business does not produce sufficient taxable income to absorb it in the relevant carry forward period.

2-102.   In such a situation, the enterprise may wish to minimize the loss carry forward amount by revising the capital cost allowance taken in the previous year. Such revisions are only permitted when they do not change the taxes payable for the previous year. In general, this will only happen when the downward revision in capital cost allowance is accompanied by an equivalent increase in the amount of loss being carried back to that year.

Appeals

Consent Form

2-103.   At the initial stages of any dispute, a taxpayer may wish to represent himself. However, if complex issues are involved, or if the dispute progresses to a later stage where procedures require more formal representation, a taxpayer is likely to authorize some other party to act as their representative.

2-104.   In order to provide this authorization, the taxpayer must file Form T1013, "Authorizing Or Canceling A Representative" with the CRA. If a signed Consent Form is not on file, the CRA will not discuss the issue under dispute with anyone other than the involved taxpayer.

Informal Request For Adjustments

2-105.   If a taxpayer disagrees with an assessment or reassessment, the usual first step in the process of disputing the assessment is to contact the CRA immediately. In some cases the proposed change or error can be corrected or resolved through telephone contact or by letter.

Notice Of Objection
General Rules

2-106.   If the informal contact does not resolve the issue in question, ITA 165(1) gives the taxpayer the right to file a notice of objection. While its use is not required, Form T400A, "Objection", can be used for this purpose. This form simply requires a statement of the relevant facts along with the reasons for the objection. It is addressed to the Chief of Appeals in the Tax Services Office, or to any Taxation Centre.

2-107.   For corporations and inter vivos trusts, a notice of objection must be filed within 90 days of the date on which the notice of assessment was mailed. For individuals and testamentary trusts, the rules are more generous. For these taxpayers, the notice of objection must be filed before the later of:

- 90 days from the date of mailing of the notice of assessment or reassessment; or
- one year from the filing due date for the return under assessment or reassessment.

   Example   An individual required to file on April 30, 2012, files on March 26, 2012. A notice of assessment is mailed on May 14, 2012.

   Analysis   For this individual, a notice of objection could be filed up to the later of August 12, 2012 (90 days after the mailing) and April 30, 2013 (one year after the filing due date). In this case, the relevant date would be April 30, 2013, without regard for the fact that the return was actually filed on March 26, 2012.

2-108.   When an individual dies after October of the assessment year and before May of the following year, you will recall that the filing date for the return is extended to six months after the date of death, thereby extending the date for filing a notice of objection by the same number of months.

2-109.   Under ITA 166.1(1), a taxpayer can request an extension of the filing deadline for the notice of objection. However, under ITA 166.1(7) the application or request will not be granted unless:

(a) the application is made within one year after the expiration of the time otherwise limited by this Act for serving a notice of objection or making a request, as the case may be; and

(b) the taxpayer demonstrates that

    (i) within the time otherwise limited by this Act for serving such a notice or making such a request, as the case may be, the taxpayer
        (1) was unable to act or to instruct another to act in the taxpayer's name, or
        (2) had a bona fide intention to object to the assessment or make the request,

    (ii) given the reasons set out in the application and the circumstances of the case, it would be just and equitable to grant the application, and

    (iii) the application was made as soon as circumstances permitted.

2-110.   If the request is denied by the Minister, the taxpayer has 90 days to appeal for a time extension to the Tax Court of Canada. This is provided for under ITA 166.2.

2-111.   Once the notice of objection is filed, the Minister is required to reply to the taxpayer:

- vacating the assessment,
- confirming it (i.e., refusing to change it),
- varying the amount, or
- reassessing.

2-112.   Unresolved objections are subject to review by the Chief of Appeals in each Tax Services Office. These appeals sections are instructed to operate independently of the assessing divisions and should provide an unbiased second opinion. If the matter remains unresolved after this review, the taxpayer must either accept the Minister's assessment or, alternatively, continue to pursue the matter to a higher level of appeal.

Rules For Large Corporations

2-113.   The Department of Finance appears to believe that it has been the practice of certain corporate taxpayers to delay the dispute process by filing vague objections in the first instance, and subsequently bringing in fresh issues as the appeal process goes forward.

2-114.   To prevent this perceived abuse, the Department has issued ITA 165(1.11). This legislation requires that, in filing a notice of objection, a corporation must specify each issue to be decided, the dollar amount of relief sought for each particular issue, and the facts and reasons relied on by the corporation in respect of each issue.

2-115.   If the corporation objects to a reassessment or additional assessment made by the CRA, or appeals to the Tax Court of Canada, the objection or appeal can be only with respect to issues and dollar amounts properly dealt with in the original notice of objection. There is an exception to this general rule for new issues that are raised by the CRA on assessment or reassessment. These limitations are only applicable to "large corporations", defined as a corporation with Taxable Capital Employed In Canada that is in excess of $10 million at the end of the current year and at the end of the previous year.

Exercise Two - 10

Subject: Notice Of Objection

Jerry Fall filed his 2012 tax return as required on April 30, 2013. He receives his notice of assessment during June, 2013. However, on June 1, 2014, he receives a reassessment indicating that he owes additional taxes, as well as interest on the unpaid amounts. The reassessment was mailed on May 15, 2014. What is the due date for filing a notice of objection to this reassessment? Explain your answer.

End of Exercise.   Solution available in Study Guide.

Tax Court Of Canada

Deadline For Appeal

2-116.   A taxpayer who does not find satisfaction through the notice of objection procedure may then proceed to the next level of the appeal procedure, the Tax Court of Canada. Appeals to the Tax Court of Canada can be made within 90 days of the mailing date of the Minister's response to the notice of objection which would confirm the assessment or reassessment, or 90 days after the notice of objection has been filed if the Minister has not replied. It is not possible to bypass the Tax Court of Canada and appeal directly to the Federal Court level, except in very limited circumstances.

Informal Procedure

2-117.   On appeal to the Tax Court of Canada, the general procedure will automatically apply unless the taxpayer elects to have his case heard under the informal procedure. The informal procedure can be elected for appeals in which the total amount of federal tax and penalty involved for a given year is less than $12,000, or where the loss in question is less than $24,000. There is a proposal to raise these amounts to $25,000 and $50,000 respectively. Cases involving larger amounts can use this informal procedure, provided the taxpayer restricts the appeal to these limits.

2-118.   Advantages of the informal procedure include:

- The rules of evidence remain fairly informal, allowing the taxpayer to represent himself, or be represented by an agent other than a lawyer.
- Under the informal procedure, even if the taxpayer is unsuccessful, he cannot be asked to pay court costs.
- The informal procedure is designed as a fast-track procedure that is usually completed within 6 or 7 months whereas the general procedure may take many years.

2-119.   The major disadvantage of the informal procedure is that the taxpayer generally gives up all rights to further appeals if the Court decision is unfavourable.

General Procedure

2-120.   If the general procedure applies, formal rules of evidence must be used, resulting in a situation where the taxpayer has to be represented by either himself, or legal counsel. In practical terms, this means that for cases involving substantial amounts, lawyers will usually be involved.

2-121.   Under the general procedure, if the taxpayer is unsuccessful, the Court may require that costs be paid to the Minister. Under either procedure, if the taxpayer is more than 50 percent successful (e.g., if he is claiming $10,000 and is awarded more than $5,000), the judge can order the Minister to pay all or part of the taxpayer's costs.

Appeals By The Minister

2-122.   There are situations in which the Minister may pursue a matter because of its general implications for broad groups of taxpayers. The individual taxpayer is given protection from the costs associated with this type of appeal by the requirement that the Minister be responsible for the taxpayer's reasonable legal fees when the amount of taxes payable in question does not exceed $12,000 or the loss in dispute does not exceed $24,000. This is without regard to whether the appeal is successful.

Resolution

2-123.   Prior to the hearing by the Tax Court of Canada, discussions between the taxpayer and the Department are likely to continue. It would appear that, in the majority of cases, the dispute will be resolved prior to the actual hearing. However, if a hearing proceeds, the Court may dispose of an appeal by:

- dismissing it; or
- allowing it and
    - vacating the assessment,
    - varying the assessment, or
    - referring the assessment back to the Minister for reconsideration and reassessment.

Federal Court And The Supreme Court Of Canada

2-124.   Either the Minister or the taxpayer can appeal a general procedure decision of the Tax Court of Canada to the Federal Court of Appeal. The appeal must be made within 30 days of the date on which the Tax Court of Canada makes its decision.

2-125.   It is possible to pursue a matter beyond the Federal Court to the Supreme Court of Canada. This can be done if the Federal Court of Appeal refers the issue to the higher Court, or if the Supreme Court authorizes the appeal. These actions will not usually happen unless there are new issues or legal precedents to be dealt with and, as a result, such appeals are not common. However, when tax cases do reach the Supreme Court, they often attract a great deal of public attention.

Tax Evasion, Avoidance And Planning

Tax Evasion

2-126.   The concept of tax evasion is not difficult to understand. It is described on the CRA web site (in their Tax Alert) as follows:

> **Tax evasion** typically involves deliberately ignoring a specific part of the law. For example, those participating in tax evasion may under-report taxable receipts or claim expenses that are non-deductible or overstated. They might also attempt to evade taxes by willfully refusing to comply with legislated reporting requirements.

> Tax evasion, unlike tax avoidance, has criminal consequences. Tax evaders face prosecution in criminal court.

2-127.   There is little ambiguity in this description as it involves deliberate attempts to deceive the taxation authorities. The most common of the offenses that fall under this description of tax evasion is probably the failure to report revenues that are received in cash (e.g., individual in the construction trades doing renovations to private residences).

Tax Avoidance And Tax Planning

A Fuzzy Concept

2-128.   Despite the fact that disputes may arise with respect to its implementation, the concept of tax evasion is clear — tax evasion involves deliberately breaking the law. Working from this concept, it could be argued that any tax arrangement that is within the law should be considered tax planning.

2-129.   However, there is a longstanding view within the government that there are tax arrangements that, while they do not break the law, violate the "spirit" of the law. Such transactions are commonly referred to as avoidance transactions. In an attempt to support this view, the CRA web site describes the difference between tax planning and tax avoidance as follows:

> **Effective tax planning** occurs when the results of these arrangements are consistent with the intent of the law. When tax planning reduces taxes in a way that is inconsistent with the overall spirit of the law, the arrangements are referred to as **tax avoidance**. The Canada Revenue Agency's interpretation of the term "tax avoidance" includes all unacceptable and abusive tax planning. Aggressive tax planning refers to arrangements that "push the limits" of acceptable tax planning.

2-130.   It is our view that the use of such terms as "spirit of the law" and "abusive tax planning" provides a very fuzzy conceptual basis for making such an important distinction.

Stubart Investments
2-131.   Prior to 1984, this issue was approached by applying a business purpose test. The Department assessed on the basis that a transaction which had no business purpose other than the avoidance or reduction of taxes was a sham and should not be considered acceptable for tax purposes. However, this approach was struck down by the Supreme Court in the Stubart Investments Ltd. case (84 DTC 6305).

2-132.   The case involved a transfer of the assets of a profitable subsidiary to the books of a sister subsidiary which had large accumulated losses. There was no reason for the transaction other than the desire to have the losses of the latter subsidiary absorbed before their carry forward period expired. The Supreme Court upheld the right of Stubart Investments to undertake this transaction, thereby eliminating the judicial basis for a business purpose test.

General Anti-Avoidance Rule (GAAR)
2-133.   With the Supreme Court decision in the Stubart Investments case removing the CRA's ability to assess general tax avoidance arrangements, the Department began to call for a new general anti-avoidance rule (GAAR). This was provided in the 1988 tax reform legislation in Section 245. The basic provision here is as follows:

> **Paragraph 245(2)** Where a transaction is an avoidance transaction, the tax consequences to a person shall be determined as is reasonable in the circumstances in order to deny a tax benefit that, but for this section, would result, directly or indirectly, from that transaction or from a series of transactions that includes that transaction.

2-134.   The Section goes on to describe an avoidance transaction as follows:

ITA 245(3)   An avoidance transaction means any transaction

(a) that, but for this section, would result, directly or indirectly, in a tax benefit, unless the transaction may reasonably be considered to have been undertaken or arranged primarily for bona fide purposes other than to obtain the tax benefit; or

(b) that is part of a series of transactions, which series, but for this section, would result, directly or indirectly, in a tax benefit, unless the transaction may reasonably be considered to have been undertaken or arranged primarily for bona fide purposes other than to obtain the tax benefit.

2-135.   Note that the preceding provisions provide a basic defense against the GAAR in that it does not apply to transactions which have a bona fide non-tax purpose. An additional line of defense is found in ITA 245(4) as follows:

ITA 245(4)   Subsection (2) applies to a transaction only if it may reasonably be considered that the transaction

(a) would, if this Act were read without reference to this section, result directly or indirectly in a misuse of the provisions of any one or more of

(i) this Act,
(ii) the Income Tax Regulations,
(iii) the Income Tax Application Rules,
(iv) a tax treaty, or
(v) any other enactment that is relevant in computing tax or any other amount payable by or refundable to a person under this Act or in determining any amount that is relevant for the purposes of that computation; or

(b) would result directly or indirectly in an abuse having regard to those provisions, other than this section, read as a whole.

2-136.   Taken together, these provisions mean that the GAAR will apply to any transaction other than those where there is a bona fide non-tax purpose, or where there is no misuse or abuse of the *Act*. If a transaction is judged to be an avoidance transaction, the Section goes on to indicate that the determination of the tax consequences will be as follows:

ITA 245(5) Without restricting the generality of subsection (2), and notwithstanding any other enactment,

(a) any deduction, exemption or exclusion in computing income, taxable income, taxable income earned in Canada or tax payable or any part thereof may be allowed or disallowed in whole or in part,

(b) any such deduction, exemption or exclusion, any income, loss or other amount or part thereof may be allocated to any person,

(c) the nature of any payment or other amount may be recharacterized, and

(d) the tax effects that would otherwise result from the application of other provisions of this Act may be ignored,

in determining the tax consequences to a person as is reasonable in the circumstances in order to deny a tax benefit that would, but for this section, result, directly or indirectly, from an avoidance transaction.

2-137.   The GAAR has been heavily criticized for creating considerable uncertainty in many tax planning arrangements. Some relief from this uncertainty was provided by the issuance of IC 88-2. This Information Circular was issued in 1988, with Supplement 1 issued in 1990. These publications provide fairly detailed guidance with respect to the application of ITA 245. For example, they indicate that the following would not be considered avoidance transactions:

• the use of flow through shares
• gifts to adult children, except where the related income is given back to the parent
• most types of estate freezes (these transactions will be discussed in Chapter 19)

2-138.   In contrast, the following transactions would fall under the provisions of ITA 245:

• transitory arrangements (i.e., issuance and redemption of shares) not carried out for bona fide non-tax purposes
• a sale to an intermediary company to create a reserve, followed by a sale to a third party
• conversion of salary to capital gains by issuing preferred stock to employees entitled to profits, followed by a sale of the preferred stock

2-139.   The CRA has a GAAR Committee that reviews potential GAAR actions. As of March, 2011, 944 cases have been referred to this committee. The GAAR was approved for application in 689 (73%) of these cases. The most common issues involved in these cases are as follows:

• surplus strips (155 cases)
• tax on split income, a.k.a. kiddie tax (81 cases)
• loss creation via stock dividends (64 cases)
• capital and non-capital losses (55 cases)
• Part I.3 tax (49 cases)
• debt forgiveness (43 cases)

- interest deductibility (35 cases)
- capital gains (33 cases)
- indirect loans (31 cases)

Reasonable Expectation Of Profit (REOP)
Current Situation
2-140.   In addition to the use of GAAR, the CRA has attempted to replace the old business purpose test with a test for reasonable expectation of profit (commonly referred to as REOP). In particular, they have attempted to disallow the deduction of losses on arrangements that do not have a reasonable expectation of profit. This approach has been rejected at the Supreme Court level under existing legislation. In both the Stewart case (2002 DTC 6969) and the Walls case (2002 DTC 6960), the Supreme Court indicated that, under existing legislation, expenses and losses could not be generally disallowed because there was no reasonable expectation of a profit.

2-141.   However, a note of caution is appropriate with respect to these decisions. If the undertaking involves a personal benefit or hobby element (e.g., losses incurred by a riding stable that is used extensively by the taxpayer or his family), the taxpayer will still have to show that the activities that generated the losses were undertaken in pursuit of profit.

Proposed Change
2-142.   The CRA is not a good loser. Having the administrative application of the REOP criteria severely restricted by the Supreme Court, the government concluded that they would solve the problem with legislation. In a release dated October 31, 2003, a new ITA 3.1(1) was proposed to apply to taxation years beginning after 2004. This proposed legislation had the objective of applying a new "reasonable expectation of profit" rule.

2-143.   This proposal was subject to a significant amount of well founded criticism. While there was some discussion of attempting to modify the proposal to deal with this criticism, nothing has been done. Further, it is our understanding that the government has no intention of doing further work on this provision. Given this, we have removed our coverage of the proposed ITA 3.1(1).

Collection And Enforcement

Taxpayer Property
2-144.   The CRA has enforcement powers under the provisions of ITA 231.1, "Inspections" and ITA 231.2, "Requirement To Provide Documents Or Information".

2-145.   Tax officials or other persons authorized by the Minister of National Revenue have the right to enter a taxpayer's place of business, locations where anything is done in connection with the business, or any place where records related to the business are kept. Tax officials may also examine any document of another taxpayer that relates, or may relate to, the information that is, or should be, in the books and records of the taxpayer who is being audited. However, in those cases where the place of business is also a dwelling, the officials must either obtain the permission of the occupant or have a court issued warrant. In this process, the officials may audit the books and records, examine all property, and require that the taxpayer answer questions and provide assistance.

2-146.   Seizure of books and records requires a court issued warrant. If this occurs, a taxpayer may apply to have the records returned. Also requiring judicial authorization is demands for information about unnamed persons from third parties. This could include information from the files of the taxpayer's lawyer or accountant. There are additional confidentiality rules in this area that protect solicitor/client communications. However, accountant/client privilege is not protected unless they are part of the solicitor/client privilege. This usually occurs when a lawyer directs the activities of the accountant.

Collections

2-147.   As noted earlier in the Chapter, the due date for the payment of personal income taxes for a taxation year is April 30 of the following year. The due date for corporate income taxes is two months after the corporate year end (three months for qualifying Canadian controlled private corporations). Additional taxes may become payable as a result of an assessment or reassessment. If this is the case, these taxes are due at the time the notice of assessment is mailed.

2-148.   Initial collection procedures will not normally extend beyond communicating with the taxpayer about his liability and the related interest that will be charged. In the case of taxes resulting from an assessment or reassessment, the CRA cannot exercise its collection powers until:

- 90 days after the assessment or reassessment date when no objection is filed;
- 90 days from the date of the notice from the CRA appeals division confirming or varying the assessment or reassessment where an objection has been filed and no further appeal has been made; or
- 90 days after a court decision has been made and there are no further appeals.

2-149.   If informal procedures fail to result in payment of the tax owing by the defaulter, ITA 224 allows the CRA to order a taxpayer owing money to the defaulter to make payments to the Receiver General in settlement of the defaulter's liability. A common example of this would be garnishment of a defaulter's wages to pay income taxes owed. ITA 223 goes even further, allowing the CRA to obtain a judgment against a tax defaulter that can be enforced by seizure and sale of the taxpayer's property.

Other Penalties

Examples

2-150.   We have previously discussed the penalties associated with the late payment of taxes and the late filing of tax returns. There are a number of other penalties that are specified in tax legislation. Examples of such penalties would be as follows:

Repeated Failure To Report Income Penalty   This penalty applies when there is a failure to report an amount in income, and there has been a previous failure to report an amount in any of the preceding three years. The federal penalty is 10 percent of the unreported amount (not the taxes owing). There is also a provincial penalty equal to 10 percent of the unreported amount.

False Statements Or Omissions   This penalty applies in cases of gross negligence where there is an intention to disregard the *Income Tax Act*. The penalty is the greater of $100 and 50 percent of the understated tax.

Evasion   Penalties here range from 50 percent to 200 percent of the relevant tax and, in addition, imprisonment for a period not exceeding two years.

Tax Advisers And Tax Return Preparers

2-151.   Civil penalties for tax advisers and tax return preparers who encourage or assist clients with tax evasive practices are found in ITA 163.2, titled "Misrepresentation of a Tax Matter by a Third Party". The penalty of most concern to accountants is found in ITA 163.2(4). The penalty for participating in a misrepresentation in the preparation of a return is the greater of $1,000 and the penalty assessed on the tax return preparer's client under ITA 163(2) for making the false statement or omission. The penalty on the client is equal to 50 percent of the amount of tax avoided as a result of the misrepresentation. The total amount of the penalty is capped at $100,000, plus the gross compensation to which the tax return preparer is entitled to receive.

2-152.   IC 01-1, "Third-Party Civil Penalties", is an extensive Information Circular that contains 18 examples of the application of third-party penalties. While the examples cited in the IC and the technical notes to ITA 163.2 illustrate clear cut abuses, there are many situations in which it is to the taxpayer's advantage to pursue a more aggressive stance in claiming deductions. It is believed that these penalties discourage tax return preparers from suggesting or condoning this type of approach, out of fear that they may be liable for the third party penalties if the returns are audited. In addition, there is evidence that an increasing number of tax return preparers are refusing to service certain types of high risk clients.

Promoters Of Tax Planning Arrangements

2-153.   A penalty for misrepresentations in tax planning arrangements is specified under ITA 163.2(2). It is applicable when a person makes a statement that they either know to be false or could be reasonably expected to know to be false unless they are involved in "culpable conduct". Culpable conduct is defined in the Section as follows:

> **Culpable Conduct** means conduct, whether an act or a failure to act, that
>
> (a) is tantamount to intentional conduct;
> (b) shows an indifference as to whether the Act is complied with; or
> (c) shows a wilful, reckless or wanton disregard of the law.

2-154.   The Section makes it clear that "culpable conduct" does not generally arise when a tax adviser has relied in good faith, on information provided by the taxpayer. However, this "good faith" defense does not apply to false statements made in the course of an excluded activity. These excluded activities are described as follows:

> **Excluded Activity** in respect of a false statement means, generally, the activity of
>
> (a) promoting or selling (whether as principal or agent or directly or indirectly) an arrangement where it can reasonably be considered that the arrangement concerns a flow-through share or a tax shelter or is an arrangement one of the main purposes for a person's participation in which is to obtain a tax benefit; or
> (b) accepting (whether as principal or agent or directly or indirectly) consideration in respect of the sale of, or participation in, such an arrangement.

2-155.   When ITA 163.2(2) is applicable, the penalty is specified under ITA 163.2(3) as the greater of $1,000 and the total of the adviser's "gross entitlements" as determined at the time the notice of assessment of the penalty is sent to that person. Gross entitlements are defined as follows:

> **Gross Entitlements** of a person from a planning activity or a valuation activity, means all amounts to which the person is entitled, either absolutely or contingently, to receive or obtain.

Statistics

2-156.   At a 2010 round table, the CRA indicated that, as of December 31, 2009, third party civil penalties had been applied in 27 completed audits. These audits resulted in $4.7 million in planner penalties, as well as $1.6 million in preparer penalties. Examples cited include:

* RRSP strips (tax free removal of RRSP balances);
* creation of fictitious business expenses; and
* creation of fictitious expenses for an inactive business.

Taxpayer Relief Provisions (Fairness Package)

Basic Rules

2-157.   There is a widespread perception that the application of some of the CRA's rules on interest and penalties, as well as certain other rules, can result in individuals and other taxpayers being treated in an unfair manner. Reflecting this concern, a "fairness package" was introduced in 1991. The implementation of this package required a number of changes in the *Income Tax Act*, specifically the addition of ITA 220(3.1) and (3.2) and IC 07-1, "Taxpayer Relief Provisions". In general terms, the content of IC 07-1 is as follows:

Part I This first Part of the IC describes the relevant legislation and limits claims to 10 years from the end of the calendar year in which the tax issue occurred.

Part II - Guidelines For The Cancellation Or Waiver Of Penalties And Interest This Part indicates that penalties or interest may be waived in the following situations:

- **Extraordinary Circumstances** - Examples include natural disasters or serious illness.

- **Actions Of The CRA** - Examples here include processing delays and errors in materials made available to the public

- **Inability To Pay Or Financial Hardship** - Example here included the need to provide extended payment arrangements or the inability of an individual to provide basic necessities for his family.

Part III - Guidelines for Accepting Late, Amended, or Revoked Elections While the *Act* contains numerous elections, there is rarely any provision for revoking, amending, or making them after the specified time period has passed. The Appendix to IC 07-01 provides a fairly long list of prescribed elections for which the Minister has discretionary authority to extend the statutory time limit for their filing, amending, or revoking.

Part IV - Guidelines For Refunds Or Reduction In Amounts Payable Beyond The Normal Three Year Period The *Act* sets a three year limitation period from the end of the tax year of an individual to file an income tax return to claim a tax refund and a three year limitation period from the date of the original Notice of Assessment to ask for an adjustment to an assessment issued for a previous tax year. The information in Part IV of this IC deals with the Minister's discretion to relieve an individual (other than a trust) and a testamentary trust from the limitation period and, in certain circumstances, to accept late requests to give the individual or testamentary trust a refund or reduction in tax.

Part V - Rules and Procedures When Relief is Granted or Denied This is a more technical section, setting out the procedures related to granting relief, as well as the procedures associated with administrative and judicial reviews of fairness decisions.

Application

2-158. Very little has been written about the application of the taxpayer relief provisions. Perhaps the most useful information is a guide that was prepared by the CRA for internal use. This *Taxpayer Relief Guide,* which is available as the result of a request made under the Federal *Access To Information Act*, provides a very extensive discussion of the application of the taxpayer relief provisions.

2-159. We would note that it has become commonplace for decisions made under the authority of the taxpayer relief legislation to be challenged in court through an application for judicial review. This may result in the decision being returned to the CRA for reconsideration (see *Robertson vs. MNR 2003* DTC 5068, or *Cayer vs. CRA 2009* DTC 5191).

2-160. We would also note that the CRA has taken a number of steps that are designed to ensure that taxpayers are, in fact, treated fairly. These include the publication of a fairness pledge as well as a taxpayer bill of rights. More information about this subject is available on the CRA web site.

Key Terms Used In This Chapter

2-161. The following is a list of the key terms used in this Chapter. These terms, and their meanings, are compiled in the Glossary Of Key Terms located at the back of the separate paper Study Guide.

Assessment	Prescribed Rate
Consent Form	Reasonable Expectation Of Profit (REOP)
EFILE	Reassessment
Fairness Package	Small CCPC
GAAR	Source Deductions
Information Return	Tax Avoidance
Instalment Threshold	Tax Court Of Canada
Instalments	Tax Evasion
Net Tax Owing	Tax Planning
NETFILE	Taxpayer
Notice Of Assessment	Taxpayer Relief Provisions
Notice Of Objection	TELEFILE
Penalties	

References

2-162.   For more detailed study of the material in this Chapter, we would refer you to the following:

ITA 150	Filing Returns Of Income - General Rule
ITA 151	Estimate Of Tax
ITA 152	Assessment
ITA 153(1)	Withholding
ITA 156	Other Individuals (Instalments)
ITA 156.1	Definitions (Instalments)
ITA 157	Payment By Corporation (Instalments)
ITA 161	Interest (General)
ITA 162-163.1	Penalties
ITA 163.2	Misrepresentation Of A Tax Matter By A Third Party
ITA 164(1)	Refunds
ITA 165	Objections To Assessment
ITA 169-180	Appeals To The Tax Court Of Canada And The Federal Court Of Appeal
ITA 220	Minister's Duty
ITA 221	Regulations
ITA 222	Definitions (Collections)
ITA 223	Definitions (Seizure Of Property)
ITA 224	Garnishment
ITA 227	Withholding Taxes
ITA 230	Records And Books
ITA 231.1	Inspections
ITA 231.2	Requirement To Provide Documents Or Information
ITA 261	Definitions (Functional Currency)
ITA 245-246	Tax Avoidance
ITR Part II	Information Returns
ITR 4301	Prescribed Rate of Interest
ITR 5300	Instalments (Individuals)
ITR 5301	Instalments (Corporations)
ITR 5800	Retention Of Books And Records
IC 71-14R3	The Tax Audit
IC 75-6R2	Required Withholding From Amounts Paid To Non-Resident Persons Providing Services In Canada

IC 75-7R3   Reassessment Of A Return Of Income
IC 78-10R5   Books And Records Retention/Destruction
IC 84-1   Revision Of CCA Claims And Other Permissive Deductions
IC 88-2   General Anti-Avoidance Rule: Section 245 Of The Income Tax Act
IC 98-1R3   Collection Policies
IC 00-1R2   Voluntary Disclosures Program
IC 01-1   Third-Party Civil Penalties
IC 07-1   Taxpayer Relief Provisions

P148   Resolving Your Dispute: Objection And Appeal Rights Under The Income Tax Act

Problems For Self Study

(The solutions for these problems can be found in the separate Study Guide.)

Self Study Problem Two - 1 (Individual Tax Instalments)

In January, 2012, you are asked to provide tax advice to Mr. Lester Gore. He has provided you with the following information about his combined federal and provincial taxes payable and the income taxes withheld by his employer for the 2010 and 2011 taxation years:

Year	Taxes Payable	Taxes Withheld
2010	$15,000	$11,500
2011	10,800	11,750

For 2012, he estimates that his combined federal and provincial taxes payable will be $17,000 and that his employer will withhold a total of $13,000 in income taxes.

He has asked you whether it will be necessary for him to pay instalments in 2012 and, if so, what the minimum amounts that should be paid are, and when they should be paid.

Required: Provide the information requested by Mr. Gore. Note that, in answering this question, you should state a conclusion on whether or not instalments are required, even if the amount of the instalments is nil. Also indicate the required due dates, even if no instalments are required.

Self Study Problem Two - 2 (Corporate Tax Instalments)

Amalmor Inc. is not a small CCPC. For its fiscal year ending December 31, 2010, the Company had Taxable Income of $250,000 and paid taxes of $62,500. In 2011, the corresponding figures were $320,000 and $80,000. It is estimated that for the current year ending December 31, 2012, the Company will have Taxable Income of $380,000 and taxes payable of $95,000.

Required:

A. Determine the amount of the minimum instalments that must be made by Amalmor Inc. during 2012 and when they would be due.

B. How would your answer differ if Amalmor Inc. was a small CCPC?

Self Study Problem Two - 3 (Individual And Corporate Tax Instalments)

For the three years ending December 31, 2012, the taxpayer's combined federal and provincial taxes payable were as follows:

Year Ending December 31	Taxes Payable
2010	$23,540
2011	11,466
2012 (Estimated)	25,718

Case One   The taxpayer is an individual whose employer withholds combined federal and provincial taxes of $18,234 in 2010, $7,850 in 2011, and $27,346 in 2012.

Case Two   The taxpayer is an individual whose employer withholds combined federal and provincial taxes of $21,720 in 2010, $6,250 in 2011, and $21,833 in 2012.

Case Three   The taxpayer is a small CCPC with a taxation year that ends on December 31.

Case Four The taxpayer is a publicly traded corporation with a taxation year that ends on December 31. Assume that its combined federal and provincial taxes payable for the year ending December 31, 2011 were $32,560, instead of the $11,466 given in the problem.

Required: For each of the preceding independent Cases determine:

- Whether instalments are required for the 2012 taxation year (you should indicate the requirement to make instalments, even if one of the methods results in instalments of nil). Explain your conclusion.

- If instalments are required, indicate the best alternative for calculating the instalments, as well as the amount of the instalments under that alternative.

- If instalment payments must be made, indicate the dates on which the payments will be due.

Self Study Problem Two - 4 (Individual And Corporate Tax Instalments)

For the year ending December 31, 2010, the taxpayer's combined federal and provincial taxes payable amounted to $18,000, while for the year ending December 31, 2011, the amount payable was $14,400. It is estimated that federal and provincial taxes payable for the year ending December 31, 2012 will be $13,500.

Required: For each of the following independent Cases, indicate whether instalments are required for the 2012 taxation year (you should indicate the requirement to make instalments, even if one of the methods results in instalments of nil). Explain your conclusion. sIn addition, if instalments are required, indicate the best alternative for calculating the instalments, as well as the amount of the instalments under that alternative. Also, if instalment payments must be made, indicate the dates on which the payments will be due.

A. The taxpayer is an individual whose employer withholds combined federal and provincial taxes of $12,000 in 2010, $10,000 in 2011, and $10,000 in 2012.

B. The taxpayer is an individual whose employer withholds combined federal and provincial taxes of $7,000 in 2010, $15,000 in 2011, and $9,000 in 2012.

C. The taxpayer is a small CCPC with a December 31 year end.

D. The taxpayer is a publicly traded corporation with a December 31 year end. Assume that its combined federal and provincial taxes payable for the year ending December 31, 2012 are estimated to be $16,000, instead of the $13,500 given in the problem.

Self Study Problem Two - 5 (Canadian Taxable Entities)

List the three types of entities that are subject to federal income taxation in Canada and, for each, state:

- how their taxation year is established;
- the filing deadlines for their respective income tax returns;
- how frequently income tax instalments must be made; and
- the dates on which the instalment payments must be made.

Self Study Problem Two - 6 (Assessment Disputes)

Mr. Coffee is one of your major clients. He is extremely wealthy and has paid his very sizable tax payable over the years without complaint.

On August 15th of the current year, Mr. Coffee receives a notice from the CRA indicating that he is being reassessed for the preceding taxation year. The additional amount of taxes involved is $5,000, and he feels that the position of the CRA is completely unjustified.

Mr. Coffee has approached you for advice on dealing with the matter.

Required: Indicate the procedures that may be used in dealing with this dispute between the CRA and Mr. Coffee.

Assignment Problems

(The solutions for these problems are only available in
the solutions manual that has been provided to your instructor.)

Assignment Problem Two - 1 *(Individual Tax Instalments)*

For the three years 2010, 2011, and 2012, Mr. George Grafton provides the following information on his combined federal and provincial taxes payable, along with information on withholdings by his employer:

Year	Taxes Payable	Taxes Withheld
2010	$31,500	$29,800
2011	14,600	6,200
2012 (Estimated)	27,400	24,300

In January, 2012, you are asked to provide tax advice to Mr. Grafton. He has asked you whether it will be necessary for him to pay instalments in 2012 and, if so, what the minimum amounts that should be paid are, along with the dates on which these amounts are due.

Required: Provide the information requested by Mr. Grafton.

Assignment Problem Two - 2
(Instalments, Interest And Penalties For Corporations)

For both tax and accounting purposes Lanterna Inc. has a July 31 year end. Lanterna is a publicly traded Canadian company.

For the three years ending July 31, 2012, it provides the following information with respect to its federal Tax Payable:

2010	$32,650
2011	41,720
2012 (Estimated)	39,460

Required:

A. Calculate the instalment payments that are required for the year ending July 31, 2012 under the alternative methods available. Indicate which of the alternatives would be preferable.

B. If the Company did not make any instalment payments towards its 2012 taxes payable, and did not file its corporate tax return or pay its taxes payable on time, indicate how the interest and penalty amounts assessed against it would be determined (a detailed calculation is not required).

Assignment Problem Two - 3 *(Individual Tax Instalments)*

For the three years ending December 31, 2012, George Shivraj had combined federal and provincial Tax Payable as follows:

2010	$13,500
2011	16,200
2012 (Estimated)	18,400

Using this information consider the following three independent cases.

Case One   Mr. Shivraj's employer withholds $11,200 in 2010, $12,900 in 2011, and $15,100 in 2011.

Case Two   Mr. Shivraj's employer withholds $9,200 in 2010, $10,300 in 2011, and $14,900 in 2012.

Case Three   Mr. Shivraj's employer withholds $9,800 in 2012, $16,300 in in 2011, and $14,700 in 2012.

Required: For each of the preceding independent Cases, calculate the minimum instalment payments that are required to be made towards the settlement of the taxes payable for the year ending December 31, 2012. If instalments must be paid, include in your answer the date that each instalment is due. Note that, in answering this question, you should state a conclusion on whether or not instalments are required, even if the amount of the instalments is nil.

Assignment Problem Two - 4 *(Corporate Tax Instalments)*

For the three taxation years ending December 31, 2012, a corporation's combined federal and provincial tax payable are as follows:

Year Ending December 31	Taxes Payable
2010	$ 86,500
2011	101,400
2012 (Estimated)	94,600

Case One   The taxpayer is a small CCPC.

Case Two   The taxpayer is a small CCPC. Assume that its combined federal and provincial taxes payable for the year ending December 31, 2011 were $92,100, instead of the $101,400 given in the problem.

Case Three   The taxpayer is a publicly traded corporation.

Case Four   The taxpayer is a publicly traded corporation. Assume that its combined federal and provincial taxes payable for the year ending December 31, 2011 were $92,100, instead of the $101,400 given in the problem.

Required: For each of the preceding independent Cases, provide the following information:

1. Indicate whether instalments are required during 2012. Provide a brief explanation of your conclusion.

2. Calculate the amount of instalments that would be required under each of the acceptable methods available.

3. Indicate which of the available methods would best serve to minimize instalment payments during 2012. If instalments must be paid, indicate the dates on which they are due.

Assignment Problem Two - 5 (Filing Dates)

In addition to interest charges on any late payment of taxes, penalties may be assessed for failure to file a return within the prescribed deadlines. These deadlines vary depending on the taxpayer.

Required: Indicate when income tax returns must be filed for each of the following types of taxpayers:

    A. Living individuals.
    B. Deceased individuals.
    C. Trusts.
    D. Corporations.

Assignment Problem Two - 6 (Appeals)

Mr. James Simon has asked for your services with respect to dealing with a reassessment notice requesting additional tax for the 2008 taxation year which he says he has just received. Your first interview takes place on March 15, 2012, and Mr. Simon informs you that he has had considerable difficulty with the CRA in past years and, on two occasions in the past five years, he has been required to pay penalties as well as interest.

With respect to the current reassessment, he assures you that he has complied with the law and that there is a misunderstanding on the part of the assessor. After listening to him describe the situation, you decide it is likely that his analysis of the situation is correct.

Required: Indicate what additional information should be obtained during the interview with Mr. Simon and what steps should be taken if you decide to accept him as a client.

Assignment Problem Two - 7 (Tax Preparer's Penalty)

For each of the following independent cases, indicate whether you believe a penalty would be assessed against the tax return preparer under ITA 163.2. Explain your conclusion.

    A. Accountant X is asked by Client A to prepare a tax return including a business financial statement to be used in the return. In response to a request by Accountant X for business related documents, Client A supplies information to Accountant X, which includes a travel expense receipt. Accountant X relies on this information provided by Client A and prepares the business statement that is filed with the return. The CRA conducts a compliance audit and determines that Client A's travel expense was a non-deductible personal expense.

    B. Accountant X has several clients that have been reassessed in respect of a tax shelter. Accountant X knows that the CRA is challenging the tax effects claimed in respect of the tax shelter on the basis that the shelter is not a business, is based on a significant overvaluation of the related property and is technically deficient in its structure. The Tax Court of Canada, in a test case (general procedures), denies deductions claimed in respect of the tax shelter in a previous year by Client B (a client of Accountant X). Client B's appeal is dismissed. The case is not appealed and Accountant X is aware of the Court's decision. Accountant X prepares and files a tax return on behalf of Client C that includes a claim in respect of the same tax shelter that the Tax Court denied deductions for.

    C. Taxpayer Z approaches Tax-preparer X to prepare and EFILE Z's tax return. Taxpayer Z provides X with a T4 slip indicating that Z has $32,000 of employment income. Taxpayer Z advises X that he made a charitable donation of $24,000 but forgot the receipt at home. Z asks that X prepare and EFILE the tax return. In fact, Z never donated anything to a charity. X prepares Z's tax return without obtaining the receipt.

CHAPTER 3

Income Or Loss From An Office Or Employment

Employment Income Defined

General Rules

3-1. Income or loss from an office or employment (employment income, hereafter) is covered in Part I, Division B, Subdivision a of the *Income Tax Act*. This relatively short Subdivision is made up of Sections 5 through 8, the general contents of which can be described as follows:

Section 5 contains a definition of employment income.

Section 6 provides detailed information on what amounts must be included in the determination of employment income.

Section 7 is a more specialized Section that provides the tax rules associated with stock options granted to employees.

Section 8 provides detailed information on what amounts can be deducted in the determination of employment income.

3-2. The basic description of employment income is as follows:

ITA 5(1) Subject to this Part, a taxpayer's income for a taxation year from an office or employment is the salary, wages and other remuneration, including gratuities, received by the taxpayer in the year.

3-3. While ITA 5(2) contemplates the possibility of a loss from an office or employment, the limited amount of deductions that can be made against employment income inclusions would make such an event unusual.

3-4. "Employment" is generally defined in ITA 248(1) as the position of an individual in the service of some other person. Similarly, "office" is defined as the position of an individual entitling him to a fixed or ascertainable stipend or remuneration. As will be discussed later, determining whether an individual is, or is not, an employee can be a contentious issue.

3-5. As to what is included in employment income, the terms "salary" and "wages" generally refer to monetary amounts provided in return for employment services. However, the term "remuneration" is somewhat broader and includes any type of reward or benefit associated with employment services. With the specific inclusion of gratuities, it is clear that employment income includes not only payments from an employer but, in addition, includes any other payments or benefits that result from a taxpayer's position as an employee.

3-6.   While it would not be common, it is possible that an individual could receive a payment from an employer that is not related to the quantity or quality of services performed as an employee. For example, if the employee made a personal loan to the employer, any interest paid by the employer to the employee on the loan would not be considered employment income.

Cash Basis And The Use Of Bonus Arrangements

Amounts Received

3-7.   As presented in Paragraph 3-2, the definition of an employee's income states that it is made up of amounts "received by the taxpayer in the year". This serves to establish that employment income must be reported on a cash basis, not on an accrual basis.

Tax Planning Opportunity

3-8.   This fact, when combined with the fact that business income for tax purposes is calculated on an accrual basis (see Chapter 6), provides a tax planning opportunity. A business can declare a bonus to one of its employees and, because it is on an accrual basis, deduct it for tax purposes by simply recognizing a firm obligation to pay the amount. In contrast, the employee who has earned the bonus will not have to include it in employment income until it is actually received.

> **Example**   A business with a December 31 year end declares a bonus to one of its employees in December, 2012, but stipulates that it will not be paid until January, 2013.

> **Analysis**   While the business would get the deduction in 2012, the employee would not have to include the amount in income until the 2013 taxation year. If the bonus had been paid in December, 2012, the employee would have had to include it in income in 2012. In effect, this arrangement defers the taxation applicable to the employee by one taxation year.

Limits On Deferral

3-9.   There are, however, limits to this procedure. ITA 78(4) indicates that, where such a bonus is not paid within 180 days of the employer's year end (note that this is not always December 31), the employer will not be able to deduct the amount until it is paid.

> **Example**   An employer with a June 30 year end declares a bonus for an employee on June 30, 2012 that is payable on January 1, 2013.

> **Analysis**   As January 1, 2013 is more than 180 days after the employer's year end, the employer will not be able to deduct the bonus in the fiscal year ending June 30, 2012. It will have to be deducted in the fiscal year ending June 30, 2013.

3-10.   A further problem arises when a "bonus" will not be paid until more than three years after the end of the calendar year in which the employee's services were rendered. In this case, the "bonus" may become a "salary deferral arrangement", resulting in the employee being taxed on the relevant amounts in the year in which the services were rendered. This type of arrangement is discussed in more detail in Chapter 10.

3-11.   The tax consequences associated with the three types of bonus arrangements are summarized in the following Figure 3-1:

Figure 3 - 1 Bonus Arrangements	
Type Of Bonus Arrangement	**Tax Consequences**
Standard Bonus (Paid within 180 days of business year end.)	The employer deducts when declared. The employee includes when received.
Other Bonus (Paid more than 180 days after the employer's year end, but prior to three years after the end of the year in which the bonus was earned.)	The employer deducts when paid. The employee includes when received.
Salary Deferral Arrangement (Paid more than three years after the end of the year in which it was earned.)	The employer deducts when earned. The employee includes when earned. (See Chapter 10)

Exercise Three - 1

Subject: Bonus

Neelson Inc. has a September 30 year end. On September 30, 2012, it declares a bonus of $100,000 payable to Mr. Sam Neelson, an executive of the Company. The bonus is payable on May 1, 2013. Describe the tax consequences of this bonus to both Neelson Inc. and Mr. Neelson.

End of Exercise. Solution available in Study Guide.

Net Concept

3-12.   Employment income is a net income concept. That is, it is made up of both inclusions (e.g., salaries and wages) and deductions (e.g., registered pension plan contributions and union dues). In conjunction with this, we would point out that the deductions that are described in ITA 8 can only be deducted against employment income inclusions. Given the limited deductions available in the determination of employment income, it would be very rare for these deductions to exceed the inclusions.

3-13.   If an employment loss were to occur, the excess ITA 8 deductions could not be applied against any other source of income. However, if other sources of income are available, the same result can be accomplished by deducting the net employment loss under ITA 3(d) as per the calculation of Net Income For Tax Purposes that is described in Chapter 1.

> **Example** An individual has employment income of $3,000 and employment expenses of $4,500 (as indicated this is unlikely to occur in the real world).

> **Analysis**   This would result in an employment loss of $1,500 ($4,500 - $3,000). Provided the individual has at least a $1,500 balance after ITA 3(c), this amount can be deducted in the determination of Net Income For Tax Purposes.

Employee Versus Self-Employed

Introduction

3-14.   An individual doing work for an organization will be undertaking this activity in one of two possible roles. He may be working as an employee. If this is the case, he is earning employment income and is subject to the rules discussed in this Chapter.

3-15.   In contrast, he may be working as a self-employed individual, often referred to as an independent contractor (from the point of view of the organization using the individual's services, such arrangements are referred to as contracting out). The payments made to such self-employed individuals are classified as business income and are subject to the rules that are covered in Chapter 6, Business Income.

3-16.   This distinction is of considerable importance, both to the individual worker and to the organization using his services. Given this importance, the following material describes the tax features of these alternatives, both from the point of view of the worker and from the point of view of the organization using his services.

3-17.   In terms of tax planning, structuring a working relationship to achieve the desired classification of the individual doing the work may result in tax avoidance for both parties. For the worker, being classified as a self-employed individual will generally result in larger deductions against income, thereby reducing Tax Payable.   From the point of view of the organization using the individual's services, the independent contractor classification can reduce the costs of using those services.

Employee Perspective
Deductions Available

3-18.   As will be discussed later in this Chapter, an individual's ability to deduct expenses from employment income is quite limited when compared to self-employed individuals. If an individual is self-employed, any income that he earns is classified as business income, making it eligible for the wider range of deductions that is available under the business income provisions of the *Income Tax Act*. For example, a self-employed professional can deduct the costs of driving to work. If this individual were classified as an employee, this deduction would not be available.

CPP And EI Contributions

3-19.   If an individual is an employee, his employer will be required to withhold a portion of his pay for Canada Pension Plan (CPP) contributions and Employment Insurance (EI) premiums. With respect to CPP contributions, for 2012 both the employee and the employer are required to contribute 4.95 percent of up to $50,100 of gross wages in excess of a basic exemption of $3,500. This results in maximum contributions by both the employee and employer of $2,307, or a total of $4,614. With respect to EI premiums, the amount paid by the employee amounts to 1.83 percent of the first $45,900 in gross wages, with a maximum annual value of $840. The employer is assessed 1.4 times this amount, an effective rate of 2.56 percent.

3-20.   In contrast, if an individual is self-employed, there will be no withholding of either CPP or EI from the amounts received as business income. However, this does not mean that this individual can completely escape these costs. With respect to CPP contributions, a self employed individual must make contributions on the same basis as an employee. Further, self-employed individuals are required to pay both an employee share and an employer share, resulting in a potential maximum payment of $4,614.

3-21.   Prior to 2010, self-employed individuals could not participate in the EI program. However, as of January, 2010, individuals can opt into this program on a voluntary basis for special (restricted) EI benefits. They must opt in at least 12 months prior to making a claim, but once they opt in, they are committed for the taxation year. Further, if a claim is made under this program, the individual is committed for life, or until they stop being self employed. The good news is that self-employed individuals do not have to pay the employer's share of EI premiums. This means the maximum cost for 2012 would be $840.

3-22.   Although CPP contributions and EI premiums are not part of net tax owing, as noted in Chapter 2, CPP and EI amounts for the self-employed are collected by the CRA. They are calculated on the T1 tax return where they become part of the amount owing. Further, the CRA includes them in the instalment base when instalments are required. This, of course, means that they may be a factor in determining the size of quarterly instalments. However, this could be viewed as a modest advantage of being self employed as there is some deferral of the required payments over payroll deductions.

3-23.   With respect to CPP contributions, any benefit resulting from deferral of the required payments is clearly offset by the fact that the self-employed individual has to pay both the employee and the employer share. There is clearly an overall disadvantage to the self-employed individual.

3-24. This is not the case with EI. There is some deferral of payment here. Further, participation is voluntary, suggesting that the self-employed individual will not pay these amounts unless he has concluded that it is to his advantage. Finally, unlike the situation with CPP contributions, the self-employed individual does not have to pay the employer's share of these amounts. The EI rules appear to be advantageous to the self-employed individual.

Fringe Benefits

3-25. A significant disadvantage of being classified as an independent contractor rather than an employee is the fact that independent contractors do not receive fringe benefits. An employee may receive a wide variety of benefits such as dental and drug plans, membership in a registered pension plan, vacation pay, or life insurance coverage. These benefits may, in some cases, add as much as 20 percent to an employee's remuneration. The fact that such benefits are not available to a self-employed individual means that he will have to receive significantly higher basic remuneration to be in the same economic position as an individual working as an employee who has generous benefits.

Opportunity For Tax Evasion

3-26. While we certainly do not condone this, as a practical matter, being self-employed can offer significantly larger opportunities for tax evasion. When employment income is received from a business, there are stringent reporting requirements that make it difficult for an employee to avoid detection if he fails to report employment income.

3-27. In contrast, self-employment income is sometimes received partially or wholly in cash, depending on the clients. Usually when cash is received, the work is being done for an individual who cannot deduct the cost of the work and does not require a receipt to be issued. A common example of this would be the owner of a residence who hires a self-employed contractor to do renovations.

3-28. If the self-employed individual is willing to evade taxes by not reporting these revenues, then the lack of withholding on self-employment earnings becomes a permanent reduction in taxes. Although it is a clearly illegal form of behavior, for some individuals, not reporting earnings received in cash is one of the main motivations behind being self-employed.

Conclusion

3-29. As the preceding indicates, the desirability of self-employed status is not clear cut. For an individual with limited deductible expenses, self-employment may not be advantageous from an economic point of view. Alternatively, if an individual's work is such that large amounts of business expenses are generated, it is probably desirable to be taxed as a self-employed contractor.

3-30. Non-tax advantages could include the ability to set work schedules and the freedom to choose the amount and type of work accepted. The added cost of accounting for the business and the implications of the GST/HST would also have to be considered. As noted in Chapter 21, in most cases, a self-employed individual would have to register for the GST/HST if he is not a small supplier.

Employer Perspective

3-31. There are several advantages to a business from using the services of self-employed individuals as opposed to employees. One of the major advantages associated with the hiring of these independent contractors (a.k.a. contracting out) is that the employer avoids payments for Canada Pension Plan (CPP), Employment Insurance (EI), Workers' Compensation, and Provincial Health Care (where applicable).

3-32.　　The amounts involved here are consequential. CPP and EI payments alone can add more than 7 percent to the wage costs. Provincial payroll taxes can push the total of these costs above 10 percent of wage costs. Further cost savings result from the fact that the employer will avoid the administrative costs associated with having to withhold and remit income taxes and the employee's share of CPP and EI payments.

3-33.　　Also in favour of using independent contractors is the fact that the business will avoid the costs of any fringe benefits that it normally extends to its employees. A less measurable benefit is that employers are freed from ongoing commitments to individuals because there is generally no long-term contract with self-employed workers.

3-34.　　An additional and less direct advantage of using independent contractors is that the business is not legally responsible for their work. If an employee does work that results in some type of legal liability for damages, it is the employer that will be responsible for any costs that arise. In contrast, if such work is carried out by an independent contractor, the organization may escape any legal responsibility.

3-35.　　Given all of these advantages, it is not surprising to find more businesses contracting out in order to control labour costs and limit liability.

Making The Distinction

Intent

3-36.　　The general approach to distinguishing between an employee and an independent contractor is the question of whether an employer/employee relationship exists. As there is no clear definition of employer/employee relationships, disputes between taxpayers and the CRA are very common. To avoid such disputes, and to assist taxpayers in determining whether or not an individual is an employee, the CRA provides a Guide titled "Employee Or Self-Employed?" (RC4110).

3-37.　　As described in this pamphlet, the first step in making this distinction is to determine the intent of both parties. Both the worker and the payer must be clear as to whether there is a contract of service (employee/employer) or alternatively, a contract for services (business relationship). This intent may or may not be in the form of a written agreement.

Other Factors

3-38.　　In many cases, the intent may be clear. However, the worker and payer must ensure that their intent is reflected in the actual terms and conditions of their relationship. In making this determination, the Guide indicates that the following factors will be considered by the CRA:

Control　　In an employer/employee relationship, the employer usually controls, directly or indirectly, the way the work is done and the work methods used. The employer assigns specific tasks that define the real framework within which the work is to be done.

Ownership Of Tools And Equipment　　In an employer/employee relationship, the employer usually supplies the equipment and tools required by the employee. In addition, the employer covers the following costs related to their use: repairs, insurance, transport, rental, and operations (e.g., fuel).

In some trades, however, it is customary for employees to supply their own tools. This is generally the case for garage mechanics, painters, and carpenters. Similarly, employed computer scientists, architects, and surveyors sometimes supply their own software and instruments.

Ability To Subcontract Or Hire Assistants　　If the individual must personally perform the services, he is likely to be considered an employee. Alternatively, if the individual can hire assistants, with the payer having no control over the identity of the assistants, the individual is likely to be considered self-employed.

Financial Risk In general, employees will not have any financial risks associated with their work. In contrast, self-employed individuals can have risk and can incur losses. Responsibility for fixed monthly costs is a good indicator that an individual is self-employed.

Responsibility For Investment And Management If the individual has no capital investment in the business and no presence in management, he is likely to be considered an employee. Alternatively, if the individual has made an investment and is active in managing the business, he should be considered self-employed.

Opportunity For Profit In an employer/employee relationship, the employer alone normally assumes the risk of loss. The employer also usually covers operating costs, which may include office expenses, employee wages and benefits, insurance premiums, and delivery and shipping costs. The employee does not assume any financial risk, and is entitled to his full salary or wages regardless of the financial health of the business.

Correspondingly, an employee will have little or no opportunity for profit. While there may be productivity bonuses for exceptional work, such amounts are not generally viewed as profit.

3-39. The CRA Guide includes a long list of indicators for each of the preceding factors that could affect whether an individual was considered an employee or self-employed. This Guide can be quite helpful if more detailed information in this area is required.

3-40. We would point out that it is extremely important for a business to be sure that any individual who is being treated as a self-employed contractor qualifies for that status. Actions that can be taken to ensure self-employed status for the individual include:

- Having the individual register for the GST.
- Having the individual work for other businesses.
- Having the individual advertise his services.
- To the extent possible, having the individual cover his own overhead, including phone service, letterhead, equipment, and supplies.
- Having the individual prepare periodic invoices, preferably on an irregular basis.
- Having a lawyer prepare an independent contractor agreement.
- If feasible, having the individual incorporate.

3-41. A failure to take these steps could prove to be very costly to a business using the services of that individual. It is possible that, if the CRA judges the individual to be an employee, the business could be held liable for CPP and EI amounts that should have been withheld from the individual's earnings, as well as the employer's share of these amounts.

Inclusions - Salaries And Wages

3-42. We have noted that ITA 5 specifies that employment income includes salaries, wages, and other remuneration. When only salaries or wages are involved, there is little need to elaborate on employment income inclusions. Such amounts clearly must be included in the determination of employment income. However, for a variety of reasons, employers make use of many benefits other than salaries or wages. These alternative forms of compensation are commonly referred to as fringe benefits and they create additional complexity in the determination of employment income for income tax purposes.

Inclusions - Fringe Benefits

ITA 6(1) - Amounts To Be Included In Income

3-43. ITA 6 contains several Subsections dealing with inclusions in employment income. The first of these, ITA 6(1), contains a number of Paragraphs that either list specific items to be included in employment income (e.g., standby charge for automobiles), or describe a type of item that must be incorporated into this determination (e.g., personal or living expenses).

3-44.   The first of these Paragraphs, ITA 6(1)(a), contains a general provision which states that all benefits received or enjoyed by an individual by virtue of an office or employment must be included in income. However, this same Paragraph also notes a number of important items that can be excluded. These include

- employers contributions to:
  - registered pension plans;
  - group sickness or accident insurance plans, provided that any benefits received under the plan will be taxed under ITA 6(1)(f);
  - private health services plans;
  - supplementary unemployment benefit plans;
  - deferred profit sharing plans;
  - employee life and health trusts.

- counseling services related to the mental or physical health of the employee or a related party, or related to re-employment or retirement of the employee; and,

- benefits under a retirement compensation arrangement, employee benefit plans (e.g. death benefit plans), and employee trusts. However actual payments or allocations from such plans or arrangements are taxable elsewhere.

- benefits resulting from reduced tuition provided to the children of teachers at private schools, provided the teacher is dealing at arm's length with the school and the reduction is not a substitute for salary or other remuneration from the school.

  Note   If you were to read ITA 6(1)(a), you would find that the listed exclusions include both group term life insurance, as well as benefits related to automobiles. This sounds like these items are not taxable benefits. However, this is not the case. In a somewhat awkward approach to this issue, these benefits are excluded under ITA 6(1)(a), but included under other provisions. Automobile benefits are included under ITA 6(1)(e) and (k) as listed in the following paragraph, and group term life insurance premiums are included under ITA 6(4).

3-45.   Other Paragraphs under ITA 6(1) provide additional guidance in the form of specific items that must be included in employment income. These are:

- ITA 6(1)(b)   amounts received as an allowance for personal or living expenses or as an allowance for any other purpose;
- ITA 6(1)(c)   director's or other fees;
- ITA 6(1)(d)   allocations under profit sharing plans;
- ITA 6(1)(e)   standby charge for automobiles;
- ITA 6(1)(f)   wage loss replacement plans, provided they are received on a periodic basis and are intended to replace employment income;
- ITA 6(1)(g)   employee benefit plan benefits;
- ITA 6(1)(h)   allocations under employee trusts;
- ITA 6(1)(i)   salary deferral arrangement payments;
- ITA 6(1)(j)   reimbursements and awards; and
- ITA 6(1)(k)   automobile operating expense benefit.

CRA Administrative Practice On Fringe Benefits (IT-470R)
Inclusions Under IT-470R
3-46.   At a less formal level, an important Interpretation Bulletin provides guidance with respect to fringe benefits. This Bulletin, IT-470R (Consolidated), indicates that the following benefits should be considered as part of employment income:

- board and lodging that is provided free or at an unreasonably low rate
- rent free and low rent housing
- travel benefits
- personal use of an automobile furnished by an employer
- gifts (see Paragraph 3-47)

- holiday trips, other prizes and incentive awards
- points used for personal travel that were earned in frequent flyer programs while traveling on employer paid business trips (see Paragraph 3-51)
- travel expenses of the employee's spouse if there is no business reason for the travel
- premiums that are allocated to specific employees under provincial hospitalization and medical care insurance plans, and certain Government of Canada plans
- employer paid educational costs (see paragraph 3-56)
- employer reimbursement for the cost of tools required to perform work
- wage loss replacement plans
- amounts related to interest free or low interest loans
- financial counseling and income tax preparation

Gifts

3-47.   Employers commonly provide both gifts and awards to their employees. These items are clearly benefits to the recipient employees and, in the absence of some type of special provision, would be taxable. This view is reflected in the list of taxable items that is found in IT-470R.

3-48.   Despite the clarity of the legislation applicable to this situation, the CRA has, for many years, attempted to provide some room for providing a limited amount of such benefits on a tax free basis. The current policy was issued in Income Tax Technical News No. 40 (June, 2009). The discussion which follows is based entirely on the content of this publication.

3-49.   As found in Technical News No. 40, the current policy is as follows:

- Non-cash gifts and non-cash awards to an arm's length employee, regardless of number, will not be taxable to the extent that the total aggregate value of all non-cash gifts and awards to that employee is less than $500 annually. The total value in excess of $500 annually will be taxable.

- In addition to the preceding, a separate non-cash long service/anniversary award may also qualify for non-taxable status to the extent its total value is $500 or less. The value in excess of $500 will be taxable. In order to qualify, the anniversary award cannot be for less than five years of service or for five years since the last long service award had been provided to the employee. For the purposes of applying the $500 thresholds, the annual gifts and awards threshold and the long service/anniversary awards threshold are separate. In other words, a shortfall in value under one policy cannot be used to offset an excess value of the other.

- The employer gift and award policy will not apply to non-arm's length employees (e.g., relative of proprietor, shareholders of closely held corporations) or related persons of the non-arm's length employee.

- For clarification purposes, items of an immaterial or nominal value, such as coffee, tea, T-shirts with employer logos, mugs, plaques, trophies, etc., will not be considered a taxable benefit to employees. There is no defined monetary threshold that determines an immaterial amount. Factors that may be taken into account include the value, frequency, and administrative practicability of accounting for nominal benefits.

3-50.   Two additional points are made with respect to the nature of gifts that qualify under these rules:

- Performance related rewards (e.g., rewards for being the month's top salesperson) do not qualify for treatment as gifts and will be taxable to the recipient.

- Cash and near cash rewards (e.g., gift certificates that can be redeemed for a wide selection of items) do not qualify for treatment as gifts and will be taxable to the recipient.

Exercise Three - 2

Subject: Gifts To Employees

During the current year, Jeffrey's employer provides him with a number of gifts and awards. Describe the tax consequences for Jeffrey that result from each of the following gifts and awards.

Gift	Fair Market Value
T-shirt with employer logo	$ 15
Birthday gift (gift certificate at The Bay)	75
Reward for exceeding sales targets	400
10 year anniversary award (Seiko watch)	275
Wedding gift (crystal vase)	300
Weight loss award (tickets to sporting event)	250
Holiday season gift (gourmet food basket)	150

End of Exercise. Solution available in Study Guide.

Loyalty Programs (Frequent Flyer Points)

3-51.   It is not uncommon for employees to earn points in loyalty programs as a result of expenditures made when involved in employment related activities. Perhaps the most important of these situations involves individuals who earn points in airline or other loyalty programs as the result of business travel.

Example   Ms. Gerri Donat flies 250,000 miles on Air Canada during the current year. All of this travel was related to her employment. The $150,000 cost of the airline tickets was charged to her credit card. However, her employer reimbursed all of these costs. As a result of her travel and the fact that her credit card also provided Aeroplan miles, Ms. Donat has 650,000 Aeroplan miles.

3-52.   In general, in situations such as this, employers have allowed their employees to use their Aeroplan miles for personal travel. Under IT-470R, the employee was required to include the value of such personal travel in their Net Income For Tax Purposes.

3-53.   This rule created significant difficulties for employees in that they were required to determine the fair market value of the travel. Further, they had to segregate points accumulated through employment from points accumulated through personal expenditures. The rule also created significant difficulties for the CRA in that its enforcement was nearly impossible.

3-54.   Given these considerations, the CRA changed its administrative practice in this area. As noted in Income Tax Technical News No. 40 (June, 2009), the CRA no longer requires that the cost of personal benefits related to points earned through employment activity be included in income provided:

• the points are not converted to cash;
• the plan is not an alternative form of remuneration; and
• the plan is not for tax avoidance purposes.

3-55. Two other considerations are noted:

• If the employer controls the points (e.g., they are earned using a company credit card, with the points accruing to the employee), use of the points will create a taxable benefit.

• If the employee is allowed to use a personal credit card to pay the expenses of other employees or other general business costs in order to maximize point accumulation, and is reimbursed for these costs, use of the points will create a taxable benefit.

Tuition Fees

3-56.   The basic idea here is that employer-paid educational costs are not a taxable benefit if the learning experience is primarily for the benefit of the employer. If the costs are primarily for the benefit of the employee, it will be considered a taxable benefit. To assist in making this distinction, IT-470R describes three different situations:

- **Specific Employer-Related Training**   Courses that are taken for maintenance or upgrading of employer-related skills will generally be considered to primarily benefit the employer and therefore be non-taxable. An example of this would be an employer who provides bookkeeping services paying the tuition fees for an employee to take an accounting course.

- **General Employment-Related Training**   Other business-related courses, even if not directly related to the employer's business, will generally be considered non-taxable. Examples of non-taxable general training would include stress management, employment equity, first-aid, and language skills.

- **Personal Interest Training**   Employer-paid courses for personal interest or technical skills that are not related to the employer's business are considered of primary benefit to the employee and thus taxable. For example, fees paid for a self-interest music course would result in a taxable benefit.

3-57.   Note that the employer will be able to deduct these costs, without regard to whether they create a taxable benefit for the employee. The Bulletin also indicates that the relevant costs could include meals, travel, and accommodation as required by the educational program, again without regard to whether the employee is receiving a taxable benefit. If the tuition fees create a taxable benefit, the employee will be able to claim any related tuition fee tax credit (see Chapter 4).

Non-Taxable Benefits (IT-470R)

3-58.   Also found in IT-470R is a list of non-taxable benefits that are not included in employment income. These include:

- discounts on merchandise, other than big ticket items such as homes or appliances, and the waiving of commissions on sales of merchandise or insurance for the personal use of the employee
- subsidized meals provided in employer facilities
- uniforms and special clothing
- subsidized school services in remote areas
- transportation to the job in employer vehicles in specific circumstances
- use of employer recreational facilities
- membership fees in non-employer social or athletic clubs, provided it is an advantage to the employer for the employee to belong to such organizations
- reimbursement of certain moving expenses (See Chapter 9 for a detailed discussion of moving costs.)
- premiums under private health services plans [as noted in Paragraph 3-44, this is specifically excluded from employment income under ITA 6(1)(a)]
- employer's required contributions under certain provincial hospitalization and medical care insurance plans where remittances are based on some percentage of total payroll
- transportation passes for employees of bus or rail companies, and certain passes for employees of airline companies
- the costs of providing counseling services related to the mental or physical health of the employee, his re-employment, or his retirement [this item is also explicitly excluded from employment income under ITA 6(1)(a)]
- the cost of an employee's professional membership fees where the professional association is related to an employee's duties and membership is a requirement of employment

Other ITA 6 Inclusions

3-59. ITA 6(1) is the most broadly based Subsection in ITA 6. There are, however, a number of other Subsections that deal with specific items. These Subsections and where their coverage begins are as follows:

- ITA 6(2) and (2.1) **"Reasonable Standby Charges"** - Paragraph 3-86.

- ITA 6(3) and (3.1) **"Payments By Employer To Employee"**, which requires the inclusion of amounts paid either immediately before employment begins, or subsequent to the period of employment - Paragraph 3-181.

- ITA 6(4) **"Group Term Life Insurance"** - Paragraph 3-141.

- ITA 6(6) **"Employment At Special Work Site Or Remote Location"** - Paragraph 3-75.

- ITA 6(7) **"Cost Of Property Or Service"**, which requires the addition of applicable GST/HST/PST to the amount of some taxable benefits - Paragraph 3-73.

- ITA 6(9) **"Amount In Respect Of Interest On Employee Debt"** - Paragraph 3-150.

- ITA 6(11) **"Salary Deferral Arrangements"** are covered in Chapter 10, Retirement Savings And Other Special Income Arrangements.

- ITA 6(15) and (15.1) **"Forgiveness Of Employee Debt And Forgiven Amount"**, which require that employee debt forgiven by an employer must be included in employment income - Paragraph 3-182.

- ITA 6(19) through (22) **"Housing Loss And Eligible Housing Loss"** limit the amount that can be reimbursed on a tax free basis to an employee who has suffered a housing loss as the result of a required move. These Subsections are covered in this Chapter beginning in Paragraph 3-183, as well as in Chapter 9 as part of our discussion of moving expenses.

Exercise Three - 3

Subject: Employee Benefits

John Nilson is an employee of a high end furniture store. During the current year, John receives a number of benefits from his employer. Describe the tax consequences for John that result from receiving each of the following benefits.

- A 35 percent discount on merchandise with a total value of $10,000.
- Reimbursement of $2,000 in tuition fees for a course in creative writing.
- Business clothing with a value of $8,500 to be worn during working hours. (John's employer felt he needed a better image in dealing with clients.)
- A set of china on the occasion of John's wedding anniversary costing $450, including taxes.
- A private health care plan for John and his family. The employer pays an annual premium of $780 for this plan.

End of Exercise. Solution available in Study Guide.

Tax Planning Considerations

Salary The Benchmark

3-60. As previously discussed, some of the benefits provided to employees are fully taxable while other benefits can be extended without creating a taxable benefit. This has important implications in planning employee compensation.

3-61. As the bulk of compensation for most employees is in the form of wages or salaries, such payments provide the benchmark against which other types of compensation must be evaluated. From an income tax point of view, these benchmark payments are fully deductible to the employer in the year in which they are accrued and fully taxable to the employee in the year in which they are received. There is no valid tax reason for using a type of fringe benefit that has these same characteristics.

3-62. For example, if an employer rewards a valued employee with a holiday trip, the cost of the trip will be fully deductible to the employer. Further, the trip's cost will be fully taxable to the employee on the same basis as if the amount had been paid in the form of additional salary. This means that, while there may be a motivational reason for using a holiday trip as a form of compensation, there is no significant income tax advantage in doing so.

Tax Avoidance

3-63. The most attractive form of non-salary compensation involves benefits that are deductible to the employer, but are received tax free by the employee. Since IT-470R indicates that private health care benefits are not taxable, an employer can provide employees with, for example, a dental plan without creating any additional tax liability for the employee.

3-64. From a tax point of view, this type of compensation should be used whenever practical, provided it is desirable from the point of view of the employee. For example, although providing a dental plan to an employee is a tax free benefit, if the employee's spouse has already been provided with an identical dental plan by her employer, this benefit is of no value to the employee.

Tax Deferral

3-65. Also attractive are those benefits that allow the employer to deduct the cost currently, with taxation of the employee deferred until a later period. We have already considered an example of this involving the use of bonus arrangements. A further important example of this would be contributions to a registered pension plan. The employer can deduct the contributions in the period in which they are made, while the employee will not be taxed until the benefits are received in the form of pension income. This will usually involve a significant deferral of taxation for the employee.

Club Dues And Recreational Facilities

3-66. In the preceding cases, the tax planning considerations are very clear. There are no tax advantages associated with benefits that are fully and currently taxable to the employee. In contrast, advantages clearly arise when there is no taxation of the benefit, or when the taxation of the employee is deferred until a later point in time.

3-67. There is, however, a complicating factor in the case of certain employer provided recreational facilities or employer payment of club dues. While IT-470R indicates that such benefits are not taxable to the employee, the employer is not allowed to deduct the cost of providing such benefits (see Chapter 6 for a more detailed description of these rules). This means that the advantage of no taxes on the employee benefit is offset by the employer's loss of deductibility.

3-68. Whether this type of benefit is tax advantageous has to be evaluated on the basis of whether the tax savings to the employee are sufficient to offset the extra tax cost to the employer of providing a non-deductible benefit. The decision will generally be based on the relative tax rates applicable to the employee and the employer. If the employee's tax rate is higher than the employer's, this form of compensation may be advantageous from a tax point of view. There are also other non-tax factors that may be important, such as employee loyalty.

Two Problem Benefits - Automobiles and Loans

3-69. Before leaving this general discussion of tax planning considerations related to employee benefits, we would note that two important types of benefits present significant difficulties with respect to determining their desirability. These two benefits are employer provided automobiles and loans to employees.

3-70.   The basic problem in both cases is that the benefit to the employee is not based on the cost to the employer. In the case of the employee benefit associated with having the use of an employer supplied car, it is partially based on an arbitrary formula, under which the cumulative assessed benefit can exceed the cost of the car. In the case of employee loans, the taxable benefit is assessed using the prescribed rate of interest, not the cost of the funds to the employer.

3-71.   Because of this lack of reciprocity in the measurement of the cost and benefit, a case-by-case analysis is required. In each situation, it must be determined whether the cost to the employer is greater than, or less than, the benefit to the employee. If the cost is greater, the employer may wish to consider some alternative, and more tax effective, form of compensation. This makes these benefits considerably more difficult to administer.

3-72.   The taxable benefits associated with both employer provided automobiles and employer provided loans are discussed in detail at a later point in this chapter.

Exercise Three - 4

Subject: Planning Employee Benefits

As part of her compensation package, Jill Tyler is offered the choice of: a dental plan for her family, an annual vacation trip for her family, or an annual birthday gift of season's tickets to the ballet for her and her spouse. The alternative benefits are each worth about $4,000 per year. Indicate which benefit would be best for Jill from a tax point of view and explain your conclusion.

End of Exercise. Solution available in Study Guide.

Inclusions - GST/HST/PST On Taxable Benefits

3-73.   Many benefits included in employment income are goods and services on which an employee would have to pay GST, HST, or PST if he personally acquired the item or service. For example, if an employer provides a free domestic airline ticket to reward an employee for outstanding service, this is an item on which the employee would have to pay such taxes if he purchased the ticket on his own. This means that the taxable benefit should also include a tax component as the employee has received a benefit with a real value that includes both the price of the ticket and the related taxes.

3-74.   Given this situation, ITA 6(7) requires the calculation of employee benefits on a basis that includes PST, HST, or GST that was paid by the employer on goods or services that are included in the benefit. In situations where the employer is exempt from these taxes, a notional amount is added to the benefit on the basis of the amounts that would have been paid had the employer not been exempt.

Exercise Three - 5

Subject: GST On Taxable Benefits

Ms. Vicki Correli, as the result of an outstanding sales achievement within her organization, is awarded a two week vacation in the Bahamas. Her Alberta employer pays a travel agent $4,500, plus GST of $225 for the trip. What is the amount of Ms. Correli's taxable benefit?

End of Exercise. Solution available in Study Guide.

Inclusions - Board And Lodging

3-75.　Two aspects of this fringe benefit require further explanation. The first relates to valuation. Under IT-470R, any board and/or lodging benefit received is valued at fair market value, less any amounts recovered from the employee. Also of note is that subsidized meals do not have to be included as long as the employee is required to pay a reasonable charge. This puts subsidized meals provided in conjunction with free or subsidized lodging on a similar tax footing as subsidized meals in general. There is a difference, however, in that any benefit associated with lodging is based on fair market value, while any benefit related to meals is valued at the cost to the employer.

3-76.　As an exception to this general approach to employer provided meals and housing, ITA 6(6) indicates that under certain circumstances, these benefits will not be considered employment income. Two such situations are described in ITA 6(6):

Employment At A Temporary Special Work Site　If the work site is at such a distance from the employee's principal residence that it would not be reasonable to expect daily commuting, the benefit is not taxable.

Employment At A Remote Work Site　If the work site is at such a distance from an established community that it would not be reasonable to expect the employee to establish and maintain a domestic establishment, the benefit is not taxable.

3-77.　In general, taxable benefits should be computed on a GST/HST/PST included basis. However, as explained in Chapter 21, long-term (one month or more) residential rents and provision of lodging at remote work sites are not subject to GST/HST/PST. As a result, no GST/HST/PST amount would be associated with this type of employee benefit.

Inclusions - Automobile Benefits

Employees And Automobiles

Influence On Employment Income

3-78.　Automobiles have an influence on the determination of an individual's employment income in three different situations. These situations can be described as follows:

Employer Provided Automobiles　It is fairly common for a business to provide an automobile to an employee in order to assist the individual in carrying out his employment duties. In most cases, the employee will be able to make some personal use of the vehicle that is provided. If this is the case, the employee will have a taxable benefit which must be added to his employment income.

Allowances　As an alternative to providing an employee with an automobile, some employers pay an allowance to the employee for business use of his personally owned automobile. This allowance may be included in employment income and, when this is the case, the employee will be able to deduct some portion of the automobile's costs against such inclusions.

Deductible Travel Costs　Under certain circumstances, employees can deduct various travel costs. If the employee uses his personally owned automobile for travel related to his employment, a portion of the costs associated with this vehicle can be deducted in the determination of employment income.

3-79.　In this Chapter, we will give detailed attention to the benefit resulting from employer provided automobiles, as well as to the appropriate treatment of allowances for automobile costs. With respect to automobile related travel costs, the rules for these deductions are the same for both employees and businesses. Because of this, we will defer some of our coverage of this subject to Chapter 6 which deals with business income.

Tax Benefit - Employer Provided Automobile

3-80.   There are two types of costs that can be associated with ownership of an automobile. First, there is a fixed cost that accrues from simply owning the vehicle over time. As you are all aware, if you own a car, its value will decline, even if you do not drive the vehicle a single kilometre. For an average vehicle, this "depreciation" takes place on something close to a 25 percent declining balance basis.

3-81. In addition to this fixed cost or annual depreciation, there will be costs associated with operating the vehicle. These costs will tend to have a direct relationship to the number of kilometres driven. However, they will vary significantly, depending on the type of vehicle that is being operated.

3-82.   Tax legislation reflects this economic analysis. The two benefits that can be assessed to an employee who is provided with an employer owned or leased automobile can be described as follows:

Standby Charge   This benefit is assessed under ITA 6(1)(e). This benefit reflects the fixed cost of owning an automobile. However, we will find that the amount assessed can vary with the amount of personal, non-employment usage of the vehicle.

Operating Cost Benefit   This benefit is assessed under ITA 6(1)(k) and, as the name implies, it reflects the costs of operating the vehicle. You should note, however, that it is not based on the employer's actual costs. It is assessed at a fixed rate for each kilometre that the employee drives for personal or non-employment usage.

3-83.   As discussed in Paragraph 3-73, a GST/HST/PST component must be included when taxable benefits provided to employees involve goods or services that would normally be subject to the GST, PST, or HST. Personal use of an automobile falls into this category. Both the standby charge benefit and the operating cost benefit that are discussed in the following material are calculated in a manner that includes a GST/HST/PST component.

Allowances And Deductible Travel Costs

3-84.   Both allowances and deductible travel costs involve the determination of amounts that can be deducted by an employee who owns or leases his own automobile. As you may be aware, tax legislation places limits on the amounts that can be deducted for automobile costs (e.g., for 2012, lease payments in excess of $800 per month before taxes are not deductible and tax depreciation (capital cost allowance or CCA) cannot be deducted on automobile costs in excess of $30,000 before taxes). As these limits are the same for an employee who owns or leases a vehicle that is used in employment activities, and for a business that owns or leases a vehicle that is used in business activities, they are given detailed coverage in Chapter 6 on business income.

3-85.   However, it is important to note here that the limits that are placed on the deductibility of automobile costs have no influence on the amount of the taxable benefit that will be assessed to an employee who is provided with a vehicle by his employer. The taxable benefit to the employee will be the same, without regard to whether the employer can deduct the full costs of owning or leasing the vehicle. This means that if an employer provides an employee with an automobile that costs $150,000, the employee's benefits will be based on the full $150,000, despite the fact that the employer will be able to deduct capital cost allowance on only $30,000.

Taxable Benefits - Standby Charge

Employer Owned Vehicles

3-86.   While ITA 6(1)(e) requires the inclusion of a standby charge in income, ITA 6(2) provides the formulas for calculating this amount. If the employer owns the automobile, the basic standby charge is determined by the following formula:

[(2%)(Cost Of Car)(Periods Of Availability)]

3-87.   The components of this formula require some additional explanation:

Cost Of Car   The cost of the car is the amount paid, without regard to the list price of the car. It includes all related GST/PST/HST amounts.

Periods Of Availability   Periods of availability is roughly equal to months of availability. However, it is determined by dividing the number of days the automobile is "made available" by 30 and rounding to the nearest whole number. Oddly, a ".5" amount is rounded down rather than up.

Made Available   One would think that if an employee simply returned the automobile and its keys to an employer's premises it would not be considered "available for use". For example, if an employee was traveling out of the country for 2 months, you might assume that, if he left the vehicle and keys with his employer during this period, it would not be considered available for his use. However, this is not the case. In a 2011 Income Tax Ruling (#040922), the CRA has indicated that the employee must be "required" to return the vehicle to the employer's premises to avoid the accrual of a taxable benefit. This means that it is not sufficient to voluntarily return the vehicle. It must be the policy of the employer to require this return.

3-88.   If we assume that a vehicle was available throughout the year and cost $33,900, including $3,900 in HST, the standby charge would be $8,136 [(2%)($33,900)(12)]. If the vehicle continues to be available to the employee throughout the year for subsequent years, the benefit would be the same each year, without regard to the age of the car.

3-89.   You should note that the application of this formula can result in a situation where the cumulative standby charge will exceed the cost of the automobile.

Example   An employee has use of an automobile that cost $56,500, including HST. This availability continues for five years (60 months).

Analysis   The taxable benefit resulting from the standby charge calculation would be $67,800 [(2%)($56,500)(60)]. This taxable benefit is 20 percent larger than the cost of the car to the employer.

Employer Leased Vehicles

3-90.   In those cases where the employer leases the automobile, the basic standby charge is determined by the following formula:

[(2/3)(Lease Payments For The Year Excluding Insurance)(Availability Factor)]

3-91.   As was the case with the formula for employer owned vehicles, the components of this formula require additional explanation:

Lease Payments   The amount to be included here is the total lease payments for the year, including any relevant GST/PST/HST. This total would be reduced by any amounts that have been included for insuring the vehicle. The insurance costs are excluded as the CRA considers them to be part of the operating cost benefit.

Availability Factor   This is a fraction in which the numerator is the number of days during the year the vehicle is available to the employee and the denominator is the number of days during the year for which lease payments were made. If the employee had the use of the vehicle throughout the lease period, the value of this fraction would be 1. When the car is owned by the employer, the *Act* clearly requires the availability period to be based on the days of availability, rounded to the nearest number of 30 day periods. In contrast, when the car is leased, a strict reading of the *Act* requires the availability period to be based on the days available as a fraction of the days in the lease period. However, the Employers' Guide: Taxable Benefits (T4130), uses the 30 day rounding rule for both purchase and lease situations. We will be using this latter approach in our examples and problems.

3-92.   An example will illustrate these procedures:

Example   A vehicle is leased for 3 months at a rate of $750 per month, including HST.   The $750 includes a monthly insurance payment of $75 per month.   An employee has use of the vehicle for 85 of the 92 days in the lease term.

Analysis   Since both (85 ÷ 30) and (92 ÷ 30) would round to 3, the standby charge would be $1,350 [(2/3)(3)($750 - $75)(3 ÷ 3)].   If the calculation in the *Act* was strictly followed, the benefit would be $1,247 [(2/3)(3)($750 - $75)(85 ÷ 92)].

3-93.   Unlike the situation with an employer owned vehicle, it is unlikely that the taxable benefit associated with a leased vehicle will exceed the value of the automobile.   While we have seen no comprehensive analysis to support this view, it seems clear to us that, in most normal leasing situations, the taxable benefit on a leased vehicle will be significantly less than would be the case if the employer purchased the same vehicle.

Example   In the real world, a $55,000 (HST inclusive) vehicle could be leased for 48 months with a lease payment of $800 per month (HST inclusive).

Analysis - Vehicle Purchased   If the car is purchased, the standby charge will be $13,200 per year [(2%)($55,000)(12)].

Analysis - Vehicle Leased   If the vehicle is leased, the standby charge will be $6,400 per year [(2/3)(12)($800)(12 ÷ 12)].

3-94.   This example illustrates what we believe to be a fairly general result.   For a given automobile, the taxable benefit for the employee will be lower in situations where the employer leases the vehicle, rather than purchasing the vehicle.   It is our opinion that the only exceptions to this would occur when the lease has a very short term.

Reduced Standby Charge

3-95.   When an employer provides an automobile to an employee, it is usually used by that employee for a combination of personal activities and employment related activities.   Among different employees, there are significant variations in the mix of these activities.   Employees of some organizations may use the car almost exclusively in carrying out employment related activities.   In other situations, particularly when the employer and the employee are not at arm's length (e.g., the employee is related to the owner of the business), the car may be used almost exclusively for personal travel.

3-96.   This would suggest that there should be some modification of the basic standby charge in situations where there is only limited personal use of the automobile.   This, in fact, is the case.   The ITA 6(2) standby charge formula provides for a reduction based on the amount of personal usage of the vehicle.

3-97.   The reduction involves multiplying the regular standby charge for either an employer owned or an employer leased vehicle by the following fraction:

Non - Employment Kilometers (Cannot Exceed Denominator)

1,667 Kilometers Per Month Of Availability *

*The number of months of availability is calculated by dividing the number of days that the employee is in possession of the keys to the vehicle by 30, and rounding to the nearest whole number.

3-98.   In applying this formula, the numerator is based on the number of kilometers driven for personal or non-employment activities.   To prevent the fraction from having a value in excess of one, the numerator is limited to the value in the denominator.   The denominator is based on the idea that, if the employee uses the automobile for as much as 1,667 kilometers of personal activities in a month (20,004 kilometers per year), the vehicle has fully replaced the need for a personally owned vehicle.

3-99.   This fraction can be used to reduce the basic standby charge provided two conditions are met:

- The employee is required by the employer to use the automobile in his employment duties.

- The use of the automobile is "primarily" employment related. In general, "primarily" is interpreted by the CRA to mean more than 50 percent. Note that this standby charge reduction formula is not completely fair to everyone, in that it fails to distinguish between an employee who uses the employer's automobile 49 percent for employment related activity from an employee who uses the automobile exclusively for personal travel. Despite the significant difference in personal usage, they would each be assessed the same standby charge on a given vehicle.

3-100.   While the fraction is still applicable when personal use is more than 1,667 kilometers per month (20,004 kilometers for the year), it will be equal to 1 (20,004 ÷ 20,004) and will not provide for any reduction in the basic standby charge.

Operating Cost Benefit
Basic Calculation
3-101.   In those cases where the employer pays the operating costs for an automobile that is available to an employee, that employee is clearly receiving a benefit related to the portion of these costs that are associated with his personal use of the automobile. An obvious approach to assessing an operating cost benefit would be to simply pro rate operating costs paid by the employer between personal and employment related usage. The problem with this, however, is that the employer would be required to keep detailed cost and mileage records for each employee. This approach is further complicated by the fact that some operating costs incur GST or HST (e.g., gasoline), while other operating costs are exempt from GST or HST (e.g., insurance and licenses).

3-102.   Given these problems, ITA 6(1)(k) has provided an administratively simple solution. The operating cost benefit is determined by multiplying a prescribed amount by the number of personal kilometers driven. For 2012, this prescribed amount is $0.26. This amount includes a notional GST or HST component and, as a consequence, no further GST or HST benefit has to be added to this amount.

3-103.   Note that this amount is applicable without regard to the level of the actual operating costs, resulting in favourable treatment for employees driving cars with high operating costs and unfavourable treatment for employees using vehicles with low operating costs.

Alternative Calculation
3-104.   There is an alternative calculation of the operating cost benefit. Employees who use an employer provided automobile "primarily" (i.e., more than 50 percent) in the performance of the taxpayer's office or employment can elect to have the operating cost benefit calculated as one-half of the standby charge by notifying their employer. This alternative calculation does not have to be used and, in many situations, it will not be a desirable alternative as it will produce a higher figure for the operating cost benefit.

3-105.   It should be noted that ITA 6(1.1) specifically excludes any benefit related to employer provided parking from the automobile benefit. This does not mean that employer provided parking is not a taxable benefit. While it is not considered to be a component of the automobile benefit calculation, it would still have to be included in the employee's income under ITA 6(1)(a). The logic of this is that parking may be provided to employees who are not provided with an automobile and, as a consequence, it should be accounted for separately in the employee benefit calculation.

3-106.   Figure 3-2 summarizes the calculations that relate to the taxable benefit arising from employer provided automobiles.

Figure 3 - 2   Summary Of Automobile Benefit Calculations

The **full** standby charge calculation on an employer owned or leased vehicle is:

Owned $[(2\%)(\text{Cost Of Car}^*)(\text{Days Available} \div 30 \text{ Rounded})]$

Leased $\left[\left(\dfrac{2}{3}\right)(\text{Lease Payments For The Year}^*)\left(\dfrac{\text{Days Available} \div 30 \text{ Rounded}}{\text{Days Leased} \div 30 \text{ Rounded}}\right)\right]$

* Including GST/HST/PST, but excluding any insurance in lease payment

---

A **reduced** standby charge is available if employment related usage is greater than 50%. The calculation is as follows:

$$\left[(\text{Full Standby Charge})\left(\dfrac{\text{Personal Use Kilometers (Cannot Exceed Denominator)}}{1{,}667 \text{ Kilometers Per Month Of Availability}}\right)\right]$$

The **regular** operating cost benefit for 2012 is $[(\$0.26)(\text{Personal use kilometers})]$.

An **alternative** operating cost benefit calculation is available if employment related usage is greater than 50%. It is $[(1/2)(\text{Standby Charge, reduced if applicable})]$.

Payments By Employee For Automobile Use

3-107.   Under ITA 6(1)(e), the standby charge benefit can be reduced by payments made by the employee to the employer for the use of the automobile. In corresponding fashion under ITA 6(1)(k), the operating cost benefit can be reduced by such payments.

3-108.   Note, however, that if the employee pays part of the operating costs (e.g., the employee personally pays for gasoline), it does not reduce the basic $0.26 per kilometer benefit. This is not a desirable result and, if the employee is going to be required to pay a portion of the operating expenses, the employer should pay for all of the costs and have the employee reimburse the employer for the appropriate portion. Under this approach, the payments will reduce the operating cost benefit.

Example - Employer Owned Automobile

3-109.   The following data will be used to illustrate the calculation of the taxable benefit where an employee is provided with a vehicle owned by an employer in 2012.

Cost Of The Automobile ($30,000 + $3,900 HST)	$33,900
Days Available For Use	310
Months Owned By The Employer	12
Total Kilometers Driven	30,000
Personal Kilometers Driven	16,000

3-110.   The 310 days of availability would have to be rounded to 10 months (310 ÷ 30 rounded). The basic standby charge benefit to be included in employment income would be calculated as follows:

Standby Charge $= [(2\%)(\$33,900)(10)] = \underline{\$6,780}$

3-111.   As less than 50 percent $[(30,000 - 16,000) \div 30,000 = 46.7\%]$ of the driving was related to the employer's business, no reduction in the basic standby charge is available. Also note that the cost figure used in the preceding calculation includes the HST.

3-112.   The operating cost benefit to be included in employment income is as follows:

Operating Cost Benefit = [($0.26)(16,000)] = $4,160

3-113. As the employment related use of the car was less than 50 percent, there is no alternative calculation of the operating cost benefit.

3-114. As the employee does not make any payments to the employer for the personal use or operation of the automobile, the total taxable benefit to be included in employment income is as follows:

Total Taxable Benefit = ($6,780 + $4,160) = $10,940

Exercise Three - 6

Subject: Taxable Benefits - Employer Owned Automobile

Mrs. Tanya Lee is provided with an automobile by her employer. The employer acquired the automobile in 2011 for $25,000, plus $1,250 GST and $2,000 PST. During 2012, Ms. Lee drives the automobile a total of 28,000 kilometers, 16,000 of which were related to employment duties. The automobile is available to Mrs. Lee throughout the year. Calculate Mrs. Lee's minimum 2012 taxable benefit for the use of the automobile.

End of Exercise. Solution available in Study Guide.

Example - Employer Leased Vehicle

3-115. To provide a direct comparison between the employer owned and employer leased cases, this example will be based on the same general facts that were used in the ownership example. If the employer was to lease a $30,000 car with a 36 month lease term, the lease payment, calculated using normal lease terms, would be approximately $822 per month, including HST (this cannot be calculated with the information given). With the exception of the fact that the car is leased rather than purchased by the employer, all of the other facts are the same as in the Paragraph 3-109 example. The standby charge benefit would be calculated as follows:

Standby Charge = [(2/3)(12)($822)(10/12*)] = $5,480

* The availability factor is calculated as [(310 ÷ 30 rounded)/(365 ÷ 30 rounded)].

3-116. As was the case when the car was owned by the employer, there is no reduction for actual business kilometers driven because the car was driven less than 50 percent for employment related purposes. Also note that the benefit is based on the lease payment including HST.

3-117. The operating cost benefit is the same as the employer owned case and is as follows:

Operating Cost Benefit = [($0.26)(16,000)] = $4,160

3-118. As in the case where the employer owned the car, with the employment related use of the car at less than 50 percent, there is no alternative calculation of the operating cost benefit.

3-119. As the employee does not make any payments to the employer for the personal use or operation of the automobile, the total taxable benefit is as follows:

Total Taxable Benefit = ($5,480 + $4,160) = $9,640

3-120. Note that the total benefit is significantly less ($9,640 as compared with $10,940) when the employer leases the car as opposed to purchasing it. As indicated in our earlier discussion in Paragraph 3-94, this would be the anticipated result.

Exercise Three - 7

Subject: Taxable Benefits - Employer Leased Automobile

Mr. Michael Forthwith is provided with a car that is leased by his employer. The monthly lease payments for 2012 are $525, plus $68 HST. During 2012, he drives the automobile a total of 40,000 kilometers, of which 37,000 kilometers are employment related. The automobile is used by him for 325 days during the year. When he is not using the automobile, company policy requires that it be returned to their premises. Calculate Mr. Forthwith's minimum 2012 taxable benefit for the use of the automobile.

End of Exercise. Solution available in Study Guide.

Employer Provided Cars And Tax Planning

3-121.   Providing employees with cars is not a clearly desirable course of action. As is discussed in Chapter 6, there are limits on the ability of the employer to deduct the costs of owning or leasing the vehicle (e.g., leasing costs in excess of $800 per month before taxes are not deductible). Further, the taxable benefit calculations are such that they may produce a taxable benefit that exceeds the value to the employee of having the car.

3-122.   This means that a decision by an employer to provide an employee with a car requires a careful analysis of all of the relevant factors. While a complete analysis of all of these issues goes beyond the scope of this material on employment income, some general tax planning points can be made.

Require The Car Be Returned   In many situations, there will be periods of time when an employee does not use an employer provided vehicle. Examples would include vacation periods, extensive periods of travel for work, or confinement because of illness. During such periods, the vehicle will be considered available for use unless the employer **REQUIRES** it to be returned to their premises. Given this, the employer should have a policy of requiring vehicles to be returned during periods of non-use by the employee.

Record Keeping   In the absence of detailed records, an employee can be charged with the full standby charge and 100 percent personal usage. To avoid this, it is essential that records be kept of both employment related and personal kilometers driven.

Leasing Vs. Buying   As was previously noted, in most cases, a lower taxable benefit will result when the employer leases the car rather than purchases it. One adverse aspect of leasing arrangements should be noted. Lease payments are made up of a combination of both interest and principal payments on the car. As the taxable benefit is based on the total lease payment, the interest portion becomes, in effect, a part of the taxable benefit.

Minimizing The Standby Charge   This can be accomplished in a variety of ways including longer lease terms, lower trade-in values for old vehicles in purchase situations, larger deposits on leases, and the use of higher residual values in leasing arrangements. However, this minimization process is not without limits. As is explained in Chapter 6, refundable deposits in excess of $1,000 on leases can reduce the deductible portion of lease costs.

Cars Costing More Than $30,000   With the taxable benefit to the employee based on the full cost of the car and any portion of the cost in excess of $30,000 not being deductible to the employer (this limit on the deductibility of automobile expenses is discussed in Chapter 6), it is difficult to imagine situations in which it would make economic sense for a profit oriented employer to provide any employee with a luxury car. As the taxable benefit to the employee is based on the actual cost of the car, while the deductible amount is limited to $30,000, a situation is created in which the employee is paying taxes on an amount which can be significantly larger than the amount that is deductible to the employer. For example, the standby charge on a $150,000 Mercedes-Benz is $36,000 per year [(2%)($150,000)(12)], an amount that may be fully taxable to the employee. In contrast, the employer's deduction for capital cost allowance (tax depreciation) in the first year of ownership is limited to only $4,500 [($30,000)(30%)(1/2)]. The only winner in this type of situation is the CRA.

Consider The Alternative   The alternative to the employer provided automobile is to have the employer compensate the employee for using his own automobile. In many cases this may be preferable to providing an automobile. For example, in those situations where business use is less than 50 percent, the provision of an automobile to an employee will result in a benefit assessment for the full standby charge. If business use was 45 percent, for example, it is almost certain that the amount assessed will exceed the actual benefit associated with 55 percent personal use of the vehicle. If, alternatively, the employee is reasonably compensated for using his own personal vehicle, there is no taxable benefit.

Inclusions - Allowances

Allowance Vs. Reimbursement

3-123.   A reimbursement is an amount paid to an employee to compensate that individual for amounts that he has disbursed in carrying out his employment duties. An example of this would be an employee who purchases an airline ticket for travel on behalf of his employer. The employee will present the receipt to the employer who reimburses the employee for the amount shown on the receipt. In such cases the employee will have no net cost and will have neither an income inclusion nor a deduction. The employer will, of course, be able to deduct the amount reimbursed.

3-124.   The situation is more complex with allowances. These are amounts that are paid, usually to provide a general level of compensation, for costs that an employee incurs as part of his employment activities. However, as there is no direct, dollar-for-dollar relationship with the actual costs incurred, the tax treatment of these items is more complicated. These complexities are dealt with in the material that follows.

General Rules

3-125.   The term allowance is used to refer to amounts received by employees from an employer other than salaries, wages, benefits, and reimbursements. In practice, allowances generally involve payments to employees as compensation for travel costs, use of their own automobile, or other costs that have been incurred by employees as part of their efforts on behalf of the employer. A mileage allowance for a traveling salesperson or a technician who does service calls would be typical examples of such an allowance.

3-126.   ITA 6(1)(b) provides a general rule which requires that allowances for personal or living expenses must be included in an employee's income. However, many of the items for which employees receive allowances are costs that an employee can deduct against employment income under ITA 8. (See the discussion of deductions later in this Chapter for a full explanation of these amounts.) Examples of such deductible items are as follows:

- ITA 8(1)(f)   salesperson's expenses
- ITA 8(1)(h)   traveling expenses other than motor vehicle expenses
- ITA 8(1)(h.1)   motor vehicle traveling expenses
- ITA 8(1)(i)   professional dues, office rent, salaries, and supply costs
- ITA 8(1)(j)   motor vehicle capital costs (interest and capital cost allowance)

3-127.   If allowances for these items are included in the employee's income, a circular process is involved in which they are added under ITA 6(1)(b) and then subtracted under

ITA 8. In view of this, ITA 6(1)(b) indicates that there are exceptions to the rule that allowances must be included in income. While there is a fairly long list of such items, the most important of these exceptions involve allowances paid for the types of costs that would be deductible under ITA 8. Specifically, the following allowances are among those that do not have to be included in an employee's income:

- ITA 6(1)(b)(v) - Reasonable allowances for traveling expenses paid during a period in which the employee was a salesperson (includes allowances for the use of a motor vehicle).

- ITA 6(1)(b)(vii) - Reasonable allowances for traveling expenses for employees other than salespersons, not including allowances for the use of a motor vehicle.

- ITA 6(1)(b)(vii.1) - Reasonable allowances for the use of a motor vehicle for employees other than salespersons.

Taxable Vs. Non-Taxable Allowances

3-128.   The preceding general rules mean that there are two possible treatments of allowances paid to employees for travel and motor vehicle costs.

Non-Taxable Allowances   If a reasonable allowance is paid to an employee, it will not be included in the employee's income records (T4 Information Return). However, when such allowances are not included in income, the employee will not be able to deduct his actual costs. For example, if an individual received $150 per day of travel to cover hotel costs, this would probably be considered reasonable and not included in his income. If the employee chose to stay at a luxury hotel for $400 per day, he would not be able to deduct the additional cost associated with this choice. Alternatively, if he chose to stay at a hostel for $50 per day, he would pocket the excess allowance on a tax free basis.

Taxable Allowances   If an allowance is not considered to be reasonable, it will be included in the employee's T4 Information Return for the period. To the extent the employee can qualify for the deduction of business travel or commission salespersons expenses, related expenses incurred by the employee can be deducted in the determination of his net employment income. If the employee's actual costs exceed the allowance, having the allowance included in his income will be advantageous. Conversely, if his actual costs are less than the allowance, the result will be a net inclusion in employment income.

3-129.   It is not clear what constitutes a reasonable amount in the case of the general costs of travel. It appears that, as long as an allowance appears to be in line with actual costs for food, lodging, and miscellaneous costs, the allowance that is provided is likely to be viewed as reasonable.

3-130.   However, if a junior employee was given $30,000 a month for food and lodging and he was known to be staying at budget motels and eating fast food, it is likely that the allowance would have to be included in income and reduced, to the extent possible, by actual costs incurred (while this example sounds unrealistic, it might be attempted in an owner-managed business where the employee was not dealing at arm's length with the employer).

3-131.   Although it may be more difficult to administer, reimbursement of actual costs is less likely to cause this type of tax problem than providing an arbitrarily determined general allowance to cover all possible costs.

Reasonable Allowances For Motor Vehicles

3-132.   In Paragraph 3-127, we noted that ITA 6(1)(b)(v) and 6(1)(b)(vii.1) indicate that "reasonable allowances" for an employee's use of a motor vehicle do not have to be included in the employee's income. While the *Act* is not specific as to what constitutes a reasonable allowance for the use of a motor vehicle, it does point out that an allowance will be deemed not to be reasonable:

- if it is not based solely on the number of kilometers for which the vehicle is used in employment duties [ITA 6(1)(b)(x)]; or

- if the employee, in addition to the allowance, is reimbursed for all or part of the expenses of using the vehicle [(ITA 6(1)(b)(xi)].

3-133.   With respect to the first of these conditions, it is clear that an allowance of $200 per month would have to be included in the employee's income. Any allowance that is not specifically based on kilometers is deemed to be unreasonable. This, however, does not answer the question as to what constitutes a reasonable allowance.

3-134.   On the upper end, the CRA has indicated that if a per kilometer allowance exceeds the prescribed amount that is deductible for a business, it will be considered unreasonable, resulting in its inclusion in the employee's income. For 2012, the relevant amounts are $0.53 per kilometer for the first 5,000 kilometers driven by a given employee, and $0.47 for each additional kilometer.

3-135.   If the per kilometer allowance is less than this prescribed amount, it appears that the administrative practice of the CRA is to view the allowance as reasonable. This means that, unless an employee is willing to pursue the matter, he does not have the option of including a non-taxable allowance in income and deducting his actual costs. While there has been one case (Brunet vs. H.M.Q.) where an employee was allowed to include a $0.15 per kilometer allowance and deduct actual costs, there have been other cases where this was not allowed.

Exercise Three - 8

Subject: Deductible Automobile Costs

Ms. Lauren Giacomo is required by her employer to use her own automobile in her work. To compensate her, she is paid an annual allowance of $3,600. During the current year, she drove her automobile a total of 24,000 kilometers, of which 6,500 kilometers were employment related. Her total automobile costs for the year, including lease costs, are $7,150. What amounts should Ms. Giacomo include and deduct in determining net employment income for the current year?

Exercise Three - 9

Subject: Automobile Allowances

During the current year, Jacob Lorenz leases an automobile for $450 per month, a total for the year of $5,400. He drives a total of 60,000 kilometers, of which 35,000 are employment related. His total operating costs for the year are $15,000. His employer pays him $0.10 for each employment related kilometer driven, a total of $3,500. What amounts should Mr. Lorenz include and deduct in determining net employment income for the current year?

End of Exercises. Solutions available in Study Guide.

Employer's Perspective Of Allowances

3-136.   From the point of view of the employer, paying taxable allowances is the easiest solution. All amounts paid will be included in the income of the employees and, as a consequence, there is no necessity for the employer to maintain detailed records of actual costs. It is up to the employee to keep these records and to claim the relevant deductible costs against the allowances included in their T4 Information Return.

3-137.   Somewhat more onerous is an approach which uses direct reimbursements of the employee's actual costs. Some efficiencies are available here in that the CRA will generally accept a modest per diem for food without requiring detailed documentation from either the employer or the employee. However, for more substantial costs, the reimbursement approach involves more detailed record keeping than is the case with the use of taxable allowances.

3-138.   In the case of employee owned automobile costs, the use of non-taxable allowances is particularly complex. As we have noted, the 2012 amounts that can be deducted by an employer for automobile costs are generally limited to $0.53 per kilometer for the first 5,000 kilometers driven by a given employee, and $0.47 for each additional kilometer. If a non-taxable allowance is based on these rates, the employer will have to keep detailed employee-by-employee mileage records to support the deduction of automobile costs.

Employee's Perspective Of Allowances

3-139.   From the employee's point of view, the receipt of a non-taxable allowance represents a very simple solution to the problem. While records may have to be kept for the information needs of the employer, the employee has the advantage of simply ignoring the allowance and the related costs when it comes time to file a tax return.

3-140.   In real economic terms, however, the non-taxable allowance approach may or may not be advantageous. If the employee's actual deductible costs exceed the allowance, the non-inclusion of the allowance in income eliminates the deductibility of the additional costs. Alternatively, if the actual costs are less than the allowance, the employee has, in effect, received a tax free benefit.

Exercise Three - 10

Subject: Travel Allowances

Sandra Ohm travels extensively for her employer. Her employer provides an allowance of $200 per day to cover hotel costs. In addition, she is paid $0.41 per kilometer when she is required to use her automobile for travel. For her work, during the current year, she traveled a total of 82 days and drove 9,400 kilometers. Her employer paid her $16,400 for lodging [(82)($200)], as well as $3,854 dollars for mileage [(9,400)($0.41)]. Her actual lodging costs were $18,300, while her total automobile costs were $7,200, including monthly lease payments. Her total mileage on the car during the year was 23,500 kilometers. What amounts should Ms. Ohm include and deduct in determining net employment income for the current year?

End of Exercise.   Solution available in Study Guide.

Inclusions - Employee Insurance Benefits

Life Insurance

3-141.   The cost of providing life insurance benefits to employees is a taxable benefit under ITA 6(4). This means that any premiums paid on a life insurance policy by the employer must be included in employment income. In the event of the employee's death, the benefit payment received by his estate would not be taxable. No GST (or HST) amount would be included in this benefit as insurance services are exempt from GST (see Chapter 21).

Disability Insurance
(a.k.a. Group Sickness Or Accident Insurance Plan)

3-142.   The basic rules rules for group disability insurance plans are as follows:

Contributions By Employee   Without regard to whether the employer makes contributions to the plan, contributions made by an employee are not deductible by the employee.

Contributions By Employer ITA 6(1)(a) indicates that these contributions do not create a taxable benefit to the employee. This is conditional on the benefits received by an employee being taxable under ITA 6(1)(f). If they are not taxable, the employer's contribution will be treated as a taxable benefit (see below).

Benefits Received (Employer Does Not Contribute To Plan) In the unusual situation where the employee makes all of the contributions to the plan, benefits will be received tax free.

Benefits Received (Employer Makes All Or Part Of The Contributions) Under ITA 6(1)(f), benefits received are taxable to an employee provided they are (1) paid on a periodic basis, and (2) paid to compensate the individual for loss of employment income. If plan benefits do not meet both of these criteria, the employer contributions to the plan will be considered a taxable benefit to the employee. Note that, if benefits are taxed under ITA 6(1)(f), the employee will be able to offset the income inclusion by the amount of contributions that he has made to the plan prior to receiving the benefits.

3-143. These rules give rise to three possible situations:

Employee Pay All Plans If the employee makes 100 percent of the contributions to the plan, the contributions will not be deductible and any benefits received will not be taxed.

Employer Contributes - Benefits Not Taxed If the employer makes all or part of the contributions to the plan and benefits received are not taxed (because they are not periodic or do not replace employment income), the employer contributions to the plan will be treated as a taxable benefit to the employee. Any employee contributions to the plan are not deductible.

Employer Contributes - Benefits Taxed If the employer makes all or part of the contributions to the plan and benefits received by the employee are taxed, the employer's contributions do not create a taxable benefit. Any employee contributions to the plan are not deductible by the employee. However, the cumulative amount of such contributions can be used to offset the benefit inclusion.

3-144. The most common of these situations is the one in which the employer makes contributions that do not create a taxable benefit for the employee, with any benefits received being taxed in the hands of the employee. Most of our examples and problems will be based on this type of situation.

3-145. You should note that these rules only apply to group disability plans. If the plan is not a group plan, any contributions made by an employer will be treated as a taxable benefit to the employee.

Example Jane Forthy's employer provides a disability insurance plan which provides periodic benefits to compensate her for lost employment income. During the current year, the premiums on Jane Forthy's disability insurance plan totaled $1,600. The plan is a group plan sponsored by Jane's employer who pays one-half of the annual cost of premiums. Jane pays the remaining one-half. As the result of a car accident during the current year, Jane received disability benefits of $16,000. In previous years, Jane has contributed a total of $3,600 towards the disability insurance premiums.

Analysis Jane's income inclusion for the current year would be $11,600 [$16,000 - (1/2)($1,600) - $3,600].

3-146. As noted in the previous section on life insurance, insurance services are exempt from GST/HST, and no GST/HST amount is associated with taxable benefits related to disability insurance.

Exercise Three - 11

Subject: Disability Insurance Benefits

Mr. Lance Bardwell is a member of a group disability plan sponsored by his employer. The plan provides periodic benefits that compensate Mr. Bardwell for lost employment income. During 2012, his employer's share of the annual premium was $1,800. Beginning in 2011, Mr. Bardwell was required to contribute $300 per year to this plan. The 2011 and 2012 contributions were withheld from his wages by his employer. During 2012, he was incapacitated for a period of six weeks and received $5,250 in benefits under the plan. What amount will Mr. Bardwell include in his 2012 employment income?

End of Exercise. Solution available in Study Guide.

Health Care Insurance

3-147.   Where an employer pays the individual premiums on provincial or Government of Canada health care plans (e.g., Alberta and British Columbia), the amounts are considered taxable benefits of the employees. Where provincial health care is funded by an employer payroll tax or other general levy (e.g., Manitoba and Quebec) and there are no individual premiums, these payments are not allocated to employees as a taxable benefit.

3-148.   Payments made for private health services plans, for instance a dental plan, are specifically excluded from treatment as a taxable benefit under guidelines provided in ITA 6(1)(a)(i). The benefits received under such plans are not taxable and, in addition, any contributions made by the employee to such private health care plans can be treated as a medical expense eligible for a credit against taxes payable. (See Chapter 4.)

3-149.   As was the case with other types of insurance benefits, there is no GST amount associated with taxable health care benefits.

Loans To Employees

General Rules

3-150.   If an employer extends a loan to an employee that is either interest free or has a rate that is below the going market rate, the employee is clearly receiving a benefit that should be taxed. This view is reflected in ITA 6(9), which requires the assessment of a taxable benefit on all interest free or low interest loans to employees. This provision applies whether the loan is made as a consequence of prior, current, or future employment.

3-151.   As specified in ITA 80.4(1), which describes how this benefit is calculated, the taxable benefit would equal imputed interest calculated at a rate specified in the *Income Tax Regulations*. This rate, as determined by ITR 4301, is referred to as the prescribed rate. It is established for each calendar quarter on the basis of Government Of Canada Treasury Bill yields. In general, the taxable benefit is calculated using the prescribed rate that is applicable to each calendar quarter. The amount of the benefit is reduced by any interest paid on the loan by the employee during the year or within 30 days of the end of the year.

Example On January 1 of the current year, Ms. Brooks Arden borrows $50,000 from her employer at an annual rate of 1 percent. Assume that during this year, the prescribed rate is 3 percent during the first two quarters, and 4 percent during the last two quarters. Ms. Arden pays the required 1 percent interest on December 31.

Analysis The taxable benefit to be included in Ms. Arden's net employment income would be calculated as follows:

Imputed Interest:		
Quarters I and II [(3%)($50,000)(2/4)]		$ 750
Quarters III and IV [(4%)($50,000)(2/4)]		1,000
Total Imputed Interest		$1,750
Interest Paid [(1%)($50,000)]		(500)
Taxable Benefit		$1,250

In general, interest calculations that are made for tax purposes are based on the number of days the principal is outstanding. However, IT-421R2, in its illustration of employee loan interest calculation, uses calendar quarters and treats each calendar quarter as one-quarter of the year. In situations where full calendar quarters are involved we will use this approach in our text and problem material.

3-152.   Several additional points should be made with respect to these loans:

- If the rate negotiated with the employer is at least equal to (or greater than) the rate that the employee could have negotiated himself with a bank, then under ITA 80.4(3), no benefit will be assessed to the employee regardless of subsequent changes to the prescribed rate. However, this is rarely applicable as the prescribed rate is consistently lower than rates available on loans to individuals.

- ITA 80.4(2) contains a different set of rules that is applicable to loans made to certain shareholders of a company. The different rules that are applicable to shareholders are described in Chapter 15, "Corporate Taxation And Management Decisions".

- Proceeds from a loan to an employee could be used to invest in assets that produce business or property income. In general, interest paid on loans to finance investments is deductible against the income produced. ITA 80.5 clearly states that an imputed interest benefit assessed under ITA 80.4(1) or 80.4(2) is deemed to be interest paid for the purposes of determining net business or property income. Referring to the example in Paragraph 3-151, if Ms. Arden had invested the $50,000 loan proceeds in income producing assets, her deductible interest would total $1,750, the $500 that she paid, plus the assessed $1,250 taxable benefit.

- When the purpose of the loan is to assist an employee with a home purchase or home relocation (see Paragraph 3-153), ITA 80.4(4) indicates that the annual amount of interest used in the benefit calculations cannot exceed the annual amount determined using the prescribed rate in effect when the loan was extended. Note that this rule is applied on an annual basis, not on a quarter by quarter basis.

This provides a ceiling for the benefit and, at the same time, allows the taxpayer to benefit if the prescribed rate becomes lower. This ceiling on the benefit is only available for the first five years such loans are outstanding. ITA 80.4(6) indicates that, after this period of time, the loan will be deemed to be a new loan, making the calculation of the benefit subject to the prescribed rate in effect at this point in time. This new rate will again serve as a ceiling for the amount of the benefit for the next five years.

Example   On January 1 of the current year, an employee receives a $200,000, interest free home purchase loan from his employer. Assume that the prescribed rate is 4 percent for the first quarter, 3 percent during the second and third quarters and 7 percent in the fourth quarter.

Analysis   If interest is calculated on a quarterly basis, the benefit would be $8,500 [($200,000)(4%)(1/4) + ($200,000)(3%)(2/4) + ($200,000)(7%)(1/4)]. Alternatively, using the prescribed rate in effect at the time the loan was made, the amount is $8,000 [($200,000)(4%)]. As this is lower, the taxable benefit would be $8,000.

Home Relocation Loans

3-153.   If an employer provides a home purchase loan when an employee moves to a new work location, it is referred to as a home relocation loan if certain conditions are met. If this is an interest free or low interest loan, the ITA 80.4(1) rules apply as outlined in the preceding section. However, in the case of a home relocation loan, there is an offsetting deduction.

3-154.   This deduction is equal to the benefit associated with an interest free home relocation loan of up to $25,000. Note, however, the deduction is applied in the calculation of Taxable Income. This being the case, the usual ITA 80.4(1) imputed interest benefit will be included in net employment income, a figure that will not be changed by the home relocation loan deduction. The deduction will be applied after net employment income has been added to other sources in the determination of Net Income For Tax Purposes. The details of this deduction from Taxable Income are covered in Chapter 4.

3-155.   There is no GST benefit on imputed interest on a low or no interest loan. This reflects the fact that no GST is charged on financial services (see Chapter 21).

Exercise Three - 12

Subject: Housing Loan

On January 1, 2012, Mrs. Caldwell receives a $100,000 loan from her employer to assist her in purchasing a home. The loan requires annual interest at a rate of 1 percent, which she pays on December 31, 2012. Assume that the relevant prescribed rate is 2 percent during the first quarter of 2012, 3 percent during the second quarter, and 1 percent during the remainder of the year. Calculate Mrs. Caldwell's taxable benefit on this loan for the year (1) assuming that the loan qualifies as a home relocation loan and (2) assuming that it does not qualify as a home relocation loan.

End of Exercise. Solution available in Study Guide.

Tax Planning For Interest Free Loans

General Approach

3-156.   Tax rules result in a taxable benefit to the employee if the interest rate on the loan is lower than the prescribed rate. Given this, the question arises as to whether the use of employee loans is a tax effective form of providing employee benefits. As with other types of benefits, the question is whether it is better that the employer supplies the benefit or, alternatively, provides sufficient additional salary to allow the employee to acquire the benefit directly. In the case of loans, this additional salary would have to be sufficient to allow the employee to carry a similar loan at commercial rates.

3-157.   To determine whether a loan is an effective form of employee compensation, several factors have to be considered:

- the employer's rate of return on alternative uses for the funds
- the employer's tax rate
- the employee's tax rate
- the prescribed rate
- the rate available to the employee on a similar arm's length loan

3-158.   In analyzing the use of loans to employees, we begin with the assumption that we would like to provide a requested benefit to one or more employees and we are looking for the most cost effective way of providing the benefit. As noted, the alternative to providing an employee with a loan is to provide that employee with sufficient after tax income to carry an equivalent loan at commercial rates of interest.

3-159.   It then becomes a question of comparing the cash flows associated with the employer providing the loan (this would have to include sufficient additional income to pay the taxes on any loan benefit that will be assessed), with the cash flows required for the employer to provide the employee with sufficient income to carry an equivalent loan acquired from a commercial lender.

Example Of Interest Free Loan Benefit

3-160.   The following example will illustrate the calculations that are required in determining whether the use of a low interest or no interest loan is a tax effective form of employee compensation.

> **Example** In 2012, a key executive asks for a $100,000 interest free housing loan. The loan does not qualify as a home relocation loan. At this time, the employer has an investment opportunity that is expected to provide a rate of return of 12 percent before taxes. Assume the prescribed rate is 2 percent, while the rate for home mortgages is 5 percent. The employee is subject to a marginal tax rate of 45 percent, while the employer pays corporate taxes at a marginal rate of 28 percent.

> **Alternative 1 - Provide Additional Salary**   In the absence of the interest free loan, the employee would borrow $100,000 at 5 percent, requiring an annual interest payment of $5,000. In determining the amount of salary required to carry this loan, consideration has to be given to the fact that additional salary will be taxed at 45 percent. In terms of the algebra that is involved, we need to solve the following equation for X:

$$\$5,000 = [(X)(1 - 0.45)]$$

> You will recall that this type of equation is solved by dividing both sides by (1 - 0.45), resulting in a required salary of $9,615:

$$X = [\$5,000 \div (1 - 0.45)] = \$9,091$$

> Using this figure, the employer's after tax cash flow required to provide sufficient additional salary for the employee to carry a conventional $100,000 mortgage would be calculated as follows:

Required Salary [$5,000 ÷ (1 - 0.45)]	$9,091
Tax Savings From Deducting Salary [($9,091)(28%)]	(2,545)
Employer's After Tax Cash Flow - Additional Salary	**$6,546**

> **Alternative 2 - Provide The Loan**   If the loan is provided, the employee will have a taxable benefit of $2,000 [(2% - Nil)($100,000)], resulting in additional taxes payable of $900 [(45%)($2,000)]. To make this situation comparable to the straight salary alternative, the employer will have to provide the executive with both the loan amount and sufficient additional salary to pay the $900 in taxes on the benefit that will be assessed. The required amount would be $1,636 [$900 ÷ (1 - 0.45)].

> The employer's cash flow associated with the after tax cost of providing the additional salary as well as the after tax lost earnings on the $100,000 loan amount would be calculated as follows:

Required Salary [$900 ÷ (1 - 0.45)]	$1,636
Tax Savings From Deducting Salary [($1,636)(28%)]	(458)
After Tax Cost Of Salary To Cover Taxes On Benefit	$1,178
Employer's Lost Earnings [(12%)(1 - 0.28)($100,000)]	8,640
Employer's After Tax Cash Flow - Loan	**$9,818**

> **Conclusion**   Given these results, payment of additional salary appears to be the better alternative. However, the preceding simple example is not a complete analysis of the situation. Other factors, such as the employee's ability to borrow at going rates and the employer's ability to grant this salary increase in the context of overall salary policies, would also have to be considered.

Exercise Three - 13

Subject: Loans To Employees - Tax Planning

In 2012, a key executive asks for a $125,000 interest free housing loan that does not qualify as a home relocation loan. At this time, the employer has investment opportunities involving a rate of return of 7 percent before taxes. Assume the relevant prescribed rate is 2 percent, while the market rate for home mortgages is 5 percent. The employee is subject to a marginal tax rate of 42 percent, while the employer pays corporate taxes at a marginal rate of 26 percent. Determine whether the employer should grant the loan or, alternatively, provide sufficient salary to carry an equivalent loan from a commercial lender.

End of Exercise. Solution available in Study Guide.

Inclusions - Stock Option Benefits

The Economics Of Stock Option Arrangements

3-161. Stock options allow, but do not require, the holder to purchase a specified number of shares for a specified period of time at a specified acquisition price. Because of tax considerations, at the time of granting, the option price is usually at or above the market price of the shares. For example, options might be issued to acquire shares at a price of $10 at a time when the shares are trading at that same $10 value.

3-162. At first glance, such an option would appear to have no value as it simply allows the holder to acquire a share for $10, at a time when that share is only worth that amount. In reality, however, this option could have significant value, in that it allows the holder to participate in any upward price movement in the shares without any obligation to exercise the option if the price stays at, or falls below, $10. Stated alternatively, the option provides full participation in gains on the option shares, with no downside risk. Further, for an employee receiving such options, they provide this participation with no real investment cost until such time as the options are exercised.

Example Because of his excellent work, Andrew Chang is given options to buy 1,000 shares of his employer's stock at a price of $10 per share. At this time, the shares are trading at $10 per share. One year later, he exercises the options and immediately sells the acquired shares for $12 per share.

Analysis Andrew has enjoyed a gain of $2,000 [(1,000)($12 - $10)] with no initial investment. This clearly illustrates why the options have a value, even when they are not issued "in-the-money". The expression "in-the-money" refers to situations where the option price ($10 in this example) is below current market value. In this example, the options are in-the-money when the market value is greater than $10.

3-163. Stock options are granted to employees in the belief that, by giving an employee an interest in the stock of the company, he has an incentive to make a greater effort on behalf of the enterprise. In some companies, use of this form of compensation is restricted to senior executives. In contrast, other corporations make options available to larger groups of employees.

3-164. Prior to 2004, a very significant advantage to the use of stock options was that the cost of issuing such options was not recorded in the financial statements of the issuing corporation. Because of an inability of accountants to agree on the appropriate value for options that are not "in-the-money", corporations were able to issue huge quantities of stock options without recording any compensation expense.

3-165. However, this is no longer the situation. Beginning in 2004, Canadian GAAP has required the recognition of a compensation expense when stock options are issued.

3-166.   In contrast to their accounting treatment under Canadian GAAP, the issuance of stock options has no current tax consequences, either for the issuer or the recipient. The issuer cannot deduct any amount to reflect the economic value of the issued options. Further, the recipient does not have any income inclusion when the options are issued.

Overview Of The Tax Rules

3-167.   This is a difficult subject to present in that it involves several different areas of tax legislation. In addition to issues related to employment income, stock options influence the determination of Taxable Income and the calculation of taxable capital gains. While it would be possible to present this material on a piecemeal basis, we have found this to be confusing to our readers. An alternative would be to defer any discussion of this issue until all of the relevant material has been covered.

3-168.   However, this fails to reflect the fact that stock option issues relate most directly to employment income. As a consequence, most of our material on stock options will be presented in this Chapter. As this involves some material that will not be covered until later Chapters, an overview of the stock option material that will be presented in this Chapter is useful. (Note that the Student CD-ROM contains Supplementary Reading No. 2, "Stock Option Shares Deemed Not Identical Properties".) The basic points here are as follows:

Value At Issue   As noted previously, the tax rules give no recognition to the fact that stock options have a positive value at the time of issue. The issuing employer can make no deduction and the recipient employee has no income inclusion.

Employment Income Inclusion - Measurement   The employment income inclusion will be measured on the date that the options are exercised. The amount will be equal to the excess of the per share fair market value on the exercise date over the option price, with the difference multiplied by the number of shares acquired. This amount will never be negative as the employee would only exercise the options in situations where the value of the shares are equal to, or exceed, the option price.

Employment Income Inclusion - Recognition   While the employment income inclusion will always be measured at the time the options are exercised, it may not be recognized until the shares are sold. Whether the inclusion will be recognized at the time of exercise or at the time of sale will depend on the type of corporation that is issuing the stock options. Note that when the appropriate event triggers recognition of this income inclusion, it will be classified as employment income, even if the taxpayer is no longer an employee.

Taxable Income Deduction   As many of you are aware, gains on dispositions of securities are considered to be capital gains, subject to taxation on only one-half of their total amount. In the absence of some mitigating provision, the full amount of the employment income inclusion that arises on the exercise of options or the sale of option shares would be subject to tax. As this would not be an equitable situation, tax legislation permits a deduction in the calculation of Taxable Income equal to one-half of the employment income inclusion. While general coverage of Taxable Income is found in Chapters 4 and 11, this deduction will be covered here as part of our discussion of stock options. Note, however, this deduction does not influence the calculation of Net Employment Income. This means that, if you are solving a problem that requires the calculation of Net Employment Income, you will NOT include this deduction in your calculation.

Capital Gains   With the difference between fair market value at the exercise date and the option price being treated as an employment income inclusion, fairness requires that the adjusted cost base of the acquired shares be based on their fair market value, not the actual cost to the employee. This means that, when the shares are eventually sold, there will be a capital gain or loss based on the difference between the sale price and the fair market value of the shares at the time of exercise. As is discussed more fully in Chapter 8, only one-half of capital gains are subject to tax (the "taxable capital gain"). One-half of capital losses are deductible (the "allowable capital loss"), but only to the extent that there are taxable capital gains in the year.

3-169.   A simple example will serve to illustrate the relevant calculations:

Example An executive receives options to acquire 1,000 of his employer's common shares at an option price of $25 per share. At this time, the common shares are trading at $25 per share. He exercises the options when the shares are trading at $40 per share. In the following year, he sells the shares for $50 per share.

Analysis   Assuming that the employment income inclusion must be recognized when the options are exercised, the tax consequences for the year of exercise would be as follows:

Employment Income [(1,000)($40 - $25)]	$15,000
Taxable Income Deduction (One-Half)	(7,500)
Taxable Income In Year Of Exercise	**$ 7,500**

When the shares are sold, the additional tax consequences to the employee would be as follows:

Proceeds Of Disposition [(1,000)($50)]	$50,000
Adjusted Cost Base [(1,000)($40)]	(40,000)
Capital Gain	$10,000
Inclusion Rate	1/2
Taxable Capital Gain In Year Of Sale	**$ 5,000**

3-170.   Several points should be made with respect to this example:

• The employment income inclusion will always be measured at the time the options are exercised. However, its recognition for tax purposes may be deferred until the acquired shares are sold. This will be discussed in more detail in the material that follows.

• The $7,500 deduction is from Net Income For Tax Purposes in the calculation of Taxable Income, not from employment income. The net employment income that will be included in the executive's current or future Net Income For Tax Purposes, as well as his Earned Income inclusion for RRSP purposes (see Chapter 10), is $15,000.

• The availability of the $7,500 deduction requires that certain conditions be met. These conditions will be discussed in detail in the material that follows.

• As we have noted, when the $15 per share employment income benefit is included in employment income, this amount will be added to the adjusted cost base of the shares, increasing their value to $40 per share ($25 + $15). This inclusion is provided for under ITA 53(1)(j).

CCPCs Vs. Public Companies

3-171.   As is discussed more fully in Chapter 12, a Canadian controlled private corporation (CCPC) is generally a corporation that is controlled by Canadian residents and does not have its shares traded on a prescribed stock exchange. This is an important distinction in many areas of tax work. However, our concern here is with the difference between the tax treatment of stock options issued by public companies and the tax treatment of stock options issued by private companies.

3-172.   In very simplified terms, for options issued by public companies, the general rule is that the employment income inclusion will be taxed when the options are exercised. In contrast, for options issued by Canadian controlled private corporations, the employment income inclusion is still measured when the options are exercised, but the benefit is not taxed until the acquired shares are sold.

3-173.   This clearly places individuals receiving stock options to acquire shares of public companies at a disadvantage. They are required to pay taxes on an unrealized amount of income, sometimes resulting in a need to dispose of some portion of the acquired shares. For a short period of time, relief was provided in the form of an election that allowed the deferral of some of the employment income inclusion until the option shares were actually sold. However, this election is no longer available and will be given no further attention in this text.

Rules For Public Companies

3-174.   Under ITA 7(1)(a), when options to acquire the shares of a publicly traded company are exercised, there is an employment income inclusion equal to the excess of the fair market value of shares acquired over the price paid to acquire them. A deduction from Taxable Income, equal to one-half of the employment income that is included under ITA 7(1)(a), can be taken under ITA 110(1)(d).

3-175.   Note, however, this ITA 110(1)(d) deduction in the calculation of Taxable Income is only available if, at the time the options are issued, the option price was equal to, or greater than, the fair market value of the shares at the option grant date. If the option price is less than the fair market value of the shares at the time of issue, the deduction will not be available and the individual will be subject to tax on the full amount of the employment income inclusion.

> **Example** On December 31, 2010, John Due receives options to buy 10,000 shares of his employer's common stock at a price of $25 per share. The employer is a publicly traded company and the options are exercisable as of their issue date. At this time, the shares are trading at $25 per share.
>
> On July 31, 2012, Mr. Due exercises all of these options. At this time, the shares are trading at $43 per share. On September 30, 2013, Mr. Due sells the shares that he acquired with his options. The proceeds from the sale are $45 per share.
>
> **Analysis** The tax consequences of the preceding events and transactions are as follows:
>
> - **Issue Date** (December 31, 2010)   Despite the fact that the options clearly have a positive value at this point in time, there are no tax consequences resulting from the issuance of the options.
>
> - **Exercise Date** (July 31, 2012)   As the option price was equal to the fair market value of the shares at the option grant date, Mr. Due can use the ITA 110(1)(d) deduction in calculating his Taxable Income. The tax consequences resulting from the exercise of the options would be as follows:

> | | |
> |---|---:|
> | Fair Market Value Of Shares Acquired [(10,000)($43)] | $430,000 |
> | Cost Of Shares [(10,000)($25)] | (250,000) |
> | ITA 7(1)(a) Employment Income Inclusion | |
> | = **Increase In Net Income For Tax Purposes** | **$180,000** |
> | ITA 110(1)(d) Deduction [(1/2)($180,000)] | (90,000) |
> | **Increase In Taxable Income** | **$ 90,000** |

> - **Disposition Date** (September 30, 2013)   The tax consequences resulting from the sale of the shares would be as follows:

> | | |
> |---|---:|
> | Proceeds Of Disposition [(10,000)($45)] | $450,000 |
> | Adjusted Cost Base [(10,000)($43)] | (430,000) |
> | Capital Gain | $ 20,000 |
> | Inclusion Rate | 1/2 |
> | **Taxable Capital Gain** | **$ 10,000** |

Note that, in the 2013 calculation, the adjusted cost base of the shares has been bumped up to the value of the shares at the time of exercise, reflecting the fact that the difference between the $43 per share value on that date and the $25 option price has already been included in the taxpayer's Net Income For Tax Purposes.

Also note that, if the taxpayer had sold the shares for less than the bumped up value of $43 in 2012, he would have an allowable capital loss. If this was the case, the taxpayer would not be able to deduct the loss in 2012, unless he had taxable capital gains from some other source. This creates a situation that could be viewed as unfair in that the taxpayer has had to include gains up to the $43 value, but might not be able to deduct the loss resulting from a subsequent decline in value in the same year. He cannot deduct the capital loss against the $43 per share increase in value because that increase was classified as employment income.

Exercise Three - 14

Subject: Stock Options - Public Company

During 2010, Mr. Gordon Guise was granted options to buy 2,500 of his employer's shares at a price of $23.00 per share. At this time, the shares are trading at $20.00 per share. His employer is a large publicly traded company. During July, 2012, he exercises all of the options when the shares are trading at $31.50 per share. In September, 2012, the shares are sold for $28.00 per share. What is the effect of the exercise of the options and the sale of the shares on Mr. Guise's 2012 Net Income For Tax Purposes and Taxable Income? Where relevant, identify these effects separately.

End of Exercise. Solution available in Study Guide.

Rules For Canadian Controlled Private Corporations

3-176.   The basic public company rules that we have just described require the recognition of a taxable benefit when the options are exercised, prior to the realization in cash of any benefit from the options granted. This may not be an insurmountable problem for employees of publicly traded companies, in that they can sell some of the shares or use them as loan collateral if they need to raise the cash to pay the taxes on the benefit.

3-177.   However, for employees of a Canadian controlled private corporation (CCPC), a requirement to pay taxes at the time an option is exercised could create severe cash flow problems. As a consequence, a different treatment is permitted for stock options issued by CCPCs. The employment income inclusion is still measured at the time the options are exercised, but it is not taxed until the shares are sold.

3-178.   For CCPCs, the employment income inclusion is determined under ITA 7(1)(a) and 7(1.1). The ITA 110(1)(d) deduction from Taxable Income is also available to CCPCs provided the option price was equal to, or more than, the fair market value of the shares at the option grant date.   However, if this condition is not met, an additional provision under ITA 110(1)(d.1) allows the taxpayer to deduct one-half of the employment income inclusion, provided the shares are held for at least two years after their acquisition.

3-179.   Using the same information that is contained in the example in Paragraph 3-175, altered only so that the employer is a CCPC, the tax consequences would be as follows:

Analysis For CCPC Example

- **Issue Date** (December 31, 2010)   Despite the fact that the options clearly have a positive value at this point in time, there are no tax consequences resulting from the issuance of the options.

- **Exercise Date** (July 31, 2012)   While the amount of the employment income inclusion would be measured on this date, it would not be included in income at this point.

Based on the increase in share value from $25 to $43 per share, the benefit would be measured as $180,000 [($43 - $25)(10,000 Shares)]. This benefit, along with the related $90,000 Taxable Income deduction, would be deferred until such time as the shares are sold.

- **Disposition Date** (September 30, 2013)   The tax consequences resulting from the sale of the shares would be as follows:

Deferred Employment Income [($43 - $25)(10,000)]		$180,000
Proceeds Of Disposition [(10,000)($45)]	$450,000	
Adjusted Cost Base [(10,000)($43)]	(430,000)	
Capital Gain	$ 20,000	
Inclusion Rate	1/2	10,000
Increase In Net Income For Tax Purposes		**$190,000**
ITA 110(1)(d) Deduction [(1/2)($180,000)]		(90,000)
Increase In Taxable Income		**$100,000**

3-180.   Note that this is the total increase in Taxable Income that would have resulted from simply purchasing the shares at $25 and later selling them for $45 [(10,000)(1/2)($45 - $25) = $100,000]. The structuring of this increase is different and, in some circumstances, the difference could be significant. For example, the fact that the $180,000 increase in value has been classified as employment income rather than capital gains means that it is not eligible for the lifetime capital gains deduction (see Chapter 10), but it will increase Earned Income for RRSP purposes (see Chapter 9). Although the timing is different, the $100,000 total increase in Taxable Income is the same as in the public company example in Paragraph 3-175.

Exercise Three - 15

Subject: Stock Options - CCPC

In 2008, Ms. Milli Van was granted options to buy 1,800 of her employer's shares at a price of $42.50 per share. At this time, the shares have a fair market value of $45.00 per share. Her employer is a Canadian controlled private corporation. In June, 2011, when the shares have a fair market value of $75.00 per share, she exercises all of her options. In September, 2012, Ms. Van sells her shares for $88,200 ($49.00 per share). What is the effect of the exercise of the options and the sale of the shares on Ms. Van's 2011 and 2012 Net Income For Tax Purposes and Taxable Income? Where relevant, identify these effects separately.

End of Exercise. Solution available in Study Guide.

Other Inclusions

Payments By Employer To Employee

3-181.   As noted in Paragraph 3-59, ITA 6(3) deals with employment related payments made prior to, or subsequent to, the employment period. This includes payments for accepting employment, as well as payments for work to be completed subsequent to the termination of employment. ITA 6(3) requires that all such amounts be included in employment income.

Forgiveness Of Employee Loans

3-182.   There may be circumstances in which an employer decides to forgive a loan that has been extended to an employee. As noted in Paragraph 3-59, ITA 6(15) requires that the forgiven amount be included in the income of the employee in the year in which the forgiveness occurs. The forgiven amount is simply the amount due, less any payments that have been made by the employee.

Housing Loss Reimbursement

3-183.   When an employee is required to move, employers often provide various types of financial assistance. As is discussed in Chapter 9, an employer can pay for the usual costs of moving (e.g., shipping company costs) without tax consequences to the employee. In recent years, particularly when an employee is moved from an area with a weak housing market, it has become more common for employers to reimburse individuals for losses incurred in the disposition of their principal residence.

3-184.   Initially this type of reimbursement was allowed, with no limits on the amount that could be received by the employee on a tax free basis. However, the current rules limit the amount of housing loss that can be reimbursed without tax consequences. This is accomplished in ITA 6(19) by indicating that amounts paid to employees for housing losses, except for amounts related to "eligible housing losses", must be included in income.

3-185.   ITA 6(22) defines an "eligible housing loss" as a loss that is related to a move that qualifies for the deduction of moving expenses. While this issue is discussed in more detail in Chapter 9, we would note here that an employee is generally allowed to deduct moving expenses when he moves at least 40 kilometers closer to a new work location.

3-186.   ITA 6(20) limits the amount of housing loss reimbursement that can be received by indicating that one-half of any amount received in excess of $15,000 as an eligible housing loss must be included in the employee's income as a taxable benefit. Stated alternatively, the tax free amount of housing loss reimbursement is limited to the first $15,000, plus one-half of any amount paid in excess of $15,000.

Discounts On Employer's Merchandise

3-187.   When an employee is allowed to purchase merchandise which is ordinarily sold by an employer, any discount given to the employee is not generally considered to be a taxable benefit. If discounts are extended by a group of employers, or if an employer only extends the discounts to a particular group of employees, a taxable benefit may arise. In addition, this administrative position is not intended to apply to big-ticket items (e.g., a contractor giving an employee a discount on a new home).

3-188.   A further interesting note is that the CRA has indicated that, in the case of airline employees, a benefit is assessed if the employee travels on a space confirmed basis and pays less than 50 percent of the economy fare. The benefit is the difference between 50 percent of the economy fare and the amount paid.

3-189.   When a benefit must be included in income as the result of merchandise discounts, it will include any GST/HST that is applicable to these amounts.

Club Dues And Recreational Facilities

3-190.   With respect to employer provided recreational facilities, IT-470R notes that they are not considered a taxable benefit to the employee. In the case of employers paying membership fees in social or recreational clubs, the IT Bulletin indicates that as long as the facilities are used to the advantage of the employer, they would not be considered a taxable benefit to the employee.

3-191.   While this would seem to indicate that such fees do become a taxable benefit unless they are used primarily to further the business interests of the employer, the CRA has not pursued this approach with any rigour. As a consequence, employer payments for social or recreational club memberships generally do not result in a taxable benefit to the employee. As noted previously, the attractiveness of this type of employee benefit is reduced by the fact that, in general, employers cannot deduct the cost of club dues or recreational facilities in the determination of business income.

Specific Deductions

Overview

3-192.   The provisions covering deductions that can be made against employment income are found in ITA 8. In addition, ITA 8(2) contains a general limitation statement that makes it clear that unless an item is listed in ITA 8, it cannot be deducted in the calculation of employment income.

3-193.   We have noted previously that the ITA 8 list of deductions is very limited, particularly in comparison with the list of deductions available to self-employed individuals earning business income. Despite the shortness of its list, the application of ITA 8 is fairly complex. This results from the fact that there are restrictions on the type of employee that can deduct certain items, restrictions on the items that can be deducted, and additional restrictions against simultaneous usage of some of the statutory provisions. Given this complexity, a listing and brief description of the more significant deductions available is a useful introduction to this material.

ITA 8(1)(b) Legal Expenses allows an employee to deduct any legal costs paid to collect or establish the right to salary or wages owed by an employer or former employer. Also deductible are legal costs incurred to recover benefits, such as health insurance, that are not paid by an employer or former employer, but that are required to be included in employment income when received.

ITA 8(1)(f) Sales Expenses covers the deductions available to individuals who earn commission income. It covers travel expenses, motor vehicle expenses, and other types of expenses associated with earning commissions (e.g., licenses required by real estate salespersons).

ITA 8(1)(h) Travel Expenses covers deductions available to all employees for travel expenses, other than motor vehicle expenses. An employee earning commissions can deduct travel costs under ITA 8(1)(f) or ITA 8(1)(h), but cannot use both provisions simultaneously.

ITA 8(1)(h.1) Motor Vehicle Travel Expenses covers deductions available to all employees for motor vehicle expenses. An employee earning commissions can deduct motor vehicle costs under ITA 8(1)(f) or ITA 8(1)(h.1), but cannot use both provisions simultaneously.

ITA 8(1)(i) Dues And Other Expenses Of Performing Duties covers a variety of deductions available to all employees, such professional dues, office rent paid or costs of maintaining a home office, salaries to an assistant and the cost of supplies used in employment related activities.

ITA 8(1)(j) Motor Vehicle And Aircraft Costs In general, employees cannot deduct capital costs. This includes tax depreciation (capital cost allowance or CCA) and interest on funds borrowed to acquire capital assets This Paragraph creates an exception for motor vehicles and aircraft.

While generally less important, we would note that ITA 8(1)(p) allows the deduction of CCA on musical instruments required by employment activities. Note, however, this provision does not include the deduction of interest related to the financing of such instruments.

ITA 8(1)(m) Employee's Registered Pension Plan (RPP) Contributions As was noted previously, ITA 6(1)(a) excludes employer's contributions to an RPP from treatment as a taxable benefit. Adding to the attractiveness of these arrangements is the fact that ITA 8(1)(m) provides for the employee's contributions to be treated as a deduction. This deduction is given detailed attention in Chapter 10 which provides comprehensive coverage of the various retirement savings arrangements.

ITA 8(1)(r) Apprentice Mechanic's Tool Costs provides for the deduction of tools that are required by an apprentice mechanic. This is a very complex provision that allows for a deduction of costs in excess of an annual threshold amount. The threshold is the lesser of $500 plus the Canada employment credit amount (see Chapter 4), and 5 percent of an adjusted income figure.

ITA 8(1)(s) Tradesperson's Tool Expenses provides for the deduction of up to $500 for tools that are required by a tradesperson. Only costs in excess of $1,095 can be deducted.

ITA 8(4) Meals Both ITA 8(1)(f) and ITA 8(1)(h) refer to travel costs. As such costs could include meals, ITA 8(4) specifies when meals can be considered a part of travel costs. This Subsection notes that, for meals to be deductible as travel costs under ITA 8(1)(f) or ITA 8(1)(h), the meal must be consumed when the taxpayer is required, by his employment duties, to be away from the municipality or metropolitan area where his employer's establishment is located for at least 12 hours.

We would also note here that ITA 67.1(1) limits the deductibility of food and entertainment costs to 50 percent of the amount paid. This limitation applies without regard to whether the individual is working as an employee, or as a self-employed individual earnings business income.

ITA 8(13)   Work Space In Home provides rules for an employee deducting the costs of a work space in his home.

3-194.   Most of these provisions will be given more detailed attention in the material in this Chapter. The Employee and Partner GST Rebate available on deductible expenses is covered in Chapter 21. Other, less commonly used Paragraphs such as ITA 8(1)(e) which allows the deduction of certain expenses of railway employees, will not be given coverage.

Salesperson's Expenses Under ITA 8(1)(f)

3-195.   Individual employees who are involved with the selling of property or the negotiating of contracts are permitted to deduct all expenses that can be considered necessary to the performance of their duties. As stated in ITA 8(1)(f), to be eligible to deduct salesperson's expenses, all of the following conditions must be met:

1. The salesperson must be required to pay his own expenses. The employer must sign Form T2200 certifying that this is the case. While the form does not have to be filed, it must be available if requested by the CRA.

2. The salesperson must be ordinarily required to carry on his duties away from the employer's place of business.

3. The salesperson must not be in receipt of a travel allowance that was not included in income.

4. The salesperson must receive at least part of his remuneration in the form of commissions or by reference to the volume of sales.

3-196.   Item that can be deducted under ITA 8(1)(f) include:

• advertising and promotion
• meals and entertainment (subject to the previously noted 50 percent limit)
• lodging
• motor vehicle costs (other than CCA and interest)
• parking (which is not considered a motor vehicle expense)
• work space in the home costs (property taxes and insurance in addition to maintenance costs - see Paragraph 3-213).
• training costs
• transportation costs
• licences (e.g., for real estate sales)
• bonding and liability insurance premiums
• computers and office equipment (leased only - see following Paragraph)

3-197.   Except in the case of an automobile or aircraft, an employee who is a salesperson cannot deduct CCA or interest on funds borrowed to acquire capital assets. This means that if a salesperson purchases a computer to maintain customer records, he will not be able to deduct CCA on it. Alternatively, if the computer is leased, the lease payments are deductible.

3-198.   In order to deduct 50 percent of the cost of meals, the salesperson must be away from the municipality or metropolitan area where the employer's establishment is located for at least 12 hours. As is the case in the determination of business income, no deduction is permitted for membership fees for clubs or recreational facilities. A salesperson is permitted to deduct motor vehicle costs, supplies, salaries to an assistant, office rent and the cost of maintaining an office in his home. However, these costs can also be deducted by other types of employees and, as a consequence, will be dealt with later in this Chapter.

3-199.   The amount of qualifying expenses that can be deducted under ITA 8(1)(f) is limited to the commissions or other sales related revenues received during the year. This limitation does not, however, apply to CCA or interest on a motor vehicle or aircraft. These costs are deductible under ITA 8(1)(j) (see Paragraph 3-210). The deduction under ITA 8(1)(j) is not limited to commission income and, because it can be used in conjunction with ITA 8(1)(f), the salesperson's total deductions can exceed commission income.

Travel Expenses And Motor Vehicle Costs Under ITA 8(1)(h) and 8(1)(h.1)

3-200.   The conditions for deducting expenses under ITA 8(1)(h) and (h.1) are similar to those for deductions under ITA 8(1)(f), except that there is no requirement that some part of the employee's remuneration be in the form of commissions. The conditions are as follows:

1. The person must be required to pay his own travel and motor vehicle costs. As was the case with commission salespersons, the employee must have Form T2200, signed by the employer, certifying that this is the case.

2. The person must be ordinarily required to carry on his duties away from the employer's place of business.

3. The person must not be in receipt of an allowance for travel costs that was not included in income.

3-201.   There is one further condition that will be discussed more fully beginning at Paragraph 3-205. Both ITA 8(1)(h) and (h.1) state that, if a deduction is made as a salesperson under ITA 8(1)(f), no deduction can be made under these Paragraphs.

3-202.   ITA 8(1)(h) provides for the deduction of travel costs such as accommodation, airline or rail tickets, taxi fares, and meals. As was the case with salespersons' expenses, only 50 percent of the cost of meals is deductible. Here again, the deductibility of meals is conditional on being away from the municipality or metropolitan area in which the employer's establishment is located for at least 12 hours.

3-203.   ITA 8(1)(h.1) provides for the deduction of motor vehicle costs, other than CCA and financing costs, when an employee uses his own vehicle to carry out employment duties. Note that these are the same costs that could be deducted by a salesperson under ITA 8(1)(f).

3-204.   These deductions can be claimed by any employee who meets the specified criteria. Further, they are not limited by employment income. The deductions can be used to create a net employment loss which, if not usable against other types of income in the current year, is subject to the carry forward provisions that are discussed in Chapter 11.

The Salesperson's Dilemma

3-205.   All of the travel and motor vehicle costs that a salesperson could deduct under ITA 8(1)(h) and (h.1) could also be deducted using ITA 8(1)(f). However, the use of ITA 8(1)(f) involves both good news and bad news:

- **Good News** The good news is that, if the salesperson uses ITA 8(1)(f), he can deduct expenses related to sales activity that are not deductible under any other provision (e.g., advertising and promotion).

- **Bad News** The bad news is that, if a salesperson uses ITA 8(1)(f), the amount that he can deduct is limited to the amount of commission income.

3-206.   At first glance, the logical course of action here would be to use ITA 8(1)(h) and (h.1) for the travel and motor vehicle costs (this deduction would not be limited by commission income), and to then use ITA 8(1)(f) to deduct the maximum amount of other items that are available under this latter Paragraph (subject to the commission income limitation). However, this cannot be done — the *Income Tax Act* prohibits the use of ITA 8(1)(h) or (h.1), if a deduction is made under ITA 8(1)(f).

3-207.   The result is, in situations where potential deductions under ITA 8(1)(f) exceed commission income, the salesperson must undertake an additional calculation to determine whether the total travel costs under ITA 8(1)(h) and (h.1) would be greater than the commission limited amount of deductions under ITA 8(1)(f). Should this be the case, the salesperson would deduct the larger amount that is available under ITA 8(1)(h) and (h.1). It is difficult to understand the tax policy goal that is achieved through this complexity.

3-208.   Note that this choice does not influence the amount of other deductions available to the salesperson. The amounts deducted under other ITA 8(1) Paragraphs will be unchanged by whether the salesperson uses ITA 8(1)(f) or the combination of ITA 8(1)(h) and (h.1).

Exercise Three - 16

Subject: Commission Salesperson Expenses

Mr. Morton McMaster is a commission salesperson. During 2012, his gross salary was $82,000 and he received $12,200 in commissions. During the year he had advertising costs of $8,000 and expenditures for entertainment of clients of $12,000. His travel costs for the year totaled $13,100. He is required to pay his own expenses and does not receive any allowance from his employer. What is Mr. McMaster's maximum expense deduction for 2012?

End of Exercise. Solution available in Study Guide.

Other Expenses Of Performing Duties Under ITA 8(1)(i)

3-209.   ITA 8(1)(i) contains a list of other items that can be deducted in the determination of employment income by all employees. The major items included here are as follows (see IT-352R for more detailed coverage):

- Annual professional membership dues, if their payment was necessary to maintain a professional status recognized by statute.
- Union dues that are paid pursuant to the provisions of a collective agreement.

In order to deduct the following amounts, the employee must be required to incur the costs under a contract of employment. This must be supported by Form T2200, signed by the employer and certifying that the requirement exists.

- Office rent and/or certain costs of maintaining a home office (see Paragraph 3-213)
- Salary paid to an assistant or a substitute.
- The cost of supplies consumed in the performance of employment duties. Supplies include stationery, long distance telephone calls and cell phone airtime, but not the basic monthly charge for a telephone or amounts paid to connect or license a cell phone.

Automobile And Aircraft Expenses Under ITA 8(1)(j)

3-210.   Under either ITA 8(1)(f) or ITA 8(1)(h.1) an employee can deduct the operating costs of an automobile used in employment duties. With respect to operating costs, this would include an appropriate share (based on the proportion the employment related kilometers are of the total kilometers driven) of such costs as fuel, maintenance, normal repair costs, insurance, and licensing fees.

3-211.   In addition, under ITA 8(1)(j), an employee can deduct CCA and interest costs on an automobile or an aircraft that is used in employment related activities. The deductible amounts for CCA are calculated in the same manner as they would be for a business. CCA would be calculated on a 30 percent declining balance basis on automobiles and a 25 percent declining balance basis on aircraft, while deductible interest would be based on actual amounts paid or payable. (See Chapter 5 for complete coverage of CCA calculations.) With respect to interest calculations, there is a difference in that, while a business can deduct accrued interest, an employee can only deduct interest that has been paid.

3-212.   However, there are limits on the amounts that can be deducted here for business purposes, and these limits are equally applicable to the calculation of employment income deductions. While these limits are discussed more completely in Chapter 6 on Business Income, we would note that for 2012 there is no deduction for CCA on the cost of an automobile in excess of $30,000 (before GST/HST/PST), that deductible interest is limited to $300 per month, and that deductible lease payments are limited to $800 per month (before GST/HST/PST). With respect to employees, their deduction would be based on the fraction of these costs, subject to the preceding limits, that reflects the portion of employment related kilometers included in the total kilometers driven.

Home Office Costs For Employees

3-213.   We have noted that salespersons can deduct the costs associated with an office in their home under ITA 8(1)(f), and that any employee who is required by his employment contract to maintain an office can make a similar deduction under ITA 8(1)(i). Because of the obvious potential for abuse in this area, ITA 8(13) establishes fairly restrictive conditions with respect to the availability of this deduction. Under the provisions of this Subsection, costs of a home office are only deductible when the work space is either:

- the place where the individual principally performs the duties of the office or employment, or

- used exclusively during the period in respect of which the amount relates for the purpose of earning income from the office or employment and used on a regular and continuous basis for meeting customers or other persons in the ordinary course of performing the duties of the office or employment.

3-214.   Once it is established that home office costs are deductible, it becomes necessary to determine what kind of costs can be deducted. We have noted previously that, for employees, the only assets on which CCA and interest can be deducted are automobiles and aircraft (CCA only can be deducted on musical instruments). This means that no employee can deduct CCA or mortgage interest related to an office that is maintained in their residence. (Chapter 6 contains a comparison of deductible home office costs for employees and for self-employed contractors.)

3-215.   With respect to other costs, IT-352R2 indicates that an employee making a deduction under ITA 8(1)(i) can deduct an appropriate portion (based on floor space used for the office) of maintenance costs such as fuel and electricity, light bulbs, cleaning materials, and minor repairs.

3-216.   For commissioned salespersons making a deduction for a home office under ITA 8(1)(f), IT-352R2 indicates that they can deduct the items listed in the preceding paragraph, plus an appropriate portion of property taxes and house insurance premiums.

3-217.   If the home office is in rented property, the percentage of rent and any maintenance costs paid related to the home office are deductible.

3-218.   The amount deductible for home office costs is limited to employment income after the deduction of all other employment expenses. Stated alternatively, home office costs cannot be used to create or increase an employment loss. Any home office costs that are not deductible in a year can be carried forward to the following year. They become part of the home office costs for that year and, to the extent that this total cannot be deducted in that year, the balance can be carried forward to the following year. This, in effect, provides an indefinite carry forward of these costs.

Key Terms Used In This Chapter

3-219.   The following is a list of the key terms used in this Chapter. These terms, and their meanings, are compiled in the Glossary Of Key Terms located at the back of the separate paper Study Guide.

Allowance	Operating Cost Benefit
Bonus Arrangement	Prescribed Rate
Canadian Controlled Private Corporation	Public Corporation
Employee	Salary
Employer/Employee Relationship	Self-Employed Individual
Employment Income	Standby Charge
Fringe Benefits	Stock Option
Home Relocation Loan	Taxable Allowance
Imputed Interest	Taxable Benefit
In-The-Money	

References

3-220.   For more detailed study of the material in this Chapter, we would refer you to the following:

ITA 5	Income From Office Or Employment
ITA 6	Amounts To Be Included As Income From Office Or Employment
ITA 7	Agreement To Issue Securities To Employees
ITA 8	Deductions Allowed
ITA 80.4	Loans
ITA 80.5	Deemed Interest
ITR 4301	Interest Rates [Prescribed Rate Of Interest]
IC 73-21R9	Claims for Meals and Lodging Expenses of Transport Employees
IT-63R5	Benefits, Including Standby Charge For An Automobile, From The Personal Use Of A Motor Vehicle Supplied By An Employer - After 1992
IT-85R2	Health And Welfare Trusts For Employees
IT-91R4	Employment At Special Or Remote Work Locations
IT-99R5	Legal And Accounting Fees (Consolidated)

IT-103R	Dues Paid To A Union Or To A Parity Or Advisory Committee
IT-113R4	Benefits To Employees - Stock Options
IT-158R2	Employees' Professional Membership Dues
IT-196R2	Payments By Employer To Employee
IT-202R2	Employees' Or Workers' Compensation
IT-352R2	Employee's Expenses, Including Work Space in Home Expenses
IT-389R	Vacation Pay Trusts Established Under Collective Agreements
IT-421R2	Benefits To Individuals, Corporations And Shareholders From Loans Or Debt
IT-428	Wage Loss Replacement Plans
IT-470R	Employees' Fringe Benefits (Consolidated)
IT-504R2	Visual Artists And Writers (Consolidated)
IT-514	Work Space In Home Expenses
IT-518R	Food, Beverages And Entertainment Expenses
IT-522R	Vehicle, Travel and Sales Expenses of Employees
IT-525R	Performing Artists
RC4110	CRA Guide - Employee Or Self-Employed?

Income Tax Technical News No. 40, "Administrative Policy Changes for Taxable Employment Benefits"

Guide T4044, "Employment Expenses"

Problems For Self Study

(The solutions for these problems can be found in the separate Study Guide.)

Self Study Problem Three - 1 (Bonus Arrangements)

Empire Inc. has an October 31 year end. On October 31, 2012, the Company accrues a bonus of $250,000, payable to Joan Betz, the president of the Company.

Required: For each of the following cases, indicate the taxation year in which the Company could deduct the bonus, as well as the taxation year in which Ms. Betz would have to include it in her taxable income.

Case A The bonus is paid on November 1, 2012.

Case B The bonus is paid on January 1, 2013.

Case C The bonus is paid on June 30, 2013.

Case D The bonus is paid on December 31, 2015.

Self Study Problem Three - 2 *(Taxable Automobile Benefits)*

Ms. Tamira Vines is a salesperson for Compudata Ltd., a Regina based software company. As her work requires her to travel extensively throughout southern and central Saskatchewan, the Company provides her with an automobile. The provincial sales tax rate for Saskatchewan is 5 percent.

From January 1, 2012 through May 31, 2012, the Company provided her with an Acura TL. This car was purchased by the Company on January 1, 2012 at a cost of $39,000, plus $1,950 in provincial sales tax and $1,950 in GST. During the period January 1, 2012 through May 31, 2012, the car was driven 38,800 kilometers for employment related purposes and 3,400 kilometers for personal use. The Company paid all operating costs during the period, an amount of $3,656, including applicable provincial sales tax and GST.

On June 1, 2012, following a late evening sales conference at the Shangri La Hotel in Moose Jaw, Ms. Vines was involved in an accident in which the Acura was destroyed. Ms. Vines was hospitalized and was not able to return to work until July 1, 2012. Compudata's insurance company paid $27,500 to the Company for the loss of the car.

When she returned to work on July 1, 2012, the Company provided Ms. Vines with a Ford Crown Victoria. The Company leased this vehicle at a monthly cost of $699 per month, including applicable provincial sales tax and GST. This monthly payment also includes a $100 per month charge for insurance.

For the period July 1, 2012 through December 31, 2012, operating costs, other than insurance, totaled $3,456, including applicable provincial sales tax and GST. These were paid for by the Company. During this period, Ms. Vines drove the car 15,600 kilometers for employment related purposes and 14,600 kilometers for personal use.

Ms. Vines paid to the Company $0.10 per kilometer for the personal use of the cars owned or leased by the Company for the year.

Required: Calculate the minimum taxable car benefit that will be included in Ms. Vines' employment income for the year ending December 31, 2012.

Self Study Problem Three - 3 *(Taxable Automobile Benefits)*

During the current year, the Carstair Manufacturing Company provides automobiles for four of its senior executives, with the value of the cars being in proportion to the salaries which they receive. While each of the individuals uses their car for employment related travel, they also use them for personal matters. The portion of personal use varies considerably among the four individuals. When the car is not being used by the employee, the Company requires that it be returned to the corporate premises.

The details related to each of these cars, including the amount of personal and employment related travel recorded by the executives, are as follows:

Mr. Sam Stern   Mr. Stern is the president of the Company and is provided with a Mercedes which has been purchased by the Company at a cost of $78,000. The car was new last year and, during the current year, it was driven a total of 38,000 kilometers. Of this total, only 6,000 kilometers were for employment related purposes, while the remaining 32,000 were for personal travel. Operating costs totaled $.50 per kilometer and, because Mr. Stern made an extended trip outside of North America, the car was used by Mr. Stern for 8 months during the current year.

Ms. Sarah Blue   Ms. Blue is the vice president in charge of marketing and has been provided with a Corvette. The Company leases this vehicle at a cost of $900 per month. During the current year, the car was driven a total of 60,000 kilometers, with all but 5,000 of these kilometers being for employment related purposes. The car was used by Ms. Blue throughout the current year, and total annual operating costs amount to $18,000.

Mr. John Stack   Mr. Stack is the vice president in charge of finance and he has been provided with an Acura that was purchased by the Company in the preceding year at a cost of $48,000. During the current year, Mr. Stack drove the car 42,000 kilometers for employment related purposes and 10,000 kilometers for personal travel. Operating costs for the year were $20,800, and the car was used by Mr. Stack throughout the current year. In order to reduce his taxable benefit, Mr. Stack made a payment of $7,000 to the Company for the use of this car.

Mr. Alex Decker   Mr. Decker, the vice president in charge of industrial relations, chose to drive a Lexus. This car was leased by the Company at a cost of $500 per month. The lease payment was significantly reduced by the fact that the Company made a refundable deposit of $10,000 to the leasing Company at the inception of the lease. During the current year, Mr. Decker drove the car 90,000 kilometers for employment related purposes and 8,500 kilometers for personal use. The operating costs were $0.35 per kilometer and, because of an extended illness, he was only able to use the car for the first 10 months of the year.

Required: Calculate the minimum amount of the taxable benefit for the current year that will accrue to each of these executives as the result of having the cars supplied by the Company. In making these calculations, ignore GST/HST/PST considerations. From the point of view of tax planning for management compensation, provide any suggestions for the Carstair Manufacturing Company with respect to these cars.

Self Study Problem Three - 4 (Loans To Employees)

Mr. Thomas Malone is employed by Technocratic Ltd. in a management position. Because of an outstanding performance in his division of the Company, he is about to receive a promotion accompanied by a large increase in compensation. He is discussing various possible ways in which his compensation might be increased without incurring the same amount of taxation as would be assessed on an increase in his salary. He has suggested that it might be advantageous for the Company to provide him with a five year interest free loan in the amount of $200,000 as part of any increase in compensation.

The funds will either be used to purchase a cottage in which case any interest on related loans will not be deductible to Mr. Malone, or used to purchase investments in which case any interest on related loans will be deductible to Mr. Malone.

Other relevant information is as follows:

- Given Mr. Malone's present salary, any additional income will be taxed at 45 percent.
- Technocratic Ltd. is able to invest funds at a before tax rate of 18 percent. It is subject to taxation at a 40 percent rate.
- Mr. Malone can acquire a similar term, $200,000 loan at an annual rate of 5 percent.
- Assume that the relevant Regulation 4301 rate for imputing interest on various tax related balances is 2 percent.

Required: Evaluate Mr. Malone's suggestion of providing him with an interest free loan in lieu of salary from the point of view of the cost to the Company. How will the deductibility of the interest affect your conclusion?

Self Study Problem Three - 5 (Employee Stock Options)

During 2010, Ms. Sara Wu's employer, Imports Ltd., granted her stock options that allowed her to acquire 12,000 shares of the Company's common stock at a price of $22 per share. At this time, the shares have a fair market value of $20 per share.

On June, 1, 2011, Ms. Wu exercises all of these options. At this time, Imports Ltd. shares have a fair market value of $31 per share.

Problems For Self Study

On January 31, 2012, Ms. Wu sells the 12,000 Imports Ltd. shares at a price of $28 per share.

Required   For each of the following Cases, calculate the tax consequences of the transactions that took place during 2010, 2011, and 2012 on both the Net Income For Tax Purposes and the Taxable Income of Ms. Wu. Where relevant, identify these effects separately.

    Case A   Imports Ltd. is a public company.
    Case B   Imports Ltd. is a Canadian controlled private corporation.

Self Study Problem Three - 6 (Employment Income - No Commissions)

For the last three years, Sam Jurgens has been employed in Halifax as a loan supervisor for Maritime Trust Inc. Maritime Trust is a large public company and, as a consequence, Mr. Jurgens felt that he did not have the opportunity to exhibit the full range of his abilities. To correct this situation, Sam decided to accept employment in Toronto effective July 1, 2012 as the general manager of Bolten Financial Services, a Canadian controlled private corporation specializing in providing financial advice to retired executives.

In April, 2012, prior to leaving Maritime Trust, Mr. Jurgens exercised options to purchase 5,000 shares of the public company's stock at a price of $15 per share. At the time the Maritime Trust options were granted, the shares were trading at the option price of $15 per share. At the time that he exercised these options, the shares were trading at $16 per share. He is still holding these shares on December 31, 2012.

Mr. Jurgens had an annual salary at Maritime Trust of $105,000, while in his new position in Toronto, the salary is $90,000 per year. However, he has the option of acquiring 1,000 shares per year of Bolten stock at a price of $20 per share. On July 1, when he was granted the option, Bolten stock had a fair market value of $14 per share. On December 1, 2012, when the Bolten stock has a fair market value of $22 per share, Mr. Jurgens exercises these options and acquires 1,000 shares. It is his intent to hold these shares for an indefinite period of time.

Because there is extensive travel involved in the position with Bolten Financial Services, the Company has provided Mr. Jurgens with a $40,000 company car. Between July 1 and December 31, 2012, Mr. Jurgens drove this car a total of 25,000 kilometers, of which 15,000 kilometers were clearly related to his work with Bolten Financial Services. The operating costs associated with the car for this period, all of which were paid for by the Company, amount to $5,000. Because of extensive repairs resulting from a manufacturer's recall, the car had to be returned to the Company for the months of October and November, 2012.

At the time of his move to Toronto, Bolten Financial Services provided Mr. Jurgens with a $200,000 home relocation loan to purchase a personal residence near the center of town. No interest was charged on this loan.

During the year, Mr. Jurgens earned $15,000 in interest and received $45,000 in dividends from taxable Canadian corporations.

Assume that the relevant prescribed rate through all of 2012 is 2 percent.

Required: Compute Sam Jurgens' minimum net employment income for the year ending December 31, 2012.

Self Study Problem Three - 7 (Employment Income - No Commissions)
(This Problem Is Continued In Self Study Problem Four-4)

Mr. John Barth has been employed for many years as a graphic illustrator in Kamloops, British Columbia. His employer is a large publicly traded Canadian company. During 2012, his gross salary was $82,500. In addition, he was awarded a $20,000 bonus to reflect his outstanding performance during the year. As he was in no immediate need of additional income, he arranged with his employer that none of this bonus would be paid until 2017, the year of his expected retirement.

Other Information:

For the 2012 taxation year, the following items were relevant.

1. Mr. Barth's employer withheld the following amounts from his income:

Federal Income Tax	$16,000
Employment Insurance Premiums	840
Canada Pension Plan Contributions	2,307
United Way Donations	2,000
Registered Pension Plan Contributions	3,200
Payments For Personal Use Of Company Car	3,600

2. During the year, Mr. Barth is provided with an automobile owned by his employer. The cost of the automobile was $47,500. Mr. Barth drove the car a total of 10,000 kilometers during the year, of which only 4,000 kilometers were related to the business of his employer. The automobile was used by Mr. Barth for ten months of the year. During the other two months, he was out of the country he was required to leave the automobile with one of the other employees of the corporation.

3. During the year, the corporation paid Mega Financial Planners a total of $1,500 for providing counseling services to Mr. Barth with respect to his personal financial situation.

4. In order to assist Mr. Barth in purchasing a ski chalet, the corporation provided him with a five year loan of $150,000. The loan was granted on October 1 at an interest rate of 1 percent. Mr. Barth paid the corporation a total of $375 in interest for 2012 on January 20, 2013. Assume that, at the time the loan was granted and throughout the remainder of the year, the relevant prescribed rate was 2 percent.

5. Mr. Barth was required to pay professional dues of $1,800 during the year.

6. On June 6, 2012, when Mr. Barth exercised his stock options to buy 1,000 shares of his employer's common stock at a price of $15 per share, the shares were trading at $18 per share. When the options were issued, the shares were trading at $12 per share. During December, 2012, the shares were sold at $18 per share.

Required: Calculate Mr. Barth's minimum net employment income for the year ending December 31, 2012. Provide reasons for omitting items that you have not included in your calculations. Ignore GST and PST considerations.

Self Study Problem Three - 8 (Employment Income With Commissions)

Ms. Sandra Firth is a commission salesperson who has been working for Hadley Enterprises, a Canadian public corporation, for three years. During the year ending December 31, 2012, her gross salary, not including commissions or allowances, was $72,000. Her commissions for the year totalled $14,000. The following amounts were withheld by Hadley Enterprises from Ms. Firth's gross salary:

Federal and provincial income taxes	$22,000
Registered pension plan contributions (Note One)	3,200
Payments for group disability insurance (Note Two)	250
Payments for personal use of company car (Note Three)	2,400
Payments for group term life insurance (Note Four)	450
Interest on home purchase loan (Note Five)	3,000
Purchase of Canada Savings Bonds	2,060

Note One Hadley Enterprises made a matching $3,200 contribution to Ms. Firth's registered pension plan.

Note Two Ms. Firth is covered by a comprehensive disability plan which provides periodic benefits during any period of disability to compensate for lost employment income. Prior to 2012, Hadley Enterprises paid all of the $500 per year premium on this plan.

However, as of 2012, Ms. Firth is required to pay one-half of this premium, the $250 amount withheld from her gross salary. During 2012, Ms. Firth was hospitalized for the month of March. For this period, the disability plan paid her $500 per week, for a total of $2,000.

Note Three   Hadley Enterprises provides Ms. Firth with a Lexus that was purchased in 2011 for $58,000. During 2012, she drove the car 92,000 kilometers, 7,000 of which were personal in nature. Ms. Firth paid all of the operating costs of the car, a total of $6,200 for the year ending December 31, 2012. However, the Company provides her with an annual allowance of $7,200 to compensate her for these costs. While Ms. Firth was hospitalized during the month of March (see Note Two), her employer required that the car be returned to their premises.

Note Four   Ms. Firth is covered by a group term life insurance policy that pays her beneficiary $160,000 in the event of her death. The 2012 premium on the policy is $1,350, two-thirds of which is paid by her employer.

Note Five   On January 1, 2012, the Company provided Ms. Firth with a $400,000 loan to assist with the purchase of a new residence. The loan must be repaid by December 31, 2012. All of the interest that is due on the loan for 2012 is withheld from Ms. Firth's 2012 salary. This loan does not qualify as a home relocation loan.

Other Information:

1. At Christmas, the Company gives all of its employees a BlackBerry. Each BlackBerry costs the Company $350, including all applicable taxes. The Company deducts this amount in full in its corporate tax return.

2. During 2011, Ms. Firth received stock options from Hadley to acquire 1,000 shares of its common stock. The option price is $5.00 per share and, at the time the options are issued, the shares are trading at $4.50 per share. In June, 2012, the shares have increased in value to $7.00 per share and Ms. Firth exercises her options to acquire 1,000 shares. She is still holding them at the end of the year and has no intention of selling them.

3. The Company provides Ms. Firth with a membership in the Mountain Tennis Club. The cost of this membership for the year is $2,500. During the year, Ms. Firth spends $6,500 entertaining clients at this club. The Company does not reimburse her for these entertainment costs.

4. Ms. Firth had travel costs related to her employment activities as follows:

Meals	$1,300
Lodging	3,500
Total	$4,800

Her employer provides her with a travel allowance of $300 per month ($3,600 for the year) which is included on her T4 for the year.

5. Assume that the relevant prescribed rate for the entire year is 2 percent.

Required: Calculate Ms. Firth's minimum net employment income for the year ending December 31, 2012. Provide reasons for omitting items that you have not included in your calculations. Ignore any GST or PST implications.

Self Study Problem Three - 9
(Employment Income With Commissions, Car CCA)

Mr. Jones is a salesman handling a line of computer software throughout Western Canada. During 2012, he is paid a salary of $25,800 and receives sales commissions of $47,700. He does not receive an allowance from his employer for any of his expenses. During the year, Mr. Jones made the following employment related expenditures:

Airline Tickets	$ 2,350
Office Supplies And Postage	415
Purchase Of Laptop Computer	2,075
Client Entertainment	1,750
Cost Of New Car	24,000
Operating Costs Of Car	7,200

The new car was purchased on January 5, 2012, and replaced a car which Mr. Jones had leased for several years. During 2012, Mr. Jones drove the car a total of 50,000 kilometers, of which 35,000 kilometers were for employment related purposes. The capital cost allowance for the car (100 percent) is $3,600.

In addition to expenditures to earn employment income, Mr. Jones has the following additional disbursements:

| Alberta Blue Cross Medical Insurance Premiums | $435 |
| Group Life Insurance Premiums | 665 |

Mr. Jones indicates that he regularly receives discounts on his employer's merchandise and, during the current year, he estimates that the value of these discounts was $1,300.

One of the suppliers of his employer paid $2,450 to provide Mr. Jones with a one week vacation at a northern fishing lodge.

Required: Determine Mr. Jones' net employment income for the 2012 taxation year. Ignore all GST and PST implications.

Self Study Problem Three - 10
(Employment Income With Commissions And Home Office Costs)

Mr. Worthy is a commissioned salesman and has asked for your assistance in preparing his 2012 income tax return. He has provided you with the following information:

Employment Income		
Salary		$65,000
Commissions		$11,000
Telephone Charges		
Monthly Charge For Residential Line	$ 250	
Long Distance To Clients		
From Home Office	400	
Cellular Phone Airtime To Clients	800	$ 1,450
Office Supplies And Postage At Home Office		$ 295
Cost of Tickets To Basketball Games With Clients		$ 2,550
Travel Expenses		
Car Operating Costs	$2,700	
Meals	900	
Hotels	2,850	$ 6,450
Capital Cost Allowance On Car (100%)		$ 2,450
Cost Of Maintaining Home Office		
(Based On A Proportion Of Space Used)		
House Utilities	$485	
House Insurance	70	
House Maintenance	255	
Capital Cost Allowance - House	750	
Capital Cost Allowance - Office Furniture	475	
Mortgage Interest	940	
Property Taxes	265	$ 3,240

Interest		
On Loan To Buy Office Furniture	$1,700	
On Loan To Buy Car	2,300	$ 4,000

Mr. Worthy's car was purchased, used, several years ago for $28,000. Twenty percent of the milage on the car is for personal matters. He is required by his employer to maintain an office in his home and is eligible to deduct home office costs. Mr. Worthy has received no reimbursement from his employer for any of the amounts listed.

Required: Ignore GST and PST implications in your solutions.

A. Calculate Mr. Worthy's minimum net employment income for 2012.

B. Assume Mr. Worthy had only $4,000 in commission income in addition to his $65,000 salary. Calculate Mr. Worthy's minimum net employment income for 2012.

Assignment Problems

(The solutions for these problems are only available in
the solutions manual that has been provided to your instructor.)

Assignment Problem Three - 1 (Bonus Arrangements)

Mr. Carl Lange is the president of Lange Enterprises Inc., a Canadian controlled private company. The Company has a September 30 year end. On September 30, 2012, the Company declares a bonus of $175,000, payable to Mr. Lange.

Required: For each of the following cases, indicate the taxation year in which the Company can deduct the bonus, as well as the taxation year in which Mr. Lange will have to include it in his taxable income.

Case A   The bonus is paid on October 1, 2012.

Case B   The bonus is paid on January 31, 2013.

Case C   The bonus is paid on July 30, 2013.

Case D   The bonus is paid on December 31, 2015.

Assignment Problem Three - 2 (Employee Vs. Self-Employed)

Farnham Ltd. is interested in acquiring the services of a highly qualified engineering professional. This individual has agreed to become an employee at a salary of $250,000 per year. For employees, the cost of providing benefits (pension plan and extended health care) is about 8 percent of gross wages.

In addition to CPP and EI, the province levies a 2 percent payroll tax to provide for health care. The tax applies to all wages and salaries with no upper limit.

This individual's work is such that a contract could be arranged that would make him an independent contractor. However, because he likes the security and benefits associated with being an employee, the contract would have to provide income of $280,000 in order for him to find it acceptable.

Required   Advise the company as to the preferable alternative.

Assignment Problem Three - 3 (Taxable Automobile Benefits)

Jordan Ltd. owns a car with an original cost of $28,500. The car has been owned by the company for over three years, with the Company deducting maximum CCA in each year. Jordan Ltd. requires that cars be returned to the corporate premises when they are not being used by the employee.

During 2012, the car has been used by Ms. Rachel Smith, the Company's regional marketing manager. During this year, she drove the car a total of 52,000 kilometers, with all of the operating expenses being paid for by the Company. These operating expenses averaged $0.12 per kilometer, a total of $6,240.

Required: Ignore all GST/PST/HST implications. Indicate the minimum taxable benefit that would be allocated to Ms. Smith in each of the following Cases:

Case A Ms. Smith has use of the car for the entire year and drives it a total of 18,000 kilometers for personal purposes.

Case B Ms. Smith has use of the car for 10 months of the year and drives it a total of 11,000 kilometers for personal purposes.

Case C Ms. Smith has use of the car for 6 months of the year and drives it a total of 28,300 kilometers for personal purposes.

Assignment Problem Three - 4 (Taxable Automobile Benefits)

Three employees of the Cancar Company were given the use of company cars on January 1 of the current year. The three cars are identical. Each car was driven 16,000 kilometers during the year and the operating costs were $2,400 for each car during the year, all of which were paid by the company. When the car is not being used by the employee, the Company requires that it be returned to its premises.

Required: Ignore all GST/PST/HST implications. For each of the following cars, calculate the minimum taxable benefit to the employees for the current year ending December 31.

Car A is purchased for $30,000. It is used by Aaron Abbott for the whole year. He drives it for personal purposes for a total of 9,000 kilometers.

Car B is leased for $635 per month. It is used by Babs Bentley for 11 months of the year. She drives it for personal purposes for a total of 6,000 kilometers and pays Cancar Company $500 for the use of the car.

Car C is purchased for $30,000. It is used by Carole Cantin for 10 months of the year. She drives it for personal purposes for a total of 7,000 kilometers.

Assignment Problem Three - 5 (Taxable Automobile Benefits)

The Martin Distributing Company provides cars for four of its senior executives. While the cars are used for employment related travel, the executives also use them for personal matters. The personal use varies considerably among the four individuals. When the car is not being used by the employee, the Company requires that it be returned to the corporate premises.

The details related to each of these cars, including the amount of personal and employment related travel recorded by the executives, are as follows:

Mr. Joseph Martin Mr. Martin is the president of the Company and is provided with a Mercedes that has been leased by the Company for $2,100 per month. During the current year, the car was driven a total of 42,000 kilometers, of which 19,000 could be considered employment related travel. Operating costs averaged $0.80 per kilo-meter. Because of an extended illness which required hospitalization, the car was only used by Mr. Martin for the first seven months of the year.

Mrs. Grace Martin   Mrs. Martin, the vice president in charge of marketing, is provided with a Lexus that the Company has purchased for $78,000. During the current year, this car was driven a total of 15,000 kilometers, of which all but 2,000 kilometers were employment related. Operating costs for the year amounted to $3,500 and the car was used by to Mrs. Martin throughout the year.

Mr. William Martin   William Martin, the vice president in charge of finance, is provided with a Ford that the Company leases for $600 per month. The total milage during the current year amounted to 38,000 kilometers, of which 32,000 kilometers related to personal matters. Operating costs for the year were $7,400 and the car was used by Mr. Martin throughout the year. William Martin paid the Company $300 per month for the use of the car.

Mrs. Sharon Martin-Jones   Mrs. Martin-Jones, the vice president in charge of industrial relations, is provided with a Nissan that the Company purchased for $39,000. During the current year, the car was driven 24,000 kilometers on employment related matters and 9,500 kilometers on personal matters. The operating costs average $0.40 per kilometer and, as the result of considerable travel outside of North America, the car was only used by Mrs. Martin-Jones for nine months of the year.

Required: Calculate the minimum taxable benefit that will accrue to each of these executives as the result of having the cars supplied by the Company.   Ignore all GST/PST/HST implications.

Assignment Problem Three - 6 (Loans To Employees)

Alan Cheng is negotiating a large increase in his compensation. As he is interested in using any tax advantaged form of compensation, he has suggested that his employer give him a $250,000 interest free loan.   He will be using the proceeds of this loan for a variety of investments.

Other information that is relevant to this decision is as follows:

- Mr. Cheng's various sources of income are such that any additional income will be taxed at a rate of 44 percent.
- Mr. Cheng can acquire a similar term, $250,000 loan at an annual rate of 4 percent.
- His employer is subject to tax at a combined federal/provincial rate of 32 percent. The company has alternative investment opportunities that earn a pre-tax rate of 8 percent.
- The relevant prescribed rate for all periods under consideration is 3 percent.
- Mr. Cheng's investment projects are expected to provide a pre-tax return of 12 percent.

Required: Evaluate Mr. Cheng's suggestion of providing him with an interest free loan in lieu of sufficient salary to carry a commercial loan at the rate of 5 percent. Note that, because he is using the loan for income producing purposes, any interest on related loans will be deductible to Mr. Cheng.

Assignment Problem Three - 7 (Employee Stock Options)

During 2010, her first year as an employee of Borden Ltd., Ms. Marcia Balzac was granted options to purchase 2,500 of the Company's shares at a price of $8.00 per share.

When Ms. Balzac exercises the options, the shares are trading at $8.30 per share.

On November 1, 2012, Ms. Balzac sells all of her shares at a price of $8.55 per share.

Required: Indicate the tax effect on Ms. Balzac of the transactions that took place during 2010, 2011, and 2012 under each of the following independent Cases. Your answer should include the effect on both Net Income For Tax Purposes and Taxable Income.

A. Borden Ltd. is a Canadian controlled private corporation. At the time the options were granted, the Company's shares had a fair market value of $7.50 per share. The options were exercised on October 1, 2011.

B. Borden Ltd. is a Canadian public company. At the time the options were granted, the shares were trading at $7.50 per share. The options were exercised on October 1, 2011.

C. Borden Ltd. is a Canadian public company. At the time the options were granted, the shares were trading at $8.25 per share. The options were exercised on October 1, 2011.

D. Borden Ltd. is a Canadian controlled private corporation. At the time the options were granted, the Company's shares had a fair market value of $9.00 per share. The options were exercised on October 1, 2010.

Assignment Problem Three - 8 (Employment Income - Simple)

Mr. Siegfried Karson is employed by a publicly traded Canadian corporation. His 2012 salary was $82,500. In addition, he earned commission of $8,400. For the 2012 year, his employer withheld the following amounts from his income:

Federal And Provincial Income Taxes	$18,600
CPP Contributions	2,307
EI Premiums	840
United Way Contributions	250
Registered Pension Plan Contributions	4,200
Union Dues	375

Mr. Karson's employer made a matching contribution of $4,200 to the registered pension plan.

Other Information:

1. During 2012, the employer provided Mr. Karson, as well as all other employees of the corporation, with non-cash gifts with a total value of $450.

2. In 2010, the company provided all of its employees with stock options that allowed them to acquire 500 shares at $26 per share. At this time, the shares were trading at $25 per share. During 2012, when the shares were trading at $37 per share, Mr. Karson exercised all of his options. Before the end of the year, he sold one-half of these shares for $39 per share.

3. Mr. Karson is provided with an automobile that is leased by the company for $725 per month. The lease payment includes $75 per month to cover insurance on the vehicle. The car is used by Mr. Karson for 10 months during 2012 and, when it is not being used by him, he is required to return the vehicle to the premises of the Company. During 2012, he drove the car 46,000 kilometers, of which 11, 000 were not related to employment activities. He reimburses his employer $0.45 per kilometer for his personal use of the vehicle.

4. Mr. Karson is required to pay all travel and promotional expenses with no reimbursement from the Company. He had the following employment related expenses during 2012:

Advertising	$4,200
Client Entertainment	3,100
Traveling Costs (Hotels, Airlines And 50 Percent of Meals)	9,200

Required: Calculate Mr. Karson's minimum net employment income for the year ending December 31, 2012. Ignore all GST and PST considerations.

Assignment Problem Three - 9 *(Employment Income With Commissions)*

Mr. Carlos Segovia is a very successful salesperson and is employed by a large Canadian public company. For 2012, his base salary is $252,000. In addition, he earns commissions of $18,500. Other information relevant to Mr. Segovia's 2012 employment income is as follows:

1. Mr. Segovia is required by his employer to pay all of his own employment related expenses. He is also required to provide his own office space. Mr. Segovia has a Form T2200 signed by his employer that certifies this.

2. His travel costs for 2012, largely airline tickets, food, and lodging, total $29,000. This includes $9,500 spent on business meals.

3. His annual dues to the Salesperson's Association (a trade union) were $450.

4. He is a member of his employer's registered pension plan. During 2012, his employer contributed $5,500 to this plan on his behalf. In addition, $5,500 was withheld from his salary and contributed to the plan.

5. During 2012, Mr. Segovia was billed a total of $13,500 by his golf club. Of this amount, $3,300 was the annual membership fee, with the remainder being charges for meals and drinks with clients.

6. During 2012, Mr. Segovia used 35 percent of his personal residence as an office. The designated space is where he principally performs his employment duties. Interest payments on his mortgage totalled $11,500 for the year and property taxes were $4,800. Utilities paid for the house totalled $2,600 and house insurance paid for the year was $1,250. Other maintenance costs associated with the property amounted to $1,450. Mr. Segovia does not intend to deduct CCA on the home office portion of the house.

7. For business travel, Mr. Segovia drives a car that he purchased in 2011 for $49,000. He financed the purchase of the car through his local bank and, for 2012, the interest on the loan was $2,250. During 2012, he drives the car a total 60,000 kilometers, 45,000 of these being for employment related travel. His accountant has advised him that, if the car were used 100 percent for employment related activities, the CCA (tax depreciation) for 2012 would be $7,650. The costs of operating the car during the year totaled $7,500.

8. During 2012, Mr. Segovia received three non-cash awards, none of which were performance related. The first, a spa weekend at a local hotel, had a fair market value of $300. The second was a $400 gift-certificate at a men's clothing store. The third award, a bottle of 1995 Haut Brion, had a fair market value of $450.

9. In 2011, his employer granted him options to buy 1,000 shares of the company's stock at $20 per share. At the time of the grant, the shares were trading at $19 per share. On June 1, 2012, all of these options are exercised. At this time the shares are trading at $31 per share. He does not sell the shares in 2012.

Required: Calculate Mr. Segovia's minimum net employment income for the 2012 taxation year. Ignore GST and PST considerations.

Assignment Problem Three - 10 *(Employment Income)*
(This Problem Is Continued In Assignment Problem Four-4)

For the past five years, Mr. Brooks has been employed as a financial analyst by a large Canadian public firm located in Winnipeg. During 2012, his basic gross salary amounts to $53,000. In addition, he was awarded an $11,000 bonus based on the performance of his division. Of the total bonus, $6,500 was paid in 2012 and the remainder is to be paid on January 15, 2013.

During 2012, Mr. Brooks' employer withheld the following amounts from his gross wages:

Federal Income Tax	$3,000
Employment Insurance Premiums	840
Canada Pension Plan Contributions	2,307
Registered Pension Plan Contributions	2,800
Donations To The United Way	480
Union Dues	240
Payments For Personal Use Of Company Car	1,000

Other Information:

1. Due to an airplane accident while flying back from Thunder Bay on business, Mr. Brooks was seriously injured and confined to a hospital for two full months during 2012. As his employer provides complete group disability insurance coverage, he received a total of $4,200 in payments during this period. All of the premiums for this insurance plan are paid by the employer. The plan provides periodic benefits that compensate for lost employment income.

2. Mr. Brooks is provided with a car that the company leases at a rate of $678 per month, including both GST and PST. The company pays for all of the operating costs of the car and these amounted to $3,500 during 2012. Mr. Brooks drove the car a total of 35,000 kilometers during 2012, 30,000 kilometers of which were carefully documented as employment related travel. While he was in the hospital (see Item 1), his employer required that the car be returned to company premises.

3. On January 15, 2011, Mr. Brooks received options to buy 200 shares of his employer's common stock at a price of $23 per share. At this time, the shares were trading at $20 per share. Mr. Brooks exercised these options on July 6, 2012, when the shares were trading at $28 per share. He does not plan to sell the shares for at least a year.

4. In order to assist Mr. Brooks in acquiring a new personal residence in Winnipeg, his employer granted him a five year, interest free loan of $125,000. The loan qualifies as a home relocation loan. The loan was granted on October 1, 2012 and, at this point in time, the interest rate on open five year mortgages was 5 percent. Assume the relevant ITR 4301 rate was 2 percent on this date. Mr. Brooks purchases a house for $235,000 on October 2, 2012. He has not owned a home during any of the preceding four years.

5. Other disbursements made by Mr. Brooks include the following:

Advanced financial accounting course tuition fees	$1,200
Music history course tuition fees	
(University of Manitoba one week intensive course)	600
Fees paid to financial planner	300
Payment of premiums on life insurance	642

    Mr. Brooks' employer reimbursed him for the tuition fees for the accounting course, but not the music course.

Required: Calculate Mr. Brooks' net employment income for the taxation year ending December 31, 2012.

Assignment Problem Three - 11 *(Alternative Employment Offers)*
Alicia Arden has established herself as a very effective sales representative for products related to health care services. While she has worked independently for a number of years, she has received two very attractive offers of employment. Both of these offers would require that she begin work on January 2, 2012.

Offer One

This offer would provide her with a fixed salary of $225,000 per year with no commissions on her sales. The employer would provide an allowance of $30,000 per year to cover hotel, meals, and airline costs. The employer believes that the CRA will consider this allowance to be reasonable in the circumstances. With respect to advertising and promotion expenses, no allowance or reimbursement would be provided.

This employer would provide her with an automobile which would be leased at a cost of $850 per month, including a $75 per month payment for insurance. The employer will pay all of the operating costs of the automobile.

This employer would provide her with a $200,000 interest free loan in order to facilitate her investment activities. The loan will have to be repaid after five years.

Offer Two

This offer would provide her with a fixed salary of $175,000 per year, plus a commission on all of her sales. Ms. Arden estimates that for 2012, these commissions will total $85,000. The employer would reimburse her hotel, meal, and airline costs. With respect to advertising and promotion expenses, no allowance or reimbursement would be provided.

While this employer will not provide her with an automobile, the business will provide her with an allowance for using her own automobile of $1,500 per month. Ms. Arden estimates that for 2012 the total costs associated with driving her own vehicle will be as follows:

Operating Costs	$10,600
Capital Cost Allowance (Tax Depreciation) (100%)	4,500
Financing Costs	1,800
Total	$16,900

Other Information

The following information is applicable to either of the alternative offers.

1. She estimates that her employment related expenses during 2012 would be as follows:

Travel Costs (Hotel And Airline Costs)	$18,000
Travel Costs (Meals)	8,500
Advertising And Promotion	23,000

2. Whether it is the employer's automobile or her own personal vehicle, she would use the car throughout 2012. She expects to drive this vehicle a total of 53,000 kilometers during 2012, with 37,000 of these kilometers required by her employment activities.

3. Both offers include a group disability insurance plan for which the company will pay all of the premiums. The plan provides periodic benefits that compensate for lost employment income. This will cost the employer $4,500 per year.

4. Both offers include a $1,000,000 face value life insurance policy. All of the premiums, which will total $3,800 per year, will be paid by the employer.

5. Assume that the prescribed rate is 2 percent throughout 2012.

Required:

A. Based on the estimates made by Ms. Arden, calculate Ms. Arden's minimum 2012k Net Employment Income for each of the two offers. Ignore PST and GST considerations.

B. Discuss the factors that Ms. Arden should consider in deciding between the two alternatives.

Assignment Problem Three - 12 (Comprehensive Employment Income)

Ms. Matilda Bracken is a Certified Financial Planner (CFP) with many years of successful experience. In 2011, she decided that she was not adequately appreciated in her current position with a large financial institution in Windsor, Ontario. Given this, she resigned on November 1, 2011.

After several months of investigation, she decided to take a position with Retirement Planners Ltd. (RPL), a Canadian controlled private corporation located in London, Ontario. She commenced working for RPL on May 1, 2012.

She owned a home in Windsor which she had acquired several years ago for $375,000. Because of the depressed real estate market in this area, she was eventually forced to sell the property for $275,000, resulting in a $100,000 loss on this property.

Because of the uncertainty surrounding the sale of her Windsor property, she moves into an apartment when she arrives in London on May 1, 2012. The apartment is rented on a monthly basis until November 30, 2012. After she accepts an offer to purchase her Windsor house, she finds a home in London that she purchases on November 1, 2012 for $420,000. She moves into this new home on December 1, 2012.

Matilda's new job requires her to meet with clients outside of regular office hours, seven days a week. She has set aside space in her home to be used exclusively to meet with clients. RPL will sign form T2200 stating that she is required to pay for certain employment expenses without reimbursement and use a portion of her home for work. Matilda is also provided with an automobile to use in her work.

Matilda is compensated by salary with a bonus and stock option arrangement. The bonus is based on overall company profits. The stock option is available to all employees depending upon level of service and overall job evaluation.

Other Information:

1. Because of her strong professional reputation, RPL paid her a signing bonus of $12,000. The signing bonus was paid on June 1, 2012.

2. During the period May 1, 2012 through December 31, 2012, Matilda earned salary of $124,000. Of these earnings, $120,125 was paid during this period with the remainder paid in the first pay period of 2013. The Company withheld the following amounts from her salary:

Income Taxes	$18,650
CPP	2,307
EI	840
RPP Contributions	3,700
Payment For Personal Use Of Automobile	880

3. RPL contributed $3,500 on Matilda's behalf to the Company's RPP.

4. RPL provides group medical coverage to all of its employees. The private health plan premiums paid by RPL on Matilda's behalf cost $562.

5. On December 12, 2012, a bonus of $10,600 was accrued for Matilda. Matilda received $5,300 of this bonus on December 29, 2012, with the remainder being paid on January 17, 2013.

6. As was RPL's policy, Matilda received non-cash gifts during the year. The total value of the gifts was $650.

7. Because of the need to invest some of her additional income, RPL provided Matilda with financial counseling services. The value of these services was $1,200.

8. In order to assist her move, RPL agreed to compensate her for one-half of the $100,000 loss on the sale of her Windsor home. The $50,000 payment was made on December 1, 2012.

9. RPL has a stock option plan for its employees. Under this plan, employees are permitted to acquire a limited number of option shares at 10 percent below their fair market value on December 1 of each year. The company hires valuators to determine the fair market value at each of those dates. Matilda acquires 200 shares on December 1, 2012 for cash of $7,200. On December 15, she sells 100 of these shares for $4,100.

10. Matilda paid $1,600 in CFP dues in 2012. RPL's policy is to reimburse 50 percent of such professional dues. RPL reimbursed her $800 in December, 2012.

11. RPL provides its professional employees with a membership in the London Curling Club. They believe this is a useful venue for entertaining clients of the Company. The cost of this annual membership was $1,300.

12. In order to help Matilda with financing her new London residence, RPL provided her with a $220,000 interest free housing loan. The funds are provided to Matilda on November 1, 2012. Assume that the prescribed rate for all of 2012 is 2 percent.

13. Matilda received an allowance of $325 per month for eight months to cover the costs of maintaining an office in her home.

14. RPL provides Matilda with a vehicle that was purchased in 2012 for $45,200, including HST. The vehicle was used by Matilda for all months during the period May 1, 2012 through December 31, 2012. During this period, she drove the vehicle a total of 52,000 kilometers, of which 40,000 were related to her employment duties. RPL pays all operating and maintenance costs, a total of $8,900 during the period that Matilda used the car. RPL withheld $110 per month from her salary to pay for her personal use of the vehicle.

15. Matilda used a separate room in her apartment exclusively as a home office. She used this office space between May 1 and November 30, 2012. This home office occupied 150 square feet of the 1,250 square feet available in her apartment. The home office in the residence she moved into on December 1, 2012 will not be available for use until 2013. Home office related costs are as follows:

Monthly Rent	$2,200
Office Furniture	3,400
Computer Purchase	896
Stationery And Office Supplies Purchased	147
Monthly Phone Line Charge (For 7 Months)	210
Employment Related Long Distance Calls (For 7 Months)	110
Electricity Charge (For 7 Months)	350
Paint For Apartment	165
Property Insurance (7 Months)	175

Required: Determine Matilda's net employment income for 2012.

Assignment Problem Three - 13 (Comprehensive Employment Income)

Mitch Lesner, after years of considerable effort, met all the requirements and was admitted to the Association of Certified General Accountants in early 2012 at the age of 26. He immediately applied for a number of jobs and accepted a position as a junior financial officer with Oxford Associates Ltd., an employer offering financial consulting services in Ottawa, Ontario. Oxford Associates Ltd. is a large Canadian controlled private corporation (CCPC) incorporated in Ontario in 1982 employing more than two hundred people.

Prior to accepting employment with Oxford Associates, Mitch had always lived in Red Deer, Alberta. Once he had signed the contract with Oxford Associates, plans were made to sell the house he owned in Red Deer. Unfortunately the home remained unsold when he moved on March 8, 2012. It was sold in late May, 2012 for $125,000. He had purchased the home several years before for $147,000.

He arrived in Ottawa on March 16 and moved into an apartment he had rented on a monthly basis until he could arrange to purchase a home. Rent payments were required from April 1.

Mitch began work on April 1, 2012 and eagerly awaited the arrival of his long-time girlfriend Janice Masters from Alberta. Shortly after her arrival in Ottawa, Mitch and Janice were married on November 29, 2012. Mitch had purchased a house just outside of Ottawa for $235,000 that they moved into on December 1, 2012.

Mitch's new job requires him to meet with existing and prospective clients outside of regular office hours and, at times, on weekends. As a result, Oxford Associates will sign form T2200 stating Mitch is required to pay for certain employment expenses without reimbursement and use a portion of his home for work. He has set aside a small room in his rented apartment which is used exclusively to meet with clientele. Mitch is also provided with an automobile to use in his work.

Mitch is compensated by salary with a bonus and stock option arrangement. The bonus is based on overall company profits. The stock option is available to all employees depending upon level of service and overall job evaluation.

Other Information:

1. Given Mitch's high grades in the CGA examinations, Oxford Associates offered Mitch $10,000 to convince him to sign a five year employment contract. After Mitch accepted, he received the cheque in February, 2012. During the period April 1, 2012 through December 31, 2012, Mitch earned salary of $63,700. Of these earnings, $62,550 was paid during this period as Oxford Associates holds back one week's pay. The Company withheld the following amounts from his salary:

Income Taxes	$11,400
CPP	2,307
EI	840
RPP Contributions	1,200
Payment For Personal Use Of Automobile	600

2. On December 16, 2012, a bonus of $7,450 was accrued for Mitch. Mitch received $2,000 of this bonus on December 21, 2012, with the remainder being paid on February 17, 2013.

3. A few months into the new job Mitch became quite depressed. His employer suggested he take advantage of the company assistance program. He went to four appointments in October and November and felt much better. Oxford Associates paid $700 for Mitch's counselling services.

4. Oxford Associates provides group medical coverage to all of its employees without charge. The premiums paid by Oxford Associates on Mitch's behalf cost $410.

5. Oxford Associates contributed $1,200 on Mitch's behalf to the Company's RPP.

6. Mitch paid $785 in CGA dues in 2012. Oxford Associates's policy is to reimburse 80 percent of such annual professional dues. Oxford Associates reimbursed him $628 in November 2012.

7. When Mitch was married in December he received non-cash wedding gifts valued at $850. Half of the amount was contributed by his employer and the balance from other employees.

8. Oxford Associates discovered years ago that many existing clients frequent certain recreational and sporting clubs. To encourage contacts with potential clients, employees have their choice among five such clubs. Since Mitch enjoys squash, he chose a free membership at a local squash club. The annual membership fee is $915.

9. Oxford Associates reimbursed Mitch for 80 percent of the $22,000 ($147,000 - $125,000) loss that he experienced on the sale of his Red Deer home.

Assignment Problems

10. Mitch had $35,000 for a down-payment on his new Ottawa home. Since he had no previous work experience, the banks were reluctant to provide him a mortgage at favourable terms. His employer stepped in and agreed to an interest-free housing loan of $200,000 beginning on December 1. Mitch agreed to reduce his salary slightly with respect to this benefit. The loan requires annual payments of $7,500 due at the end of November beginning in 2013. The loan is required to be paid if Mitch dies, sells the home or terminates his employment. Assume that the prescribed interest rates for such benefits are 2 percent in each of the first two quarters of 2012 and 1 percent in the third and fourth quarters.

11. Oxford instituted a stock option plan for its employees in 2011. The plan eligibility requires six months of service. Employees are permitted to acquire a limited number of option shares at 20 percent below their fair market value on either May 1 or November 1. The company hires valuators to determine the fair market value at each of those dates. Mitch acquires 200 shares November 1, 2012 for $12,800. Low on cash and wanting to buy Janice a nice wedding ring, he is forced to sell 80 of the shares. He sells them on December 16, 2012 for $8,960.

12. Oxford Associates has an arrangement with a local dealership to lease a minimum number of new automobiles each year at favourable rates. Mitch receives his leased automobile May 1, 2012. It has 162 kilometres on it when it is received. The odometer reads 19,414 kilometres on December 31, 2012. Mitch estimates that he drove 5,198 kilometres for personal purposes, including drives to and from home to the office. Oxford Associates pays monthly lease payments (including HST) of $430. The cost of gas, oil, insurance, repairs and maintenance and other charges total $2,175 for 2012. Oxford Associates requires each employee provided with an automobile to pay $75 each month for the use of the automobile which is withheld directly from their pay.

13. Mitch prepared a separate room in his apartment to be used exclusively for a home office. He used the office space between June 1 and November 30, 2012. A home office was not ready in his newly purchased home until February, 2013. The apartment office space is exactly 100 square feet. The total apartment space is 1,176 square feet. Home office related costs are as follows:

Monthly Rent	$ 960
Office Furniture	1,344
Computer Purchase	1,739
Stationery And Office Supplies Purchased	129
Monthly Phone Line Charge	416
Employment Related Long Distance Calls (June to November)	74
Electricity Charge (March 16 to November 30)	870
Paint for apartment	253
Property insurance (March 16 to November 30)	175

14. Mitch received an allowance of $250 per month for six months to cover the costs of maintaining an office in his home.

Required: Determine Mitch's net employment income for the year 2012. Provide explanations for all amounts including reasons for omitting items not included in your calculations.

CHAPTER 4

Taxable Income And Tax Payable For Individuals

Introduction

4-1. As discussed in Chapter 1, Taxable Income is Net Income For Tax Purposes, less a group of deductions that are specified in Division C of Part I of the *Income Tax Act*. Also noted in the Chapter 1 material was the fact that Net Income For Tax Purposes is made up of several different income components. These components are employment income, business and property income, taxable capital gains, other sources, and other deductions.

4-2. Some tax texts defer any coverage of Taxable Income and Tax Payable until all of the income components that make up Net Income For Tax Purposes have been given detailed consideration. Despite the fact that the only component of Taxable Income that we have covered to this point is employment income, we have decided to introduce material on Taxable Income and Tax Payable for individuals at this point in the text.

Major Reason The major reason for this approach is that it allows us to introduce the many tax credits that go into the calculation of Tax Payable at an earlier stage in the text. We believe that this will enhance the presentation of the material in subsequent Chapters on business income, property income, and taxable capital gains. For example, in our discussion of property income, we can deal with after tax rates of return, as well as provide a meaningful discussion of the economics of the dividend gross up/tax credit procedures.

Other Reasons Other reasons for this organization of the material are more pedagogical in nature.

- Leaving the coverage of tax credits until after the completion of the material on all of the components of Taxable Income places this complex subject in the last weeks of most one semester tax courses which can create significant difficulties for students.

- By introducing Taxable Income and Tax Payable at this earlier stage in the text, instructors who wish to do so can make more extensive use of the tax software programs provided with the text.

4-3. Since a significant portion of the material on Taxable Income and Tax Payable can be best understood after covering the other types of income that make up Net Income For Tax

Purposes, we require a second Chapter dealing with the subject of Taxable Income and Tax Payable. In addition, a few of the credits that are available in the calculation of Tax Payable require an understanding of additional aspects of business income, property income, and taxable capital gains. Given this, Chapter 11 is devoted to completing the necessary coverage of Taxable Income and Tax Payable for individuals. For corporations, these subjects are covered in Chapters 12 and 13.

Taxable Income Of Individuals

Available Deductions

4-4.   The deductions that are available in calculating the Taxable Income of an individual can be found in Division C of Part I of the *Income Tax Act*. As indicated in the introduction to this Chapter, some of these deductions will be dealt with in this Chapter. However, coverage of the more complex items is deferred until Chapter 11. The available deductions, along with a description of their coverage in this text, are as follows:

ITA 110(1)(d), (d.01), and (d.1) - Employee Stock Options   Our basic coverage of stock options and stock option deductions is included in Chapter 3. This coverage will not be repeated here. We would note, however, that Supplementary Reading No. 2 - *Stock Option Shares Deemed Not Identical Property*, provides coverage of a more advanced issue in this area. The Supplementary Readings can be found on the Student CD-ROM which accompanies this text.

ITA 110(1)(f) - Deductions For Payments   This deduction, which is available for social assistance and workers' compensation received, is covered beginning in Paragraph 4-6.

ITA 110(1)(j) - Home Relocation Loan   We refer to this deduction in Chapter 3 as it is related to a taxable benefit that is included in employment income. However, more detailed coverage is found in this Chapter beginning in Paragraph 4-9.

ITA 110.2 - Lump Sum Payments   This Section provides a deduction for certain lump-sum payments (e.g., an amount received as a court-ordered termination benefit and included in employment income). It provides the basis for taxing this amount as though it were received over several taxation years (i.e., income averaging). Because of its limited applicability, no additional coverage is given to this provision.

ITA 110.6 - Lifetime Capital Gains Deduction   The provisions related to this deduction are very complex and require a fairly complete understanding of capital gains. As a consequence, this deduction is covered in Chapter 11.

ITA 110.7 - Residing In Prescribed Zone (Northern Residents Deductions)   These deductions, which are limited to individuals living in prescribed regions of northern Canada, are covered in Paragraph 4-13.

ITA 111 - Losses Deductible   This is a group of deductions that is available for carrying forward or carrying back various types of losses. The application of these provisions can be complex and requires a fairly complete understanding of business income, property income, and capital gains. Coverage of this material is deferred until Chapter 11.

Ordering Of Deductions

4-5.   ITA 111.1 specifies, to some degree, the order in which individuals must subtract the various deductions that may be available in the calculation of Taxable Income. As our coverage of these deductions is not complete in this Chapter, we will defer coverage of this ordering provision until Chapter 11.

Deductions For Payments - ITA 110(1)(f)

4-6.   ITA 110(1)(f) provides for the deduction of certain amounts that have been included in the calculation of Net Income For Tax Purposes. The items listed here are amounts that are exempt from tax in Canada by virtue of a provision in a tax treaty or agreement with another country, workers' compensation payments received as a result of injury or death, income from employment with a prescribed international organization, and social assistance payments made on the basis of a means, needs, or income test and included in the taxpayer's income.

4-7.   At first glance, this seems to be a fairly inefficient way of not taxing these items. For example, if the government does not intend to tax social assistance payments, why go to the trouble of including them in Net Income For Tax Purposes, then deducting an equivalent amount in the calculation of Taxable Income?

4-8.   There is, however, a reason for this. There are a number of items that influence an individual's tax obligation that are altered on the basis of the individual's Net Income For Tax Purposes. For example, we will find later in this Chapter that the amount of the age tax credit is reduced by the individual's Net Income For Tax Purposes in excess of a specified amount (a.k.a. the threshold amount or the income threshold). In order to ensure that income tests of this type are applied on an equitable basis, amounts are included in Net Income For Tax Purposes, even in situations where the ultimate intent is not to assess tax on these amounts.

Home Relocation Loan - ITA 110(1)(j)

4-9.   As discussed in Chapter 3, if an employer provides an employee with a loan on which interest is payable at a rate that is less than the prescribed rate, a taxable benefit must be included in the employee's income. Under ITA 80.4(1), the benefit will be measured as the difference between the interest that would have been paid on the loan at the prescribed rate and the amount of interest that was actually paid. This taxable benefit must be included in income, even in situations where the loan qualifies as a "home relocation loan".

4-10.   A home relocation loan is defined in ITA 248(1) as a loan made by an employer to an employee in order to assist him in acquiring a dwelling. This acquisition must be related to employment at a new work location, and the new dwelling must be at least 40 kilometers closer to the new work location. As is discussed more completely in Chapter 9, the distance is the same 40 kilometer test that is used in determining whether or not an individual can deduct moving expenses.

4-11.   Provided the loan qualifies as a home relocation loan, ITA 110(1)(j) provides a deduction in the calculation of the individual's Taxable Income equal to the lesser of:

- **The Benefit Included In Income Under ITA 80.4(1)**   As presented in detail in Chapter 3, the benefit on employee provided loans is determined by applying the prescribed rate to the principal amount of the loan on a quarterly basis. The amount of the benefit is then reduced by any interest payments made by the employee. When the loan is a home purchase loan or a home relocation loan, ITA 80.4(4) limits the benefit to the amount that would be determined by applying the prescribed rate that was applicable when the loan was made to the principal amount on an annual basis. This limit is in place for the first five years the loan is outstanding.

- **The Amount That Would Been Calculated Under ITA 80.4(1)(a) On A $25,000 Loan** This deduction is calculated using the same rules that are applicable to housing loans in general, except for the fact that it is:

  (1) based on $25,000 rather than the actual amount of the loan, and
  (2) the amount is not reduced by interest payments made by the employee.

  By not deducting interest payments made by the employee, this effectively bases the calculation of the amount on an interest free loan of $25,000. If this amount exceeds the benefit included under ITA 80.4(1), the deduction will equal the taxable benefit and the net effect will be nil.

4-12. This deduction is available for a period of up to five years. However, as the deduction is designed to offset a benefit that is included in employment income, the deduction will not be available after the loan has been paid off and there is no longer an employment income inclusion. While the calculation of the benefit and the deduction can be based on the number of days in each quarter, an example in IT-421R2 makes it clear that treating each calendar quarter as one-quarter of a year is an acceptable procedure.

Exercise Four - 1

Subject: Home Relocation Loan

On January 1 of the current year, in order to facilitate an employee's relocation, Lee Ltd. provides her with a five year, $82,000 loan. The employee pays 2 percent annual interest on the loan on December 31 of each year. Assume that at the time the loan is granted the prescribed rate is 4 percent. However, the rate is increased to 5 percent for the third and fourth quarters of the current year. What is the effect of this loan on the employee's Taxable Income for the current year?

End of Exercise. Solution available in Study Guide.

Northern Residents Deductions - ITA 110.7

4-13. Residents of Labrador, the Territories, as well as parts of some of the provinces, are eligible for deductions under ITA 110.7. To qualify for these deductions, the taxpayer must be resident in these prescribed regions for a continuous period of six months beginning or ending in the taxation year. The amount of the deductions involves fairly complex calculations that go beyond the scope of this text. The purpose of these deductions is to compensate individuals for the high costs that are associated with living in such prescribed northern zones.

Calculation Of Tax Payable

Federal Tax Payable Before Credits

4-14. The calculation of federal Tax Payable for individuals requires the application of a group of progressive rates to marginal increments in Taxable Income. The rates are progressive, starting at a low rate of 15 percent and increasing to rates of 22 percent, 26 percent, and 29 percent as the individual's Taxable Income increases. In order to maintain fairness, the brackets (i.e., income segments) to which these rates apply are indexed to reflect changes in the Consumer Price Index. Without such indexation, taxpayers could find themselves effectively subject to higher rates without having an increased level of real, inflation adjusted income.

4-15. For 2012, the brackets to which these four rates apply are as follows:

Taxable Income In Excess Of	Federal Tax	Marginal Rate On Excess
$ -0-	$ -0-	15%
42,707	6,406	22%
85,414	15,802	26%
132,406	28,020	29%

4-16. Note that the average rate for an individual just entering the 22 percent bracket is 15 percent ($6,406 ÷ $42,707). For an individual just entering the highest 29 percent bracket, the average rate is 21.2 percent ($28,020 ÷ $132,406).

4-17. There is a common misconception that once Taxable Income reaches the next tax bracket, all income is taxed at a higher rate. This is not the case as each rate is a marginal rate. For example, if Taxable Income is $132,407, only $1 is taxed at 29 percent.

4-18.   The preceding table suggests that individuals are taxed on their first dollar of income. While the 15 percent rate is, in fact, applied to all of the first $42,707 of Taxable Income, a portion of this amount is not really subject to taxes. As will be discussed later in this Chapter, every individual resident in Canada is entitled to a personal tax credit. For 2012, this tax credit is $1,623 [(15%)($10,822)]. In effect, this means that no taxes will be paid on at least the first $10,822 of an individual's Taxable Income. The amount that could be earned tax free would be even higher for individuals with additional tax credits (e.g., the age credit).

4-19.   As an example of the calculation of federal Tax Payable before credits, consider an individual with Taxable Income of $92,300. The calculation would be as follows:

Tax On First $85,414	$15,802
Tax On Next $6,886 ($92,300 - $85,414) At 26%	1,790
Federal Tax Payable Before Credits	$17,592

4-20.   A surtax is an additional tax calculated on the basis of the regular Tax Payable calculation. While such additional taxes are not assessed at the federal level, they are used in two provinces, most notably in Ontario. For 2012, Ontario has a surtax of 56 percent on amounts of Ontario Tax Payable in excess of $5,392. This significantly increases the highest rate in Ontario from the stated 11.16 percent to 17.41 percent.

Provincial Tax Payable Before Credits
Provincial Rates

4-21.   As is the case at the federal level, provincial Tax Payable is calculated by multiplying Taxable Income by either a single tax rate or a group of progressive rates. In general, the provinces other than Quebec use the same Taxable Income figure that is used at the federal level.

4-22.   With respect to rates, Alberta uses a single flat rate of 10 percent applied to all levels of income. All of the other provinces use either 3, 4, or 5 different rates which are applied in tax brackets that are similar to those established at the federal level. In addition, two provinces (Ontario and P.E.I.) apply surtaxes when the provincial Tax Payable figure reaches a certain level.

4-23.   To give you some idea of the range of provincial rates, the 2012 minimum and maximum rates for provinces other than Quebec are as found in the following table. The maximum rates include surtaxes where applicable. These rates are correct as of a specific point in time. You may see other rates as provincial budgets are introduced.

Province	Minimum Tax Rate	Maximum Tax Rate
Alberta	10.00%	10.00%
British Columbia	5.06%	14.70%
Manitoba	10.80%	17.40%
New Brunswick	9.10%	14.30%
Newfoundland and Labrador	7.70%	13.30%
Nova Scotia	8.79%	21.00%
Ontario (including 56% surtax)	5.05%	17.41%
Prince Edward Island (including 10% surtax)	9.80%	18.37%
Saskatchewan	11.00%	15.00%

4-24.   You should note the significant differences in rates between the provinces. The maximum 21 percent rate in Nova Scotia is more than double the flat 10 percent rate in Alberta. This amounts to extra taxes of $11,000 per year on each additional $100,000 of income. This can make provincial tax differences a major consideration when an individual decides where he should establish provincial residency.

4-25.   When these provincial rates are combined with the federal rate schedule, the minimum combined rate varies from a low of 20.05 percent in Ontario (15 percent federal, plus 5.05 percent provincial), to a high of 26 percent in Saskatchewan (15 percent federal, plus 11 percent provincial).

4-26.   Maximum combined rates are lowest in Alberta where the rate is 39 percent (29 percent federal, plus 10 percent provincial). They are highest in Nova Scotia where the combined rate is 50 percent (29 percent federal, plus 21 percent provincial). Because the calculations are completely different, we have not included Quebec in this list of rates. We would note however, the overall rate in Quebec ranges from a low of 28.53 percent to a high of 48.22 percent.

Exercise Four - 2

Subject: Calculation Of Tax Payable Before Credits

During 2012, Joan Matel is a resident of Ontario and has calculated her Taxable Income to be $46,700. Assume that Ontario's rates are 5.05 percent on Taxable Income up to $42,707, 9.15 percent on the next $42,707, and 11.50 percent on the excess. Calculate her 2012 federal and provincial Tax Payable before consideration of credits, and her average rate of tax.

End of Exercise. Solution available in Study Guide.

Provincial Residence

4-27.   Given the significant differences in provincial tax rates on individuals, it is somewhat surprising that the rules related to where an individual will pay provincial taxes are fairly simple. With respect to an individual's income other than business income, it is subject to tax in the province in which he resides on the last day of the taxation year. This means that, if an individual moves to Ontario from Nova Scotia on December 30 of the current year, any income for the year, other than business income, will be taxed in Ontario.

Types Of Income

4-28.   In terms of the effective tax rates, the income accruing to Canadian individuals can be divided into three categories:

Ordinary Income   This would include employment income, business income, property income other than dividends, and other sources of income. In general, the effective tax rates on this category are those presented in the preceding tables. For example, the marginal rate for an individual living in Alberta and earning more than $132,406, would be 39 percent (29 percent federal, plus 10 percent provincial).

Capital Gains   As will be discussed in detail in Chapter 8, capital gains arise on the disposition of capital property. Only one-half of such gains are included in Net Income For Tax Purposes and Taxable Income. This means that the effective tax rate on this category of income is only one-half of the rates presented in the preceding tables. Returning to our Alberta resident who is earning more than $132,406, his effective marginal rate on capital gains would be 19.5 percent [(1/2)(29% + 10%)].

Dividends   As will be explained in Chapter 7, dividends from taxable Canadian companies are subject to a gross up and tax credit procedure which reduces the effective tax rate on this type of income. Also in that Chapter, we explain the difference between eligible dividends and non-eligible dividends. Continuing with our Alberta example, maximum federal/provincial tax rates on dividends are as follows:

Eligible Dividends	19.3%
Non-Eligible Dividends	27.7%

4-29.   A more complete discussion of the different effective tax rates mentioned here is provided in Chapter 7 (dividends) and Chapter 8 (capital gains).

Taxes On Income Not Earned In A Province

4-30.   As will be discussed in Chapter 20, International Issues In Taxation, it is possible for an individual to be considered a resident of Canada for tax purposes, without being a resident of a particular province or territory. This would be the case, for example, for members of the Canadian Armed Forces who are stationed outside of Canada. It is also possible for non-residents to earn income in Canada that is not taxed in a particular province (e.g. Canadian employment income).

4-31.   Income that is not subject to provincial or territorial tax is subject to additional taxation at the federal level. This additional tax is a surtax of 48 percent on federal tax payable. This gives a maximum rate of 42.9 percent [(29%)(148%)] This additional tax is paid to the federal government.

Calculating Tax Credits

Federal Amounts

4-32.   The most direct way of applying a tax credit system is to simply specify the amount of each tax credit available. In 2012, for example, the basic personal tax credit could have been specified to be $1,623. However, the Canadian tax system is based on a less direct approach. Rather than specifying the amount of each credit, a base amount is provided, to which the minimum federal tax rate (15 percent) is applied. This means that, for 2012, the basic personal tax credit is calculated by taking 15 percent of $10,822 (we will refer to this number as the tax credit base), resulting in a credit against Tax Payable in the amount of $1,623.

4-33.   Note that the legislation is such that, when the minimum federal tax rate of 15 percent is changed, the new rate will be used in determining individual tax credits. In our tax credit examples and problems, we will generally use the tax credit base in our calculations and apply the 15 percent rate to the subtotals and totals. This approach makes the relationships between the various credits easier to see and reduces calculation errors.

4-34.   As was the case with the tax rate brackets, in order to avoid having these credits decline in value in terms of real dollars, the base for the tax credits needs to be adjusted for changing prices. While it is not a common occurrence, there may be adjustments to tax credit bases for amounts that do not simply reflect the rate of inflation. For example, in 2009, the base for the basic personal credit was increased to $10,320, $220 more than would have been required by a simple inflation adjustment.

4-35.   A technical problem in calculating credits will arise in the year a person becomes a Canadian resident, or ceases to be a Canadian resident. As discussed in Chapter 20, such individuals will only be subject to Canadian taxation for a part of the year. Given this, it would not be appropriate for them to receive the same credits as an individual who is subject to Canadian taxation for the full year. This view is reflected in ITA 118.91, which requires a pro rata calculation for personal tax credits, the disability tax credit and tax credits transferred from a spouse or a person supported by the taxpayer. Other tax credits, for example the tax credits for charitable donations and adoption expenses, are not reduced because of part year residence. This is because these credits reflect actual amounts paid or costs incurred during the period of Canadian residency.

Provincial Amounts

4-36.   In determining provincial tax credits, the provinces use the same approach as that used at the federal level. That is, the minimum provincial rate is applied to a base that is indexed each year. In most cases, the base used is different from the base used at the federal level. For 2012, the basic personal tax credit at the federal level is $1,623 [(15%)($10,822)]. Comparative 2012 figures for selected provinces are as follows:

Province	Base	Rate	Credit
Alberta	$17,282	10.00%	$1,782
British Columbia	11,354	5.06%	574
Newfoundland And Labrador	8,237	7.70%	634
Ontario	9,405	5.05%	475

Personal Tax Credits - ITA 118(1)

A Note On The Family Caregiver Amount

4-37.   The 2011 budget introduced what is referred to as the family caregiver amount (FCA). This is a provision which is applicable to 2012 and subsequent years. The FCA for 2012 is $2,000. However, it will be indexed beginning in 2013.

4-38.   The FCA becomes available when an individual is claiming one or more of five different credits. These credits are:

- The spouse or common-law partner amount.
- The amount for an eligible dependant.
- The amount for children under the age of 18.
- The amount for infirm dependants age 18 or older.
- The caregiver amount.

4-39.   The FCA is added to each of these credits, subject to the following conditions:

- If the credit is claimed for an individual age 18 or older, the individual must be dependent on the taxpayer by reason of physical or mental infirmity.

- If the credit is claimed for a child under the age of 18, the child must have a medical or physical infirmity and as a result of that infirmity is, and is likely to be for a long continued period of indefinite duration, dependent on others for significantly more assistance in attending to the child's personal needs and care when compared to children of the same age.

  It would appear that this does not require a disability so severe that the child would qualify for the disability tax credit. However, it is a stronger requirement than that applicable to dependants who are 18 years of age or older.

4-40.   We would also note the following with respect to the FCA:

- While not a standard requirement, the CRA can require a signed statement from a medical doctor certifying that the dependant is eligible for the FCA.
- The FCA can be claimed for each dependant that qualifies, i.e., it can be claimed for multiple dependants.
- In those cases where both the eligible dependant credit and the child under 18 credit is claimed for the same individual, only the amount for a child under 18 will be increased by the FCA.

Individuals With A Spouse Or Common-Law Partner - ITA 118(1)(a)

Basic Personal Plus Spousal Tax Credits

4-41.   For individuals with a spouse or common-law partner filing tax returns in 2012, ITA 118(1)(a) provides for two tax credits — one for the individual (sometimes referred to as the basic personal credit) and one for his or her spouse or common-law partner (sometimes referred to as the spousal credit). The credit for the individual is calculated as follows:

$$\text{Basic Personal Credit} = [(15\%)(\$10,822)] = \$1,623$$

Calculation Of Spousal Tax Credit

4-42.   If the individual's spouse is not dependent because of a mental or physical infirmity, the spousal credit is calculated using the same base as the basic personal credit. However, it must be reduced by the spouse or common-law partner's Net Income For Tax Purposes. The calculation is as follows:

Spousal Credit = [(15%)($10,822 - Spouse Or Common-Law Partner's Net Income)]

4-43.   As discussed beginning in Paragraph 4-37, the FCA may be added to this credit in situations where a spouse or common-law partner is dependent because of a physical or mental infirmity. Note, if the spouse or common-law partner is dependent simply because they have little or no income, the FCA is not available. The dependency must be the result of an infirmity.

4-44.   If the spouse or common-law partner qualifies for the FCA, the calculation of the spousal credit is as follows:

[(15%)($10,822 + $2,000 - Spouse Or Common-Law Partner's Net Income)]

4-45.   As an example, consider an individual with a spouse who had Net Income For Tax Purposes of $5,200. The total personal credits under ITA 118(1)(a) if the spouse (1) was not eligible for the FCA and (2) was eligible for the FCA, would be calculated as follows:

	No FCA	With FCA
Basic Personal Amount	$ 10,822	$ 10,822
Spousal Amount ($10,822 - $5,200)	5,622	
Spousal Amount ($10,822 + $2,000 - $5,200)		7,622
Credit Base	$16,444	$18,444
Rate	15%	15%
Personal Tax Credits	$ 2,467	$ 2,767

4-46.   There are several other points to be made with respect to the credits for an individual with a spouse or common-law partner:

Spouse Or Common-Law Partner's Income   The income figure that is used for limiting the spousal amount is Net Income For Tax Purposes, with no adjustments of any sort.

Applicability To Either Spouse Or Common-Law Partner   The ITA 118(1)(a) provision is applicable to both spouses and, while each is eligible to claim the basic amount of $10,822, IT-513R specifies that only one spouse or common-law partner may claim the spousal amount. IT-513R indicates that the spouse making the claim should be the one that supports the other (support is defined in Appendix A of IT-513R).

Eligibility   The additional credit can be claimed for either a spouse or a common-law partner. There is no definition of spouse in the *Income Tax Act*, so it would appear that the usual dictionary definition would apply. That is, a spouse is one of a pair of persons who are legally married. With respect to common-law partner, ITA 248(1) defines such an individual as a person who cohabits with the taxpayer in a conjugal relationship and:

• has so cohabited for a continuous period of at least one year; or
• is the parent of a child of whom the taxpayer is also a parent.

There is no requirement in the income tax legislation that either a spouse or a common-law partner be a person of the opposite sex. One can, however, assume that they must be of the same species (e.g., you can't claim your dog).

Multiple Relationships   Based on these definitions, it would be possible for an individual to have both a spouse and a common-law partner. ITA 118(4)(a) makes it clear that, if this is the case, a credit can only be claimed for one of these individuals. In such cases, determining your tax credits may be the least of your problems.

Year Of Separation Or Divorce   In general, ITA 118(5) does not allow a tax credit based on the spousal amount in situations where the individual is making a deduction for the support of a spouse or common-law partner (spousal support is covered in Chapter 9). However, IT-513R indicates that, in the year of separation or divorce, an individual can choose to deduct amounts paid for spousal support, or claim the additional tax credit for a spouse.

Exercise Four - 3

Subject: Spousal Tax Credit

Mr. Johan Sprinkle is married and has 2012 Net Income For Tax Purposes of $35,450. His spouse has 2012 Net Income For Tax Purposes of $2,600. Assuming that Johan's spouse does not have a mental or physical infirmity, determine Mr. Sprinkle's personal tax credits for 2012. How would your answer differ if Johan's spouse was dependent because of a mental or physical infirmity?

End of Exercise. Solution available in Study Guide.

Individuals Supporting A Wholly Dependent Person - ITA 118(1)(b)

Eligibility And Eligible Dependant Defined

4-47.   The ITA 118(1)(b) credit is available to an individual who is not claiming the spousal credit and who supports a wholly dependent person who lives with them in a self-contained domestic establishment (we will refer to this person as an eligible dependant). To qualify for this credit, the individual must be:

- unmarried;
- not living in a common-law partnership; or
- a person who is married or has a common-law partner but neither supports nor lives with that spouse or common-law partner.

4-48.   To claim this credit, the eligible dependant must be "related" to the individual making the claim and "wholly dependent". ITA 251(2) defines related individuals as those who are related by blood, marriage, common-law partnership, or adoption. IT-419R2 indicates that this would exclude aunts, uncles, nieces, nephews, and cousins. To be "wholly dependent" would mean that the individual provides all means of support (food, clothing, shelter), as well as all financial support. For example, a young child would normally be wholly dependent on a parent. The death of a spouse or common-law partner severs all marriage and common-law relationships. For example, a taxpayer is no longer related to his deceased wife's mother.

4-49.   In view of today's less stable family arrangements, the question of exactly who is considered a child for tax purposes requires some elaboration. As explained in IT-513R, the credit may be taken for natural children, children who have been formally adopted, as well as for natural and adopted children of a spouse or common-law partner.

Calculation Of Eligible Dependant Tax Credit

4-50.   If the eligible dependant is not mentally or physically infirm, this credit is calculated as follows:

$$[(15\%)(\$10,822 - \text{Eligible Dependant's Net Income})]$$

4-51.   We have noted that the FCA may be added to this credit. For the FCA to be added to the base for this credit, two conditions must present:

- The eligible dependant must be mentally or physically infirm.

- The eligible dependant will not receive the FCA if they are a child under the age of 18. The reason for this condition is that a taxpayer is allowed to take both the eligible dependant tax credit and the child tax credit for the same child. As the FCA is generally available on both of these credits, there could be a double application of this amount. To prevent this, ITA 118(1)(b) does not allow the FCA to be added when the eligible dependant is a child under 18. This ensures that only one FCA can be claimed for a specific child.

4-52. If these conditions are met, the eligible dependant credit includes the FCA and is calculated as follows:

$$[(15\%)(\$10,822 + \$2,000 - \text{Eligible Dependant's Net Income})]$$

4-53. Assume that an unmarried person was supporting an adult eligible dependant who has Net Income For Tax Purposes of $5,200. The total personal credits under ITA 118(1)(a) if the dependant (1) was not eligible for the FCA and (2) was eligible for the FCA, would be calculated as follows:

	No FCA	With FCA
Basic Personal Amount	$ 10,822	$ 10,822
Eligible Dependant Amount		
($10,822 - $5,200)	5,622	
($10,822 + $2,000 - $5,200)		7,622
Credit Base	$16,444	$18,444
Rate	15%	15%
Personal Tax Credits	$ 2,467	$ 2,767

4-52. Note that this credit provides for the same total credits that would be available to an individual with a spouse who had Net Income For Tax Purposes of $5,200 (see Paragraph 4-45). For this reason, it is sometimes referred to as the equivalent to married tax credit.

Application

4-55. This credit is most commonly claimed by single parents who are supporting a minor child. More generally, this credit is available to individuals who are single, widowed, divorced, or separated, and supporting a dependant who is:

- related to the individual by blood, marriage, adoption or common-law relationship;
- wholly dependent on the individual for support;
- under 18 at any time during the year, or mentally or physically infirm, or the individual's parent or grandparent;
- living with the individual in a home that the individual maintains (this would not disqualify a child who moves away during the school year to attend an educational institution as long as the home remains the child's home); and
- residing in Canada (this requirement is not applicable to an individual's child as long as they are living with the individual).

4-56. The eligible dependant credit cannot be claimed by an individual:

- if the individual is claiming the spousal credit;
- if the individual is living with, supporting, or being supported by a spouse (the claim is only available for individuals who are either single, or living separately from their spouse);
- for more than one person;
- if the dependant's Net Income exceeds $10,822 or $12,822 if the FCA is applicable;
- if someone other than the individual is making this claim for the same individual; or
- for the individual's child, if the individual is making child support payments to another individual, for that child. As is noted in Chapter 9, when child support is being paid, only the recipient of such payments can claim this tax credit. This is the case without regard to whether or not the individual making the child support payments is able to deduct the payments in determining Net Income For Tax Purposes.

Child Tax Credit - ITA 118(1)(b.1)

4-57. An individual is eligible for a tax credit for each child who is under 18 years of age at the end of the taxation year. The credit has a 2012 value of $329 per child [(15%)($2,191)]. In addition, if the child is mentally or physically infirm, the parent can claim the FCA, which brings the total value of the credit to $629 [(15%)($2,191 + $2,000)]. Somewhat surprisingly, it is not reduced by the child's income or family income.

4-58. Also surprising is the fact that this credit can be claimed for a particular child, even when the ITA 118(1)(b) eligible dependant credit is being claimed for that same child. For example, if a single mother was supporting a child under 18 in a self-contained domestic establishment, she could claim both the eligible dependant tax credit and the child tax credit for that one child. We would remind you, however, that if that child was eligible for the FCA, she would receive the extra $2,000 only on the child tax credit. It would not be available on both credits.

4-59. Other relevant points are as follows:

- Provided the child resides with both parents throughout the year, it can be claimed by either parent. The phrase "throughout the year" is defined to include the fraction of the year subsequent to the birth or adoption of the child and the fraction of the year prior to the death of a child.

- If the parents are living separately, this credit can only be claimed by the parent who claims the eligible dependant credit for the child, or who would have been able to claim the eligible dependant credit for the child if not for the one person restriction. However, unlike the eligible dependant credit, the child tax credit can be claimed for more than one child.

Single Persons (Basic Personal Tax Credit) - ITA 118(1)(c)

4-60. Individuals living with a spouse, common-law partner or eligible dependant receive a credit for themselves and their spouse or common-law partner under ITA 118(1)(a), or themselves and their eligible dependant under ITA 118(1)(b). For individuals who do not have a spouse, common-law partner or eligible dependant, a basic personal tax credit is received under ITA 118(1)(c). For 2012, this credit is equal to $1,623 [(15%)($10,822)].

Caregiver Tax Credit - ITA 118(1)(c.1)

4-61. ITA 118(1)(c.1) allows for a caregiver tax credit to an individual who provides in home care for a related adult (18 years or older). To qualify, the related adult must be:

- the parent or grandparent of the individual or the individual's spouse or common-law partner who is a resident of Canada and is 65 years of age or older, regardless of whether there is dependency due to a mental or physical infirmity, or

- the adult child or grandchild of the individual who is dependent because of a mental or physical infirmity, regardless of whether the (grand)child is a resident of Canada; or

- the adult brother, sister, aunt, uncle, nephew or niece of the individual, or of the individual's spouse, or of the individual's common-law partner, who is a resident of Canada and is dependent because of a mental or physical infirmity.

4-62. A credit may be claimed for each individual who qualifies.

4-63. For 2012, the basic credit has a value of $660 [(15%)($4,402)]. As we have noted, this is one of the credits where the FCA is added when dependency is based on mental or physical infirmity. If this is the case, the credit has value of $960 [(15%)($4,402 + $2,000)].

4-64. The base for the credit is reduced by the amount of the dependant's Net Income in excess of $15,033. This means that this tax credit is not available once the dependant's Net Income is more than $19,435 ($15,033 + $4,402), or $21,435 if the FCA is available.

4-65. As dependency based on mental or physical infirmity is one of the general criteria for this credit, the FCA would usually be added to the caregiver credit. The one exception would be when the related adult is a parent or grandparent who is 65 or over. Such individuals qualify for the caregiver credit, without having to be mentally or physically infirm.

Exercise Four - 4

Subject: Caregiver Tax Credit

Joan Barton lives with her husband. Two years ago her father, who is 69 years old and very active, moved in with her. His Net Income For Tax Purposes for 2012 is $15,600. Determine the amount of Joan's caregiver tax credit, if any, for 2012. How would your answer differ if her father was mentally or physically infirm?

End of Exercise. Solution available in Study Guide.

Infirm Dependant Over 17 Tax Credit - ITA 118(1)(d)

4-66.   ITA 118(1)(d) specifies a credit for dependants who are age 18 or older prior to the end of the year, provided they are dependent by reason of mental or physical infirmity. For purposes of this credit, the *Income Tax Act* defines dependant as follows:

ITA 118(6)   Definition of "dependant" — ..."dependant" of an individual for a taxation year means a person who at any time in the year is dependent on the individual for support and is

(a) the child or grandchild of the individual or of the individual's spouse or common-law partner; or

(b) the parent, grandparent, brother, sister, uncle, aunt, niece or nephew, if resident in Canada at any time in the year, of the individual or of the individual's spouse or common-law partner.

4-67.   Note that this definition is not the same as that applicable to the ITA 118(1)(b) credit for a wholly dependent person, a.k.a. eligible dependant (see Paragraph 4-47). The definition here includes aunts, uncles, nieces, and nephews. These relatives could not be considered eligible dependants for purposes of the ITA 118(1)(b) credit.

4-68.   For 2012, the FCA has been added to this credit. Unlike the situation with the other credits where the FCA is available, the FCA will always be included with this credit as criteria for this credit and the FCA are the same. Both credits are available for dependants who are mentally or physically infirm.

4-69.   For 2012, this credit has a value of $960 [(15%)($6,402)]. The base for the credit is reduced by the amount of the dependant's Net Income in excess of $6,420. This means that this tax credit is not available once the dependant's Net Income is more than $12,822 ($6,420 + $6,402).

4-70.   The ITA 118(1)(d) infirm dependant over 17 credit should not be confused with the mental and physical impairment credit (a.k.a., disability tax credit) that is available to disabled individuals under ITA 118.3. The ITA 118.3 disability credit requires a doctor to certify that there is a prolonged impairment that severely restricts basic living activities. The disability credit is claimed by the disabled person, but can be transferred to a supporting person if it cannot be fully utilized (see Paragraph 4-144).

4-71.   In contrast, the ITA 118(1)(d) credit can only be claimed by the supporting person and a doctor's certification of the mental or physical infirmity is not required. For example, a daughter would be eligible to claim this credit if her mother is living in a nursing home because she is too frail to live alone, and her mother has income of less than $12,822 during the year.

4-72.   Note that because the disability credit can be transferred to a supporting person, the supporting person may be able to claim both the credit for an infirm dependant over 17, and the disability tax credit for the same person.

Exercise Four - 5

Subject: Infirm Dependant Over 17 Tax Credit

Harold Reed is married. His 70 year old mother has severe arthritis and lives in a nursing home. Her Net Income For Tax Purposes for 2012 is $7,600 and she relies on Harold for support. Determine the amount of Harold's caregiver and infirm dependant over 17 tax credit for 2012.

End of Exercise. Solution available in Study Guide.

Interaction: Eligible Dependant Credit Vs. Caregiver Or Infirm Dependant Over 17 Credits

4-73.   In reading through the material related to these three tax credits, it may have occurred to you that a taxpayer could have a dependant who was eligible for both the ITA 118(1)(b) eligible dependant credit and either the caregiver credit or infirm dependant over 17 credit. This did not happen in either Exercise Four-4 or Four-5 because both Joan Barton and Harold Reed were living with their spouses, making them ineligible to claim the eligible dependant credit.

4-74.   In contrast, assume a single individual has a disabled child over 17 years of age. In the absence of some restriction, this individual could claim both the eligible dependant credit and the infirm dependant over 17 credit. ITA 118(4)(c) provides such a restriction. This paragraph indicates that, if a taxpayer is eligible for the ITA 118(1)(b) eligible dependant credit for a particular individual, he cannot claim either the caregiver credit or the infirm dependant over 17 credit for that individual. Note that ITA 118(4)(c) refers to "entitled to", without regard to whether the credit is actually taken.

4-75.   ITA 118(4)(c) requires careful interpretation. If a taxpayer has only one dependant and that dependant is eligible for both the eligible dependant credit and either the caregiver or infirm dependant credits, the taxpayer must take the eligible dependant credit. However, if you add a second dependant who also qualifies for the eligible dependant credit, the situation changes. If the eligible dependant credit is claimed for the second dependant, the first dependant is no longer entitled to the eligible dependant credit because only one claim can be made for this credit. This means the caregiver or infirm dependant credit could be claimed for the first dependant.

4-76.   Because the eligible dependant base has no income threshold, it is reduced if the dependant has any Net Income For Tax Purposes. It is completely eliminated when the dependant's Net Income For Tax Purposes is equal to or greater than $10,822. In contrast, both the caregiver and infirm dependant over 17 credits are only reduced by the dependant's Net Income For Tax Purposes in excess of a threshold amount. Given this difference, the ITA 118(4)(c) restriction could have the unintended result of reducing the amount of tax credits.

4-77.   ITA 118(1)(e) provides a solution to this problem. This provision allows an additional credit to be taken based on the excess of what the caregiver or infirm dependant over 17 credit would have been, over the amount available under the eligible dependant credit.

Exercise Four - 6

Subject: Eligible Dependant Vs. Caregiver Tax Credits

Barry Litvak is a single individual with a 67 year old mother. While his mother is not mentally or physically infirm, she lives with Barry. She has Net Income For Tax Purposes for 2012 of $7,500. Calculate the tax credits that will be available to Barry as a result of his mother living with him.

End of Exercise. Solution available in Study Guide.

Interaction: Caregiver Vs. Infirm Dependant Over 17 Credits

4-78.   It is likely that you have noted that a single individual may qualify for both the caregiver and infirm dependant over 17 tax credits. In terms of qualifying individuals, there are two differences:

- In general, both credits require the qualifying individual to be mentally or physically infirm. However, the caregiver credit makes an exception for parents and grandparents who are over 64. These individuals may qualify for the caregiver credit, but not the infirm dependant over 17 credit.

- The caregiver credit requires that the qualifying individual live with the taxpayer. The infirm dependant over 17 credit does not have this requirement.

4-79.   Despite these differences, it is clear that in many cases, an individual who qualifies for the caregiver credit would also qualify for the infirm dependant over 17 credit. This means that, in the absence of some type of restrictive provision, both credits could be claimed for the same individual.

4-80.   ITA 118(4)(d) provides such a restriction. This paragraph indicates that, if a taxpayer is entitled to the caregiver credit for a particular individual, that individual is deemed not to be a dependant and, therefore, not eligible for the infirm dependant over 17 credit. This prevents the taxpayer from claiming both credits for the same individual and, in effect, requires the use of the caregiver credit in situations where a single individual is eligible for both credits.

4-81.   With the exception of non-infirm parents and grandparents over 64 who are not eligible for the FCA, both credits have a 2012 maximum value of $960 [(15%)($6,402)]. However, there is a difference in the income thresholds, with the caregiver amount being significantly higher, $15,033 vs. $6,420. Because of this, the caregiver credit will be more desirable. This means that, in effect, ITA 118(4)(d) forces the taxpayer to make the more advantageous decision on this issue.

Exercise Four - 7

Subject: Caregiver Vs. Infirm Dependant Over 17 Tax Credits

Suki Leonard is married, lives with her husband, and has a 28 year old son. He lives with her and is dependent because of a physical infirmity. For 2012, the son has investment income of $8,250. Suki would like to know whether she should take the caregiver tax credit for her son or, alternatively, the infirm dependant over 17 tax credit and how much tax the correct credit will save her.

End of Exercise. Solution available in Study Guide.

Exercise Four - 8

Subject: Multiple Credits For Dependants

Ms. Jane Forest is 48 years old and divorced from her husband. She has retained the family home and both of the children of the marriage live with her. Her son is 20 years old and suffers from Down Syndrome. He does not qualify for the disability tax credit. Her daughter is 16 years old and in good health. Her son has no income during 2012, while her daughter has Net Income For Tax Purposes of $1,800. Determine Ms. Forest's maximum federal tax credits for 2012.

End of Exercise. Solution available in Study Guide.

Other Tax Credits For Individuals

Age Tax Credit - ITA 118(2)

4-82.   For individuals who attain the age of 65 prior to the end of the year, ITA 118(2) provides an additional tax credit of $1,008 [(15%)($6,720)]. However, the base for this credit is reduced by 15 percent of the individual's Net Income For Tax Purposes in excess of $33,884. This means that, at an income level of $78,684 [($6,720 ÷ 15%) + $33,884], the reduction will be equal to $6,720 and the individual will not receive an age credit. Note that the reduction is only 15% of the income above the threshold, not a dollar for dollar reduction.

> **Example**   A 67 year old individual has 2012 Net Income For Tax Purposes of $35,000.

> **Analysis**   An age credit of $983 {[15%][$6,720 - (15%)($35,000 - $33,884)]} will be available to this individual.

4-83.   As we shall see when we consider the transfer of credits to a spouse, if an individual does not have sufficient Tax Payable to use this credit, it can be transferred to a spouse.

Exercise Four - 9

Subject: Age Tax Credit

Joshua Smythe is 72 years old and has 2012 Net Income For Tax Purposes of $51,500. Determine Mr. Smythe's age credit for 2012.

End Of Exercise. Solution available in Study Guide.

Pension Income Tax Credit - ITA 118(3)

General Rules

4-84.   The pension income credit is equal to 15 percent of the first $2,000 of eligible pension income. This results in a maximum value of $300 [(15%)($2,000)]. The base for this credit is not indexed for inflation.

4-85.   The credit is only available with respect to "eligible pension income". Specifically excluded from this definition are:

- payments under the Old Age Security Act or Canada Pension Plan;
- payments under certain provincial pension plans;
- payments under salary deferral arrangements;
- payments under retirement compensation arrangements;
- payments under an employee benefit plan; and
- death benefits.

4-86.   Like the age credit, if an individual does not have sufficient Tax Payable to use this credit, it can be transferred to a spouse.

Individuals 65 Or Over

4-87.   For an individual who has reached age 65 before the end of the year, this credit is available on "pension income" as defined in ITA 118(7). This includes payments that are:

- periodic (not lump sum) payments from a registered pension plan (RPP);
- an annuity payment out of a Registered Retirement Savings Plan (RRSP);
- a payment out of a Registered Retirement Income Fund (RRIF);
- an annuity payment from a Deferred Profit Sharing Plan (DPSP); and
- the interest component of other annuities.

Individuals Under 65

4-88.   For an individual who has not reached age 65 during the year, the credit is based on "qualified pension income", also defined in ITA 118(7). In general, this only includes the periodic payments from a registered pension plan. However, if the other types of pension income described in Paragraph 4-87 are received as a consequence of the death of a spouse or common-law partner, these amounts are also qualified, regardless of the age of the recipient.

Canada Employment Tax Credit - ITA 118(10)

4-89.   This credit is available to all individuals who have Canadian employment income. From a conceptual point of view, it is designed to provide limited recognition of the fact that there are costs associated with earning employment income. As only limited deductions are available against employment income, this would appear to be an appropriate form of relief.

4-90.   For 2012, the amount of the credit is equal to 15 percent of the lesser of:

- $1,095; and
- the individual's Net Employment Income, calculated without the deduction of any employment related expenses.

4-91.   For most employed individuals, this will produce a credit of $164 [(15%)($1,095)].

Adoption Expenses Tax Credit - ITA 118.01

4-92.   The adoption expenses tax credit is available to a taxpayer who adopts an "eligible child". As defined in ITA 118.01(1), an eligible child means a child who has not attained the age of 18 years at the time that an adoption order is issued or recognized by a government in Canada in respect of the adoption of that child.

4-93.   The 2012 credit is based on up to $11,440 in eligible adoption expenses, resulting in a maximum of $1,716 [(15%)($11,440)].   The expenses can only be claimed in the year in which the adoption is finalized. The total amount of eligible expenses is reduced by any assistance that is received and not included in that taxpayer's income. Note, however, if an employer makes a provision for an employee's adoption expenses, this amount will normally be treated as a taxable benefit. Given this, such amounts will not be deducted from the adoption expenses that form the basis for this credit.

4-94.   An "adoption period" is defined in ITA 118.01(1). It begins at the earlier of:

- the time that the eligible child's adoption file is opened with a provincial ministry responsible for adoption (or with an adoption agency licensed by a provincial government), and
- the time that an application related to the adoption is made to a Canadian court.

It ends at the later of:
- the time an adoption order is issued by, or recognized by, a government in Canada in respect of that child, and
- the time that the child first begins to reside permanently with the individual.

4-95.   Eligible adoption expenses must be incurred during the adoption period and include:

(a) fees paid to an adoption agency licensed by a provincial government;
(b) court costs and legal and administrative expenses related to an adoption order in respect of that child;
(c) reasonable and necessary travel and living expenses of the child and the adoptive parents;
(d) document translation fees;
(e) mandatory fees paid to a foreign institution;
(f) mandatory expenses paid in respect of the immigration of the child; and
(g) any other reasonable expenses related to the adoption required by a provincial government or an adoption agency licensed by a provincial government.

4-96.   In the usual situation, a child will be adopted by a couple, either legally married or co-habiting on a common-law basis. The legislation points out that, while both parties are eligible for this credit, the $11,440 limit must be shared by the couple. The claim can be made by either party or split at their discretion.

Exercise Four - 10

Subject: Adoption Expenses Tax Credit

Ary Kapit and his spouse have adopted an infant Chinese orphan. The adoption process began in June, 2011 when they traveled to China to discuss the adoption and view available children. The cost of this trip was $4,250. Their provincial government opens the adoption file on February 13, 2012, and the adoption order is issued on August 27, 2012. In September, the couple returns to China to pick up their new daughter. The happy family returns to Canada on September 18, 2012. The cost of this trip is $6,420.

Additional expenses paid during the first week of September, 2012 were $1,600 paid to the Chinese orphanage and $3,200 paid to a Canadian adoption agency. Legal fees incurred during the adoption period were $2,700. After arrival in Canada, an additional $2,500 in medical expenses were incurred for the child prior to the end of 2012. Mr. Kapit's employer has a policy of providing reimbursement for up to $5,000 in adoption expenses eligible for the adoption expenses tax credit. This amount is received in September, 2012 and will be considered a taxable benefit to Mr. Kapit. Calculate the maximum adoption expenses tax credit that can be claimed by the couple?

End of Exercise. Solution available in Study Guide.

Public Transit Passes Tax Credit - ITA 118.02

4-97.   This credit is equal to 15 percent of the cost of eligible public transit passes attributable to the use of an individual, his spouse or common-law partner, and his children who have not attained the age of 19 during the year.

4-98.   Eligible public transit passes are defined as follows:

• Passes that provide for unlimited travel for an uninterrupted period of at least 28 days (monthly passes).

• Passes that provide for unlimited travel for an uninterrupted period of at least 5 days, provided a sufficient number of such passes are acquired that at least 20 days will be covered in a period of 28 days (a group of weekly passes).

4-99.   The credit is also available with respect to the costs of "eligible electronic payment cards". These must provide for at least 32 one-way trips during an uninterrupted period that does not exceed 31 days.

4-100.   The passes must be for use on "public commuter transit services" which means services offered to the general public, ordinarily for a period of at least five days per week, of transporting individuals, from a place in Canada to another place in Canada, by means of bus, ferry, subway, train or tram, and in respect of which it can reasonably be expected that those individuals would return daily to the place of their departure.

4-101.   As was the case with adoption expenses, the costs that are eligible for the credit must be reduced by any amounts that are reimbursed and not included in the taxpayer's income. Note, however, that employer reimbursements are generally included in an employee's income and, as a consequence, would not reduce the base for this credit.

Child Fitness Tax Credit - ITA 118.03 And Children's Arts Tax Credit - ITA 118.031

General Rules

4-102.   The child fitness and children's arts credits are two tax credits available to parents who enrol their children in eligible programs. They are very similar except for the definition of the relevant eligible activities.

4-103.   Both credits are equal to 15 percent of the lesser of $500 and the eligible fees paid. This provides a maximum credit of $75 [(15%)($500)]. The base for these credits is not subject to indexation. Both credits can be claimed by either parent or may be shared between them.

4-104.   For both credits, there is an additional credit of $75 [(15%)($500)] available for children who qualify for the Disability Tax Credit (see discussion beginning in Paragraph 4-144) and who are under 18 at the beginning of the year. While these credit supplements are not based on actual costs, their availability requires a minimum of $100 in eligible fees to be paid. The base for these supplements is not subject to indexation.

4-105.   To qualify for these credits, the costs must be related to a child who is under 16 years of age at the beginning of the year (under 18 if the child qualifies for the disability tax credit).

Eligible Programs And Fees

4-106.   In order to be eligible for the child fitness credit an activity must:

- require significant physical activity that contributes to cardiorespiratory endurance, plus one or more of:

  - muscular strength,
  - muscular endurance,
  - flexibility, and/or
  - balance.

4-107.   In order to be eligible for the children's arts credit an activity must:

- help children develop particular intellectual skills, creative skills or expertise in an artistic or cultural activity;
- substantially focus on wilderness and the natural environment;
- provide enrichment or tutoring in academic subjects; or
- include interaction among children where supervisors teach or help children develop interpersonal skills.

4-108.   Eligible fees include registration and membership fees in a program that includes a significant amount of eligible activities. The program must be ongoing, supervised, suitable for children, not part of a school's curriculum and a minimum of:

- for general programs – eight consecutive weeks with at least one session per week; or
- for camps – five consecutive days.

4-109. The eligible costs do not include the cost of accommodation, travel or food. The eligible costs must be reduced by any reimbursements received unless the reimbursed amount is included in the taxpayer's income.

No Double Counting For Fitness Credit, Arts Credit Or Child Care Costs

4-110.   It is possible that a program could have activities eligible for both the fitness credit and the arts credit. Both credits can be claimed for a specific child, but the same fees cannot be used as a base for both credits.

4-111.   Where both credits could be applicable, the fitness credit should be claimed first as the definition of eligible costs for the arts credit excludes any amounts that have been claimed for another credit.

4-112.   An additional point here is that some costs that would be eligible for either of these credits may also be eligible for deduction as child care costs (see Chapter 9). To avoid the possibility of such amounts being double counted, the definition of eligible costs for both credits excludes any amounts that have been deducted as child care costs.

First Time Home Buyer's Tax Credit - ITA 118.05

4-113.   A tax credit is available for first-time home buyers who acquire a qualifying home. The credit is equal to 15 percent of the first $5,000 of the cost of a qualifying home, resulting in a maximum credit of $750. To be eligible for the credit, the buyer must intend to occupy the home no later than one year after its acquisition.

4-114.   An individual will be considered a first-time home buyer if neither the individual nor the individual's spouse or common-law partner, owned and lived in another home in the calendar year of the home purchase or in any of the four preceding calendar years.

4-115.   The credit may be claimed by the individual who acquires the home or by that individual's spouse or common-law partner. For the purpose of this credit, a home is considered to be acquired by an individual only if the individual's interest in the home is registered in accordance with the applicable land registration system.

Volunteer Firefighters Tax Credit - ITA 118.06

4-116.   There is a tax credit for volunteer firefighters who perform at least 200 hours of volunteer firefighting services during a taxation year. The base for the non-refundable credit will be $3,000. This amount is not indexed.

4-117.   If the individual provides paid services to a particular fire department, volunteer hours at that department will not count towards the required 200. There is an exemption under ITA 81(4)(b) for up to $1,000 in compensation received for volunteer firefighting duties. This exemption is not available to individuals who claim the tax credit for volunteer firefighters.

Charitable Donations Tax Credit - ITA 118.1

Extent Of Coverage In This Chapter

4-118.   For tax purposes, donations, even in the form of cash, are segregated into categories, each with a different set of rules. Additional complications arise when non-cash donations are made. To be able to deal with gifts of depreciable capital property, a full understanding of capital gains and CCA procedures is required. Given these complications, a comprehensive treatment of charitable gifts is deferred until we revisit Taxable Income and Tax Payable in Chapter 11. However, limited coverage of charitable donations is included in this Chapter.

Eligible Gifts

4-119.   In our coverage of donations in this Chapter, we will deal only with gifts of cash or monetary assets. Donations of other types of property are covered in Chapter 11.

4-120.   In this Chapter, our coverage will be limited to what is referred to in ITA 118.1 as total charitable gifts. These include amounts donated to entities such as:

- a registered charity;
- a registered Canadian amateur athletic association;
- a Canadian municipality;
- the Canadian government;
- a university outside of Canada which normally enrolls Canadian students; and
- a charitable organization outside of Canada to which the Canadian government made a gift in the current or preceding taxation year.

Limits On Amount Claimed

4-121.   It is the policy of the government to limit the amount of charitable donations that are eligible for the tax credit to a portion of a taxpayer's Net Income For Tax Purposes. Note that, while corporations deduct their donations from Taxable Income as opposed to receiving a credit against Tax Payable, the limits on the amount of eligible donations are the same for corporations as they are for individuals.

4-122.   The general limit on eligible amounts of charitable gifts is 75 percent of Net Income For Tax Purposes. For individuals, this limit is increased to 100 percent of Net Income For Tax Purposes in the year of death and the preceding year.

Calculating The Credit

4-123.   Once the contribution base is established, the credit is equal to 15 percent of the first $200, and 29 percent of any additional donations. The charitable donations credit is the only credit that features two rates for determining the allowable credit. The reason for this approach was concern that, because charitable donations are voluntary, an overall credit at the lowest bracket rate of 15 percent would have resulted in a decline in donations from individual with high incomes. The 29 percent credit on donations over $200 was added in order to encourage larger donations.

4-124.   While the same level of total giving could probably have been achieved with a compromise rate somewhere between 15 and 29 percent, this would have changed the composition of sources for donations. Such a compromise rate would have been an incentive for low income donors and would have increased donations to organizations such as churches that rely on this sector of the population. In contrast, high income donors would have less incentive to contribute, and this would have reduced donations to such beneficiaries as educational institutions. The government did not view this as a desirable result and, as a consequence, we have a two rate system for charitable donations.

4-125.   The following example illustrates the calculation of the charitable donations tax credit, including the determination of eligible amounts:

> **Example**   Nancy Hart has 2012 Net Income For Tax Purposes of $100,000 and Taxable Income of $40,000. On the receipt of a large inheritance, she makes a charitable donation of $15,000. She chooses to claim only $2,000 in donations in 2012.
>
> **Analysis**   The total for all eligible gifts is limited to 75 percent of her Net Income For Tax Purposes, or $75,000. As her gift is less than $75,000, she could have claimed all of it. However, since she has chosen to claim $2,000, $13,000 ($15,000 - $2,000) in donations are carried forward. Her 2012 tax credit would be calculated as follows:

15 Percent Of $200	$ 30
29 Percent Of $1,800 ($2,000 - $200)	522
Total Credit	$552

4-126.   For couples, the CRA's administrative practices permit either spouse or common-law partner to claim all of the donations made by both spouses or common-law partners. Given the dual rates on the credit, there is a small advantage in combining the donations. In addition, this may be an important consideration when one spouse has a sufficiently low income that it is limiting the use of his or her donations.

Carry Forward Of Charitable Donations

4-127. With the limit set at 75 percent of Net Income, individuals will normally be able to claim all of the donations that they make in a year. However, if their donations exceed the 75 percent limit, or they choose not to claim all of the donations that year, any unused amounts can be carried forward and used in the subsequent five year period.

4-128. A further point here is that this limit is based on Net Income For Tax Purposes. This means that an individual could have eligible donations in excess of Taxable Income. This could occur, for example, if the individual deducted a large loss carry forward from a previous year. In situations such as this, it is important to recognize that the charitable donations tax credit is non-refundable. Given this, only the amount of donations required to reduce Tax Payable to nil should be claimed. Any additional amounts should be carried forward to future periods. Any claim that does not serve to reduce Tax Payable will simply be lost.

Example Barry Mann has Net Income For Tax Purposes of $80,000. This is reduced to a Taxable Income of $20,000 because of a large business loss carry forward from a previous year. Because of a fortuitous lottery win, he chooses to make a charitable donation of $100,000.

Analysis The potential base for Barry's charitable donations tax credit is $60,000 [(75%)($80,000)]. However, if he were to claim this amount, the credit of $17,372 [(15%)($200) + (29%)($59,800)] would be far in excess of the Tax Payable on only $20,000 of Taxable Income. Claiming the maximum amount would result in simply losing the greater part of the available credit. The preferable alternative would be to claim only enough to reduce his Tax Payable to nil and carry the remainder forward.

4-129. Determining the specific amounts to be used and carried forward will be discussed in Chapter 11.

Exercise Four - 11

Subject: Charitable Donations Tax Credit

Marion Scalpal has Net Income For Tax Purposes of $65,000 in 2012 and 2013. After years of losses at her local casino, her luck changes and she wins over $200,000 in 2012. As she had promised in her prayers, she immediately donates $100,000 to her church. She chooses to claim $10,000 of her donations in 2012. Determine her charitable donations tax credit for 2012, as well as the maximum amount of the donation that she can use in 2013. Until what year can she claim any unused portions of her 2012 donation?

End of Exercise. Solution available in Study Guide.

Medical Expenses Tax Credit - ITA 118.2

Qualifying Medical Expenses

4-130. There are many types of medical expenses which qualify for the credit under ITA 118.2. (For a detailed list see IT-519R2 Consolidated.) The list of qualifying medical expenses has been repeatedly extended in various budgets and includes amounts paid for:

- the services of licenced medical practitioners, dentists and registered nurses,
- artificial limbs, aids and other devices and equipment,
- products required because of incontinence,
- prescription eyeglasses or contact lenses,
- oxygen tents,
- guide and hearing-ear dogs and other specially trained animals,

- the costs of arranging a bone marrow or organ transplant,
- the costs of home modifications for those with severe mobility restrictions, and to allow individuals confined to a wheelchair to be mobile within their home,
- the cost of rehabilitative therapy to adjust for speech or hearing loss,
- devices and equipment listed in ITR 5700 and prescribed by a medical practitioner,
- preventive, diagnostic and other laboratory work,
- prescribed drugs, medicaments and other preparations or substances,
- dentures, and
- premiums to private health services plan

4-131. Although payments for attendants, nursing home care and care in an institution are qualifying medical expenses, there are many complications with claiming these expenses. They will be briefly covered after we have dealt with the disability tax credit.

4-132. Not all budget changes have expanded the list of qualifying expenditures. Costs incurred for purely cosmetic reasons no longer qualify for the medical expense tax credit. Examples of non-qualifying procedures include liposuction, hair replacement procedures, Botox injections and teeth whitening. Cosmetic procedures continue to qualify if they are required for medical or reconstructive purposes (e.g., facial surgery required due to a car accident). Somewhat amusingly, the CRA refused to deal with the question of whether male infant circumcision was, or was not, cosmetic.

Determining The Credit

4-133. Qualifying medical expenses of an individual do not include any expense for which the individual has been, or is entitled to be, reimbursed unless the amount is required to be included in income. An amount reimbursed under a public or private medical, dental or hospitalization plan would not qualify for purposes of the medical expense tax credit.

4-134. The amount of the medical expense tax credit is determined by the following formula:

$$A [(B - C) + D]$$

Where:

A is the appropriate percentage for the taxation year (15 percent).

B is the total of an individual's medical expenses for himself, his spouse or common-law partner, and any of his children who have not reached 18 years of age at the end of the year.

C is the lesser of 3 percent of the individual's Net Income For Tax Purposes and $2,109 (2012 figure).

D is the total of all amounts each of which is, in respect of a dependant of the individual (other than a child of the individual who has not attained the age of 18 years before the end of the taxation year), the amount determined by the formula

$$E - F$$

Where:

E is the total of the dependant's medical expenses

F is the lesser of 3 percent of the dependant's Net Income For Tax Purposes and $2,109 (2012 figure).

4-135. If the taxpayer has no dependants who are 18 years of age or older, components D, E and F in the formula are not relevant. In this case, the credit base is equal to the total of the qualifying medical expenses of the individual taxpayer, his spouse or common-law partner, and his minor children. This balance is reduced by the lesser of 3 percent of the taxpayer's income and an indexed figure which for 2012 is equal to $2,109. This latter figure will be the limiting factor once an individual's 2012 Net Income For Tax Purposes reaches $70,300 ($2,109 ÷ 3%).

4-136.   If the taxpayer has dependants who are 18 years of age or older, a separate credit base calculation is required for each of these dependants. This credit base is equal to the dependant's qualifying medical expenses, reduced by the lesser of 3 percent of the dependant's Net Income For Tax Purposes and $2,109 (E and F in the formula). The taxpayer adds the total of these amounts to the credit base calculated for the taxpayer, his spouse or common-law partner and his minor children.

4-137.   A further point here relates to who actually pays for medical expenses. The credit is only available to the individual who pays the eligible amounts. For an individual to claim the medical expenses of a child or other dependant, he must have paid them. If the individual makes the payment, the child or dependant cannot claim the payment for the credit.

Twelve Month Period

4-138.   Medical expenses can be claimed for any period of 12 months that ends in the taxation year. This provision is extended to 24 months in the year of death. The ability to claim expenses for a 12 month period ending in the year is advantageous for individuals with large expenses in a 12 month period other than a calendar year.

> **Example**   Alex Lau has Net Income For Tax Purposes of $60,000 in both 2011 and 2012. In July, 2011, he began a year long (and very painful) corrective dental surgery program. During July to December, 2011 he paid $10,000 in dental fees. During January to June, 2012 he paid $12,000 in dental fees.
>
> **Analysis**   The 2011 claim could be deferred and the $22,000 total could be claimed in full in the 2012 taxation year. The advantage of doing this is that the threshold amount reduction would be applied only once in 2012. If medical expenses had to be claimed in the year in which they were incurred, Mr. Lau would have to apply the threshold reduction of $1,800 [(3%)($60,000)] in both years. If the full amount is claimed in 2012, federal tax savings would total $270 [(15%)($1,800)].

Example Of Medical Expense Tax Credit Calculation

4-139.   The following example will serve to illustrate the application of the medical expense tax credit formula:

> **Example** Sam Jonas and his dependent family members had the following Net Income For Tax Purposes and medical expenses for 2012. Sam paid for all of the medical expenses.
>
> | Individual | Net Income | Medical Expenses |
> | --- | --- | --- |
> | Sam Jonas | $100,000 | $ 5,000 |
> | Kelly (Sam's Wife) | 12,000 | 4,400 |
> | Sue (Sam's 16 Year Old Daughter) | 8,500 | 4,100 |
> | Sharon (Sam's 69 Year Old Mother) | 6,000 | 16,500 |
> | Martin (Sam's 70 Year Old Blind Father) | 12,000 | 4,000 |
> | Total Medical Expenses | | $34,000 |

Analysis Sam's 2012 medical expense tax credit, using the formula in Paragraph 4-134, would be calculated as follows:

Amount B Qualifying Expenses ($5,000 + $4,400 + $4,100) $13,500

Amount C
Lesser Of:
- [(3%)($100,000)] = $3,000
- 2012 Threshold Amount = $2,109   (2,109)

Subtotal	$11,391

Amount D

Sharon's Medical Expenses	$16,500	
Reduced By The Lesser Of:		
• $2,109		
• [(3%)($6,000)] = $180	(180)	16,320
Martin's Medical Expenses	$ 4,000	
Reduced By The Lesser Of:		
• $2,109		
• [(3%)($12,000)] = $360	(360)	3,640

Allowable Amount Of Medical Expenses	$31,351
Amount A The Appropriate Rate (Minimum Rate)	15%
Medical Expense Tax Credit	$ 4,703

Exercise Four - 12

Subject: Medical Expense Tax Credit

Ms. Maxine Davies and her spouse, Lance Davies, have 2012 medical expenses which total $4,330. While Ms. Davies has 2012 Net Income For Tax Purposes in excess of $150,000, Lance has no income during the year. They have two children. Their 12 year old daughter, Mandy, has 2012 medical expenses of $4,600 and no Net Income For Tax Purposes. Their 21 year old son, Max, has 2012 medical expenses of $8,425 and Net Income For Tax Purposes of $8,250. Ms. Davies pays all of the medical expenses. Determine Ms. Davies' medical expense tax credit for 2012.

End of Exercise. Solution available in Study Guide.

Refundable Medical Expense Supplement - ITA 122.51

4-140.   The tax credits that we have discussed to this point are referred to as non-refundable. This means that, if the individual does not have sufficient Tax Payable to use the credit, it is of no benefit to the taxpayer. In contrast, there are a limited number of refundable credits. In the case of these credits, if the individual does not have sufficient Tax Payable to use the credit, the government will issue a cheque for the unused amount. The ITA 122.51 refundable medical expense supplement is this type of credit.

4-141.   To be eligible for the 2012 medical expense supplement, the individual must be 18 or over at the end of the year, and must have earned income (employment or business) of at least $3,268. The credit is the lesser of $1,119 and 25/15 of the medical expense tax credit that can be claimed for the year. This can also be described as 25 percent of the expenses eligible for the medical expense tax credit plus 25 percent of the disability supports deduction (see Paragraph 4-154).

4-142.   The lesser amount is reduced by 5 percent of "family net income" in excess of an indexed threshold amount. Family net income is the sum of the income of the taxpayer and his spouse or common-law partner, but not that of an eligible dependant. For 2012, the income threshold is $24,783 and the credit is completely eliminated when family net income reaches $47,163. A simple example will serve to illustrate this provision:

Example   For 2012, Mr. Larry Futon and his spouse have medical expenses that total $4,650. His Net Income For Tax Purposes is $26,900, all of which qualifies as earned income. His spouse has Net Income For Tax Purposes of $500. Mr. Futon claims the caregiver tax credit for his mother who has Net Income of $8,000. She is not mentally or physically infirm.

Analysis   Mr. Futon's allowable medical expenses for tax credit purposes would be $3,843 [$4,650 - (3%)($26,900)], resulting in a tax credit of $576 [(15%)($3,843)]. Given this, 25/15 of the credit, or alternatively, 25 percent of the allowable medical expenses, would equal $961. Since this is less than the maximum of $1,119, his refundable credit would be $961 less a reduction of $131 [(5%)($26,900 + $500 - $24,783)], leaving a balance of $830 ($961 - $131).

4-143.   The receipt of this refundable credit does not affect an individual's ability to claim a tax credit for the same medical expenses that are used to calculate the refundable credit. Assuming he has no tax credits other than the basic personal, spousal, caregiver, and medical expense, his federal Tax Payable would be reduced to nil [(15%)($26,900 - $10,822 - $10,822 - $500 - $4,402 - $3,843)]. This means that he will be able to claim the entire $830 as a refund.

Exercise Four - 13

Subject: Refundable Medical Expense Supplement

During 2012, Ms. Lara Brunt and her common-law partner, Sara, have medical expenses that total $6,250. Her Net Income For Tax Purposes is $26,400, all of which qualifies as earned income. Sara has no income of her own. Determine Lara's minimum Tax Payable for 2012.

End of Exercise. Solution available in Study Guide.

Disability Tax Credit - ITA 118.3
Calculation
4-144.   The disability credit is available under ITA 118.3 and, for 2012, it is equal to $1,132 [(15%)($7,546)]. In addition, there is a supplement to this amount for a disabled child who is under the age of 18 at the end of the year. For 2012, the base for the supplement is $4,402, providing a total credit for a disabled minor of $1,792 [(15%)($7,546 + $4,402)]. Note, however, that the supplement amount of $4,402 is reduced by child care and attendant care costs in excess of $2,578. This means that once such costs reach $6,980 for the year, the supplement is completely eliminated.

4-145.   To qualify for this credit, the requirement has been that the impairment must be such that there is a "marked" restriction of the activities of daily living. In addition, it must have lasted, or be expected to last, for at least 12 months. This has been amended to include situations where there is a "significant" restriction in more than one activity (while both terms are undefined, it appears that significant is less severe than marked).

4-146.   In general, a medical doctor, or optometrist, must certify on Form T2201 that a severe physical or mental impairment exists. In the case of restrictions on the ability to walk, recent amendments allow a physiotherapist to make the required certification.

4-147.   ITA 118.4(1) tries to make the conditions for qualifying for this credit as clear as possible. This Subsection points out that an individual clearly qualifies if they are blind. They also qualify if 90 percent of the time they cannot perform, or take an inordinate amount of time to perform, a basic activity of daily living. The following are listed as basic activities:

- mental functions necessary for everyday life;
- feeding oneself or dressing oneself;

- speaking such that the individual can be understood in a quiet setting by someone familiar with the individual;
- hearing such that the individual can, in a quiet setting, understand someone familiar with the individual;
- bowel or bladder functions; or
- walking.

4-148.   There have been several attempts to provide improved guidance in this area. However, many practitioners feel that the CRA is, perhaps, overly aggressive in its interpretation of the terms "markedly restricted" and an "inordinate amount of time" (e.g., the credit was denied for an individual with cerebral palsy because he was able to walk with braces).

Disability Credit Transfer To A Supporting Person

4-149.   In many cases, an individual who is sufficiently infirm to qualify for the disability credit will not have sufficient Tax Payable to use it. In this situation, all or part of the credit may be transferred to a spouse, or a supporting person who claimed the disabled individual as:

- a dependant under the eligible dependant provision [ITA 118(1)(b)];
- a dependant for purposes of the caregiver tax credit [ITA 118(1)(c.1)]; or
- a disabled dependant over 17 [ITA 118(1)(d)].

4-150.   In order to make the disability credit transfer available in situations where there is a disabled dependant who does not qualify for one of these credits, the transfer is extended by a somewhat awkward measure to situations in which the supporting person:

- could have claimed the eligible dependant credit, if neither the supporting person nor the disabled dependant were married; or
- could have claimed the disabled dependant over 17, or the caregiver credit, if the dependant had been 18 years of age or older and had no income.

4-151.   The amount that can be transferred is the same $1,132 (or $1,792 if the full under 18 supplement is available) that could be claimed by the disabled individual. However, if the disabled individual has Tax Payable in excess of his credits under ITA 118, 118.06 (adoption expenses), 118.02 (public transit passes), 118.03 (child fitness), 118.05 (first time home buyer), 118.06 (volunteer firefighters), and 118.7 (CPP and EI), the credit must first be applied to reduce the disabled individual's Tax Payable to nil. If a balance remains after all Tax Payable has been eliminated, it can then be transferred to the supporting person.

Exercise Four - 14

Subject: Disability Tax Credit

John Leslie lives with his wife and 21 year old blind son, Keith, who qualifies for the disability tax credit. Keith has no income of his own. During 2012, John paid medical expenses of $16,240 for Keith. None of these expenses involve attendant care. John's Taxable Income for 2012 was $100,000. Determine the total amount of tax credits related to Keith that will be available to John.

End of Exercise. Solution available in Study Guide.

Other Credits And Deductions Related To Disabilities

4-152.   For disabled individuals who earn employment or business income, the "working income tax benefit supplement" provides an additional amount for individuals who qualify for the disability tax credit. This benefit is covered beginning at Paragraph 4-202.

4-153.   Disabled individuals, or a supporting person, may have paid significant medical expenses involving attendant care and/or nursing home care. The availability of the medical expenses credit for these costs is limited by the following considerations:

- Neither the individual, nor a supporting person, can claim the disability credit if a medical expense credit is claimed for a full time attendant, or for full time care in a nursing home. However, the individual or supporting person can claim either of the two amounts.

- The disability credit can be claimed if a medical expense credit is claimed for a part-time attendant. Part-time is defined as expenses claimed of less than $10,000 for the year ($20,000 in the year of death). Note that part-time attendant care can only be claimed as a medical expense credit if no part of that care is claimed as child care costs or for attendant care required to produce income.

4-154.   For disabled individuals who work, or who attend a designated educational institution or secondary school, the disability supports deduction provides tax relief for a number of medical expenses, including attendant care, which would assist a disabled person to work or go to school. (See Chapter 9, Other Income, Other Deductions And Other Issues for coverage of this deduction.)

4-155.   There are complications and restrictions related to claiming these and many other types of medical expenses. Complete coverage of all the relevant rules goes beyond the scope of this text. For those interested in this subject, we refer you to IT-519R2 (Consolidated), *Medical Expense and Disability Tax Credits and Attendant Care Expense Deduction*.

Education Related Tax Credits
Tuition Fees Tax Credit - ITA 118.5(1) To ITA 118.5(4)
4-156.   Under ITA 118.5, individuals receive a credit against Tax Payable equal to 15 percent of qualifying tuition fees paid with respect to the calendar year, regardless of the year in which they are actually paid. The fees must total at least $100, but there is no upper limit on this credit. The following tuition fees qualify:

- Tuition fees paid to a university, college, or other institution for post-secondary courses located in Canada.

- Tuition fees paid to an institution certified by the Minister of Human Resources and Skills Development for a course that developed or improved skills in an occupation (the individual must be 16 or older).

- Tuition fees paid to a university outside Canada. To qualify the course must have a minimum duration of 3 weeks.

- For individuals who live near the U.S. border and commute, tuition fees paid to a U.S. college or university for part-time studies.

Examination Fees Included In Tuition Fees Tax Credit
4-157.   To qualify for this credit, the fees must exceed $100. The credit base includes ancillary fees such as the cost of examination materials or required identification cards. It does not include the costs for travel, parking, or required equipment (e.g., computers).

4-158.   In addition to fees for university examinations, the credit base includes fees for professional examinations such as bar examinations and examinations required by the CGAs, CAs, or CMAs. It does not, however, include fees for examinations required for entrance to professional programs (e.g., the CMA entrance examination).

Ancillary Fees Included In Tuition Fees Tax Credit
4-159.   It has been noted that universities are relying more heavily on ancillary fees for such items as health services, athletics, and various other services. As a reflection of this situation, ITA 118.5(3) extends the tuition fees tax credit to cover all mandatory ancillary fees that are imposed by universities on all of their full time, or all of their part-time students. In addition, ITA 118.5(3)(d) allows up to $250 in such ancillary fees to be added to the total, even if they do not meet the condition of being required for all full or part-time students.

Education Tax Credit - ITA 118.6(2)

4-160. Under ITA 118.6(2), there is a credit for 2012 equal to $60 [(15%)($400)] per month of full time attendance at a designated educational institution or enrollment in a "qualifying educational program". For this purpose, designated educational institutions include universities, colleges, and institutions certified by the Minister of Human Resource And Skills Development for a course that develops or improves skills in an occupation.

4-161. Enrollment in a qualifying educational program is described in IT-515R2 as a program that must run for at least 3 consecutive weeks, and must require instruction or work in the program of at least 10 hours a week throughout its duration. Both of these descriptions can be thought of as full time pursuit of educational activities.

4-162. An alternative education credit of $18 [(15%)($120)] per month is available for attendance in a "specified educational program". In general terms, this is defined as a program that, were it not for the 10 hours per week requirement, would be a qualifying educational program. This means that, while a specified educational program must run for at least 3 consecutive weeks, there is no minimum hours of work required to comply with the definition. This credit is normally claimed by part-time students.

4-163. A further modification of the general rules for the education credit is available to individuals who either qualify for the disability tax credit or, because of a mental or physical disability, cannot pursue educational activities on a full time basis. The full education credit of $60 per month is available to such individuals, without regard to whether their attendance is full or part-time.

Textbook Tax Credit - ITA 118.6(2.1)

4-164. While this credit is described as a "textbook" tax credit, it is not based on an actual purchase of such books. Rather, it is simply an addition to the education credit. This "textbook" credit is equal to $10 [(15%)($65)] for each month in which the student is entitled to claim the education credit as a full-time student, or $3 [(15%)($20)] for each month in which the student is entitled to claim the education credit as a part-time student.

4-165. This credit is added to the tuition and education credits as part of the amount that is eligible for a carry forward by the student (see Paragraph 4-167). It is also added to these credits in determining the amount that can be transferred to a spouse, parent or grandparent (see Paragraph 4-171). As was the case with the education credit, students who qualify for the disability tax credit or, because of mental or physical disability, cannot pursue full time education activities, will receive the full $10 per month textbook credit.

Interest On Student Loans Tax Credit - ITA 118.62

4-166. There is a credit available under ITA 118.62 if a student or a related person has paid interest on student loans. The credit for the student is equal to 15 percent of interest paid in the year, or in any of the five preceding years. The interest paid must be on a loan under the *Canada Student Loans Act*, the *Canada Student Financial Assistance Act*, or a provincial statute governing the granting of financial assistance to students at the post-secondary school level.

Exercise Four - 15

Subject: Education Related Tax Credits

During 2012, Sarah Bright attends university for four months of full time study and two months of part-time study. Her total tuition for the year, including all ancillary fees, is $3,200 of which she prepaid $1,000 in 2011. The amount paid in 2012 includes $400 in fees that are only charged to students in her geology program. Interest paid for the year on her student loan was $325. Determine the total amount of education related tax credits that would be available for Ms. Bright for 2012.

End of Exercise. Solution available in Study Guide.

Carry Forward Of Tuition, Education, And Textbook Credits - ITA 118.61

4-167.   There are situations in which a student does not have sufficient Tax Payable to use their tuition, education, and textbook credits and, in addition, has not transferred them to a spouse, parent, or grandparent (see Paragraph 4-171). To deal with this type of situation, ITA 118.61 allows a carry forward of unused tuition, education, and textbook credits. There is no time limit on this carry forward. In addition, ITA 118.62 provides for a 5 year carry forward of unused interest on student loans.

4-168.   Unfortunately, the calculation of the amount that is carried forward can be complex. Although the *Income Tax Act* uses Tax Payable and credit amounts to calculate carry forwards and transfers, Schedule 11 in the personal tax return uses Taxable Income and credit base amounts in its calculations. We will explain the *Income Tax Act* approach in the text, but illustrate both approaches in the example in Paragraph 4-175.

4-169.   To carry amounts forward, the total available credits must be reduced by the student's Tax Payable, calculated using the following credits (note the medical expenses tax credit is not included in the list):

- ITA 118 (Personal)
- ITA 118.01 Through ITA 118.06 (Various)
- ITA 118.3 (Disability)
- ITA 118.7 (CPP And EI)

4-170.   The available amount is also reduced by transfers to other individuals. The resulting balance can be carried forward and is available for the student's personal use in any subsequent year.   However, once it is carried forward, it cannot be transferred to another individual.

Transfer Of Tuition, Education, And Textbook Credits - ITA 118.9

4-171.   ITA 118.9 provides for a transfer of these tax credits to a parent or grandparent. ITA 118.8 provides for a transfer of these credits (plus several others), to a spouse or common-law partner. ITA 118.81 limits the total amount of tuition, education, and textbook credits that can be transferred under either of these provisions. The transfer is at the discretion of the student and the legislation states that he must indicate in writing the amount that he is willing to transfer.

4-172.   The maximum transfer for an individual student is the lesser of the available credits and $5,000 multiplied by the tax rate for the minimum tax bracket (referred to as the "appropriate percentage"). This amount is $750 [(15%)($5,000)].

4-173.   This $750 maximum amount must be reduced by the student's Tax Payable calculated after the same credits used to calculate the carry forward of education related credits. As described in Paragraph 4-169, these are the credits available under ITA 118 through ITA 118.06, 118.3 and 118.7. Added to the list for this purpose are any education related credits carried forward from a previous year under ITA 118.61. If these credits reduce the student's Tax Payable to nil, the full $750 is available for transfer.

4-174.   The $750 limit is on a per student basis. A parent or grandparent could have $750 transfers from any number of children or grandchildren. For obvious reasons, transfers from more than one spouse would not be acceptable for tax purposes (tax considerations might be the least of such an individual's problems). If the student is married, the supporting parent or grandparent can make the claim only if the student's spouse did not claim the spousal credit, or any unused credits transferred by the student (see Paragraph 4-183).

4-175.   An example will serve to illustrate both the ITA 118.9 transfer, as well as the ITA 118.81 limits on this transfer.

   Example   Megan Doxy has 2012 Taxable Income of $12,000, all of which is rental income. She attends university full time for 8 months of the year, paying a total amount for tuition of $8,000. This gives her a tuition amount of $8,000, an education amount of $3,200 [(8)($400)], and a textbook amount of $520 [(8)($65)], a total of

$11,720. Her only other tax credit is her personal amount of $1,623 [(15%)($10,822)]. She would like to transfer the maximum credits to her father.

Analysis - Income Tax Act Approach   Megan's education related credits total $1,758 [(15%)($8,000 + $3,200 + $520)], well in excess of the maximum transfer of $750. However, this maximum of $750 would have to be reduced by Megan's Tax Payable after the deduction of her personal amount. This amount would be $177 [(15%)($12,000 - $10,822)], leaving a maximum transfer of $573 ($750 - $177). This would leave Megan with remaining unused credits of $1,008 ($1,758 - $177 - $573) which can be carried forward to future years, for her own use. These calculations are the result of using the approach presented in the *Income Tax Act*.

Analysis - Tax Return Approach   The alternative calculation approach that is used in the tax return would begin with the total education related amount of $11,720. The maximum transfer amount in this approach is $5,000. This would be reduced by $1,178 ($12,000 - $10,822), the excess of Megan's Taxable Income over her basic personal amount. This results in a maximum transfer of $3,822 ($5,000 - $1,178). Megan's carry forward amount is $6,720 ($11,720 - $1,178 - $3,822). Multiplying these amounts by the 15 percent minimum rate will give you the same $1,008 of unused credits as the calculations using the preceding *Income Tax Act* approach.

Exercise Four - 16

Subject: Carry Forward Of Education Related Credits

At the beginning of 2012, Kerri Holmes has a carry forward of education credits from 2011 of $300 [(15%)($2,000)]. During 2012, she is in full time attendance at a Canadian university for 8 months of the year. Her tuition fees total $4,800 for the year. Her Taxable Income for 2012 is $24,000. Other than education related tax credits, her only tax credit is her basic personal credit. Determine Kerri's total education related tax credits and any available carry forward.

Exercise Four - 17

Subject: Transfer And Carry Forward Of Education Related Credits

Jerry Fall has 2012 Taxable Income of $11,250. He is a student at Indiana University in the U.S. on a full time basis for 11 months of the year, paying a total amount for tuition of $23,500 (Canadian dollars). His only tax credits, other than education related credits, are his basic personal credit and a medical expense credit of $233 [(15%)($1,555)]. Determine Jerry's total education related tax credits and indicate how much of this total could be transferred to a parent and how much would be carried forward.

End of Exercises. Solutions available in Study Guide.

Employment Insurance (EI) And
Canada Pension Plan (CPP) Tax Credits - ITA 118.7

4-176.   ITA 118.7 provides a tax credit equal to 15 percent of the Employment Insurance (EI) premiums paid by an individual, all of the Canada Pension Plan (CPP) contributions paid on employment income, and half of the CPP contributions paid on self-employed income.

4-177.   For 2012, an employee's CPP contributions are based on maximum pensionable earnings of $50,100, less a basic exemption of $3,500. The rate for 2012 is 4.95 percent, resulting in a maximum contribution of $2,307 [(4.95%)($50,100 - $3,500)]. This provides for a maximum 2012 credit against federal Tax Payable of $346 [(15%)($2,307)]. The employer matches the contributions made by the employee. However, this matching payment has no tax consequences for the employee.

4-178.   A self-employed individual earning business income must make a matching CPP contribution for himself, effectively paying twice the amount he would as an employee. As discussed in Chapter 9, the matching contribution is a deduction from Net Income For Tax Purposes under ITA 60(e) (a Division B, Subdivision e deduction). This treatment for the matching CPP contribution as a deduction is analogous to the treatment used by employers. This means that a self-employed individual will have a tax credit equal to one-half of his CPP contributions for self-employed income, and a deduction for the remaining one-half.

4-179.   For 2012, EI premiums are based on maximum insurable earnings of $45,900. The employee's rate is 1.83 percent, resulting in a maximum annual premium of $840. This results in a maximum credit against federal Tax Payable of $126 [(15%)($840)].

4-180.   Employers are also required to pay EI premiums, the amount being 1.4 times the premiums paid by the employee. However, these employer paid premiums have no tax consequences for the employee. While self-employed individuals can elect to participate in the EI program, unlike for the CPP, they do not have to remit the employer share. Their premiums will be limited to the same $840 that is applicable to employees.

Overpayment Of EI Premiums And CPP Contributions

4-181.   It is not uncommon for employers to withhold EI and CPP amounts that are in excess of the amounts required. This can happen through an error on the part of the employer's payroll system. Even in the absence of errors, overpayments can arise when an individual changes employers. We would note that the CRA's form T2204 is designed to assist taxpayers in calculating the amount of any overpayment.

4-182.   A refund of these excess amounts is available when an individual files his tax return. While any CPP or EI overpayment is not part of the base for the tax credit, it will increase the refund available or decrease the tax liability that is calculated in the return.

Example   Jerry Weist changed employers during 2012 and, as a consequence, the total amount of EI premiums withheld during the year was $910. In a similar fashion, the total amount of CPP contributions withheld by the two employers was $2,520. His employment income was well in excess of the maximum insurable and pensionable earnings.

Analysis   In filing his 2012 tax return, Jerry will claim a refund of $283, calculated as follows:

EI Premiums Withheld	$ 910	
2012 Maximum	(840)	$70
CPP Contributions Withheld	$2,520	
2012 Maximum	(2,307)	213
Refund		$283

Transfers To A Spouse Or Common-Law Partner - ITA 118.8

4-183.   In the preceding material, we have covered several tax credits that can be claimed by either spouse, such as the child fitness credit. There are also a number of tax credits that can usually be transferred to a spouse or common-law partner under ITA 118.8. They are:

- the child tax credit (see Paragraph 4-57)
- the age tax credit (see Paragraph 4-82),
- the pension income tax credit (see Paragraph 4-84),
- the disability tax credit (see Paragraph 4-144), and
- the current year tuition, education, and textbook tax credits to a maximum of $750 (see material beginning in Paragraph 4-171).

4-184.   The maximum amount that can be transferred is based on the sum of these credits, reduced by a modified calculation of the spouse or common-law partner's Tax Payable.   While the legislation is based on Tax Payable, the T1 tax return uses a simplified approach based on Taxable Income. This approach starts with the sum of the base for all of the preceding credits. From this amount is subtracted the spouse's taxable income, reduced by the bases of: the basic personal credit, CPP and EI credits, Canada employment credit, public transit credit, child fitness credit, children's arts credit, adoption expenses credit, first time home buyers' credit, volunteer firefighter credit and the tuition, education and textbook credits. The resulting remainder is the amount that can be transferred to a spouse or common-law partner.

Exercise Four - 18

Subject: Transfer Of Credits From A Spouse

Mr. Martin Levee is 68 years old and has Net Income For Tax Purposes of $42,000. Of this total, $24,000 was from a life annuity that he purchased with funds in his RRSP. His spouse is 66 years old, has no income of her own as she is ineligible for OAS, and is attending university on a full time basis. Her tuition fees for the year were $2,200 and she was in full time attendance for 4 months of the year. Determine Mr. Levee's maximum federal tax credits for 2012. Ignore the possibility of splitting his pension income with his spouse.

End of Exercise. Solution available in Study Guide.

Political Contributions Tax Credits - ITA 127(3)
Federal Accountability Act
4-185.   While no changes have been made in the *Income Tax Act*, the *Federal Accountability Act* limits the ability to make political contributions to individuals only. More specifically, this *Act* contains the following provisions:

- There is a total ban on contributions by corporations, trade unions and unincorporated associations.

- The amount that can be contributed annually by an individual:
    - to a registered party is limited to $1,100,
    - to a candidate or a leadership contestant is limited to $1,100, and
    - to a nomination contestant is limited to $1,100.

Income Tax Rules
4-186.   A federal tax credit is available on political contributions made to a registered federal political party, or to candidates at the time of a federal general election or by-election. The maximum value is $650 and it is available to both individuals and corporations. However, as discussed in the preceding Paragraph, the *Federal Accountability Act* totally bans contributions by corporations. The credit is calculated as follows:

	Contributions	Credit Rate	Tax Credit
First	$ 400	3/4	$300
Next	350	1/2	175
Next	525	1/3	175
Maximum Credit	$1,275		$650

4-187.   The $650 credit is achieved when contributions total $1,275. Contributions in excess of this amount do not generate additional credits. Also note that most provinces have a similar credit against provincial Tax Payable. There is a difference, however, in that the eligible contributions must be made to a registered provincial political party.

Exercise Four - 19

Subject: Political Contributions Tax Credit

Ms. Vivacia Unger contributes $785 to the Liberal New Conservative Democratic Party, a registered federal political party. Determine the amount of her federal political contributions tax credit.

End of Exercise. Solution available in Study Guide.

Labour Sponsored Funds Tax Credit - ITA 127.4

4-188.   The government wishes to encourage investment in small and medium sized enterprises. To that end, ITA 127.4 provides a credit for individuals investing in the shares of prescribed labour sponsored venture capital corporations.

4-189.   For purposes of this Section, these corporations must be set up under the appropriate legislation and managed by a labour organization. The assets of the corporation must be invested in small and medium sized businesses. In addition, under proposed legislation, the province in which the corporation is registered must provide a similar credit.

4-190.   The federal credit is based on 15 percent of the cost of the labour sponsored venture capital corporation shares purchased by the individual. To be eligible for the credit, the investor must be the first registered holder of the shares. In addition, the maximum credit for a year is $750. This limits the net cost of investments eligible for the credit to $5,000.

Exercise Four - 20

Subject: Labour Sponsored Funds Credit

On June 30, 2012, Mr. Brad Clintor purchases newly issued shares in a prescribed labour sponsored venture capital corporation at a cost of $3,000. The province in which Mr. Clintor lives provides a provincial tax credit for this investment. Determine the amount of the federal tax credit that will result from this purchase.

End of Exercise. Solution available in Study Guide.

Dividend Tax Credit

4-191.   The dividend tax credit is covered in Chapter 7 as part of our discussion of property income.

Foreign Tax Credits

4-192.   The credits that are available for taxes paid in foreign jurisdictions are covered in Chapters 7 and 11.

Investment Tax Credits

4-193.   When taxpayers make certain types of expenditures, they become eligible for investment tax credits. These credits reduce federal Tax Payable. While these credits can be claimed by individuals as well as corporations, they are much more commonly used by corporations and, as a consequence, we cover investment tax credits in Chapter 14.

Refundable Credits

Introduction

4-194.   With the exception of the refundable medical expense supplement, the credits that we have encountered to this point can be described as non-refundable. This means that, unless the taxpayer has Tax Payable for the current taxation year, there is no current benefit from the credit. Further, with the exception of the charitable donations credit and education related credits, there is no carry forward of these non-refundable credits to subsequent taxation years. This means that, if the credits are not used in the current year, they are permanently lost.

4-195.   In this section we will describe three refundable credits:

- the GST/HST tax credit;
- the working income tax benefit (WITB); and
- the Canada child tax benefit.

4-196.   With respect to the GST/HST credit and child tax benefit, our coverage will be limited. This reflects the fact that, unlike non-refundable credits, taxpayers do not calculate the eligible amount of these credits in their tax returns. Rather, the CRA calculates the credits from the tax returns that the taxpayer has filed in previous years and pays these amounts to the eligible taxpayers. Given this, there is no need to provide coverage of the detailed calculation of these credits.

Refundable GST/HST Credit - ITA 122.5

4-197.   One of the major problems with the goods and services tax (GST) is the fact that it is a regressive tax. In order to provide some relief from the impact of the GST on low income families, there is a refundable GST credit available under ITA 122.5.

4-198.   The GST credit is determined by the CRA on the basis of eligibility information supplied in the individual's tax returns for previous years. Because of this, it is only paid to individuals who file tax returns.

4-199.   For 2012, the system provides for a total credit that is calculated as follows:

- $260 for the "eligible individual". An eligible individual includes a Canadian resident who is 19 years of age or over during the current taxation year, or is married or living common-law, or is a parent who resides with their child. In the case of a married couple, only one spouse can be an eligible individual.

- $260 for a "qualified relation". A qualified relation is defined as a cohabiting spouse or common-law partner. If the eligible individual does not have a qualified relation, he is entitled to an additional credit that is the lesser of $137 and 2 percent of the individual's Net Income For Tax Purposes in excess of $8,439.

- $260 for a dependant eligible for the eligible dependant tax credit.

- $137 for each "qualified dependant". A "qualified dependant" is defined as a person who is the individual's child or is dependent on the individual or the individual's cohabiting spouse or common-law partner for support. In addition, the child or dependent person must be under 19 years of age, reside with the individual, have never had a spouse or common-law partner, and have never been a parent of a child he has resided with.

4-200.   The total of these amounts must be reduced by 5 percent of the excess of the individual's "adjusted income" over an indexed threshold amount. For 2012, this threshold amount is $33,884. "Adjusted Income" is defined as total income of the individual and his qualified relation, if any.

4-201.   The refundable GST credit is available to all eligible individuals, without regard to whether they have Tax Payable. The amount of the credit is calculated by the CRA on the basis of information included in the individual's tax return for a particular year, and the amounts are automatically paid to the taxpayer in subsequent years.

Working Income Tax Benefit - ITA 122.7
The Welfare Wall

4-202.   Despite the rantings of ostensibly virtuous individuals of a right-wing persuasion, many individuals who are receiving various types of social assistance are not necessarily lazy or lacking in motivation. The simple fact is that, given the types of wages such individuals receive, they are often better off economically if they do not work. The types of wages that such individuals can earn are typically at the legal "minimum" (e.g., $10.25 per hour in Ontario). The amounts earned at this wage are typically offset by reductions in social assistance payments. Additional negative effects flow from loss of subsidized housing, prescription drug assistance, and other benefits that flow to individuals with little or no income.

4-203.   It has been demonstrated that, if such individuals find employment, the result can be a reduction in their real income. Instead of rewarding their efforts, our current system can actually punish individuals who make an effort to improve their economic status. This is commonly referred to as the welfare wall.

Calculation Of The Basic Working Income Tax Benefit (WITB)

4-204.   To assist eligible working low income individuals, ITA 122.7 provides for a working income tax benefit (WITB). This refundable tax credit is available to "eligible" individuals who are 19 years of age or older and who were not full-time students for more than 13 weeks in the year, or in prison for 90 days or more during the year. Note that, if the individual has an eligible dependant, they qualify for the benefit, even if they are a full time student.

4-205.   The benefit is paid on the basis of working income. Working income is defined as gross employment income (i.e., no employment expenses deducted), business income, scholarships, and research grants. The amount of the benefit will depend on whether the individual is single or, alternatively, has a spouse or an eligible dependant. For this purpose, an eligible dependant is a child who lives with the individual and who is under the age of 19 at the end of the year. For 2012 the benefit is calculated as follows:

Single Individual   In this case, the benefit is equal to the lesser of:

- 25 percent of the individual's working income in excess of $3,000; and
- $970.

This means that the benefit reaches a maximum value of $970 when working income is $6,880 [$3,000 + ($970 ÷ 25%)]. The benefit remains at this level until working income reaches $11,011. The benefit is reduced by 15 percent of working income in excess of $11,011. It disappears completely when working income reaches $17,477.

Family (Eligible Spouse Or Eligible Dependant)   In this case, the benefit is equal to the lesser of:

- 25 percent of the family working income in excess of $3,000; and
- $1,762.

Family working income is the working income of the individual plus that of his spouse or common-law partner, but not that of an eligible dependant. The benefit reaches a maximum value of $1,762 when family working income is $10,048 [$3,000 + ($1,762 ÷ 25%)]. The benefit remains at this level until family working income reaches $15,205. The benefit is reduced by 15 percent of family working income in excess of $15,205. It disappears completely when family working income reaches $26,952.

WITB Disability Supplement

4-206.   For individuals qualifying for the disability tax credit, a WITB disability supplement is available. For a single individual, the amount is the lesser of $485 and 25 percent of working income in excess of $1,150. For details of the phase out of this benefit, we would refer you to the CRA web site.

Exercise Four - 21

Subject: Working Income Tax Benefit (WITB)

Both Angelina and her common-law partner are employed during 2012. Angelina is an eligible individual and her common-law partner is an eligible spouse for the purposes of the working income tax benefit. Angelina earns $13,000 (including tips) working at a restaurant while her partner earns $6,000 in a part-time sales position. Neither Angelina nor her partner is entitled to the disability tax credit for the year. Angelina makes a claim for the WITB for 2012. Determine the amount of her claim.

End of Exercise. Solution available in Study Guide

Canada Child Tax Benefit

Basic Amount

4-207. The Canada Child Tax Benefit is in the form of a non-taxable monthly payment. Similar to the refundable GST credit, the amount of this benefit is calculated by the CRA. The benefits are subject to indexation and are reduced if family net income for the preceding year is over a threshold amount. For 2012, the benefits are as follows:

- $1,405 per year (paid monthly) for each qualified dependant, basically a child who is under 18; and
- an additional $98 per year (paid monthly) for each dependant in excess of two.

4-208. This basic benefit is reduced when 2011 family net income reaches $42,707. The phase out rate is dependent on the number of children in the family.

National Child Benefit Supplement

4-209. In addition to the regular Child Tax Benefit, there is also a National Child Benefit Supplement. The amount of the supplement is $2,177 per year for the first child, $1,926 per year for the second, and $1,832 per year for the third and subsequent child. All of these benefits are paid monthly.

4-210. The benefit is reduced when 2011 family Net Income reaches $24,863. The phase out rate is dependent on the number of children in the family.

Universal Child Care Benefit

4-211. While this is not part of the child tax benefit system, we would note here that there is also a taxable Universal Child Care Benefit. This benefit is paid to the lower income spouse or common-law partner and is included in their Net Income For Tax Purposes (see Chapter 9).

Social Benefits Repayment (OAS And EI)

Basic Concepts

Clawbacks

4-212. Many Canadian tax credits and benefits are available on a universal basis, without regard to the income level of the recipient. However, both Old Age Security payments (OAS) and Employment Insurance payments (EI) are reduced for higher income individuals.

4-213. With respect to OAS payments, the government assesses a Part I.2 tax on OAS benefits received by individuals with an adjusted Net Income above a threshold amount. In similar fashion, the *Employment Insurance Act* requires that individuals with an adjusted Net Income above a specified threshold amount repay a portion of any Employment Insurance (EI) benefits received. These required repayments are commonly referred to as "clawbacks".

Treatment In Net And Taxable Income

4-214.   Both OAS payments received and EI payments received must be included in an individual's Net Income For Tax Purposes. However, in situations where all or part of these amounts must be repaid, it would not be appropriate to allow the full amounts received to flow through to Taxable Income and have an influence on Tax Payable.

4-215.   This problem is dealt with by providing a deduction for amounts repaid. You may recall from Chapter 1 that one of the components of Net Income For Tax Purposes was Other Deductions (subdivision e of the *Income Tax Act*). While we will not provide detailed coverage of this subdivision until Chapter 9, we need to note here that ITA 60(v.1) provides a deduction for repayments of EI, and ITA 60(w) provides a deduction for repayment of OAS amounts received.

4-216.   As both the EI and OAS repayments are calculated on the basis of the individual's income in excess of a threshold amount, the question arises as to whether these tests should be applied using income figures which include the full amount received or, alternatively, income figures from which the repayments have been deducted. The solution to this problem will be discussed in the two sections which follow.

Employment Insurance (EI) Benefits Clawback

4-217.   The *Employment Insurance Act* requires the partial repayment of benefits received if the recipient's threshold income is greater than $57,375 (1.25 times the 2012 maximum insurable earnings of $45,900). This $57,375 income figure includes all of the components of Net Income For Tax Purposes except the deductions for repayment of EI benefits [ITA 60(v.1)] and the deduction for the repayment of OAS benefits [ITA 60(w)]. As the EI clawback is deducted from the threshold income used for determining the OAS clawback, the EI clawback must be determined prior to calculating the amount of the OAS clawback.

4-218.   Once the amount of threshold income over $57,375 is determined, it must be compared to the EI benefits included in the current year's Net Income For Tax Purposes. The lesser of these two amounts is multiplied by 30 percent and this becomes the amount that must be repaid for the year as a social benefits repayment. This amount can then be deducted under ITA 60(v.1) in the determination of Net Income For Tax Purposes for the year.

Old Age Security (OAS) Benefits Clawback

4-219.   The OAS clawback is the lesser of the OAS payments included in income and 15 percent of the taxpayer's income in excess of the $69,562 income threshold. For this purpose, income is equal to Net Income For Tax Purposes computed after any EI clawback, but before consideration of the deduction for the OAS clawback.

4-220.   For the second quarter of 2012, the OAS benefit is $540.12 per month. If this rate did not change during the year, the 2012 total would be $6,481.44. Based on this figure, the benefit would disappear at an income level of $112,772.

4-221.   For higher income seniors, OAS benefits are clawed back on a regular basis, with some individuals receiving no benefits under this program during their lifetime. Given this, the government has an administrative procedure under which they withhold payments that they expect to be clawed back. Expectations are based on tax returns filed in the two previous years.

Example   In her tax returns for both 2010 and 2011, Sally Leung has reported Taxable Income in excess of $200,000 per year.   Despite the fact that Sally is 70 years of age, she would receive no OAS payments in 2012.

4-222.   Interestingly, once an individual has applied for OAS, the government will issue an information slip [T4A(OAS)] indicating that they have received the full benefit, even in cases where no OAS was paid and the full amount has been withheld. The information slip will show any amount that is clawed back. This means the full benefit must be included in income, accompanied by a deduction for the amount "repaid". For an individual who reaches age 65 with the expectation that they will have very high income for the foreseeable future, this process can be avoided by not applying for OAS.

Exercise Four - 22

Subject: EI and OAS Clawbacks

For 2012, Ms. Marilyn Jacobi has net employment income of $60,000, receives EI payments of $10,000, and receives $6,500 in Old Age Security (OAS) payments. No amount was withheld from the OAS payments because she had very low income in the previous two years due to large rental losses. Determine Ms. Jacobi's Net Income For Tax Purposes for 2012.

End of Exercise. Solution available in Study Guide.

Comprehensive Example

4-223.   While this Chapter has provided a reasonably detailed description of the determination of Tax Payable for individuals, including small examples of some of the issues that arise in this process, a more comprehensive example is appropriate at this point. To simplify calculations, we have ignored provincial income taxes and income tax withholdings on employment income. In the separate paper Study Guide, there is an additional example containing a completed tax return, as well as a Tax Software Self Study Problem, both of which include provincial income taxes.

Basic Data

Mr. Thomas Baxter is 66 years of age and his 2012 income is made up of net employment income of $73,800 and Old Age Security benefits of $6,500 (because of large business losses during the previous two years, no amount was withheld from these payments). For 2012, Mr. Baxter's employer withheld maximum CPP and EI contributions. Other information pertaining to 2012 is as follows:

1. Mr. Baxter's spouse is 49 years old and qualifies for the disability tax credit. Her only income for the year is $5,000 in Canadian source interest. The investment funds were inherited from her father at the time of his death.

2. Mr. and Mrs. Baxter have two daughters and, at the end of the year, their ages were 14 and 17. Kim, the younger daughter, has income of $2,700, none of which was employment income. Lori, the older daughter, had net income of $2,000, none of which was employment income. In September, 2012, Lori began full time attendance at a Canadian university. Mr. Baxter paid her tuition fees of $5,000, of which $2,500 was for the fall, 2012 semester.

3. The family medical expenses for the year, all of which were paid by Mr. Baxter, totalled $2,843. Of this amount, $900 was paid for Lori.

4. During the year, Mr. Baxter made cash donations to registered Canadian charities in the amount of $3,000.

5. During the year, Mr. Baxter made contributions to federal political parties totalling $800.

6. During the year, Mr. Baxter paid $960 for monthly public transit passes.

7. Because of an ongoing problem with her weight, Mr. Baxter enrolled his daughter, Kim, in an eligible fitness program. The annual cost of this program is $1,800.

Net And Taxable Income

Net Employment Income	$73,800
OAS Benefits	6,500
Net Income Before Clawback	$80,300
OAS Clawback (Note One)	(1,611)
Net Income For Tax Purposes And Taxable Income	$78,689

Note One   The required repayment of OAS is the lesser of:

- $6,500, the OAS payments included in income, and
- $1,611 [(15%)($80,300 - $69,562)].

Tax Payable/Federal Balance Owing

Federal Tax On First $42,707			$ 6,406
Federal Tax On Next $35,982 ($78,689 - $42,707) At 22 Percent			7,916
Gross Tax			$14,322
Tax Credits:			
Basic Personal Amount	($10,822)		
Spousal ($10,822 - $5,000)	(5,822)		
Child - Kim	(2,191)		
Child - Lori	(2,191)		
Age (Note Two)	Nil		
Public Transit Passes	(960)		
Child Fitness (Note Three)	(500)		
Medical Expenses (Note Four)	(734)		
Mrs. Baxter's Disability Transferred	(7,546)		
Lori's Tuition, Education, And Textbook Transferred (Note Five)	(4,360)		
EI Premiums (Maximum)	(840)		
CPP Contributions (Maximum)	(2,307)		
Canada Employment	(1,095)		
Total	($39,368)		
Rate	15%		(5,905)
Charitable Donations {[(15%)($200)] + [(29%)($3,000 - $200)]}			(842)
Political Contributions Tax Credit - Lesser Of:			
• $650 (Maximum)			
• [($400)(3/4) + ($350)(1/2) + ($50)(1/3)] = $492			(492)
Federal Tax Payable			$ 7,083
Social Benefits Repayment (Note One)			1,611
Federal Balance Owing			$ 8,694

Note Two   Mr. Baxter's age credit would be calculated as follows:

Full Base Amount		$6,720
Reduction - Lesser Of:		
• [(15%)($78,689 - $33,884)] = $6,721		
• Full Base Amount = $6,720		(6,720)
Age Credit		Nil

Note Three   While Mr. Baxter paid $1,800 for this program, the maximum credit base is $500.

Note Four   Medical expenses eligible for the credit are the lesser of $734 (the actual expenditures of $2,843, less the maximum of $2,109) and $2,361 (3 percent of Mr. Baxter's Net Income of $78,689). Since both daughters are under 18 at the end of the year, their expenses can be aggregated with those of Mr. Baxter for the purposes of this calculation.

Note Five   Lori's total education related amount is calculated as follows:

Tuition For 2012 Semester ($5,000 - $2,500)	$2,500
Education (Four Months At $400)	1,600
Textbook (Four Months At $65)	260
Total Amount Available For Transfer Or Carry Forward	$4,360

Since Lori has no Tax Payable before consideration of her education related credits, the solution assumes that they are all transferred to her supporting parent as they total less than the $5,000 transfer limit. Alternatively, she could choose to carry forward these credits to apply against her own Tax Payable in a subsequent year.

Key Terms Used In This Chapter

4-224.   The following is a list of the key terms used in this Chapter. These terms, and their meanings, are compiled in the Glossary Of Key Terms located at the back of the separate paper Study Guide.

Adoption Expenses Tax Credit	Infirm Dependant Over 17 Tax Credit
Age Tax Credit	Labour Sponsored Funds Tax Credit
Canada Employment Credit	Medical Expense Tax Credit
Canada Pension Plan (CPP)	Non-Refundable Tax Credit
Canada Pension Plan Tax Credit	Northern Residents Deductions
Caregiver Tax Credit	OAS Clawback
Charitable Donations Tax Credit	Old Age Security (OAS) Benefits
Charitable Gifts	Pension Income Tax Credit
Child Tax Benefit	Personal Tax Credits
Child Tax Credit	Political Contributions Tax Credit
Child Fitness Tax Credit	Progressive Tax System
Children's Arts Tax Credit	Public Transit Pass Tax Credit
Clawback	Refundable Medical Expense Supplement
Common-Law Partner	Refundable Tax Credit
Dependant	Regressive Tax System
Disability Tax Credit	Social Benefits Repayment
Disability Tax Credit Supplement	Spousal Tax Credit
Education Tax Credit	Spouse
Eligible Dependant Tax Credit	Student Loan Interest Tax Credit
Employment Insurance (EI)	Tax Credit
Employment Insurance Tax Credit	Taxable Income
Family Caregiver Tax Credit	Textbook Tax Credit
First Time Home Buyer's Tax Credit	Tuition Fees Tax Credit
GST Tax Credit	Volunteer Firefighters Tax Credit
Home Relocation Loan	Wholly Dependent Person
Indexation	Working Income Tax Benefit

References

4-225.   For more detailed study of the material in this Chapter, we would refer you to:

ITA 110	Deductions Permitted
ITA 111.1	Order Of Applying Provisions
ITA 117	Tax Payable Under This Part
ITA 117.1	Annual Adjustment
ITA 118(1)	Personal Credits
ITA 118(2)	Age Credit
ITA 118(3)	Pension Credit
ITA 118(10)	Canada Employment Credit
ITA 118.01	Adoption Expense Credit
ITA 118.02	Public Transit Pass Credit
ITA 118.03	Child Fitness Credit
ITA 118.031	Children's Arts Tax Credit (Proposed)
ITA 118.05	First-Time Home Buyers' Credit
ITA 118.06	Volunteer Firefighters Tax Credit (Proposed)
ITA 118.1	Definitions (Charitable Gifts)
ITA 118.2	Medical Expense Credit
ITA 118.3	Credit For Mental Or Physical Impairment
ITA 118.5	Tuition And Other Education Related Credits
ITA 118.6	Education Credit And Textbook Credit
ITA 118.61	Unused Tuition And Education Tax Credits
ITA 118.62	Credit For Interest On Student Loan
ITA 118.7	Credit for EI and QPIP premiums and CPP contributions
ITA 118.8	Transfer Of Unused Credits To Spouse Or Common-Law Partner
ITA 118.81	Tuition, Textbook, And Education Tax Credits Transferred
ITA 118.9	Transfer To Parent Or Grandparent
ITA 122.5	Definitions (GST Credit)
ITA 122.51	Definitions (Refundable Medical Expense Supplement
ITA 122.6-6.4	Canada Child Tax Benefit
ITA 122.7	Working Income Tax Benefit
ITA 127(3)	Federal Political Contributions Tax Credit
ITA 127.4	Labour Sponsored Funds Tax Credit
ITA 180.2	OAS Clawback
ITR 5700	Prescribed Device Or Equipment
ITR 9400	Prescribed Program Of Physical Activity
IC 75-2R8	Contributions To A Registered Political Party Or To A Candidate At A Federal Election
IC 75-23	Tuition Fees And Charitable Donations Paid To Privately Supported Secular and Religious Schools
IC 84-3R6	Gifts To Certain Organizations Outside Canada
IT-110R3	Gifts And Official Donation Receipts
IT-113R4	Benefits To Employees — Stock Options
IT-226R	Gift To A Charity Of A Residual Interest In Real Property Or An Equitable Interest In A Trust
IT-244R3	Gifts By Individuals Of Life Insurance Policies As Charitable Donations
IT-407R4	Dispositions Of Cultural Property To Designated Canadian Institutions (Consolidated)
IT-513R	Personal Tax Credits
IT-515R2	Education Tax Credit
IT-516R2	Tuition Tax Credit
IT-519R2	Medical Expense And Disability Tax Credits And Attendant Care Expense Deduction (Consolidated)
IT-523	Order Of Provisions Applicable In Computing An Individual's Taxable Income And Tax Payable

Sample Tax Return For Chapter 4

The Sample Tax Return for Chapter 4 can be found in the Study Guide beginning on page S-48.

Problems For Self Study

(The solutions for these problems can be found in the separate Study Guide.)

NOTE   The **Tax Software Self Study Problem** for Chapter 4 is available in the separate Study Guide.

Self Study Problem Four - 1 (Individual Tax Payable - 5 Cases)

Ms. Wanda Sykes is 42 years old. The following five independent Cases make varying assumptions for the 2012 taxation year with respect to Ms. Sykes' marital status, number of dependants, and type of income. In all Cases, Ms. Syke had Net Income For Tax Purposes of $78,000.

Case A   Ms. Sykes is a single mother. She has a son, John, who is 10 years old and lives with her. John had no income. During 2012, Ms. Sykes attends university for 10 months of the year on a part time basis. Her tuition fees total $5,640. All of Ms. Sykes' income is from spousal support payments.

Case B   Ms. Sykes is not married and has no dependants. All of her income is from employment. In December, she wins $2,000,000 in the provincial lottery. She donates $150,000 of this amount to the church where she prayed for a winning lottery ticket. She plans to claim $35,000 of this donation for a tax credit in 2012.

Case C   Ms. Sykes is married and her husband, Buff has Net Income For Tax Purposes of $7,600. All of her income is from investments. They have one child, Martin. He is 10 years old, has no income of his own, and qualifies for the disability tax credit. Buff's 73 year old father, Harry, lives with them. His Net Income For Tax Purposes was $17,600. He is not mentally or physically infirm.

Case D   Ms. Sykes is married and her husband, Buff has Net Income For Tax Purposes of $2,540. All of her income is employment income. Wanda and Buff have two children, Janice who is 10 years of age, and Mark who is 20 years of age. Both children are in good health. As Mark has been unable to find full-time employment, he still lives at home. While Mark had Net Income For Tax Purposes of $2,460 from part-time employment, Janice had no income during the year. During 2012 Ms. Sykes paid for the following medical expenses:

Ms. Sykes	$ 2,100
Buff	360
Janice	3,645
Mark	4,520
Total	$10,625

Case E   Ms. Sykes is married and her husband, Buff is 66 years old. All of her income is from employment. Wanda and Buff have two children, a son aged 12 and a daughter aged 14. Both children are in good health and have no income of their own. Buff is disabled and qualifies for the disability tax credit. His only income is $9,600 in pension income from his former employer as he is not eligible for OAS. He attends university on a full time basis for 8 months of the year and his tuition costs for 2012 are $8,450.

Required: In each Case, calculate Ms. Sykes' minimum federal Tax Payable for 2012. Indicate any carry forwards available to her and her dependants and the carry forward provisions. Ignore any tax amounts that Ms. Sykes might have had withheld or paid in instalments.

Self Study Problem Four - 2 (Individual Tax Payable - Simple)

Mr. Dennis Lane has been a widower for several years. For 2012, both his Net Income For Tax Purposes and Taxable Income were equal to his net employment income of $70,000. Mr. Lane's employer withheld $10,100 in federal income taxes, $840 for Employment Insurance premiums and $2,342 in Canada Pension Plan contributions. Because of an error by his employer, an overcontribution of $35 was made for the Canada Pension Plan.

Other Information:

1. Mr. Lane made political contributions to federal political parties in the amount of $450.

2. Mr. Lane has three children, aged 10, 12, and 15. They all live with him in his principal residence and, other than his 15 year old son, have no income of their own. Mr. Lane paid no medical expenses other than $4,400 for hospital care for his 15 year old son. His son had 2012 Net Income For Tax Purposes of $8,200.

3. Mr. Lane buys public transit passes for his oldest son and himself. The monthly cost of these passes is $75 for each individual. Because of a family vacation, no passes were purchased in the month of July.

4. His two younger children are enrolled in an eligible fitness program. The annual cost for each child is $425.

Required: Calculate Mr. Lane's federal tax payable (refund) for 2012.

Self Study Problem Four - 3 (Individual Tax Payable - 7 Cases)

The following seven independent Cases make varying assumptions with respect to Stanley Murphy and his 2012 tax status. In all Cases, where Stanley earned employment income, his employer withheld the maximum EI premium and CPP contribution.

Case A   Stanley Murphy is 48 years of age and has employment income of $55,000. During the year, Stanley makes contributions to federal political parties in the amount of $1,000. Stanley is not married and has no dependants.

Case B   Stanley Murphy is 48 years of age and has income from employment of $55,000. His wife, Helen, is 43 years of age and has Net Income For Tax Purposes of $4,650. They have one child, Eileen, who is 11 years of age and has income of $3,000. During the year, the family had eligible medical expenses of $1,050 for Stanley, $1,800 for Helen, and $300 for Eileen.

Case C   Stanley Murphy is 48 years old and his wife, Helen, is 43. Stanley has rental income of $55,000 and Helen has investment income of $9,400. They have a 19 year disabled son, Albert, who lives with them. His disability qualifies him for the disability tax credit and he has no income of his own. During the year, Stanley and Helen have medical expenses of $1,250. Medical expenses for Albert during the year total $8,350.

Case D   Stanley Murphy is 48 years of age and his wife, Helen, is 43. Stanley has income from employment of $55,000. Helen has employment income of $12,000. Helen's 68 year old father, Ahmed, and her 70 year old aunt, Jaleh, live with them. Both are in good health. Ahmed's Net Income For Tax Purposes is $9,200 and Jaleh's Net Income For Tax Purposes is $11,000. Stanley paid $375 in interest related to his student loan during the year.

Case E   Stanley Murphy is 48 years of age and his common-law partner Bob is 43. Stanley has employment income of $55,000. Bob has Net Income For Tax Purposes of $4,500. They have two adopted children, Barry aged 7 and Don aged 9. After living in rented premises for the last 7 years, Stanley and Bob decide to purchase a residence. They acquire a 3 bedroom house in the suburbs at a cost of $245,000 and move into the house during the year.

Case F Stanley Murphy is 48 years of age and his wife, Helen, is 43. Stanley has income from employment of $55,000. Helen has Net Income For Tax Purposes of $5,050. They have a son, Albert, who is 19 years old and lives at home. He attends university on a full time basis during 8 months of the year. Stanley pays $5,400 for Albert's tuition for two semesters during the 2012 calendar year and $525 for required textbooks. Albert had employment income of $3,000 that he earned during the summer. He will transfer any unused credits to his father.

Case G Stanley Murphy is 67 and his wife Helen is 68. Helen has been completely disabled for a number of years and the extent of her disability qualifies her for the disability tax credit. The components of Stanley and Helen's income are as follows:

	Stanley	Helen
Interest	$ 300	$ 50
Canada Pension Plan Benefits	4,400	200
Old Age Security Benefits	6,500	6,500
Income From Registered Pension Plan	31,150	450
Total Net Income	$42,350	$7,200

Required: In each Case, calculate Stanley Murphy's minimum federal Tax Payable for 2012. Indicate any carry forwards available to him and his dependants and the carry forward provisions. Ignore any amounts Stanley might have had withheld or paid in instalments and the possibility of pension splitting.

Self Study Problem Four - 4 (Tax Payable With Employment Income)
Extension of Self Study Problem Three-7

Mr. John Barth has been employed for many years as a graphic illustrator in Kamloops, British Columbia. His employer is a large publicly traded Canadian company. During 2012, his gross salary was $82,500. In addition, he was awarded a $20,000 bonus to reflect his outstanding performance during the year. As he was in no immediate need of additional income, he arranged with his employer that none of this bonus would be paid until 2017, the year of his expected retirement.

Other Information:
For the 2012 taxation year, the following items were relevant.

1. Mr. Barth's employer withheld the following amounts from his income:

Federal Income Tax	$16,000
Employment Insurance Premiums	840
Canada Pension Plan Contributions	2,307
United Way Donations	2,000
Registered Pension Plan Contributions	3,200
Payments For Personal Use Of Company Car	3,600

2. During the year, Mr. Barth is provided with an automobile owned by his employer. The cost of the automobile was $47,500. Mr. Barth drove the car a total of 10,000 kilometers during the year, of which only 4,000 kilometers were related to the business of his employer. The automobile was used by Mr. Barth for ten months of the year. During the other two months, he was out of the country and left the automobile with one of the other employees of the corporation.

3. During the year, the corporation paid Mega Financial Planners a total of $1,500 for providing counseling services to Mr. Barth with respect to his personal financial situation.

4. In order to assist Mr. Barth in purchasing a ski chalet, the corporation provided him with a five year loan of $150,000. The loan was granted on October 1 at an interest rate of 1 percent. Mr. Barth paid the corporation a total of $375 in interest for the year on January

20, 2013. Assume that, at the time the loan was granted and throughout the remainder of the year, the relevant prescribed rate was 2 percent.

5.   Mr. Barth was required to pay professional dues of $1,800 during the year.

6.   On June 6, 2012, when Mr. Barth exercised his stock options to buy 1,000 shares of his employer's common stock at a price of $15 per share, the shares were trading at $18 per share. When the options were issued, the shares were trading at $12 per share. During December, 2012, the shares were sold at $18 per share.

7.   Mr. Barth lives with his wife, Lynda. Lynda is blind and qualifies for the disability tax credit. She has Net Income For Tax Purposes of $1,250.

8.   His 22 year old dependent daughter, Marg, is a full time student at the University of British Columbia for 8 months of the year. She lives in Vancouver and has Net Income For Tax Purposes and Taxable Income of $13,400. She had withheld from her employment income EI premiums of $245 [(1.83%)($13,400)] and CPP contributions of $490 [(4.95%)($13,400 - $3,500)]. Mr. Barth paid Marg's tuition for 2012 of $6,300. She has agreed to transfer the maximum credit available to her father.

9.   Mr. Barth paid the following medical costs:

For Himself	$ 200
For His Wife	3,550
For Marg	720
Total	$4,470

Required: Calculate, for the 2012 taxation year:

A.   Marg's minimum federal Tax Payable and any carry forward amounts available to her at the end of the year.

B.   Mr. Barth's minimum Taxable Income and federal Tax Payable (Refund).

Self Study Problem Four - 5 (Tax Payable With Multiple Credits)

Ms. Eleanor Victoria's husband died two years ago. After her husband died, she moved from her house in Prince George, B.C., to a rented house in Victoria, B.C.

Ms. Victoria's widowed mother, Marjorie Toshiro, lives with Ms. Victoria and takes care of the house, Ms. Victoria's younger daughter, Amy, and all of the household cooking. In addition to OAS benefits, Marjorie has a small income from her deceased husband's life insurance policy. She has never filed a tax return and she is not infirm.

Diane Victoria, Eleanor's older daughter, is studying psychology at McGill University in Montreal. Her field is addiction research with a special emphasis on gambling. She does volunteer work at a gambling addiction treatment centre in Montreal in the summers. As Eleanor has paid for her tuition and living costs, Diane has agreed that any credits available should be transferred to her mother.

Diane has decided not to file a tax return this year as she is too busy with her studies and volunteer work. Her income was earned driving for a client of the addiction treatment centre who had lost his licence after being charged with impaired driving.

Other information concerning Ms. Victoria for 2012 is as follows:

1.   Eleanor was born on May 15, 1964.

2.   The birth dates and Net Income For Tax Purposes for the year of her dependants are as follows:

	Birth Date (Y/M/D)	Net Income
Diane	1992-05-14	$2,300
Amy	2000-10-11	Nil
Marjorie	1931-05-21	$8,000

3. Eleanor's T4 for 2012 showed the following:

Salary	$60,202
Employee's EI Premiums	840
Employee's CPP Contributions	2,307
RPP Contributions	2,406
Pension Adjustment	7,829
Union Dues	749
Charitable Donations	175
Income Tax Withheld	Assume Nil

4. Eleanor and her family had the following medical expenses for 2012, all of which Eleanor paid for:

Patient	Medical Expenses	Description	Amount
Eleanor	Grace Hospital	Ambulance Charge	$ 392
Eleanor	Paramed Home Health	Nursing Care	1,350
Marjorie	Dr. Zhang (Optometrist)	Contact Lenses	110
Marjorie	Pharmacy	Prescription	75
Diane	Dr. Glassman	Physiotherapist	100
Amy	Walk Right Foot Clinic	Orthotics	450
Amy	Dr. Tamo	Dental	1,120
Total			$3,597

5. In addition to the $175 in charitable contributions withheld by Eleanor's employer, Eleanor and Diane had the following charitable donations for 2012:

Donor	Charitable Donation Receipts	Amount
Eleanor	Heart And Stroke	$ 375
Eleanor	Terry Fox Foundation	50
Diane	Addiction Research Council Of Canada	100

6. During 2012, Diane was in university full time for 8 months and part time for an additional 2 months. Her tuition fees for the year were $7,000.

Required: Calculate Eleanor's minimum federal Tax Payable. List any assumptions you have made, and any notes and tax planning issues you feel should be discussed with Eleanor.

Self Study Problem Four - 6
(Comprehensive Tax Payable With Employment Income)

Mr. Lance Strong is a skilled carpenter who is employed by a large public company. For 2012, his annual salary is $72,000. He is required to pay for his own tools, but is reimbursed for out-of-pocket travel costs when he is required to work away from his employer's municipality for more than 12 hours.

During 2012, Mr. Strong's employer withheld the following amounts from his compensation:

EI Premiums	$ 840
CPP Contributions	2,307
RPP Contributions	4,200
Contributions To Disability Plan (Employer Makes Matching Contribution)*	430

*This plan provides periodic benefits that are designed to compensate for lost employment income.

Mr. Strong is married and has two children aged 14 and 16. Neither child has any income during 2012. His spouse has 2012 income of $5,600. Mr. Strong's 67 year old mother lives with the family. Her Net Income For Tax Purposes of $7,000 consists of OAS payments and investment income. She is not mentally or physically infirm.

Other Information:

1. Mr. Strong is provided with an automobile by his employer. During 2012, it is driven 32,000 kilometres, of which only 15,000 are employment related. The automobile is leased by the employer at a monthly rate of $565, including HST of $65. The monthly rate also includes a payment for insurance of $40 per month. The automobile was used by Mr. Strong for 10 months during 2012. During the two that he did not use the automobile, he was required to return it to his employer's garage.

2. During 2012, Mr. Strong was required to buy $1,800 in carpentry tools in order to carry out his employment duties.

3. Mr. Strong's employer encourages its employees to take university courses by paying their tuition fees. During 8 months of 2012, Mr. Strong was in part time attendance for two university courses. The first course was devoted to 16th century liturgical chants and the second was a course in spoken French. The tuition for each course was $600, with the employer paying the full amount. The employer was particularly interested in the French course as it would allow Mr. Strong to deal more effectively with francophone clients.

4. Mr. Strong incurred $4,600 in travel costs during 2012, all of which were reimbursed by his employer.

5. During 2012, Mr. Strong sold his house and purchased a heritage home 50 kilometres closer to his employer's main office. To assist with the relocation, on April 1, 2012, his employer provided an interest free loan of $150,000. It must be repaid in full on April 1, 2017. Assume that during the first two quarters of 2012 the prescribed rate was 2 percent and that during the last two quarters it declined to 1 percent.

6. During 2012, Mr. Strong pays for the following eligible medical costs:

For Himself	$1,250
For His Spouse	2,300
For His Two Children	850
For His Mother	1,960
Total Medical Costs	$6,360

7. During 2012, Mr. Strong gives cash of $1,200 to his church. He also donates carpenter services with a market value of $1,500.

8. Mr. Strong buys monthly transit passes for both of his children during the school year. The cost is $60 per month per child. The passes covered 10 months during 2012.

Required:

A. Determine Mr. Strong's minimum Net Income For Tax Purposes for the 2012 taxation year.

B. Determine Mr. Strong's minimum Taxable Income for the 2012 taxation year.

C. Based on your answer in Part B, determine Mr. Strong's federal Tax Payable for the 2012 taxation year. Ignore any amounts that might have been withheld by his employer or paid in instalments.

Self Study Problem Four - 7
(Comprehensive Tax Payable With Employment Income)

Mr. Andrew Bosworth is married and has two children. His 19 year old son attends a local university and lives at home. His tuition for the 8 months of attendance during 2012 was $7,650. His father paid the tuition and, in addition, paid $560 in ancillary fees and $425 for textbooks. The ancillary fees were charged to all students attending the university. The son had 2012 Net Income For Tax Purposes of $12,450 resulting from investments he inherited from his grandfather. The son's only tax credit is the basic personal credit for single persons. He has agreed to transfer any unused education related credits to his father.

Mr. Bosworth's daughter is 12 years old and has been blind since birth. As Mr. Bosworth's spouse is responsible for her care, she has not taken a full-time position of employment. However, she has Net Income For Tax Purposes of $6,450 resulting from part-time employment.

Mr. Bosworth works for a publicly traded company. During 2012, his base salary was $180,000. In addition, he received commissions totaling $11,500 and a bonus of $38,000. None of the bonus will be paid until January, 2013.

During 2012, his employer withholds the following amounts from his salary:

Registered Pension Plan Contributions	$5,200
EI Premiums	840
CPP Contributions	2,307
Contributions To The Local United Way	2,400
Life Insurance Premiums (The Employer Makes A Matching Contribution)	460

Other Information

1. Mr. Bosworth's employer provides him with an automobile that is leased for $925 per month, including a $75 per month payment for insurance. During 2012, the automobile is driven a total of 62,000 kilometers, of which 41,000 involve employment related activities. Mr. Bosworth paid all of the $10,300 in 2012 operating costs and is not reimbursed by his employer. The automobile was used by Mr. Bosworth throughout 2012.

2. In 2009, Mr. Bosworth received options to acquire 5,000 shares of his employer's common stock at a price of $9.75 per share. This was the market price of the shares at the time the options were granted. On July 1, 2012, when the shares were trading at $12.35, Mr. Bosworth exercises all of these options. He is still holding the acquired shares at the end of the current year.

3. Mr. Bosworth is not reimbursed for advertising, entertainment or travel costs. In addition to the operating costs for his vehicle, he paid for the following employment related costs:

Meals While Traveling	$ 6,420
Hotels	10,350
Advertising	12,400
Entertainment	6,500
Total	$35,670

4. Mr. Bosworth's employer provides all employees with a luxury weekend at a local resort. The cost of the gift is $2,500 for each employee.

5. Mr. Bosworth enrolls both of his children in fitness programs. The cost for his son is $450 for the year. For his daughter the cost is $400 for the year.

6. Mr. Bosworth pays for the following medical expenses during 2012:

For Andrew	$ 1,200
For His Spouse	2,250
For His Son	2,340
For His Daughter	11,250
Total	**$17,040**

7. Because of his ongoing interest in Elizabethan drama, Mr. Bosworth enrolls in a course on Shakespeare's tragedies at the local university. His tuition for this part-time attendance was $1,670 and his required textbooks cost $165. The duration of the course was 4 months.

Required:

A. Determine Mr. Bosworth's minimum Net Income For Tax Purposes for the 2012 taxation year.

B. Determine Mr. Bosworth's minimum Taxable Income for the 2012 taxation year.

C. Based on your answer in Part B, determine Mr. Bosworth's federal Tax Payable for the 2012 taxation year. Ignore any amounts that might have been withheld by his employer, any amount paid in instalments, as well as any considerations related to HST, GST, or PST.

Assignment Problems

(The solutions for these problems are only available in
the solutions manual that has been provided to your instructor.)

Assignment Problem Four - 1 (Personal Tax Credits - 5 Cases)

In each of the following independent Cases, determine the maximum amount of 2012 personal tax credits, including transfers from a spouse or dependant, that can be applied against federal Tax Payable by the taxpayer.

A calculation of Tax Payable is not required, only the applicable credits.

1. Jack Brown has Net Income For Tax Purposes of $97,000, all of which is employment income. He is married to Janice Brown whose Net Income For Tax Purposes is $7,250. They have three children aged 7, 9, and 11. All of the children are in good health. None of them have income of their own.

2. Marion Barkin was divorced from her husband several years ago. She has custody of their three children, ages 9, 12, and 15. Her Net Income For Tax Purposes consists of spousal support payments totaling $48,000 per year. The children are all in good health. The oldest child has Net Income For Tax Purposes of $9,500 during the year.

3. John Appleton has Net Income For Tax Purposes of $86,500, none of which is employment income or income from self-employment. His spouse has Net Income For Tax Purposes of $5,650. Their daughter is 15 years old, lives with them, and has Net Income For Tax Purposes of $1,550. Their son is 22 years old and, because of a physical disability, continues to live with them. He has no income of his own. His disability is not severe enough to qualify for the disability tax credit.

4. Sarah Pale is 67 years old and has Net Income For Tax Purposes of $52,500. This total is made up of OAS payments and pension income from her former employer. Her husband is 62 years old and has Net Income For Tax Purposes of $4,840. Ignore the possibility of splitting Sarah's pension income.

5. Martin Land has Net Income For Tax Purposes of $126,420, all of which is rental income. His wife has no income of her own. They have three children, ages 14, 16, and 19. All of these children are in good health and continue to live at home. The 19 year old child has Net Income For Tax Purposes of $7,240. During the current year, Mr. Land pays the following medical expenses:

Himself	$ 2,450
His Spouse	3,240
14 Year Old Child	2,620
16 Year Old Child	1,450
19 Year Old Child	4,560
Total	$14,320

Assignment Problem Four - 2 (Individual Tax Payable - 7 Cases)

There are seven independent cases which follow. Each case involves various assumptions as to the amount and type of income earned by Mr. Bob Barnes during 2012, as well as to other information that is relevant to the determination of his 2012 Tax Payable. In those cases where we have assumed that the income was from employment, the employer withheld the maximum EI premium and CPP contribution.

Case 1   Bob Barnes is 52 years old, has employment income of $75,000, and makes contributions of $4,500 to registered charities. He is not married and has no dependants.

Case 2   Bob Barnes is 58 years old and has employment income of $75,000. His common-law partner is 53 years old and has income of $6,480. They have an adopted child who is 19 years old and lives at home. Bob and his partner have medical expenses of $4,300. Medical expenses for the son total $5,600. The son has Net Income For Tax Purposes of $4,200.

Case 3   Bob Barnes is 58 years old and has income from investments of $95,000. He is divorced and has been awarded custody of his 21 year disabled son. The son quali- fies for the disability tax credit. He has Net Income For Tax Purposes of $8,000, and is dependent on his father for support. Bob paid $900 for a 3 month art appreciation course for his son, as well as $1,500 for a 6 month fitness program.

Case 4   Bob and his wife Barbra are both 67 years of age. Barbra is sufficiently disabled that she qualifies for the disability tax credit. The components of the 2012 income earned by Bob and Barbra are as follows:

	Bob	Barbra
Interest	$ 750	$ 750
Canada Pension Plan Benefits	8,600	Nil
Old Age Security Benefits	6,500	6,500
Income From Registered Pension Plan	34,500	1,450
Total Net Income	$50,350	$8,700

Case 5   Bob Barnes is 46 years old and has employment income of $142,000. His wife Barbra is 41 years old and has Net Income For Tax Purposes of $8,400. They have a 20 year old son who lives at home. He is dependent because of a physical infirmity. However, he is able to attend university on a full time basis for 8 months during 2012. Bob pays his tuition fees of $7,900, as well as $725 for the textbooks that he requires in his program. The son has Net Income For Tax Purposes of $10,000.

Case 6 Bob Barnes is 43 years old and has rental income of $95,000. His wife died last year. He has two children. Martin is 15 and is physically infirm, but not sufficiently to qualify for the disability tax credit. He has income from part time work as a graphic artist of $12,250. The other child, Sarah, is 12 and is in good health. She has no income of her own.

Case 7 Bob Barnes is 45 years old and has employment income of $75,000. His wife Barbra is 37 years old and has Net Income For Tax Purposes of $4,600. They have no children. However, they provide in home care for Barbra's father who is 66 years old, dependent because of a physical infirmity and has no income of his own. Also living with them is Bob's 67 year old father. He is in good physical and mental health and has Net Income For Tax Purposes of $18,300.

Required: In each Case, calculate Bob Barnes' minimum federal Tax Payable for 2012. Indicate any carry forwards available to him and his dependants and the carry forward provisions. Ignore any amounts Bob might have had withheld or paid in instalments and the possibility of pension splitting.

Assignment Problem Four - 3 *(Individual Tax Payable - 5 Cases)*

Mr. William Norris is 45 years old. The following five independent Cases make varying assumptions for the 2012 taxation year with respect to Mr. Norris' marital status and number of dependants. In all Cases, Mr. Norris earned employment income of $51,000 and his employer withheld the required EI premiums and CPP contributions.

Case A Mr. Norris is married and his wife, Susan, has Net Income For Tax Purposes of $8,800. Susan's 73 year old mother, Bernice, lives with them. Bernice, an avid skier, had Net Income For Tax Purposes of $16,000 for the year.

Case B Mr. Norris is married and his wife, Susan, has Net Income For Tax Purposes of $4,410. They have one child, Martha, who is 10 years of age. Martha had no income during the year. During the year, the family had medical expenses as follows:

William	$1,200
Susan	1,600
Martha	350
Total	$3,150

Case C Mr. Norris is married and his wife, Susan, has Net Income For Tax Purposes of $4,500. They have a son, Allen, who is 19 years old and lives at home. He attends university on a full time basis during 8 months of the year. Mr. Norris pays $4,000 for Allen's tuition and $900 for required textbooks. Allen had employment income during the summer months of $2,200. He will transfer any unused credits to his father.

Case D Mr. Norris is not married and has no dependants. On receipt of a $300,000 inheritance in December, he donates $50,000 to his local hospital, a registered charity. He chooses to claim $15,000 in 2012. In addition, he makes contributions to federal political parties in the amount of $1,000.

Case E Mr. Norris is a single father. He has a daughter, Mary, who is 8 years old and lives with him. Mary had no income for the year. Two years ago, Mr. Norris graduated from a Canadian university. He currently has a Canada Student Loan outstanding. Mr. Norris pays back this loan in monthly instalments of $300. During the year, he paid $450 in interest on this loan.

Required: In each Case, calculate Mr. Norris' minimum federal Tax Payable for 2012. Indicate any carry forwards available to him and his dependants and the carry forward provisions. Ignore any tax amounts that Mr. Norris might have had withheld or paid in instalments.

Assignment Problem Four - 4 *(Tax Payable With Employment Income)*

Extension of Assignment Problem Three-10

For the past five years, Mr. Brooks has been employed as a financial analyst by a large Canadian public firm located in Winnipeg. During 2012, his basic gross salary amounts to $53,000. In addition, he was awarded an $11,000 bonus based on the performance of his division. Of the total bonus, $6,500 was paid in 2012 and the remainder is to be paid on January 15, 2013.

During 2012, Mr. Brooks' employer withheld the following amounts from his gross wages:

Federal Income Tax	$3,000
Employment Insurance Premiums	840
Canada Pension Plan Contributions	2,307
Registered Pension Plan Contributions	2,800
Donations To The United Way	480
Union Dues	240
Payments For Personal Use Of Company Car	1,000

Other Information:

1. Due to an airplane accident while flying back from Thunder Bay on business, Mr. Brooks was seriously injured and confined to a hospital for two full months during 2012. As his employer provides complete group disability insurance coverage, he received a total of $4,200 in payments during this period. All of the premiums for this insurance plan are paid by the employer. The plan provides periodic benefits that compensate for lost employment income.

2. Mr. Brooks is provided with a car that the company leases at a rate of $678 per month, including both GST and PST. The company pays for all of the operating costs of the car and these amounted to $3,500 during 2012. Mr. Brooks drove the car a total of 35,000 kilometers during 2012, 30,000 kilometers of which were carefully documented as employment related travel. While he was in the hospital (see Item 1), his employer required that the car be returned to company premises.

3. On January 15, 2011, Mr. Brooks received options to buy 200 shares of his employer's common stock at a price of $23 per share. At this time, the shares were trading at $20 per share. Mr. Brooks exercised these options on July 6, 2012, when the shares were trading at $28 per share. He does not plan to sell the shares for at least a year.

4. In order to assist Mr. Brooks in acquiring a new personal residence in Winnipeg, his employer granted him a five year, interest free loan of $125,000. The loan qualifies as a home relocation loan. The loan was granted on October 1, 2012 and, at this point in time, the interest rate on open five year mortgages was 5 percent. Assume the relevant ITR 4301 rate was 2 percent on this date. Mr. Brooks purchases a house for $235,000 on October 2, 2012. He has not owned a home during any of the preceding four years.

5. Other disbursements made by Mr. Brooks include the following:

Advanced financial accounting course tuition fees	$1,200
Music history course tuition fees	
(University of Manitoba one week intensive course)	600
Fees paid to financial planner	300
Payment of premiums on life insurance	642

   Mr. Brooks' employer reimbursed him for the tuition fees for the accounting course, but not the music course.

6. Mr. Brooks is a widower. His wife was killed in a car accident in 2009 that injured his 8 year old son, Harold, so badly that he qualifies for the disability tax credit. Mr. Brooks' mother, Grace, lives with Mr. Brooks and cares for Harold. Harold has no Net Income For Tax Purposes. Grace is 67 years old and her Net Income For Tax Purposes is $7,500.

Assignment Problems

Grace refused to take any payments for caring for Harold as she received a large inheritance in the previous year. As a result, Mr. Brooks did not pay any child care or attendant costs for Harold.

7. Mr. Brooks paid the following eligible medical costs:

For Himself	$ 7,300
For Harold	4,450
For Grace	1,265
Total	$13,015

8. Mr. Brooks buys public transit passes for his son, his mother and himself. The monthly cost of these passes is $26 (son), $50 (mother) and $60 (himself). He purchased these passes for 10 months of the year.

Required: Calculate, for the 2012 taxation year, Mr. Brooks' minimum Taxable Income and federal Tax Payable (Refund).

Assignment Problem Four - 5
(Comprehensive Tax Payable With Employment Income)

Phil Cousteau is an accountant. He works for ModFam Company and was paid a salary of $70,000 in 2012. He also earned a bonus of $5,000 in 2012, with one-fifth of the bonus to be paid each year from 2012 to 2016.

During 2012 he received a briefcase worth $800 as an award for being the "employee of the year" and a Christmas basket from the company worth $600. All of the Company's employees received a similar basket.

Phil is 47 years old and is married to Claire who is 45 years old and blind. She has no income in 2012 other than $9,000 in interest on investments she inherited from her mother ago.

Phil and Claire have two children, a 15 year old daughter, Haley, and a 19 year old son, Manny. Both Haley and Manny live at home.

Haley earned $800 during 2012 baby-sitting and spent it all on clothes. During 2012, her parents paid for dance classes that cost $1,000.

Manny has a disability that is not severe enough for his doctor to sign off on the T2201 form. Manny inherited investments from his grandmother and received $15,000 in interest income from them during 2012.

Phil's brother, Cameron, lives in the basement of Phil's Toronto home. Cameron is 50 years old and his only income for 2012 was EI benefit payments totaling $3,000.

Phil also supports his 85 year old father, Jay, who is physically infirm and lives in a retirement home. Jay had Net Income For Tax Purposes of $8,500 for 2012. His income consisted of OAS and payments from a registered pension plan.

ModFam transferred Phil from their Toronto office to their Vancouver office in 2012. On April 1, Phil moved his family out of the house they had rented in Toronto for the last 10 years and into a brand new house in Vancouver that cost $800,000.

Although Jay was to stay at the retirement home in Toronto, Cameron moved with the family to Vancouver. Phil was reimbursed by his employer for all of his moving costs. As a consequence, he has no deductible moving costs.

To help finance the new house, ModFam Company lent Phil $500,000 on April 1 at 1 percent interest. Phil would have paid 5 percent interest on a similar loan from the bank.

ModFam provides Phil with a company car. While he was at the Toronto office, he had a Toyota Highlander that the company leased for $875 per month ($50 of which was for insurance). The company paid $1,600 for the Highlander's other operating costs from January 1 to

March 31. During that period, Phil drove the car 9,000 kilometers of which 6,000 kilometers were employment related.

On April 1, the Vancouver office gave Phil the keys to a Toyota Camry Hybrid that was purchased for $31,300. The company paid $4,500 for the Camry's operating costs from April 1 to December 31. During that period, Phil drove the car 24,000 kilometers of which 10,000 kilometers were employment related.

During 2012, the following amounts were deducted from Phil's pay:

Federal Income Tax	$8,500
CPP	2,307
EI	840
Group Life Insurance Premiums	600
Registered Pension Plan	1,200
Canada Savings Bonds	1,800
United Way Donations	1,500

The company matched the life insurance and RPP amounts.

During 2012, Phil paid the following amounts of eligible medical expenses:

Himself	$ 650
Claire	1,940
Haley	860
Manny	1,250
Cameron	480
Jay	990

Phil paid $900 for his 2012 CMA dues. Claire made a $500 donation to their church during 2012.

Assume that the prescribed interest rates for 2012 were 2 percent for the first and fourth quarter and 3 percent for the second and third quarter.

Required: For the 2012 taxation year, calculate Mr. Cousteau's minimum:

1. Net Income For Tax Purposes,
2. Taxable Income,
3. Federal Tax Owing.

In determining these amounts, ignore GST, PST and HST considerations.

Assignment Problem Four - 6
(Comprehensive Tax Payable With Employment Income)

Margarita Dalvi is a financial analyst employed by a large public company. Her 2012 salary is $143,000 and, in addition, she was awarded an incentive bonus of $34,500. Two-thirds of this bonus was paid during 2012, with the balance due in September, 2013.

Ms. Dalvi's employer withheld the following amounts from her earnings:

EI Premiums	$ 840
CPP Contributions	2,307
RPP Contributions	6,400
Federal Income Taxes	29,000
Contributions To United Way	4,000
Professional Association Dues	1,200

Ms. Dalvi is 55 years old and married to Jonathan Dalvi who has been legally blind since an automobile accident that occurred several years ago. Jonathan is 66 years old. He has 2012 income from OAS and various investments of $7,200. The couple have three children:

Martha is 15 years old. She has 2012 income from various part time jobs of $11,000.

Mary is 19 years old and has mental health problems that prevent her from working on a full time basis. She lives with her mother and father and has 2012 income from part time jobs of $4,800.

Mark is 21 years old and attends university on a full time basis for 10 months of the year. His tuition fees are $9,400. As he has no income of his own, he has agreed to transfer all of his education related credits to his mother.

The family's 2012 medical expenses, all of which were paid by Ms. Dalvi, were as follows:

Ms. Dalvi And Her Husband	$ 6,200
Martha	1,800
Mary	11,300
Mark	2,500

Other Information:

1. Ms. Dalvi buys monthly transit passes for Mark and Martha. The cost is $75 per month per child. The passes covered 10 months during 2012.

2. Ms. Dalvi is provided with an automobile by her employer. The automobile is leased at a rate of $728 per month, including applicable HST. This payment also includes a payment of $50 per month for insurance coverage. During 2012, the automobile is driven 57,000 kilometers, of which 42,000 were employment related. The automobile was used by Ms. Dalvi for 11 months during 2012. She was required to return the automobile to her employer's garage during the month that she did not use it.

3. During 2012, Ms. Dalvi spent $14,800 on employment related meals and entertainment with clients. Her employer reimbursed $9,500 of these costs.

4. Throughout their marriage, the Dalvi's have always lived in rented premises. Seeing the current level of mortgage rates as presenting an opportunity to acquire a residence, they purchase a 4 bedroom bungalow in the same neighbourhood for $422,000 on July 1, 2012. On this date, her employer provides Ms. Dalvi with a $250,000 loan that will facilitate this acquisition. The loan does not require any payment of interest. However, the balance must be paid on July 1, 2017. Assume that the prescribed rate is 1 percent throughout 2012.

5. During 2012, Ms. Dalvi receives several gifts from her employer:

   • As is the case for all of her employer's senior staff, she receives a $400 gift certificate that can be used for merchandise at a local clothing store.

   • In recognition of 10 years of continuous service, she receives an engraved wrist watch. The retail value of this watch is $1,200.

   • At Christmas all of the employees of her employer receive a gift basket containing gourmet food items. The retail value of this basket is $300.

6. During 2011, Ms. Dalvi received options to purchase 1,200 shares of her employer's stock at a price of $37 per share. At the time the options were granted, the market price of the shares was $40 per share. During July, 2012, when the shares are trading at $45 per share, Ms. Dalvi exercises all of these options. She is still holding these shares on December 31, 2012.

Required:

A. Determine Ms. Dalvi's minimum Net Income For Tax Purposes for the 2012 taxation year.

B. Determine Ms. Dalvi's minimum Taxable Income for the 2012 taxation year.

C. Based on your answer in Part B, determine Ms. Dalvi's federal Tax Payable and amount owing (refund) for the 2012 taxation year.

Tax Software Assignment Problems

(The solutions for these problems are only available in
the solutions manual that has been provided to your instructor.)

Tax Software Assignment Problem Four - 1

This problem is continued in Chapter 11.

DISCLAIMER: All characters appearing in this problem are fictitious. Any resemblance to real persons, living or dead, is purely coincidental.

Mr. Buddy Musician (SIN 527-000-061) was born in Vancouver on August 28, 1944. He has spent most of his working life as a pianist and song writer. He and his family live at 1166 West Pender Street, Vancouver, B.C. V6E 3H8, phone (604) 669-7815.

Mr. Musician's wife, Natasha (SIN 527-000-129), was born on June 6, 1986. She and Mr. Musician have four children. Each child was born on April 1 of the following years, Linda; 2006, Larry; 2007, Donna; 2008, and Donald; 2009. Natasha's only income during 2011 is $4,800 [(4)($100)(12)] in universal child care benefits.

Buddy and Natasha Musician have two adopted children. Richard (SIN 527-000-285) was born on March 15, 1994 and has income of $2,800 for the year. Due to his accelerated schooling, he started full time attendance at university in September of 2011 at the age of 17. His first semester tuition fee is $3,000 and he requires books with a total cost of $375. These amounts are paid by Mr. Musician.

The other adopted child, Sarah, was born on September 2, 1991, and is in full time attendance at university for all of 2011 (including a four month summer session). Her tuition is $9,600 and she requires textbooks which cost $750. These amounts are also paid by Mr. Musician. Sarah has no income during the year.

Neither Richard nor Sarah will have any income in the next three years. Any unused credits of either child are available to be transferred to their father.

Mr. Musician's mother, Eunice, was born on April 10, 1924 and his father, Earl, was born on November 16, 1922. They both live with Mr. Musician and his wife.

While his father is still physically active, his mother is blind. Eunice Musician had income of $9,500 for the year, while Earl Musician had income of $7,500.

Other information concerning Mr. Musician and his family for 2011 is as follows:

1. Mr. Musician earned $16,500 for work as the house pianist at the Loose Moose Pub. His T4 showed that his employer withheld $500 for income taxes and $294 for EI. No CPP was withheld.

2. During the year, Mr. Musician made $3,000 in donations to Planned Parenthood Of Canada, a registered Canadian charity.

3. Mr. Musician has been married before to Lori Musician (SIN 527-000-319). Lori is 52 years old and lives in Fort Erie, Ontario.

4. Mr. Musician has two additional children who live with their mother, Ms. Dolly Holt (SIN 527-000-582), in Burnaby, British Columbia. The children are Megan Holt, aged 12 and Andrew Holt, aged 14. Neither child has any income during 2011. While Ms. Holt and Mr. Musician were never married, Mr. Musician acknowledges that he is the father of both children. Although Buddy has provided limited financial aid, the children are not dependent on Buddy for support.

5. Mr. Musician wishes to claim all his medical expenses on a calendar year basis. On December 2, 2011, Mr. Musician paid dental expenses to Canada Wide Dental Clinics for the following individuals:

Himself	$1,200
Natasha (wife)	700
Richard (adopted son)	800
Sarah (adopted daughter)	300
Linda (daughter)	100
Earl (father)	1,050
Lori (ex-wife)	300
Dolly Holt (mother of two of his children)	675
Megan Holt (daughter of Dolly Holt)	550
Total	$5,675

6. Mr. Musician paid four quarterly instalments of $1,000 each (total of $4,000) for 2011, as requested on his Instalment Reminders from the CRA.

7. Assume that Mr. Musician has not applied to receive either OAS or CPP benefits.

Required: With the objective of minimizing Mr. Musician's Tax Payable, prepare his 2011 income tax return using the ProFile tax software program. List any assumptions you have made, and any notes and tax planning issues you feel should be placed in the file.

Tax Software Assignment Problem Four - 2
This problem is continued in Chapter 11.

DISCLAIMER: All characters appearing in this problem are fictitious. Any resemblance to real persons, living or dead, is purely coincidental.

George Pharmacy is a pharmaceutical salesman who has been very successful at his job in the last few years. Unfortunately, his family life has not been very happy. Three years ago, his only child, Anna, was driving a car that was hit by a drunk driver. She and her husband were killed and their 13 year old son, Kevin, was blinded in the accident. He also suffered extensive injuries to his jaw that have required major and prolonged dental work.

George and his wife, Valerie, adopted Kevin. Valerie quit her part-time job to care for him. She also cares for her mother, Joan Parker. Joan suffers from diabetes and severe depression and lives with George and Valerie.

Valerie's parents separated two years ago in Scotland after her father, David Parker, suffered enormous losses in the stock market. They were forced to sell their home and David moved to South America. David phones periodically to request that money be deposited in his on-line bank account.

Joan does not meet the residency requirements necessary to qualify for Canadian Old Age Security payments.

George's brother, Martin, completed an alcohol rehabilitation program after being fired for drinking on the job. He is also living with George and Valerie while he is enrolled as a full time student at the Northern Alberta Institute of Technology.

George is paying his tuition and Martin has agreed to transfer any available education related amounts to George. Although Martin plans to file his 2011 tax return, he has not done so yet.

In addition to George's salary, he also earns commissions. His employer requires him to have an office in his home and has signed the form T2200 each year to this effect.

Other information concerning George for 2011 is given on the following pages.

Required: Prepare the 2011 income tax return of George Pharmacy using the ProFile tax software program.   List any assumptions you have made, and any notes and tax planning issues you feel should be placed in the file. Ignore GST implications in your solutions.

Personal Information	Taxpayer
Title	Mr.
First Name	George
Last Name	Pharmacy
SIN	527-000-509
Date of birth (Y/M/D)	1947-07-02
Marital Status	Married
Canadian citizen?	Yes
Provide information to Elections Canada?	Yes
Own foreign property of more than $100,000 Canadian?	No

Taxpayer's Address
97 Jasper Avenue, Apt 10, Edmonton, Alberta   T5J 4C8
Phone number (780) 495-3500

Family Members	Spouse	Child	Mother-In-Law
First Name	Valerie	Kevin	Joan
Last Name	Pharmacy	Pharmacy	Parker
SIN	527-000-483	527-000-517	None
Date of birth (Y/M/D)	1946-12-30	1995-10-17	1926-02-24
Net income	$5,800 in CPP	Nil	$500

Family Members	Father-In-Law	Brother
First Name	David	Martin
Last Name	Parker	Pharmacy
SIN	None	527-000-533
Date of birth (Y/M/D)	1927-01-12	1964-06-02
Net income	Nil	$8,300

T2202A - (Martin)	Box	Amount
Tuition fees - for Martin Pharmacy (brother)	A	6,000
Number of months in school - part-time	B	0
Number of months in school - full-time	C	8

Tax Software Assignment Problems

T4	Box	Amount
Issuer - Mega Pharma Inc.		
Employment income	14	378,000.00
Employee's CPP contributions	16	2,217.60
Employee's EI premiums	18	786.76
Income tax deducted	22	114,000.00
Employment commissions	42	82,000.00
Charitable donations	46	400.00

During 2011, Mega reimbursed George $3,788 for meals and entertainment with clients, $2,268 for hotels and $4,925 for airline tickets.

Donor	Charitable Donation Receipts	Am't
Valerie	Mothers Against Drunk Drivers (MADD)	1,000
George	Canadian Institute For The Blind (CNIB)	3,000

(Y/M/D)	Patient	Medical Expenses	Description	Am't
2011-12-31	George	Johnson Inc.	Out of Canada insurance	731.30
2011-08-31	George	Dr. Smith	Dental fees	155.40
2011-09-19	George	Optician	Prescription glasses	109.00
2011-11-07	Valerie	Pharmacy	Prescription	66.84
2011-06-07	Joan	Dr. Wong	Psychiatric counseling	2,050.00
2011-03-22	David	Tropical Disease Centre	Prescription	390.00
2011-12-20	Martin	Dr. Walker	Group therapy	6,000.00
2011-10-01	Kevin	Dr. Takarabe	Orthodontics and Dental	30,000.00

George paid $800 for the care and feeding of Kevin's seeing eye dog, Isis, during 2011.

House Costs	
Area of home used for home office (square feet)	650
Total area of home (square feet)	5,000
Telephone line including high speed internet connection	620
Hydro	3,200
Insurance - House	4,000
Maintenance and repairs	3,800
Mortgage interest	6,200
Mortgage life insurance premiums	400
Property taxes	6,700

During 2011, George purchased a new computer and software that will be used solely in his home office for employment related uses. The computer cost $3,600 and the various software programs cost $1,250.

Tax Software Assignment Problem Four - 3

This problem is continued in the Tax Software Assignment Problem for Chapter 6.

DISCLAIMER: All characters appearing in all versions of this problem are fictitious. Any resemblance to real persons, living or dead, is purely coincidental.

This Tax Software Assignment Problem is introduced in this Chapter and is continued in Chapters 6 through 11. More information is provided in subsequent chapters that is related to the material covered in that Chapter. Each Tax Software Assignment Problem must be completed in sequence. The information in each problem is applicable to all subsequent problems.

Seymour Career and Mary Career are your tax clients. They have been married for two years. In late December, 2011, Mary comes to your office with the tax information for 2011 which she has managed to obtain before the end of the year.

Mary has progressed quickly in MoreCorp, the large, publicly traded firm she is working for due to her strong tax and accounting background. She has been rewarded with a large bonus in 2011. Her firm has an excellent health and dental plan that reimburses 100 percent of all medical expenses.

Although Seymour has been working, his increasing ill health makes it likely that he will not be able to continue to work in 2012. He is contemplating a return to university as a student of music.

In order to estimate her possible financial position in 2012, she would like you to prepare her 2011 tax return assuming that Seymour has no income for 2011. She would also like you to compare her 2011 tax liability in the different provinces assuming Seymour has no income for 2011.

Personal Information	Taxpayer	Spouse
Title	Ms.	Mr.
First Name	Mary	Seymour
Last Name	Career	Career
SIN	527-000-129	527-000-079
Date of birth (Y/M/D)	1973-12-08	1952-01-29
Marital status	Married	Married
Canadian citizen?	Yes	Yes
Provide information to Elections Canada?	Yes	Yes
Own foreign property of more than $100,000 Cdn?	No	No

Taxpayer's Address
126 Prince William Street, Saint John, N.B.   E2L 4H9
Phone number (506) 636-5997
Spouse's address same as taxpayer? Yes

Dependant	Child
First Name	William
Last Name	Career
SIN	527-000-319
Date of Birth (Y/M/D)	2004-02-24
Net Income	Nil

T4 - Mary	Box	Amount
Issuer - MoreCorp		
Employment Income	14	152,866.08
Employee's CPP Contributions	16	2,217.60
Employee's EI Premiums	18	786.76
RPP Contributions	20	Nil
Income Tax Deducted	22	48,665.11
Charitable Donations	46	1,000.00

Donor	Charitable Donation Receipts	Amount
Seymour	Canadian Cancer Foundation	500
Seymour	Salvation Army	250

Required:

A.　With the objective of minimizing Mary's Tax Payable, prepare, but do not print, her 2011 income tax return using the ProFile tax software program. Assume that Seymour has no income in 2011. **Hint:** On her "Info" page, answer "Yes" to the question in the spousal information box "Is spouse's net income zero?". List any other assumptions you have made and provide any explanatory notes and tax planning issues you feel should be placed in the files.

B.　Access and print Mary's summary (Summary on the Form Explorer, not the T1Summary). This form is a two column summary of the couple's tax information. In this version, the second column is blank.

C.　Create and print a separate table (not in ProFile) that compares the total federal and provincial Tax Payable (Refund) for Mary for all the territories and provinces other than Quebec. **Hint**: On the "Info" screen, you can change the province of residence. (You must press the "Enter" key for the change to take effect.) The data monitor at the bottom of the screen should show the new balance/refund. The difference can also be seen on the "Summary" form. To see a detailed analysis of the effect of various changes such as province of residence, use the "Snapshot/Variance" feature (information on this feature is available from the Help menu) to create a separate snapshot of the finished return for Mary. Then open the Auditor <Ctrl+F9> and select the Variance tab.

CHAPTER 5

Capital Cost Allowances And Cumulative Eligible Capital

Capital Cost Allowance System

General Rules

5-1. In Chapter 6, we will give consideration to the calculation of business income as described in Subdivision b of the *Income Tax Act*. As was the case with employment income, business income is based on a group of inclusions and deductions that are combined to arrive at a net income or loss for the taxation year.

5-2. In Subdivision b, ITA 18(1) lays out a group of general limitations with respect to what can be deducted in the determination of net business income. In Paragraph 18(1)(b), it is noted that a taxpayer cannot deduct capital expenditures except as expressly permitted in the *Act*. In this same Subdivision b, ITA 20(1) provides a list of specific items that can be deducted in the determination of net business income. Paragraph 20(1)(a) notes that taxpayers can deduct such part of the capital cost of property "as is allowed by regulation". Taken together, these two Paragraphs provide the basis for the deduction of the tax equivalent of what financial accountants refer to as amortization. This tax "amortization" is referred to as capital cost allowance (CCA).

5-3. While ITA 20(1)(a) provides the legislative basis for deducting CCA, all of the detailed rules for determining the amounts to be deducted are found in the *Income Tax Regulations* (ITR). More specifically, ITR Part XI lists the items to be included in the various CCA classes, while ITR Schedules II through VI provide the rates for each of these classes.

Tax And Accounting Procedures Compared

Introduction

5-4. There are many similarities between the capital cost allowance system that is used for tax purposes and the amortization procedures that are used by financial accountants. In fact, the general goal of both sets of procedures is to allocate the cost of a depreciable asset to the expenses (deductions) of periods subsequent to its acquisition. However, there are a number of differences that are described in the material which follows.

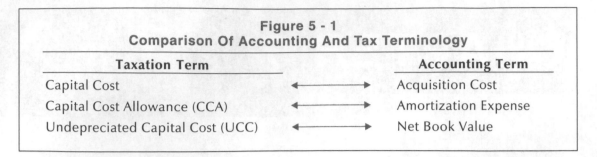

Figure 5 - 1
Comparison Of Accounting And Tax Terminology

Taxation Term		Accounting Term
Capital Cost	←————→	Acquisition Cost
Capital Cost Allowance (CCA)	←————→	Amortization Expense
Undepreciated Capital Cost (UCC)	←————→	Net Book Value

Terminology

5-5.   The two sets of procedures use different terms to describe items that are analogous. While the amounts involved will be different, the underlying concepts are the same. For example, both Undepreciated Capital Cost (UCC) and Net Book Value refer to the original cost of a depreciable asset, less amounts that have been deducted in the calculation of income. A general comparison of these analogous terms is found in Figure 5-1.

5-6.   However, one technical difference in the use of the terms is that where Net Book Value at the end of the year is reduced by the amortization expense for the year, UCC is reduced by CCA deducted in preceding years only. In other words, the December 31, 2012 UCC is not reduced by the 2012 CCA. The 2012 CCA is deducted in the calculation of the January 1, 2013 UCC.

5-7.   With respect to dispositions of depreciable assets, the accounting and tax procedures are very different and, as a result, the related terminology cannot be directly compared. For accounting purposes, a disposition will simply result in a gain or loss. For tax purposes, this transaction could result in no tax effect, a capital gain, recapture of CCA, or a terminal loss. There is no real equivalency between these two sets of terminology.

Acquisitions

5-8.   The accounting and tax procedures for acquisitions can be described as follows:

Accounting   In general, accountants record an acquisition cost for each material asset acquired. The acquisition cost that will be recorded in individual asset records is the amount of consideration given up to acquire the asset. This would include all costs directly attributable to the acquisition, including installing it at the relevant location and in the condition necessary for its intended use.

Tax   In general, the capital cost of acquired assets will be allocated to what is referred to as a class. These classes are, in most cases, broadly defined (e.g., Class 10 contains most types of vehicles acquired by an enterprise).

In general, the amount of capital cost to be recorded is the same number that would be recorded as the acquisition cost in the accounting records. A difference can arise, however, when non-arm's length transactions are involved. In accounting, the acquired asset will consistently be recorded at the fair value of the consideration given up. As will be discussed in Chapter 8, this is not always the case when tax procedures are applied to non-arm's length transactions.

Dispositions

5-9.   The accounting and tax procedures for dispositions can be described as follows:

Accounting   For accounting purposes, the Net Book Value of the asset being disposed of is subtracted from the proceeds resulting from that disposition. If the result is positive, a gain is recorded. Alternatively, if the result is negative, a loss is recorded. It would be extremely unusual for a disposition to have no effect on accounting Net Income.

Tax   Tax procedures require that the lesser of the proceeds of disposition and the capital cost of the specific asset be deducted from the UCC balance of its class. While in the majority of cases this procedure will have no current tax consequences, there are several other possibilities. There may be a capital gain, recapture of CCA, or a terminal loss. These more complex concepts will be explained in detail at a later point in this Chapter. Note that, while CCA is based on classes of assets, for the purpose of dealing with dispositions, records must be kept of the capital cost of each individual asset.

Amortization And Capital Cost Allowance

5-10. The accounting and tax procedures for allocating the cost of depreciable assets to income can be described as follows:

Accounting Accounting amortization is based on the consistent application of generally accepted accounting principles (GAAP). While these principles would encompass a wide variety of methods, including those used for calculating the maximum CCA for tax purposes, the straight-line method is by far the most widely used method for accounting purposes.

Once a method is chosen, it is generally applied to individual assets. The adopted method must be applied consistently, with the full amount that results from its application being charged as an expense in the determination of accounting Net Income for the current period.

Tax The *Income Tax Regulations* specify the method that must be applied to each class. Two methods are used for this purpose — the straight-line method and the declining balance method. The required method will be applied to calculate a maximum deduction for the taxation year.

While taxpayers will generally wish to deduct this maximum amount, they are not required to do so. They can deduct all of it, none of it, or any value in between. While the regulations specify consistency in the calculation method used, there is no requirement for year-to-year consistency in the portion of the maximum amount deducted.

5-11. We have noted that, for accounting purposes, most companies use straight-line amortization. In contrast, the *Income Tax Regulations* require the use of declining balance procedures on the majority of important CCA classes. Given that most enterprises will deduct the maximum amount of CCA, the amount of CCA deducted is usually larger than the amount of accounting amortization charged to expense. Because of this, most companies will have accounting values for their depreciable assets that are significantly larger than the corresponding tax values. These differences are referred to as temporary differences and, as many of you are aware, GAAP may require the recording of Future Income Tax Liabilities to reflect such differences.

Additions To Capital Cost

Determination Of Amounts

General Rules

5-12. To be added to a CCA class, an asset must be owned by the taxpayer and, in addition, it must be used for the purpose of producing income from business, property, or in certain limited circumstances, employment. To qualify for inclusion in a CCA class, the asset must be a capital asset rather than inventory. This means that whether an asset should be added to a CCA class depends on the nature of the business. A drill press is a capital asset for a taxpayer using it in a manufacturing process. However, it would be treated as inventory by a taxpayer in the business of selling that type of equipment.

5-13. Capital cost means the full cost to the taxpayer of acquiring the property and would include all freight, installation costs, duties, non-refundable provincial sales taxes, legal, accounting, appraisal, engineering, or other fees incurred to acquire the property. Note that any refundable GST or HST would not be added to the capital cost (see Paragraph 5-20).

5-14.   In the case of property constructed by the taxpayer for use in producing income, it would include material, labour, and an appropriate allocation of overhead. If the property is paid for in a foreign currency, the Canadian dollar capital cost would be determined using the exchange rate on the date of acquisition.

Capitalization Of Interest

5-15.   In addition to the direct costs described in the two preceding Paragraphs, ITA 21(1) allows a taxpayer to elect to add the cost of money borrowed to acquire depreciable property to its capital cost. This election is in lieu of deducting the interest in the current taxation year and will usually be an undesirable choice.

5-16.   However, if the deduction of the interest in the current year would result in a non-capital loss, this election may be desirable. By adding the interest to the capital cost of the asset, the amount can be deducted as part of the CCA on the asset's class for an unlimited number of future years. Alternatively, if it serves to increase the non-capital loss for the year, it would become part of the loss carry forward or loss carry back for the year. It would then be subject to the business and property loss carry over time limits of 3 years back and 20 years forward.

Government Assistance

5-17.   Another consideration in determining the capital cost of an addition to a CCA class is government assistance. Under ITA 13(7.1), any amounts received or receivable from any level of government for the purpose of acquiring depreciable assets must be deducted from the capital cost of those assets. This would include grants, subsidies, forgivable loans, tax deductions, and investment tax credits.

5-18.   This tax requirement is consistent with the requirements of IAS 20, *Accounting For Government Grants And Disclosure Of Government Assistance*, which, in general, requires government assistance, including investment tax credits, to be deducted from the cost of assets for accounting purposes.

Non-Arm's Length Acquisitions

5-19.   If transfers of depreciable property between persons not dealing at arm's length are not made at fair market value, they are subject to very unfavourable tax treatment. This may result in the capital cost of the asset not being equal to the amount of consideration given for the asset. This point is discussed in more detail in Chapter 8.

GST, HST And PST Considerations

5-20.   GST, PST (Provincial Sales Tax), or HST (Harmonized Sales Tax) is usually paid on depreciable asset acquisitions. While we will not provide detailed coverage of GST/HST until Chapter 21, you should be aware of the following:

- GST paid by businesses on the acquisition of assets will, in general, be refunded as input tax credits. Note that there are many complications related to this rule and they will be discussed in Chapter 21.
- HST is the term used to refer to the combined GST and PST amounts that are collected in Ontario and British Columbia, and all of the Atlantic provinces except Prince Edward Island. In general, HST paid on the acquisition of depreciable assets is refunded as input tax credits.
- The Quebec PST is integrated with the GST system and, as a consequence, these amounts are refunded on much the same basis as GST.
- The PST that is paid in other provinces, such as Manitoba, is not refunded and, as a consequence, it is included in the capital cost of acquired assets.

5-21.   From a technical point of view, all amounts of GST/HST/PST are, at least initially, included in the capital cost of depreciable assets. However, to the extent that these amounts are refunded as input tax credits, they are defined in ITA 248(16) as a form of government assistance and, as a consequence, the refunds are deducted from the capital cost of depreciable assets in the same manner as other government assistance. In somewhat simplified terms, GST/HST/PST amounts that are refunded are not included in the capital cost of depreciable assets.

> **Example** An enterprise acquires a depreciable asset in Ontario at a cost of $11,300. The basic cost of this asset is $10,000, with the extra $1,300 reflecting Ontario's 13 percent HST.

> **Analysis** Provided the enterprise is an HST registrant, the $1,300 will be refunded as an input tax credit. This means that the CCA base for this asset is the pre-HST amount of $10,000.

Summary

5-22. In reviewing the detailed tax rules applicable to depreciable asset acquisitions, it is clear that these rules will produce capital costs for depreciable assets that are almost always identical to the acquisition costs produced when GAAP is applied. While differences between amortization amounts and the corresponding CCA deductions will cause these values to diverge significantly as the assets are used, the initial amounts recorded for depreciable assets will normally be the same for both accounting and tax purposes.

Available For Use Rules

5-23. For many types of assets, the available for use rules do not present a problem. Most acquired assets are put into use immediately and the acquirer is allowed to deduct CCA in the year of acquisition. For other assets, the rules can make CCA calculations quite complicated. Real estate assets, especially those that require several years to develop, can be particularly hard hit by the fact that there can be a deferral of the right to deduct CCA for two years, or until the structure is considered available for its income producing use.

5-24. The basic rules are found in ITA 13(26) through 13(32). In simplified terms, properties are considered to be available for use, and thereby eligible for CCA deductions, at the earliest of the following times:

- For properties other than buildings, when the property is first used by the taxpayer for the purpose of earning income.
- For buildings, including rental buildings, when substantially all (usually 90% or more) of the building is used for the purpose for which it was acquired.
- The second taxation year after the year in which the property is acquired. This maximum two year deferral rule is also referred to as the rolling start rule.
- For public companies, the year in which amortization is first recorded on the property under generally accepted accounting principles.
- In the case of motor vehicles and other transport equipment that require certificates or licences, when such certificates or licences are obtained.

5-25. The preceding is a very incomplete description of the available for use rules. There are other special rules for particular assets, as well as significant complications in the area of rental properties. Detailed coverage of these rules goes beyond the scope of this text.

Segregation Into Classes

General Rules

5-26. Part XI and Schedules II through VI of the *Income Tax Regulations* provide a detailed listing of classes and rates for the determination of CCA. There are over 40 classes that vary from extremely narrow (Class 26 which contains only property that is a catalyst or deuterium enriched water) to extremely broad (Class 8 refers to property that is a tangible capital asset and not included in another class). As the applicable rates vary from a low of 4 percent to a high of 100 percent, the appropriate classification can have a significant impact on the amount of CCA that can be taken in future years. This, in turn, has an impact on Taxable

Income and Tax Payable.

5-27.   Assets do not belong in a class unless they are specifically included in the ITR description of that class. While there are a large number of classes and, as we have noted, Class 8 contains a provision for tangible property not listed elsewhere, some assets are specifically excluded from depreciable property status by ITR 1102. Most importantly, inventories and land cannot be added to any CCA Class. This means, in dealing with real property, the land component of the total cost must be separated from the building component.

5-28.   For your convenience in working with CCA problems, the Appendix to this Chapter provides an alphabetical list of common assets, indicating the appropriate CCA class as well as the rate applicable to that class.

Separate Classes

5-29.   The general rule is that all of the assets that belong in a particular class are allocated to that class, resulting in a single class containing all of the assets of a particular type. There are, however, a number of exceptions to this general rule that are specified in ITR 1101. Some of these exceptions, for instance the requirement of a separate Class 30 for each telecommunication spacecraft, are not of general importance. However, some of the other exceptions are applicable to a large number of taxpayers. These important exceptions are as follows:

Separate Businesses An individual may be involved in more than one unincorporated business. While the income of all of these businesses will be reported in the tax return of the individual, separate CCA classes will have to be maintained for each business. For example, an individual might own both an accounting practice and a coin laundry. Both of these unincorporated businesses would likely have Class 8 assets. However, a separate Class 8 would have to be maintained for each business.

Rental Properties Of particular significance in the tax planning process is the requirement that each rental property acquired after 1971 at a cost of $50,000 or more be placed in a separate CCA class. When the property is sold, the lesser of the proceeds of disposition and the cost of the asset will be removed from the particular class. This will commonly result in a negative balance in the class and this amount will have to be taken into income by the taxpayer (see later discussion of recapture of CCA). If it were not for the separate class requirement, this result could be avoided by adding other properties to a single rental property class.

Luxury Cars The separate class rules apply to passenger vehicles that have a cost in excess of a prescribed amount. While this prescribed amount was expected to be changed periodically, it has been $30,000 from 2001 through 2012. Given the degree to which car prices have increased during this period, it is difficult to view a $30,000 automobile as a luxury vehicle.

Elections For the assets described in the preceding three paragraphs, separate classes must be used. The taxpayer has no choice in the matter. There are other situations where a taxpayer is allowed to elect having a separate class. One of these situations involves non-residential buildings where the election to use a separate class can result in an additional amount of CCA (see Paragraph 5-32). Another situation involves assets subject to high rates of technological obsolescence (e.g., photocopiers). In this case a separate class election can provide for the recognition of terminal losses. This is discussed starting at Paragraph 5-69.

Capital Cost Allowances

General Overview

Methods

5-30.   Once capital assets have been allocated to appropriate classes, these amounts form the base for the calculation of CCA. The maximum CCA is determined by applying a rate that is specified in the Regulations to either the original capital cost of the assets in the class (straight-line classes) or, more commonly, to the end of the period UCC for the class (declining balance classes). The following example will illustrate this difference:

Example   A particular CCA class contains assets with a capital cost of $780,000 and an end of the period UCC balance of $460,000. There have been no additions to the class during the year. The rate for the class is 10 percent.

Declining Balance Class   If we assume that this is a declining balance class, the rate would be applied to the $460,000 end of the period UCC balance. This would result in a maximum CCA for this class of $46,000 [(10%)($460,000)].

Straight-Line Class   If we assume that this is a straight-line class, the rate would be applied to the $780,000 cost of the assets. This would result in a maximum CCA for this class of $78,000 [(10%)($780,000)].

5-31.   This relatively simple process is complicated by the following:

Half-Year (a.k.a. First Year) Rules   For most classes, one-half of any excess of additions for acquisitions over deductions for dispositions to a class for the year must be subtracted prior to the application of the appropriate CCA rate.

Class Changes   When the government wishes to change the rate applicable to certain types of assets, they normally implement this decision by allocating such assets to a new or different class. This means that the same type of asset may be found in more than one class, depending on when it was acquired (e.g., manufacturing and processing equipment acquired before March 19, 2007 is in Class 43 with a 30 percent declining balance CCA rate, manufacturing and processing equipment acquired after March 18, 2007 is in Class 29 with a 50 percent straight line write off).

Rental Property CCA Restriction   In general, taxpayers are not permitted to create or increase a net rental loss by claiming CCA on rental properties. This topic is covered in detail in Chapter 7, Property Income.

Rates For Commonly Used CCA Classes

5-32.   The following is a brief description of the more commonly used CCA classes, including the items to be added, the applicable rates, and the method to be used:

Class 1 - Buildings (4%, 6%, or 10%)   In general, Class 1 is a 4 percent declining balance class, applicable to buildings acquired after 1987.   This class also includes bridges, canals, culverts, subways, tunnels, and certain railway roadbeds.

Each rental building with a cost of $50,000 or more must be allocated to a separate Class 1.

If a new building, acquired after March 18, 2007 is allocated to a separate Class 1, the general 4 percent rate is increased as follows:

- to 10 percent if it is used 90 percent or more for manufacturing and processing,
- to 6 percent if it does not qualify for the manufacturing and processing rate, but is used 90 percent or more for non-residential purposes.

Class 3 - Buildings Pre-1988 (5%)   Class 3 is a 5 percent declining balance class. It contains most buildings acquired before 1988. As is the case for Class 1 rental properties, separate classes were required for each rental building with a cost of $50,000 or more. This class also includes breakwaters, docks, trestles, windmills, wharfs, jetties, and telephone poles.

Class 8 - Various Machinery, Equipment, and Furniture (20%)   Class 8 is a 20 percent declining balance class. It includes most machinery, equipment, structures such as kilns, tanks and vats, electrical generating equipment, advertising posters, bulletin boards, and furniture not specifically included in another class. As will be discussed at a later point in the Chapter, individual photocopiers, fax machines, and pieces of telephone equipment purchased for $1,000 or more can be allocated to a separate Class 8 at the election of the taxpayer.

Class 10 - Vehicles (30%)   Class 10 is a 30 percent declining balance class. It includes most vehicles (excluding certain passenger vehicles that are allocated to Class 10.1), automotive equipment, trailers, wagons, contractors' movable equipment, mine railway equipment, various mining and logging equipment, and TV channel converters and decoders acquired by a cable distribution system.

Class 10.1 - Luxury Cars (30%)   Class 10.1 is a class established for passenger vehicles with a cost in excess of an amount prescribed in ITR 7307(1)(b). For cars acquired in 2001 through 2012, the prescribed amount is $30,000. Like Class 10, where most other vehicles remain, it is a 30 percent declining balance class. However, each vehicle must be allocated to a separate Class 10.1. Also important is that the amount of the addition to the separate class is limited to the prescribed amount of $30,000. This, in turn, limits the base for CCA to this same amount.

On the positive side, in the year in which the vehicle is retired, one-half of the normal CCA for the year can be deducted, despite the fact that there will be no balance in the class at the end of the year. A further difference is that, in the year of retirement, neither recapture nor terminal losses are recognized for tax purposes.

Class 12 - Computer Software and Small Assets (100%)   Class 12 includes computer software that is not systems software, books in a lending library, dishes, cutlery, jigs, dies, patterns, uniforms and costumes, linen, motion picture films, and videotapes. Dental and medical instruments, kitchen utensils, and tools are included, provided they cost less than $500. This class is subject to a 100 percent write-off in the year of acquisition. As will be noted when we discuss this issue, the half-year rule must be applied to some, but not all, Class 12 assets. When this rule is applicable, the relevant Class 12 assets are effectively subject to a two year write off at 50 percent per year.

Class 13 - Leasehold Improvements (Straight-Line)   In general, only assets that are owned by the taxpayer are eligible for CCA deductions. However, an exception to this is leasehold improvements which are allocated to Class 13. For Class 13, the Regulations specify that CCA must be calculated on a straight-line basis for each capital expenditure incurred. The maximum deduction will be the lesser of:

- one-fifth of the capital cost of the improvement; and
- the capital cost of the lease improvement, divided by the lease term (including the first renewal option, if any).

The lease term is calculated by taking the number of full 12 month periods from the beginning of the taxation year in which the particular leasehold improvement is made until the termination of the lease. For purposes of this calculation, the lease term is limited to 40 years. Note that, in the case of such straight-line classes, the application of the half-year rules (see later discussion) will mean that the maximum CCA in the first and last years will be based on one-half of the straight-line rate.

Class 14 - Limited Life Intangibles (Straight-Line, No Half-Year Rules) Class 14 covers the cost of intangible assets with a limited life. These assets are subject to straight-line amortization over their legal life. IT-477 indicates that CCA should be calculated on a pro rata per diem basis. Because of this, neither the half-year rule nor the short fiscal period rule applies to Class 14. In both the first and last years of the asset's life, the per diem approach would be used. Note, however, if there is a disposition of Class 14 assets, the usual recapture and terminal loss procedures would apply.

Classes 29 And 43 - Manufacturing and Processing Assets   Manufacturing and processing assets acquired before March 19, 2007 are included in Class 43 where the rate is 30 percent applied to a declining balance. Manufacturing and processing assets acquired after March 18, 2007 are allocated to Class 29 where CCA is calculated on a 50 percent straight-line basis. While this allocation was scheduled to end in 2012, the 2011 budget extended the relevant period to assets acquired prior to 2014. The half-year rules are applicable to Class 29.

Class 44 - Patents (25%)   At one point in time, patents were allocated to Class 14 where they were amortized over their legal life of 20 years. This approach failed to recognize that the economic life of this type of asset was usually a much shorter period. To correct this problem, patents are now allocated to Class 44, where they are subject to write-off at a 25 percent declining balance rate. Note, however, that a taxpayer can elect to have these assets allocated to Class 14. This would be a useful alternative if a patent was acquired near the end of its legal life.

Class 45, 50 And 52 - Computer Hardware And Systems Software   CCA classes and rates for computer hardware and systems software are as follows:

Acquisition Date	Class	Rate
After March 22, 2004, Before March 19, 2007	45	45% Declining Bal.
After March 18, 2007, Before Jan. 28, 2009	50	55% Declining Bal.
After Jan. 27, 2009, Before Feb. 1, 2011*	52	100% Write-Off
After January 31, 2011	50	55% Declining Bal.

* No application of the half-year rules.

The fact that there are different classes for computers provides a good example of the government's approach to changing CCA rates. Prior to March 23, 2004, computer hardware was included in Class 10 (30 percent rate). The government concluded that this rate was too low. Rather than change the rate on Class 10 (which includes vehicles), they dealt with this problem by indicating that computer hardware acquired after March 22, 2004 should be allocated to new Class 45 (45 percent rate), computer hardware acquired after March 18, 2007 should be allocated to new Class 50, (55 percent rate) and computer hardware acquired between January 28, 2009 and January 31, 2011 should be allocated to new Class 52 with a 100 percent write-off.

Since the 2011 budget did not extend the use of Class 52 beyond January 31, 2011, computer hardware is once again allocated to Class 50. The advantage of this approach is that it avoids having to apply the new rates on a retroactive basis to computers that were acquired before the changes took place.

Exercise Five - 1

Subject: Segregation Into CCA Classes

For each of the following depreciable assets, indicate the appropriate CCA Class. (The Appendix to this Chapter contains a listing of CCA classes.)

- Taxicab
- Manufacturing and processing equipment acquired in 2012
- Franchise with a limited life
- Automobile (i.e., passenger vehicle) with a cost of $120,000
- Water storage tank
- Photocopy machine
- Leasehold improvements
- Residential rental property acquired in 2007 for $150,000 (Land Value = $50,000)

End of Exercise. Solution available in Study Guide.

Half-Year Rules (a.k.a. First Year Rules)
General Rules

5-33.   At one time, a taxpayer was permitted to take a full year's CCA on any asset acquired during a taxation year. This was true even if the asset was acquired on the last day of the year. This was not an equitable situation and the most obvious solution would have been to base CCA calculations on the proportion of a taxation year that the asset was used. Despite the fact that this pro rata approach is widely used for accounting purposes, the government decided that this would be too difficult to implement and an alternative approach was chosen.

5-34.   The approach adopted is based on the arbitrary assumption that assets acquired during a particular taxation year were in use for one-half of that year. Stated simply, in determining the end of period UCC for the calculation of maximum CCA, one-half of the excess, if any, of the additions to UCC for acquisitions over the deductions from UCC for dispositions is removed. As established by the use of the phrase "if any", this adjustment is only made when the net amount is positive.

5-35.   The following example is a simple illustration of the half-year adjustment for additions to most CCA classes. It has not been complicated by the presence of capital gains, recapture of CCA, or terminal losses.

> **Example**   Radmore Ltd., with a taxation year that ends on December 31, has a Class 10 (30 percent) UCC balance on January 1, 2012 of $950,000. During 2012, it acquires 15 cars at a cost of $20,000 each, for a total addition of $300,000, and disposes of 18 cars for total proceeds of $144,000. In no case did the proceeds of disposition exceed the capital cost of the vehicle being disposed of. The maximum CCA for 2012 and the January 1, 2013 UCC balance are calculated as follows:

January 1, 2012 UCC Balance		$ 950,000
Add: Acquisitions During The Year	$300,000	
Deduct: Dispositions During The Year	(144,000)	156,000
Deduct: One-Half Net Additions [(1/2)($156,000)]		(78,000)
Base Amount For CCA Claim		$1,028,000
Deduct: 2012 CCA [(30%)($1,028,000)]		(308,400)
Add: One-Half Net Additions		78,000
January 1, 2013 UCC Balance		**$ 797,600**

Exceptions To Half-Year Rules

5-36.   There are some classes, or parts of classes, to which the half-year rules do not apply. For the classes that we have described in this Chapter, the exceptions are as follows:

- All assets included in Class 14 (limited life intangibles).
- Some Class 12 assets such as medical or dental instruments and tools costing less than $500, uniforms, and chinaware. Other Class 12 assets such as certified Canadian films, computer software, and rental video cassettes, are subject to the half-year rules.

5-37.   A further exception is available for some property transferred in non-arm's length transactions. Specifically, depreciable property acquired in non-arm's length transactions is generally exempt from the half-year rule if, prior to the transfer, the property was depreciable property that was owned for at least one year and was used to produce business or property income. The property remains in the CCA class that it was in prior to its transfer. This prevents the double application of this rule in situations where there is no real change in the ownership of the property.

> **Example**   Amber Bailey has an unincorporated business that owns Class 8 assets with capital cost of $200,000 and a UCC of $75,000. The assets are sold to her sister for their fair market value of $250,000. Her sister plans to continue operating the unincorporated business.

Analysis This is a non-arm's length transfer and, both before and after the transfer, the Class 8 assets will be used to produce business income. In this situation, the half-year rule would not be applicable. As the half-year rule was applicable when Ms. Bailey acquired the assets, this exception prevents a double application of this rule to the same assets.

Exercise Five - 2

Subject: CCA Error

During the taxation year ending December 31, 2012, your company acquired a depreciable asset for $326,000 and you included this asset in Class 1 for the year (it was not allocated to a separate Class 1). Early in 2013, you discover that the asset should have been allocated to Class 10. What was the impact of this error on your company's 2012 deductions from business income?

Exercise Five - 3

Subject: Class 13 And Half-Year Rule

Vachon Ltd. has a December 31 year end. The Company leases its office space under a lease that was signed on January 1, 2007. The lease term is 10 years, with an option to renew at an increased rent for an additional five years. In 2007, the Company spends $52,000 renovating the premises. In 2012, changing needs require the Company to spend $31,000 renovating the space. Determine the maximum amount of Class 13 CCA that the Company can deduct for 2012.

Exercise Five - 4

Subject: Class 8 And Half-Year Rule

Justin Enterprises, an unincorporated business with a December 31 year end, has a Class 8 UCC balance on January 1, 2012 of $212,000. During 2012, it acquires additional Class 8 assets at a cost of $37,400. Also during 2012, it deducts $18,300 from the UCC balance for dispositions. Determine the maximum CCA for 2012 and the January 1, 2013 UCC balance.

Exercise Five - 5

Subject: Class 14 - No Half-Year Rule

Arnot has a December 31 year end. On March 31, 2012, Arnot Ltd. pays $375,000 to enter a franchise agreement. The life of the franchise is 10 years with rights commencing on April 1, 2012. Determine the maximum CCA for 2012 and the January 1, 2013 UCC balance.

End of Exercises. Solutions available in Study Guide.

Short Fiscal Periods

5-38. The previous material noted that a half-year assumption has been built into the capital cost allowance system to deal with assets that are acquired or disposed of during a given taxation year. In contrast to this somewhat arbitrary provision for dealing with part year ownership, a more precise rule has been included in the Regulations for dealing with short fiscal periods.

5-39.   In the first or last years of operation of a business, or in certain other types of situations that will be covered in later chapters, a taxation year with less than 365 days may occur. Under these circumstances, the maximum CCA deduction for most classes must be calculated using a proration based on the relationship between the days in the actual fiscal year and 365 days.

5-40.   For example, assume that a business with a taxation year that ends on December 31 begins operations on November 1. On December 1, $100,000 of Class 8 assets (20 percent declining balance) are purchased.   There are no further additions or dispositions in December. The CCA for the first fiscal year, taking into consideration the half-year rules, would be calculated as follows:

$$[(1/2)(20\%)(\$100,000)(61/365)] = \underline{\$1,671}$$

5-41.   As is illustrated in the preceding calculation, the half-year rules also apply in these short fiscal period situations. Note it is the length of the taxation year for the business, not the period of ownership of the asset, which determines the proration.

5-42.   Two additional points are relevant here:

• As noted previously and illustrated in Exercise Five-5, Class 14 assets are subject to pro rata CCA calculations, based on the number of days of ownership in the year. This obviates the application of the short fiscal period rules.

• When an individual uses assets to produce property income (e.g., rental income), the full calendar year is considered to be the taxation year of the individual. This means that the short fiscal period rules are not applicable in these situations.

Exercise Five - 6

Subject: Short Fiscal Periods

Olander Inc. is incorporated on August 1, 2012. On September 15, 2012, the Company acquires $115,000 in Class 8 assets. The Company has a December 31 year end and no other depreciable assets are acquired before December 31, 2012. Determine the maximum CCA for the year ending December 31, 2012.

End of Exercise.   Solution available in Study Guide.

Tax Planning Considerations

5-43.   As previously noted, the tax rules on capital cost allowances are expressed in terms of maximum amounts that can be deducted. There is, however, no minimum amount that must be deducted, and this leaves considerable discretion as to the amount of CCA to be taken in a particular year. In fact, under certain circumstances, a taxpayer is even allowed to revise the CCA for the previous taxation year. This can, in effect, create a "negative" CCA for the current year. The guidelines for this type of amendment are found in IC 84-1. Note, however, that a revision of CCA for a previous year is only permitted if there is no change in the Tax Payable of any year.

5-44.   If the taxpayer has Taxable Income and does not anticipate a significant change in tax rates in future years, tax planning for CCA is very straightforward. The optimum strategy will generally be to take the maximum CCA allowed in order to minimize Taxable Income and Tax Payable.

5-45.   The situation becomes more complex in a loss year. If a taxpayer wishes to minimize a loss for tax purposes, one approach is to reduce the amount of CCA taken for the year (whether or not the taxpayer will wish to minimize a loss is affected by the loss carry over provisions that are discussed in Chapter 11). In these circumstances, it is necessary to decide on which class or classes the CCA reduction should be applied.

5-46. The general rule is that CCA reductions should be allocated to the classes with the highest rates, while taking full CCA on those classes with the lowest rates.

Example A taxpayer has a $100,000 loss he would like to eliminate by reducing his CCA by $100,000. The UCC of Class 1 (4 percent) is $2,500,000 and the UCC of Class 10 (30 percent) is $333,333. Both classes would have maximum CCA of $100,000.

Analysis If $100,000 in CCA is taken on Class 1, the following year's maximum CCA will be reduced by only $4,000, from $100,000 [(4%)($2,500,000)] to $96,000 [(4%)($2,400,000)]. In contrast, taking the $100,000 CCA on Class 10 would reduce the following year's maximum CCA by $30,000, from $100,000 [(30%)($333,333)] to $70,000 [(30%)($233,333)]. It would clearly be preferable to take the CCA on Class 1, so that the taxpayer has the option of taking higher CCA in the following year.

5-47. Similar opportunities arise when current tax rates are below those expected in the future. For example, some provinces institute periodic tax holidays for certain types of businesses. As taxes will be applied in future years, it may be advantageous to stop taking CCA in order to maximize Taxable Income during the years of tax exemption.

Exercise Five - 7

Subject: CCA And Tax Planning

Monlin Ltd. has determined that, for the current year, it has Taxable Income before the deduction of CCA of $45,000. It is the policy of the Company to limit CCA deductions to an amount that would reduce Taxable Income to nil. At the end of the year, before the deduction of CCA, the following UCC balances are present:

Class 1 (4%)	$426,000
Class 8 (20%)	126,000
Class 10 (30%)	89,000
Class 10.1 (30%)	21,000

There have been no additions to these classes during the year. Which class(es) should be charged for the $45,000 of CCA that will be required to reduce Taxable Income to nil? Explain your conclusion.

End of Exercise. Solution available in Study Guide.

Dispositions Of Depreciable Assets

Overview Of Procedures

Basic Rule

5-48. The basic rule for dealing with dispositions of capital assets is as follows:

Basic Rule For Dispositions When there is a disposition of a depreciable property, an amount will be deducted from the UCC balance in the relevant CCA Class. The deduction will be equal to the lesser of:

- The proceeds of disposition.
- The capital cost of the individual asset.

5-49. Note that, while we do not need the value of individual assets for purposes of determining maximum CCA, it is necessary to track the value of individual assets in order to apply this basic disposition rule.

Dispositions With No Immediate Tax Consequences

5-50. In the majority of cases, the proceeds of disposition for a depreciable asset will be less than its capital cost. In applying the basic rule, this means that the proceeds of disposition will be subtracted from the balance in the relevant CCA Class.

5-51.   Given the broadly based nature of most CCA Classes, it is likely that a business would have additional assets in the Class subsequent to the disposition. Further, it is also likely that a balance will remain in the Class after the proceeds of disposition have been deducted. In such situations, there are no immediate tax consequences associated with the disposition. While the balance in the Class will be reduced and this will result in smaller CCA deductions in current and future years, the disposition does not give rise to any immediate income inclusion or deduction.

5-52.   For students who are used to working with accounting procedures, this tends to be an uncomfortable result. The accounting procedures for dispositions require that we compare the proceeds of disposition for the individual asset with the net book value of that asset. It would be very unusual for these procedures not to result in either a gain (the proceeds exceed the net book value) or a loss (the proceeds are less than the net book value). In contrast, many, perhaps a majority, of depreciable asset dispositions have no immediate tax consequences.

Dispositions With Tax Consequences

5-53.   As noted in the previous section, the disposition of a depreciable asset will have no immediate tax consequences, provided that:

- The proceeds of disposition are less than the capital cost of the asset.
- There are additional assets in the CCA Class.
- There is a positive balance in the CCA Class, subsequent to the subtraction of the proceeds of disposition. Even if the balance is negative at the time of the disposition, there will still be no tax consequences, provided additions to the Class prior to the end of the year leave a positive balance.

5-54.   While many dispositions meet these conditions, there will also be situations where one or more of these conditions is not present. When this happens, immediate tax consequences will arise. While we will discuss each of these results in more detail, in general terms the various possible consequences can be described as follows:

Capital Gain   A capital gain will arise on the disposition of a depreciable asset if the proceeds of disposition exceed the capital cost of the asset.

Recapture Of CCA   Subtraction of the proceeds of disposition from the UCC may result in the creation of a negative balance in the class. This can occur whether or not there are any assets left in the class. If this negative balance is not eliminated by new acquisitions prior to the end of the taxation year, this negative amount must be included in income as recapture of CCA. The amount will also be added to the UCC for the class, thereby setting the balance to nil for the beginning of the next year.

Terminal Loss   This occurs only when there are no assets left in the class at the end of the year. If, when the proceeds from the disposition of the last asset(s) are deducted from the UCC for the class, a positive balance remains, this balance can be deducted as a terminal loss. Note that it is not a capital loss. A terminal loss is 100 percent deductible against any other income. The amount of the terminal loss will also be deducted from the UCC for the class, thereby leaving the balance at nil.

No Capital Losses   It is important to note that there is no possibility of a capital loss arising on the disposition of a depreciable asset. When a depreciable asset is acquired for use in a business, there is an expectation that it will decline in value as it is used to produce income. This is reflected in the fact that its tax value will be written down by taking fully deductible CCA. Given this, it would not be equitable to record a capital loss, only one-half of which would be deductible. The only type of loss that can arise on the disposition of a depreciable asset is a fully deductible terminal loss.

Capital Gains

5-55.   The tax rules related to capital gains are fairly complex and will be covered in detail in Chapter 8. However, in order to fully understand the tax procedures related to dispositions of depreciable assets, some understanding of this component of Net Income For Tax Purposes is required. The basic idea is that, if a capital asset is sold for more than its capital cost, the excess of the proceeds of disposition over the capital cost of the asset is a capital gain. As many of you are aware, only one-half of this gain will be included in the taxpayer's Net Income For Tax Purposes. As we have noted, this one-half of the capital gain is referred to as the taxable capital gain.

5-56. The more important point to remember when calculating CCA is that this excess amount will not be deducted from the UCC. When the proceeds of disposition exceed the capital cost of the asset, the amount deducted from the UCC on the disposition is limited to its capital cost. This is reflected in the basic rule for dispositions that was presented in Paragraph 5-48.

Exercise Five - 8

Subject: Capital Gains On Depreciable Assets

Vaughn Ltd. has a Class 8 balance of $275,000. During the current year, an asset with a capital cost of $18,000 is sold for $23,000. There are no other dispositions during the year and there are over 100 assets left in Class 8. What are the tax consequences of this disposition?

End of Exercise. Solution available in Study Guide.

Recapture Of Capital Cost Allowance
Procedures
5-57. Recapture of capital cost allowance refers to situations in which a particular class contains a negative, or credit, balance at the end of the taxation year. As previously described, the UCC ending balance for a particular class is calculated by starting with the opening balance of the class, adding the cost of acquisitions, and subtracting the lesser of the proceeds of disposition and the capital cost of any assets sold (CCA is subtracted at the beginning of the following taxation year). If the disposal subtraction exceeds the balance in the class, a negative balance will arise.

5-58. Note, however, that a disposition that creates a temporary negative balance at some point during the year does not create recapture. If additions to the class that are made later in the year eliminate this negative balance prior to year end, no recapture will have to be included in income.

5-59. It is important to note that acquiring additional assets of a particular class will not eliminate negative balances in those situations where each individual asset has to be allocated to a separate class (e.g., rental buildings costing $50,000 or more). As was intended by policy makers, when individual assets must be allocated to separate classes, a disposition that creates a negative balance at any time during the taxation year will result in recapture. This result cannot be eliminated as no subsequent acquisitions can be added to this separate class.

Economic Analysis
5-60. Recapture of CCA arises when deductions from the class exceed additions and this generally means that the proceeds of the dispositions, when combined with the CCA taken, exceed the cost of the assets added to the class. In effect, recapture is an indication that CCA has been deducted in excess of the real economic burden of using the assets (cost minus proceeds of disposition). As a reflection of this situation, ITA 13(1) requires that the recaptured CCA be added back to income. The recapture amount is also added to the UCC balance, leaving a balance of nil at the beginning of the next taxation year.

Exercise Five - 9

Subject: Recapture of CCA

At the beginning of 2012, Codlin Inc. has two assets in Class 8. The cost of each asset was $27,000 and the Class 8 UCC balance was $24,883. On June 30, 2012, one of the assets was sold for $28,500. There are no other additions or dispositions prior to the Company's December 31, 2012 year end. What is the effect of the disposition on the Company's 2012 net business income? In addition, determine the January 1, 2013 UCC balance.

End of Exercise. Solution available in Study Guide.

Terminal Losses

Procedures

5-61.   When there is a disposition of the last asset in a CCA class, or the disposition of the only asset when a separate class is used, the resulting balance may be positive or negative. As discussed in the previous section, a negative balance will have to be included in income as recapture. Alternatively, if a positive balance remains, this balance is referred to as a terminal loss.

5-62.   A terminal loss occurs only when there are no assets in the class at the end of the period. If there is a positive balance in the class at some point during the year, but no assets in the class, there is no terminal loss if additional assets are acquired prior to the end of the year.

5-63.   Terminal losses are fully deductible in the determination of business or property income. In addition, the amount of the loss is subtracted from the CCA class, leaving a nil balance at the beginning of the following year.

5-64.   An additional point here relates to employment income. While employees can deduct CCA on automobiles and aircraft and are subject to the usual rules with respect to recapture, IT-478R2 indicates that terminal losses cannot be deducted on such assets. The reason for this position is that ITA 8(2) indicates that employees can only deduct items that are listed in ITA 8. As terminal losses are not covered by this Section, no deduction is available.

Economic Analysis

5-65.   The presence of a positive balance subsequent to the sale of the last asset in the class is an indication that the taxpayer has deducted less than the full cost of using the assets in this class. Under these circumstances, ITA 20(16) allows this terminal loss to be deducted in full. As we have previously noted, this is not a capital loss. While it is possible to have capital gains on assets that are subject to CCA, it is not possible to have a capital loss on the disposition of a depreciable asset.

Exercise Five - 10

Subject: Terminal Losses

At the beginning of 2012, Codlin Inc. has two assets in Class 8. The cost of each asset was $27,000 and the Class 8 UCC balance was $24,883. On June 30, 2012, both of these assets are sold for a total of $18,000. There are no other additions or dispositions prior to the Company's December 31, 2012 year end. What is the effect of the disposition on the Company's 2012 net business income? In addition, determine the January 1, 2013 UCC balance.

End of Exercise. Solution available in Study Guide.

Exercise Five - 11

Subject: Depreciable Asset Dispositions

Norky Ltd. disposes of a Class 8 asset for proceeds of $126,000. The capital cost of this asset was $97,000 and it had a net book value of $43,500. The Company's Class 8 contains a number of other assets and the balance for the Class prior to this disposition was $2,462,000. Describe briefly the accounting and tax treatments of this disposition.

End of Exercise. Solution available in Study Guide.

Summary Of Tax Consequences

5-66.   Figure 5-2 provides a summary of the various tax consequences that can result from dispositions of depreciable assets, along with a description of the conditions that lead to each possible consequence.

Figure 5 - 2
Dispositions Of Depreciable Assets - Summary of Tax Consequences

Result	Conditions
Capital Gain	If the proceeds of disposition exceed the capital cost of the asset. Will normally be accompanied by recapture of CCA.
Recapture Of CCA	If a deduction resulting from a disposition exceeds the balance in the CCA Class and a negative balance remains at the end of the taxation year. There may or may not be assets remaining in the Class
Terminal Loss	If the last asset in a CCA Class is disposed of and a positive balance remains in the Class at the end of the taxation year.
No Immediate Tax Consequences	If the proceeds of disposition are less than the capital cost of the asset (no capital gain), the disposition does not leave a negative balance in the CCA Class at the end of the taxation year (no recapture), and there are assets left in the CCA Class at the end of the taxation year (no terminal loss).

CCA Schedule

5-67.   At this point, it is useful to summarize the CCA calculations in a schedule.   A commonly used format is illustrated in the following example.

Example   The fiscal year end of Blue Sky Rentals Ltd. is December 31. On January 1, 2012, the UCC balance for Class 8 is $155,000. During the year ending December 31, 2012, $27,000 was spent to acquire Class 8 assets. During the same period, used Class 8 assets were sold for $35,000. The capital cost of these assets was $22,000.

UCC Of The Class At The Beginning Of The Year		$155,000
Add: Acquisitions During The Year	$27,000	
Deduct: Dispositions During The Year - Lesser Of:		
• Capital Cost = $22,000		
• Proceeds Of Disposition = $35,000	(22,000)	5,000
Deduct: One-Half Net Additions [(1/2)($5,000)]*		(2,500)
Amount Subject To CCA		$157,500
Deduct: CCA For The Year [(20%)($157,500)]		(31,500)
Add: One-Half Net Additions		2,500
UCC Of The Class At The Beginning Of The Subsequent Year		$128,500

*This adjustment for one-half of the excess of additions over disposal deductions is only made when the net amount is positive.

5-68.   While this schedule is not designed to show this value, there is also a taxable capital gain of $6,500 [(1/2)($35,000 - $22,000)] resulting from the sale of assets.

CCA Determination - Special Situations

Separate Class Election

The Problem

5-69.   In our discussion of CCA procedures we noted that, in general, all assets of a particular type must be allocated to a single CCA class. However, we also noted that there were a number of exceptions to this general approach. For example, the *Income Tax Regulations* require that a separate class be used for each rental property with a cost in excess of $50,000.

5-70.   As a further point, we noted that for certain other types of assets, the taxpayer could elect to use a separate CCA class for each individual asset. Now that you have an understanding of the procedures associated with dispositions of depreciable assets, we can meaningfully discuss the reasons for making such an election for certain types of assets.

5-71.   Consider a $25,000 colour photocopier that would normally be allocated to Class 8. After two years, the UCC balance would be calculated as follows:

Capital Cost	$25,000
CCA Year One [(20%)(1/2)($25,000)]	(2,500)
CCA Year Two [(20%)($25,000 - $2,500)]	(4,500)
UCC - Beginning Of Year Three	$18,000

5-72.   Given the rate of technological change in this area, it is possible that this photocopier would be replaced after two years. Further, the value of the old photocopier would likely be relatively small. If, for example, the photocopier was disposed of for proceeds of $5,000, there would be a terminal loss equal to $13,000 ($18,000 - $5,000).

5-73.   There are two problems with this analysis:

• Most businesses will have more than one asset in Class 8. This disposition would leave other assets in the Class and no terminal loss could be recognized.

• Even if the photocopier is the only Class 8 asset, if the photocopier is replaced, the replacement would likely be acquired within the same taxation year, again resulting in a situation where no terminal loss could be recognized because there are remaining assets in the Class.

5-74.   The election to allocate this photocopier to a separate Class 8 balance alleviates these problems. When the photocopier is retired, a terminal loss can be recognized, even if the business replaces it prior to year end or has other Class 8 assets.

Eligible Assets (Rapidly Depreciating Electronic Equipment)

5-75. There are a number of high tech or electronic products that are normally included in Class 8 (20 percent declining balance) that have actual service lives that are significantly shorter than the rates applicable to that Class would imply. Under ITR 1101(5p), some of these assets are eligible for separate class treatment. The following Class 8 assets are eligible, provided they have a capital cost of $1,000 or more:

- photocopiers (Class 8)
- electronic communications equipment, such as telephone equipment (Class 8)
- computer software (only if included in Class 8 rather than Class 10, 12, or 50)

5-76. As noted in our earlier discussion, the purpose of this separate class election is to provide for the recognition of terminal losses on the disposition of certain short-lived assets. Under the usual single class procedures, such recognition is not usually possible, either because there are assets remaining in the particular CCA class, or because the retired assets are being replaced on a regular and ongoing basis.

Exercise Five - 12

Subject: Separate Class Election

In January, 2012, Edverness Inc. acquires 10 photocopiers at a cost of $20,000 each. In December, 2012, two of these photocopiers are traded in on faster machines with more features. The new photocopiers cost $22,000 each, and the Company receives a trade-in allowance for each old machine of $3,000. Indicate the amount(s) that would be deducted from 2012 business income if no election is made to put each photocopier in a separate class. Contrast this with the deduction(s) that would be available if the separate class election is used.

End of Exercise. Solution available in Study Guide.

Other Special Situations

5-77. There are a number of other situations which involve special rules that are applicable to real and deemed dispositions of depreciable assets. Briefly described, they are as follows:

Sale Of Real Properties (Land And Buildings) When real properties are sold, it is not uncommon that the result is a capital gain on the land, combined with a terminal loss on the building. Given that the loss is fully deductible, while only one-half of the capital gain is subject to tax, it is not surprising that special rules are applicable to such transactions.

Replacement Properties When an involuntary disposition (a disposition resulting from events such as fire or expropriation) occurs, it may result in large capital gains and recapture of CCA. Similarly, when there is a voluntary disposition (e.g., a business sells its assets to move to a new location), such taxable amounts may also arise. In such situations, the *Income Tax Act* has provisions that provide relief, provided the assets are replaced within a specified period of time.

Changes In Use When the use of a property is changed from personal to income producing (e.g., an individual converts a principal residence to a rental property), the *Income Tax Act* views the change as a deemed disposition, combined with a deemed re-acquisition. These deemed transactions have tax consequences which may, in particular circumstances, be very important.

5-78. While all of these special situations require an understanding of the concepts introduced in this Chapter 5, they also require a sound understanding of the taxation of capital gains and losses. Given this situation, we will defer our coverage of these situations to Chapter 8, Capital Gains And Losses.

Cumulative Eligible Capital (CEC)
Eligible Capital Expenditures Defined

5-79.   IT-123R6, "Transactions Involving Eligible Capital Property", describes eligible capital property as "intangible capital property, such as goodwill and other 'nothings', the cost of which neither qualifies for capital cost allowance nor is deductible in the year of its acquisition as a current expense". IT-143R3, "Meaning Of Eligible Capital Expenditures", lists the following items to be included in eligible capital expenditures:

- Goodwill purchased as one of the assets of a business.
- Customer lists purchased and not otherwise deductible.
- The cost of trademarks, patents, licences, and franchises with unlimited lives. (In general, if these expenditures have limited lives they are Class 14 or Class 44 assets.)
- Expenses of incorporation, reorganization, or amalgamation.
- Appraisal costs associated with valuing eligible capital property, such as a government right. Also appraisal costs on an anticipated property purchase that does not take place.
- The costs of government rights.
- Initiation or admission fees to professional or other organizations for which the annual maintenance fees are deductible.
- Some payments made under non-competition agreements.

5-80.   To clarify the matter further, IT-143R3 specifically excludes the following from the definition:

- The cost of non-depreciable tangible assets (land).
- The cost of depreciable intangibles (such as Class 14 patents).
- Payments made to produce exempt income.
- Payments made to creditors for redemption or cancellation of bonds or other debt instruments.
- Payments by a corporation to a person as a shareholder of the corporation (dividends, payments to redeem shares, or for appropriations of property).
- The cost of acquiring or issuing shares, bonds, mortgages, notes, or an interest in a trust or partnership.

Terminology

5-81.   While eligible capital expenditures are treated in much the same manner as expenditures for depreciable assets, the terminology is sufficiently different that some explanation would be useful. The term, "eligible capital expenditure", is the equivalent of capital cost for depreciable capital assets. When these expenditures are made, three-quarters of the cost is added to a cumulative balance designated "cumulative eligible capital" (CEC). This CEC balance is the equivalent of the UCC balance for a particular class of depreciable capital assets. As such, it is reduced by amounts deducted, as well as by three-quarters of the proceeds of any dispositions, without regard to their cost.

5-82.   For tax purposes, amortization of depreciable capital assets is called capital cost allowance (CCA) and is deducted under ITA 20(1)(a) at a variety of rates that are prescribed in the *Income Tax Regulations*. Amortization of CEC is deducted under ITA 20(1)(b) at the 7 percent rate specified in that Paragraph. The term "CEC amount" is usually applied to this deduction.

5-83.   The terminology for dispositions is more complex. We will find that there will be results that are similar to capital gains, recapture of CCA, and terminal losses on depreciable capital assets.

Additions, Amortization, And Dispositions
General Procedures

5-84.   All acquisitions and dispositions of eligible capital expenditures are accounted for in a single cumulative eligible capital account for each business. The ending balance in this account is used to calculate the deductible amortization. The rules for dealing with eligible capital expenditures are similar to the procedures used for depreciable capital assets. There are, however, important differences that will be described in the following material.

Applicability

5-85.   The depreciable property rules are applicable to business income, property income, and, in somewhat more limited circumstances, employment income (see Chapter 6 for an explanation of the difference between business income and property income). In contrast, the rules for dealing with eligible capital expenditures are only applicable to business income calculations. The ITA 20(1)(b) deduction of CEC cannot be made against either property income or employment income.

Additions

5-86.   When an eligible capital expenditure is acquired, three-quarters of its cost is added to the CEC account. The probable reason for limiting the inclusion to three-quarters of the cost is because the other party to the expenditure will often record a capital gain on the disposition. For example, when an individual sells a business including its goodwill, the goodwill will usually not have a tax value. This means that the total amount allocated to goodwill will be treated as proceeds from the disposal of CEC and given treatment similar to that accorded to capital gains (i.e., only 50 percent of the amount will be subject to tax.)

5-87.   Based on the preceding analysis, it would logical to expect that the inclusion rate for CEC additions would be adjusted when the inclusion rate for capital gains is changed. This, in fact, happened in 1990. In that year, when the capital gains inclusion rate was changed from one-half to three-quarters, the inclusion rate for CEC additions was also increased from one-half to three-quarters.

5-88.   For reasons that have not been clearly explained by the Department of Finance, a similar adjustment did not accompany the changes in the capital gains inclusion rate that occurred in 2000. When the capital gains inclusion rate was reduced from three-quarters to one-half in 2000, the inclusion rate for CEC additions was left at three-quarters.

Amortization

5-89.   Amortization is deducted under ITA 20(1)(b). The write-off procedures for the cumulative eligible capital account are similar to those used for declining balance UCC classes. As noted previously, the rate is specified in ITA 20(1)(b) as 7 percent. This rate is applied to the end of the period balance in the cumulative eligible capital account.

5-90.   As with CCA, any amount up to the maximum can be claimed and deducted from the account. For CEC, there is no equivalent of the half-year rules that can apply to CCA calculations. However, ITA 20(1)(b) indicates that, in situations where there is a short fiscal period, the amount deducted must be prorated on the basis of the number of days in the short fiscal period.

Dispositions

5-91.   When there is a disposition of cumulative eligible capital, three-quarters of the proceeds of disposition are deducted from the CEC account. There are two things of note here. First, as was the case with the inclusion rate for additions to CEC, the amount to be deducted on a disposition was not changed by the 2000 budget. It remains at three-quarters of the proceeds of disposition, as opposed to the one-half inclusion rate for capital gains.

5-92.   Also note that, unlike the situation with depreciable asset dispositions, three-quarters of the proceeds will be deducted even in cases where this amount exceeds three-quarters of the original cost of the asset. For cumulative eligible capital dispositions, the deduction is always based on the proceeds of disposition. This is in contrast to the situation with depreciable capital assets where we deduct the lesser of the proceeds of disposition and the capital cost. This difference eliminates the need to track the cost of individual eligible capital expenditures. However, as will be discussed beginning in Paragraph 5-99, there is an election available that may make this cost information useful.

5-93.   If a positive CEC balance remains after making the deduction for the disposition, the business continues to deduct a CEC amount at the rate of 7 percent applied to the remaining balance. This is without regard to whether any of the assets that were added to the balance are still present. As long as the business continues to operate, the 7 percent will be applied to any remaining balance. An ongoing business will never record a terminal loss on CEC balances.

5-94.   Alternatively, if the deduction creates a negative balance, we have a situation that is analogous to recapture. Prior to the 2000 budget, this negative balance was taken into income as an inclusion under ITA 14(1), and added back to the CEC balance to begin the next taxation year with a nil balance. As there was no need to limit the deduction from the CEC balance on the basis of the cost of the eligible capital expenditure, this ITA 14(1) income inclusion was made up of a combination of previously deducted CEC (the equivalent of recapture), as well as possible capital gains.

5-95.   As long as the capital gains inclusion rate was at three-quarters, the same rate that was used for CEC additions, this was an equitable situation. As additions to, and deductions from, the CEC balance were also based on this fraction, any capital gain that was included in the negative balance was, in effect, included in income at the same three-quarters rate that was applicable to capital gains in general.

5-96.   However, since 2000, we have had a situation where the CEC amounts have remained at the three-quarters level, while capital gains are being included at a lower one-half rate. As part of a negative CEC balance may reflect amounts that are similar to capital gains, following the pre-2000 budget procedures would result in these amounts being taxed on a three-quarters basis. To deal with this problem, ITA 14(1) has been modified to require that any negative balance be divided into two components. These components, along with their tax treatment, are as follows:

- To the extent that there have been CEC deductions in the past, the negative amount will be added to income under ITA 14(1). This is the equivalent of recapture for depreciable assets.

- Any excess of the negative amount over past CEC deductions will be viewed as similar to a capital gain. To give this excess amount treatment analogous to that given to capital gains, it will be multiplied by two-thirds prior to its inclusion in the taxpayer's income. This factor reduces the amount from a three-quarters inclusion to a one-half inclusion [(3/4)(2/3) = 1/2].

Example - Cumulative Eligible Capital

5-97.   The example that follows will help clarify the procedures used to deal with CEC:

Example   A corporation begins operations on March 1, 2011 and acquires goodwill for $40,000 on May 24, 2011. In July, 2013, the goodwill is sold for $46,000. The company's fiscal year ends on December 31.

Analysis   The analysis of the cumulative eligible capital account would be as follows:

	CEC Balance	CEC Deductions
Addition, May, 2011 [(3/4)($40,000)]	$30,000	
CEC Amount [($30,000)(7%)(306/365)]	(1,761)	$1,761
Balance, January 1, 2012	$28,239	
CEC Amount [($28,239)(7%)]	(1,977)	1,977
Balance, January 1, 2016	$26,262	
Proceeds Of Sale [(3/4)($46,000)]	(34,500)	
Balance After Sale	($ 8,238)	$3,738

An amount of $3,738 that represents recapture of previous CEC deductions would be added to income.

The $4,500 excess ($8,238 - $3,738) would be multiplied by two-thirds to arrive at an income inclusion of $3,000. The logic behind this approach becomes clear when you recognize that $3,000 is one-half of the $6,000 ($46,000 - $40,000) gain on the sale of the goodwill, demonstrating that these procedures give capital gains treatment to gains on the disposition of CEC balances.

5-98.   As a final point on dispositions, an income inclusion under ITA 14(1) only occurs when the CEC balance is negative at the end of the year. As was the case with recapture, the income inclusion would not occur if there are additions to the balance that eliminate the negative amount prior to the end of the taxation year.

Exercise Five - 13

Subject: Cumulative Eligible Capital With Disposition

On January 1, 2010, Keddy Inc. purchases another business and pays $85,600 for goodwill. At this time, the cumulative eligible capital of the Company is nil. There are no additions to this balance in 2011 or 2012. On June 30, 2012, the business acquired in 2010 was sold and the sale price included a payment for goodwill of $93,400. The Company has a December 31 year end and takes the maximum deduction for cumulative eligible capital in both 2010 and 2011. What amount, if any, will be included in the Company's 2012 income as a result of this sale?

End of Exercise. Solution available in Study Guide.

CEC Disposal Election

5-99.   Unlike CCA calculations where the deduction of the proceeds of disposition is limited to the cost of the asset, three-quarters of the entire proceeds from any disposition is normally deducted from the CEC balance. This requirement has the effect of deducting amounts which are, in effect, capital gains from the CEC balance. For companies that wish to recognize capital gains (e.g., companies with capital losses), this is not a totally equitable situation.

5-100.   To correct this, ITA 14(1.01) provides for an election that effectively allows for separate treatment of individual dispositions. Under this election, the amount deducted from the CEC balance is limited to three-quarters of the cost of the individual item being disposed of. The excess is then treated as an ordinary capital gain.

Example   On January 1, 2012, Marq Ltd.'s CEC balance was nil. During 2012, Marq Ltd. acquires two eligible capital expenditures, one for $80,000 and the other for $140,000. For the taxation year ending December 31, 2012, the Company deducts the maximum CEC amount. In early 2013, the $80,000 asset is sold for $120,000.

Analysis The following table compares the balance in the CEC account assuming the election is not made, with the balance assuming the election is made:

	No Election	With Election
2012 Addition [(3/4)($80,000 + $140,000)]	$165,000	$165,000
CEC Amount [($165,000)(7%)]	(11,550)	(11,550)
January 1, 2013 CEC Balance	$153,450	$153,450
Proceeds Of Sale [(3/4)($120,000)]	(90,000)	Nil
Deemed Proceeds Of Sale [(3/4)($80,000)]	Nil	(60,000)
Balance After Sale	$ 63,450	$ 93,450

If no election is made in 2013, there will be no income inclusion and the only tax consequence of the disposition is a reduction in the 2013 and future CEC amounts.

If an election is made under ITA 14(1.01), Marq Ltd. is deemed to have disposed of a capital property with an adjusted cost base equal to the cost of $80,000 for proceeds of disposition equal to the actual proceeds of $120,000. This results in a capital gain of $40,000 ($120,000 - $80,000), with a taxable amount of $20,000 [(1/2)($40,000)].

5-101.   ITA 14(1.03)(a) does not allow the use of the election with respect to goodwill, regardless of whether it has been purchased or generated internally. Further, this election can only be used for eligible capital expenditures that have a cost that can be determined. The election cannot be used to recognize a loss in situations where the fair market value of the item is less than its cost.

Exercise Five - 14

Subject: Cumulative Eligible Capital Election

On January 1, 2011, Que Industries Ltd. has no CEC balance. During the taxation year ending December 31, 2011, it has made the following eligible capital expenditures:

Government License	$206,000
Payment For Non-Competition Agreement	85,000
Customer List	223,000
Total	$514,000

The Company deducts the maximum amount of CEC for 2011. In November, 2012, the customer list is sold for $296,000. Compare the tax consequences associated with the sale of the customer list assuming: (1) no election is made and (2) an election is made under ITA 14(1.01) to treat the disposition of the customer list separately.

End of Exercise. Solution available in Study Guide.

Special Situations

Business Terminations

5-102.   When a business is terminated, a positive balance may remain in the CEC account. If this is the case, the situation is similar to that involving terminal losses on depreciable capital assets. With respect to terminal losses, the balance remaining can be deducted in the computation of Net Income For Tax Purposes. In similar fashion, any CEC balance that is left when a business terminates can also be deducted.

5-103.   However, an important difference from the terminal loss situation on depreciable assets is that the deductible amount of any loss on CEC is only three-quarters of the actual amount of the real economic loss. As is the case with terminal losses, any amount deducted from income is also deducted from the CEC balance in order to leave a balance of nil.

5-104.   A limitation on this involves situations where a taxpayer ceases doing business and the business is continued by the taxpayer's spouse, common-law partner, or a corporation controlled by the taxpayer. Under these circumstances, ITA 24(2) prohibits the deduction of a loss, requiring that the balance must be transferred to the opening CEC balance of the continuing business.

Death Of A Taxpayer

5-105.   ITA 70(5.1) provides that when a taxpayer dies, and the taxpayer's eligible capital property is acquired by a beneficiary who continues to carry on the business, he is deemed to have disposed of it immediately before death at proceeds that are equal to the cumulative eligible capital balance. This would mean that no income inclusion or terminal loss occurs at this time.

Key Terms Used In This Chapter

5-106. The following is a list of the key terms used in this Chapter. These terms, and their meanings, are compiled in the Glossary Of Key Terms located at the back of the separate paper Study Guide and on the Student CD-ROM.

Capital Cost	First Year Rules
Capital Cost Allowance (CCA)	Half-Year Rules (a.k.a. First Year Rules)
Capital Gain	Non-Depreciable Capital Property
Class	Recapture Of CCA
Cumulative Eligible Capital (CEC)	Separate Class Rules
Declining Balance Method	Straight-Line Method
Depreciable Capital Property	Taxable Capital Gain
Disposition	Terminal Loss
Eligible Capital Expenditure	Undepreciated Capital Cost (UCC)

References

5-107. For more detailed study of the material in this Chapter, we would refer you to the following:

ITA 13(1)	Recaptured Depreciation
ITA 13(7.1)	Deemed Capital Cost Of Certain Property
ITA 13(26) to ITA 13(32)	Available For Use Rules
ITA 14(1)	Eligible Capital Property - Inclusion In Income From Business
ITA 14(1.01)	Election Re Capital Gain
ITA 20(1)(a)	Capital Cost Of Property
ITA 20(1)(b)	Cumulative Eligible Capital Amount
ITA 20(16)	Terminal Loss
ITR Part XI	Capital Cost Allowances
ITR II-VI (Schedules)	Capital Cost Allowances
IC-84-1	Revision Of Capital Cost Allowance Claims And Other Permissive Deductions
IT-79R3	Capital Cost Allowance - Buildings Or Other Structures
IT-123R6	Transactions Involving Eligible Capital Property
IT-128R	Capital Cost Allowance - Depreciable Property
IT-143R3	Meaning Of Eligible Capital Expenditure
IT-147R3	Capital Cost Allowance - Accelerated Write Off Of Manufacturing And Processing Machinery And Equipment
IT-190R2	Capital Cost Allowance - Transferred And Misclassified Property
II-195R4	Rental Property - Capital Cost Allowance Restrictions
IT-206R	Separate Businesses
IT-220R2	Capital Cost Allowance - Proceeds Of Disposition Of Depreciable Property
IT-285R2	Capital Cost Allowance - General Comments
IT-313R2	Eligible Capital Property - Rules Where A Taxpayer Has Ceased Carrying On A Business Or Has Died
IT-386R	Eligible Capital Amounts
IT-418	Capital Cost Allowance - Partial Dispositions Of Property
IT-472	Capital Cost Allowance - Class 8 Property
IT-478R2	Capital Cost Allowance - Recapture And Terminal Loss

Appendix - CCA Rates For Selected Assets

This Appendix lists the CCA Class and rate for assets commonly used in business. Restrictions and transitional rules may apply in certain situations. ITR Part XI contains detailed descriptions of the CCA Classes.

Asset	Class	Rate
Aircraft (including components)	**9**	**25%**
Airplane runways	17	8%
Automobiles, passenger		
• Cost < or = Prescribed amount ($30,000 in 2012)	10	30%
• Cost > Prescribed amount	10.1	30%
Automotive equipment	10	30%
Bar code scanners	**8**	**20%**
Billboards	8	20%
Boats, canoes and other vessels	7	15%
Bridges, canals, culverts and dams	1	4%
Buildings Acquired Before 1988	3	5%
Buildings Acquired After 1987 - No Separate Class	1	4%
Buildings (New Only) Acquired After March 18, 2007:		
• Manufacturing and Processing In Separate Class 1	1	10%
• Non-Residential In Separate Class 1	1	6%
Buses	10	30%
Calculators	**8**	**20%**
Cash registers	8	20%
China, cutlery and tableware	12	100%
Computer hardware and systems software, acquired:		
• After March 18, 2007, Before Jan. 28, 2009	50	55%
• After Jan. 27, 2009, Before Feb. 1, 2011	52	100%
• After January 31, 2011	50	55%
Computer software (applications)	12	100%
Copyrights	14	Straight-line
Data network infrastructure equipment	**46**	**30%**
Dies, jigs, patterns, and molds	12	100%
Docks, breakwaters and trestles	3	5%
Electrical advertising billboards	**8**	**20%**
Electronic point-of-sale equipment	8	20%
Equipment (not specifically listed elsewhere)	8	20%
Fences	**6**	**10%**
Films	10	30%
Franchises (limited life)	14	Straight-line
Franchises (unlimited life)	CEC	N/A
Furniture and fixtures		
(not specifically listed elsewhere)	8	20%
Goodwill	**CEC**	**N/A**
Instruments, dental or medical (See Tools)		
Kitchen utensils (See Tools)		

Asset	Class	Rate
Land	N/A	N/A
Landscaping	N/A	Deductible
Leasehold improvements	13	Straight-line
Licences (limited life)	14	Straight-line
Licences (unlimited life)	CEC	N/A
Linen	12	100%
Machinery and equipment		
(not specifically listed elsewhere)	8	20%
Manufacturing and processing equipment		
• acquired before March 19, 2007	43	30%
• acquired after March 18, 2007 and before 2014	29	50%
		Straight-line
Office equipment (not specifically listed elsewhere)	8	20%
Outdoor advertising billboards	8	20%
Parking area and similar surfaces	17	8%
Patents (limited life)	44	25%
Patents (unlimited life)	CEC	N/A
Photocopy machines	8	20%
Portable buildings and equipment	10	30%
Power operated movable equipment	38	30%
Radio communication equipment	8	20%
Railway cars		
• acquired after February 27, 2000	7	15%
• acquired before February 28, 2000	35	7%
Roads	17	8%
Sidewalks	17	8%
Software (applications)	12	100%
Software (systems)	10	30%
Storage area	17	8%
Storage tanks, oil or water	6	10%
Tangible Capital Assets		
(not specifically listed elsewhere)	8	20%
Taxicabs	16	40%
Telephone systems	8	20%
Television commercials	12	100%
Tools		
• acquired after May 1, 2006 (under $500)	12	100%
• acquired after May 1, 2006 ($500 or over)	8	20%
Trailers	10	30%
Trucks and tractors for hauling freight	16	40%
Trucks (automotive), tractors and vans	10	30%
Uniforms	12	100%
Video games (coin operated)	16	40%
Video tapes	10	30%
Video tapes for renting	12	100%
Wagons	10	30%

Problems For Self Study

(The solutions for these problems can be found in the separate Study Guide.)

Self Study Problem Five - 1 (CCA Calculations)

Mr. Marker has been the sole proprietor of Marker Enterprises since its establishment in 1999. This business closes its books on December 31 and, on January 1, 2012, the following information on its assets was contained in the records of the business:

Type Of Asset	Undepreciated Capital Cost	Original Capital Cost	CCA Rate
Building (Class 1)	115,000	190,000	4 Percent
Equipment (Class 8)	96,000	130,000	20 Percent
Vehicles (Class 10)	6,700	30,000	30 Percent
Equipment (Class 29)*	$ 75,000	$100,000	50 Percent

*The manufacturing and processing equipment was acquired in 2011.

Other Information:

1. During the year ending December 31, 2012, Mr. Marker's business acquired additional Class 8 equipment at a total cost of $52,000. This new equipment replaced equipment that had an original cost of $75,000, which was sold during the year for total proceeds of $35,000.

2. During the year ending December 31, 2012, Mr. Marker acquired a used automobile to be used in his business for a total cost of $8,000. Also during this year, Mr. Marker sold one of the trucks that was used in his business for proceeds of $25,000. This truck, which had an original capital cost of $20,000, had achieved a high value as the result of its extra features, which were no longer available on later models.

3. As the result of a decision to lease its premises in future years, Mr. Marker sold his building for total proceeds of $260,000. Of the $260,000 received, $150,000 is for the land on which the building is situated. The adjusted cost base of the land was equal to the $150,000 proceeds of disposition.

Required: Calculate the total effect of all of the preceding information on Mr. Marker's Net Income For Tax Purposes for the year ending December 31, 2012. Your answer should include the maximum CCA that can be deducted by Mr. Marker for each class. In addition, calculate the January 1, 2013 UCC balance for each Class.

Self Study Problem Five - 2 (CCA Calculations Over 5 Years)

Golden Dragon Ltd. begins operations in Vancouver on September 1, 2007. These operations include an elegant sit down restaurant specializing in northern Chinese cuisine, as well as a take out operation that provides home delivery throughout the city. To facilitate this latter operation, on October 12, 2007, the Company acquires 20 small cars to be used as delivery vehicles. The cost of these cars is $12,000 each and, for purposes of calculating CCA, they are classified as Class 10 assets.

During the first year of operations, the Company establishes a fiscal year ending on December 31. In the fiscal periods 2008 through 2012, the following transactions take place with respect to the Company's fleet of delivery cars:

2008   The Company acquires five more cars at a cost of $12,500 each. In addition, three of the older cars are sold for total proceeds of $27,500.

2009   There are no new acquisitions of cars during this year. However, four of the older cars are sold for total proceeds of $38,000.

2010   In December, 2010, 13 of the original cars and 3 of the newer cars are sold for $128,000. It was the intent of the Company to replace these cars. However, because of a delay in delivery by the car dealer, the replacement did not occur until January, 2011.

2011   In January of 2011, the Company takes delivery of 25 new delivery cars at a cost of $16,000 each. No cars are disposed of during 2011.

2012   In March, 2012, there is a change in management at Golden Dragon Ltd. They conclude that the Company's take out operation is not in keeping with the more elegant image that the sit down restaurant is trying to maintain. As a consequence, the take out operation is closed, and the 27 remaining delivery cars are sold. Because of the large number of cars being sold, the total proceeds are only $268,000.

Golden Dragon Ltd. takes maximum CCA in each of the years under consideration.

Required: For each of the fiscal years 2007 through 2012, calculate CCA, recapture, or terminal loss for Golden Dragon's fleet of cars. In addition, indicate the January 1 UCC for each of the years 2008 through 2013.

Self Study Problem Five - 3 (CCA And Tax Planning)

For its taxation year ending December 31, 2012, Marion Enterprises has determined that its operating Net Income For Tax Purposes before any deduction for CCA amounts to $53,000. The Company does not have any Division C deductions, so whatever amount is determined as Net Income For Tax Purposes will also be the amount of Taxable Income for the taxation year.

On January 1, 2012, the Company has the following UCC balances:

Class 1 (Building Acquired in 2004)	$876,000
Class 8	220,000
Class 10	95,000
Class 10.1 (Cadillac)	25,500
Class 10.1 (Porsche)	17,850

During 2012, the cost of additions to Class 10 amounted to $122,000, while the proceeds from dispositions in this class totalled $87,000. The capital cost of the assets retired totaled $118,000, and there were still assets in Class 10 on December 31, 2012.

There were no acquisitions or dispositions in Class 1, 8 or 10.1 during 2012. During the preceding three taxation years, the Company reported Taxable Income totalling $39,000 for the three years.

Required:

A. Calculate the maximum CCA that could be taken by Marion Enterprises for the taxation year ending December 31, 2012. Your answer should include the maximum that can be deducted for each CCA class.

B. As Marion Enterprises' tax advisor, indicate how much CCA you would advise the Company to take for the 2012 taxation year, and the specific classes from which it should be deducted. Provide a brief explanation of the reasons for your recommendation. In determining your solution, ignore the possibility that 2012 losses can be carried forward to subsequent taxation years.

Self Study Problem Five - 4 (Cumulative Eligible Capital)

On January 1, 2009, Miss Nash acquires an unincorporated business operation for a total price of $2,500,000. While most of this amount can be allocated to specific identifiable assets, an amount of $500,000 is left and must be allocated to goodwill.

Miss Nash operates the business until October 15, 2012. At that point, she receives an offer of $3,800,000 for the business and decides to sell it. Of the total sales price, an amount of

$780,000 is allocated to goodwill.

Required: Prepare a schedule showing the cumulative eligible capital amount that can be deducted in each year of business and the tax effect related to the sale of goodwill by Miss Nash.

Self Study Problem Five - 5 (CCA And CEC Calculations)

The following information relates to Bartel Ltd. for its fiscal year that ends on December 31, 2012:

1. The Company has UCC balances on January 1, 2012 for its tangible assets as follows:

Class 1 (All Buildings Acquired In 2005)	$590,000
Class 8	570,000
Class 10	61,000

2. During 2012, the Company purchased office furniture for $14,000.

3. During 2012, the Company purchased a truck from its majority shareholder for $22,000. The truck was four years old, had a fair market value of $22,000, and the shareholder's UCC for the truck was $26,000.

4. On January 1, 2010, the Company expanded its operations by purchasing another business. The purchase price for this business included a payment of $92,000 for goodwill, $120,000 for a franchise with a six year life, and $28,000 for a franchise with an unlimited life.

5. During 2012, one of the Company's buildings was sold for proceeds of $440,000, of which $150,000 represented the value of the land on which the building was situated. The Building had a capital cost of $475,000, of which $175,000 represented the value of the land at the time of the acquisition.

    The building was replaced during 2012 with a new building that cost $500,000, of which $125,000 represented the value of the land. The use of this building is 100 percent office space and it is allocated to a separate Class 1.

6. During 2011, the Company sold part of its original operations. The proceeds of disposition included a payment for goodwill of $59,000.

7. Bartel Ltd. has always deducted the maximum CCA and the maximum write-off of cumulative eligible capital allowable in each year of operation.

Required: Calculate the maximum total CCA and the maximum write-off of cumulative eligible capital that can be deducted for 2012. Your answer should include the maximum that can be deducted for each CCA class.

Self Study Problem Five - 6 (CCA And CEC Calculations)

The fiscal year of the Atlantic Manufacturing Company, a Canadian public company, ends on December 31. On January 1, 2012, the UCC balances for the various classes of assets owned by the Company are as follows:

Class 1 - Building (Note 1)	$625,000
Class 8 - Office Furniture And Equipment	155,000
Class 10 - Vehicles	118,000
Class 13 - Leasehold Improvements	61,750
Class 29 - Manufacturing Equipment	217,000

Note 1 The Class 1 building was acquired in 2005.

During the year ending December 31, 2012, the following acquisitions of assets were made:

Class 8 - Office Furniture And Equipment	$ 27,000
Class 10 - Vehicles (Note 2)	33,000
Class 12 - Tools (Note 3)	34,000
Class 13 - Leasehold Improvements	45,000
Class 50 - Computer Hardware	28,000

Note 2   The acquired vehicle was a delivery truck.

Note 3   None of the tools that were acquired during the year cost more than $500.

During this same period, the following dispositions occurred:

Class 8 - Used office furniture and equipment was sold for cash proceeds in the amount of $35,000. The original cost of these assets was $22,000.

Class 10 - A delivery truck with an original cost of $23,000 was sold for $8,500.

Class 29 - Since the manufacturing operations will be done by subcontractors in the future, all of the manufacturing equipment was sold for total proceeds of $188,000. Its original cost was $752,000.

Other Information:

1.   The Company leases a building for $27,000 per year that houses a portion of its manufacturing operations. The lease was negotiated on January 1, 2009 and has an original term of eight years. There are two renewal options on the lease. The term for each of these options is four years. The Company made $78,000 of leasehold improvements immediately after signing the lease. No further improvements were made until the current year.

2.   On February 24, 2012, one of the Company's cars was totally destroyed in an accident. At the time of the accident, the fair market value of the car was $12,300. The proceeds from the Company's insurance policy amounted to only $8,000. The original cost of the car was $17,000.

3.   The Atlantic Manufacturing Company was organized in 2007 and has no balance in its cumulative eligible capital account on January 1, 2012. During March, 2012, the Company granted a manufacturing licence for one of its products to a company in southern Ontario. This licensee paid $87,000 for the right to manufacture this product for an unlimited period of time.

4.   It is the policy of the Company to deduct maximum CCA in all years.

Required: Calculate the maximum 2012 CCA that can be taken on each class of assets, the January 1, 2013 UCC balance for each class, and any other 2012 income inclusions or deductions resulting from the information provided in the problem.

Self Study Problem Five - 7 *(CEC With Disposal Election)*

On January 1, 2010, Crown Resources Inc. (CRI) has a CEC balance of $2,345,000. During the taxation year ending December 31, 2010, the Company acquires an unlimited life franchise for consideration of $400,000.

During the taxation year ending December 31, 2011, CRI sells one of its operating divisions. The sales price included a $240,000 payment for goodwill. As this goodwill was internally developed, its presence was not reflected in the Company's CEC balance. Also during this year, an unlimited life franchise with an original cost of $300,000 was sold for $160,000.

During 2012, the unlimited life franchise that was acquired in 2010 was sold for $560,000.

It is the policy of CRI to deduct maximum amounts of CCA and CEC.

Required:

A.   What is the maximum deduction that CRI can claim for amortization of cumulative eligible capital in 2010, 2011, and 2012? Assume that no elections are made with respect to the CEC dispositions in any of these years.

B. Calculate the amounts that will be included in CRI's 2011 and 2012 Net Income For Tax Purposes as a result of the CEC dispositions. Assume that no elections are made with respect to the CEC dispositions.

C. How would the results in Parts A and B differ if CRI makes all possible CEC disposal elections under ITA 14(1.01)? Explain why a taxpayer might want to make this election.

Assignment Problems

(The solutions for these problems are only available in
the solutions manual that has been provided to your instructor.)

Assignment Problem Five - 1 *(CCA For M&P Assets)*

Gold Mountain Manufacturing Ltd. has a taxation year that ends on December 31. On May 1, 2011, Gold Mountain purchased equipment for $500,000 that is to be used in manufacturing and processing in Canada. It had been leasing its equipment prior to this purchase.

Gold Mountain has two buildings in Class 1 and is planning to purchase a new building in 2012. The building's use would be allocated in one of the following ways:

1. 100 percent for manufacturing.
2. 60 percent for manufacturing and 40 percent for office space.
3. 40 percent for manufacturing, 30 percent for office space and 30 percent for long-term residential rentals.

Required:

A. For the equipment, calculate the maximum amount of CCA that Gold Mountain can deduct for 2011, 2012, and 2013, as well as the January 1, 2014 UCC balance.

B. For the new building, determine the CCA rate that would be applicable under each of the three alternative uses described. Briefly explain your conclusions.

Assignment Problem Five - 2 *(CCA On Rental Properties)*

On March 1, 2011, Ms. Fox acquires a residential duplex for a total cost of $725,000. Of this total, it is estimated that the land has a value of $150,000 at the time of the acquisition. The two units are identical in size and, for purposes of allocation to a CCA Class, the property is considered to be a single unit.

Before the end of March, 2011, both units were rented. The tenant occupying one of the units asked that, in return for an additional amount of rent, Ms. Fox furnish the unit. Furniture and appliances for the unit were acquired by Ms. Fox on April 1, 2011 at a cost of $18,500.

During the year ending December 31, 2011, rents on the two units totaled $43,500. Expenses, other than CCA, totaled $28,000.

Late in 2012, the tenants in the furnished unit moved out. As Ms. Fox did not wish to continue renting the unit on a furnished basis, she sold the furniture and appliances to the departing tenants for $14,000.

During 2012, the two units generate total rent of $45,000. Expenses, other than CCA, totaled $32,000.

Ms. Fox deducts the maximum CCA allowable in both years.

Required: Calculate the maximum CCA that can be deducted by Ms. Fox in each of the years 2011 and 2012. Also, determine her UCC balances on January 1, 2013. Include in your solution any tax consequences associated with the sale of the furniture and appliances.

Assignment Problem Five - 3 (CCA Calculations)

Opening Balances   The taxation year of Burton Steel Ltd. ends on December 31. On January 1, 2012, the UCC balances for the various classes of assets owned by the Company are as follows:

Class 3 - Building	$1,562,000
Class 8 - Office Furniture And Equipment	278,000
Class 10 - Vehicles	204,000
Class 13 - Leasehold Improvements	106,250
Class 29 - Manufacturing Equipment	126,000
Class 50 - Computer Hardware	11,000

Acquisitions   During the year ending December 31, 2012, the following acquisitions of assets were made.

Class 1 - Building (Note 1)	$258,000
Class 8 - Office Furniture And Equipment	72,000
Class 10 - Vehicles (Note 2)	63,000
Class 13 - Leasehold Improvements	58,000
Class 50 - Computer Hardware	17,000

Note 1   The $423,000 total cost of the Building was allocated $258,000 to the building itself, and $165,000 to the land. The Building will be used 100 percent for non-residential activity, none of which involves manufacturing and processing activity. It will be allocated to a separate Class 1.

Note 2   The addition to Class 10 was made up of three passenger vehicles, with a cost of $21,000 each.

Dispositions   During this same period, the following dispositions occurred:

Class 8 - Office furniture and equipment were sold for cash proceeds of $42,000. The original cost of these assets totalled $38,000.

Class 10 - A delivery truck with an original cost of $37,000 was sold for $12,000.

Class 29 - Since Burton Steel Ltd. will only be involved in retail operations in the future, all of the manufacturing equipment was sold for total proceeds of $89,000. The original cost of the equipment was $504,000.

Other Information:

1. The Company leases its main office building for $47,000 per year. The lease was negotiated on January 1, 2010 and had an original term of eight years. There are two renewal options on the lease, each for a period of two years. The Company made $125,000 of leasehold improvements immediately after signing the lease. No further improvements were made until the current year.

2. During the year ending December 31, 2012, some of the Company's office furniture and equipment was destroyed in a small fire. At the time of the accident, the fair market value of the destroyed property was $19,000. However, proceeds from the Company's insurance policy amounted to only $11,000. The original cost of the destroyed property was $18,000.

3. Maximum CCA has always been taken by Burton Steel.

Required: Calculate the maximum CCA that can be taken by Burton Steel Ltd. on each class of assets for the year ending December 31, 2012, and calculate the UCC for each class of assets on January 1, 2013. Indicate any other inclusions or deductions from Taxable Income resulting from the preceding information.

Assignment Problem Five - 4 (CCA Calculations Over 4 Years)

Barbara's Messenger Service begins operations on November 1, 2009. It operates an intra-city service which guarantees delivery of important documents within 3 hours. Barbara Good is the sole owner of this unincorporated business. The business will have a taxation year that ends on December 31. Barbara indicates that she plans to take maximum CCA every year.

On November 15, 2009, the business acquires 10 small cars to be used for deliveries. These vehicles have a cost of $18,000 each.

During the year ending December 31, 2010, the business acquires 5 additional cars at a cost of $22,000 each. In addition, 4 of the original cars are sold for proceeds of $5,000 each.

During the year ending December 31, 2011, 8 additional cars are acquired at a cost of $25,000 each. The remaining 6 cars that were purchased in 2009 are sold for $2,000 each.

Barbara has found that when particularly important, high value packages are involved, some of her clients require the package to be hand delivered in an awe-inspiring style. These clients are willing to pay a very hefty surcharge for this service. In order to accommodate this, the business acquires two S Class Mercedes at a cost of $160,000 each.

Early in 2012, Barbara receives a proposal of marriage from her wealthiest client. Barbara accepts this proposal and, because she will be moving to a different city, she decides to terminate her business. The 13 remaining small cars are sold for $6,000 each. The S Class Mercedes are sold for $95,000 each.

Required: For each of the taxation years 2009 through 2012, calculate the maximum available CCA deduction. In addition, determine the amount of any capital gain, recapture, or terminal loss that arises on any of the transactions that occurred during these years. Ignore GST/HST/PST considerations.

Assignment Problem Five - 5 (CCA Calculations Over 3 Years)

Ken's Kouriers is an unincorporated business which provides courier services within the city of Halifax. It has a taxation year that ends on December 31.

Ken's Kouriers began operating on May 1, 2010 by acquiring a new building at a total cost of $326,000. Of this total, $53,000 is allocated to the land on which the building is situated. As it will be used 100 percent for non-residential purposes, it is allocated to a separate Class 1.

Furnishings for the building are acquired on June 1, 2010 at a cost of $85,000.

Also on June 1, 2010, the business acquires 12 vehicles to be used by its couriers. The cost of these vehicles is $23,000 each for a total of $276,000.

During 2011, the business trades in 5 of its old vehicles for more fuel efficient vehicles. The replacement vehicles cost $27,000 per vehicle. The company receives a trade-in allowance of $16,000 for each old vehicle. Also during 2011, the Company acquires a luxury vehicle to be used by Ken, the owner of the business. The cost of this vehicle is $103,000.

During 2012, Ken and five of his drivers are charged with smuggling counterfeit goods. Ken's Kouriers is closed down and Ken sells the assets as follows:

- The building is sold for $342,000, with $53,000 of this amount being attributed to the land.
- The remaining 7 vehicles that were purchased in 2010 are sold for $73,000. The 5 vehicles that were acquired in 2011 are sold for $62,500.
- The furniture is sold for $12,300.
- The luxury vehicle is sold for $63,800.

Required: Determine the maximum CCA that can be taken in each of the years 2010 through 2012. In your calculations, include and identify the UCC balances for January 1, 2011, January 1, 2012, and January 1, 2013. In addition, indicate any tax effects resulting from the 2011 and 2012 dispositions. Ignore GST/HST/PST considerations.

Assignment Problem Five - 6 (CCA, CEC And Tax Planning)

For the taxation year ending December 31, 2012, Kreton Inc. has determined that its Net Income For Tax Purposes, before any deductions for CCA or CEC, amounts to $51,000. As the Company does not have any Division C deductions, Taxable Income, before any deductions for CCA or CEC, would also amount to $51,000.

On January 1, 2012, the Company has the following UCC and CEC balances:

Class 8	$220,000
Class 10	152,000
Class 12	56,000
Class 13	272,000
CEC	210,000

During 2012, the cost of additions to Class 8 amount to $42,000, while the proceeds from dispositions in this class totaled $16,000. In no case did the proceeds of disposition exceed the capital cost of the assets retired, and there were still assets in the class as of December 31, 2012.

All of the Class 12 assets were acquired in 2011.

The leasehold improvements were made in 2010 at a cost of $320,000.

There were no 2012 acquisitions or dispositions in Classes 10, 12, or 13. There were no eligible capital expenditures acquired during 2012 and no dispositions of cumulative eligible capital.

In previous years, the Company has always deducted the maximum amount of CCA and CEC.

Required:

A. Calculate the maximum CCA and CEC write-off that could be taken by Kreton Inc. for the taxation year ending December 31, 2012.

B. As Kreton's tax advisor, indicate how much CCA and CEC you would advise them to take for the 2012 taxation year and the specific classes from which it should be deducted. Provide a brief explanation of the reason for your recommendation. In providing this advice, do not take into consideration the possibility that losses can be carried either back or forward.

Assignment Problem Five - 7 (CEC With Disposal Election)

On January 1, 2010, Altec Ltd. has no balance in its CEC account. The Company has a taxation year that ends on December 31.

During the 2010 taxation year, Altec acquires the assets of another business at a cost of $4,250,000. The identifiable assets of this business have a fair value of $4,000,000, indicating that Altec has acquired $250,000 of goodwill. In addition, the identifiable assets of Altec included an unlimited life franchise with a fair value of $175,000.

The unlimited life franchise proved to be incompatible with the Altec's other operations and, during the 2011 taxation year, it is sold for proceeds of $225,000.

During the 2012 taxation year, Altec sells one of its business divisions. The consideration received included a $350,000 payment for the division's goodwill.

It is the policy of Altec Ltd. to deduct maximum amounts of CCA and CEC.

Required:

A. What is the maximum deduction that Altec can claim for amortization of cumulative eligible capital in 2010, 2011, and 2012? Assume that no elections are made with respect to the CEC dispositions in any of these years.

B. Calculate the amounts that will be included in Altec's 2011 and 2012 Net Income For Tax Purposes as a result of the CEC dispositions. Assume that no elections are made with respect to the CEC dispositions.

C. How would the results in Parts A and B differ if Altec makes all possible CEC disposal elections under ITA 14(1.01)? Explain why a taxpayer might want to make such elections.

Assignment Problem Five - 8 (CCA And CEC Calculations)

The following information relates to Andorn Ltd. for its taxation year that ends on December 31, 2012:

1. The Company has UCC balances on January 1, 2012 for its tangible assets as follows:

Class 1 (A single building acquired in 2008)	$478,695
Class 8	243,000
Class 10	126,000
Class 13	127,500

2. During 2012, the building that was acquired in 2008 was sold for cash of $650,000. Of this total, $125,000 represented the value of the land on which the building was situated. The building had a capital cost of $625,000, of which $80,000 represented the value of the land at time the building was acquired.

    The building was replaced during 2012 with a new building at a cost of $745,000, of which $125,000 represented the value of the land.

    The old building was used 100 percent for office space and was allocated to a separate Class 1. The new replacement building is also used 100 percent for office space and is allocated to a separate Class 1.

3. During 2012, the Company purchased office furnishings for $74,000. They traded in older furnishings and received an allowance of $17,000. The capital cost of the furnishings that were traded in was $56,000.

4. Andorn conducts some of its business out of a building which it leases. The lease was signed on January 1, 2010 and had an initial term of 7 years. It has an option to renew for 3 years. At the time the lease was signed, Andorn spent $150,000 on leasehold improvements.

5. The only vehicle purchased during the year was a Lexus to be used by the president of the Company. The cost of this car was $93,000. The president drives it 23,000 kilometers during the year, of which 5,750 kilometers are for employment related purposes.

6. During 2010, the Company purchased two franchises. The first, which was purchased on August 1, 2010, had cost $62,000 and a legally limited life of 8 years. The second, purchased on July 5, 2010, cost $84,000 and had an unlimited life. This second franchise was sold during 2012 for $65,000.

7. Andorn Ltd. has always deducted the maximum CCA and the maximum write-off of cumulative eligible capital allowable in each year of operation.

Required: Calculate the maximum CCA and the maximum write-off of cumulative eligible capital that can be deducted for 2012. Your answer should include the maximum that can be deducted for each CCA class. In addition, indicate the amount of any recapture or terminal loss that results from dispositions during 2012.

CHAPTER 6

Income Or Loss From A Business

Overview

Net Income For Tax Purposes

Where We Are At

6-1.   In Chapter 1, we indicated that much of this volume would be devoted to the concepts and procedures associated with determining Net Income For Tax Purposes. In terms of the *Income Tax Act*, this subject is covered in Part I, Division B. This Division, titled Computation Of Income, contains 11 Subdivisions, with the first three dealing with specific types of income. They are as follows:

Subdivision a   Income Or Loss From An Office Or Employment

Subdivision b   Income Or Loss From A Business Or Property

Subdivision c   Taxable Capital Gains And Allowable Capital Losses

6-2.   At this point, we have provided fairly comprehensive coverage of the first of these Subdivisions. In Chapter 3, we discussed in detail the inclusions and deductions that go into the calculation of employment income or loss.

6-3.   While we could have followed the discussion of employment income with coverage of the other components of Net Income For Tax Purposes, we chose to devote Chapter 4 to an introduction to Taxable Income and Tax Payable for individuals. While most texts leave this subject until the end of their coverage of all components of Net Income For Tax Purposes, we provided this introduction so that we could include comprehensive problems at an early stage in the text.

6-4.   Again in contrast to some other texts, we introduced CCA calculations in Chapter 5, prior to our coverage of business income. As you are now aware, this is a very technical subject which involves what is often one of the most important deductions in the determination of business income. It was included prior to our coverage of business income in order to facilitate the presentation of complete examples of the determination of business income.

Where We Are Going

6-5.   Chapters 6, 7, and 8 will provide coverage of the remaining specific types of income that go into the determination of Net Income For Tax Purposes. While business income and property income are dealt with in a single Subdivision of the *Income Tax Act*, these two types of income are subject to somewhat different rules. In addition, in some circumstances, they are subject to significantly different rates of tax. Given this, we will deal with Subdivision b in two separate Chapters. This Chapter 6 will cover business income, with Chapter 7 dealing with property income.

6-6.   The final major component of Net Income For Tax Purposes, taxable capital gains and allowable capital losses, will be dealt with in Chapter 8.

Classification Of Income
A Net Determination
6-7.   We have then, four basic types of income:

- employment income;
- business income;
- property income; and
- capital gains.

6-8.   Each of these basic types is determined on a net basis. That is, each amount that is to be included in Net Income For Tax Purposes is based on a specific group of inclusions that will usually be reduced by a specific group of deductions.

6-9.   In general, the deductions applicable to one type of income cannot be deducted against the inclusions in a different type. However, if a loss is created in a particular year by an excess of deductions over inclusions, that loss can generally be applied against other types of income. The exception to this is a current year net capital loss. While such losses can be carried back or forward to other taxation years, they cannot be applied against other types of income that have been recognized during the current year. In fact, even in carry over years, allowable capital losses can only be deducted to the extent that taxable capital gains are present.

Applicable Taxpayers
6-10.   Employment income is unique in that only individuals can earn this type of income. In contrast, business income, property income, and capital gains can be recognized by all taxpayers. This would include individuals, corporations, and trusts.

Classification And The Use Of Property
6-11.   Business income, property income, and capital gains generally involve the use of property. Further, it is usually the manner in which the property is being used that determines the classification of the resulting income. Because of this, it is important to understand the use of this term in the *Income Tax Act*.

6-12.   Property is defined very broadly in ITA 248(1) as "property of any kind whatever whether real or personal or corporeal or incorporeal". This would include both depreciable and non-depreciable property. The definition also encompasses both tangible and intangible property.

6-13.   In terms of classifying the various types of income, it is useful to identify four categories of property on the basis of the manner in which they are used.

Property Acquired For Use In A Business   These are assets acquired to be used in a business. Examples would be factory and store buildings, the land underlying such buildings, furniture and fixtures in a retail store, and equipment used in manufacturing. While these assets are held, the income produced will be classified as business income. If the taxpayer disposes of such assets, classification of the income that is produced will depend on the type of asset.

Non-Depreciable Capital Assets   A disposition will result in a capital gain or a capital loss.

Figure 6 - 1 Classification Of Income		
Use Of Property	Income While Held	Income At Disposition
Used In Business		
Depreciable	Business Income	Capital Gain, Recapture, Or Terminal Loss
Non-Depreciable	Business Income	Capital Gain (Loss)
Acquired As Investment		
Depreciable	Property Income	Capital Gain, Recapture, Or Terminal Loss
Non-Depreciable	Property Income	Capital Gain (Loss)
Acquired For Resale	Generally None	Business Income (Loss)
Acquired For Personal Use	None	Capital Gain (In General, Losses Are Not Deductible)

Depreciable Capital Assets   A disposition will result in recapture, a capital gain and recapture, or a terminal loss (capital losses cannot arise on depreciable assets). As noted in Chapter 5, both recapture and terminal losses are components of business income when the asset is used in the business.

Property Acquired And Held As An Investment   These assets are acquired to be held while they produce income. They are distinguished from business assets in that they produce income with little or no effort on the part of the acquirer. Examples would be holdings of debt securities, holdings of equity securities, and ownership of rental properties. While they are held, these investment assets produce property income. As was the case with assets acquired for use in a business, the classification of income that results from a disposition of such assets will depend on whether the asset is depreciable or non-depreciable.

Non-Depreciable Assets   A disposition will result in a capital gain or a capital loss.

Depreciable Assets   A disposition will result in recapture, a capital gain and recapture, or a terminal loss. Both recapture and terminal losses are components of property income when the asset is used to produce property income.

Property Acquired For Resale At A Profit   These assets are acquired with the objective of reselling them at a profit. Examples would be the typical inventory balances that are held by most businesses. Any gain or loss that arises on their disposition will be treated as a business income or loss, not as a capital gain or loss. In most cases, such assets will not produce income while they are held. If they do, it would be classified as business or property income.

Property Acquired By Individuals For Personal Use   These are assets acquired by individuals for personal use. Examples would be personal use automobiles, personal use boats, and real property that is not held to produce income. While these assets are held they do not produce income. However, if they are sold at a value in excess of their adjusted cost base, the excess will be subject to tax as a capital gain. Alternatively, if they are sold for less than their adjusted cost base, the resulting loss will generally not be deductible (see the discussion of personal use property in Chapter 8).

6-14.   As you can see, this categorization of the various ways a property can be used serves to outline how the various types of income are classified. The types of income produced by the various categories of property are summarized in Figure 6-1.

Areas Of Controversy

6-15.   In many situations, classification presents no problems.

- An individual being paid an hourly rate on the General Motors assembly line is clearly earning employment income.

- An individual operating a Second Cup franchise is clearly earning business income.

- An investor receiving interest on Canada Savings Bonds is clearly earning property income.

6-16.   However, this is not always the case. As the manner in which income is classified can have significant tax consequences, it is not surprising that classification is a controversial issue in some situations. In general terms, there are three types of problems that can arise:

Business Income Vs. Employment Income   For some individuals, it is not clear whether they are working as an employee or, alternatively, as an independent contractor earning business income (a.k.a., self-employed individual). The tax consequences and classification guidelines related to this issue were discussed, in detail, in Chapter 3.

Business Income Vs. Property Income   While income producing assets are being held, there may be a question as to whether they are producing business income or, alternatively, property income. The tax consequences and classification guidelines related to this issue will be discussed in this Chapter.

Business Income Vs. Capital Gains   On dispositions of property, it is sometimes difficult to establish whether the resulting gain is business income or, alternatively, a capital gain. The tax consequences and classification guidelines related to this issue will also be discussed in this Chapter.

Business Income Vs. Property Income

Tax Consequences Of Classification

Rates

6-17.   For individuals, both business income and property income will generally be subject to tax at the rates that were discussed in Chapter 4. This will require the application of a progressive rate structure, beginning at the low federal rate of 15 percent and increasing to the maximum federal rate of 29 percent. In terms of applicable rates, the business vs. property classification is not a significant issue for individuals.

6-18.   This is not the case for corporations. If a corporation is Canadian controlled and its shares are not publicly traded, the first $500,000 of its business income is eligible for a small business deduction that, in effect, can lower the corporate tax rate by 17 percentage points. Property income earned by such corporations is not eligible for this deduction and, as a result, will be much more heavily taxed. This makes the business vs. property classification a very important consideration for Canadian controlled private corporations.

Other Considerations

6-19.   Other tax considerations related to the business vs. property income classification are as follows:

- **CCA Calculations**   When property income is being earned, the deduction of capital cost allowance (CCA) cannot be used to create or increase a net loss for the period. In addition, when property income is being earned by individuals, there is no requirement for a pro rata CCA reduction to reflect a short fiscal period. If business income is being earned, CCA can be used to create a loss. However, CCA deductions must be prorated for short fiscal periods.

- **Attribution Rules**   When property income is being earned, the income attribution rules (see Chapter 9) are applicable. This is not the case when business income is being earned.

- **Earned Income Calculations** Property income is generally not included in the determination of earned income, either with respect to RRSP contributions or the limit on child care cost deductions. Business income is included in these figures.

- **Expense Deductions** Certain expenses can be deducted against business income, but not property income. These include write-offs of cumulative eligible capital and travel expenses. In contrast, for individuals, there is a deduction for foreign taxes on property income in excess of 15 percent that is not available against foreign business income.

Business Income Defined

General Rules

6-20. ITA 9 indicates a taxpayer's business income is his profit from a business. While profit is not defined in the *Act*, it is generally understood that it is a net amount resulting from the application of generally accepted accounting principles, modified by the rules found in Subdivision B. Business is defined in the *Act* as follows:

> **ITA 248(1)** Business includes a profession, calling, trade, manufacture or undertaking of any kind whatever and, except for the purposes of paragraph ..., an adventure or concern in the nature of trade ...

6-21. While this definition lists some of the things that might be considered to be a business, it does not provide a description of the characteristics that identify these activities as a business. A more useful definition can be found in Abstract No. 124 from the CICA's Emerging Issues Committee (now withdrawn):

> A business is a self-sustaining integrated set of activities and assets conducted and managed for the purpose of providing a return to investors. A business consists of (a) inputs, (b) processes applied to those inputs, and (c) resulting outputs that are used to generate revenues.

6-22. Some of the other principles involved in making the distinction between business and property income are as follows:

- Whether income is from a business or property is a question of fact. The fact that property is used to earn income is not determinative.

- Where a corporation has a specific investment business object in its incorporation documents, its investment income will likely be characterized as income from a business.

- Where funds are employed and risked by a business and the investment of these funds is necessary for the taxpayer to conduct its business, the income from this investment activity will likely be considered income from a business.

- Income from property does not require active and extensive business-like intervention to produce it; it is passive income resulting from the mere ownership of property, without a significant commitment of time, labour, or attention.

- Income from business requires organization, systematic effort, and a certain degree of activity.

Adventure Or Concern In The Nature Of Trade

6-23. When a person habitually does a thing that is capable of producing a profit, then he is carrying on a trade or business, notwithstanding that these activities may be quite separate and apart from his ordinary occupation. An example of this would be a dentist who habitually buys and sells real estate.

6-24. Where such a thing is done only infrequently, or possibly only once, it still is possible to hold that the person has engaged in a business transaction if it can be shown that he has engaged in "an adventure or concern in the nature of trade". If this is the case, the ITA 248(1) definition of a business makes it clear that any income that is produced will be considered business income. In addition, any gain or loss arising on the disposition of any property acquired as part of this adventure or concern will be considered business income, rather than a capital gain or loss.

6-25. As described in IT-459, factors that would identify a transaction as an adventure or concern in the nature of trade are as follows:

Taxpayer's Conduct If the taxpayer's actions in regard to the property in question were essentially what would be expected of a dealer in such a property, it would be considered to be an adventure or concern in the nature of trade.

Nature Of The Asset If the asset in question was not capable of producing income, this would indicate an adventure or concern in the nature of trade.

Taxpayer's Intention If the taxpayer acquired the asset with an intention to sell, this would be evidence of an adventure or concern in the nature of trade.

Property Income Defined

6-26. While the *Income Tax Act* does not define income from property, it can be thought of as the return on invested capital in situations where little or no effort is required by the investor to produce the return. Falling into this category would be rents, interest, dividends, and royalties earned for the right to use property. In terms of tax legislation, capital gains are not treated as a component of property income, even in cases where they arise on investments being held to produce property income (e.g., capital gains on dividend paying shares).

6-27. In cases where a great deal of time and effort is directed at producing interest or rents, such returns can be considered business income. For example, while rent is generally viewed as a type of property income, the rents earned by a large real estate holding company would be treated as a component of business income.

Exercise Six - 1

Subject: Business Vs. Property Income

Joan Bullato, because of her great fondness for his music, has purchased the rights to one of the songs written by John Clapton. She estimates that the royalties from the song will total about $35,000 per year for the next few years. She has no plans to buy any additional song rights. Explain whether the royalties she receives would be treated as business income or property income. In addition, indicate how any gain or loss on a disposition of the rights would be taxed.

End of Exercise. Solution available in Study Guide.

Business Income Vs. Capital Gains

Tax Consequences Of Classification

6-28. The tax consequences associated with the classification of a disposition as a capital transaction vs. a business income transaction can be described as follows:

- Only one-half of a capital gain is taxed and only one-half of a capital loss is deductible. If a gain transaction can be classified as capital in nature, the savings to the taxpayer is very significant. Alternatively, if a loss is involved, classification as a capital transaction reduces the value of this loss by one-half.

- Allowable capital losses (i.e., the deductible one-half) can only be deducted against taxable capital gains (i.e., the taxable one-half). This can be of great importance, particularly to individual taxpayers and smaller business enterprises. It may be years before such taxpayers realize taxable capital gains, resulting in a situation where there is significant deferral of the tax benefits associated with allowable capital losses.

6-29. These are, of course, very significant tax consequences. Not surprisingly, this has resulted in thousands of disputes related to this classification, many of which wind up in the various levels of our court system.

Capital Gains Defined

6-30. The business income vs. property income issue arises while an asset is being held. Using the criteria discussed in the previous section, during the period of ownership the taxpayer must determine whether the income that is produced by the asset is business income or, alternatively property income.

6-31. In contrast, the business income vs. capital gains issue is only applicable when there is a disposition of an asset. If the disposition is of a non-depreciable capital asset, the result will be a capital gain or loss. If the asset is a depreciable capital asset, no capital loss can occur and there may be other outcomes such as recapture of CCA or a terminal loss. If the disposition is of an asset that is not a capital asset, the result will be a business income or loss.

6-32. The basic concept is a simple one — capital assets are acquired and held to produce income through their use. If an asset is acquired not to be held but, rather, to be resold for a profit, it is not a capital asset.

6-33. As a simple example, consider the assets of a retail store. These will include inventories of purchased merchandise that are being held for resale. Such assets are not part of the capital assets of the business, and any income related to their sale would be classified as business income. However, the building in which the merchandise is being offered for sale, as well as the furniture and fixtures necessary to the operation of the business, are capital assets. This would mean that if the operation were to sell these assets for more than their capital cost, any resulting gain would be capital in nature.

6-34. In general, capital assets are somewhat analogous to the accounting classification of non-current assets, while non-capital assets are somewhat analogous to the accounting classification of inventories.

6-35. An additional analogy, sometimes applied in court cases, is with a fruit bearing tree. The tree itself is a capital asset and its sale would result in a capital gain or loss. In contrast, the sale of the fruit from the tree would generate business income.

6-36. The actual use of the asset often determines the appropriate classification. A particular type of asset can be classified as capital by one business and as inventory by another. Consider a piece of equipment such as a backhoe. For a construction company using this asset for excavating construction sites, it would clearly be a capital asset. Alternatively, if it were held for sale by a dealer in construction equipment, it would be classified as inventory, with any gain on its sale being taxed as business income.

6-37. It should be noted that you cannot always equate capital property with income producing property. Consider a real estate developer who is holding an inventory of properties for sale. If he chooses to rent some of these properties on a short term basis, they would be producing income. However, this would not alter the fact that the developer's primary intent is to sell these properties, making inventory the appropriate classification.

Criteria For Identifying Capital Gains
Primary And Secondary Intention

6-38. As implied in the previous discussion, the determination of whether a property is a capital property is based on the intent of the taxpayer when the asset was acquired. If his primary intention was to use the property to produce income it is a capital property and its disposition will result in a capital gain or capital loss. If the intent was to resell the property as quickly as possible, its disposition will result in business income.

6-39.   There may be situations where a property is originally acquired for income producing purposes but is sold because the acquirer's primary goal cannot be met. It is possible to argue that the taxpayer's secondary intention was to sell in the event his primary intention was frustrated.

6-40.   Unfortunately, only the taxpayer has unequivocal knowledge of his intention at the time a property is acquired. Because of this, other, more objectively measurable factors have to be considered in making this determination.

Other Considerations

6-41.   Other factors that have been considered in attempting to establish whether an asset should be considered capital property include the following:

Length Of The Ownership Period   The longer the period of ownership, the more likely it is that the taxpayer's intent was to hold the asset to produce income.

Number And Frequency Of Transactions   A large number of closely spaced transactions in a given period of time would be an indication that the investor was in the business of dealing in this type of asset, not holding it to produce income.

Relationship To The Taxpayer's Business   If the transaction is related to the taxpayer's business, this may be sufficient to disqualify any gain or loss from capital gains treatment. For example, a gain on a mortgage transaction might be considered business income to a real estate broker.

Supplemental Work On The Property   Additional work on the property, directed at enhancing its value or marketability, would indicate an adventure in the nature of trade resulting in business income.

Nature Of The Assets   The conventional accounting distinction between fixed assets and working capital has been used in some cases to determine whether income was business or capital in nature. Also, whether the asset is capable of producing income would be a consideration.

Objectives Declared In Articles Of Incorporation   Gains and losses on transactions that fall within the corporation's declared objectives may be considered business income. However, as most corporations state their objectives in a very broad manner, this criterion is not frequently used.

6-42.   For more specific guidance with respect to transactions in securities, IT-479R, "Transactions In Securities" provides a list of factors that the courts have considered in making the capital gains/business income distinction. A similar list for the classification of real estate transactions can be found in IT-218R, "Profit, Capital Gains And Losses From The Sale of Real Estate, Including Farmland And Inherited Land And Conversion Of Real Estate From Capital Property To Inventory And Vice Versa".

Exercise Six - 2

Subject: Business Income Vs. Capital Gain

During 2012, Sandra Von Arb acquired a four unit apartment building for $230,000. While it was her intention to operate the building as a rental property, one month after her purchase she received an unsolicited offer to purchase the building for $280,000. She accepts the offer. Should the $50,000 be treated as a capital gain or as business income? Justify your conclusion.

End of Exercise. Solution available in Study Guide.

Business Income And GAAP

6-43.   Financial statements requiring audit opinions must be prepared in accordance with generally accepted accounting principles, or GAAP. These principles have had a significant influence on the development of the tax concept of business income. This is reflected in the fact that, for tax purposes, business income is usually an accrual, rather than a cash based calculation. Further, it is a net rather than a gross concept. In addition, GAAP continues to be influential in that income as computed under these principles is usually required for tax purposes, unless a particular provision of the *Act* specifies alternative requirements.

6-44.   This means that business income under the *Income Tax Act* will not be totally unfamiliar to anyone who has had experience in applying GAAP. However, there are a number of differences between GAAP based Net Income and net business income for tax purposes. While many of these will become apparent as we cover specific provisions of the *Act*, it is useful to note some of the more important differences at this point. They are as follows:

Amortization (Depreciation)   As was noted in Chapter 5, the *Income Tax Regulations* provide the methods and rates to be used in determining the maximum CCA that can be deducted in a given taxation year. However, there is no requirement that this maximum amount be deducted, nor is there any requirement that a consistent policy be followed as long as the annual amount involved is no greater than the maximum amount specified in the *Act*. In contrast, GAAP allows management to choose from a variety of amortization methods. However, once a method is adopted, it must be used consistently each year to deduct the full amount as calculated by that method.

Because of these different approaches, CCA deducted will be different and usually larger, than the corresponding amortization expense under GAAP. This is the most common and, for most enterprises, the largest difference between accounting Net Income and Net Income For Tax Purposes.

Other Allocations   There are other items, similar to amortization charges, where the total cost to be deducted will be the same for tax and accounting purposes. However, they will be deducted using different allocation patterns. Examples would be pension costs (funding payments are deducted for tax purposes), warranty costs (cash payments are deducted for tax purposes), and scientific research and experimental development expenditures (some capital costs are fully deductible for tax purposes in the year of acquisition).

Permanent Differences   There are some differences between tax and accounting income that are permanent in nature. For example, 100 percent of capital gains are included in accounting Net Income, while only one-half of this income is included in Net Income For Tax Purposes. Other examples of this type of difference would be the non-deductible 50 percent of business meals and entertainment and the non-deductible portion of automobile lease payments (see discussion later in this Chapter).

Unreasonable Expenses   In applying GAAP, accountants are generally not required to distinguish between expenses that are reasonable and those that are not. If assets were used up in the production of revenues of the period, they are expenses of that period. This is not the case for tax purposes. ITA 67 indicates that only those expenditures that may be considered reasonable in the circumstances may be deducted in the computation of Net Income For Tax Purposes. If, for example, a large salary was paid to a spouse or to a child that could not be justified on the basis of the services provided, the deduction of the amount involved could be disallowed under ITA 67. The fact that this salary could be deducted in the determination of accounting Net Income would not alter this conclusion.

Non-Arm's Length Transactions   ITA 69 deals with situations involving transactions between non-arm's length parties and provides special rules when such non-arm's length transactions take place at values other than fair market value (see Chapter 8 for a complete discussion of these rules). For example, if a taxpayer acquired an asset with a fair market value of $2,000 from a related party for $2,500 (a value in excess of its fair market value), the transferee is deemed to have acquired it at its fair market value of $2,000, while the transferor is taxed on the basis of the $2,500 consideration received. If the transferee was a business, no similar adjustment would be required under GAAP. Note, however, there are requirements under GAAP for disclosing related party transactions.

6-45.   As many of you are aware, the financial reporting rules applicable to accounting for taxes focus on temporary differences. Canadian GAAP defines these differences with reference to Balance Sheet items. However, in determining business income (for tax purposes), the normal approach is to reconcile accounting Net Income with Net Income For Tax Purposes. As a consequence, individuals working in the tax area will focus on Income Statement differences, as opposed to Balance Sheet differences.

Business Income - Inclusions (Revenues)

Inclusions In Business Income - Income Tax Act Provisions
ITA 12
6-46.   In subdivision b of the *Income Tax Act*, inclusions in business and property income are covered in Sections 12 through 17.   The focus in this Chapter will be on Section 12 where we find the tax treatment of most of the items that we commonly think of as operating revenues for a business.

6-47.   We would note, however, that ITA 12(1)(c) deals with interest income and ITA 12(1)(j) and (k) deal with dividends received. As these inclusions most commonly relate to property income, they will be discussed in Chapter 7, Income From Property.

6-48.   In addition, ITA 12(1)(l) requires the inclusion of business and property income from a partnership, and ITA 12(1)(m) requires the inclusion of benefits from trusts. These inclusions will be dealt with in Chapters 18 and 19 which deal, respectively, with partnerships and trusts.

ITA 13 Through 17
6-49.   Sections 13 and 14, which deal with recapture of CCA and CEC inclusions, were covered in Chapter 5. Section 15, which deals with benefits conferred on shareholders of corporations, will be covered in Chapter 15, Corporate Taxation And Management Decisions. Sections 16 and 17 deal with specialized issues that will not be covered in this text.

Amounts Received And Receivable
6-50.   The most important inclusion in business income is found in ITA 12(1)(b) which requires the inclusion of amounts that have become receivable during the year for property sold or services rendered. This provision clearly establishes that, in general, business income is determined on an accrual basis.

6-51.   ITA 12(1)(b) also notes that amounts generally become receivable on the day on which the services were rendered. You will note that this is consistent with the accountant's point of sale approach to revenue recognition.

6-52.   However, in a departure from the usual GAAP definition of revenue, ITA 12(1)(a) requires the inclusion of amounts received for goods to be delivered in the future. Under GAAP such advances from customers are treated as a liability, rather than as a revenue. While this would appear to create a difference between accounting Net Income and business income for tax purposes, we will find that this difference is eliminated through the use of a reserve for undelivered goods.

6-53.   In the following material we will examine how reserves are used to modify the amount of revenues recorded under ITA 12(1)(a) and (b). While, at first glance, these procedures are somewhat different than those used under GAAP, they will generally result in a final inclusion that is identical to the amount of revenue that is recognized under GAAP.

Reserves
The General System
6-54.   In tax work, the term "reserve" is used to refer to a group of specific items that can be deducted in the determination of net business income. Unlike most deductions that relate either to cash outflows or the incurrence of liabilities, these items are modifications of amounts received (reserve for undelivered goods) or amounts receivable (reserve for doubtful debts and reserve for unpaid amounts).

6-55. With respect to the use of such reserves, the basic rules are as follows:

Deductible Reserves   ITA 18(1)(e) indicates that a particular reserve cannot be deducted unless it is specifically provided for in the *Act*. This means that, for example, when estimated warranty costs are deducted as an accounting expense in the year in which the related product is sold, no reserve can be deducted for tax purposes, as a reserve for estimated warranty costs is not specified in the *Act*. Note that while ITA 20(1)(m.1) does refer to a manufacturer's warranty reserve, careful reading shows that amounts can only be deducted under this provision when they are for an extended warranty covered by an insurance contract.

Addition To Income   When a reserve is deducted in a particular taxation year, it must be added back to income in the immediately following year. These additions are required under various Paragraphs in ITA 12 (e.g., ITA 12(1)(d) requires the addition of reserves deducted for doubtful debts in the preceding year).

6-56.   The most common reserves that can be deducted from business income are as follows:

- ITA 20(1)(l) - **Reserve For Doubtful Debts (Bad Debts)**
- ITA 20(1)(m) - **Reserve For Undelivered Goods And Services**
- ITA 20(1)(n) - **Reserve For Unpaid Amounts**

6-57.   The more specific details of these reserves will be covered in the following material.

Reserve For Doubtful Debts - ITA 20(1)(l)
6-58.   While specific tax procedures for dealing with bad debts differ from those used under GAAP, the alternative procedures will normally produce identical results. The required tax procedures are as follows:

- Under ITA 20(1)(l), a year end deduction is permitted for anticipated bad debts.

- During the subsequent year, actual bad debts may be deducted under ITA 20(1)(p).

- At the end of this subsequent year, the old reserve is included in business income under ITA 12(1)(d), and a new reserve is established under ITA 20(1)(l).

Example   On December 31, 2011, at the end of its first year of operations, Ken's Print Shop estimates that $5,500 of its ending Accounts Receivable will be uncollectible. For 2011, an Allowance For Bad Debts is established for this amount for accounting purposes (by debiting Bad Debt Expense and crediting Allowance For Bad Debts). In addition, a reserve of $5,500 is deducted under ITA 20(1)(l). During the year ending December 31, 2012, $6,800 in accounts receivable are written off. At December 31, 2012, estimated uncollectible accounts total $4,800.

6-59.   For accounting purposes, the 2011 estimate of bad debts would be charged to expense and credited to an Allowance For Bad Debts (a contra account to Accounts Receivable). For tax purposes, the same amount would be deducted from net business income as a reserve.

6-60.   During 2012, the accountant for Ken's Print Shop would credit Accounts Receivable and debit Allowance For Bad Debts for the actual write offs of $6,800. This would leave a debit (negative) balance in this account of $1,300 ($5,500 - $6,800), indicating that the 2011 estimate was too low. This error would be corrected by adding the $1,300 to the Bad Debt Expense for 2012. The total expense for 2012 would be as follows:

2012 Estimate Of Future Bad Debts (Credit Allowance)	$4,800
Increase In Expense To Eliminate Debit Balance In Allowance	1,300
2012 Bad Debt Expense For Accounting Purposes	$6,100

6-61.   For tax purposes, the total Bad Debt Expense would be the same $6,100. However, the calculation follows a different pattern:

Add: 2011 Reserve For Tax Purposes		$ 5,500
Deduct:		
2012 Actual Write-Offs	($6,800)	
2012 Reserve For Tax Purposes	(4,800)	(11,600)
2012 Net Deduction For Tax Purposes		($ 6,100)

Exercise Six - 3

Subject: Bad Debts And Reserve For Doubtful Accounts

On December 31, 2011, Norman's Flowers estimates that $16,000 of its ending Accounts Receivable will be uncollectible. A reserve for this amount is deducted for tax purposes. During the year ending December 31, 2012, $17,200 in bad accounts are written off. At December 31, 2012, estimated uncollectible accounts total $18,400. What is the 2012 Bad Debt Expense for accounting purposes? By what amount will the 2012 net business income (for tax purposes) of Norman's Flowers be increased or decreased by the preceding information with respect to bad debts?

End of Exercise. Solution available in Study Guide.

Reserve For Undelivered Goods And Services - ITA 20(1)(m)

6-62.   It was previously noted that, unlike the situation under GAAP, amounts received for goods or services to be delivered in the future must be included in the calculation of revenues for tax purposes. However, this difference is offset by the ability to deduct, under ITA 20(1)(m), a reserve for goods and services to be delivered in the future. This means that, while the procedures are somewhat different, the treatment of amounts received for undelivered goods and services is the same under both the *Income Tax Act* and GAAP.

    Example   During the taxation year ending December 31, 2012, Donna's Auto Parts has receipts of $275,000. Of this amount, $25,000 is a prepayment for goods that will not be delivered until 2013.

    Analysis   While the $275,000 will be considered an inclusion in 2012 net business income, Donna will be able to deduct a reserve of $25,000 under ITA 20(1)(m). This $25,000 amount will have to be added back to her 2013 net business income, reflecting the fact that the goods have been delivered and the revenue realized.

Exercise Six - 4

Subject: Reserve For Doubtful Accounts And Undelivered Services

As an unincorporated business, Barbra's Graphic Design keeps its records on a cash basis. During 2012, its first year of operation, the business has cash sales of $53,400. At the end of the year, an additional $26,300 of revenues was receivable. Of the amounts received, $5,600 was for services that will be delivered during 2013. Barbra estimates that $425 of the end of year receivable amounts will be uncollectible. By what amount will the 2012 net business income of Barbra's Graphic Design be increased by the preceding information?

End of Exercise. Solution available in Study Guide.

Reserve For Unpaid Amounts - ITA 20(1)(n)

6-63.   When a business sells goods with the amount being receivable over an extended period (i.e., instalment sales), ITA 20(1)(n) permits the deduction of a reasonable reserve based on the profit on the sale. Note that this type of reserve should not be confused with capital gains reserves which are covered in Chapter 8.

6-64.   While this appears to provide for the recognition of revenue on a cash basis, there are two significant constraints:

ITA 20(1)(n) indicates that no reserve can be deducted unless at least some part of the proceeds will not be received until at least two years after the date the property is sold (this two year requirement does not apply to sales of real property inventory).

ITA 20(8) specifies that no reserve can be deducted in a year, for any type of property, if the sale took place more than 36 months before the end of that year (i.e., the reserve is limited to a maximum of 3 years). In addition, the reserve is not available if the purchaser is a corporation controlled by the seller, or a partnership in which the seller has a majority interest.

Exercise Six - 5

Subject: Reserve For Unpaid Amounts

During November, 2012, Martine's Jewels Ltd. sells a necklace for $120,000. The cost of this necklace was $55,000, resulting in a gross profit of $65,000. The $120,000 sales price is to be paid in four equal annual instalments on December 31 in each of the years 2013 through 2016. Martine's Jewels Ltd. has a December 31 year end. Indicate the amount of the reserve that can be deducted, and the net business income, for each of the years 2012 through 2016.

End of Exercise. Solution available in Study Guide.

Other Inclusions

6-65.   There are a number of other inclusions in business income. While some are of limited interest in a text such as this [e.g., ITA 12(1)(z.4) requires the inclusion of eligible funeral arrangements], several of these inclusions warrant additional comment:

Damage Payments Received   Damages are usually received as the result of non-performance of a contractual arrangement. As they will generally serve to offset deductible costs, they are included in income.

Profits From Betting Or Gambling   Generally speaking, these items are not included in net business income. As lotteries are a form of gambling, lottery winnings would be received on a tax free basis.

However, if a taxpayer's gambling activities were so extensive as to constitute a business, such income could become taxable (e.g., a professional poker player). This would also suggest that losses would be fully deductible.

Profits From An Illegal Business   Many people are aware that the famous American gangster Al Capone was sent to jail, not for his illegal activities involving alleged robbery and murder, but rather for his failure to pay taxes on the resulting profits. As illegal revenues must be included in business income, related expenses are generally deductible. This can lead to interesting conclusions as evidenced by a 1999 publication of the New Zealand Inland Revenue Department. This publication provided a detailed list of items that could be deducted by what was referred to as "sex workers". Without going into detail, we would note that see-through garments and whips were on the list, provided they were used in delivering services to a client.

Debt Forgiveness   Situations arise in which outstanding debt is forgiven, often by a related taxpayer. When this happens, ITA 80 contains a complex set of rules that apply when the debtor has been able to deduct the interest expense on the forgiven debt. These rules may require the amount of debt forgiven to be applied to reduce loss carry over balances, the tax cost of certain properties and, in some situations, to be included in income in the year of forgiveness. The details of these rules are beyond the scope of this text.

Government Assistance   Whether or not government assistance will be included in current income depends on the nature of the assistance. The tax rules here largely reflect the accounting rules that are found in Canadian GAAP. That is, assistance related to current revenues and expenses will be included in current income while, in contrast, assistance related to the acquisition of capital assets will be deducted from the cost of these assets.

Inducement Receipts   Businesses may receive payments that induce them to undertake some activity. An example of this would be a payment received by a lessor to induce him to undertake leasehold improvements. The taxpayer has several alternatives here. The amount received can be included in current income, used to reduce the cost of any related assets, or used to reduce any required expenses. These are the same alternatives that are available under GAAP.

Restrictive Covenant Receipts   A restrictive covenant is an agreement entered into, an undertaking made, or a waiver of an advantage or right by a taxpayer. A proposed ITA 56.4 would, in general, require that these payments be included in income. There are a limited number of exceptions, one of which would allow the receipt to be allocated to cumulative eligible capital.

Limitations On Deductions From Business And Property Income

General Approach - Restrictions In ITA 18 Through ITA 19.1

6-66.   It would be extremely difficult to provide a detailed list of all of the items that might possibly be considered a business expense. While ITA 20 spells out many such items, it is often necessary to have more general guidance when new types of items arise. ITA 18 through ITA 19.1 gives this guidance in a somewhat backwards fashion by providing guidelines on what should not be deducted in computing business income. However, this negative guidance frequently provides assistance in determining what should be deducted in computing business income.

6-67.   Note, however, that if an item is specifically listed in the *Act* as a deduction, the specific listing overrides the general limitation. For example, Section 18 prohibits the deduction of capital costs, thereby preventing the immediate write-off of a capital asset. The fact that ITA 20(1)(aa) permits the deduction of landscaping costs, some of which would be capital expenditures, overrides the general prohibition found in Section 18.

6-68.   The restrictions contained in ITA 18 through ITA 19.1 apply only to deductions from business and property income. There are other restrictions, for example the cost of business meals and entertainment, which apply to deductions from both business and property income, as well as to deductions from employment income. Most of these more general restrictions are found in Subdivision f, "Rules Relating To Computation Of Income", and are discussed later in this Chapter.

Specific Limiting Items Under ITA 18
Incurred To Produce Income
6-69.   One of the most important of the limiting provisions is as follows:

ITA 18(1)(a)   No deduction shall be made in respect of an outlay or expense except to the extent that it was made or incurred by the taxpayer for the purpose of gaining or producing income from the business or property.

6-70.   When there is a question as to the deductibility of an item not covered by a particular provision of the *Act*, it is usually this general limitation provision that provides the basis for an answer. As a consequence, there are many Interpretation Bulletins dealing with such matters as legal and accounting fees (IT-99R5) and motor vehicle expenses (IT-521R). In addition, there have been hundreds of court cases dealing with particular items. For example, with respect to insurance costs, there have been cases in the following areas:

- Damage insurance on business assets (deductible)
- Life insurance when required by creditor (deductible, if interest on loan is deductible)
- Life insurance in general (not deductible)
- Partnership insurance on partners' lives (not deductible)
- Insurance against competition (deductible)

6-71.   As can be seen from the preceding list, this is a complex area of tax. If there is doubt about a particular item's deductibility, it will sometimes be necessary to do considerable research to establish whether it is dealt with in an Interpretation Bulletin or a court case.

6-72.   In applying this provision, it is not necessary to demonstrate that the expenditure actually produced income. It is generally sufficient to demonstrate that it was incurred as part of an income earning process or activity.

Capital Expenditures
6-73.   ITA 18(1)(b) prohibits the deduction of any expenditure that is designated as a capital expenditure. However, deductions are permitted under ITA 20(1)(a) for capital cost allowances. The limitations on this deduction were discussed in detail in Chapter 5.

Exempt Income Expenditures
6-74.   ITA 18(1)(c) prohibits the deduction of any expenditures that were incurred to produce income that is exempt from taxation. For a business, this would have limited applicability as few sources of business income are tax exempt.

Personal And Living Expenses
6-75.   ITA 18(1)(h) prohibits the deduction of an expenditure that is a personal or living expense of the taxpayer. An example of this would be a situation where a business pays for the travel costs of one of its employees or owners. If the travel is business related, the costs would be deductible. Alternatively, if no business purpose was involved, the travel would be classified as a non-deductible personal or living expense.

6-76.   This can create a very unfortunate tax situation in that, not only will the costs of such travel be non-deductible to the business, the beneficiary of the trip may have to include the value of the trip in their income as a shareholder or employee benefit. Clearly, it would be preferable to simply pay additional salary equal to the value of the trip. Using this alternative, the tax consequences to the employee or owner would be the same. However, the business would benefit from being able to deduct the amount paid.

6-77.   Somewhat indirectly, ITA 18(1)(h) introduces an additional rule with respect to the deductibility of costs. The ITA 248(1) definition of "personal or living expenses" indicates that the expenses of properties maintained for the use of an individual or persons related to that individual are personal unless the properties maintained are connected to a business that is either profitable, or has a reasonable expectation of being profitable. This could result in some deductions being denied for a cottage that was rented during the year, but was used by the taxpayer for a part of that year.

Deferred Income Plans

6-78.   ITA 18(1)(i) restricts the deductibility of contributions under supplementary unemployment benefit plans to the amount specified in ITA 145. ITA 18(1)(j) and 18(1)(k) provide similar limitations for contributions to deferred profit sharing plans and profit sharing plans. ITA 18(1)(o) prohibits the deduction of contributions to an employee benefit plan. Finally, under ITA 18(1)(o.1) and (o.2), limits are placed on the deductibility of amounts paid to salary deferral arrangements and retirement compensation arrangements. These amounts are only deductible as specified under ITA 20(1)(r) and (oo). All of these provisions are discussed in detail in Chapter 10, Retirement Savings And Other Special Income Arrangements.

Recreational Facilities And Club Dues

6-79.   ITA 18(1)(l) prohibits the deduction of amounts that have been incurred to maintain a yacht, camp, lodge, golf course or facility, unless the taxpayer is in the business of providing such property for hire. Because of the fairly specific wording of this provision, it would appear that the costs of providing other types of recreational benefits would be deductible. For example, a corporation could deduct the costs of providing a general fitness center for their employees, provided it was made available to all employees.

6-80.   A similar prohibition is made against the deduction of membership fees or dues to dining, sporting, or recreational facilities. Note, however, that there is no prohibition against deducting the cost of legitimate entertainment expenses incurred in such facilities, subject to the 50 percent limitation that will be described shortly.

Political Contributions

6-81.   ITA 18(1)(n) prohibits the deduction of political contributions in the determination of business or property income. Given the restrictions on the making of political contributions that are found in the *Federal Accountability Act*, this is not a costly provision for business. You may recall from Chapter 4 that this *Act* limits individual contributions to an annual amount of $1,100 for a party or contestant and completely prohibits contributions by corporations.

Expenses Of A Personal Services Business

6-82.   A personal services business is a corporation that has been set up by an individual to provide personal services that are, in effect, employment services. ITA 18(1)(p) restricts the deductible expenses of such a corporation to those that would normally be deductible against employment income. Chapter 12, Taxable Income And Tax Payable For Corporations, provides coverage of this subject.

Automobile Mileage Payments

6-83.   As is discussed in Chapter 3, a business may pay its employees or shareholders a per kilometer fee for having them use their own automobile on behalf of the business. The amount of such payments that can be deducted by a business is limited by ITA 18(1)(r) to an amount prescribed in ITR 7306. For 2012, this amount is 53 cents for the first 5,000 kilometers and 47 cents for additional kilometers driven by an employee.

6-84.   Amounts paid in excess of these limits will only be deductible to the payer to the extent that they are included in the income of the recipient.

Interest And Property Taxes On Land

6-85.   Many businesses pay interest and property taxes on land. To the extent that the primary purpose of holding this land is to produce income, these payments clearly represent amounts that can be deducted as part of the costs of carrying the land while it is producing income.

6-86.   In contrast, when land is vacant or generating insignificant amounts of income, ITA 18(2) restricts the deduction for property taxes and interest to the amount of net revenues produced by the land. For example, if a parcel of land that is being held as a future plant site is producing some revenues by being rented for storage, interest and property taxes on the land can only be deducted to the extent of the net revenues from the rent. ITA 53(1)(h) allows the non-deductible interest and property taxes to be added to the adjusted cost base of the property, thereby reducing any future capital gain resulting from the disposition of the property.

6-87. In the case of land that is being held as inventory, ITA 10(1.1) permits the non-deductible interest and property taxes to be added to the cost of the land.

6-88. The preceding general rules could be viewed as too restrictive for those companies whose "principal business is the leasing, rental or sale, or the development for lease, rental or sale, of real property". As a consequence, these real estate companies are allowed to deduct interest and property tax payments to the extent of net revenues from the property, plus a "base level deduction".

6-89. This base level deduction is defined in ITA 18(2.2) as the amount that would be the amount of interest, computed at the prescribed rate, for the year, in respect of a loan of $1,000,000 outstanding throughout the year. This means that, if the prescribed rate for the year was 2 percent, real estate companies could deduct interest and property taxes on the land that they are carrying to the extent of net revenues from the land, plus an additional $20,000 [(2%)($1,000,000)].

Soft Costs

6-90. Costs that are attributable to the period of construction, renovation, or alteration of a building, or in respect of the ownership of the related land, are referred to as soft costs. These costs could include interest, legal and accounting fees, insurance, and property taxes. In general, ITA 18(3.1) indicates that such costs are not deductible and must be added to the cost of the property.

Appraisal Costs

6-91. While these costs are not covered in ITA 18, there are limitations on their deductibility that are discussed in IT-143R3, *Meaning Of Eligible Capital Expenditures*. As discussed in that Bulletin, the treatment of appraisal costs on capital property will depend on the reason for their incurrence:

- If they are incurred on a capital property for the purpose of its acquisition or disposition, they are generally added to the adjusted cost base of the property.
- If they are incurred with respect to a proposed acquisition that does not take place, they should be treated as eligible capital expenditures (see Chapter 5).
- If they are incurred for the purpose of gaining or producing income from a business (e.g., the cost of an appraisal required for insurance purposes), they are deductible in computing income for the year.

Interest In Thin Capitalization Situations

6-92. In general, interest paid on debt is deductible to a business, whereas dividends paid on outstanding shares are not. Given this, there is an incentive for a non-resident owner of a Canadian resident corporation to take back debt rather than equity for the financing that he provides to the corporation. This could result in a situation where the payment of the interest is deductible in Canada and, at the same time, is not taxable to the non-resident recipient due to an international tax treaty (see Chapter 20).

6-93. To prevent this from happening, ITA 18(4) through 18(6) limit the deductibility of interest paid in such "thin capitalization" situations. Interest paid or payable to the non-resident specified shareholder is disallowed if it is paid on amounts of debt in excess of 2.0 times the sum of the shareholder's share of contributed capital, plus 100 percent of the corporation's Retained Earnings at the beginning of the year. Note that, for taxation years beginning after 2012, the 2.0 will be reduced to 1.5. For this purpose, a specified shareholder is defined in ITA 18(5) as a person who holds shares that give him 25 percent or more of the votes that would be cast at the annual meeting of the shareholders, or 25 percent or more of the fair market value of all issued and outstanding shares. A simple example will serve to clarify these rules:

Limitations On Deductions From Business And Property Income

Example   Throughout 2012, Mr. Lane, a resident of the U.S., owns 45 percent of the shares and holds $3,000,000 of the long-term debt securities of Thinly Ltd.   The capital structure of Thinly Ltd. throughout the year is as follows:

Long-Term Debt (11% Rate)	$5,000,000
Common Stock	200,000
Retained Earnings	300,000
Total Capital	$5,500,000

Analysis Mr. Lane is clearly a specified shareholder as he holds 45 percent of the corporation's shares. His relevant equity balance is $390,000 [(45%)($200,000) + (100%)($300,000)].   His debt holding is clearly greater than 2 times this relevant equity balance. As a consequence, there would be disallowed interest of $265,650 calculated as follows:

Total Interest Paid To Mr. Lane [(11%)($3,000,000)]	$330,000
Maximum Deductible Interest [(11%)(2.0)($390,000)]	(85,800)
Disallowed Interest	$244,200

Exercise Six - 6

Subject: Interest In Thin Capitalizations

On January 1, 2011, a new Canadian corporation is formed with the issuance of $8,600,000 in debt securities and $2,400,000 in common shares. On this date, Ms. Sally Johnson, who is a resident of Mexico, acquires $4,500,000 of the debt securities and 30 percent of the common shares. The debt securities pay interest at 9 percent. The company has a December 31 year end. On January 1, 2012, the Retained Earnings balance of the company is $900,000. How much, if any, of the interest paid on Ms. Johnson's holding of debt securities during 2012 would be disallowed under the thin capitalization rules in ITA 18(4)?

End of Exercise. Solution available in Study Guide.

Prepaid Expenses

6-94.   ITA 18(9) prevents the deduction of amounts that have been paid for goods or services that will be delivered after the end of the taxation year. This Subsection also prohibits the deduction of interest or rents that relate to a subsequent taxation year. As a result, the tax treatment of these items is the same as their treatment under GAAP.

Home Office Costs (Workspace-In-Home Costs)

6-95.   As you may recall from Chapter 3, individuals who are employees are permitted, under certain conditions, to deduct the costs associated with a home office. Self-employed individuals earning business income are also eligible for such deductions. For employees, the criteria for deducting these costs are specified under ITA 8(13). For self-employed individuals, analogous criteria are specified under ITA 18(12). Both of these provisions restrict the deductibility of home office costs to those situations where:

- the work space is the individual's principal place of business; or
- the space is used exclusively for the purpose of earning income from business and is used on a regular and continuous basis for meeting clients, customers, or patients of the individual.

6-96.   If an individual qualifies for this deduction because it is his principal place of business, the space does not have to be used exclusively for business purposes. If, for example, a dining room table is used to run a mail order business and that room qualifies as the principal

	Employee - No Commissions	Employee - With Commissions	Self-Employed Business Income
Rent (if tenant)	Yes	Yes	Yes
Utilities	Yes	Yes	Yes
Repairs, Maintenance	Yes	Yes	Yes
Telephone*	Yes	Yes	Yes
Supplies	Yes	Yes	Yes
Property Taxes	No	Yes	Yes
Home Insurance	No	Yes	Yes
Mortgage Interest	No	No	Yes
CCA On House	No	No	Yes

Figure 6 - 2
Deductibility Of Home Office Costs

*The amount that can be deducted includes employment or business related long distance charges and cellular phone airtime. If applicable, it would also include charges for a telephone used exclusively for employment or business activities.

place of business for the operation, home office costs can be deducted for the dining room space. Note, however, that in determining the appropriate amount of costs, consideration would have to be given to any personal use of that space.

6-97. If the work space is not the principal place of business, it must be used exclusively for the purpose of earning income. This requires that some part of the home must be designated as the home office and not be used for any other purpose. In addition, this second provision requires that the space be used on a regular and continuous basis for meeting clients, customers, or patients. IT-514, "Work Space In Home Expenses", indicates that a work space for a business that normally requires infrequent meetings, or frequent meetings at irregular intervals, would not meet this requirement.

6-98. When the conditions for deductibility are met, expenses must be apportioned between business and non-business use in a reasonable manner, usually on the basis of floor space used. Pro rata deductions may be available for utilities, repairs and maintenance, property taxes, house insurance, mortgage interest, and CCA. The extent to which these items can be deducted is dependent on whether the taxpayer is an employee with no commission income, an employee with commission income, or a self-employed individual earning business income. The specific items that can be deducted by each of these types of taxpayer are summarized in Figure 6-2.

6-99. You will note in Figure 6-2 that individuals earning business income can deduct CCA on their home. While this deduction would result in a lower Taxable Income for the current year, tax professionals generally advise people not to make this deduction. The reason for this relates to the fact that gains on an individual's principal residence can generally be received on a tax free basis (see Chapter 8 for a full discussion of the principal residence exemption). If an individual deducts CCA on this property as a self-employed individual, the result can be that part of the gain on the sale of the residence will be taxable.

6-100. Regardless of the types of costs deducted, home office costs cannot create or increase a business or employment loss. As a result, the total deduction will be limited to the amount of net business or employment income calculated without reference to the home office costs (IT-514). Any expenses that are not deductible in a given year because they exceed the business or employment income in that year, can be carried forward and deducted in a subsequent year against income generated from the same business. In effect, there is an indefinite carry forward of unused home office costs. This carry forward is conditional on the work space continuing to meet the test for deductibility in future years.

Exercise Six - 7

Subject: Home Office Costs

During 2012, Jobul Krist has the following costs related to his home office:

Utilities	$2,400
Maintenance And Repairs	4,600
Telephone:	
Monthly Charge	360
Personal Long Distance Charges	375
Employment/Business Related Long Distance Charges	590
Office Supplies	425
Property Taxes	5,200
House Insurance	2,300
Interest On Mortgage	7,800

Mr. Krist estimates that he uses 25 percent of the residence for employment/business related purposes. Maximum CCA on 100 percent of the house would be $12,000. Determine the maximum deduction that would be available to Mr. Krist assuming:

A.   He is an employee with $50,000 in income (no commissions).
B.   He is an employee with $50,000 in commission income.
C.   He is self-employed and earns $50,000 in business income.

End of Exercise.   Solution available in Study Guide.

Foreign Media Advertising - ITA 19 And 19.1

6-101.   In order to provide some protection to Canadian media, the *Income Tax Act* places limitations on the deductibility of advertising expenditures in foreign media. For print media, this limitation is found in ITA 19, with ITA 19.1 containing a corresponding provision for broadcast media. In general, these provisions deny a deduction for expenditures made in foreign print or foreign broadcast media in those cases where the advertising message is directed primarily at the Canadian market. It does not apply where such foreign media expenditures are focused on non-Canadian markets.

6-102.   ITA 19.01 modifies the general non-deductibility rule by exempting certain foreign periodicals. Canadian businesses can deduct 100 percent of advertising costs in these publications, without regard to whether it is directed at the Canadian market, provided 80 percent or more of its non-advertising content is "original editorial content". Original editorial content is defined as non-advertising content:

- the author of which is a Canadian citizen or a permanent resident of Canada and, for this purpose, "author" includes a writer, a journalist, an illustrator and a photographer; or

- that is created for the Canadian market and has not been published in any other edition of that issue of the periodical published outside Canada.

6-103.   If the periodical cannot meet the 80 percent criteria, only 50 percent of such advertising costs will be deductible. Note that ITA 19.01 applies to periodicals only, and not to other foreign media.

Provincial Capital And Payroll Taxes

6-104.   In the late 1980s and early 1990s, several provinces switched from having individual premiums for health care to a payroll tax applicable to all wages and salaries. This change had significant implications for the federal government because, as you may recall from Chapter 3, when an employer pays for individual provincial health care premiums, it is considered a taxable benefit to the employee. Given that many employers did, in fact, pay the individual provincial health care premiums, the switch to a non-individualized payroll tax resulted in a significant loss of revenues for the federal government.

6-105.   In response to such changes, the 1991 federal budget proposed limiting the deduction of provincial capital and payroll taxes to an annual amount of $10,000. This proposal proved to be very controversial and, as a consequence, is still pending. While the government has indicated that, as an interim measure, it will deny deductibility to any increases in provincial payroll or capital taxes, at present these amounts continue to be fully deductible.

Limitations On Deductions From Business, Property, And Employment Income

Introduction
6-106.   The restrictions that are found in ITA 18 through ITA 19.1 are applicable only to business and property income. For the most part, they involve expenses that would only be deductible against this type of income and so the restriction has no influence on the determination of other types of income. The exception to this is home office costs, which can be deducted in the calculation of either employment or business income. Note, however, that in this case, different ITA Sections are applicable to each type of income.

6-107.   Other types of expenses, for example business meals and entertainment, can be deducted against either employment or business income. The restrictions on deductions of these more general types of expenses are applicable to business, property, or employment income and, as a consequence, they are found in other Sections of the *Act*. More specifically, Division B's Subdivision f, "Deductions In Computing Income", covers these restrictions.

Reasonableness
6-108.   Subdivision f begins with a broad, general rule which limits deductible expenses to those that are "reasonable in the circumstances". This general limitation, which is applicable to the determination of business, property, or employment income, is as follows:

> **ITA 67**   In computing income, no deduction shall be made in respect of an outlay or expense in respect of which any amount is otherwise deductible under this Act, except to the extent that the outlay or expense was reasonable in the circumstances.

6-109.   This general rule is most commonly applied in non-arm's length situations. For example, it is not uncommon for the sole owner of a small private company to attempt income splitting through salary payments to a spouse or children. While there is a considerable amount of latitude for making such arrangements, the owner should be able to demonstrate that the individual who received the payment provided services that had a value that could reasonably be associated with the amount received.

> **Example**   The sole shareholder of a private corporation appoints his 6 month old daughter vice president of the corporation and pays her a salary of $100,000. (While this sounds absurd, similar arrangements have been attempted.)

> **Analysis**   As the services of a 6 month old are unlikely to have any value, the $100,000 would be disallowed on the grounds of being unreasonable in the circumstances.

Meals And Entertainment
General Rules - ITA 67.1
6-110.   It can be argued that business expenditures for food, beverages, or entertainment involve an element of personal living costs and, to the extent that this is true, such amounts should not be deductible in calculating Net Income For Tax Purposes. This idea is embodied in ITA 67.1(1) which restricts the amount that can be deducted for the human consumption of food or beverages, or the enjoyment of entertainment. The amount of these costs that can be

deducted is equal to 50 percent of the actual costs. The Subsection makes it clear that this limit does not apply to meals related to moving costs, child care costs, amounts eligible for the medical expense tax credit or amounts eligible for the adoption expenses tax credit. Further exceptions to this general rule are described in the next section of this Chapter.

Exceptions

6-111.   ITA 67.1(1.1) provides an exception to the 50 percent for meal costs incurred by long-haul truck drivers during eligible travel periods (i.e., away from home for at least 24 continuous hours). Since 2011, individuals who are long-haul truck drivers and their employers can deduct 80 percent of the cost of eligible meals.

6-112.   ITA 67.1(2) provides a number of additional exceptions for food and entertainment. Situations where the 50 percent rule does not apply include:

- Hotels, restaurants, and airlines provide food, beverages, and entertainment in return for compensation from their customers. The costs incurred by these organizations in providing these goods and services continue to be deductible. However, when the employees of these organizations travel or entertain clients, their costs are subject to the 50 percent limitation.

- Meals and entertainment expenses relating to a fund raising event for a registered charity are fully deductible.

- Where the taxpayer is compensated by someone else for the cost of food, beverages, or entertainment and the amount is separately identified in writing. Such amounts will be fully deductible against this compensation. For example, if Mr. Spinner was a management consultant and was reimbursed by his client for separately billed meals and entertainment, he could deduct 100 percent of these costs. However, his client would only be able to deduct 50 percent of the reimbursements.

- When amounts are paid for meals or entertainment for employees and, either the payments create a taxable benefit for the employee, or the amounts do not create a taxable benefit because they are being provided at a remote work location, the amounts are fully deductible to the employer.

- When amounts are incurred by an employer for food, beverages, or entertainment that is generally available to all individuals employed by the taxpayer, the amounts are fully deductible. Note, however, this exception applies to no more than six special events held by an employer during a calendar year.

6-113.   In addition to the preceding exceptions, ITA 67.1(3) provides a special rule for meals that are included in conference or convention fees. When the amount included in the fee for meals and entertainment is not specified, the Subsection deems the amount to be $50 per day. In these circumstances, it is this $50 per day that is subject to the 50 percent limitation.

6-114.   Airline, bus, and rail tickets often include meals in their price. It appears that the government views the value of such meals as being fairly immaterial. This is reflected in the fact that ITA 67.1(4) deems the food component of the ticket cost to be nil. Individuals who have been subjected to these "meals" are likely to agree with this assessment!

"Luxury" Automobile Costs

6-115.   When a business provides an automobile to an employee or shareholder, it is clear that these individuals have received a taxable benefit to the extent that they make any personal use of the vehicle. This fact, along with the methods used to calculate the benefit, was covered in detail in Chapter 3. As you will recall, the amount of the benefit is based on the cost of cars purchased or, alternatively, the lease payments made on cars that are leased.

6-116.   A different issue relates to the costs that can be deducted by a business in the determination of its net business income, or by any employee in the determination of net employment income. For a number of years, it has been the policy of the government to discourage the deduction of costs related to the use of what is perceived to be luxury automobiles. This has been accomplished by limiting the amounts that can be deducted for:

- CCA on cars owned by the taxpayer;
- interest costs on cars owned by the taxpayer and financed with debt; and
- lease payments on cars that are leased by the taxpayer.

6-117.   Before describing these limitations, we would again remind you that the taxable benefit that results from a business providing an automobile to an employee or shareholder is calculated without regard to restrictions on the deductibility of its costs. For example, if an employee has the exclusive personal use of a $150,000 passenger vehicle that is owned by his employer, his standby charge for the year would be $36,000 [(2%)(12)($150,000)]. The calculation of this amount will not be affected by the fact that the employer's deduction for CCA on this automobile is limited to $30,000.

Automobiles Owned By The Taxpayer
Limits On CCA - ITA 13(7)(g)
6-118.   With respect to cars that are owned by a business, ITA 13(7)(g) limits the deductibility of capital costs to a prescribed amount. From 2001 through 2012, this prescribed amount has been unchanged at $30,000, plus GST/HST and PST. This amount would be reduced by any GST/HST and PST that was recoverable as input tax credits.

Limits On Interest - ITA 67.2
6-119.   When the automobile is owned by the business, there may be interest costs associated with related financing. If this is the case, ITA 67.2 restricts the amount of interest that can be deducted to an amount determined by the following formula:

$$(A \div 30)(B), \text{ where}$$

A   is a prescribed amount ($300 from 2001 through 2012)
B   is the number of days in the period during which interest is paid or payable

6-120.   While the popular press sometimes describes this limit as $300 per month, you can see from the formula that this is not correct. The correct limit is currently $10 per day.

Exercise Six - 8

Subject: Deductible Automobile Costs (Business Owns Automobile)

On September 15, 2012, Ms. Vanessa Lord purchased an automobile to be used exclusively in her newly formed unincorporated business that commenced operations on September 15, 2012. The cost of the automobile was $45,000, before GST and PST. She finances a part of the purchase price and, as a consequence, has financing charges for the year of $1,200. In calculating her net business income for 2012, how much can Ms. Lord deduct for CCA and interest? Ignore GST and PST considerations and the fact that 2012 is a leap year.

End of Exercise. Solution available in Study Guide.

Automobile Leasing Costs - ITA 67.3
Basic Formula (Cumulative)
6-121.   When a business leases a passenger vehicle, ITA 67.3 restricts the deductibility of the lease payments to a prescribed amount. The basic formula that is used to implement this limitation is as follows:

Limitations On Deductions From Business, Property, And Employment Income

$$\text{Basic Cumulative Formula} = \left[A \times \frac{B}{30} \right] - C - D - E, \text{ where}$$

A   is a prescribed amount ($800 for vehicles leased in 2001 through 2012);

B   is the number of days from the beginning of the term of the lease to the end of the taxation year (or end of the lease if that occurs during the current year);

C   is the total of all amounts deducted in previous years for leasing the vehicle;

D   is a notional amount of interest since the inception of the lease, calculated at the prescribed rate on refundable amounts paid by the lessee in excess of $1,000;

E   is the total of all reimbursements that became receivable before the end of the year by the taxpayer in respect of the lease.

6-122.   In simplified language, this Section restricts, for leases entered into in 2001 through 2012, the deductibility of lease payments to $800 (Item A), plus GST/HST and PST, per 30 day period from the inception of the lease through the end of the current taxation year (some of the GST/HST may be recoverable through input tax credits as discussed in Chapter 21). Note that this is a cumulative amount over the entire lease term and this means that the prescribed amount for the year in which the lease is signed is applicable throughout the lease term. That is, if the $800 limit was increased after 2012, the change would have no effect on the leasing cost limit calculations for leases entered into in 2012.

6-123.   The formula also contains components that:

• remove lease payments that were deducted in previous taxation years (Item C);
• require the deduction of imputed interest on refundable deposits that could be used by the lessee to reduce the basic lease payments (Item D);
• remove reimbursements that are receivable by the taxpayer during the year (Item E).

6-124.   In applying this formula, it is important to note that all of the components are cumulative from the inception of the lease.

Anti-Avoidance Formula

6-125.   While the basic concept of limiting the deductible amount to a prescribed figure is fairly straightforward, it would be very easy to avoid the intended purpose of the preceding formula. Almost any vehicle can be leased for less than $800 per 30 day period through such measures as extending the lease term, or including a required purchase by the lessee at the end of the lease term at an inflated value. Because of this, a second formula is required. This second formula is based on the manufacturer's suggested list price for the vehicle and is as follows:

$$\text{Anti} - \text{Avoidance Formula} = \left[A \times \frac{B}{.85\,C} \right] - D - E, \text{ where}$$

A   is the total of the actual lease charges paid or payable in the year;

B   is a prescribed amount ($30,000 for vehicles leased in 2001 through 2012);

C   is the greater of a prescribed amount ($35,294 for vehicles leased in 2001 through 2012) and the manufacturer's list price for the vehicle (note that this is the original value, even when a used vehicle is leased);

D   is a notional amount of interest for the current year, calculated at the prescribed rate on refundable amounts paid by the lessee in excess of $1,000;

E   is the total of all reimbursements that became receivable during the year by the taxpayer in respect of the lease.

6-126.   Note that, unlike the calculations in the basic cumulative formula, the components of this formula are for the current year only. Also note that the .85 in the denominator is based on the assumption of a standard 15 percent discount off the manufacturers' list price. When the list price is $35,294, 85 percent of this amount is $30,000, leaving the (B ÷ .85C) component equal to one. This means that this component only kicks in when the list price exceeds $35,294, a vehicle that the formula assumes has been acquired for $30,000.

Deductible Amount

6-127.   ITA 67.3 indicates that, when lease payments are being deducted, the amount cannot exceed the lesser of the two formula based amounts. This means that the deductible amount is the least of:

- the actual amount of the lease payments;
- the amount determined using the basic cumulative formula; and
- the amount determined using the anti-avoidance formula.

Example

6-128.   The following example will serve to illustrate the application of these rules.

Example   A car with a manufacturer's list price of $60,000 is leased on December 1, 2011 by a company for $1,612 per month, payable on the first day of each month. The term of the lease is 24 months and a refundable deposit of $10,000 is made at the inception of the lease. In addition, the employee who drives the car pays the company $200 per month for personal use. Assume that the prescribed rate is 2 percent per annum for all periods under consideration. Ignoring GST and PST implications and the fact that 2012 is a leap year, determine the maximum deductible lease payments for 2011 and 2012.

2011 Solution   For 2011, the D component in the ITA 67.3 cumulative formula is $15 [(2%)($10,000 - $1,000)(31/365)] and the E component is $200 [($200)(1)].   The maximum deduction for 2011 is $612, the least of the following amounts:

- $[(\$1,612)(1)] = \underline{\$1,612}$

- $\left[\$800 \times \dfrac{31}{30}\right] - \$0 - \$15 - \$200 = \underline{\$612}$ (Basic cumulative formula)

- $\left[\$1,612 \times \dfrac{\$30,000}{(85\%)(\$60,000)}\right] - \$15 - \$200 = \underline{\$733}$ (Anti-avoidance formula)

2012 Solution   Because the lease was entered into during 2011, the 2011 limit of $800 applies for the life of the lease. For 2012, the D components in the ITA 67.3 formula are $195 [(2%)($10,000 - $1,000)(396/365)] in the basic formula and $180 [(2%)($10,000 - $1,000)(365/365)] in the anti-avoidance formula.

The 2012 E components are $2,600 [($200)(13)] in the basic formula, and $2,400 [($200)(12)] in the anti-avoidance formula.

The maximum deduction for 2012 is $7,153, the least of the following amounts:

- $[(\$1,612)(12)] = \underline{\$19,344}$

- $\left[\$800 \times \dfrac{396}{30}\right] - \$612 - \$195 - \$2,600 = \underline{\$7,153}$ (Basic cumulative formula)

- $\left[\$19,344 \times \dfrac{\$30,000}{(85\%)(\$60,000)}\right] - \$180 - \$2,400 = \underline{\$8,799}$ (Anti-avoidance formula)

Exercise Six - 9

Subject: Deductible Automobile Costs (Business Leases Automobile)

On August 1, 2012, Mr. Sadim Humiz leases an automobile to be used 100 percent of the time in his unincorporated business. The lease cost is $985 per month. The manufacturer's suggested list price for the automobile is $78,000. Mr. Humiz makes no down payment and no refundable deposits. Determine his maximum deduction for lease payments for 2012. Ignore GST and PST considerations.

End of Exercise.   Solution available in Study Guide.

Illegal Payments, Fines And Penalties - ITA 67.5 And 67.6

6-129.   Under ITA 67.5, payments made to government officials that constitute an offence under either the *Corruption of Public Foreign Officials Act* or Canada's *Criminal Code* are not deductible. This would be the case, even if the related income was taxable.

6-130.   It is not uncommon for fines and penalties to be incurred in the process of carrying on business activity (e.g., the driver for a courier company receives a parking ticket while making a delivery). While some uncertainty existed with respect to the deductibility of these amounts in the past, the issuance of ITA 67.6, "Non-Deductibility Of Fines And Penalties", eliminated this uncertainty. This Section states that no deduction can be made for any fine or penalty imposed under a law of a country or of a political subdivision of a country.

Leasing Property

6-131.   While, from a legal perspective, leasing a property is a distinctly different transaction than purchasing the same property, the economic substance of many long-term leases is that they are arrangements to finance the acquisition of assets. From the perspective of the CRA, the problem with such long-term leases is that they may be structured to provide the enterprise with accelerated deductions in comparison with the CCA schedule that would have been applicable had the assets in question been purchased.

6-132.   At one time, a CRA Interpretation Bulletin required that taxpayers look through the legal form of some leases and treat them as a purchase (lessee perspective) or sale (lessor perspective). However, this Interpretation Bulletin was overruled by a Supreme Court decision, resulting in its cancellation. This means that leases must now be accounted for as leases, without regard to whether the lease terms suggest that they are, essentially, instalment purchases.

6-133.   This creates a significant difference between the accounting and tax rules for dealing with leasing arrangements. As many of you are aware, Canadian GAAP requires the capitalization of long-term leases that meet certain criteria, such as a lease term that is a substantial part of the asset's economic life. These accounting rules focus on economic substance and, if the usual risks and rewards of ownership are transferred to the lessee, the lease must be treated as a sale and purchase. In contrast, the tax rules focus on legal form. Under these rules, a lease arrangement cannot be treated as a purchase, without regard to the question of whether it transfers the risks and rewards of ownership.

Exercise Six - 10

Subject: Leases: Tax vs. GAAP Treatment

Markit Ltd. signs a 10 year lease for an asset with an economic life of 11 years. The lease payments are $23,000 per year. Compare the tax treatment of the lease with its treatment under Canadian GAAP.

End of Exercise.   Solution available in Study Guide.

Business Income - Specific Deductions

Inventory Valuation (Cost Of Sales)
General Procedures
6-134.   IT-473R points out that ITA 10 and ITR 1801 allow two alternative methods of inventory valuation. They are:

- valuation at lower of cost or fair market value for each item (or class of items if specific items are not readily distinguishable) in the inventory;
- valuation of the entire inventory at fair market value.

6-135.   The selected method must be applied consistently from year to year, and cannot normally be changed. IT-473R indicates that, in exceptional circumstances, the CRA will allow a change, provided it can be shown that the new method is more appropriate, it is used consistently in future periods, and the taxpayer uses the new method for financial statement purposes.

6-136.   IT-473R indicates that fair market value can mean either replacement cost or net realizable value. The Bulletin also notes that the method used in determining "fair market value" for income tax purposes should normally be the same as the method used to determine "market" for financial statement purposes.

6-137.   IT-473R indicates that cost can be determined through specific identification, an average cost assumption, a First In, First Out (FIFO) assumption, or through the use of the retail method. However, the Bulletin specifically prohibits the use of a Last In, First Out (LIFO) assumption for the determination of inventory costs. Since Canadian GAAP no longer allows LIFO for accounting purposes, it cannot be used for either tax or accounting purposes.

Overhead Absorption
6-138.   While not discussed in ITA 10, IT-473R indicates that, in the case of the work in process and finished goods inventories of manufacturing enterprises, an applicable share of overhead should be included. The CRA will accept either direct costing, in which only variable overhead is allocated to inventories, or absorption costing, in which both variable and fixed overhead is added to inventories. The Bulletin does indicate, however, that the method used should be the one that gives the truer picture of the taxpayer's income.

6-139.   Under absorption costing, amortization will generally be a component of the overhead included in beginning and ending inventories. In calculating net business income, the amounts recorded as accounting amortization will be replaced by amounts available as CCA deductions. This process will require adjustments reflecting any amounts of amortization included in beginning and ending inventories. While these adjustments go beyond the scope of this text, interested readers will find that they are illustrated in an Appendix to IT-473R.

Tax Vs. GAAP
6-140.   Canadian GAAP rules for inventories can be compared to current tax rules as follows:

Inventory Valuation For tax purposes, inventories can be valued at either lower of cost and fair market value, or at fair market value. Both IFRS No. 2 and Section 3031 of the *Private Enterprise Handbook* require that inventories be valued at the lower of cost and net realizable value.

Determination Of Market For tax purposes, market can be determined using either replacement cost or net realizable value. The accounting rules require the use of net realizable value.

Determination Of Cost For tax purposes, cost can be determined using specific identification, a First In, First Out (FIFO) or average cost assumption, or through the use of the retail method. The accounting rules permit the use of the same methods, but is more prescriptive with respect to when each method must be used.

Use Of Direct Costing The use of direct costing is not permitted by either IFRS No. 2 or Section 3031 of the *Private Enterprise Handbook*. We have noted that, with respect to this issue, IT-473R does permit the use of direct costing provided it is the method that gives a "truer picture" of the taxpayer's income. However, with the accounting rules prohibiting the use of direct costing, it would be difficult to argue that this method provides such a picture.

6-141. While there are some differences between the tax rules and the accounting requirements, we would expect that differences between cost of sales for tax purposes and cost of sales for accounting purposes would be fairly unusual.

Special Rule For Artists

6-142. When artists are required to apply normal inventory valuation procedures, it prevents them from writing off the cost of their various works until they are sold. Given the periods of time that such works are sometimes available for sale, this can result in hardship for some artists. As a consequence, ITA 10(6) allows artists to value their ending inventories at nil, thereby writing off the costs of producing a work prior to its actual sale.

Exercise Six - 11

Subject: Inventory Valuation

Brandon Works sells a single product which it buys from various manufacturers. It has a December 31 year end. During 2012, purchases of this item were as follows:

Date	Quantity	Price
February 1	50,000	$2.50
May 23	35,000	2.85
August 18	62,000	2.95
October 28	84,000	3.05

On December 31, 2012, 102,000 of these items are on hand. Their replacement cost on this date is $3.10 and they are being sold for $4.50. It is estimated that selling costs average 10 percent of the sales price. It is not possible to identify the individual items being sold. Calculate all the values that could be used for the 102,000 remaining units for tax purposes, identifying the method you used for each value.

End of Exercise. Solution available in Study Guide.

Other Deductions

6-143. Earlier in this Chapter we described some of the many restrictions that the *Income Tax Act* places on the deduction of items in the determination of net business income. In considering these restrictions, it becomes clear that they also serve to provide general guidance on the items that are deductible.

6-144. In addition to this general guidance, ITA 20 contains a detailed list of specific items that can be deducted in computing net business income. If an item falls clearly into one of ITA 20's deduction categories, it is not subject to the restrictions listed in ITA 18. Some of the more important deductions described in ITA 20 are as follows:

- 20(1)(a) - **Capital Cost Of Property** This Paragraph provides for the deduction of a portion of the cost of capital assets as capital cost allowances. The detailed provisions related to this deduction are covered in Chapter 5.

- 20(1)(b) - **Cumulative Eligible Capital Amount** This relates to the write-off of certain long-lived assets, including goodwill and other intangibles as discussed in Chapter 5.

- 20(1)(c) and (d) - **Interest** These two Paragraphs cover both current and accrued interest, provided the borrowed money was used to earn business or property income. Chapter 7 contains a detailed discussion of some of the problems that arise in this area.

- 20(1)(e) - **Expenses Re Financing** In general, costs related to the issuance of shares or incurred on the borrowing of funds must be deducted on a straight-line basis over five years. Any undeducted financing costs can be written off when the loan is repaid.

- 20(1)(f) - **Discount On Certain Obligations** For tax purposes, bond discount cannot be amortized over the life of the bonds, the normal accounting treatment. This means that only the amount of interest actually paid can be deducted in the determination of business income. It also means that, since the discount balance is not being amortized, it will have to be deducted when the bonds are retired. If the bonds are issued for not less than 97 percent of their maturity amount and, if the effective yield is not more than 4/3 of the coupon rate, the full amount of the discount can be deducted when the bonds are retired. If these conditions are not met, the payment of the discount at maturity is treated in the same manner as a capital loss, with only one-half of the payment being deductible. Note that the tax treatment of bond premiums also differs from the normal accounting treatment. We would note here that, for tax purposes, bond premiums will not normally be amortized over the life of the bond. This issue is discussed in more detail in Chapter 7 which deals with property income.

- 20(1)(j) - **Repayment Of Loan By Shareholder** As is explained in Chapter 15, if a loan to a shareholder is carried on the Balance Sheet of a corporation for two consecutive year ends, the principal amount must be added to the income of the borrower. This Paragraph provides for a deduction when such loans are repaid.

- 20(1)(l) - **Reserves For Doubtful Debts** See Paragraphs 6-58 to 6-61.

- 20(1)(m) - **Reserves For Goods And Services To Be Delivered In Future Taxation Years** See Paragraph 6-62.

- 20(1)(m.1) - **Reserves For Warranties** This provision only applies to amounts paid to third parties to provide warranty services. It does not apply to so-called "self warranty" situations where the business that sold the warrantied item assumes the risk of providing warranty services.

- 20(1)(n) - **Reserve For Unpaid Amounts** This reserve provides for limited use of cash based revenue recognition in computing net business income. See Paragraphs 6-63 to 6-64.

- 20(1)(p) - **Actual Write Offs Of Bad Debts** See Paragraphs 6-58 to 6-61.

- 20(1)(q) - **Employer's Contributions To Registered Pension Plans** This deduction is subject to the limitations described in Chapter 10. At this point we would note that, unlike the accrual approach to pension costs that is used for financial reporting purposes, this deduction is on a cash basis. For tax purposes, the deduction for pension costs is based entirely on funding payments made during the year.

- 20(1)(y) - **Employer's Contributions Under A Deferred Profit Sharing Plan** Only amounts that are paid during the year can be deducted.

- 20(1)(z) and (z.1) - **Costs Of Cancellation Of A Lease** This deduction, in effect, requires amounts paid by a lessor to cancel a lease to be treated as a prepaid expense. Such amounts can be deducted on a pro rata per diem basis over the remaining term of the lease, including all renewal periods. If the property is sold subsequent to the cancellation, the remaining balance can be deducted at that time. If the property is a capital property, only one-half of the remaining balance can be deducted.

- 20(1)(aa) - **Costs For Landscaping Of Grounds** In the absence of this provision, landscaping costs would have to be treated as a capital expenditure. While this provision allows for an immediate deduction, it is based on amounts paid in the year. Costs accrued at the end of the taxation year cannot be deducted.

- 20(1)(cc) - **Expenses Of Representation**

- 20(1)(dd) - **Costs Of Investigation Of A Site To Be Used In The Business**

- 20(1)(oo) - **Amounts Deferred Under A Salary Deferral Arrangement**

- 20(1)(qq) and (rr) - **Disability Related Costs** These two paragraphs allow the costs of disability related building modifications and acquisitions of disability related equipment to be treated as current deductions, rather than as capital assets. Like the similar provision for landscaping costs, the deduction is only available for amounts paid during the year.

- 20(4) - **Uncollectible Portion Of Proceeds From Disposition Of A Depreciable Property**

- 20(10) - **Convention Expenses** This allows the taxpayer to deduct the costs of attending no more than two conventions held during the year, provided they are in a location that is consistent with the territorial scope of the organization.

- 20(11) - **Foreign Taxes On Income From Property Exceeding 15 Percent** This provision is only applicable to individuals and reflects the fact that an individual's credit for foreign taxes paid is limited to 15 percent. This matter is discussed in Chapters 7 and 11.

- 20(16) - **Terminal Losses** This deduction was explained in Chapter 5.

Reconciliation Schedule

6-145.   While it would be possible to calculate net business income starting with a blank page, adding inclusions, and subtracting deductions, this approach is rarely used. Since most businesses have an accounting system that produces an accounting Net Income figure, the normal approach to determining net business income is to start with accounting Net Income, then add and deduct various items that are different for tax purposes. Note, however, that some smaller businesses that do not require audited financial statements base their regular accounting system on tax rules. In such cases, no reconciliation is needed.

6-146.   For those businesses that base their accounting system in whole or part on GAAP, a reconciliation between accounting Net Income and net business income is required. While there are many other items that could require adjustment, the items shown in Figure 6-3 (following page) are the common reconciliation items for most taxpayers.

6-147.   In working with this schedule, several general points are relevant:

- Accounting Net Income is an after tax concept. This means that the Tax Expense that is recorded in the accounting records must be added back in this reconciliation schedule.

Figure 6 - 3
Conversion Of Accounting Net Income To Net Income For Tax Purposes

Additions To Accounting Income:
- Income tax expense
- Amortization, depreciation, and depletion of tangible and intangible assets (accounting amounts)
- Recapture of CCA
- Tax reserves deducted in the prior year
- Losses on the disposition of capital assets (accounting amounts)
- Pension expense (accounting amounts)
- Scientific research expenditures (Accounting amounts)
- Warranty expense (accounting amounts)
- Amortization of discount on long-term debt issued (see discussion in Chapter 7)
- Foreign tax paid (accounting amounts)
- Excess of taxable capital gains over allowable capital losses
- Interest and penalties on income tax assessments
- Non-deductible automobile costs
- 50 percent of business meals and entertainment expenses
- Club dues and cost of recreational facilities
- Non-deductible reserves (accounting amounts)
- Charitable donations
- Asset write-downs including impairment losses on intangibles
- Fines, penalties, and illegal payments

Deductions From Accounting Income:
- Capital cost allowances (CCA)
- Amortization of cumulative eligible capital (CEC)
- Terminal losses
- Tax reserves claimed for the current year
- Gains on the disposition of capital assets (accounting amounts)
- Pension funding contributions
- Deductible scientific research expenditures
- Deductible warranty expenditures
- Amortization of premium on long-term debt issued
- Foreign non-business tax deduction [ITA 20 (12)]
- Allowable business investment losses
- Landscaping costs

This addition would include both the current tax expense and any future tax expense recorded under GAAP.

- The amounts deducted in the accounting records for amortization, scientific research, and resource amounts will generally be different from the amounts deducted for tax purposes. While it would be possible to simply deduct the net difference (the tax amount is normally larger than the accounting amount), the traditional practice here is to add back the accounting amount and subtract the tax amount (e.g., we add back accounting amortization and subtract CCA).

- Accounting gains on the disposition of capital assets will be deducted and losses added in this schedule. With these amounts removed, they will be replaced by the relevant tax amounts. As explained in Chapter 5, the disposition of capital assets can result in capital gains, recapture, or terminal losses. These amounts are listed separately in Figure 6-3.

- As was noted in Chapter 1, allowable capital losses can only be deducted against taxable capital gains. As a consequence, only the excess of taxable capital gains over allowable capital losses is included in this schedule. If there is an excess of allowable capital losses over taxable capital gains in the current year, the excess can be carried forward or carried back, but it cannot be deducted in the current year. As a consequence, such amounts are not included in this reconciliation schedule.

- You will note that there are no adjustments related to either Sales or Cost Of Sales. With respect to sales, this simply reflects the fact that the tax and accounting rules produce, in the great majority of situations, identical results. With respect to Cost Of Sales, differences between the *Income Tax Act* and Canadian GAAP are not common and were covered in Paragraph 6-140.

Business Income - Example

Example Data

6-148.   The Markee Company has a December 31 accounting and taxation year end and, for the year ending December 31, 2012, its GAAP determined income before taxes amounted to $1,263,000. You have been asked to calculate the Company's 2012 Net Income For Tax Purposes, and have been provided with the following additional information concerning the 2012 fiscal year:

1. Accounting amortization expense totalled $240,000. For tax purposes, the Company intends to deduct CCA of $280,000.

2. Accounting income includes a gain on the sale of land in the amount of $20,000. For tax purposes, one-half of this amount will be treated as a taxable capital gain.

3. During December, the Company spent $35,000 on landscaping costs. These costs were capitalized in the Company's accounting records. As the expenditure was near the end of the year, no amortization was recorded.

4. The Company's Interest Expense includes $5,000 in bond discount amortization.

5. Financing costs, incurred on January 1, to issue new common stock during the year totaled $60,000. All of these costs were charged to expense in the accounting records.

6. Accounting expenses include $48,000 in business meals and entertainment.

7. During the year, the Company begins selling a product on which it provides a five year warranty. At the end of the year, it recognizes a warranty liability of $20,000.

8. In the accounting records, the Company recognized a Pension Expense of $167,000. Contributions to the pension fund totaled $150,000.

9. The Company leased a car beginning on June 1, 2011 that is used by the sales manager. The lease payments are $750 per month on a car with a manufacturer's suggested list price of $33,000. No refundable deposit was paid.

Example Analysis

6-149.   The following points are relevant to the Net Income calculation:

- Item 1 - The accounting amortization has to be added back and replaced with the CCA deduction.

- Item 2 - The accounting gain has to be removed and replaced by the taxable capital gain.

- Item 3 - Despite the fact that landscaping costs are usually capital costs, ITA 20(1)(aa) specifically permits their immediate deduction.

- Item 4 - The bond discount has to be added back to income.

- Item 5 - Financing costs must be amortized over five years on a straight-line basis under ITA 20(1)(e). As a result, only $12,000 is deductible in the current year and $48,000 must be added back to income.

- Item 6 - Only 50 percent of business meals and entertainment can be deducted.

- Item 7 - Warranty costs can only be deducted as incurred.

- Item 8 - Pension costs can only be deducted when they are funded.

• Item 9 - The lease payments are not limited by the restrictions described beginning in Paragraph 6-121. As a result, the payments are fully deductible and no adjustment is needed.

6-150. Based on the preceding analysis, the calculation of 2012 Net Income For Tax Purposes would be as follows:

Accounting Income Before Taxes		$1,263,000
Additions (Identified By Item Number):		
1 - Accounting amortization	$240,000	
2 - Taxable capital gain on land sale [(1/2)($20,000)]	10,000	
4 - Bond discount amortization	5,000	
5 - Financing costs [(80%)($60,000)]	48,000	
6 - Meals and entertainment [(50%)($48,000)]	24,000	
7 - Warranty liability	20,000	
8 - Unfunded pension expense ($167,000 - $150,000)	17,000	364,000
Deductions (Identified By Item Number):		
1 - Capital Cost Allowance (CCA)	($280,000)	
2 - Accounting gain on sale of land	(20,000)	
3 - Landscaping costs	(35,000)	(335,000)
Net Income For Tax Purposes		$1,292,000

Taxation Year

General Rules

6-151. The *Act* defines a taxation year as follows:

ITA 249(1) For the purpose of this Act, a "taxation year" is

(a) in the case of a corporation, a fiscal period, and

(b) in the case of an individual, a calendar year,

and when a taxation year is referred to by reference to a calendar year, the reference is to the taxation year or years coinciding with, or ending in, that year.

6-152. For corporations, ITA 249.1(1) defines a fiscal period as a period that does not exceed 53 weeks. The 53 week designation provides for situations where a corporation wishes to have a fiscal period that ends in a specified week within a month. For example, if the corporate year end is the last Friday in January, the fiscal year will, in some years, include 53 weeks.

6-153. A new corporation can select any fiscal year end. However, subsequent changes require the approval of the Minister. In most situations, corporations will have a fiscal year for tax purposes that coincides with the fiscal period used in their financial statements.

Unincorporated Businesses - Non-Calendar Fiscal Year

6-154. Unincorporated businesses such as proprietorships and partnerships are not, for income tax purposes, separate taxable entities. The income of such businesses is included in the tax return of the individual proprietor or partner.

6-155. While unincorporated businesses are not required to file an income tax return, they are required to calculate an annual business income figure to be included in the tax returns of their owners. Given that the individuals who are the owners of proprietorships and partnerships must use a taxation year based on the calendar year, it would seem logical to require that these unincorporated businesses also base their taxation year on a calendar year.

6-156. This logic is overridden, however, by the fact that there can be important reasons, unrelated to income tax, for the use of a non-calendar fiscal year (e.g., having the year end at a low point in the activity of the business). As a consequence, under ITA 249.1(4), a proprietorship or partnership can elect to have a fiscal year that does not end on December 31.

6-157. This election is available to any new unincorporated business. However, it must be made on or before the filing date for the individual proprietor or partner. This would be June 15 of the year following the year in which the business commences. The election cannot be made in a subsequent year.

6-158. If the election is made, ITA 34.1(1) requires taxpayers to include an amount of income for the period between the end of their normal fiscal year and December 31 of that year. This income is referred to as "additional business income" and, in simple terms, it is a pro rata extrapolation of the income earned during the non-calendar fiscal period that ends in the year. It is used to create an estimate of the income that will be earned from the end of the non-calendar fiscal period to the end of the calendar year. A simple example will illustrate this process.

> **Example** Jack Bartowski forms a new business on November 1, 2011. It has a fiscal year end of January 31 and had the following net business income:
>
> | Period | Number Of Days | Net Business Income |
> |---|---|---|
> | November 1, 2011 to January 31, 2012 | 92 | $25,000 |
> | February 1, 2012 to January 31, 2013 | 334* | 80,000 |
>
> *Ignoring the fact that 2012 is a leap year.

> **2012 Analysis** The "additional business income" that must be added for 2012 is calculated as follows:
>
> $$[(\$25,000)(334 \text{ Days} \div 92 \text{ Days})] = \underline{\$90,761}$$
>
> The income that will be reported by Mr. Bartowski in his 2012 personal tax return is calculated as follows:
>
> | | |
> |---|---|
> | Actual Income - November 1, 2011 To February 1, 2012 | $ 25,000 |
> | Additional Business Income | |
> | February 1, 2012 To December 31, 2012 | 90,761 |
> | 2012 Business Income | $115,761 |

Note that he will be taxed on his estimated income for 14 months. There is an election available that would alleviate this situation by allowing him to report the November and December 2011 income in 2011, and not 2012.

> **2013 Analysis** The "additional business income" that must be added for 2013 is calculated as follows:
>
> $$[(\$80,000)(334 \text{ Days} \div 365 \text{ Days})] = \underline{\$73,205}$$
>
> The 2013 business income will be calculated by taking the actual figure for February 1, 2012 through January 31, 2013, deducting the additional business income that was included in his 2012 tax return, and adding the new additional business income for the period February 1, 2013 through December 31, 2013. The calculations are as follows:
>
> | | |
> |---|---|
> | Actual Business Income - February 1, 2012 To January 31, 2013 | $80,000 |
> | Additional Business Income: | |
> | Reversal Of Estimated Amount Added In 2012 | (90,761) |
> | Addition Of Estimate Of Income for Feb. 1 to Dec. 31 2013 | 73,205 |
> | 2013 Business Income | $62,444 |

Exercise Six - 12

Subject: Additional Business Income - Non-Calendar Fiscal Year

Mr. Morgan Gelato starts a business on March 1, 2012. Because it will be a slow time of year for him, he intends to have a fiscal year that ends on June 30. During the period March 1, 2012, through June 30, 2012, his business has income of $12,300. What amount of business income will Mr. Gelato report in his personal tax return for the year ending December 31, 2012?

End of Exercise. Solution available in Study Guide.

Special Business Income Situations

Income For Farmers

Farm Losses

6-159.   For an individual who looks to farming as his chief source of activity and income, farm losses are fully deductible against other types of income. The difficulty with farm losses is that there are various levels of interest in farming activity, ranging from a full time endeavour to produce profits from farming, through situations where an individual acquires a luxury home in a rural setting, allows three chickens to run loose in the backyard, and then tries to deduct all the costs of owning and operating the property as a "farm loss". In the latter case, the ownership of a "farm" is nothing more than a hobby or a means to enhance the individual's lifestyle.

6-160.   For such hobby farmers, engaged in farming activity as merely an attractive addition to a lifestyle and with no serious intent to produce a profit from this type of activity, the costs of farming must be viewed as personal living expenses. This means that no portion of farm losses should be considered deductible by hobby farmers.

Restricted Farm Losses

6-161.   The more complex situation is an individual who expects to make a profit from farming, but for whom farming is not his chief source of income. This individual is described in IT-322R, "Farm Losses", as:

> **Paragraph 1(b)**   A taxpayer whose chief source of income is not farming or a combination of farming and some other source of income, but who still carries on a farming business. Such a taxpayer must operate the farm with a reasonable expectation of profit but devotes the major part of his or her time and effort to other business or employment.

> **Note**   This IT bulletin was written in 1978 and does not reflect subsequent court decisions. These decisions suggest the use of a pursuit of profit test, as opposed to the more stringent reasonable expectation of a profit.

6-162.   In this situation, ITA 31 comes into effect. This Section limits the amount of farm losses that can be deducted against other sources of income to the first $2,500 of such losses, plus one-half of the next $12,500, for a total deduction of $8,750 on the first $15,000 of farm losses.

6-163.   Any amount of the farm loss that is not deductible in the current year is commonly referred to as a "restricted farm loss" and is subject to carry over provisions. These carry over provisions are given detailed consideration in Chapter 11.

6-164.   While the preceding distinctions between various types of farming activity may appear to be reasonably clear, this is not the case in actual practice. It is rare that a month goes by without a case involving these distinctions being heard at some stage of the assessment appeals process.

Exercise Six - 13

Subject: Farm Losses

Ms. Suzanne Morph is a high school teacher. In her spare time she grows vegetables for sale in the local farmers' market. While in most years she has shown a profit, she incurred a loss in 2012 of $18,700. How much of this loss is deductible in her 2012 tax return?   Calculate any farm loss carry over available to her.

End of Exercise. Solution available in Study Guide.

Losses And Cash Basis Accounting

6-165.   As previously noted in this Chapter, business income is generally computed on the basis of accrual accounting. A major exception to this applies to taxpayers engaged in a farming or fishing business. ITA 28 permits an election for a farming or fishing business to determine income on a cash basis. This is in contrast to the required use of accrual accounting in the computation of other types of business income.

6-166.   As most farmers will have receivables and inventories in excess of their payables, the ability to calculate income on a cash basis has a general tendency to defer the payment of tax. While it is clear that the original intent of ITA 28 was to provide this form of relief to the farming industry, the government became concerned that taxpayers were using even bona fide farms, in contrast to those described previously as hobby farms, as tax shelters, particularly in years when losses were incurred.

6-167.   The remedy to this problem that has evolved is to require an inventory adjustment in those cases where the use of the cash basis produces a loss. This requires the lesser of the amount of the cash basis loss and the value of purchased inventories to be added back to the cash basis income.

6-168.   Although the procedures involved are complicated by a number of factors, a simple example will illustrate the basic calculation:

Example   Garfield Farms begins operations on January 1, 2012. At this time, it has no Accounts Receivable, Accounts Payable, or Inventories. The Loss on a cash basis for the year ending December 31, 2012 amounted to $600,000. On December 31, 2012, Garfield Farms has the following:

- Accounts Receivable of $2,000,000
- Inventories that total $1,400,000
- Accounts Payable of $750,000

Inventory Adjustment   A mandatory inventory adjustment of $600,000 (lesser of the $600,000 loss and $1,400,000 in inventories) would be added to the cash basis loss of $600,000, resulting in a final income figure for tax purposes of nil.

Accrual Basis Income   If cash basis accounting was not used, normal accrual basis income for the year ending December 31, 2012 would amount to $2,050,000 (-$600,000 + $2,000,000 + $1,400,000 - $750,000).

Capital Gains Deduction

6-169.   One of the most important tax benefits available to Canadian residents is the lifetime capital gains deduction. This deduction essentially provides for a significant amount (up to $750,000) of capital gains on dispositions of qualified farm properties, qualified fishing properties, and shares of a qualified small business corporation, to be received tax free. This provision is discussed in detail in Chapter 11.

Professional Income (Billed Basis Of Recognition)

6-170.   When a business involves the delivery of professional services, clients are billed on a periodic basis, normally after a block of work has been completed. This block of work may be task defined (e.g., billing when a client's tax return is finished), time defined (e.g., billing on a monthly basis), or on some other basis. However, in the majority of professional income situations, billing does not occur until after the work has been completed.

6-171.   If the normal accrual approach was applied to this type of business income, the inclusion in net business income would be recorded at the time work is being done. This would require the inclusion of work in progress (i.e., unbilled receivables) in net business income.

6-172.   However, ITA 34 contains a special rule that is applicable to accountants, dentists, lawyers, medical doctors, veterinarians, and chiropractors. These professionals can elect not to include unbilled work in progress in their income. This so-called "billed basis of income recognition" is not available to other professionals such as architects, engineers, and management consultants.

> **Example**   Ms. Shelly Hart begins her new accounting practice on January 1, 2012. During her first year of operation, she records 2,050 billable hours. Her regular billing rate is $100 per hour and, at the end of her first year, she has billed 1,750 hours, or a total of $175,000. Of this amount, $32,300 is uncollected at the end of the year.

> **Analysis**   As Ms. Hart is an accountant, she can elect the use of the billed basis. If she does so, her inclusion in Net Income For Tax Purposes will be $175,000. Alternatively, if she used the normal accrual approach, the inclusion would be $205,000 [($100)(2,050)]. It would clearly be to her advantage to use the billed basis.

Exercise Six - 14

Subject: Professional Income (Billed Basis Of Recognition)

Jack Winters is a lawyer and, at the beginning of the current year, he had unbilled work in process of $35,000, as well as uncollected billings of $57,000. During the year, he bills the remaining work in process and collects all of these new receivables, as well as the uncollected amounts that were present at the beginning of the year. His work during the year totals potential billings of $245,000. Of this amount, $185,000 has been billed and $160,000 of these billings have been collected. Calculate his inclusion in net business income for the year using:

- the cash basis;
- the billed basis; and
- accrual accounting.

End of Exercise. Solution available in Study Guide.

Sale Of A Business

General Rules

6-173.   ITA 22 through 25 contain a group of provisions that apply when a person sells substantially all of the assets that have been used to carry on a business. The need for special provisions here reflects the fact that, because the business in its entirety is considered to be a capital asset, the gains or losses that result from the sale would be considered to be capital in nature.

6-174.   While this capital gains treatment may be appropriate with respect to many of the assets of a business, gains and losses on the sale of some assets would not be considered capital in nature. In particular, a separate sale of either inventories or accounts receivable would normally result in business income or loss, not a capital gain or loss. Because of this anomaly, there are special provisions with respect to gains and losses on the disposition of these assets when they are sold as part of a business disposition.

Inventories

6-175.   ITA 23 provides that when inventories are included in the sale of a business, the sale will be viewed as being in the ordinary course of carrying on the business. This means that any gain or loss resulting from a sale of inventory will be treated as business income or loss. No election is required to produce this result.

Accounts Receivable - ITA 22 Election

6-176.   In dealing with the sale of accounts receivable as part of the disposition of a business, there are two basic problems. The first is that, if the receivables are worth less than their carrying value, the difference will be considered to be a capital loss. This means that only one-half of the amount of the loss will be deductible, and that the deduction can only be made against taxable capital gains.

6-177.   The second problem is that bad debts cannot be deducted, or a reserve established, unless the receivables have been previously included in income. In the case of the sale of a business, this would create a problem for the purchaser in that the purchased receivables would never have been included in his income.

6-178.   To deal with these two problems, ITA 22 provides for a joint election by the vendor and purchaser of the accounts receivable. The following example illustrates the application of this election.

> **Example**   Mr. Whitney agrees to buy Mr. Blackmore's business. As part of the trans-action, Mr. Whitney acquires Mr. Blackmore's trade receivables for $25,000. These receivables have a face value of $30,000 and Mr. Blackmore has deducted a $4,000 reserve for doubtful debts with respect to these receivables.

> **Analysis - Vendor**   Whether or not the election is made under ITA 22, Mr. Blackmore will have to include the $4,000 reserve in business income. If no election is made, he will then record an allowable capital loss of $2,500 [(1/2)($30,000 - $25,000)]. Assuming Mr. Blackmore has taxable capital gains against which the $2,500 loss can be deducted, the transaction will result in a net inclusion in income of $1,500 ($4,000 - $2,500).

> In contrast, if the ITA 22 election is made, Mr. Blackmore would still have to include the $4,000 reserve in income. However, it will be offset by a business loss of $5,000 on the sale of the receivables, a distinct improvement over the results with no elec-tion. Under this approach, there will be a net deduction from income of $1,000.

> **Analysis - Purchaser**   From the point of view of Mr. Whitney, if no election is made, he will record the receivables as a $25,000 capital asset. If more or less than $25,000 is actually collected, the difference will be a capital gain or a capital loss.

> If, however, the ITA 22 election is made, he will have to include the $5,000 difference between the face value and the price paid in income, in the year the receivables are acquired. Subsequent to the sale, any difference between the $30,000 face value of the receivables and amounts actually collected will be fully deductible in the calcula-tion of net business income. Mr. Whitney could establish a new reserve for doubtful debts related to the purchased receivables that are still outstanding at the year end. If the amount collected is equal to $25,000, Mr. Whitney will be in exactly the same position, whether or not the election is made. If more than $25,000 is collected, he will be worse off with the election because 100 percent rather than one-half of the excess will be taxable. Correspondingly, if less than $25,000 is collected, he will be better off with the election as the shortfall will be fully deductible.

Exercise Six - 15

Subject: Sale Of Receivables

Mr. Donato Nero is selling his unincorporated business during 2012. Included in his assets are accounts receivable with a face value of $53,450. He and the purchaser of the business, Mr. Labelle, have agreed that the net realizable value of these receivables is $48,200. In 2011, Mr. Nero deducted a reserve for doubtful debts of $3,800. Determine the tax consequences of the sale of these receivables for Mr. Nero and Mr. Labelle, provided that they jointly elect under ITA 22.

End of Exercise. Solution available in Study Guide.

Scientific Research And Experimental Development

6-179.   In an effort to encourage expenditures in this area of business activity, special provisions for scientific research and experimental development (SR&ED) expenditures are provided in ITA 37 as well as other Sections of the *Income Tax Act*.

6-180.   SR&ED expenditures generate some of the most generous investment tax credits that are available under today's tax legislation. As SR&ED expenditures are usually made by corporations, our coverage of them is found in Chapter 14, "Other Issues In Corporate Taxation".

Key Terms Used In This Chapter

6-181.   The following is a list of the key terms used in this Chapter. These terms, and their meanings, are compiled in the Glossary Of Key Terms located at the back of the separate paper Study Guide.

Accrual Basis	Net Business Income
Allowable Capital Loss	Net Income
Billed Basis	Property Income
Business	Reserve
Business Income	Restricted Farm Loss
Capital Asset	Restrictive Covenant
Capital Gain/Loss	Soft Costs
Cash Basis	Specified Non-Resident Shareholder
Fiscal Period	Specified Shareholder [ITA 18(5)]
GAAP	Taxable Capital Gain
Hobby Farmer	Taxation Year
Inventory	Thin Capitalization

References

6-182.   For more detailed study of the material in this Chapter, we would refer you to the following:

ITA 9	Income
ITA 10	Valuation Of Inventory
ITA 12	Income Inclusions
ITA 18	General Limitations [On Deductions]
ITA 20	Deductions Permitted In Computing Income From Business Or Property
ITA 22	Sale Of Accounts Receivable
ITA 23	Sale Of Inventory

References

ITA 24	Ceasing To Carry On Business
ITA 28	Farming Or Fishing Business
ITA 31	Loss From Farming Where Chief Source Of Income Not Farming
ITA 34	Professional Business
ITA 67	General Limitation Re Expenses
ITA 67.1	Expenses For Food
ITA 67.2	Interest On Money Borrowed For Passenger Vehicle
ITA 67.3	Limitation Re Cost Of Leasing Passenger Vehicle
ITA 67.5	Non-Deductibility Of Illegal Payments
ITA 67.6	Non-Deductibility Of Fines And Penalties
IC 86-4R3	Scientific Research And Experimental Development
IT-51R2	Supplies On Hand At The End Of A Fiscal Period
IT-99R5	Legal And Accounting Fees (Consolidated)
IT-104R3	Deductibility Of Fines Or Penalties
IT-148R3	Recreational Properties and Club Dues
IT-151R5	Scientific Research And Experimental Development Expenditures (Consolidated)
IT-154R	Special Reserves
IT-185R	Losses From Theft, Defalcation, Or Embezzlement (Consolidated)
IT-188R	Sale Of Accounts Receivable
IT-218R	Profit, Capital Gains And Losses From The Sale Of Real Estate, Including Farmland And Inherited Land And Conversion Of Real Estate From Capital Property To Inventory And Vice Versa
IT-256R	Gains From Theft, Defalcation Or Embezzlement
IT-287R2	Sale Of Inventory
IT-322R	Farm Losses
IT-357R2	Expenses Of Training
IT-359R2	Premiums And Other Amounts With Respect To Leases
IT-364	Commencement Of Business Operations
IT-417R2	Prepaid Expenses And Deferred Charges
IT-433R	Farming Or Fishing - Use Of Cash Method
IT-442R	Bad Debts And Reserves For Doubtful Debts
IT-457R	Election By Professionals To Exclude Work In Progress From Income
IT-459	Adventure Or Concern In The Nature Of Trade
IT-473R	Inventory Valuation
IT-475	Expenditures On Research And For Business Expansion
IT-479R	Transactions In Securities
IT-487	General Limitation On Deduction of Outlays or Expenses
IT-514	Work Space In Home Expenses
IT-518R	Food, Beverages And Entertainment Expenses
IT-521R	Motor Vehicle Expenses Claimed By Self-Employed Individuals
IT-525R	Performing Artists (Consolidated)

Income Tax Technical News #30 (contains restricted farm loss guidance)

Problems For Self Study

(The solutions for these problems can be found in the separate Study Guide.)

Self Study Problem Six - 1 (Bad Debts)

Dr. Allworth is a dentist with an office in one of the less prosperous sections of Vancouver. While he has very large gross billings, his patients are such that he often has trouble collecting the amounts that are due to him. As a consequence, he takes great care in keeping track of outstanding balances in accounts receivable and in making estimates of the amounts that he expects will not be collectible.

At the end of 2011, his accounts receivable balance was $104,000 and, for tax purposes, he deducted a reserve for doubtful debts of $11,500. The corresponding balances at the end of 2012 were $208,000 in total receivables, with a reserve for doubtful debts of $15,900. Both of the reserves were established on the basis of a detailed aging schedule, applied on a receivable by receivable basis.

During 2011, there were recoveries of amounts written off as uncollectible in the amount of $190.

During 2012, $8,800 in accounts receivable were written off as uncollectible. However, $700 of this amount related to a patient where there was some hope of collecting the amount due. As the patient was a personal friend of Dr. Allworth, no real effort had been made to collect the amount and further dental services had been extended on a credit basis. In addition, accounts totalling $1,500 that had been written off in 2011 were recovered during 2012.

Required: How would the preceding information affect the calculation of Dr. Allworth's business income for 2012?

Self Study Problem Six - 2 (Reserves)

Olga Sadowski produces silk flower arrangements that are purchased by both individuals and businesses. In 2012, her first year of operation, she has cash sales of $112,000 and sales on account of $96,000. In addition, she has received $12,000 for arrangements that will not be delivered until 2013. Olga does not include advances in her sales figures.

On December 31, 2012, she has an outstanding Accounts Receivable balance of $42,000. She estimates that $11,000 of this balance will be uncollectible.

During 2013, Olga's cash sales increase to $146,000 and sales on account increase to $123,000. With respect to the $12,000 in 2012 advances from customers, she delivered all of the required arrangements. In 2013, she receives $16,000 for arrangements to be delivered in 2014.

Actual write-offs of Accounts Receivable during 2013 totaled $13,000. On December 31, 2013, outstanding Accounts Receivable total $51,000. Olga estimates that $10,000 of this balance will be uncollectible.

Required: How would the preceding information affect the calculation of Olga Sadowski's business income for the 2012 and 2013 taxation years? Include the full details of your calculations, not just the net result for each year.

Self Study Problem Six - 3 (Home Office Costs And CCA)

Billy Jow is a music instructor at a local high school in your area. He is employed by the school board and earns approximately $50,000 annually. To supplement his income, Billy started to teach music on April 1, 2012, to a number of children in the neighbourhood in the evenings and on weekends.

Billy comes to you for advice on how he should report this supplementary teaching income and what expenses are deductible. Billy does not mind paying his fair share of income taxes, but he wants to pay no more than he has to. From discussions with friends, he understands that he may be entitled to claim a portion of the costs of his home.

Since he was not using the den in his home, he decided to use it for this supplementary teaching. His home is approximately 2,000 square feet in size. The den is approximately 200 square feet.

From April 1, 2012 to December 31, 2012, Billy earned $3,700 in music fees. He has chosen December 31 as his year end and has incurred the following costs since April 1:

Purchase Of Music Books	$ 250
Supplies (Paper, Pens, Etc.)	1,000
Tuxedo For Students' Performances	350
Snacks For Students (Cookies, Pretzels, Candies, Milk, Etc.)	250
Utilities For Home (Heat, Light, And Water)	3,500
Mortgage Interest Paid	11,000
Repairs And Maintenance For Home	2,600
Software Program To Assist In Teaching Music	300
Electric Piano And Bench	5,000
Total	$24,250

Billy is currently using the software program on an old computer that he uses mainly to watch YouTube videos. He is considering the purchase of a new computer solely for teaching purposes if the teaching generates enough income.

Required:

A. Briefly explain when expenses for work space in the home are deductible.

B. Based on the information given, compute the minimum net business income or loss that Billy should report in his 2012 personal income tax return. Ignore the fact that 2012 is a leap year.

C. Briefly describe any issues that should be discussed with Billy concerning his home office and business costs.

Self Study Problem Six - 4 (Business Income - Employee Vs. Self-Employed)

Ms. Wise is a very successful salesperson. She pays all of her own business expenses and provides the following information related to her taxation year ending December 31, 2012.

1. Travel costs, largely airline tickets, food, and lodging on trips outside the area in which she resides, totaled $23,000. Included in this amount is $8,000 of business meals.

2. During the year, she used 40 percent of her personal residence as an office. She has owned the property for two years. It is her principal place of business and it is used exclusively for meeting clients on a regular basis throughout the year. Interest payments on the mortgage on this property totalled $13,500 and property taxes for the year were $4,700. Utilities paid for the house totalled $3,550 and house insurance paid for the year was $950. Other maintenance costs associated with the property amounted to $1,500. The January 1, 2012 UCC of the 40 percent portion of the residence that is used for business is $140,000.

3. For business travel, Ms. Wise drove a car that she purchased for $53,000 on October 15, 2011. During 2012, she drove a total of 50,000 kilometers, 35,000 of these being for business purposes. The business usage of her car varies from 60 to 80 percent each year. The total operating costs for the year were $6,000. In addition, there were financing costs

of $2,500 on a bank loan used to purchase the car. She has always taken maximum CCA on her car.

4. She paid dues to the Salesperson's Association (a trade union) of $600.

5. She was billed a total of $12,000 by a local country club. Of this amount, $2,500 was a payment for membership dues and the remaining $9,500 was for meals and drinks with clients.

Required:

A. Calculate the maximum amount of expenses that would be deductible by Ms. Wise for 2012 assuming:

   i.   She is an employee of a manufacturing company. Her employment income of $137,000 includes $15,000 in commissions.

   ii. She represents a group of manufacturers with a diversified product line. During 2012, she earned total commissions of $137,000.

   In making these calculations, ignore GST and PST considerations.

B. Comment on the desirability of taking CCA on Ms. Wise's personal residence.

Self Study Problem Six - 5 (Deductible Automobile Costs And Taxable Benefit)

Borris Industries is a Canadian controlled private corporation with a taxation year that ends on December 31. Mr. John Borris is the president of the Company and an employee of Borris Industries.

On December 1, 2011, Borris Industries leases a new Mercedes to be used by Mr. Borris. The lease calls for monthly payments of $1,800 per month, payable on the first day of each month for a period of three years. At the time the lease is signed, the Company is required to make a refundable deposit of $10,000. The manufacturer's suggested list price for the car is $85,000. Mr. Borris will pay the Company $500 per month for his personal use of the car. This is the only automobile that is leased by Borris Industries.

During December, 2011, Mr. Borris drives the car a total of 2,500 kilometers, none of which are related to his Company's business activities. Operating costs for this period, all of which are paid by the Company, totaled $1,100.

During 2012, Mr. Borris drives the car 45,000 kilometers, of which 23,000 were related to his Company's business. Operating costs for this period, all of which are paid by the Company, totaled $10,200.

During the period December 1, 2011 through December 31, 2012, the automobile was always available to Mr. Borris.

Assume that the prescribed rate is 2 percent for the period December 1, 2011 through December 31, 2012. Ignore the fact that 2012 is a leap year.

Required: Determine the following:

A. The maximum deduction for automobile lease payments that Borris Industries can take in each of the two years 2011 and 2012.

B. The minimum amount of the taxable benefit that Mr. Borris will have to include in his Net Income For Tax Purposes for each of the two years 2011 and 2012 as a result of having the Mercedes available for his personal use. Note that the prescribed operating cost benefit per kilometer is equal to $0.24 in 2011.

Ignore GST and PST considerations in both parts of this question.

Self Study Problem Six - 6 *(Valuation Of Business Inventories)*

Jasper Retailers Inc. began business on January 1 of the current year. Purchases during the year are as follows:

Date	Quantity	Price	Total Cost
January 1	15,000	$10.00	$ 150,000
March 1	35,000	$11.00	385,000
June 15	42,000	$11.50	483,000
September 1	27,000	$12.00	324,000
October 1	17,000	$12.50	212,500
Totals	136,000		$1,554,500

On December 31, the end of the Company's taxation year, the inventory on hand amounts to 22,000 units. It is estimated that these units have a replacement cost of $10.50 per unit and a net realizable value of $11.75 per unit.

Required: Calculate the various closing inventory values that could be used to determine business income for tax purposes. Your answer should indicate the valuation method being used, as well as the resulting value.

Self Study Problem Six - 7 *(Proprietorship - Comprehensive Business Income)*

Yossarian Tools is a successful proprietorship that John Yossarian has owned and operated for five years. It sells and services power tools of all types.

The accountant for the business has calculated a Net Income for the year ending December 31, 2012 of $298,000 using generally accepted accounting principles. The following information relates to this calculation:

1.   The increase in the reserve for warranties during the year was $14,500. This amount is based on a self-insurance warranty program.

2.   Parking tickets received by Mr. Yossarian and his employees totalled $980. Since they were incurred in the course of deliveries and meetings with clients, they were paid for by Yossarian Tools and deducted in the accounting records.

3.   During the year, Yossarian Tools spent $15,600 landscaping the grounds of its retail store. This amount was deducted as an expense in the determination of Net Income.

4.   The Net Income figure was after the deduction of Amortization Expense of $53,750. CCA has been correctly calculated to total $62,000.

5.   Because of a failure to pay its municipal property taxes on their due date, Yossarian Tools was charged interest of $975.

6.   A contribution of $4,300 was made to a registered charity during the year.

7.   Included in revenues was a payment of $31,200 from an insurance company to compensate for loss of profits when Yossarian Tools was closed for two weeks because of a fire.

8.   Yossarian Tools follows a policy of providing various types of volume discounts to its regular customers. During the year, such discounts amounted to $21,250.

9.   Yossarian Tools paid $1,400 for membership in a local golf and country club. The total of all meals charged at the club by Mr. Yossarian and paid by Yossarian Tools during the fiscal year was $3,400. These meals were all business related and his guests were always important clients or suppliers.

10. Yossarian Tools incurred and expensed appraisal costs of $7,400 in order to determine the current market value of certain capital assets that it intends to sell.

11. As Mr. Yossarian's 6 year old son is very popular with his peers at his school, he was paid a monthly fee of $1,000 ($12,000 for the year) to promote Yossarian Tools to the students in his school. This fee was deducted in the accounting records.

12. As a firm believer in the universal right to bear arms, Mr. Yossarian buys guns from various sources and sells them to special clients. Although this business is illegal, Mr. Yossarian insists that his accountant include his gun sale profits of $28,500 in the Net Income of Yossarian Tools as Mr. Yossarian believes he will have a large loss in the next year which he plans to deduct.

13. Yossarian Tools leased a car in 2011 that Mr. Yossarian uses 100 percent for business purposes. The car was available to him throughout 2012. The lease payments were $650 per month, the manufacturer's suggested list price was $35,000 and no refundable amounts were paid on the lease. The car was driven 30,200 kilometers during 2012. Operating costs averaging $0.73 per kilometer, or $22,046 were paid.

14. As the business is unincorporated, no taxes were deducted in calculating Net Income.

Required: Calculate the minimum net business income for Yossarian Tools that will be included in Mr. Yossarian's tax return for the year ending December 31, 2012. Indicate why you have not included any of the preceding items in your calculations. Ignore GST and PST considerations.

Self Study Problem Six - 8 (Comprehensive Business Income)

Barnes Industries Ltd. is a Canadian private company located in Nova Scotia. Mike Barnes, the majority shareholder of the Company, devotes all of his time to managing the operations of this enterprise. Over the years, the business has consistently shown a profit and, for the taxation year ending December 31, 2012, Mike has determined that the Company's Net Income After Income Taxes is $340,000.

In determining this income figure, Mike has used generally accepted accounting principles. Other information with respect to the determination of accounting income before taxes for 2012 is as follows:

1. The Income Tax Expense deducted by Barnes Industries Ltd. for the year is $86,000, including $13,000 in future income taxes.

2. During the year, the Company has deducted donations to various registered charities in the amount of $3,500.

3. The Company recorded amortization expense for the year of $241,000.

4. The maximum CCA for the year has been correctly determined to be $389,000.

5. After attending a seminar on the tax advantages of income splitting among family members, Mike hires his unemployed cousin to do filing in the office. She proves to be totally incapable of doing the job and is asked to leave after only one day. In the interests of family harmony, he pays her $10,000, which is deducted in the accounting records of the Company.

6. The Company has deducted $23,000 for advertising in newspapers in the New England states. The advertising is directed towards selling the Company's products in that region.

7. The Company provides warranties on several of the products that it sells. For its accounting records, it estimates the cost of providing these warranties and records a liability on the basis of these estimates. The liability at the beginning of the year was $18,000 and the corresponding figure at the end of the fiscal year was $27,000.

8. At the end of 2011, the Company estimated that its bad debts on ending accounts receivable would total $31,000. Actual write-offs during 2012 amounted to $35,000. At the end of 2012, the estimate of bad debts on ending accounts receivable was $33,000. The accounting estimates are considered appropriate for tax purposes.

Problems For Self Study

9. On December 31, 2012, the Company issued new common shares. The legal and accounting fees related to this issue of shares were $8,000. For accounting purposes, these costs were added to the intangible asset, organization costs. As the issue of shares was on December 31, there was no 2012 amortization of this amount for accounting purposes.

10. In January, 2012, the Company paid landscaping costs of $11,000 that were expected to have a useful life of 10 years. These costs were capitalized for accounting purposes and are being amortized on a straight line basis over a period of ten years. (This amortization is included in the amortization expense of $241,000 listed in Part 3.)

11. As a result of Mike's business travel, the Company incurred costs for meals and entertainment in the amount of $13,500. All of these costs were deducted in the determination of accounting income.

12. Amortization of bond discount for the year was $1,800.

13. On January 1, 2012, the Company leases a Mercedes for five years for Mike to use in his business travels. The total 2012 lease payments amount to $18,000 and, in addition, the Company pays all of the operating costs. These operating costs total $6,200 for the year. There are no refundable deposits associated with the lease and the lease payments do not include any amounts for insurance or licensing. All of these amounts are expensed in the determination of the Company's accounting income. The manufacturer's suggested list price for the car is $128,000. Mike has use of the car throughout the year. He drives it a total of 92,000 kilometers, of which 38,000 kilometers were employment related.

Required: For Barnes Industries Ltd.'s 2012 taxation year, determine Net Income For Tax Purposes. Indicate why you have not included any of the preceding items in your calculations. Ignore any GST or PST implications and ignore the fact that 2012 is a leap year.

Self Study Problem Six - 9
(Partnership - Business Income, Employee vs. Self-Employed)

The Montpetit Fashion Group is a partnership that custom designs and retails high-fashion clothing in Calgary. The partnership commenced operations on February 1, 2012.

Part I The three partners have sought your advice on a number of issues related to the tax procedures to be used by their business. Provide the requested advice on each of the following issues:

A. Explain to the partners how business income from partnerships is taxed in Canada.

B. The partners have not picked a partnership year end and would like to know what options they have.

C. Designer gowns, for which there are no production economies of scale, are designed and made by private seamstresses who work in their own homes. Montpetit supplies the fabric and accessories, and pays a previously agreed fixed amount upon satisfactory completion of each gown. The partners are uncertain as to the need for source deductions (income tax, EI and CPP contributions) on these amounts.

Part II The partners would like you to review the following transactions that occurred during their first fiscal year of business ending on December 31, 2012. Advise the partners on the taxability of income amounts in the calculation of net business income for the year. Similarly, for expenditures, provide advice on the specific deductions (with amounts) that can be claimed.

A. Legal fees of $800 were paid for the drafting of a partnership agreement.

B.   Five industrial sewing machines were acquired at the beginning of the year at a cost of $1,100 each. Sewing accessories (thread, needles, scissors, etc.) were also acquired for a total of $850.

C.   Each partner contributed $10,000 to get the business off the ground. On July 1, 2012, each partner loaned the partnership $15,000. Interest of 4 percent per year on the loans was paid by the partnership for the last six months of the year. In addition to the interest, the partners are planning to deduct the $10,000 payments on their personal income tax returns for the current year.

D.   At year-end, designer clothes with a retail price of $26,000 are held on consignment by boutiques throughout the city. The cost of making these clothes was $5,000 in labour and $4,500 in fabric.

E.   Montpetit paid $15,000 for the exclusive right to distribute Dali sweaters for five years.

F.   During 2012, payments totalling $3,250 were made to the Champs Elysee Club. Of this amount, $1,100 was for the annual membership fee and the remaining $2,150 was for charges in the Crepe Suzette Diner. Of the dining charges, $1,500 was spent for entertaining clients and the remainder was for the personal use of the three partners.

Self Study Problem Six - 10 (Proprietorship - Business Income With CCA)

Christine Powell is a visual designer. Until May, 2012, she worked as an employee for a printing supply firm. In June, she became self-employed when she started up "Design Power". Through this business, Christine works with several advertising agencies in the design and desktop publishing of promotional materials.

In January, 2013, she comes to you for tax advice. Being vaguely aware of the complexity of the tax laws, she has kept meticulous track of all business related costs for the period from June 1 to December 31, 2012. Christine's fiscal year end for the business is December 31.

Christine works out of her home. Her studio occupies 20 percent of the useable space in the house. Christine does not intend to claim any CCA on the house. The total operating costs related to the house during the period June 1, 2012 through December 31, 2012 are:

Utilities	$1,500
Home Insurance	700
Mortgage Interest	1,600
Property Taxes	2,600
Total Home Operating Costs	$6,400

On June 1, 2012, Christine bought a used car for business and personal use. The total purchase price of the car was $18,000, financed with a $3,000 cash down-payment and a $15,000 term loan. Her detailed records show that she uses the car 70 percent for business. The automobile costs include:

Down Payment On Car Purchase	$3,000
Gasoline And Oil	1,100
Licence And Registration	200
Insurance	800
Interest On Car Loan	700
Total Automobile Costs	$5,800

On July 15, 2012, Christine purchased computer equipment for $5,000 and various applications software for $1,200. On August 1, she purchased several pieces of office furniture for $2,000. All of these assets were acquired solely for business use.

Her revenues and other costs for the period June 1, 2012 to December 31, 2012 were as follows:

Revenues

Collected	$22,000
Billed, but not collected	4,000
Unbilled work-in-progress	1,500

Costs

Legal and business licence fees	$1,000
Business meals and entertainment with clients	500
Office and computer supplies	650
Printing sub-contract fees	1,800

Required: Calculate the minimum net business income Christine would include in her 2012 personal income tax return.   In preparing your solution, ignore GST/HST/PST implications.

Self Study Problem Six - 11 (Proprietorship - Business Income With CCA)

Carla Jensen is Chartered General Management Accountant who is employed as an internal auditor by a Canadian public company. The constant, unrelenting stress of her employment has resulted in a dependency on recreational drugs. This, in turn, has resulted in the need for additional funds. Because of this need for additional income, she operates an unincorporated tax and accounting services business.

This business has a December 31 year end and has been in operation for several years. The business operates out of a building which Carla purchased, new, in 2009. She uses this building exclusively for non-residential purposes. It has been allocated to a separate Class 1.

On January 1, 2012, Carla had unbilled work-in-progress of $28,000, along with billed receivables of $37,000. During 2012, her cash receipts total $105,000. On December 31, 2012, the unbilled work-in-progress has increased to $35,000 and the billed receivables have increased to $42,000.

On January 1, 2012, the business has the following UCC balances:

Class 1 Building	$226,000
Class 8 Furniture And Fixtures	46,500
Class 10 Vehicle (Purchased For $20,300)	17,255

During January 2012, Carla acquires a new computer for $1,800, along with applications software for $725.

During March, 2012, the Class 10 vehicle is involved in a serious accident, requiring it to be permanently taken off the road. The insurance proceeds are $12,300. On April 1, Carla replaces it with a vehicle with a manufacturer's list price of $32,000 that is leased for $475 per month. Both vehicles are used exclusively for business purposes.

During July, 2012, Carla replaces some of the furniture in her office. The old furniture has a capital cost of $18,000, while the new items cost $34,000. Carla receives a trade in allowance for the old furniture of $6,000.

During September, 2012, Carla acquires a client list from an accountant who is retiring. The cost of this list is $47,000.

During 2012, the various costs of operating her business, determined on an accrual basis, are as follows:

Building Operating Costs	$24,500
Costs Of Operating Leased Vehicle	7,200
Payments To Assistants	13,500
Miscellaneous Office Costs	3,750
Meals With Clients	4,200

Required: Calculate the minimum net business income Carla would include in her 2012 personal income tax return. In preparing your solution, ignore GST and PST implications.

Self Study Problem Six - 12 (ITA 22 Accounts Receivable Election)

Beckett Enterprises is an unincorporated business that has operated successfully for a number of years under the direction of its owner, Ms. Joan Close. However, in early 2012, she decides to dispose of the business and retire. She will sell all of the assets of the business to an unrelated party, Mr. John Phar.

The date of the disposition is February 1, 2012 and, on that date, the business has accounts receivable with a face value of $120,000. Because of anticipated bad debts, the realizable value of these receivables is estimated to be $107,000. In 2011, Ms. Close deducted a reserve for doubtful debts in the amount of $8,000.

Beckett Enterprises has a December 31 year end. Mr. Phar will continue the business on an unincorporated basis and will also have a December 31 year end.

During the year ending December 31, 2012, $100,000 of the accounts receivable are collected, with the remainder being written off as non-recoverable.

Both Ms. Close and Mr. Phar have heard of an election under ITA 22 that may have some influence on the tax treatment of the transfer of accounts receivable. They would like to have your advice on this matter. They will both have significant capital gains in 2012.

Required: Indicate the tax effects, for both Ms. Close and Mr. Phar, of the disposition of the accounts receivable and the subsequent 2012 collections and write-offs, assuming:

A. that no election is made under ITA 22.

B. that they make an election under ITA 22.

Self Study Problem Six - 13 (Business Income With CCA)

Darlington Inc. has a fiscal year ending December 31. For the year ending December 31, 2012, the Company's accounting Net Income, determined in accordance with generally accepted accounting principles, was $596,000. Other information related to the preparation of its 2012 tax return is as follows:

1. The income tax expense was $55,000, including $7,000 in future income tax expense.

2. The Company spent $95,000 on landscaping for its main office building. This amount was recorded as an asset in the accounting records and, because the work has an unlimited life, no amortization was recorded on this asset.

3. The Company spent $17,000 on advertisements in *Fortune* Magazine, a U.S. based publication. Approximately 90 percent of its non-advertising content is original editorial content. The advertisements were designed to promote sales in Canadian cities located on the U.S. border.

4. The amortization expense was $623,000. At the beginning of 2012, the Company has a balance in Class 1 of $1,000,000, representing the UCC of its headquarters buildings. The Company has owned this building since 2001.

   In general, other buildings are leased. However, in February, 2012, a policy change results in the acquisition of a new store building at a cost of $650,000, of which $125,000 is allocated to land. This building is used 100 percent for non-residential purposes and is allocated to a separate Class 1. None of the usage is for manufacturing and processing.

   The January 1, 2012 balance in Class 8 was $4,200,000. During 2012, there were additions to this class in the total amount of $700,000. In addition, Class 8 assets with a cost of $400,000 were sold for proceeds of $550,000. The net book value of these assets in the accounting records was $325,000, and the resulting gain of $225,000 was included in the accounting income for the year. There are numerous assets remaining in the class at the end of the 2012 taxation year.

At the beginning of 2012, the UCC in Class 10 was $800,000, reflecting the Company's fleet of cars. As the Company is changing to a policy of leasing its cars, all of these cars were sold during the year for $687,000. The capital cost of the cars was $1,200,000, and their net book value in the accounting records was equal to the sale proceeds of $687,000.

5. Included in travel costs deducted in 2012 for accounting purposes was $12,000 for airline tickets and $41,400 for business meals and entertainment.

6. The Company paid, and deducted, for accounting purposes, a $2,500 initiation fee for a corporate membership in the Highland Golf And Country Club.

7. The Company paid, and deducted, property taxes of $15,000 on vacant land that was being held for possible future expansion of its headquarters site.

Required: Calculate Darlington Inc.'s minimum Net Income For Tax Purposes for the 2012 taxation year. In addition, calculate the January 1, 2013 UCC balances for each CCA class. Indicate why you have excluded some items from your calculations.

Self Study Problem Six - 14 *(Comprehensive Case Covering Chapters 1 to 6)*

Ms. Lacy Compton is a 45 year old widow with two children:

John Her son John is 22 years old and, because he has been blind since birth, he lives with her in a residence that she owns. He qualifies for the disability tax credit and has no income of his own during 2012.

Allison Her 17 year old daughter Allison has just started university and, during 2012, she attended on a full time basis for 4 months. Her tuition fees that were paid during 2012 were $2,850. Because she has no income of her own, she intends to transfer all of her education related credits to her mother. As she is attending a local university, Allison lives in her mother's home throughout 2012. She will not reach 18 years of age prior to the end of 2012.

During 2012, her family's qualifying medical expenses are as follows:

Lacy	$ 4,220
John	11,500
Allison	2,180
Total	$17,900

The entire family purchases monthly passes to use public transit. During 2012, the cost of the pass is $60 per month for Ms. Compton, $25 per month for John, and $25 per month for Allison, payable on the first day of each month.

During 2012, Ms. Compton makes donations to registered charities of $1,250, as well as contributions to registered federal political parties in the amount of $350.

Ms. Compton is employed as a salesperson by a Canadian public company. For 2012, her salary is $68,000. In addition, she earns $13,500 in commissions during the year. For the year ending December 31, 2012, her employer withholds the following amounts from her income:

RPP Contributions*	$2,800
EI Premiums	840
CPP Contributions	2,307
Professional Association Dues	250
Payments For Personal Use Of Employer's Car	1,800

*Ms. Compton's employer makes a matching contribution of $2,800 to her RPP.

The car that she used during 2012 cost her employer $32,000. During 2012, it was used by her for 11 months of the year. It was driven a total of 27,000 kilometres, of which 22,500 was for employment related activities. During the 1 month that she did not use the car, her employer required that she return it to the company garage.

She is required by her employer to maintain an office in her home. During 2012, this office occupied 15 percent of the floor space in her home. The cost of the house (excluding the land) is $335,000. Her 2012 costs for 100 percent of the floor space were as follows:

Mortgage Interest	$5,800
Property Taxes	2,450
Utilities And Maintenance	1,100
Insurance	425
Total	$9,775

In conjunction with her sales activities, she incurred costs for meals and entertainment of $4,350. These were not reimbursed by her employer.

In addition to her employment activities, Ms. Compton owns and manages an unincorporated retail business. The fiscal year of the business ends on December 31 and, for 2012, the business had accounting Net Income of $53,500. Other information related to the business is as follows:

1. As the business is unincorporated, no taxes were deducted in calculating Net Income.

2. During 2012, the business spent $8,600 landscaping its premises. For accounting purposes, this amount is being amortized over 10 years on a straight line basis.

3. At the beginning of 2012, Ms. Compton owned depreciable assets used in the business with the following UCC balances:

	Class 1	Class 8	Class 10
January 1, 2012 UCC	$233,000	$41,500	$27,000

The Class 1 building was acquired in 2005.

In March, 2012, Class 8 assets with a cost of $12,000 were sold for $8,600. They were replaced by Class 8 assets with a cost of $13,400.

4. The Net Income figure is after the deduction of Amortization Expense of $12,800 and $6,000 in meals and entertainment with clients of the business. The Amortization Expense includes the amortization of the landscaping costs.

Required: Calculate Ms. Compton's 2012 Net Income For Tax Purposes, her 2012 Taxable Income, and her minimum 2012 federal Tax Payable without consideration of any income tax withheld by her employer. Ignore GST and PST considerations.

Assignment Problems

(The solutions for these problems are only available in
the solutions manual that has been provided to your instructor.)

Assignment Problem Six - 1 (Reserves)

Olaf Swensen owns an unincorporated business that delivers specialty food products to individuals and businesses. In 2011, his first year of operation, he had total delivered sales of $215,000, of which $85,000 were on account. In addition, he received $14,500 in advances from customers for products to be delivered in 2012. Olaf does not include advances in his sales figures.

Being unincorporated, he chooses a taxation year that ends on December 31. On December 31, 2011, he had uncollected receivables of $42,000. He estimates that $4,000 of these receivables will become uncollectible.

In 2012, Olaf's cash sales total $145,000 (not including advances from customers) and account sales total $92,000. The $14,500 of 2011 orders for which advances were received were all filled in 2012. During 2012, additional advances of $15,300 were received for deliveries in 2013.

During 2012, Olaf needed to write off $4,300 of the December 31, 2011 receivables. On December 31, 2012, the enterprise has uncollected receivables of $38,000. Olaf anticipates that $4,500 of these receivables will be uncollectible.

The December 31, 2012 receivables contain a single large order for $12,000 of Olaf's products sold to a very important customer. Because of the size of this order, Olaf has agreed to allow the customer to defer payment until January 1, 2013. The order was received on September 1, 2012.

Required: How would the preceding information affect the calculation of Olaf Swensen's business income for the 2011 and 2012 taxation years? Include the full details of your calculations, not just the net result for each year.

Assignment Problem Six - 2 *(Valuation Of Business Inventories)*

Holden's Shirts began business on January 1 of the current year. Mike Holden, the owner of the business, has always had an interest in high end clothing. Based on this interest, his business involves purchasing shirts from exclusive manufacturers and reselling them at a significant mark up. The business has a December 31 year end.

Purchases of shirts during the current year are as follows:

Date	Quantity	Price	Total Cost
January 27	400	$120	$ 48,000
April 3	1,200	130	156,000
August 15	1,500	125	187,500
October 31	800	128	102,400
Totals	3,900		$493,900

On December 31, the end of the Company's taxation year, the inventory on hand amounts to 950 shirts. It is estimated that these units have a replacement cost of $126 per unit and a net realizable value of $142 per unit.

Required: Calculate the various closing inventory values that could be used to determine business income for tax purposes. Your answer should indicate the valuation method being used, as well as the resulting value.

Assignment Problem Six - 3 *(Deductible Automobile Costs And Taxable Benefit)*

Maxine's Cleaning Services is a Canadian controlled private corporation with a December 31 year end. Maxine Brott is the sole shareholder of the corporation and actively participates in the operation of the business as an employee.

Because of the extensive travel required in supervising her employees, the Company provides Ms. Brott with a car. During the first 6 months of 2012, the provided car was a Honda Accord that had been purchased in 2011 for $29,000. During this 6 month period, she drove the car a total of 23,000 kilometres, of which 15,000 were related to her employment activities. The Class 10 UCC balance at the beginning of 2012 was $24,650.

On July 1, 2012, the Honda Accord was sold for $25,000. It was replaced with a BMW 7 Series sedan at a cost of $105,000. During the period July 1, 2012 through December 31, 2012, she drove this vehicle a total of 37,000 kilometres, of which 18,000 were related to her employment activities.

Throughout 2012, the Company paid for all of the operating costs of both vehicles, a total of $12,300.

Other than the Honda Accord and the BMW sedan, the Company did not own any other vehicles during 2012. During the period January 1, 2012 through December 31, 2012, an automobile was always available to Ms. Brott.

Required: Determine the following:

A. The tax consequences to Maxine's Cleaning Services that result from owning and selling the Honda Accord and owning the BMW sedan during 2012.

B. The minimum amount of the taxable benefit that Maxine will have to include in her Net Income For Tax Purposes for 2012.

Ignore GST and PST considerations in both parts of this question.

Assignment Problem Six - 4 (Deductible Business Expenses - Corporation)

The Vernon Manufacturing Company, a Canadian controlled private corporation, has just ended its first fiscal year. During that year, a number of outlays were made for which the Company is uncertain as to the appropriate tax treatment. You have been asked to advise them in this matter and, to that end, you have been provided with the list of outlays and expenditures that follows:

1. A part of the Company's raw materials had to be imported from Brazil. In order to obtain local financing for these inventories, the Company paid a $1,200 fee to a Brazilian financial consultant for assistance in locating the required financing.

2. Donations totalling $12,000 were given to various registered Canadian charities.

3. The Company paid $2,500 to the owner of a tract of land in return for an option to purchase the land for $950,000 for a period of 2 years. The land is adjacent to the Company's main factory and management believes it may be required for future expansion of the Company's manufacturing facilities.

4. Direct costs of $7,500, related to incorporating the Company, were incurred during the year.

5. An amount of $10,000 was paid for a franchise giving the Company the right to manufacture a Brazilian consumer product for a period of ten years.

6. Because of its rapid growth, the Company was forced to move into a building that they had originally leased to another company. In order to cancel the lease, it paid $8,000 to the tenant. In addition, $9,500 was spent to landscape the facilities and another $13,000 was spent to provide a parking lot for employees.

7. As some of its employees use public transportation, a pedestrian bridge over an adjacent highway was required to allow these employees to reach the plant from the public transportation terminal. The cost of this bridge was $12,000.

Required: Indicate which of the preceding expenditures you feel that the Vernon Manufacturing Company will be able to deduct in the calculation of business income for the current year, and the tax treatment of the non-deductible expenditures. Explain your conclusions.

Assignment Problem Six - 5 (Deductible Business Expenses - Proprietorship)

Dr. Sweet is a dentist with a well established practice in Smith Falls, Ontario. She has sought your advice regarding the deductibility of the following expenditures made during the current taxation year:

1. Insurance payments included a $680 premium for coverage of her office and contents, $1,800 for malpractice coverage, and $1,700 in life insurance premiums.

2. Payments were made to a collection agency in the amount of $1,250 for assistance in collecting past due amounts from patients.

3. Contributions of $600 were made to various registered charities.

4. Dr. Sweet paid a total of $18,000 to her husband for his services as a full time bookkeeper and receptionist.

5. Dr. Sweet paid $5,000 for a painting by a Canadian artist that has been hung in her waiting room.

6. A total of $4,600 was spent to attend a dental convention in Phoenix, Arizona. Dr. Sweet was accompanied by her husband and $1,500 of the total cost of the trip relates directly to him.

7. An amount of $1,000 was paid for membership in a racquets club. In addition, $1,300 was spent for court time, approximately 40 percent of which was for time spent playing with patients.

8. Dr. Sweet paid $1,200 in legal and accounting fees. These fees related to fighting a personal income tax reassessment for a previous tax year. The fight was not successful and, as a consequence, Dr. Sweet was required to pay additional taxes of $13,000, plus $1,600 in interest on the late payments.

9. During the year, Dr. Sweet spent $3,200 purchasing provincial lottery tickets.

Required: Advise Dr. Sweet with respect to the deductibility of the preceding expenditures in the calculation of Net Income For Tax Purposes. Explain your position on each expenditure.

Assignment Problem Six - 6 (Proprietorship - Simple Business Income)

Fairway Distribution is a proprietorship. The business distributes a wide variety of health aid products to retailers. The business is owned by John Fairway. His wife, Jane Fairway, is an avid golfer with no interest or experience in business matters.

For the taxation year ended December 31, 2012, the accountant calculated a Net Income for Fairway Distribution of $273,000. In calculating this figure, Mr. Fairway's accountant relied on generally accepted accounting principles except for the fact that no provision is made at the end of the year for anticipated bad debts. This variance from generally accepted accounting principles resulted from the accountant's belief that Mr. Fairway is a much more reasonable and pleasant person when he is presented with a higher Net Income figure.

Other Information   Other information related to the 2012 taxation year is as follows:

1. In the previous year, a reserve for bad debts was deducted for tax purposes in the amount of $15,000. Actual bad debt write-offs during 2012 amounted to $17,500 and the accountant felt that an appropriate reserve to be deducted for tax purposes at the end of 2012 would be $19,200.

2. Accounting income included a deduction for amortization in the amount of $78,500. The accountant has determined that the maximum CCA for 2012 would be $123,600.

3. The following items were included in the accounting expenses:

Cost of advertising in a foreign newspaper that is distributed in Canada	$ 3,500
Donations to registered charities	1,260
Cost of appraisal on real estate to be sold	1,470
Costs of landscaping work done on the grounds of Mr. Fairway's personal estate	5,260
Management fee to Mrs. Jane Fairway	123,000

4. As the business is unincorporated, no taxes were deducted in calculating Net Income.

Required: Calculate the minimum net business income for Fairway Distribution that will be included in Mr. Fairway's tax return for the year ending December 31, 2012.

Assignment Problem Six - 7 (Proprietorship - Business Income)

Morton Forms is a proprietorship owned by Viola Morton. For the taxation year ended December 31, 2012, Ms. Morton's daughter, Linda, who works in the business, has calculated a Net Income for Morton Forms of $193,200. In calculating this figure, Linda used generally accepted accounting principles.

Other Information:

1. During the year, Morton Forms spent $18,900 for landscaping the grounds around its Vancouver office. In accordance with generally accepted accounting principles, this amount was treated as a capital expenditure. As the work was done late in the year, no amortization was deducted for the current year.

2. The following items were included in the accounting expenses:

Amortization expense	$69,300
Cost of sponsoring local baseball teams	7,200
Reserve for inventory obsolescence	15,000
Advertising on a foreign television station (Directed at Canadian market)	9,600
Advertising circulars (Only one-quarter distributed)	12,400
Business meals and entertainment	22,000
Charitable donations	31,900
Loss from theft	16,200
Interest paid on building mortgage	24,200
Appraisal costs on land to be sold	4,200
Damages resulting from breach of contract	3,800

3. Also included in the accounting expenses were $4,000 in fees paid to Linda's 16 year old son for creating and maintaining the web site of Morton Forms. In pricing this work, Viola found that it would cost at least $8,000 to obtain the equivalent services from an outside consultant.

4. Maximum CCA has been determined to be $94,200 for the taxation year ended December 31, 2012.

5. As the business is unincorporated, no taxes were deducted in calculating Net Income.

Required: Calculate the minimum net business income for Morton Forms that will be included in Viola Morton's tax return for the year ending December 31, 2012. Indicate why you have not included any of the preceding items in your calculations.

Assignment Problem Six - 8
(Partnership - Business Income, Employee vs. Self-Employed)

Richmond Consultants is a partnership with three architects as members. The partnership provides services throughout their local region. The partnership began operations on July 1, 2012.

While the partners themselves will undertake much of the work required by their various contracts, some smaller projects may be contracted out. These outside contracts will require the architect to undertake a well defined project for a fixed fee, plus related expenses. The partners are uncertain as to the need for source deductions (income tax, EI and CPP contributions) on amounts paid to these individuals.

The partners have hired you to assist them with some of the tax issues that will arise in the operation of the partnership.

Required:

A. Explain to the partners how business income from partnerships is taxed in Canada.

B. Explain to the partners what choice they have in selecting a year end for their business.

C. Advise the partners on whether source deductions will be required on the amounts paid to the outside architects.

Assignment Problem Six - 9 (Proprietorship - Business Income With CCA)

Cody Jewel is an accountant who has not incorporated his practice. The practice has a December 31 year end.

Cody operates his practice out of a building which he owns. Cody purchased this building in 2009 for $550,000, with the estimated value of the land at that time being $125,000. His practice occupies 100 percent of the building and, because it was a new building when he acquired it, it has been allocated to a separate Class 1. On January 1, 2012, the building has a UCC of $380,000.

Because he is attracting an increasingly wealthy clientele, Cody has decided to upgrade his office. During February, 2012, he replaces all of his old furniture and fixtures. The old furniture and fixtures had a capital cost of $65,000 and a UCC of $41,000. It is sold for $22,000. The new furniture and fixtures have a capital cost of $136,000.

Other asset acquisitions during 2012 are as follows:

New Computer	$1,800
Applications Software	2,700
Client List From Retiring Accountant	32,000

Because he has started to provide in-home services for many of his clients, he has a car which is used largely for this purpose. Cody purchased this car for $56,000 on January 1, 2012. During 2012, it is driven a total of 23,000 kilometers, of which 21,000 kilometers related to providing services for his clients. Operating costs for the year totalled $4,140.

Other 2012 costs of operating his business, determined on an accrual basis, are as follows:

Building Operating Costs	$18,600
Payments To Assistants	31,200
Miscellaneous Office Costs	9,400
Meals With Clients	10,500

On January 1, 2012, Cody had unbilled work-in-progress of $52,000, along with billed receivables of $64,000. During 2012, his collections total $216,000. On December 31, 2012, the unbilled work-in-progress has increased to $61,000 and the billed receivables have increased to $72,000.

Required: Calculate the minimum net business income Cody would include in his 2012 personal income tax return. In preparing your solution, ignore GST and PST implications.

Assignment Problem Six - 10 (ITA 22 Accounts Receivable Election)

George Pentel is the owner of George's Geodes, an unincorporated business that provides distribution at the wholesale level of collectable mineral specimens. The business has a December 31 year end.

While the business has been very successful, George would like to return to his first love, research related to plate tectonics.

To accomplish this goal, he intends to sell George's Geodes to an unrelated party, Ms. Molly Stone. The transaction will take place on August 1, 2012 and will involve all of the assets of the business. Ms. Stone does not anticipate incorporating the business and will continue to use the December 31 year end.

On the date of the sale, the Accounts Receivable of the business have a face value of $352,000. George and Molly agree that the current fair market value of these receivables is $335,000. In 2011, George deducted a reserve for doubtful debts under ITA 20(1)(l) of $12,000.

Between August 1, 2012 and December 31, 2012, $337,000 of the Accounts Receivable are collected, with the remaining $15,000 being written off as uncollectible.

Both George and Molly have heard of an election under ITA 22 that may have some influence on the tax treatment of the transfer of accounts receivable. They would like to have your advice on this matter. George notes that he did not have any capital gains in the previous three years. Further, he does not expect to have capital gains in 2012 or any subsequent year.

Required:

A. Indicate the tax effects, for both George Pentel and Molly Stone, of the disposition of the accounts receivable and the subsequent 2012 collections and write-offs, assuming:

• that no election is made under ITA 22.
• that they make an election under ITA 22.

B. Indicate, from the point of view of each taxpayer, whether making the election would be a desirable course of action.

Assignment Problem Six - 11 (Home Office Costs And CCA)

In order to supplement his income working in a Calgary bookstore, Mr. Victor Larson has decided to start a home based business that will specialize in selling used textbooks to university and college students.

The business will be run out of space that he has set aside in his residence. This space involves 18 percent of the total floor space in the residence.

The residence was acquired on January 1, 2012 at a total cost of $426,000. It is estimated that $150,000 of this total value can be attributed to the land on which the residence is situated. For the year ending December 31, 2012, Mr. Larson has the following costs that can be associated with this residence:

Utilities For Home (Heat, Light, And Water)	$ 3,200
Mortgage Interest Paid	10,100
House Insurance	500
Property Taxes	4,300
Repairs And Maintenance For Home	2,600
Total	$20,700

The business begins operations on January 31, 2012. On that date, Mr. Larson acquires the following assets to be used in his new business:

Office Furniture And Storage Racks	$18,500
Computer	1,430
Business Software	570

In addition, he has a separate telephone line installed for dealing exclusively with the mail order business. The telephone charge includes charges for a toll-free number and a long distance package.

During the period January 31, 2012 through December 31, 2012, his mail order sales total $182,000. Costs associated with these sales are as follows:

Cost Of Merchandise Sold	$98,000
Unsold Merchandise (Lower Of Cost And Market)	23,500
Packaging Materials	2,400
Shipping Costs	4,600
Miscellaneous Office Supplies	560
Telephone (Total Charge For The Period)	1,100
Printing Of Posters And Brochures Distributed	420

Required:

A. Can Mr. Larson deduct home office costs? Briefly explain your conclusion.

B. Compute the minimum net business income or loss that Mr. Larson must report in his 2012 personal income tax return. Ignore the fact that 2012 is a leap year.

C. Briefly describe any issues that should be discussed with Mr. Larson concerning his home office and business costs.

Assignment Problem Six - 12 *(Comprehensive Case Covering Chapters 1 to 6)*

Ms. Alicia Archer is 48 years old and lives with a common-law partner. Her common-law partner, Maria Blair has 2012 income of $9,800.

Ten years ago, the couple adopted two children. Their 24 year daughter Helen is dependent on them because she is disabled. The disability is not severe enough to create a marked restriction in her daily activities. During 2012, Helen has income from various part time jobs of $7,200.

The couple's 18 year old son, Jeff, is in full time attendance at a Canadian university for 7 months during 2012. Jeff had 2012 Net Income For Tax Purposes of $6,400. Ms. Arden has paid his tuition fees of $7,200. In addition, Ms. Arden provided Jeff with $875 to pay for his textbooks. Jeff has agreed to transfer his education related tax credits to Ms. Arden.

Ms. Arden works for Gowan Enterprises, a large Canadian public company. For 2012, her salary is $84,000. In addition, she earns commissions for the year of $39,000. During the year ending December 31, 2012, her employer withholds the following amounts from her income:

RPP Contributions*	$5,600
EI Premiums	840
CPP Contributions	2,307
Parking Fees At Employer's Lot	600
United Way Contributions	1,200

*Ms. Arden's employer makes a matching contribution of $5,600 to her RPP.

Ms. Arden's work requires fairly extensive travel. To cover the costs of hotels and meals, her employer provides an allowance of $1,100 per month. Her actual costs during 2012 were as follows:

Hotels	$7,700
Business Meals	6,200

Ms. Arden uses her own car for her employment related travel. It was acquired on January 1, 2012 at a cost of $37,000. During 2012, she drove the car a total of 38,000 kilometers, of which 32,500 were employment related. Her total operating costs for the year were $6,800. To assist her with these costs, her employer provided an allowance of $600 per month.

In 2009, Ms. Arden's employer granted her options to acquire 2,200 shares of its common shares at a price of $4.25 per share. At the time the options were granted, the Gowan Enterprise shares were trading at $4.00 per share. In January, 2012, Ms. Arden exercises the options. At this time, the Gowan Enterprise shares were trading at $9.50 per share. Ms. Arden is still holding the acquired shares on December 31, 2012.

Because of her interest in hockey, on January 1, 2012, Ms. Arden opened a retail operation to sell hockey related merchandise. Ms. Arden invests $320,000 of her savings in this unincorporated business. Of this amount $272,000 was used to purchase a new store building, with the remaining $48,000 invested in fixtures for the store. She estimates that $78,000 of the $272,000 paid for the store represents the value of the land. The business is called The Puck Place and, as the retail operation is only a few blocks from her residence, Ms. Arden makes no use of her car in this business.

As Ms. Arden has had no formal training as an accountant, she keeps the records for The Puck Place on a cash basis. As at December 31, 2012, the business had accumulated total cash of $56,500. Ms. Arden's informal records indicate that at December 31, 2012, the business had receivables from customers of $5,200, inventories with a cost of $18,700, and liabilities to suppliers of $8,240. The business had no other debt obligations on this date.

During 2012, Ms. Arden paid medical expenses as follows:

Alicia	$ 3,940
Maria	2,450
Helen	7,250
Jeff	1,260
Total	$14,900

Required: Calculate Ms. Arden's 2012 Net Income For Tax Purposes, her 2012 Taxable Income, and her minimum 2012 federal Tax Payable without consideration of any income tax withheld by his employer. Ignore GST and PST considerations.

Assignment Problem Six - 13 (Comprehensive Case Covering Chapters 1 to 6)

Joan Galley is a salesperson for Goodship Lollipop Ltd., a Canadian public corporation. The company produces various sweets such as candy and chocolate bars.

It has been a stressful time for Joan these last 18 months. In the summer of 2011, her spouse passed away. Joan has two children: Ryan who is 13 and Julie who turned 18 on April 30, 2012.

Joan's 2012 employment contract states that she will be paid an annual base salary of $50,000 plus a commission of 1.5 percent of her annual cash sales. Her 2011 sales totaled $3,200,000, but $200,000 of such was collected by the company in 2012. Her 2012 sales amounted to $2,800,000, but the company had yet to collect $300,000 of these by December 31, 2012.

In 2012, her employer paid Joan her base salary plus her commission income. A review of her last pay stub for 2012 reveals the following was withheld from her salary:

Contributions To Her Company Pension Plan	$3,000
CPP Contributions	2,307
EI Premiums	840
Premiums For The Company's Dental And Health Plan*	1,500
Federal Income Tax Withheld	15,000

* The plan is funded 50/50 by the employees and the employer.

Joan is covered by the company's group term life insurance. Her coverage is equal to her annual base salary. The company pays a premium of $5 for every $1,000 of coverage to the Sweet Life Insurance Company.

In January of 2012, Joan detected a packaging problem with a particular line of candies before these were to be shipped. Her keen eye saved the company an estimated $360,000 in product recalls. This helped her win the employee of the year reward of an iPad2 which cost the company $900.

In September of 2011, her employer transferred her from Montreal to Toronto. She thought the change would be beneficial after the death of her spouse a few months earlier. Her employer paid for all her moving expenses. Unfortunately, due to the quick sale of her Montreal home, she incurred a $30,000 loss on its sale. Goodship Lollipop agreed to reimburse her $20,000 of the $30,000 loss, but only in January of 2012. The $20,000 was actually received by Joan on January 14, 2012.

In April of 2011, Joan's employer granted her the right to purchase up to 5,000 shares of the company for $17 per share under the employee stock option plan. At the time the option was granted, the shares were trading for $15. On February 1, 2012, when the shares were trading at $20 per share, she exercised her option on 3,000 shares. She sold 2,000 shares at $22 per share with a settlement date of December 30, 2012.

In order to purchase the 3,000 shares, Joan negotiated an interest free loan from her employer for the purchase price. The loan was received on February 1, 2012. Joan repaid the loan on December 31, 2012.

Throughout 2012 her employer provided her with an automobile, which it leases for $450 per month. The automobile was available for her personal use. During the year, Joan drove a total of 35,000 kilometers, 8,000 of which were personal. Except for $2,200 of car insurance, Goodship Lollipop did not pay for any of her automobile operating expenses as these were Joan's responsibility.

Joan is responsible for her salesperson expenses (including the automobile operating expenses). During the year she incurred the following:

Total Automobile Expenses (Excluding Insurance)	$5,400
Meals And Entertainment With Clients	2,600
Hotels	1,500

Joan is a member of the Confectioners' Association of Canada, a professional association. Her annual membership dues are $1,400.

Joan meets all of the conditions of ITA 8(1)(f) of the *Income Tax Act* (deductible salesperson expenses).

Joan has a sideline business which is called The Cup Cake Diva. She started her business venture a few years ago and has continued it in Toronto. Joan prepares and sells cupcakes and other pastries from her home. Most of her sales are made for social events which are typically held on weekends.

Joan provides you with the following information for 2012 with respect to her business:

Sales Revenues	$40,000
Supplies (Flour, Sugar, Boxes, Etc.) Purchased	12,000
Purchase Of New Commercial Oven	
(For Business Use Only)	2,200
Purchase Of New Automobile For Cash	39,000
Automobile Operating Expenses	3,000

With respect to the supplies, she had an opening inventory of $1,600. On December 31, 2012 she had $900 of supplies on hand.

Early in January, 2012, Joan sold her old automobile for $12,000. Both the old and the new automobiles were used solely for her business, as she uses the employer provided automobile for the little bit of personal travel that she does do.

Her daughter Julie helps in the business. She is making the deliveries to practice her driving and shows real aptitude for dealing with clients. Joan has not offered her any monetary compensation as Julie is just happy to be driving a new car at this point in time.

Joan uses 20 percent of the space in her home for the business. Her 2012 household expenses include the following:

All Utilities	$5,400
Property Taxes	3,800
Maintenance	1,600
Phone Line Dedicated To The Business	800
Insurance On Her Home	1,900
Mortgage Interest	12,300

The ending UCC balances at December 31, 2011 are as follows:

Class 8	$3,100
Class 10.1	9,000

Joan does not claim CCA on her home as she realizes that if she did, this would result in future recapture and capital gains implications.

Her son Ryan is in high school and reports no income. He plays inter-city soccer. Joan paid $700 in registration fees in order for Ryan to play.

Her daughter Julie, not knowing which university program she would like to enroll in, was enrolled part-time (4 months) at a local college. Joan agreed to pay her tuition of $1,600 as long as Julie transferred all of the tax benefits to her (Joan). Julie's 2012 Net Income For Tax Purposes is $7,200.

During the year, Joan paid $5,000 for orthodontic work (braces) for Ryan. She was reimbursed 50 percent of the amount through the company's dental and health plan.

During 2012, Joan made $1,600 of contributions to registered charities.

Assume the prescribed rate for benefits during all four quarters of 2012 is 1 percent.

Required:

A. For the 2012 taxation year, calculate Ms. Galley's minimum:

   1. Net Income For Tax Purposes,
   2. Taxable Income,
   3. Federal Tax Liability.

   In determining these amounts, ignore GST, PST and HST considerations.

B. Do you have any tax planning advice for Joan Galley? Discuss.

Tax Software Assignment Problem For Chapter 6

This Tax Software Assignment Problem was introduced in Chapter 4 and is continued in Chapters 6 through 11. Each Tax Software Assignment Problem must be completed in sequence. While it is not repeated in this problem, all of the information in the Chapter 4 problem (e.g., Mary's T4 content) is applicable to this problem.

If you have not prepared a tax file incorporating the Tax Software Assignment Problem information for the previous Chapter, please do so before continuing with this problem.

Tax Software Assignment Problem For Chapter 6

On December 27, 2011, Seymour Career, at the urging of his wife, Mary Career, has brought you his preliminary figures for his business. Seymour carries on a business writing and editing instruction manuals on a contract basis. He has six different clients and operates under the business name Crystal Clear Communications from an office in their home.

He knows from past experience that one of his clients will issue him a T4A for the work that he has done for them and has included this information, though he does not yet have the T4A. He is currently missing the information on interest he has paid during the year, except for interest related to his house and his car. He anticipates receiving this shortly.

During the year, Seymour is a full time student at Dalhousie University for three months. He is attending courses in child psychology in order to help deal with Mary's son, William, who has been refusing to go to school and is displaying hostile tendencies.

T2202A - Seymour	Box	Amount
Tuition fees	A	2,200
Number of months in school - part-time	B	0
Number of months in school - full-time	C	3

T4A - Seymour	Box	Amount
Issuer - 3065 Canada Inc.		
Fee For Services (Professional)	48	20,000.00

Business or Professional Income - Seymour	
Revenues without T4A	41,603.17
T4A's issued (see T4A information)	20,000.00
Membership dues - Business Writers Association	231.00
Business insurance	126.16
Bank service charges	156.20
Cell phone air time	485.27
Postage and courier charges	110.00
Supplies	2,982.17
Separate business phone line charge and long distance charges	577.86
Fees for accounting and tax advice	500.00
Air fare (business travel)	526.97
Hotels (business travel)	1,240.91
Meals when traveling on business	607.14
Meals and drinks when entertaining clients	887.12
UCC of furniture - beginning of year	2,254.94
UCC of computer application software - beginning of year	219.15
UCC of computer hardware (Class 52) - beginning of year	Nil
Application software purchased May 12, 2011	525.00
Laptop computer purchased May 12, 2011	2,048.00

House Costs	
Area of home used for business (square feet)	160
Total area of home (square feet)	1,500
Gas for heating	1,712.86
Hydro	1,641.18
Insurance - house	757.55
Snow plowing contract	440.00
Installation of new gas furnace	3,675.00
Painting of house interior	2,548.05
Mortgage interest paid to Royal Bank	8,456.22
Mortgage life insurance premiums	375.00
Mortgage principal paid	1,279.58
Property taxes	2,533.01
Interest on late property taxes	122.52

The mortgagee of Seymour's house, the Royal Bank, does not require life insurance, but given Seymour's state of health, he feels it is advisable to have life insurance on the mortgage.

Car Costs - Seymour	
Description - Subaru, cost = $35,000, bought 2008-02-15	
January 1 odometer	89,726
December 31 odometer	124,701
Business kilometers driven	8,412
Parking	321.71
Gas	2,582.12
Maintenance and repairs	458.63
Car insurance	779.00
Licence and registration fees	49.87
Interest on 4 year car loan granted on purchase date	597.89
UCC of Class 10.1 - beginning of year	15,470.00

Required:

A. Open the file that you created for the Chapter 4 version of this Software Problem and save a copy under a different name. This will enable you to check the changes between different versions of this Software Problem.

B. Create a return for Seymour that is coupled to Mary's. (Use the F5 key with Mary's return open to create Seymour's return.) Prepare and print in the following order:

i. the motor vehicle expenses worksheet for Seymour.
ii. the CCA worksheet for Crystal Clear Communications.
iii. the Statement of Business or Professional Activities (T2125) for Crystal Clear Communications.

Ignore any GST/HST implications. *Hint*: Enter all motor vehicle expenses as non-eligible for GST or HST.

C. Access and print Mary's summary (Summary on the Form Explorer, not the T1Summary). This form is a two column summary of the couple's tax information. By opening this form from Mary's return, the order of the columns is the same as the one in the previous chapter. For both returns, list the changes on this Summary form from the previous version of this Software Problem. Exclude totals calculated by the program, such as federal tax, the total for non-refundable tax credits and provincial tax from the list, but include the final Balance Owing (Refund) amount.

Sample Of Required Table

The following table is one format that could be used to list the required changes. It would contain the changes to the Summary form from the previous version, excluding calculated amounts other than Balance Owing (Refund).

Summary Line Changed	Mary	Seymour
Chapter 6		
Self-employment		
CPP (deduction from Net Income)		
Spousal credit		
Basic Personal Amount		
CPP tax credit		
Education related tax credits		
CPP contributions payable		
Balance Owing (Refund)		

CHAPTER 7

Income From Property

Introduction

7-1. Subdivision b of Division B of the *Income Tax Act* provides simultaneous coverage of both income from business and income from property. The parts of these Sections relating to business income are covered in Chapter 6, and many of these provisions are equally applicable to income from property. However, there are sufficient features that are unique to income from property that separate coverage of this subject is warranted and is provided in this Chapter. We have also included coverage of some of the basic issues related to interest deductibility in this Chapter.

Property Income: General Concept

7-2. Income from property is thought of as the return on invested capital in situations where little or no effort is required by the investor to produce the return. Falling into this category would be rents, interest, dividends, and royalties paid for the use of purchased property. In terms of tax legislation, capital gains are not treated as a component of property income, even in cases where they arise on investments being held to produce property income (e.g., capital gains on dividend paying shares). This point is made clear in ITA 9(3) which states that "income from a property does not include any capital gain ...".

7-3. In cases where a great deal of time and effort is directed at producing interest or rents, such returns can be considered business income. For example, the rents earned by a company that owns a number of shopping centers would be treated as a component of business income. As explained in Chapter 12, this is an important distinction for corporations since business income qualifies for the small business deduction, while property income generally does not.

7-4. The primary characteristic that distinguishes property income from business income is the lack of effort directed towards its production. However, in some circumstances, other factors must also be considered. Some examples of why the correct classification is important are as follows:

- When some types of property income are being earned, the deduction of capital cost allowance (CCA) cannot be used to create or increase a net loss for the period.

- When property income is being earned by individuals, there is no requirement for a pro rata CCA reduction to reflect a short fiscal period.

- When property income is being earned, the income attribution rules (see Chapter 9) are applicable. This is not the case when business income is being earned.

- Certain expenses can be deducted against business income, but not property income. These include write-offs of cumulative eligible capital and convention expenses. In contrast, for individuals, there is a deduction for foreign taxes on property income in excess of 15 percent that is not available against foreign business income.

Interest As A Deduction

The Problem

7-5.   There are differing views on the extent to which interest costs should be considered a deductible item for various classes of taxpayers. At one extreme we have the situation that, at one time, existed in the U.S. In that country it was once possible for individuals to deduct all interest costs, without regard to the purpose of the borrowing. In contrast, there are other tax regimes where the deductibility of interest is restricted to certain, very specific types of transactions.

7-6.   From a conceptual point of view, it can be argued that interest should only be deductible to the extent it is paid on funds that are borrowed to produce income that is fully taxable in the period in which the interest is paid. The application of this concept would clearly disallow the current deduction of interest when it relates to:

- the acquisition of items for personal consumption;
- the acquisition of assets which produce income that is only partially taxed (e.g., capital gains); or
- the acquisition of assets which produce income that will not be taxed until a subsequent taxation year (e.g., gains on investments in land).

7-7.   To some extent, the preceding view is incorporated into the current legislation. The real problem, however, is that there are such a multitude of provisions related to the special treatment of certain types of income and to the deferral of income, that the application of these fairly straightforward principles becomes very complex.

7-8.   As is noted in Chapter 6, the general provision for the deduction of interest is found in ITA 20(1)(c). This provision provides for the deduction of interest only if it relates to the production of business or property income. This means that, in general, interest cannot be deducted if it relates only to such other sources of income as employment income or capital gains. Note, however, that if this production of income criteria is met, the deduction is available to all types of taxpayers, including corporations, individuals, and trusts.

7-9.   As a final general point here, you will recall that when an employee receives an interest free or low interest loan from an employer, imputed interest on the loan will be included in employment income as a taxable benefit. Under ITA 80.5, this imputed interest is deemed to be interest paid and, if the loan is used to produce business or property income, the amount that was included in the employee's income will be deductible under ITA 20(1)(c).

Current Situation

7-10.   The government has made several attempts to provide more detailed guidance on the question of interest deductibility. The most recent effort occurred in 2003. On October 31 of that year, the government released an unusual document which consisted of a combination of draft legislation, along with a new Interpretation Bulletin, IT-533, *Interest Deductibility And Related Issues*. The draft legislation which is contained in a new ITA 3.1, is still listed by tax services as proposed. However, the general consensus is that these legislative proposals will never be passed.

7-11.   The government's inability to gain support for passage of these legislative proposals was made more difficult by two cases in which the Supreme Court of Canada ruled against the CRA. These were the Singleton and Ludco decisions which the Supreme Court delivered in

2001. We are left then with the precedents established in these two cases, along with the guidance provided in IT-533, *Interest Deductibility and Related Issues*. Our discussion of interest deductibility will be based on these materials and will not deal with the coverage of the 2003 proposals.

The Singleton And Ludco Court Cases

7-12. The facts in the Singleton case (The Queen vs. Singleton; 2001 DTC 5533) involved a lawyer who made a withdrawal of funds from his capital account in the law firm where he worked. These funds were used to purchase a residence for his personal use. Immediately after, he borrowed sufficient funds to replace the capital balance that he had withdrawn from his firm and then proceeded to deduct the interest on these borrowings. Mr. Singleton argued that the money borrowed was directly used to invest in the partnership and, because this was an income producing purpose, the interest should be deductible.

7-13. The CRA denied this deduction on the basis that the real purpose of the borrowings was to finance the purchase of his residence, a view that was supported by the Tax Court of Canada. However, both the Federal Court of Appeal and the Supreme Court of Canada disagreed. In making this decision, the Supreme Court noted that, in the absence of a sham or a specific provision in the *Act* to the contrary, the economic realities of a transaction cannot be used to recharacterize a clearly established legal relationship.

7-14. The facts in the Ludco case (Ludco Enterprises Ltd. vs. The Queen; 2001 DTC 5505) involved the Company borrowing $7.5 million which was used to finance investments in two offshore companies. During the period that these investments were held, Ludco paid $6 million in interest on the borrowings and received $600,000 in dividends on the shares held. When the shares were ultimately redeemed, Ludco realized a $9.2 million capital gain.

7-15. The CRA denied the deduction of the interest on the grounds that the shares were acquired for the purpose of earning a capital gain, not for the purpose of earning property income. While the Federal Court of Appeal agreed with the CRA, the Supreme Court of Canada did not. They concluded that an investment can have multiple purposes and, as long as one of these was the earning of property income, the condition that borrowing must be for the purpose of earning income was satisfied. That provision does not require either a quantitative determination of income or a judicial assessment of the sufficiency of income in order to satisfy its requirements.

IT-533 - "Interest Deductibility And Related Issues"

What Is Interest?

7-16. In order to be considered interest for tax purposes, IT-533 indicates that the amount has to satisfy three criteria:

- It must accrue on a continuous basis (note that it may be compounded using a different basis).
- It must be calculated on a principal sum.
- It must be compensation for the use of that principal sum.

7-17. IT-533 notes that participating payments meet this definition and will be deductible, provided there is an upper limit on the applicable rate and that upper limit reflects prevailing market conditions. However, payments that are contingent on some future event are not deductible until that event occurs. Further, if the event occurs in a future year, the payment would not be deductible in that year as the payment is not in respect of that year.

7-18. It is also noted that when a contract does not explicitly identify any amount as interest, deductible interest may still be present if any of the payments under the contract can reasonably be regarded as interest. An example of this would be some of the prescribed debt obligations that are discussed beginning in Paragraph 7-49.

Direct Or Indirect Use

7-19.   In order for the interest to be deductible, it must be paid on money that has been borrowed to produce income from business or property. This raises the question of whether it is the direct use, or the indirect use that is relevant. This was the issue in the Singleton court case where the direct use of the borrowings was to invest capital in the partnership, but the indirect use was to purchase a personal residence. This case, along with others, seems to make clear that it is the direct use that must be considered.   The fact that Singleton was, in economic reality, financing the purchase of his home, cannot override the fact that the direct use of the borrowed money was to invest in an income producing partnership.

7-20.   While direct use is the general rule, IT-533 does indicate, however, that there are exceptions to this rule. These exceptions include:

Filling The Hole The Bulletin uses the term "filling the hole" to describe situations where money is borrowed to pay dividends, to redeem shares, or to return capital of a corporation or partnership. The basic idea here is that the new debt replaces other forms of capital that were invested in income producing assets. In the case of dividends, this seems to be a bit of a stretch. However, the argument is that the borrowings replace the retained earnings that are being distributed in the form of dividends.

Interest-Free Loans In general, interest on money borrowed to make interest-free loans would not be deductible as the purpose of the borrowing is not to produce income. However, it can be argued that an interest-free loan to a wholly owned subsidiary has been made with a view to helping the subsidiary produce income which can ultimately be used to pay dividends. The Bulletin indicates that the interest on borrowings to make interest-free loans of this type would be deductible.

A further exception is when money is borrowed to make interest-free loans to employees. The argument here is that the interest-free loan is a form of employee compensation, the purpose of which is to encourage the employees to help the employer produce income.

Linking Interest To Current Use

7-21.   Several court decisions have made it clear that it is the current use of the borrowed money that establishes deductibility. To illustrate this point, consider the following example:

Example   An individual borrows $100,000 and invests it in an income producing property. This income producing property is subsequently sold and the proceeds invested in personal use property.

Analysis   Subsequent to the sale of the income producing investment, interest on the borrowings is no longer deductible as the current use of the property is no longer income producing.

If, alternatively, the proceeds of the sale of the income producing property had been invested in another income producing property, the interest would continue to be deductible.

Looking at this from the other direction, if the original borrowings had been to finance personal use property, the interest would not have been deductible at the time of the borrowing. However, if the personal use property was sold and the proceeds invested in an income producing property, the interest would commence being deductible at that point in time.

7-22.   A widely used technique for facilitating the linking process is referred to as "cash damming". This involves establishing two separate bank accounts, with one account receiving only deposits of borrowed funds and the other account receiving all other deposits. Management then takes steps to ensure that only expenditures which qualify for interest deductibility are made from the account that receives the borrowed funds.

7-23. A further problem with linking can arise when there is a reinvestment of proceeds that involved a gain or loss on the sale of the original investment.

Example An individual borrows $100,000 and invests it in an income producing property. This property is subsequently sold and the proceeds invested in other income producing properties.

Analysis If we assume that the original property is sold for $150,000 and invested in property A which costs $110,000 and property B which costs $40,000, the borrowed money can be allocated in any way the investor wishes. He could allocate the full $100,000 to property A or, alternatively, $40,000 to property B, with the remaining $60,000 to property A. The decision will probably be based on which property he plans to dispose of first, particularly if he does not anticipate re-investing the funds in income producing assets.

In contrast, if we assume that the original asset is sold for $90,000, with the proceeds used to acquire property A for $60,000 and property B for $30,000, IT-533 suggests that the borrowing must be allocated to the two investments on a pro rata basis. This would result in $66,667 [($60,000 ÷ $90,000)($100,000)] being allocated to property A, and $33,333 [($30,000 ÷ $90,000)($100,000)] being allocated to property B. Note that the debt allocated to each property is more than its cost. This is permitted by the disappearing source rules that are described in the following Paragraph.

Disappearing Source Rules

7-24. A problem can arise if an investment, which has been financed with debt, is sold for proceeds that are less than the debt. In such situations, the investor does not have sufficient funds to pay off all the related debt.

7-25. ITA 20.1 deals with the obvious inequity that could arise in disappearing source situations such as that illustrated in the following example:

Example An investor buys shares at a cost of $75,000, using borrowed funds to finance the purchase. At a later point in time, the investment is sold for $40,000, with the proceeds used to pay off $40,000 of the debt. The remaining $35,000 of the debt remains unpaid.

Analysis If the current use approach is used, the interest on the remaining debt would no longer be deductible as it is not currently in use to finance income producing property. However, in situations such as this, the remaining debt would be deemed under ITA 20.1 to be used in producing income and the interest would continue to be deductible.

Investments In Common Shares

7-26. IT-533 deals with a number of other issues associated with interest deductibility. Its guidance on dealing with premium and discount on the issuance of debt is discussed later in this Chapter. Most of the other issues covered are sufficiently specialized that they go beyond the scope of this text. There is, however, one other issue here of general importance.

7-27. This is the question of whether interest on funds used to invest in common shares should be considered deductible. The problem is that common shares generally do not carry a stated interest or dividend rate and, in some cases, simply do not pay dividends, either currently or for the foreseeable future. While capital gains may ultimately make such investments profitable, there are many cases where investments in common shares could be viewed as not producing property income.

7-28. Fortunately, IT-533 indicates that in most circumstances the CRA will consider interest on funds borrowed to invest in common shares to be deductible. This is on the basis of a reasonable expectation, at the time the shares are acquired, that the holder will at some time in the future receive dividends. They do, however, give an example of a situation where this expectation is not viable:

Example R Corp. is an investment vehicle designed to provide only a capital return to the investors in its common shares. The corporate policy with respect to R Corp. is that dividends will not be paid, that corporate earnings will be reinvested to increase the value of the shares, and that shareholders are required to sell their shares to a third-party purchaser in a fixed number of years in order to realize their value.

7-29. In this situation, it is not reasonable to expect income from such shareholdings and any interest expense on money borrowed to acquire R Corp. shares would not be deductible.

Discount And Premium On Long-Term Issued Debt
Economic Background
7-30. When a debt security is issued with an interest rate below the current rate, investors will react by offering a price that is less than the maturity value of the security. Such securities are said to sell at a discount and, in economic terms, this discount generally represents an additional interest charge to be recognized over the life of the security.

7-31. For example, a 10 year bond with a maturity value of $100,000 and a 10 percent stated interest rate, would sell for $88,700 to investors expecting a 12 percent interest rate. The discount of $11,300 ($100,000 - $88,700) would then be added to interest expense at the rate of $1,130 per year for the ten year period. Note that, in order simplify the presentation of this material, we are using the straight-line amortization of discount and premium. This approach is acceptable under Canadian GAAP for private enterprises. However, under international accounting standards, the effective rate method must be used.

7-32. In a corresponding fashion, a debt security that offered an interest rate above that currently expected by investors would command a premium. Such a premium would then be treated as a reduction in interest expense over the remaining life of the debt security.

7-33. The procedures described in the preceding Paragraph are, of course, well known to anyone familiar with normal accounting procedures. Surprisingly, the tax rules for dealing with bond premium and discount do not reflect these well established principles.

7-34. The required tax procedures are completely different from the accounting procedures, are inconsistent in the treatment of premium and discount, and have no conceptual basis of support. Despite this, IT-533, *Interest Deductibility And Related Issues* (previously discussed beginning in Paragraph 7-16), makes it clear that these strange procedures reflect the intent of the government.

Tax Procedures - Issuers Of Discount Bonds
7-35. From the point of view of the issuer of a discount bond, the deductible amount of interest will be based on the stated, or coupon, rate without consideration of the difference between the proceeds received from the sale of the bonds and the larger amount that must be paid when the bonds mature. This excess will be treated as a loss on the retirement of the debt (i.e., a liability is being extinguished by paying more than its carrying value for tax purposes). You may recall from Chapter 6 that, under ITA 20(1)(f), this loss will be considered a fully deductible amount, provided:

- the bonds are issued for not less than 97 percent of their maturity value; and

- the effective yield on the bonds is not more than 4/3 of the stated, or coupon, rate.

7-36. If these conditions are not met, only one-half of the loss will be deductible. This, in effect, treats the loss in the same manner as a capital loss. It would appear that the goal here is to prevent the use of deep discount bonds which, because of the failure of tax legislation to deal appropriately with bond discount, results in the investor having a part of his interest income being converted to a capital gain. A more logical solution to this problem would be to revise the relevant tax legislation to better reflect the economic substance of bond discount.

Exercise Seven - 1

Subject: Discount Bonds

On January 1, 2012, Moreau Ltd. issues bonds with a maturity value of $1,000,000 and a maturity date of December 31, 2014. The bonds pay interest on December 31 of each year at an annual coupon rate of 4 percent. They are sold for proceeds of $985,000 for an effective yield of 4.6 percent. The maturity amount is paid on December 31, 2014. What are the tax consequences related to this bond issue for Moreau Ltd. in each of the years 2012, 2013, and 2014? How would these tax consequences differ from the information included in Moreau's GAAP based financial statements? Moreau uses the straight-line method to amortize the discount on the bonds.

End of Exercise.   Solution available in Study Guide.

Tax Procedures - Issuers Of Premium Bonds

7-37.   IT-533 makes it clear that premium situations are not treated in a manner that is analogous with the treatment of discounts. This Bulletin indicates that, depending on the situation, three different possible approaches may be used by debt issuers for dealing with bond premium. These alternatives can be described as follows:

Money Lenders   The Bulletin indicates that, in situations where the borrowed money constitutes stock-in-trade for a taxpayer that is in the financing business, premium on the debt must be taken into income immediately. The Bulletin also makes it clear that this amount would not be given capital gains treatment and, as a consequence, would be 100 percent taxable. Given this treatment of the premium, the deductible amount of interest would be equal to the stated, or coupon, rate.

Other Taxpayers   In what constitutes something of a windfall for taxpayers issuing debt at a premium, the Bulletin indicates that the amount of premium received at the time of issue would be considered a non-taxable capital receipt. While IT-533 is not clear on this issue, it appears that there will be no further tax consequences related to the premium when the bonds are retired. Unlike the case with bond discount, where there is a specific ITA Paragraph which provides for the deduction of this amount at the maturity of the bonds, there is no corresponding provision that requires the premium to be treated as a gain when the bonds are retired.

Deliberate Creation Of A Premium   IT-533 introduces a third approach based on the very fuzzy concept of a "premium which arises because the debt was deliberately priced to give rise to a premium". There appears to be concern here that an enterprise might create additional tax deductions by setting an unrealistically high rate of interest on the issuance of debt. While it is not clear how "unrealistically high" will be measured, the tax consequence is that the contractual amount of interest paid will be viewed as unreasonable and will be reduced to a reasonable amount over the life of the debt. As this appears to be consistent with the premium amortization approach used in accounting, it seems the CRA's position is that only in unreasonable circumstances is it appropriate to use a reasonable approach to dealing with bond premium.

7-38.   With most conventional debt issuances, the second approach would be applicable. It is interesting to note that, in comparison with the applicable accounting procedures, this approach produces a larger interest deduction and this enhanced deduction is not offset by a gain when the bonds are retired. This permanent difference between accounting and tax income should make taxpayers who issue premium bonds very happy.

Exercise Seven - 2

Subject: Premium Bonds

On January 1 of the current year, Cannon Inc. issues 10 year bonds payable with a maturity value of $1,000,000. The bonds have a coupon rate of 18 percent, pay interest on January 1 of each year, and are sold for $1,400,000. The Company has a December 31 year end. Determine the current year tax consequences under each of the following assumptions:

- Cannon is in the business of lending money.
- Cannon is not in the business of lending money and did not make a deliberate effort to create a premium on the issuance of the bonds.
- Cannon is not in the business of lending money and made a deliberate effort to create a premium on the issuance of the bonds.

End of Exercise. Solution available in Study Guide.

Interest Income

General Provision

7-39.   ITA 12(1) lists inclusions in business and property income. Paragraph (c) of this Subsection is as follows:

> **Interest**   … any amount received or receivable by the taxpayer in the year (depending on the method regularly followed by the taxpayer in computing the taxpayer's income) as, on account of, in lieu of payment of or in satisfaction of, interest to the extent that the interest was not included in computing the taxpayer's income for a preceding taxation year.

7-40.   The wording of ITA 12(1)(c) suggests that taxpayers can use the cash basis to recognize interest income (amounts received or receivable). This is not the case. ITA 12(3) and 12(4) require the use of an accrual approach by all taxpayers. As is discussed in the following material, the accrual approach used by individuals differs from that used by corporations and partnerships.

Corporations And Partnerships - Accrual Method

7-41.   ITA 12(3) requires that corporations, partnerships, and some trusts use accrual accounting. The concept of accrual accounting that is applied to these taxpayers is the conventional one in which interest income is recorded as a direct function of the passage of time. IT-396R indicates that this calculation will generally be based on the number of days a principal amount is outstanding.

> **Example**   A corporation acquires a $5,000 debt instrument on August 15th of the current year. The instrument pays interest at an annual rate of 8 percent.

> **Analysis**   Interest for the current year would be calculated as follows:

$$[(\$5,000)(8\%)(139 \div 365)] = \$152.33$$

7-42.   For corporations and partnerships, interest income for tax purposes is, generally speaking, identical to that required under the application of generally accepted accounting principles. However, as will be explained later in this Chapter, an exception to this is interest income on bonds that have been purchased at a premium or a discount.

Individuals - Modified Accrual Method

7-43.   While ITA 12(3) requires conventional accrual accounting for corporations and partnerships, ITA 12(4) provides for a less familiar version of this concept for individuals. Under this modified version of accrual accounting, interest is not accrued on a continuous basis. Rather, ITA 12(4) requires the accrual of interest on each anniversary date of an investment contract.

7-44.   ITA 12(11) defines "investment contracts" to include most debt securities and "anniversary date" to be that date that is one year after the day before the date of issue of the security, and every successive one year interval. This would mean that, for a five year contract issued on July 1, 2012, the anniversary dates would be June 30 of each of the five years 2013 through 2017. If the holder of the investment contract disposes of it prior to its maturity, the disposal date is also considered to be an anniversary date from the point of view of that particular taxpayer.

7-45.   To the extent that the income accrued on the anniversary date has not been previously included in income, it must then be included in the individual's income, regardless of whether the amount has been received or is receivable.

> **Example** An investment contract with a maturity value of $100,000 and an annual interest rate of 10 percent is issued on July 1, 2012. The $100,000 maturity amount is due on June 30, 2017. An interest payment for the first 2.5 years of interest ($25,000) is due on December 31, 2014. The remaining interest ($25,000) is due with the principal payment on June 30, 2017. The contract is purchased by an individual at the time that it is issued.

> **Analysis** As no interest has been received in 2012 and no anniversary date has occurred during the year, no interest would have to be included in the individual's tax return for that year. As compared to the use of the full accrual method, this provides a one year deferral of $5,000 of interest.

> Annual interest of $10,000 would have to be accrued on the first two anniversary dates of the contract, June 30, 2013 and June 30, 2014. This means that $10,000 would be included in Net Income For Tax Purposes for each of these two years. When the $25,000 payment is received on December 31, 2014, an additional $5,000 would be subject to taxation for that year because it has been received, and not previously accrued. This results in taxation of $15,000 in 2014. At this point, the cumulative results are identical to those that would result from the application of the full accrual approach.

> For 2015, the June 30, 2015 anniversary date would require the accrual of $10,000. However, as $5,000 of this amount was already included in income during 2014, only $5,000 of this amount would be subject to taxation in 2015. There would be a further accrual of $10,000 on the anniversary date in 2016. In 2017, an interest payment of $25,000 will be received. As $15,000 ($5,000 + $10,000) of the amount received has been included in 2015 and 2016 income, the total for 2017 will be $10,000 ($25,000 - $15,000).

> The total interest on the investment of $50,000 [($100,000)(10%)(5 years)] is allocated as follows: 2011 - nil, 2012 - $10,000, 2013 - $15,000, 2014 - $5,000, 2015 - $10,000, and 2016 - $10,000.

7-46.   Note that the anniversary date is established by the date on which the investment contract is issued. It is not influenced by the date on which the individual investor acquires the contract.

Exercise Seven - 3

Subject: Annual Accrual Rules

On October 1, 2012, Ms. Diane Dumont acquires a newly issued debt instrument with a maturity value of $60,000. It matures on September 30, 2018 and pays interest at an annual rate of 8 percent. Payment for the first three and one-quarter years of interest is due on December 31, 2015, with interest for the remaining two and three-quarters years payable on the maturity date. What amount of interest will Ms. Dumont have to include in her tax returns for each of the years 2012 through 2018?

End of Exercise. Solution available in Study Guide.

Discount And Premium On Long-Term Debt Holdings

7-47.   Tax legislation takes the view that the taxable amount of interest is based on the accrual of the stated, or coupon, rate, without consideration of the fact that, in the case of bonds sold at a discount or premium, the investor will receive an amount at maturity that is larger or smaller than the amount that was paid for the bonds. Because tax procedures do not provide for the usual amortization of this discount or premium, it will be treated as a gain or loss at maturity by the investor.

7-48.   If the bonds are acquired at a discount, the additional amount that will be received at maturity (the discount) will be treated as a capital gain, only one-half of which will be taxable. In similar fashion, if the bonds are acquired at a premium, the receipt of just the face value at maturity will result in the premium being treated as a capital loss, only one-half of which will be deductible.

Prescribed Debt Obligations

7-49.   Over the last two or three decades, a large number of financial instruments have been developed that provide a return to investors in a less conventional manner. For example, debt obligations were developed that specified low interest payments during the early years of issue, followed by compensation in the form of higher rates during the later years. Other instruments, such as the principal component of strip bonds and zero coupon bonds, provided for no payment of interest. Investors were compensated for this lack of "interest" by maturity payments in excess of the initial issue price of the securities.

7-50.   The government responded to this situation with the issuance of more sophisticated regulations. Specifically, ITR 7000(1) identifies four types of prescribed debt obligations and indicates their required tax treatment as follows:

ITR 7000(1)(a) describes obligations that only pay a specified sum at maturity, with no interim interest payments. In the case of these obligations, referred to as zero coupon bonds, interest must be accrued by the effective rate method at the rate which will equate the original cost of the obligation to the present value of its maturity value.

ITR 7000(1)(b) describes stripped bonds in which the maturity value and the interest payments are sold separately. Interest on the maturity value component will be determined as per ITR 7000(1)(a). The interest to be recognized on the interest payment component will be based on the yield that equates the cost of that component with the present value of all future payments.

ITR 7000(1)(c) describes debt obligations that contain variable interest rate provisions. Here the interest to be accrued will be based on the greater of the maximum interest rate stipulated for the year, or the accrued interest based on the yield that equates the principal amount of the debt to the present value of the maximum future payments.

ITR 7000(1)(d) describes debt obligations in which the interest rate to be paid is contingent on a future event. In this case, the interest to be recognized must be based on the maximum rate potentially payable. For example, if an extra 1 percent interest was added to the investment's return if the obligation is held to maturity, the annual accrual would have to include this extra 1 percent.

7-51.   A comprehensive treatment of these obligations goes beyond the scope of this material. However, an example of the types of calculations that are involved would be as follows:

Example   On January 1, 2012, Albert Litton purchases a zero coupon bond with a maturity value of $10,000. The bond is issued on this date and the maturity value is due on December 31, 2014. The price paid by Mr. Litton is $7,312, providing an effective annual yield of 11 percent.

Analysis   The total interest income of $2,688 ($10,000 - $7,312) would have to be reported by Mr. Litton as follows:

Year	Opening Balance	Interest At 11%	Closing Balance
2012	$7,312	$804	$ 8,116
2013	8,116	893	9,009
2014	9,009	991	10,000
Total Interest		$2,688	

Exercise Seven - 4

Subject: Prescribed Debt Obligations

On January 1, 2012, a debt obligation is issued with a coupon interest rate of 7 percent, a maturity value of $250,000, and a maturity date of December 31, 2014. Annual interest of $17,500 is paid on December 31. The interest coupons and the maturity amount are sold separately at prices that provide an effective yield of 7 percent. The price of the maturity payment is $204,075, while the price of the interest coupons is $45,925. Calculate the amount of interest that the purchasers of these two financial instruments will have to include in their tax returns in each of the three years.

End of Exercise. Solution available in Study Guide.

Accrued Interest At Transfer

7-52.   Publicly traded debt securities are bought and sold on a day-to-day basis, without regard to the specific date on which interest payments are due. To accommodate this situation, accrued interest from the date of the last interest payment date will be added to the purchase price of the security.

7-53.   Consider, for example, a 10 percent coupon, $1,000 maturity value bond, with semi-annual interest payments of $50 on June 30 and December 31 of each year. If we assume that the market value of the bond is equal to its maturity value and it is purchased on October 1, 2012, the price would be $1,025, including $25 of interest for the three month period from June 30, 2012 through October 1, 2012.

7-54.   In the absence of a special provision dealing with this situation, the $25 would have to be included in the income of the purchaser when it is received as part of the $50 December 31, 2012 interest payment. Further, the extra $25 received by the seller would receive favourable treatment as a capital gain. To prevent this result, ITA 20(14) indicates that the seller must include the accrued interest in income and the purchaser can deduct a corresponding amount from the interest received on the bonds.

Exercise Seven - 5

Subject: Accrued Interest At Transfer

On May 1, 2012, Mr. Milford Lay purchases bonds with a maturity value of $50,000 at par. These bonds pay semi-annual interest of $3,000 on June 30 and December 31 of each year. He purchases the bonds for $52,000, including interest accrued to the purchase date. He holds the bonds for the remainder of the year, receiving both the June 30 and December 31 interest payments. What amount of interest will be included in Mr. Lay's 2012 tax return?

End of Exercise. Solution available in Study Guide.

Payments Based On Production Or Use (Royalties)

7-55.   The relevant *Income Tax Act* Paragraph here reads as follows:

ITA 12(1)(g) Payments based on production or use — any amount received by the taxpayer in the year that was dependent on the use of or production from property whether or not that amount was an instalment of the sale price of the property, except that an instalment of the sale price of agricultural land is not included by virtue of this paragraph.

7-56.   While ITA 12(1)(g), by referring only to amounts received, suggests the use of cash basis revenue recognition, this has limited application. A proposed ITA 12(2.01) indicates that ITA 12(1)(g) cannot be used to defer the inclusion of any item that would normally be included in the determination of business income. This would require the use of an accrual approach.

7-57.   ITA 12(1)(g) also requires that, except in the case of agricultural land, payments that represent instalments on the sale price of the property must also be included if their payment is related to production or use. An example will serve to illustrate this provision:

Example   The owner of a mineral deposit sells the asset with the proceeds to be paid on the basis of $2 per ton of ore removed. The total amount to be paid is not fixed by the sales agreement.

Analysis   In this situation, the owner would have to include in income the full amount received in each subsequent year, even though a portion of the payment may be of a capital nature.

Rental Income

General Rules

7-58.   Rental income is not specifically mentioned in the ITA Sections that deal with income from property. There is some merit in the view that rental receipts fall into the category of payments for production or use. However, rents are generally payable without regard to whether or not the property is used and, as a consequence, this view may not be appropriate. In any case, it is clear that rental receipts must be included in income and, given this fact, income from property would appear to be the most logical classification.

7-59.   With respect to the recognition methods to be used for rental income, the CRA's Guide, "Rental Income" (T4036) provides the following guidance:

In most cases, you calculate your rental income using the accrual method. With this method, you:

- include rents in income for the year in which they are due, whether or not you receive them in that year; and
- deduct your expenses in the year you incur them, no matter when you pay them.

However, if you have practically no amounts receivable and no expenses outstanding at the end of the year, you can use the cash method. With this method, you:

- include rents in income in the year you receive them; and
- deduct expenses in the year you pay them.

You can use the cash method only if your net rental income or loss would be practically the same if you were using the accrual method.

7-60.   Once the rental revenues are included in income, a variety of expenses become deductible against them. These would include utilities (heat, electricity, water), repairs, maintenance, interest, insurance, property taxes, management fees, and fees to rental agents for locating tenants. CCA can also be deducted. However, as discussed in the next section, this deduction is subject to several special rules.

Capital Cost Allowances
General Rules

7-61.   As noted, CCA on rental properties can be claimed. In the year of acquisition, the half-year rule is applied when calculating the maximum available amount. For individuals, the calendar year is considered the fiscal year for property income purposes. As a consequence, there is no adjustment for a short fiscal period in the year of acquisition.

7-62.   Buildings acquired after 1987 will generally fall into Class 1, where they are eligible for CCA calculated on a declining balance basis at a rate of 4 percent. However, as was noted in Chapter 5, if:

- a new building is acquired after March 18, 2007;
- it is used more than 90 percent for non-residential activities by the taxpayer or a lessee; and
- it is allocated to a separate Class 1;

it will be eligible for the enhanced CCA rates that were discussed in Chapter 5. You may recall that if the usage is 90 percent or more for manufacturing and processing, the rate is 10 percent. If this test is not met, but the building is used 90 percent or more for other types of non-residential activity, the rate is 6 percent.

7-63.   As mentioned in Chapter 5, buildings acquired prior to 1988 were allocated to Class 3, where the rate was 5 percent. This rate is still available on buildings that were allocated to Class 3 prior to 1988.

7-64.   Without regard to the CCA class to which a building is allocated, the rate is applied only to the cost of the building. This means that usually, the total cost of a real property must be segregated into land and building components. The land, of course, is not eligible for CCA deductions.

Special Rules

7-65.   There are two special rules that apply to CCA calculations on rental properties. These rules, along with a brief explanation of the reason that each was introduced, are as follows:

Separate CCA Classes   Each rental building that is acquired after 1971 at a cost of $50,000 or more must be placed in a separate class for calculating CCA, recapture, and terminal losses. In most real world situations, the amount of CCA that can be deducted on a rental property exceeds any decline in the value of the building. In fact, it is not uncommon for the value of such properties to increase over time. This means that, if an investor is required to account for each rental property as a separate item, a disposition is likely to result in recapture of CCA and an increase in Tax Payable.

In the absence of this special rule, all rental properties could be allocated to a single class. This would mean that the investor could avoid recapture for long periods of time by simply adding new properties to the class. This separate class rule prevents this from happening.

Rental Property CCA Restriction   In general, taxpayers are not permitted to create or increase a net rental loss by claiming CCA on rental properties. For this purpose, rental income is the total rental income or loss from all properties owned by the taxpayer. This amount includes any recapture, as well as any terminal losses. The reason for this restriction is a desire to limit the use of rental losses for purposes of sheltering other types of income (e.g., applying rental losses against employment income).

The fact that CCA is the only restricted deduction is probably based on the fact that, unlike most depreciable assets, the value of many rental properties does not usually decline over time. This restriction does not apply to a corporation or a corporate partnership whose principal business throughout the year is the rental or sale of real property. There are similar restrictions on CCA with respect to leasing properties other than real estate.

7-66.   Without question, these special rules make real estate less attractive as an investment. However, a number of advantages remain:

- taxation on a positive cash flow can be eliminated through the use of CCA;
- some part of the capital cost of an asset can be deducted despite the fact that real estate assets are generally not decreasing in value;
- Increases in the value of the property are not taxed until the property is sold; and
- any gain resulting from a sale is taxed as a capital gain, only one-half of which is taxable.

7-67.   These factors continue to make the tax features of investments in rental properties attractive to many individuals.

Rental Income Example

7-68.   An example will serve to illustrate the basic features involved in determining net rental income.

Example   On January 1, 2012, Mr. Bratton owns the following two rental properties:

- Property A was acquired in 1987 at a cost of $120,000, of which $20,000 was allocated to land. It has a UCC of $68,000.

- Property B was acquired in 2005 at a cost of $120,000, of which $30,000 is allocated to land. It has a UCC of $74,200. On August 28, 2012, Property B is sold for $155,000. At this time, the value of the land is unchanged at $30,000.

On December 1, 2012, Mr. Bratton acquires Property C at a cost of $200,000, of which $50,000 is allocated to land. The property is used exclusively for residential purposes.

Rents on all of the properties totaled $35,000 during 2012 and the cost of maintenance, property taxes, and mortgage interest totaled $45,400.

Net Rental Income Calculation   The maximum available CCA on the three properties would be as follows:

- Property A (Class 3) = $3,400 [(5%)($68,000)]
- Property B (Class 1) = Nil (The property was sold during the year.)
- Property C (Class 1) = $3,000 [($150,000)(1/2)(4%)]

Since a rental loss cannot be created by claiming CCA, the net rental income would be calculated as follows:

Gross Rents	$35,000
Recapture Of CCA On Property B ($90,000 - $74,200)	15,800
Expenses Other Than CCA	(45,400)
Rental Income Before CCA	$ 5,400
CCA Class 1 (Maximum)	(3,000)
CCA Class 3 (Limited)	(2,400)
Net Rental Income	Nil

7-69.   The maximum CCA was taken on Class 1, the 4 percent class, leaving the limited CCA deduction for Class 3 which has the higher rate of 5 percent. This follows the general tax planning rule that suggests that, when less than the maximum allowable CCA is taken, the CCA that is deducted should be taken from the classes with the lowest rates. However, if there had been Class 8 rental assets such as appliances, it could have been more tax advantageous to take CCA on those assets first as there is little likelihood of recapture on them. Note that the taxable capital gain of $17,500 [(1/2)($125,000 - $90,000) + (1/2)($30,000 - $30,000)] on the sale of Property B is not part of the rental income or loss calculation.

Exercise Seven - 6

Subject: Rental Income

Ms. Sheela Horne acquires a residential rental property in September, 2012 at a total cost of $185,000. Of this total, $42,000 can be allocated to the value of the land. She immediately spends $35,000 to make major improvements to the property. Rents for the year total $7,200, while rental expenses other than CCA total $5,100. This is the only rental property owned by Ms. Horne. Determine the maximum CCA that is available for 2012 and Ms. Horne's minimum net rental income for the year.

End of Exercise. Solution available in Study Guide.

Cash Dividends From Taxable Canadian Corporations

The Concept Of Integration

7-70.   While this concept will be given much more detailed attention in the Chapters dealing with corporate taxation, it is virtually impossible to understand the tax procedures associated with dividends received from taxable Canadian corporations without some elementary understanding of the concept of integration. It is fundamental, both to the procedures associated with the taxation of dividends, as well as to many other provisions related to the taxation of corporations.

7-71.   An individual who owns an unincorporated business or, alternatively, holds investments that earn property income, can choose to transfer these assets to a corporation. The various reasons for doing this will be given detailed consideration in Chapter 15. At this point, however, our concern is with the fact that, in making such a transfer, the taxpayer creates an additional taxable entity. As depicted in Figure 7-1, if the individual incorporates his source of business or property income, the corporation will be taxed on the resulting income. In addition, the individual will pay taxes on the dividends which the corporation will distribute from the corporation's after tax income.

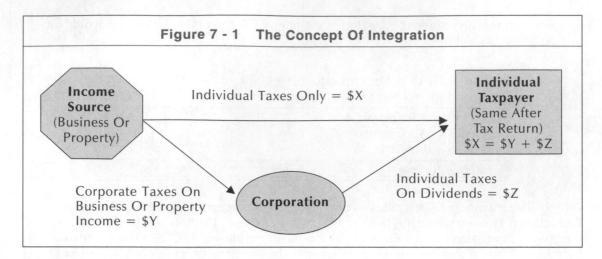

Figure 7 - 1   The Concept Of Integration

7-72.   As is also depicted in Figure 7-1, the goal of integration is to ensure that the use of a corporation does not alter the total amount of taxes that will be paid on a given stream of business or property income. Stated alternatively, the procedures associated with integration are directed at equating the total amount of taxes paid by an individual who does not incorporate an income source and pays taxes only at the individual level, with the amount of taxes that would be paid if the relevant assets were transferred to a corporation and taxed at both the corporate level and at the individual level on distribution of the after tax corporate income.

7-73.   As we will find in the various chapters dealing with corporate taxation, there are a number of procedures associated with achieving this goal. However, from the point of view of individual taxpayers, the dividend gross up and tax credit procedures are the primary tools used in building a system which integrates corporate and individual tax amounts.

Eligible Vs. Non-Eligible Dividends
The Problem
7-74.   Prior to 2006, the dividend gross up and tax credit procedures were based on the notional assumption that all corporations were taxed at a combined federal/provincial rate of 20 percent. While this rate was appropriate for Canadian Controlled Private Corporations (CCPCs) that were eligible for the small business deduction, it was significantly lower than the rate applicable to most large public companies. These companies are subject to combined federal/provincial tax rates that for 2012 range between 24 and 31 percent.

7-75.   The fact that these larger corporations were taxed at rates well above 20 percent meant that, for a given income stream, the combined taxes paid by a corporation and its shareholders were much greater than the taxes on the same stream when received directly by an individual. In these situations, the goal of integration was clearly not being achieved.

The Solution
7-76.   The May, 2006 budget dealt with this problem by introducing an enhanced dividend gross up and tax credit procedure for what it refers to as eligible dividends. In somewhat simplified terms, eligible dividends are dividends paid out of income that has been subject to high corporate tax rates (e.g., in general, dividends paid by publicly traded companies). This provision makes an effort to restore integration in such situations.

7-77.   There are many complications in the determination of which dividends are eligible and which are non-eligible. These complications will be dealt with in Chapter 14 of this text, Other Issues In Corporate Taxation.

7-78.   In this Chapter, we will focus on the procedures for determining the Tax Payable for individuals receiving eligible and non-eligible dividends. We will begin with a discussion of the dividend gross up and tax credit mechanism as it applies to non-eligible dividends. This will be followed by consideration of the modifications to this system that are required when it is applied to eligible dividends.

Gross Up And Tax Credit Procedures - Non-Eligible Dividends
The Dividend Gross Up Procedure

7-79.   For non-eligible dividends, the concepts and procedures associated with the dividend gross up can be described as follows:

> **Dividend Gross Up**   Unlike payments of interest, dividend payments cannot be deducted by the paying corporation. This means that they are paid out of a corporation's after tax income. The concept that underlies the dividend gross up is that, by adding a percentage to the actual dividends received, the grossed up amount will reflect the amount of pretax income that the corporation would need in order to have sufficient after tax income to pay that dividend.

> The gross up mechanism for non-eligible dividends requires individuals to gross up the dividends they receive by 25 percent (as all of the provinces have agreed to use the federal Taxable Income figure, the 25 percent gross up applies at both the federal and provincial levels). This percentage is based on the notional assumption that the combined federal and provincial corporate tax rate is 20 percent and, in situations where this is the case, the 25 percent gross up adjusts the taxable amount of the dividend to the pretax amount that was required at the corporate level in order to pay the dividend. This is illustrated in the following example.

> **Example**   Marin Ltd. is subject to a combined federal/provincial tax rate of 20 percent. During 2012, the company has Taxable Income of $100,000. All of the Company's after tax income is paid to Mr. Marin, its only shareholder, as a dividend.

> **Analysis**   The results at the corporate and individual levels are as follows:

Corporate Taxable Income	$100,000
Corporate Income Taxes (At 20 Percent)	(20,000)
Corporate After Tax Income And Dividends Paid	$ 80,000
25 Percent Gross Up [($80,000)(25%)]	20,000
Mr. Marin's Taxable Dividends	**$100,000**

7-80.   As demonstrated in the preceding calculation, the 25 percent gross up has resulted in a taxable dividend that is equal to the pretax corporate income that is required to pay the dividend. This is also the amount of income that Mr. Marin would have received directly had he chosen not to incorporate his source of income.

7-81.   You should note that, for non-eligible dividends, this procedure only works if the corporate tax rate is exactly 20 percent. If it was higher, Mr. Marin's Taxable Dividends would be less than the corporation's Taxable Income. If it was lower, the Taxable Dividends would be greater than the corporation's Taxable Income.

The Dividend Tax Credit Procedure

7-82.   Provided the corporate tax rate is 20 percent, the gross up procedure has served to increase the dividend recipient's Taxable Income to the $100,000 amount of corporate Taxable Income on which the non-eligible dividend payment was based. What is now required is a credit against Mr. Marin's Tax Payable to make up for the $20,000 in taxes that were paid at the corporate level. The required tax credit procedure can be described as follows:

> **Federal Dividend Tax Credit**   Since the amount of the gross up is designed to reflect the amount of taxes paid at the corporate level, it would seem logical to base the dividend recipient's credit on this figure. This, in fact, is the approach taken in the *Income Tax Act*. Under ITA 121, the individual will receive a credit against federal Tax Payable

that is equal to two-thirds of the gross up on non-eligible dividends. This credit can also be expressed as 13-1/3 percent of taxable (i.e., grossed up) dividends or as 16-2/3 percent of dividends received. In our example, this amount would be $13,333 which could be calculated as:

- 2/3 of the gross up = [(2/3)(25%)($80,000)], the calculation we will use in most of our examples, or;
- 13-1/3% of grossed up dividends = [(13-1/3%)($100,000)], or;
- 16-2/3% of dividends received = [(16-2/3%)($80,000)].

7-83.   You will note that the $13,333 dividend tax credit that we have calculated is less than the $20,000 in corporate taxes paid and, in the absence of additional credits towards this total, integration would not be working properly. The remedy to this problem lies in the fact that all of the provinces have some type of dividend gross up and credit procedure. If we assume a provincial dividend tax credit that is equal to one-third of the gross up, the combined federal/provincial dividend tax credit is equal to $20,000 [($20,000)(2/3 + 1/3)], the amount of corporate taxes paid. The following table shows the actual lowest and highest rates for 2012, as well as the average rate for the 10 provinces.

Non-Eligible Dividends - 2012	Lowest	Highest	Average
Provincial Dividend Tax Credit			
As Percentage Of 25% Gross Up	5%	40%	22%
Federal + Provincial Dividend Tax Credit	72%	107%	89%

Example Of Non-Eligible Dividends

7-84.   In the preceding section we explained how, in situations where the combined federal and provincial tax rate on corporations is 20 percent and the provincial dividend tax credit is equal to one-third of the gross up, the dividend gross up and tax credit procedures will provide for integration. This is the case, without regard to the marginal tax rate that is applicable to the individual. The example which follows illustrates the mechanics of this process.

Example   During 2012, Mr. Plummer and Ms. Black each have a business that produces $10,000 in Taxable Income. While they both live in the same province, Mr. Plummer's income is subject to a 15 percent federal tax rate and an 8 percent provincial tax rate. In contrast, Ms. Black's income is subject to a 29 percent federal tax rate and a 14.5 percent provincial tax rate. The provincial dividend tax credit is equal to one-third of the gross up and the combined federal/provincial tax rate on corporations is 20 percent.

Analysis - Direct Receipt Of Income   If Mr. Plummer and Ms. Black received the business income directly, the taxes paid and the after tax retention of the income would be as follows:

	Mr. Plummer	Ms. Black
Taxable Income	$10,000	$10,000
Total Individual Tax Payable:		
At 23 Percent (15% + 8%)	(2,300)	
At 43.5 Percent (29% + 14.5%)		(4,350)
After Tax Retention - Direct Receipt	$ 7,700	$ 5,650

Analysis - Incorporation Of Income   If the businesses were incorporated, the taxes paid and the after tax retention of the income would be as follows:

	Mr. Plummer	Ms. Black
Corporate Taxable Income	$10,000	$10,000
Corporate Taxes At 20 Percent	(2,000)	(2,000)
Available For Non-Eligible Dividends	$ 8,000	$ 8,000

Cash Dividends From Taxable Canadian Corporations

	Mr. Plummer	Ms. Black
Non-Eligible Dividends Received	$ 8,000	$ 8,000
Gross Up At 25 Percent [(25%)($8,000)]	2,000	2,000
Taxable Dividends	$10,000	$10,000

	Mr. Plummer	Ms. Black
Individual Federal Tax:		
At 23 Percent (15% + 8%)	$2,300	
At 43.5 Percent (29% + 14.5%)		$4,350
Dividend Tax Credit [(2/3 + 1/3)($2,000)]	(2,000)	(2,000)
Total Tax Payable	$ 300	$2,350

	Mr. Plummer	Ms. Black
Non-Eligible Dividends Received	$8,000	$8,000
Total Tax Payable	(300)	(2,350)
After Tax Retention - Use Of Corporation	$7,700	$5,650

7-85. The rates in this example are those that are built into the gross up and tax credit procedures applicable to non-eligible dividends. That is, the corporate tax rate is 20 percent and the provincial dividend tax credit is equal to one-third of the gross up. As you would expect with these rates, the after tax retention is the same, without regard to whether the $10,000 of income is received directly by the taxpayers or, alternatively, received indirectly after being flowed through a corporation. Note also that this conclusion is not altered by the fact that Ms. Black is in a much higher tax bracket than Mr. Plummer.

Exercise Seven - 7

Subject: Dividend Income - Non-Eligible Dividends

During 2012, Mr. John Johns receives $17,000 in non-eligible dividends from a taxable Canadian corporation. His income is such that all additional amounts will be taxed at a 29 percent federal rate and a 12 percent provincial rate. His provincial dividend tax credit is equal to 30 percent of the gross up. Determine the total federal and provincial tax that will be payable on these dividends and his after tax cash retention.

End of Exercise. Solution available in Study Guide.

Gross Up And Tax Credit Procedures - Eligible Dividends
The Problem Illustrated

7-86. As was noted in our discussion of non-eligible dividends, the assumption of a 20 percent tax rate that is inherent in the treatment of these dividends is not appropriate for publicly traded companies. These corporations are subject to combined federal/provincial tax rates that currently range between 24 and 31 percent. The problem that this creates is illustrated in the following example which applies the non-eligible dividend procedures in a situation where the corporation is taxed at 30 percent.

Example Suzanne Mills has a business with Taxable Income of $100,000. Her combined federal/provincial tax rate is 43.5 percent. In her province, the combined federal/provincial tax rate on corporations is 30 percent and the provincial dividend tax credit is equal to one-third of the gross up.

Analysis - Direct Receipt Of Income If Ms. Mills receives the income directly, she will pay taxes of $43,500 [(43.5%)($100,000)] and retain income of $56,500 ($100,000 - $43,500).

Cash Dividends From Taxable Canadian Corporations

Analysis - Use Of Corporation If Ms. Mills incorporates her business and has the corporation pay out all of its after tax income in dividends, the results are as follows:

Corporate Taxable Income	$100,000
Corporate Taxes At 30 Percent	(30,000)
Available For Dividends	$ 70,000
Dividends Received	$70,000
Gross Up At 25 Percent	17,500
Taxable Dividends	$87,500
Individual Federal Tax At 43.5 Percent	$38,063
Dividend Tax Credit [(2/3 + 1/3)($17,500)]	(17,500)
Total Tax Payable	$20,563
Dividends Received	$70,000
Total Tax Payable	(20,563)
After Tax Retention - Use Of Corporation	$49,437

7-87.   As you can see, when a realistic public corporation tax rate is used, integration does not work. In this example, there is a $7,063 ($56,500 - $49,437) advantage for the direct receipt of income.

7-88.   This problem existed for many years and, prior to 2006, it did not attract a great deal of attention. However, the importance of income trusts as an overwhelmingly popular type of investment focused attention on this issue. As is discussed in this Chapter beginning in Paragraph 7-106, income trust units are a publicly traded investment vehicle that allows an active business to avoid taxes by flowing through its income directly to investors. Because of the ability of income trusts to avoid the taxes that would be applicable to a corporation, more and more corporations were transferring their assets to income trusts, resulting in a significant reduction in taxes collected on corporate income.

7-89.   While various solutions were proposed for this problem, it was clear to anyone who understood the issues that the real problem was the fact that, for large public companies, the existing dividend gross up and tax credit procedures were based on totally unrealistic tax rates. This situation was corrected in the May, 2006 budget.

7-90.   Before proceeding to our discussion of the enhanced dividend gross up and tax credit procedures for eligible dividends, we would note that the 25 percent gross up and tax credit procedures did not disappear. They continue to apply to non-eligible dividends paid out of income that, because of some form of favourable treatment, has been taxed at a low rate. The most important example of this type of income would be the amounts of a CCPC's active business income that are eligible for the small business deduction.

Definition Of Eligible Dividends

7-91.   ITA 89(1) defines "eligible dividends" as a taxable dividend that has been designated as such by the paying corporation. To make this designation, the paying corporation simply notifies the recipient that the dividend is eligible for the enhanced gross up and tax credit procedures.

7-92.   With respect to the types of dividends that can be designated as eligible dividends, this issue will be discussed in detail in Chapter 14. However, in simplified terms, eligible dividends are made up of dividends paid to Canadian residents by:

• public corporations that are Canadian residents and subject to the general corporate tax rate,

- Canadian controlled private corporations (CCPCs), out of active business income that has been taxed at the high rate that is applicable to public corporations, and
- CCPCs, out of eligible dividends that it has received.

Gross Up And Tax Credit Procedures For Eligible Dividends

7-93.   For eligible dividends, the 2012 gross up and tax credit amounts are as follows:

- **Dividend Gross Up**   The gross up of eligible dividends received is 38 percent. Since the provinces use the federal Taxable Income figure, this 38 percent gross up applies to eligible dividends at both the federal and provincial levels.

- **Dividend Tax Credit**   The federal dividend tax credit is equal to 6/11 (54.5455%) of the dividend gross up. This could also be expressed as 15.0198% of the grossed up dividends or 20.73% of dividends received. The following table shows the actual lowest and highest rates for 2012, as well as the average rate for the 10 provinces.

Eligible Dividends - 2012	Lowest	Highest	Average
Provincial Dividend Tax Credit			
As Percentage Of 38% Gross Up	23%	44%	37%
Federal + Provincial Dividend Tax Credit	78%	98%	92%

Example   If an individual receives $100,000 in eligible dividends, the gross up would be $38,000, resulting in taxable dividends of $138,000. The federal dividend tax credit would be $20,727. This could be calculated as:

- 6/11 of the gross up = [(6/11)(38%)($100,000)], the most common calculation
- 15.0198% of grossed up dividends = [(15.0198%)($138,000)]
- 20.7273% of dividends received = [(20.7273%)($100,000)]

7-94.   For integration to work, the corporate tax rate has to be such that the 38 percent gross up will increase an individual's Taxable Income to the corporation's level of income before the application of that rate. As shown in the following calculation, the assumed corporate rate that is inherent in the 38 percent gross up is 27.53623 percent.

Pretax Corporate Taxable Income	$100,000.00
Corporate Tax At 27.53623 Percent*	(27,536.23)
Available For Dividends	$ 72,463.77
Gross Up At 38 Percent	27,536.23
Taxable Dividends	$100,000.00

* In subsequent examples, we will round this to 27.54 percent.

7-95.   The other requirement for integration to be effective is that the combined federal/provincial dividend tax credit be equal to the corporate taxes paid. This means that this combined credit must be equal to the gross up. With the 2012 federal credit at 6/11 of the gross up, the provincial credit must be set equal to 5/11 (45.5 percent) of the gross up for this condition to be met. As noted in Paragraph 7-93, the highest provincial credit is 44 percent of the gross up. This means that all of the provincial dividend tax credits are below the rate required to achieve effective integration.

7-96.   A further point that should be made here is that the assumed 27.54 percent corporate rate is higher than the combined federal/provincial tax rate on low income individuals. A typical combined rate would be 23 percent (15 percent federal and 8 percent provincial). In this situation, integration will not work because, at this rate, the credit cannot compensate for the corporate taxes paid. This is illustrated in the following example.

Example Of Eligible Dividends

7-97.   This example illustrates how integration works when the dividend gross up is 38 percent and the federal dividend tax credit is equal to 6/11 of the gross up. It uses the same situation as the example in Paragraph 7-84.

Cash Dividends From Taxable Canadian Corporations

Example   During 2012, Mr. Plummer and Ms. Black each have a business that produces $10,000 in Taxable Income. While they both live in the same province, Mr. Plummer's income is subject to a 15 percent federal tax rate and an 8 percent provincial tax rate. In contrast, Ms. Black's income is subject to a 29 percent federal tax rate and a 14.5 percent provincial tax rate. The provincial dividend tax credit is equal to 5/11 of the gross up and the combined federal/provincial tax rate on corporations is 27.54 percent.

Analysis - Direct Receipt Of Income   If Mr. Plummer and Ms. Black received the business income directly, the taxes paid and the after tax retention of the income would be as follows:

	Mr. Plummer	Ms. Black
Taxable Income	$10,000	$10,000
Total Individual Tax Payable:		
At 23 Percent (15% + 8%)	(2,300)	
At 43.5 Percent (29% + 14.5%)		(4,350)
After Tax Retention - Direct Receipt	$ 7,700	$ 5,650

Analysis - Incorporation Of Income   If the businesses were incorporated, the taxes paid and the after tax retention of the income would be as follows:

	Mr. Plummer	Ms. Black
Corporate Taxable Income	$10,000	$10,000
Corporate Taxes At 27.54 Percent	(2,754)	(2,754)
Available For Eligible Dividends	$ 7,246	$ 7,246

	Mr. Plummer	Ms. Black
Eligible Dividends Received	$ 7,246	$ 7,246
Gross Up At 38 Percent	2,754	2,754
Taxable Dividends	$10,000	$10,000

	Mr. Plummer	Ms. Black
Individual Federal Tax:		
At 23 Percent (15% + 8%)	$2,300	
At 43.5 Percent (29% + 14.5%)		$4,350
Dividend Tax Credit		
[(6/11 + 5/11)($2,754)]	(2,754)	(2,754)
Total Tax Payable	Nil	$1,596

	Mr. Plummer	Ms. Black
Eligible Dividends Received	$7,246	$7,246
Total Tax Payable	(Nil)	(1,596)
After Tax Retention - Use Of Corporation	$7,246	$5,650

7-98.   You will note that, while Ms. Black's $5,650 of after tax retention is not changed by the use of a corporation, Mr. Plummer's after tax eligible dividends are $7,246, $454 less than the $7,700 that he would have retained on the direct receipt of the business income. This reflects the fact that the assumed corporate tax rate of 27.54 percent is higher than his personal tax rate of 23 percent, a situation that cannot be corrected by a non-refundable credit against his tax payable. Note, however, if Mr. Plummer had other sources of income, this excess would offset the taxes on that income.

Exercise Seven - 8

Subject: Dividend Income - Eligible Dividends

During 2012, Ms. Ellen Holt receives $15,000 in eligible dividends from taxable Canadian corporations. Her income is such that all additional amounts will be taxed at a 29 percent federal rate and a 14.5 percent provincial rate. Her provincial dividend tax credit is equal to 30 percent of the gross up. Determine the total federal and provincial tax that will be payable on these dividends, as well as her after tax retention.

End of Exercise. Solution available in Study Guide.

Changing Rates For Eligible Dividends

7-99.   The corporate tax rate that was originally built into the gross up and tax credit procedures for eligible dividends was around 31 percent, made up of a 19 percent federal rate and a 12 percent provincial rate. As you may be aware, since 2009, the government has phased in a series of corporate tax cuts. As of 2012, the phase-in is complete as is shown in the following schedule.

Year	Federal Corporate Rate
2009	19.0%
2010	18.0%
2011	16.5%
2012 And Subsequent	15.0%

7-100.   In order to maintain some level of integration, the rate assumed in the gross up and tax credit procedures was also changed to reflect the reductions in the federal corporate rate. The changes, which reached their final level in 2012, were as follows:

Year	Gross Up Of Eligible Dividends	Dividend Tax Credit As A Fraction Of Gross Up
2009	45%	11/18 (61.1%)
2010	44%	10/17 (58.8%)
2011	41%	13/23 (56.5%)
2012 And Subsequent	38%	6/11 (54.5%)

7-101.   These changes have increased the maximum tax rate on eligible dividends. As the maximum rate on non-eligible dividends has not changed over this period, the changes have significantly reduced the difference in the rates applicable to eligible and non-eligible dividends.

Comparison Of Investment Returns

7-102.   For an individual in the maximum federal tax bracket of 29 percent, living in a province with a maximum individual rate of 14 percent, the 2012 tax rates for interest income, capital gains, non-eligible dividends, and eligible dividends are as follows:

	Interest Income	Capital Gains	Non-Eligible Dividends	Eligible Dividends
Tax Rate (In Maximum Bracket)	43.0%	21.5%	28.8%	27.2%

Note As will be discussed in Chapter 8, only one-half of capital gains is included in Taxable Income, resulting in an effective tax rate on these gains of 21.5 percent [(1/2)(43%)]. For non-eligible dividends we have assumed a provincial dividend tax credit equal to one-third of the gross up. For eligible dividends, we have assumed a provincial dividend tax credit of 30 percent of the gross up.

7-103.   While the individual rates would change, depending on the provincial tax rate on individuals and the provincial dividend tax credit, the preceding table provides a general overview of the attractiveness of various types of investment income.

7-104.   Both capital gains and dividends have always received favourable tax treatment. However, until the introduction of eligible dividends, the rates applicable to capital gains were significantly lower than the rates applicable to dividends (21.5 percent vs. 28.8 percent in our example).

7-105.   The introduction of the enhanced gross up and tax credit procedures for eligible dividends served to reduce this difference. However, this situation has been largely reversed since then by the modifications of these procedures. As we have noted, in 2012, the rate on eligible dividends is only 1.6 percent lower than the rate on non-eligible dividends.

Income Trusts

How Do Trusts Work?

7-106.   While this subject is covered in detail in Chapter 19, it is impossible to discuss the taxation of income trusts without an understanding of the basic nature of trusts. Trusts are essentially flow-through entities. What this means is that, if the income earned by a trust is distributed immediately to its beneficiaries, the trust will pay no taxes. Consistent with this, the beneficiaries of the trusts will pay taxes on that income as though they had received it directly from its source. If a trust earns $100,000 in interest and distributes the full amount to the beneficiaries, the trust will pay no income taxes and the beneficiaries will be taxed on the $100,000 of interest income.

7-107.   The other important characteristic of trusts, including publicly traded income trusts, is that, for tax purposes, various types of income retain their character as they flow through. For example, if a capital gain is earned in a trust, it will be distributed as a capital gain to the trust beneficiaries. As this point is more relevant to the taxation of mutual fund trusts, it will receive more detailed coverage in our discussion of this type of investment property.

Tax Consequences Of Investments In Publicly Traded Trusts

7-108.   The use of trusts has been common for many years for both estate planning (e.g., a deceased parent leaves his assets in a trust for his children) and for retirement savings (e.g., RRSPs are trusts). What is different here is that these trusts have been created to raise financing through the public sale of their units, with the funds being used to acquire various types of businesses.

> **Example**   The Zorin Energy Income Trust sells 1,000,000 units at a price of $50 per unit. The $50 million that was raised is used to acquire the assets and operations of Zorin Ltd., a Canadian public company. The trust is committed to distributing 100 percent of the Taxable Income from the Zorin operations to its unitholders.

7-109.   What are the tax consequences associated with this transaction? As illustrated in Figure 7-2 (following page):

• Prior to the existence of the trust, the income from the Zorin operations was subject to a corporate tax rate of 26 percent. The after tax income could then be distributed to shareholders as dividends. Assuming the dividends are eligible, and the shareholders live in a province with a maximum rate of 43 percent on ordinary income and a dividend tax credit on eligible dividends of 30 percent, they would be taxed at a rate of around 27 percent (see Paragraph 7-102). The resulting overall tax rate on the income stream channeled through Zorin Ltd. would be a maximum of 46 percent [26% + (27%)(1 - 26%)].

• In contrast, the Zorin Trust will pay no taxes if it distributes all of its income. However, the distributions to its unitholders will be taxed as ordinary income. In our example, that would be at a maximum rate of 43 percent. Unlike the situation when the income

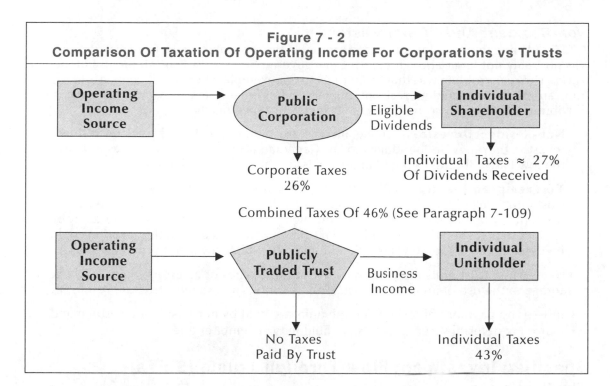

Figure 7 - 2
Comparison Of Taxation Of Operating Income For Corporations vs Trusts

from the Zorin operations was subject to corporate taxes, there will be no dividend gross up and tax credit benefits.

7-110.   This example illustrates that, in situations where normal provincial rates and dividend tax credits prevail, income that is flowed through an income trust will be subject to lower taxes than would be the case if the same stream of income was flowed through a public corporation. While the amount of the advantage may be more or less in individual provinces, results will generally favour the use of income trusts.

7-111.   You should also note that we have used 2012 rates in this example. As discussed in Paragraph 7-99, changes in the gross up and tax credit rates on eligible dividends have served to increase the effective tax rates on this type of income over the last 4 years.

Basis For Popularity
Individual Canadian Investors

7-112.   In the 1990's, most investors had never heard of income trusts, much less considered investing substantial amounts of their savings in such organizations. In the early 2000s, this changed dramatically, with billions of Canadian investment dollars flowing into the rapidly growing number of such investment entities.

7-113.   There were several reasons for this popularity:

- An overall tax savings as illustrated in the preceding example.

- In order to avoid taxes, the trust had to distribute all of its earnings to unitholders. In contrast, corporations generally retain a significant part of their income.

- Most income trusts were committed to paying out 100 percent of the cash flows from the acquired operations. As these cash flows would typically exceed both accounting and tax income, a part of the distribution was received as a tax free return of capital.

7-114.   These factors combined to provide very high rates of returns to investors in income trusts. Rates in excess of 10 percent were not uncommon. The attractiveness of these rates was enhanced by the fact that rates on most types of fixed income securities were, at that time, mired in the 4 to 5 percent range.

Non-Resident And RRSP Investors

7-115.   While there is a tax advantage present in the example that we have just presented, it was probably not large enough to result in a government effort to curtail the use of income trusts. The real problem was that, in contrast to our example where the income trust distributions are made to Canadian residents subject to full federal and provincial tax rates, some distribution recipients did not pay such taxes. More specifically:

Non-Resident Investors   If the income trust units are held by a non-resident investor, they may not be subject to any Canadian taxes. At most, the taxes will be at the low Part XIII rates. (See Chapter 20, Issues In International Income.)

Tax Exempt Entities (e.g., RPPs, RRSPs, Other Tax Exempt Entities)   If the income trust units are held inside a tax exempt entity, the distributions will not be subject to tax at the time they are received from the income trust. While they will eventually be subject to tax when they are withdrawn from the registered plan, this taxation could be deferred for 30 to 40 years. (See Chapter 10 which covers retirement savings.)

7-116.   When trust units are held by either of these types of investors, there is a large tax advantage to the use of an income trust. The use of this investment structure results in:

- little or no payment of taxes when the units are held by non-resident investors; and
- major tax deferral when the units are held in tax exempt entities.

Specified Investment Flow-Through Trusts (SIFTs)

The Problem

7-117.   Prior to changes introduced in 2006, the government was convinced that holdings of income trusts by non-residents and tax-exempt entities were resulting in an unacceptable amount of tax avoidance and deferral. Some type of solution to this problem was required.

The Solution

7-118.   The government's solution was to introduce the concept of a Specified Investment Flow-Through Trust (SIFT) in 2006. This type of entity is defined as a resident Canadian trust whose units are publicly traded and which holds non-portfolio property. Non-portfolio properties include resource property and property used to carry on business in Canada. This definition would cover most of the income trusts that Canadian investors were investing in.

7-119.   Under the legislation that accompanied the introduction of SIFTs, these entities are taxed at roughly the combined federal/provincial rate applicable to public corporations. This results in smaller distributions by the trusts. However, this is offset by the fact that the after tax distributions are treated as deemed eligible dividends. This means that they are subject to the lower individual tax rates on income that is eligible for the enhanced gross up and tax credit procedures.

7-120.   When this complex legislation was introduced in 2006, the government was aware that it would not be well received by investors. In order to allow a more comfortable transition for investors, the legislation did not apply to existing SIFTS until 2011. A further concession was that the SIFT rules would not apply to real estate investment income trusts at all.

The Current Situation

7-121.   As we are now dealing with the 2012 taxation year, most income trusts have converted to a corporate structure. However, there are many factors involved and, despite the change in taxation, some SIFTs will continue as trusts. In addition, real estate investment income trusts are not subject to the SIFT rules.

7-122.   Given this situation, income trusts will continue to be an important investment vehicle. This means that you should have a basic understanding of how investments in income trusts, other than SIFTS, are taxed. Note that coverage of the taxation of SIFTs can be found in Chapter 19, Trusts And Estate Planning.

Taxation Of Income Trusts
Distributions

7-123.　As we have noted, most income trusts are committed to distributing their net cash flow to unit holders. As you are aware from your accounting courses, this amount will not be equal to accounting income as determined under GAAP. In most cases, because of non-cash deductions for amortization, the net cash flow will exceed accounting net income. This means that trust distributions will, in general, consist of an income distribution, combined with an additional distribution that represents a return of capital (i.e., the return of amounts invested).

7-124.　To the extent that distributions reflect income that has been earned in the trust, they will be taxed in the hands of individual investors at the usual federal and provincial rates. Further, these income distributions will retain their tax characteristics. That is, if the trust earned capital gains, the distribution of these amounts will be treated as capital gains by the recipient of the distributions. Alternatively, if the amounts earned in the trust reflect business income, distributions based on these amounts will be taxed as business income in the hands of the trust unit holder.

7-125.　To the extent that the trust distribution exceeds the trust's income, the excess will be treated as a return of capital. These distributions will be received by individual investors on a tax free basis.

Adjusted Cost Base

7-126.　The determination of the adjusted cost base for income trust units is complicated by the fact that some part of its distributions may be a tax free return of capital. While such distributions are not taxed currently, they do reduce the adjusted cost base of the units held by an investor. This means that the adjusted cost base of an investment in income trust units is equal to the cost of the units to the investor, less any amounts of capital returned as part of the trust's distributions.

7-127.　A further complication relates to the fact that many income trusts have distribution reinvestment plans (DRIPs). To the extent an investor chooses to have his distributions reinvested, the amount reinvested will be an addition to the adjusted cost base of the units held. This will be accompanied by an increase in the number of units held. Note that, if the investor disposes of a part of his holding, the adjusted cost base of the units sold will be based on the average cost of all units held (see Chapter 8 on identical properties).

Example　On January 1, 2012, Joan Arden acquires 1,000 units of the Newcor Income Trust at a total cost of $100,000 or $100 per unit. During 2012, the trust distributes $6 per unit, $2 of which is a return of capital and $4 of which is a distribution of business income earned in the trust. The $6,000 distribution [($6)(1,000 units)] is reinvested in additional trust units at a cost of $110 per unit (54.55 units) which increases her holding to 1,054.55 units.

Analysis　Ms. Arden will include $4,000 in her 2012 Net Income For Tax Purposes. With respect to her adjusted cost base, the calculations are as follows:

	Adjusted Cost Base	No. Of Units
Original Investment	$100,000	1,000.00
Reinvestment Of Distribution	6,000	54.55
Tax Free Return Of Capital	(　2,000)	N/A
Adjusted Cost Base/Number Of Units	$104,000	1,054.55

This will result in an average cost for her units of $98.62 ($104,000 ÷ 1,054.55). Note that if Ms. Arden had chosen not to reinvest the distribution, she would have received $6,000 [(1,000)($6)] in cash, her Net Income would be increased by $4,000, and her 1,000 units would have an adjusted cost base of $98 per unit [($100,000 - $2,000) ÷ 1,000].

Exercise Seven - 9

Subject: Income Trust Distributions

On January 1, 2012, John Dore acquires 2,000 units of Xeron Income Trust at $55 per unit, a total cost of $110,000. During 2012, the trust distributes $5.00 per unit, $1.50 of which is a return of capital and $3.50 of which is a business income distribution. John has asked the trust to reinvest all distributions. The $5.00 per unit distribution was reinvested at a cost of $57 per additional unit. What are the tax consequences to John of the 2012 distribution and its reinvestment? What will be his adjusted cost base per unit after the reinvestment?

End of Exercise. Solution available in Study Guide.

Mutual Funds

Objective

7-128.   Mutual funds are organized to provide investment management, largely for individual taxpayers. The basic idea is that investors provide funds to these organizations which they, in turn, use to make direct investments in stocks, bonds, and other types of investment property. As will be discussed in the following material, mutual funds can be organized as either trusts or as corporations.

Organization

Mutual Fund Trusts

7-129.   In Canada, most mutual funds are organized as trusts. As was discussed in Paragraph 7-106, trusts are flow-through entities. This means that, if all of the income earned in the trust is distributed to beneficiaries, no taxes will be paid at the trust level.

7-130.   Mutual fund trusts are generally structured to make use of this flow-through feature. In most cases, the by-laws will require that the trust distribute, to the unit holders of the trust, all of the income it earns during a taxation year. This will free the mutual fund trust from any obligation to pay taxes on income earned during the year.

Mutual Fund Corporations

7-131.   Mutual fund corporations are less common than mutual fund trusts. In this case, the mutual fund will be taxed at regular corporate tax rates on the investment income that it earns. As the investors will be shareholders rather than trust unit holders, they will receive dividends and, as these dividends are paid from after tax corporate funds, they are eligible for the usual gross up and tax credit procedures. As is the case with mutual fund trusts, mutual fund corporations are usually committed to distributing all of the after tax income earned during a taxation year to their shareholders.

7-132.   There are other complications here involving capital dividends and refundable taxes on investment income that go beyond the scope of the material in this Chapter.

Distributions

Mutual Fund Trusts

7-133.   As noted in our discussion of income trusts, an important feature of the trust legal form is that various types of income retain their tax characteristics as they flow through. That is, if the mutual fund has a capital gain, the distribution of that gain will be a capital gain to the investor in the mutual fund. This means that, when a mutual fund provides an investor with an information return (a T3, if the fund is organized as a trust), it will indicate the various types of income that are included in its distributions. These types will commonly include:

- **Eligible Dividends**   These amounts will be subject to the gross up and tax credit procedures that were previously discussed in this Chapter. Eligible dividends received by the trust will be distributed as eligible dividends to the trust unit holders.

- **Canadian Interest Income**   These amounts will be taxed as ordinary interest income.

- **Capital Gains**   As with capital gains earned directly by the individual, only one-half of these amounts will be subject to taxes (this type of income is discussed in Chapter 8).

- **Foreign Non-Business (Interest And Dividend) Income**   These amounts are taxable on the same basis as Canadian interest income. As will be discussed in a later section of this Chapter, the gross amount of this income will be included in income, with amounts withheld at the foreign source being eligible for tax credit treatment.

- **Capital Distributions**   A fund can make distributions that exceed its income for the year. These are identified as a return of capital and are received tax free. They do, however, reduce the adjusted cost base of the investment.

Mutual Fund Corporations

7-134.   Shareholders in mutual fund corporations receive dividends from the after tax income earned by the corporation's investments. Unlike the situation with mutual fund trusts, the investment income earned by the mutual fund corporation does not retain its tax features when distributed to shareholders. Without regard to whether the income of the mutual fund corporation was interest, dividends, or capital gains, it is paid out as taxable dividends.

7-135.   Dividends paid by mutual fund corporations will usually be eligible dividends and these eligible dividends will qualify for the usual gross up and tax credit procedures. As was discussed earlier in this Chapter, this provides the recipient with a reduced rate of taxation.

Adjusted Cost Base

7-136.   Determining the adjusted cost base of a mutual fund trust unit uses procedures that are similar to those used in determining the adjusted cost base of an income trust unit. The balance is reduced by any amounts that represent a return of capital. Any distributions that are reinvested in the fund increase the adjusted cost base of the units (mutual fund trust) or shares (mutual fund corporation). Amounts of income that are distributed to investors do not alter the adjusted cost base of the investment.

> **Example**   On October 15, 2012, Martin Diaz purchases 1,000 units of CIC Growth Fund for $7.30 per unit. On December 1, 2012, the fund has an income distribution of $.50 per unit. At this time, the fund has a purchase price of $6 per unit. If Mr. Diaz chooses not to reinvest the distribution, he will receive $500 [(1,000 units)($0.50)] in cash. He would then have 1,000 units with his original adjusted cost base of $7.30 per unit. Alternatively, if the distribution is reinvested, he will receive 83.33 ($500 ÷ $6) additional units. This will leave him with a holding of 1,083.33 units with an adjusted cost base of $7,800 ($7,300 + $500), or $7.20 ($7,800 ÷ 1,083.33) per unit.

Exercise Seven - 10

Subject: Mutual Fund Distributions

Ms. Marissa Tiompkins owns 3,500 units of the RB Small Cap Fund, a mutual fund trust. These units were purchased at a price of $11.25 per unit, for a total value of $39,375. There have been no changes in her adjusted cost base prior to the current year. On September 1 of the current year, the Fund has an income distribution of $0.30 per unit, resulting in a reinvestment of $1,050 in Ms. Tiompkins' account. At this time, the purchase price per unit is $13. What will be her adjusted cost base per unit after the reinvestment?

End of Exercise. Solution available in Study Guide.

Other Types Of Dividends

Stock Dividends

7-137.   A stock dividend involves a pro rata distribution of additional shares to the existing shareholders of a company. For example, if the XYZ Company had 1,000,000 shares outstanding and it declared a 10 percent stock dividend, the Company would be distributing 100,000 new shares to its present shareholders on the basis of one new share for each ten of the old shares held.

7-138.   While there is no real change in anyone's financial position as a result of this transaction, in the accounting records it is accompanied by a transfer from the Company's Retained Earnings to contributed capital or paid up capital. The amount of this transfer is normally the fair market value of the shares to be issued, determined on the date of the dividend declaration.

7-139.   For tax purposes, stock dividends are dealt with in the same manner as cash dividends. The value of the dividend is based on the amount of the increase in the paid up capital of the payor. In some cases, provincial legislation requires that this amount be equal to the fair market value of the shares issued. In other provinces, the increase can be established at the discretion of the directors. Whatever the amount, it is subject to the usual gross up and tax credit procedures. As this amount has been subject to tax, it is added to the adjusted cost base of all of the shares owned by the investor.

7-140.   This approach places the investor in the position of having to pay taxes on an amount of dividends that has not been received in cash, an unfavourable situation with respect to the investor's cash flows. As a consequence, public companies make little use of stock dividends. However, they are often used in the tax planning arrangements of private companies.

Exercise Seven - 11

Subject: Stock Dividends

Morgna Inc. has 2,000,000 common shares outstanding. John Morgna acquired 10 percent of these shares at a cost of $12 per share. During the current year, the Company declares a 10 percent stock dividend. At this time the shares are trading at $15 per share. The Company transfers the amount of the stock dividend to paid up capital. What are the tax consequences to John Morgna of this transaction? Your answer should include the adjusted cost base per share of his holding.

End of Exercise. Solution available in Study Guide.

Capital Dividends

7-141.   When a corporation has a capital gain, only one-half of this amount will be taxable. However, the full amount of the proceeds of disposition is still held by the corporation. In the absence of a special provision, this full amount would be taxed if it were distributed to a shareholder as a dividend. In order to avoid this result for private companies only, one-half of the capital gain will be allocated to a balance referred to as a "capital dividend account" (as you will find in Chapter 14, several other items are allocated to this account).

7-142.   When the amounts allocated to this capital dividend account are paid out to shareholders of private companies, they will be received by Canadian resident investors on a totally tax free basis. Also to be noted here is that, for Canadian residents, such capital dividends do not have to be deducted from the adjusted cost base of the investor's shares.

Foreign Source Income

General Rules

7-143.   As Canadian taxation is based on residency, income that has a foreign source must be included in full in the calculation of Net Income For Tax Purposes of any Canadian resident. This is complicated by the fact that many foreign jurisdictions levy some form of withholding tax on such income.

7-144.   The general approach to this situation is to require Canadian residents to include 100 percent of any foreign income earned in their Net Income For Tax Purposes. They then receive a credit against Tax Payable for taxes withheld in the foreign jurisdiction. The basic idea behind this approach is to have the combined foreign and Canadian tax on this income be the same as that which would be levied on the same amount of income earned in Canada.

Example   An individual earned $1,000 in a foreign jurisdiction. As the authorities in that jurisdiction withhold $100, his net receipt is $900. The individual's marginal tax rate is 45 percent.

Analysis   The Canadian Tax Payable on the amount received would be calculated as follows:

Amount Received	$ 900
Foreign Tax Withheld	100
Increase In Taxable Income	$1,000
Rate	45%
Tax Payable Before Credit	$ 450
Foreign Tax Credit (Equal To Withholding)	(100)
Canadian Tax Payable	$ 350

Note that the combined foreign and Canadian tax equal $450, the same amount that the individual would have paid on the domestic receipt of $1,000 of income.

Foreign Non-Business (Property) Income

7-145.   Following the general rule, 100 percent of foreign source non-business income is included in Net Income For Tax Purposes. However, for individuals, the credit against Tax Payable that is provided under ITA 126(1) is limited to a maximum of 15 percent of the foreign source non-business income. If the withheld amounts exceed 15 percent, the excess can be deducted under ITA 20(11). (See example of calculation in Paragraph 7-146.)

Foreign Business Income

7-146.   In the case of foreign source business income, there is no direct limitation on the use of the amounts withheld as a credit against Tax Payable and, correspondingly, no deduction in the calculation of Net Income For Tax Purposes for any part of the amount withheld by the foreign jurisdiction. The following example compares the difference in the treatment of tax withheld on foreign non-business income and foreign business income.

Example   Mr. Grant, a taxpayer with a marginal tax rate of 45 percent, earns foreign source income of $1,000. The foreign government withholds 40 percent ($400) and he receives $600.

Analysis   The Canadian Tax Payable on the amount received assuming it is foreign non-business income or business income would be calculated as follows:

	Non-Business Income	Business Income
Amount Received	$ 600.00	$ 600.00
Foreign Tax Withheld	400.00	400.00
Inclusion For Foreign Income	$1,000.00	$1,000.00
Deduction Of Excess Withholding [$400 - (15%)($1,000)]	(250.00)	N/A
Increase In Taxable Income	$ 750.00	$1,000.00
Rate	45%	45%
Tax Payable Before Credit	$ 337.50	$ 450.00
Foreign Tax Credit [(15%)($1,000)]	(150.00)	
Foreign Tax Credit (Amount Withheld)		(400.00)
Canadian Tax Payable	$ 187.50	$ 50.00

Analysis - Foreign Non-Business Income   Income of $750 will be included in Net Income For Tax Purposes. Foreign and Canadian taxes combined would be $587.50 ($400 + $187.50), well in excess of the $450 he would have paid on $1,000 of Canadian source income. This illustrates that the availability of the deduction does not make up for the fact that the tax credit is limited to 15 percent. The value of a $1 tax credit is $1, whereas the value of a $1 deduction to Mr. Grant is only $0.45 [($1)(45%)].

Analysis - Foreign Business Income   The gross income of $1,000 will be included in Net Income For Tax Purposes. The full $400 of withholding will be used to calculate a credit against his Canadian Tax Payable of $450 [(45%)($1,000)]. This leaves $50 in Canadian Tax Payable and a total tax of $450 ($400 + $50). This is the same amount that he would have paid on the receipt of $1,000 in Canadian source income.

Exercise Seven - 12

Subject: Foreign Source Income

Norah Johns has foreign source income of $30,000 during the current year. As the foreign jurisdiction withholds 25 percent of such income, she only receives $22,500. She has other income such that this foreign source income will be taxed at the maximum federal rate of 29 percent. Determine the amount by which this foreign income would increase Norah's Taxable Income and federal Tax Payable, assuming that the foreign source income (1) is non-business income and (2) is business income.

End of Exercise. Solution available in Study Guide.

Shareholder Benefits

7-147.   Shareholders sometimes receive benefits from a corporation that are directly related to their investment in the shares of that corporation. This would include such benefits as:

- A corporation providing a shareholder with an automobile for personal use.
- A corporation building a swimming pool at a shareholder's personal residence.
- A corporation providing a shareholder with an interest free loan.

7-148.   Such benefits are taxable as property income, largely under ITA 15(1) of the *Income Tax Act*. Further, in almost all cases, the corporation is not able to deduct the cost of providing the benefit. The following simple example illustrates some of the potential tax problems related to shareholder benefits.

Example   A corporation provides a shareholder with a $10,000 holiday trip to Italy.

Analysis   ITA 15(1) requires the inclusion of the $10,000 cost of the trip in the income of the shareholder. Despite the fact that this amount is now being taxed in the hands of the shareholder, the corporation would not be able to deduct the cost of the trip.

7-149.   There are a number of complications that result from shareholder benefits, particularly those associated with low or interest free loans. These complications will be given detailed coverage in Chapter 15, Corporate Taxation And Management Decisions.

Tax Credits Revisited

Dividend Tax Credits

7-150.   Most of the credits that are available to individuals in determining their Tax Payable are discussed in Chapter 4. However, because an understanding of some amount of additional material was required, it was appropriate to defer coverage of a few of these credits to later Chapters. Given the content of this Chapter, we have added two additional credits.

7-151.   The first of these was the dividend tax credit and there are two different versions of this credit:

Eligible Dividends   For eligible dividends received from taxable Canadian corporations in 2012, the federal dividend tax credit is equal to 6/11 of a 38 percent gross up. It can also be calculated as 15.0198 percent of the grossed up amount of dividends or, alternatively, as 20.7273 percent of dividends received.

Non-Eligible Dividends   For non-eligible dividends received from taxable Canadian corporations in 2012, the credit is equal to 2/3 of a 25 percent gross up. It can also be calculated as 13-1/3 percent of the grossed up amount of dividends or, alternatively, as 16-2/3 percent of dividends received.

Foreign Income Tax Credits

7-152.   The other tax credit that was introduced in this Chapter was the credit for foreign taxes paid on foreign source income. For the purposes of this Chapter, we have indicated that this credit is equal to the amount of foreign taxes withheld, subject to the limitation that, in the case of foreign source non-business income earned by individuals, the credit is limited to 15 percent of the foreign source income.

7-153.   This, however, is not the end of the story. For both foreign source non-business income and foreign source business income, the amount of the credit may be limited by the total amount of taxes paid by the individual. This limit is based on an equation that requires an understanding of loss carry overs. As this material has not been covered at this point, we will have to return to coverage of the credits for foreign taxes paid when we revisit Taxable Income and Tax Payable For Individuals in Chapter 11.

Key Terms Used In This Chapter

7-154.   The following is a list of the key terms used in this Chapter. These terms, and their meanings, are compiled in the Glossary Of Key Terms located at the back of the separate paper Study Guide.

Accrual Basis   Foreign Taxes Paid Credit
Business Income   Income Trust
Capital Dividend   Interest Income
Capital Dividend Account   Mutual Fund
Cash Basis   Net Business Income
Cash Damming   Net Property Income
Disappearing Source Rules   Non-Eligible Dividends
Dividend Gross Up   Prescribed Debt Obligations
Dividend Tax Credit   Property Income
Dividends   Stock Dividend
Eligible Dividends

References

7-155.   For more detailed study of the material in this Chapter, we refer you to the following:

ITA 12(1)(c)	Interest
ITA 12(1)(g)	Payments Based On Production Or Use
ITA 12(3)	Interest Income
ITA 12(4)	Interest From Investment Contract
ITA 12(11)	Definitions (Investment Contract)
ITA 15	Benefits Conferred On Shareholder
ITA 20(1)(c)	Interest
ITA 20(1)(f)	Discount On Certain Obligations
ITA 20(14)	Accrued Bond Interest
ITA 20.1	Borrowed Money Used To Earn Income From Property
ITA 82(1)(b)	Taxable Dividends Received
ITA 121	Deduction For Taxable Dividends
ITA 126	Foreign Tax Deduction
ITR 7000(2)	Prescribed Debt Obligations
IT-67R3	Taxable Dividends From Corporations Resident In Canada
IT-195R4	Rental Property - Capital Cost Allowance Restrictions
IT-270R3	Foreign Tax Credit
IT-295R4	Taxable Dividends Received After 1987 By A Spouse
IT-396R	Interest Income
IT-434R	Rental Of Real Property By Individual
IT-443	Leasing Property - Capital Cost Allowance Restrictions
IT-462	Payments Based On Production Or Use
IT-506	Foreign Income Taxes As A Deduction from Income
IT-533	Interest Deductibility And Related Issues
T4036	Rental Income Guide

Problems For Self Study

(The solutions for these problems can be found in the separate Study Guide.)

Self Study Problem Seven - 1 (Interest Deductibility - 4 Cases)

Each of the following independent Cases involves the payment of interest and the issue of whether the interest will be deductible for tax purposes.

Case A   John Artho owns 1,000 shares of Bee Ltd., a publicly traded company. He also owns a personal use condominium that was financed with borrowed money. Mr. Artho sells the 1,000 shares of Bee Ltd. and uses the proceeds to pay down the mortgage on the condominium. He subsequently borrows money to acquire another 1,000 shares of Bee Ltd. Would the interest on the new loan be deductible? Explain your conclusion.

Case B   Meridee Burns borrows $100,000 and acquires an income producing property for $100,000. She subsequently sells the property for $150,000 and, without repaying the funds borrowed to acquire the first property, uses the proceeds to acquire two other properties. The cost of property A is $40,000, while the cost of property B is $110,000. How will the $100,000 in borrowing be linked to the two new properties?

Case C   Meridee Burns borrows $100,000 and acquires an income producing property for $100,000. She subsequently sells the property for $80,000 and, without repaying the funds borrowed to acquire the first property, uses the proceeds to acquire two other properties. The cost of property A is $60,000, while the cost of property B is $20,000. How will the $100,000 in borrowing be linked to the two new properties?

Case D   Jason Bridges borrows $100,000 and invests the entire amount in the shares of Loser Inc. Six months later, he sells these shares for $40,000. The proceeds of the sale are used to pay off $40,000 of the loan, leaving an ongoing balance of $60,000. Can he continue to deduct the interest payments on this $60,000 balance? Explain your conclusion.

Self Study Problem Seven - 2 (Rental Income)

On January 1 of the current year, Mr. Drake owns a total of four residential rental properties. All of the properties were acquired after 1987. The cost and UCC for the properties as at January 1 of the current year are as follows:

	Original Cost (Building Only)	UCC
Property A	$136,000	$121,500
Property B	148,000	143,000
Property C	163,000	146,000
Property D	190,000	164,000

During the year, rental revenues and cash expenses on the four properties are as follows:

	Rental Revenue	Property Taxes	Interest	Other Expenses
Property A	$ 6,200	$ 2,200	$ 1,750	$ 500
Property B	7,700	2,550	Nil	1,800
Property C	13,200	3,750	7,800	1,700
Property D	16,300	4,750	13,500	3,900

Other transactions that occurred during the year are as follows:

1. Property A was sold on July 20. The building was allocated $172,000 of the cash proceeds.

2. Property C was sold on August 24. The building was allocated $161,000 of the cash proceeds.

3. A new residential rental property, Property E, was acquired on February 1 at a cost of $292,000. Of this total, $100,000 was allocated to land and $192,000 was allocated to the building. It was not rented until late in the year and, as a result, rents for the year total only $2,000, interest charges $2,300, property taxes $2,275, and other expenses $325.

Mr. Drake wants to take the maximum CCA permitted on all of his properties and he owns no other properties.

Required: Calculate Mr. Drake's income from property and net taxable capital gains for the current taxation year.

Self Study Problem Seven - 3 (Interest Vs. Dividend Income)

Mr. James Loyt is in the middle of the 26 percent federal tax bracket and the 12 percent provincial tax bracket. The province in which he lives provides a dividend tax credit on eligible dividends equal to 30 percent of the gross up. He has $20,000 in cash to invest for a period of one year beginning January 1, 2012. Mr. Loyt is considering the following two investments:

- Bonds issued by Faxtext Ltd., a Canadian public corporation. These bonds are selling at their maturity value and pay interest at an annual rate of 7.75 percent.

- Preferred shares issued by the same corporation. These shares pay an annual eligible dividend of 5 percent on all amounts invested.

Required: Advise Mr. Loyt as to which investment he should make. As part of your recommendation, calculate the after tax income that would be generated assuming that he invested his $20,000 in:

A. the corporate bonds.
B. the preferred stock.

Self Study Problem Seven - 4 (Property Income - Alternative Investments)

On January 1, 2012, Ms. Joan Bagley has $650,000 in a bank account at ING DIRECT. While this account has great flexibility in terms of deposits and withdrawals, it pays interest at an annual rate of only 2 percent. She would like to retain $50,000 of this balance as a contingency fund, while investing the $600,000 balance for a year. After consulting with her financial advisor, she is considering the following investment alternatives:

- A $600,000 guaranteed investment certificate that will mature on December 31, 2012. The certificate will pay annual interest at a rate of 4.5 percent on December 31.

- Preferred shares of a Canadian public company with a stated value of $600,000. These shares pay an annual eligible dividend of 5.25 percent on December 15. Ms. Bagley anticipates selling these shares on December 31, 2012 for their stated value.

- Shares of a public high tech company at a cost of $600,000. While these shares do not pay dividends, Ms. Bagley anticipates selling these shares on December 31, 2012 for $675,000.

Ms. Bagley will have over $200,000 of employment income in 2012. Her provincial tax rate on any additional income is 12 percent, while the provincial dividend tax credit on eligible dividends is equal to 28 percent of the gross up.

Assume the preferred and common shares can be sold at the anticipated values on December 31, 2012.

Required: For each investment alternative, determine:

- the amount that would be included in Ms. Bagley's 2012 Taxable Income,
- the total amount of federal and provincial Tax Payable for 2012, and
- the amount of after tax cash that would be retained by Ms. Bagley in 2012.

Self Study Problem Seven - 5 (Property Income - Alternative Investments)

During December, 2011, Ms. Holmes reaches a settlement with her former husband that requires him to make a lump sum payment to her of $100,000 on January 1, 2012. While Ms. Holmes has no immediate need for the funds, she will require them on January 1, 2013 in order to finance a new business venture that she plans to launch. As a consequence, she would like to invest the funds for the year ending December 31, 2012. She is considering the following alternatives:

- Investment of the full $100,000 in a one year, guaranteed investment certificate that pays annual interest of 5.5 percent.

- Investment of the full $100,000 in the shares of Norton Ltd., a publicly traded Canadian company. Ms. Holmes expects that the Company will pay eligible dividends on these shares during 2012 of $5,000. She anticipates that by the end of 2012, the shares will be worth at least $106,000.

- Investment of the full $100,000 in a rental property with a cost of $165,000. The property currently has a tenant whose lease calls for rental payments during 2012 of $13,200. Cash expenses for the year (interest, taxes, and condominium fees) are expected to be $9,600. Of the total cost of $165,000, an amount of $15,000 can be allocated to the land on which the building is situated. Ms. Holmes believes that the property can be sold on December 31, 2012, to net her $175,000.

Ms. Holmes expects to have employment income in excess of $225,000 during 2012. Her provincial tax rate on any additional income is 15 percent, while the provincial dividend tax credit on eligible dividends is equal to 27 percent of the gross up.

Required: Write a brief memorandum providing investment advice to Ms. Holmes on the three alternatives.

Self Study Problem Seven - 6 (Income Trusts And Mutual Funds)

On January 1, 2012, Ms. Natasha Boritz acquires the following investments:

- 5,000 units of the Real Property Income Trust. The cost is $50.00 per unit for a total cost of $250,000.
- 10,000 units of the Infidelity Far East Fund, a mutual fund trust. The cost is $85.00 per unit for a total cost of $850,000.

During 2012, the Real Property Income Trust makes an annual distribution of $4.50 per unit, of which $1.25 is designated as a return of capital. The remaining $3.25 is ordinary income. Natasha has elected to use the Trust's DRIP and, as a consequence, the distribution is reinvested in new trust units at a cost of $52.00 per unit.

Also during 2012, the Infidelity Far East Fund makes a distribution of $7.00 per unit. This distribution is made up of capital gains of $2.00, eligible dividends of $2.75, and interest income of $2.25. The entire distribution is reinvested in Infidelity Far East Fund units at a cost of $83.00 per unit.

Natasha has other investment income that places her in the 29 percent federal tax bracket. Taxes on this income are sufficient to use all of her available tax credits before considering the effects of the two investments described above. She lives in a province where the maximum rate is 11 percent and the tax credit on eligible dividends is 28 percent of the gross up.

Required: Calculate the amount of Taxable Income and Tax Payable that will result from the distributions by the two trusts. In addition, indicate the per unit adjusted cost base for each of the two trust units on December 31, 2012.

Self Study Problem Seven - 7 (Comprehensive Case Covering Chapters 1 to 7)

Ms. Shelly Spring is a 48 year old widow. While her deceased husband left her financially secure, she continues to work as a course assistant at a local college. Her 2012 salary is

$64,000, from which her employer withheld the following amounts:

RPP Contributions	$2,960
EI Premiums	840
CPP Contributions	2,307
Disability Insurance Premium	250

Ms. Spring pays one-half of the total disability insurance premium to the group plan, with her employer paying the balance. The plan provides periodic benefits that compensate for lost employment income. She started making payments in 2010 and made payments of $180 in that year, $225 in 2011, and $250 in 2012. During 2012, because of an extended illness, she received benefits of $5,600.

In addition to her salary, her employer provides her with an allowance of $400 per month for maintaining an office in her home. This office is her principal work location. The office occupies 15 percent of her home and, for 2012, the costs of operating the home were as follows:

Interest On Mortgage	$4,200
Property Taxes	2,750
Electricity And Water Costs	1,340
Maintenance And Repairs	1,800
Home Insurance	820

Ms. Spring has two children and they both live with her. Her daughter, Amy, is 19 years old and, during 2012, she was in full time attendance at the local university for 8 months of the year. Her tuition fees of $8,200 were paid by Ms. Spring. Amy has Net and Taxable Income of $7,300 for the year. She has agreed to transfer the maximum education related tax credits to her mother.

Her son, Mark, is 23 years old and is dependent because of a physical disability. The disability is not severe enough, however, to qualify for the ITA 118.3 disability tax credit. Mark had no income during 2012.

The family's medical expenses, all of which have been paid by Ms. Spring, were as follows:

Ms. Spring	$ 962
Amy	2,450
Mark	8,600
Total Medical Expenses	**$12,012**

At the beginning of 2012, Ms. Spring owns two residential rental properties, both acquired in 1995. On January 1, 2012, the UCC of property A was $156,000. The cost of this property was $245,000, including $40,000 for the land. Property B had a cost of $426,000, including $100,000 for the land. Its January 1, 2012 UCC was $276,000.

On June 1, 2012, property A was sold for $201,000, including $40,000 for the land. On that same date, a new residential rental property was acquired at a cost of $322,000, including $75,000 for the land. During 2012, Ms. Spring received rents of $42,000 and had rental expenses, other than CCA, of $32,500.

On December 31, 2011, Ms. Spring purchased a zero coupon bond with a maturity value of $100,000. The bond was issued on that date and matures on December 30, 2016. She paid $68,058 for the bond, a price which provides an 8 percent effective yield.

Ms. Spring owns shares of Canadian public companies which paid eligible dividends of $9,300 during 2012. She also owns shares in a foreign company which paid dividends of $5,600 (Canadian). The government in the foreign country withheld taxes of $840, giving Ms. Spring a net receipt of $4,760.

Required: Calculate Ms. Spring's 2012 minimum Net Income For Tax Purposes, her 2012 minimum Taxable Income, and her 2012 minimum federal Tax Payable without consideration of any income tax withheld by her employer. Ignore GST/HST/PST considerations.

Self Study Problem Seven - 8 (Comprehensive Case Covering Chapters 1 to 7)

Mr. Derek Fontaine is married and has three children. His wife, Emily, works as a personal fitness trainer on a part time basis and, for 2012, her Net Income For Tax Purposes is $9,500. His two youngest children, Brad and Barbara are twins. They are 14 years old and, unfortunately, Brad has been blind since birth. Neither child has any income of their own.

His other son, Bill, is 19 years old and attends university on a full time basis for 10 months of the year. His tuition fees total $8,500. Bill has income from part time jobs of $10,000 during 2012. Bill has agreed to transfer any education related credits available to his father.

Eligible medical expenses for Derek's family, all of which were paid by Derek, are as follows:

Derek	$ 1,400
Emily	1,600
Brad	11,400
Barbara	2,300
Bill	4,600

Derek purchases transit passes for all three of his children. The cost is $60 per month for each child. In 2012 the passes were purchased for 11 months.

The twins are enrolled in a qualifying physical fitness program. The cost is $400 for each child for 2012.

The Fontaines had always lived in rented premises. However, because the current level of mortgage rates makes purchasing a home attractive, they purchase a residence at a cost of $625,000. They move in on September 1, 2012.

Derek has a management consulting business that he operates out of a building that he owns. For the taxation year ending December 31, 2012, the business has an accounting Net Income of $211,000. Other information about this business is as follows:

1. Expenses include $11,500 in business meals and entertainment.

2. Derek owns a car which is used in the business. It was purchased on January 1, 2012 for $46,000. Operating costs for 2012 totaled $4,800. All of these costs were deducted in determining the accounting Net Income of the business. During this year, the car was driven 32,000 kilometers of which 23,000 related to Derek's business activities.

3. The building that is used in the business is a new building that was purchased in 2010. It has a January 1, 2012 UCC of $450,000. Derek's business uses 100 percent of the space in the building. The furniture and fixtures in the building have a January 1, 2012 UCC of $42,000. During 2012, additional furniture was acquired at a cost of $12,000. It replaced furniture that had cost $10,000. Derek sold the used furniture for $3,000.

4. Amortization of $18,000 was deducted in determining accounting Net Income. This included amortization on the car, the furniture and fixtures, and the building.

In addition to operating his business, Derek has been an active investor in various types of securities. Information on his holdings is as follows:

Breax Common Shares On January 1, 2012, Derek holds 2,500 shares of this Company. They have an adjusted cost base of $130,000. On February 1, 2012, he sells 1,000 of these shares for $65 per share. On July 1, 2012, he acquires an additional 1,200 shares at $54 per share. During 2012 he receives eligible dividends on these shares totalling $8,000.

Realco Income Trust On January 1, 2012, Derek holds 5,000 units of this income trust. The adjusted cost base of these units is $150,000. During 2012, these units have a distribution of $2.50 per unit. Of this total, $1.00 represents a return of capital, with the other $1.50 consisting of business income. Derek uses the entire distribution to acquire additional units in the trust at $32 per unit.

Debt Security On July 1, 2011, Derek purchases a debt security with a maturity value of $100,000. The security matures on June 30, 2016 and bears interest at 8 percent per annum. Interest for the first 18 months is paid on December 31, 2012, with the remaining interest due when the security matures on June 30, 2016.

Foreign Term Deposit On January 1, 2012, Derek owns a foreign currency term deposit with a maturity value of $250,000. During the year, the term deposit earns interest of $20,000. Taxation authorities in the foreign jurisdiction withhold $8,000 of this amount. All amounts are in Canadian dollars.

Required: Calculate Mr. Fontaine's 2012 minimum Net Income For Tax Purposes, his 2012 minimum Taxable Income, and his 2012 minimum federal Tax Payable. Ignore GST/HST/PST considerations, as well as the need to make CPP contributions by Derek and Emily.

Assignment Problems

(The solutions for these problems are only available in
the solutions manual that has been provided to your instructor.)

Assignment Problem Seven - 1 (Interest Deductibility - 4 Cases)

Each of the following independent Cases involves the payment of interest and the issue of whether the interest will be deductible for tax purposes.

Case A Martin Duck borrows $300,000 and invests the entire proceeds of the loan in publicly traded securities. After 3 months, the value of the securities has fallen to $110,000. At this point, Mr. Duck sells the securities and uses the proceeds to reduce the loan to $190,000. Now that he no longer owns the securities, can he still deduct the interest on the loan? Explain your conclusion.

Case B Janet Forest owns a portfolio of securities with a current value of $190,000. Using her margin balance available from her stockbroker, she borrows $30,000 to finance the purchase of a sailboat. During the period the margin loan is outstanding, she pays interest of $900. Can she deduct this interest against the $5,000 in income earned during this period on her portfolio of securities? Explain your conclusion.

Case C Martin Brock borrows $42,000 and uses the funds to acquire an income producing property. He later sells the property for $110,000. He uses these proceeds to purchase two properties. Property A costs $45,000 and property B costs $65,000. How will the $42,000 in borrowing be linked to the two properties?

Case D Chuck Masters borrows $100,000 and uses the funds to acquire an income producing property. He later sells the property for $80,000. He uses the $80,000 to purchase two properties. Property A costs $20,000 and property B costs $60,000. How will the $100,000 in borrowing be linked to the two properties?

Assignment Problem Seven - 2 (Rental Income)

Ms. Serravalle has a firm belief in the advantages of investing in real estate. Because of this belief, she has invested most of her discretionary income in residential rental properties over the past four decades. On January 1, 2012, she owns four rental properties The relevant facts on these properties are as follows:

642 Kent Street This is a Class 3 building that has a capital cost of $722,000. Its UCC at the beginning of the year was $412,000. During the year, it generated rents of $63,000 and incurred property taxes of $7,800, interest charges of $11,700, and other expenses (excluding CCA) of $12,750.

1256 Montreal Road   This is a Class 3 building that had a capital cost of $37,000. It was sold on August 1. For CCA purposes, it was included in the same Class 3 pool as 112 Lisgar Avenue. Of the sale proceeds, $65,000 was allocated to the building. From January 1 to July 31, the building generated rents of $4,800 and incurred property taxes of $1,100, interest charges of $1,450, and other expenses (excluding CCA) of $900.

This property contained furniture that Ms. Serravalle had acquired at a cost of $8,000. On January 1, 2012, this furniture had a UCC balance of $4,200. It was sold at the same time as the rental property. The proceeds of the sale were $2,100.

112 Lisgar Avenue   This is a Class 3 building that has a capital cost of $45,000. At the beginning of the year, the UCC of the Class 3 pool, which included both 1256 Montreal Road and 112 Lisgar Avenue, was $48,000. During the year, it generated rents of $5,000 and incurred property taxes of $1,550, interest charges of $650, and other expenses (excluding CCA) of $2,500.

23 Durham Private   This Class 1 building has a capital cost of $225,000. Its UCC at the beginning of the year was $216,000. During the year, the unit generated rents of $22,000 and incurred property taxes of $3,850, interest charges of $11,500, and other expenses (excluding CCA) of $8,700.

Required: Calculate Ms. Serravalle's net rental income for 2012. Specify how much CCA should be taken for each building.

Assignment Problem Seven - 3 (Dividend vs. Interest Income)

Sarah, Sally, and Suzanne Baxter are three sisters who live in the same province. Because of their alternative career choices, they have enjoyed varying degrees of economic success.

Sarah   Sarah has devoted her life to the arts. However, the scarcity of work in her field has resulted in her being in the 15 percent federal tax bracket and the 5 percent provincial bracket.

Sally   Sally has always worked in retail and is doing well as a store manager. She is in the 26 percent federal tax bracket and the 11 percent provincial tax bracket.

Suzanne   Suzanne is a very successful attorney. Her income places her in the 29 percent federal tax bracket and the 16 percent provincial tax bracket.

The provincial dividend tax credit on eligible dividends is equal to 27 percent of the dividend gross up.

On January 1, 2012, as the result of an inheritance from a wealthy uncle, each of the sisters has $15,000 to invest. They are looking at the following alternatives:

Corporate Bonds   The issue that they are considering has a 4.5 percent coupon rate, is selling at par, and matures in 25 years.

Preferred Stock The shares that they are considering has a dividend yield of 5.6 percent. The dividend is cumulative but not participating.

The income from these investments would not move any of the three sisters to a higher federal or provincial tax bracket. Each sister has sufficient income to use all of her available tax credits.

Required: Advise each of the Baxter sisters as to which investment they should make. As part of your recommendation, calculate the after tax income that would be generated for each of the sisters, assuming that they invested their $15,000 in:

A. the corporate bonds.
B. the preferred stock.

Assignment Problem Seven - 4
(Investments In Income Trusts And Common Stock)

Late in the year 2011, Ms. Sarah Stein inherits $550,000 from an eccentric uncle. The terms of his will require that Sarah use $250,000 of this amount for luxury travel within 12 months of her receipt of the funds. Any unspent balance of this $250,000 will be returned to the uncle's estate and distributed to a specified group of charities.

With respect to the remaining $300,000, there are no restrictions on its use. Because of the time commitment related to the luxury travel, Ms. Stein would like to invest this balance for a one year period, commencing January 1. She is considering the following alternative investments and would like your advice on the appropriate choice:

> **H & R Real Estate Investment Trust**   On January 1, 2012, this trust is selling for $20 per unit. It makes a distribution of $0.0725 per unit per month. This distribution is business income only and does not include any return of capital. Ms. Stein does not expect any price appreciation over the year ending December 31, 2012.

> **Dream Spinner Tech Common Stock**   On January 1, 2012, these shares are selling for $10 each. The Company pays an annual dividend of $0.05 per share. This will be an eligible dividend. Ms. Stein anticipates that these shares will be selling for at least $10.50 per share on December 31, 2012.

In order to accommodate the required luxury travel, Ms. Stein will use her six months of accumulated vacation pay and take an unpaid leave of absence from her employer for the rest of the year. Her net employment income will be $45,000 for 2012. Taxes on this income are sufficient to use all of her available tax credits before considering the effects of the two investments described above.

Ms. Stein lives in a province that assesses a tax rate of 10 percent on all levels of income. In this province, the dividend tax credit for eligible dividends is equal to 25 percent of the gross up.

Required: Write a brief memorandum providing investment advice to Ms. Stein.

Assignment Problem Seven - 5 (Business And Property Income)

Mr. Sonny Shark is an accountant who has a well established practice in Edmonton. He uses the billed basis of income recognition.

Relevant information on his practice for the taxation year ending December 31, 2012, is as follows:

January 1 Unbilled Work In Progress	$ 42,000
Billable Hours (1,900 Hours At $250 Per Hour)	475,000
December 31 Unbilled Work In Progress	35,000
Office Supplies And Office Expenses	56,000
Travel Costs Other Than Meals And Entertainment	8,000
Business Meals And Entertainment	12,000

Mr. Shark purchased the building in which his practice is located in 2004. His practice uses 50 percent of the floor space in the building and, on January 1, 2012 the Class 1 UCC for the building is $526,000.

Since the building was purchased, the other one-half of the building had been rented to a very successful lawyer who was paying rent of $4,000 per month. This lawyer was convicted of embezzling from his clients and was jailed on July 1, 2012. Despite all his efforts, Mr. Shark could not find a new tenant and received rent for only six months during 2012.

The 2012 interest, taxes, and other expenses (other than CCA) that can be allocated to the one-half of the building that was rented total $14,400.

Mr. Shark owns the furnishings in his office. The cost of these furnishings was $24,000 and, on January 1, 2012, the Class 8 UCC for these furnishings is $11,059.

Mr. Shark is an avid investor in the stock market. During 2012, he received eligible dividends totaling $18,000. He did not dispose of any shares during the year.

Required: Determine Mr. Shark's minimum Net Income For Tax Purposes for the year ending December 31, 2012.

Assignment Problem Seven - 6
(Foreign Property Income, Income Trusts And Mutual Funds)

On January 1, 2012, Mr. Bradley Temrik acquires the following investments:

Foreign Currency Term Deposit A £225,000 term deposit which pays interest at 5 percent per annum. On December 31, 2012, interest of £11,250 is paid on this term deposit. The taxation authorities in the U.K. withhold 25 percent of this payment, with the remaining 75 percent being remitted to Bradley. Assume that throughout 2012, £1 = $1.55.

Income Trust Units 4,500 units of Canadian Realty Trust at $56 per unit. The total cost is $252,000.

Mutual Fund Units 6,200 units of Fidelitee Large Cap at $32 per unit. The total cost is $198,400.

During the year ending December 31, 2012, the following additional transactions occur:

Canadian Realty Trust This trust has a distribution of $5.20 per unit. Of this total, $2.40 represents a return of capital, with the remainder being business income. Mr. Temrik reinvests the entire amount that he receives in additional units at a cost of $59 per unit.

Fidelitee Large Cap This mutual fund has a distribution of $3.75 per unit. This is made up of capital gains of $1.00 per unit, interest of $1.25 per unit, and eligible dividends of $1.50 per unit. All of this distribution is reinvested to acquire additional units of Fidelitee at $28 per unit.

Bradley has other investment income that places him in the 29 percent federal tax bracket. Taxes on this income are sufficient to use all of his available tax credits before considering the effects of the investments described above. He lives in a province where the maximum rate is 16 percent and the tax credit on eligible dividends is 30 percent of the gross up.

Required: Calculate the amount of Taxable Income and Tax Payable that will result from the interest on the term deposit and the distributions by the two trusts. In addition, indicate the per unit adjusted cost base for each of the two trust units on December 31, 2012.

Assignment Problem Seven - 7 (Comprehensive Case Covering Chapters 1 to 7)

Mr. Jack Fox is 66 years old and while he receives significant pension income from a former employer's RPP, he is a full time employee of Jardu Enterprises Ltd. (JEL). During 2012, his gross wages were $62,000. JEL withheld the following amounts from these wages:

RPP Contributions	$3,125
EI Premiums	840
CPP Contributions	2,307
Union Dues	572
United Way Contributions	2,400

During 2012, his pension receipts totaled $42,000. He has not applied for OAS as he knows that all of it will be clawed back. Further, he has not applied for CPP as he is aware that deferring this application will result in larger benefits.

Mr. Fox has been married to the same woman, Sharon Fox, for over 30 years. Sharon is 68 years old and has Net Income For Tax Purposes of $9,900. This consists of pension income from her RRSP and OAS payments. She has not applied for CPP.

Jack has two children. His 32 year old son Jerome has been blind since birth. He lives with and is totally dependent on Jack and Sharon. He has no income of his own.

Jack's daughter Suzanne is 41 years old and is recently divorced. She and her children also live with Jack. Her only income is $36,000 in child support that she receives under a 2010 court decree. In 2012, she decided to become an accountant and, to this end, she began attending university on a full time basis in September. Jack has paid her tuition of $4,600 and Suzanne has agreed to transfer any education related credits available to her father.

The family's medical expenses, all of which have been paid by Jack, are as follows:

Jack	$ 600
Sharon	1,100
Jerome	12,250
Suzanne	1,400
Total Medical Expenses	**$15,350**

During 2012, Jack received the following dividends (all amounts in Canadian dollars):

Eligible Dividends From Taxable Canadian Corporations	$11,700
Non-Eligible Dividends On Shares In His Sister's CCPC	3,250
Dividends On Foreign Shares - Net Of 15 Percent Withholding	10,625
Total Dividends Received	**$25,575**

In addition to dividends, Jack had 2012 interest income of $2,843.

Because of the project management skills that he has acquired over the years, Jack started a management consulting business in 2009. In that year he acquired a new building to be used as an office for his business. The building cost $426,000 of which $126,000 was the estimated value of the land. On January 1, 2012, the UCC of the building is $273,540.

The building contains office furniture and fixtures that were acquired at a cost of $42,000. On January 1, 2012, they have a UCC of $30,240.

During 2012, he spends $41,000 on improving and upgrading the building. In addition, he sells the old furniture and fixtures for $18,600 and acquires replacement furniture and fixtures for $50,000.

As Jack has no reason to keep detailed accounting records, he records business income on a cash basis. For 2012, his net cash flow from operations was $123,500. Relevant figures for the beginning and end of 2012 are as follows:

	January 1	December 31
Billed Receivables	$13,400	$17,350
Unbilled Work In Process	17,470	21,250
Accounts Payable	8,670	9,272

Since the inception of the business, Jack has owned a car that is used 100 percent for business activity. The car that he acquired in 2009 was sold in 2011. He acquired a new car on January 1, 2012 at a cost of $61,500. He financed the car through his bank and, during 2012, he made payments on the loan of $13,200. All of this amount was deducted in determining his net cash flow from operations. Of the total, $4,920 represented payments for interest. Jack paid car operating costs totalling $9,260 during 2012.

Required: Calculate Jack's 2012 minimum Net Income For Tax Purposes, his 2012 minimum Taxable Income, and his 2012 minimum federal Tax Payable. Ignore GST/HST/PST considerations, the possibility of pension income splitting and the fact that 2012 is a leap year.

Assignment Problem Seven - 8 (Comprehensive Case Covering Chapters 1 to 7)

Ms. Caroline Graham is a full time employee of KLY Incorporated, an on-line clothing retailer. She has an annual salary of $75,000, from which the following amounts were withheld in 2012:

Registered Pension Plan Contributions	$3,500
CPP Contributions	2,307
EI Premiums	840
Donation to United Way	1,500
Long term disability insurance	500

The long term disability plan provides periodic benefits that compensate for lost employment income. In addition, Caroline's employer provided her with a life insurance policy at a cost of $350.

Caroline is a single parent with a 15-year-old daughter, Grace, who has no income of her own. Caroline's father lives with the family, and is financially dependent on Caroline as his only income is Old Age Security of $6,500. Caroline's father moved in with her after her mother passed away in 2011, and as a result, in January, 2012 , Caroline purchased a home for the family to live in for $350,000. Caroline and Grace had lived in a rented home for the past 6 years.

Caroline has purchased a bus pass for Grace for 10 months in 2012, costing $75 per month. She also purchased bus passes for her father for 12 months at the same rate. Grace is enrolled in figure skating lessons and Caroline has paid fees of $5,000 for skating lessons. Grace attends a private high school at a cost of $12,000 per year.

Caroline provides financial support to her sister, Kristin. Kristin has lived in France for the last 10 years. She has been in university there for the last 2 years. Caroline paid her university tuition of $15,000 for 2012 and $12,000 for medical costs related to her hospitalization after an automobile accident in March, 2012.

Caroline has provided the following information regarding the 2012 income from her investment portfolio.

Term Deposits Caroline has the following two term deposits:

- A $200,000 term deposit purchased on November 1, 2011 at 3.25 percent. Interest is payable at maturity on October 31, 2013.

- A $20,000 term deposit purchased on November 30, 2012 at 3 percent. Interest is payable at maturity in 6 months.

Treasury Bill Caroline purchased a Government of Canada Treasury Bill for $9,901 on January 1, 2012. The investment matured on December 31, 2012, and Caroline received $10,000.

Investments In Shares The income amounts from Caroline's share investments are as follows:

- Caroline owns 1,000 shares of Royal Scotia Bank. The company paid an eligible dividend of $24 per share on October 15, 2012.

- Caroline also owns 100 shares in Graham Company Limited, a corporation solely owned and operated by her brother. This company paid a non-eligible dividend of $50 per share on November 30, 2012.

- Caroline inherited 500 shares of Americo Limited, a U.S. company from her mother. In 2012, these shares paid a dividend of $20 (Canadian) per share. The U.S. government withheld 12 percent of the total dividend amount.

Future Investments In 2011, when Caroline's mother passed away, she left Caroline with a substantial sum of money which Caroline wants to invest wisely. She is planning to invest substantial funds in 2012 in one of the three following alternatives:

- term deposits,
- shares in public Canadian corporations which will pay eligible dividends, or
- additional shares in her brother's corporation which will pay non-eligible dividends.

Caroline had owned a rental property for several years, and when she received her inheritance, she sold the old property and purchased a new one.

The old rental property cost $125,000 when it was purchased in 2006, with $28,000 allocated to the land, and $2,500 allocated to appliances. UCC on this property was $90,450 on January 1, 2012 for the building and $2,145 for the appliances. The property was sold on January 1, 2012 for $120,000 with $28,000 allocated to the land and $1,000 to the appliances.

The new property was purchased on February 1, 2012, and cost a total of $200,000, with $45,000 allocated to land. Caroline collected rent for the year of $16,150. Costs to operate the property, including mortgage interest, insurance, utilities and property taxes totaled $12,500. In addition, Caroline spent the following amounts in order to make the property suitable for rental:

New windows	$14,500
Roof repairs	1,200
Carpeting and flooring replacements	7,500
Cleaning	500
Painting interior and exterior	2,000
New appliances	6,500

Required:

A. For the 2012 taxation year, calculate Caroline's minimum:

1. Net Income For Tax Purposes,
2. Taxable Income,
3. Federal Tax Liability.

B. Based on the top marginal tax rate applied to determine Caroline's tax payable, calculate the effective federal tax rate that Caroline pays on eligible dividends, non-eligible dividends and interest income (ignore provincial taxes). What advice would you give her with respect to her investment choices?

In completing the requirements of this problem, ignore GST, PST and HST considerations.

Tax Software Assignment Problem For Chapter 7

This Tax Software Assignment Problem was introduced in Chapter 4 and is continued in Chapters 6 through 11. Each Tax Software Assignment Problem must be completed in sequence. While it is not repeated in this problem, all of the information in each of the previous problems (e.g., Mary's T4 content) is applicable to this problem.

If you have not prepared a tax file incorporating the Tax Software Assignment Problem information for the previous Chapters, please do so before continuing with this problem.

Seymour was previously married and has a 19 year old daughter from the previous marriage. As part of the property settlement, he received the house that he and his family had lived in. Since Mary already owned a much nicer home, he moved in with her when they were married in 2009 and rented out the property.

On December 28, 2011, Seymour Career drops off information about his rental property and additional interest he has paid during the year. (You already have the interest related to his car and principal residence.) Mary has received data that will be on her T3 and T5 information slips from her stockbroker and bank and this is also included in the package you receive. The interest from the TD Bank is from a joint chequing account in the name of both Mary and Seymour.

Seymour believed that in June he had paid an instalment of $2,400 for 2011, but could find no record of it. You call the CRA and find that the June payment was towards his 2010 tax liability. Seymour had tax owing of more than $10,000 for 2010 and has not completely paid off the liability yet. He has paid no instalments for 2011.

Mary also paid no instalments for 2011. She has received tax refunds in the last two years.

Mary has invested in the stock market over the years and has done well. Seymour holds no securities outside of his RRSP during 2011.

During 2009, one of his clients convinced Seymour to take out a demand loan to purchase shares in the public company, XXX Art Films Ltd. for $37,000. Later that year, the company's president was indicted for fraud. In 2010, Seymour sold his shares for $2,000 and used the proceeds to pay down his demand loan. During 2011, Seymour did not have sufficient funds to pay off the demand loan, but managed to reduce the principal by $10,000.

The interest and penalties paid by Seymour during 2011 were as follows:

Interest on credit cards for business expenses	$ 627.27
Interest on loan to buy laptop and software	104.24
Interest on loan to make 2010 RRSP contribution	162.15
Interest on loan to purchase XXX Art Films securities	1,372.52
Interest on late payment of 2010 income tax	233.72
Interest on insufficient tax instalments for 2010	52.81
Interest on late GST/HST payments	212.82
Penalty for late filing of 2010 tax return	303.92
Total	$3,069.45

T5	Box	Slip 1	Slip 2
Issuer		Power Corp.	TD Bank
Recipient (Input both on Mary's return)		Mary	Joint 50% each
Actual amount of eligible dividends	24	950.00	
Taxable amount of eligible dividends	25	1,339.50	
Interest from Canadian sources	13		236.11

T3	Box	Amount
Issuer - TD Asset Management		
Recipient - Mary Career		
Foreign country - United States		
Foreign non-business income (Canadian dollars)	25	1,553.10
Foreign income tax paid - investment (Canadian dollars)	34	37.00
Other income - interest	26	214.50
Actual amount of eligible dividends	49	346.00
Taxable amount of eligible dividends	50	487.86

Tax Software Assignment Problem For Chapter 7

Real Estate Rental - Seymour	Amount
Address - 50 King Street, Moncton, NB, E1C 4M2	
Gross rents	12,000.00
Property taxes	3,610.00
Insurance	650.00
Interest on mortgage	4,207.25
Payment on principal	1,511.92
Wiring and furnace repairs	2,282.71
Snow removal and landscaping annual contract	1,070.00
Building purchased May 1, 1998 for $150,000 - UCC beginning of year	150,000.00
Appliances purchased June 6, 2009 for $1,700 - UCC beginning of year	1,350.00

Required:

A. Open the file that you created for the Chapter 6 version of this Software Problem and save a copy under a different name. This will enable you to check the changes between different versions of this Software Problem.

B. Revise and print Seymour's Statement of Business or Professional Activities (T2125) for Crystal Clear Communications after incorporating the information on interest paid.

C. Prepare and print Seymour's Statement of Real Estate Rentals and the related CCA worksheet.

D. Input the T3 and T5 information. (Note that by inputting the joint T5 on Mary's return, the T5 information will appear on Seymour's Statement Of Investment Income (Schedule 4), but not on his T5 slip screen.) Prepare and print Schedule 4 for both Mary and Seymour.

E. Review both returns with the objective of minimizing the tax liability for the family and make any changes required.

F. Access and print Mary's summary (Summary on the Form Explorer, not the T1Summary). This form is a two column summary of the couple's tax information. By opening this form from Mary's return, the order of the columns is the same as the one in the previous chapter. For both returns, list the changes on this Summary form from the previous version of this Software Problem. Exclude totals calculated by the program, but include the final Balance Owing (Refund) amount.

CHAPTER 8

Capital Gains And Capital Losses

Economic Background

Capital Assets And Income Taxation Policy

8-1.   The discussion of business income in Chapter 6 noted that capital gains and losses arise on the disposition of assets that are earning business or property income. In general, the income from the sale of such assets will be incidental to the ongoing activities that produce business income and, as a consequence, a case can be made for exempting any resulting capital gains and losses from income taxation.

8-2.   This case is reinforced during periods of high inflation. If a business is going to continue operating as a going concern, it will usually have to replace any capital assets that are sold. As gains on the sale of capital assets often reflect nothing more than inflationary price increases, such gains cannot be distributed to the owners of the business as they must be used to finance the replacement of the assets sold.

8-3.   Until 1972, Canadian tax legislation did not levy any income tax on capital gains. One of the most significant changes in the 1972 tax reform legislation was the introduction of taxation on capital gains as the government believed that the ability to completely escape taxation on this type of income was creating severe inequities in the taxation system.

8-4.   The capital gains taxation that became effective January 1, 1972, represented a compromise between the view that capital gains should be exempt from tax and the position that such freedom from taxation creates serious inequities among various classes of taxpayers. Taxation of capital gains was introduced, but on a basis that was very favourable to the taxpayer. Capital gains were considered a source of income that was not business or property income, even though capital gains and losses can only arise on the disposition of assets that earned business or property income.

8-5.   In simple terms, the 1972 rules indicated that one-half of a capital gain would be treated as a taxable capital gain and, similarly, one-half of a capital loss would be deductible against capital gains as an allowable capital loss. This meant that for a taxpayer in the 45 percent tax bracket, the effective tax rate on capital gains was an attractive 22.5 percent.

Lifetime Capital Gains Deduction

8-6.   Even though capital gains taxation was applied in a very favourable manner, there was a continuing view that any taxation of such income was not appropriate. As a reflection of this view, in 1985, the government introduced the lifetime capital gains deduction. This legislation provided that every Canadian resident could enjoy tax free treatment of up to $500,000 of capital gains on the disposition of any type of capital asset. From its introduction, this provision was heavily criticized as a gift to higher income Canadians, particularly in view of the fact that it was available on any type of capital gain. It was difficult for many analysts to see the economic justification for providing favourable tax treatment of gains on the sale of a wealthy Canadian's Florida condominium.

8-7.   As a result of such criticism, a variety of limitations were introduced over subsequent years. Without going through a detailed history, we would note that, under current legislation, a $750,000 deduction is available on gains resulting from the disposition of shares of a qualified small business corporation, or the disposition of a qualified farm or fishing property.

8-8.   It should be noted here that the provisions related to the lifetime capital gains deduction do not affect any of the material in this Chapter. The lifetime capital gains legislation did not alter the determination of the amount of taxable capital gains to be included in Net Income For Tax Purposes. Rather, the legislation provided for a deduction in the determination of Taxable Income for all or part of the taxable capital gains included in Net Income For Tax Purposes. This material is covered in Chapter 11, Taxable Income And Tax Payable For Individuals Revisited.

Changes In The Inclusion Rate

8-9.   For gains and losses on capital assets disposed of subsequent to October 17, 2000, the inclusion rate has been one-half. As the focus of this text is on the 2012 taxation year, the only relevance of alternative inclusion rates is for allowable loss carry forwards resulting from dispositions that occurred prior to October 18, 2000. As will be discussed in Chapter 11, allowable capital losses can be carried forward indefinitely. This means that if they are carried forward from dispositions prior to October 18, 2000 using an inclusion rate other than one-half, the inclusion rate will have to be adjusted.

8-10.   Given this situation, we will give only limited attention to examples involving alternative inclusion rates. For reference purposes in dealing with alternative inclusion rates when they occur, inclusion rates for the period 1972 to the present are as follows:

Period	Inclusion Rate
1972 Through 1987	1/2
1988 And 1989	2/3
1990 Through February 27, 2000	3/4
February 28, 2000 through October 17, 2000	2/3
October 18, 2000 To Present	1/2

General Rules

Capital Gains In The *Income Tax Act*

8-11.   The material in this Chapter is a continuation of our discussion of the calculation of Net Income For Tax Purposes. In Chapter 3, detailed attention was given to employment income. In terms of the *Income Tax Act*, this discussion was based on Subdivision a of Division B of the *Act*. Chapters 5, 6, and 7 dealt with Subdivision b of Division B and provided a comprehensive consideration of business and property income. This included detailed coverage of the calculations related to capital cost allowance (CCA), an important deduction in the determination of both business and property income.

8-12.   Capital gains and losses are the third major component of Net Income For Tax Purposes. This subject is covered in Subdivision c of Division B, Sections 38 through 55. Sections 38 and 39 define taxable capital gains, allowable capital losses, and other items that relate to the calculation of these amounts. Section 40 provides the general tax rules for computing these amounts. The remaining Sections 41 through 55 deal with more specific matters, such as identical properties (Section 47), adjustments to the cost base (Section 53), and various additional definitions (Section 54).

Capital Gains Defined
Capital Assets
8-13.   In general, capital gains can occur when a taxpayer disposes of a capital asset. You will recall that capital assets were described in Chapter 6 as being those assets which are capable of earning income in the form of business profits, interest, dividends, royalties, or rents. Further, the assets must be held for this income producing purpose, rather than for a quick resale at a profit.

8-14.   It was also noted in Chapter 6 that, in making the determination as to whether a particular amount of income was capital in nature, the courts would take into consideration the intent and course of the taxpayer's conduct, the number and frequency of transactions involving the type of asset under consideration, the nature of the asset, the relationship of the asset to the business of the taxpayer, and the objectives set out in the articles of incorporation.

Capital Gains Election On Canadian Securities
8-15.   Despite these guidelines, the fact that capital gains receive favourable income tax treatment has led to much controversy and litigation with respect to the distinction between capital and other assets. In the case of equity securities, it is often difficult to distinguish between those situations where a taxpayer is holding the securities in order to earn dividend income or, alternatively, holding the securities in order to generate a gain on their ultimate disposition. Fortunately, the *Income Tax Act* provides an election which keeps this issue out of the courts.

8-16.   ITA 39(4) allows taxpayers, including corporations and trusts, to elect to have all Canadian securities that they own deemed to be capital property, and all sales of such securities deemed to be dispositions of capital property. Once this election is made, it cannot be revoked and it applies to all future dispositions of Canadian securities by the taxpayer, thus assuring the taxpayer that all gains and losses will be treated as favourably taxed capital gains. However, it also prevents the taxpayer from trying to claim that a loss on the disposition of securities is a fully deductible business loss.

8-17.   ITA 39(5) indicates that this election is not available to traders or dealers in securities, financial institutions, a corporation in the business of lending money or purchasing debt obligations, or non-residents.

Dispositions
Actual Dispositions
8-18.   The definition of "disposition" in ITA 248(1) states that, in general, a disposition is any transaction or event that entitles a taxpayer to "proceeds of disposition" (see Paragraph 8-24 for an explanation of this term). The most obvious such transaction would be a simple sale of property for cash. However, as listed in this definition, there are many other transactions and events that would be considered dispositions for income tax purposes. The more common of those listed would be:

- sales of property;
- redemptions of debt securities or shares;
- cancellations of debt securities or shares;
- expirations of options;
- expropriations of capital property; and
- conversions of debt or shares.

8-19.   In general, transfers of capital assets are not considered to involve a disposition unless there is a change in beneficial ownership. For example, a transfer of property between two trusts with identical beneficiaries would not be considered a change in beneficial ownership and, as a result, the transfer would not be treated as a disposition. An exception to this general rule occurs when there is a transfer to an RRSP. Even though there is no change in beneficial ownership, the transfer would be treated as a disposition of the transferred asset.

Gifts

8-20.   While a gift between taxpayers generally involves a transfer of beneficial ownership, it is not one of the dispositions listed in the ITA 248(1) definition. However, ITA 69 indicates that where a taxpayer has disposed of anything to any person by way of a gift, the taxpayer shall be deemed to have received proceeds of disposition equal to the fair market value of the gifted property. As this provision indicates that gifts have a deemed proceeds of disposition, they qualify as a disposition under the general definition of such transactions (i.e., any transaction or event that entitles a taxpayer to proceeds of disposition).

8-21.   While most gifts are made to non-arm's length taxpayers, the ITA 69 provision cited in the preceding paragraph applies to any gift, without regard to whether the recipient is at arm's length with the person making the gift. This means that any taxpayer that has made a gift will be deemed to have proceeds equal to the fair market value of the gifted property.

8-22.   ITA 69 also indicates that where a taxpayer acquires a property by way of a gift, that taxpayer is deemed to have acquired the property at its fair market value.

Deemed Dispositions

8-23.   In addition to actual dispositions of capital property, there are a number of situations in which a disposition is deemed to have occurred. That is, even though there is no actual disposition, rules in the *Income Tax Act* require that, when certain events occur, the taxpayer must assume that a disposition and immediate re-acquisition of specified capital properties has occurred. In this Chapter we will give consideration to deemed dispositions that result from a change in the use of a property and deemed dispositions that occur when an individual departs from Canada. Deemed dispositions that arise on the death of taxpayer will be covered in Chapter 9.

Proceeds Of Disposition

Actual Proceeds Of Disposition

8-24.   The term, "proceeds of disposition", is defined in ITA 54 and ITA 13(21). Included in both of these definitions are the following:

- The sale price of property sold.
- Compensation for property unlawfully taken or for property destroyed, including related proceeds from insurance policies.
- Compensation for property that has been appropriated or injuriously affected whether lawfully or unlawfully.
- Compensation for damaged property, including amounts payable under insurance policies.

Deemed Proceeds Of Disposition

8-25.   Deemed proceeds of disposition can arise in two different ways. When there is a deemed rather than an actual disposition, the legislation that requires the deemed disposition will specify how the deemed proceeds of disposition will be determined. For example, when there is a deemed disposition for an individual departing from Canada, the deemed proceeds of disposition will generally be the fair market value of the relevant asset.

8-26.   There are other situations in which there is an actual disposition, with the *Income Tax Act* requiring the use of a deemed proceeds that is different than the actual proceeds. For example, if there is a non-arm's length transfer and the proceeds of disposition are below the fair market value of the relevant assets, ITA 69 deems the proceeds to be fair market value.

Adjusted Cost Base
Definition
8-27. The adjusted cost base of an asset is defined in ITA 54 as follows:

(i) where the property is depreciable property of the taxpayer, the capital cost to him of the property as of that time, and

(ii) in any other case, the cost to the taxpayer of the property adjusted, as of that time, in accordance with Section 53.

8-28. This definition means that, in general, the adjusted cost base of a capital asset is analogous to the accounting concept of historical cost. As with the GAAP approach to historical cost, it includes the invoice cost, delivery and setup charges, non-refundable provincial sales taxes, non-refundable GST/HST, and any other costs associated with acquiring the asset, or putting it into use.

8-29. As indicated in the adjusted cost base definition, ITA 53 specifies a number of adjustments to the cost base. Some of the more important of these adjustments can be described as follows:

Government Grants And Assistance When a taxpayer receives government grants or other types of assistance, these amounts are generally deducted from the adjusted cost base of the related asset. This is consistent with the accounting treatment of government grants under Canadian GAAP.

Superficial Losses A superficial loss occurs when a taxpayer disposes of a property and:

- within the period of 30 days before the disposition or 30 days after the disposition, the taxpayer or his spouse or common-law partner acquires the same property (referred to as the substituted property), and,
- at the end of the period (60 days), the taxpayer or his spouse or common-law partner owns the substituted property.

Any loss on the disposition of the original property is called a superficial loss. Such losses cannot be deducted, but must be added to the adjusted cost base of the substituted property.

As an example, assume that in 2008 Ms. Deffett acquires 100 shares of Norton Limited for $75 per share. On December 27, 2012 the shares are trading at $60 and, because she has realized capital gains in 2012, Ms. Deffett sells the shares on this date in order to realize a loss that can be used to offset the capital gains. One-half of the capital loss of $15 per share on the December 27, 2012 sale would be deductible, provided no Norton Limited shares are purchased between November 27, 2012 and January 26, 2013. If, however, she were to purchase 100 Norton shares on December 15, 2012 or January 15, 2013 for $65 per share, the December, 2012 loss would be disallowed. The disallowed loss would be added to the adjusted cost base of the new shares, giving these shares an adjusted cost base of $80 ($65 + $15) per share. This amount would be appropriate in that it reflects her net cash outlay per share ($75 - $60 + $65).

Other Adjustments To The Cost Base Other important adjustments would include the addition of interest and property taxes on holdings of vacant land to the adjusted cost base, the addition of subsequent capital contributions by a shareholder to a corporation to the cost base of the shares, and the requirement that under certain circumstances, forgiveness of debts on property must be deducted from the cost base of that property.

8-30. There are several other such adjustments in ITA 53. You should note, however, that in the case of depreciable property, any deductions taken for CCA do not change the adjusted cost base of the property. Capital gains are determined on the basis of the original capital cost of the asset, not the UCC.

Exercise Eight - 1

Subject: Government Assistance

On January 1 of the current year, Rotan Ltd. acquires a real property at a cost of $5,600,000. Of this amount, $600,000 represents the fair market value of the land. The building is new and will be used 100 percent for non-residential activity. Rotan allocates its cost to a separate Class 1. In order to encourage Rotan's move to this location, the local government has given them $1,500,000 to assist in the acquisition of the building. What is the maximum amount of CCA that Rotan can deduct on this building for the current year?

Exercise Eight - 2

Subject: Superficial Loss

Ms. Nadia Kinski owns 1,000 shares of Bord Ltd. They have an adjusted cost base of $23 per share. On August 20, 2012, she sells all of these shares at $14.50 per share. On August 25, 2012, she acquires 600 shares of Bord Ltd. at a cost of $13.75 per share and is still holding the shares at the end of the year. What are the tax consequences of these transactions?

End of Exercises. Solutions available in Study Guide.

Negative Adjusted Cost Base

8-31. It is possible that sufficient adjustments could be made to an adjusted cost base that its balance will become negative. When this occurs, ITA 40(3) requires that the deficiency be treated as a capital gain and the adjusted cost base of the asset be adjusted to nil. Note that, unlike the situation with recapture of CCA, this would apply even if additions to the cost base prior to the end of the taxation year were sufficient to eliminate the deficit balance.

8-32. Also note that ITA 40(3) is not applicable to most partnership interests. That is, a negative adjusted cost base for a partnership interest does not automatically trigger a capital gain and can be carried forward indefinitely. However, this exemption from ITA 40(3) does not apply to limited partners or certain inactive partners. For more details on this point, see Chapter 18, Partnerships.

GST/HST/PST Considerations

8-33. A business will pay GST, HST, or PST on most of the capital assets that it acquires. As is discussed in more detail in Chapter 21, all or part of the amounts paid can be refunded under certain circumstances. From a technical point of view, all amounts of GST/HST/PST are, at least initially, included in the capital cost of depreciable assets. However, to the extent that these amounts are refunded as input tax credits, they are defined in ITA 248(16) as a form of government assistance and, as a consequence, the refunds are deducted from the capital cost of depreciable assets in the same manner as other government assistance. In effect, this means that GST/HST/PST amounts that are refunded are not included in the capital cost of depreciable assets.

Calculating The Capital Gain Or Loss

8-34. The general formula for determining the amount of a capital gain or loss can be described very simply. The calculation, using assumed data, is as follows:

Proceeds Of Disposition		$4,750
Less - The Aggregate Of:		
Adjusted Cost Base	($3,890)	
Expenses Of Disposition	(560)	(4,450)
Capital Gain (Loss)		$ 300
Inclusion Rate		1/2
Taxable Capital Gain		$ 150

8-35.   If, as in the preceding example, there is a capital gain, one-half of the amount will be treated as a taxable capital gain. The adjective "taxable" is consistently used to indicate the portion of the total gain that will be included in income. Similarly, one-half of a negative amount (a capital loss) resulting from the application of the preceding formula would be treated as an allowable capital loss. The adjective "allowable" is consistently used to indicate the deductible portion of the total amount of the loss. For any readers who have an interest in the special rules related to pre-1972 capital assets, Supplementary Reading No. 1, "Median Rule", is included on the Student CD-ROM.

8-36. In Chapter 1 we noted that ITA 3 specifies that Net Income For Tax Purposes includes the amount, if any, by which taxable capital gains exceed allowable capital losses. At that point, we noted that the use of the phrase "if any" establishes the rule that current year allowable capital losses can only be deducted to the extent that there are current year taxable capital gains.

Detailed Application Of The Rules

Identical Properties

8-37.   A taxpayer can own a group of identical properties that have been acquired over a period of time at different costs. This would arise most commonly with holdings of securities such as common stock in a particular corporation. If part of such a group of assets is disposed of, ITA 47 requires that the adjusted cost base for the assets being disposed of be based on the average cost of the entire group. For any readers who have an interest in the complex legislation dealing with the potential identical properties problem if shares are purchased through stock options and the income benefit deferred, see Supplementary Reading No. 2.

8-38.   The following example illustrates the application of the identical property procedures, other than the procedures applicable to shares acquired through stock options:

Example   An individual has engaged in the following transactions involving the common stock of Gower Company, a Canadian public company:

Year	Number Of Shares Purchased (Sold)	Cost (Proceeds) Per Share	Total Cost (Proceeds)
1991	4,000	$10	$40,000
1993	3,000	12	36,000
1997	(2,000)	(10)	(20,000)
2005	2,500	11	27,500
2010	3,000	10	30,000
2012	(1,500)	(13)	(19,500)

Analysis   The average cost for the first two purchases was $10.86 [($40,000 + $36,000) ÷ (4,000 + 3,000)] and the loss to be recorded on the 1997 sale would be as follows:

Proceeds Of Disposition [(2,000)($10)]	$20,000
Adjusted Cost Base [(2,000)($10.86)]	(21,720)
Capital Loss	($ 1,720)
1997 Inclusion Rate (Not 1/2)	3/4
Allowable Capital Loss	($ 1,290)

This sale would leave the remaining 5,000 shares with a total cost of $54,280 ($76,000 - $21,720). The new average cost for the 2012 sale would be $10.65 [($54,280 + $27,500 + $30,000) ÷ (5,000 + 2,500 + 3,000)]. Given this, the gain on the 2012 sale would be calculated as follows:

Proceeds Of Disposition [(1,500)($13)]	$19,500
Adjusted Cost Base [(1,500)($10.65)]	(15,975)
Capital Gain	$ 3,525
Inclusion Rate	1/2
Taxable Capital Gain	$ 1,763

Exercise Eight - 3

Subject: Identical Properties

Ms. Chantal Montrose makes frequent purchases of the common shares of Comco Inc. During 2011, she purchased 650 shares at $23.50 per share on January 15, and 345 shares at $24.25 per share on March 12. She sold 210 shares on September 15, 2010 at $25.50 per share. On February 14, 2012, she purchases an additional 875 shares at $26.75 per share and, on October 1, 2012, she sells 340 shares at $29.50 per share. Determine Ms. Montrose's taxable capital gains for 2011 and 2012.

End of Exercise. Solution available in Study Guide.

Partial Dispositions

8-39. In those situations where a taxpayer disposes of part of a property, ITA 43 requires that a portion of the total adjusted cost base be allocated to the disposition on a reasonable basis. For example, if a 500 hectare tract of land had an adjusted cost base of $6,000,000 and 200 hectares of the tract were sold, it would be reasonable to allocate $2,400,000, or 40 percent (200 hectares ÷ 500 hectares), of the total adjusted cost base to the land that was sold. If, however, there was some reason that the part of the tract sold had a value that was not proportionate to the total tract, some alternative basis of allocation could be used.

Warranties On Capital Assets

8-40. If a taxpayer disposes of capital property and the proceeds include some payment for a warranty or other contingent obligation, ITA 42 requires that the full proceeds must be used in determining the capital gain. Stated alternatively, no reserve can be established to provide for any future obligations. However, one-half of any outlays related to such contingent obligations that are made in a subsequent year can be deducted as allowable capital losses, but only against taxable capital gains. Any undeducted losses are subject to the carry over provisions described in Chapter 11.

Exercise Eight - 4

Subject: Warranties On Capital Assets

During the taxation year ending December 31, 2011, Vivid Ltd. sells a capital asset with an adjusted cost base of $237,000 for proceeds of $292,000. The Company provides the purchaser with a one year warranty and the Company estimates that it will cost $4,500 to fulfill the warranty provisions. On October 1, 2012, the Company spends $4,800 to fulfill the warranty provisions. Determine the effect of these transactions on Net Income For Tax Purposes for 2011 and 2012.

End of Exercise. Solution available in Study Guide.

Capital Gains Reserves

General Principles

8-41. In some cases, a capital asset disposition may involve debt as a component of the proceeds of disposition. For example, assume Mr. Filoso sold a piece of land for a capital gain and collected only 10 percent of the total proceeds in the year of sale. In such cases, it would seem reasonable to allow him to defer recognition of a part of the capital gain. This deferral can be accomplished through the establishment of a capital gains reserve.

8-42. The general idea is that a reserve can be deducted from the total gain when not all of the proceeds are receivable in the year of the sale. The reserve would reflect the portion of the gain that is contained in the uncollected proceeds. As with other reserves, this amount must be added back to the following year's income, with a new reserve deducted to reflect any remaining uncollected proceeds. Note that the reserve is based solely on the principal amount of the debt. Accrued interest is not included in the reserve calculations.

8-43. In order to use this elective provision, individuals must file a Form T2017. Other taxpayers are not required to submit this form and can simply make this election in their return of income.

8-44. At one point in time, the deductible reserve was simply based on the portion of the proceeds of disposition that were not yet received. If a taxpayer collected only 10 percent of the proceeds, the reserve could be equal to 90 percent of the gain. It appears that this provision was being used for what the government viewed as excessive deferrals and, as a consequence, ITA 40(1)(a)(iii) limits the reserve to the lesser of two amounts.

8-45. The first of these two amounts is referred to in the *Act* as a "reasonable amount". While the *Act* does not provide a formula for this "reasonable amount", it refers to amounts that are payable after the end of the taxation year. This can be expressed as follows:

$$\bullet \left[\begin{array}{c} \text{Total} \\ \text{Gain} \end{array}\right] \left[\frac{\text{Proceeds Not Receivable Until After End Of Current Taxation Year}}{\text{Total Proceeds Of Disposition}}\right]$$

8-46. The second amount, in effect, creates a formula whereby the maximum reserve must decline by at least 20 percent each year, going from 80 percent of the proceeds in the year of disposition to nil at the end of the fourth year after the disposition. The formula is as follows:

$$\bullet \text{ [Total Gain][20\%] [4 - (Number of Preceding Taxation Years Ending After The Disposition]}$$

8-47. Under this formula, a minimum of 20 percent of the gain must be recognized in the year of the sale and each of the following four years. If the proceeds are collected faster than 20 percent per year, the reserve will be based on the actual uncollected proceeds as per the formula in Paragraph 8-45.

8-48. While this reserve is similar to the ITA 20(1)(n) reserve for uncollected amounts described in Chapter 6, the circumstances when the reserves can be used differ as follows:.

ITA 20(1)(n) Reserve   Used when there is a sale of an inventory item and part of the proceeds are not due until at least two years after the end of the current taxation year. In addition, this provision restricts the reserve to three years. However, there is no restriction on the amount of the reserve during the years that it is available.

ITA 40(1)(a)(iii) Reserve   Used when there is a capital asset disposition and all or part of the proceeds are not due until after the end of the current taxation year. In contrast to the reserve being restricted to three years under the provisions of ITA 20(1)(n), ITA 40(1)(a)(iii) allows the reserve to be used for a maximum of five years.

Example - Outstanding Balance Greater Than Formula Limit

8-49.   Assume that during 2012, Mr. Filoso sold a piece of land with an adjusted cost base of $340,000, for total proceeds of $1,000,000, resulting in a capital gain of $660,000 ($1,000,000 - $340,000) and a taxable capital gain of $330,000 [(1/2)($660,000)].   He received only $100,000 of the total amount in cash in 2012 and accepted a $900,000 note payable for the balance.   The note is payable at the rate of $100,000 per year beginning in 2013.   Interest charged at 5 percent of the outstanding balance is also paid annually.

8-50.   As he collected only 10 percent of the total proceeds, the reserve would be 90 percent under the "reasonable amount" component of ITA 40(1)(a)(iii).   As a result, the maximum reserve will be based on the second component of the formula which limits the reserve in the first year to 80 percent of the gain.   The maximum reserve would be $528,000, the lesser of:

- [($660,000)($900,000 ÷ $1,000,000)] $594,000 (Reserve)
- [($660,000)(20%)(4 - 0)] $528,000 (Reserve)

8-51.   Applying this formula, the taxable capital gain that will be recognized in 2012 is $66,000 [(1/2)($660,000 - $528,000)].   Note that, despite the fact that Mr. Filoso has only collected 10 percent of the proceeds ($100,000 ÷ $1,000,000), the application of the formula requires that he recognize 20 percent ($66,000 ÷ $330,000) of the total gain.

8-52.   In 2013, the $528,000 reserve would have to be added back to income.   The new reserve for 2013 would be $396,000, the lesser of:

- [($660,000)($800,000 ÷ $1,000,000)] $528,000 (Reserve)
- [($660,000)(20%)(4 - 1)] $396,000 (Reserve)

8-53.   Adding back the previous year's reserve of $528,000, and deducting the new maximum reserve of $396,000, gives a 2013 capital gain of $132,000.   This would result in a net addition to 2013 income of $66,000 [(1/2)($528,000 - $396,000)], or 20 percent of the $330,000 taxable capital gain.

8-54.   Based on similar calculations, the maximum reserve in 2014 would be $264,000. This would decline to $132,000 in 2015 and, at the end of 2016, no reserve would be available.   This would result in $66,000 [(1/2)($132,000)] being added to income each year.   The entire $330,000 of the taxable capital gain will have been included in income by the end of 2016.   This is despite the fact that, at the end of this five year period, $500,000 of the initial proceeds remains uncollected.

Example - Outstanding Balance Less Than Formula Limit

8-55.   In the preceding example, collections of cash were less than 20 percent in all years under consideration.   As a result, the application of ITA 40(1)(a)(iii) resulted in the recognition of 20 percent of the gain in each year.

8-56.   Situations in which the uncollected portion of the proceeds is greater than the formula limit will result in more than 20 percent of the gain being taxed in a year.   As an illustration of this possibility, assume that in the Paragraph 8-49 example, Mr. Filoso collected $250,000 in the year of the disposition, and that the required payments were $75,000 per year for the following ten years.

8-57.   Based on this information, the maximum reserve for 2012 would be $495,000, the lesser of:

- [($660,000)($750,000 ÷ $1,000,000)] $495,000 (Reserve)
- [($660,000)(20%)(4 - 0)] $528,000 (Reserve)

8-58.   This means that a taxable capital gain of $82,500 [(1/2)($660,000 - $495,000)] would be recognized in 2012.

8-59.   In 2013, the $495,000 reserve would be added back to income.   The new reserve for 2013 would be $396,000, the lesser of:

- [($660,000)($675,000 ÷ $1,000,000)] $445,500 (Reserve)
- [($660,000)(20%)(4 - 1)] $396,000 (Reserve)

8-60.   This results in the recognition of a $49,500 [(1/2)($495,000 - $396,000)] taxable capital gain in 2013. At this point, the minimum 20 percent per year recognition requirement has become the determining factor in calculating the capital gain to be included in income. As a consequence, the amount to be included in income in the years 2014, 2015, and 2016 would be as presented in Paragraph 8-54.

Exercise Eight - 5

Subject: Capital Gains Reserves

During December 2011, Mr. Gerry Goodson sells a capital property with an adjusted cost base of $293,000 for proceeds of disposition of $382,000. Selling costs total $17,200. In the year of sale, he receives $82,000 in cash, along with the purchaser's note for the balance of the proceeds. The note is to be repaid at the rate of $60,000 per year beginning in 2012. He receives the 2012 payment in full. Assume that Mr. Goodson deducts the maximum capital gains reserves. Determine his taxable capital gain for 2011 and 2012.

End of Exercise. Solution available in Study Guide.

Bad Debts On Sales Of Capital Property

8-61.   When an amount receivable results from the disposition of a capital property, the possibility arises that some of the proceeds of disposition will have to be written off as a bad debt. When this occurs, ITA 50(1) allows the seller to elect to have disposed of the receivable and immediately reacquired it at a proceeds and cost of nil. Consider the following:

Example   During 2012, a capital property with a cost of $500,000 is sold for $510,000. The proceeds are made up of $360,000 in cash, plus the purchaser's note for $150,000.

8-62.   If the vendor of the capital property does not choose to deduct a capital gains reserve for the uncollected amount, a taxable capital gain of $5,000 [(1/2)($510,000 - $500,000)] would be recognized in 2012. If, during 2012, the note received from the purchaser turns out to be uncollectible, the deemed disposition and reacquisition would result in an allowable capital loss of $75,000 [(1/2)($150,000)], $70,000 more than offsetting the $5,000 taxable capital gain on the disposition. If, at a later point in time, some amount of debt was recovered, any excess over the deemed nil proceeds would be considered a capital gain. Note, however, that the excess allowable capital loss of $70,000 can only be deducted against any taxable capital gains that are realized in 2012.

Exercise Eight - 6

Subject: Bad Debts From Dispositions Of Capital Property

During 2011, a capital property with an adjusted cost base of $125,000 is sold for $110,000. The proceeds of disposition are made up of $75,000 in cash, plus the purchaser's one-year note for $35,000. In 2012, the note proves to be uncollectible. What are the tax consequences of these events in 2011 and in 2012?

End of Exercise. Solution available in Study Guide.

Special Rule For Sales Of Real Property
The Problem
8-63.   Real property, a.k.a. real estate, is land and all appurtenances to it, such as buildings. (Although crops and mineral rights would also be included, coverage of these types of assets is beyond the scope of this material.) As only the building component qualifies for CCA deductions, it is always necessary to separate these two components. As separate market prices for the two components do not usually exist, this separation requires the use of estimates. As you are likely aware, estimates involve judgment and can vary significantly from expert to expert.

8-64.   The problem is that when there is a disposal of real property, the amounts of the proceeds that are allocated to the two components have a significant impact on any resulting Taxable Income. Larger amounts allocated to the land will create or increase a capital gain, only one-half of which is taxable. If this results in smaller amounts being allocated to the building, this could result in a fully deductible terminal loss.

Example   Martin Ltd. has only one Class 1 building. During 2012, the Company disposes of the building and replaces it with a leased property. The following information relates to this disposition:

Proceeds Of Disposition (Estimated Fair Market Value):	
Land	$300,000
Building	110,000
Total Proceeds Of Disposition	$410,000

Adjusted Cost Base Of Land	$200,000
Original Cost Of Building	175,000
UCC Class 1	150,000

8-65.   In the absence of a special rule, there would be a $50,000 taxable capital gain on the land [(1/2)($300,000 - $200,000)]. There would also be a $40,000 ($150,000 - $110,000) terminal loss on the building. The inclusion in Net Income For Tax Purposes would be $10,000 ($50,000 - $40,000).

8-66.   If, for example, $30,000 of the proceeds were shifted from the building to the land, the result would be a $15,000 increase in the capital gain, accompanied by a $30,000 increase in the terminal loss on the building. Clearly, there is an incentive to maximize the amount of the proceeds of disposition that is allocated to the land.

The Solution
8-67.   Because of this incentive, ITA 13(21.1)(a) contains a provision that can serve to limit the amount of any terminal loss that might arise on the disposition of real property. Using the example from Paragraph 8-64, this provision requires a deemed proceeds of disposition for the building to be determined as follows:

The Lesser Of:

- The FMV of the land and building $410,000
    Reduced By The Lesser Of:
    - The ACB of the land = $200,000
    - The FMV of the land = $300,000   (200,000) $210,000

- The Greater Of:
    - The FMV of the building = $110,000
    - The Lesser Of:
        The cost of the building = $175,000
        The UCC of the building = $150,000 $150,000

8-68.   In this case, the proceeds that would be allocated to the building would be $150,000, leaving $260,000 ($410,000 - $150,000) to be allocated to the land. The net result is that the

$40,000 terminal loss is completely eliminated and the capital gain is reduced by a corresponding amount to $60,000 ($260,000 - $200,000). The taxable amount of $30,000 [($60,000)(1/2)] would be included in the taxpayer's income instead of the $10,000 that would have been recorded in the absence of the special rule in ITA 13(21.1).

8-69. The effect of ITA 13(21.1)(a) on the results is summarized in the following table:

	Results Without ITA 13(21.1)(a)	Results With ITA 13(21.1)(a)
Taxable Capital Gain	$50,000	$30,000
Terminal Loss	(40,000)	Nil
Net Inclusion	$10,000	$30,000

8-70. If the potential capital gain had been less than the potential terminal loss, the terminal loss would have been reduced by the amount of the potential capital gain and the capital gain would have been eliminated. You might also note that this special rule only affects the vendor and has no tax consequences for the purchaser.

Exercise Eight - 7

Subject: Building Dispositions

On February 24, 2012, Drucker Ltd. disposed of real property for total proceeds of $1,250,000. Information with respect to this property is as follows:

Original cost of building	$930,000
UCC Class 1 (Building - only asset in class)	615,000
Fair market value of building on February 24, 2012	500,000
Adjusted cost base of land	425,000
Fair market value of land on February 24, 2012	750,000

Determine the tax consequences of this disposition assuming (1) there is no special rule for building dispositions, and (2) the ITA 13(21.1) special rule for building dispositions applies.

End of Exercise. Solution available in Study Guide.

Provisions For Special Assets

Principal Residence

Principal Residence Defined

8-71. For many individuals resident in Canada, one of the most attractive features of our tax system is the fact that, in general, capital gains arising on the disposition of a principal residence can be received free of tax. Since 1982, only one taxpayer in a family unit can designate a property as a principal residence for a particular year. For these purposes, a family unit includes a spouse or common-law partner, as well as children unless they are married or in a common-law partnership, or over 18 during the year. Special rules can apply to pre-1982 residences. Coverage of these rules can be found in Supplementary Reading No. 3, Election For Pre-1982 Residences.

8-72. ITA 54 defines a principal residence as any accommodation owned by the taxpayer that was ordinarily inhabited in the year by the taxpayer, his spouse, a former spouse, or a child, and is designated by the taxpayer as a principal residence. The definition notes that this would include land up to a limit of one-half hectare as well as a building. If the property includes additional land, it will be subject to capital gains taxation unless the taxpayer can demonstrate that the additional land was necessary for the use and enjoyment of the property.

8-73.   If a taxpayer owns more than one property that might qualify as a residence, only one property can be designated as a principal residence in any given year. From an administrative point of view, however, the CRA does not require that such a designation be made from year to year. Rather, the filing of form T2091, *Designation Of A Property As A Principal Residence By An Individual*, is generally only required when a property is disposed of, and a taxable capital gain remains after applying the reduction formula described in the following material. From an administrative point of view, this requirement is often ignored, reflecting its irrelevance in situations where the family has only one property that could be designated as a principal residence.

Gain Reduction Formula

8-74.   Technically speaking, capital gains on a principal residence are taxable. However, ITA 40(2)(b) provides a formula for reducing such gains. The formula calculates the taxable portion, which is based on the relationship between the number of years since 1971 that the property has been designated a principal residence and the number of years since 1971 that the taxpayer has owned the property. It is as follows:

$$A - \left[A \times \frac{B}{C} \right] - D, \text{ where}$$

A   is the total capital gain on the disposition of the principal residence;
B   is 1 plus the number of years since 1971 the property is designated as the taxpayer's principal residence (but cannot be greater than the denominator C);
C   is the number of years since 1971 that the taxpayer has owned the property;
D   relates to the 1994 capital gains election (not of general interest to users of this text).

8-75.   The formula in Paragraph 8-74 is applied to any capital gain resulting from the disposition of a principal residence in order to determine the amount that will be subject to taxation. For example, assume a property was purchased in 2004 and was sold in 2012 for an amount that resulted in a capital gain of $100,000. If it was designated as a principal residence for six of the nine years of ownership, the calculation of the taxable portion of the capital gain would be as follows:

$$\left[\$100,000 - (\$100,000)\left(\frac{1+6}{9}\right) \right] \left[\frac{1}{2} \right] = \$11,111$$

8-76.   If a taxpayer has only a single property that could qualify as a principal residence, that property can be designated as the principal residence for all years owned. In such situations, the use of this formula will then completely eliminate any capital gains on the disposition of that property.

8-77.   When only one residence is involved in each year, the plus one in the B component of the formula is not relevant. However, if a taxpayer sells one home and acquires another in a single year, the plus one becomes important.

Example   During 2007, Mr. Fodor acquires a principal residence at a cost of $130,000. The residence is sold in 2010 for $150,000. A replacement residence is acquired in 2010 at a cost of $170,000. In 2012, the second residence is sold for $200,000, with Mr. Fodor moving to an apartment.

Analysis   During 2010, Mr. Fodor owns two properties, only one of which can be designated as a principal residence for that year. If there was no extra year in the numerator of the reduction formula (component B), Mr. Fodor would be taxed on a portion of one of the gains. For example, assume Mr. Fodor allocates the three years 2007 through 2009 to the first property and the three years 2010 through 2012 to the second. All of the $30,000 gain on the second property would be eliminated. Since the first property was sold in 2010, the denominator in the reduction formula (component C) is 4 (2007 to 2010). If the plus one was not in the numerator, only three-quarters of the $20,000 gain would be eliminated, leaving a capital gain of

$5,000 [$20,000 - ($20,000)(3 ÷ 4)]. However, with the addition of the plus one to the years in the numerator of the reduction formula, the fraction on the first property becomes four-fourths, and there is no taxable capital gain.

Exercise Eight - 8

Subject: Sale Of Principal Residence

Mr. Norm Craft purchases his first home in 2002 at a cost of $89,000. In 2007, this home is sold for $109,500 and a second home is purchased for $152,000. In 2011, this second home is sold for $178,000 and Mr. Craft moves to a rental property. Determine the minimum tax consequences of the two property sales.

Exercise Eight - 9

Subject: Sale Of Principal Residence

Ms. Jan Sadat owns a house in Ottawa, as well as a cottage in Westport. She purchased the house in 2001 for $126,000. The cottage was gifted to her in 2004 by her parents. At the time of the gift, the fair market value of the cottage was $85,000. During June, 2012, both properties are sold, the house for $198,000 and the cottage for $143,500. She has lived in the Ottawa house during the year, but has spent her summers in the Westport cottage. Determine the minimum capital gain that she must report on the 2012 sale of the two properties.

End of Exercises. Solutions available in Study Guide.

Non-Residential Usage

8-78. A complication arises when a taxpayer either begins to rent a part of his principal residence, or begins to use it for non-residential purposes (e.g., a self-employed individual who maintains an office at home). Under the general rules for capital assets, this would be a partial disposition of the property, potentially resulting in a capital gain.

8-79. However, the CRA has indicated that it will not apply the partial disposition rules so long as the income use is ancillary to the main use as a principal residence, there is no structural change to the property, and no capital cost allowance is claimed. Given this, the standard tax planning advice to taxpayers who use a portion of their principal residence for business purposes is not to deduct CCA on this property.

Farm Properties

8-80. Many farmers have a principal residence that is a part of their farm property. This means that when the farm is sold, the farmer's principal residence will generally be included in the package that is sold. In this situation, ITA 40(2)(c) identifies two approaches that can be used in this situation.

8-81. The first approach requires that the land be divided into two components — the portion used for farming and the portion used for the use and enjoyment of the principal residence. Separate capital gains are calculated for each, with the gain on the principal residence portion being eligible for the principal residence reduction. Note that the ITA 54 definition of principal residence indicates that, as a general guideline, the land required for the use and enjoyment of the principal residence is limited to one-half hectare (i.e., 1.25 acres).

8-82. As an alternative, a farmer can elect to be taxed on the capital gain from the sale of the entire property, reduced by a fixed amount of $1,000, plus an additional $1,000 per year for every year for which the property was a principal residence.

Personal Use Property

Definition

8-83.   ITA 54 defines personal use property as any property that is owned by the taxpayer and used primarily for his personal use or enjoyment, or for the personal use or enjoyment of one or more individuals related to the taxpayer. In non-technical terms, we are talking about any significant asset owned by a taxpayer that is not used for earning business or property income. This would include personal use automobiles, principal residences, vacation homes, boats, furniture, and many other items.

Capital Gains And Losses

8-84.   In general, gains on the disposition of personal use property are taxed in the same manner as gains on other capital assets. However, there is an important difference with respect to losses. In general, losses on such property are not deductible. The reason for this is that most types of personal use property depreciate over time and to allow capital losses on the property to be deductible would, in effect, permit a write-off of the cost of normal wear and tear. As explained later, beginning in Paragraph 8-88, the exception to this is losses on listed personal property that can be deducted on a restricted basis.

8-85.   To simplify the enforcement of capital gains taxation on personal use property, ITA 46(1) provides a $1,000 floor rule. In using this rule to calculate capital gains on personal use property, the proceeds are deemed to be the greater of $1,000 and the actual proceeds. In a similar fashion, the adjusted cost base is deemed to be the greater of $1,000 and the actual adjusted cost base. This rule is illustrated in the following example involving dispositions of personal use property in four different cases:

Capital Gains (Losses) On Personal Use Property

	Case A	Case B	Case C	Case D
Proceeds Of Disposition (POD)	$300	$850	$ 500	$1,500
Adjusted Cost Base (ACB)	800	400	1,300	900
Using the $1,000 floor rule results in the following capital gain or loss:				
Greater Of Actual POD Or $1,000	$1,000	$1,000	$1,000	$1,500
Greater Of ACB Or $1,000	(1,000)	(1,000)	(1,300)	(1,000)
Gain (Non-Deductible Loss)	Nil	Nil	($ 300)	$ 500

8-86.   In situations where a taxpayer disposes of a part of an item of personal use property while retaining the remainder, the taxpayer must establish the ratio of the adjusted cost base of the part disposed of, to the total adjusted cost base of the property. Then, in applying the $1,000 floor rule, the adjusted cost base is deemed to be the greater of the portion of the adjusted cost base associated with the part disposed of, or the same portion of $1,000. In the same fashion, the proceeds would be deemed to be the greater of the actual proceeds and the appropriate portion of $1,000.

8-87.   The government perceived an abuse of this $1,000 floor rule in art donation schemes where individuals would acquire art in bulk for nominal amounts ($10 each) and would then donate them immediately to various educational institutions at values apparently determined by questionable appraisers ($1,000 or less). The capital gains would be exempt because of the $1,000 floor rule, but the individuals would receive charitable donation receipts of $1,000. As a result, ITA 46(5) excludes certain property from the $1,000 rule when it is donated as part of a scheme to receive donation receipts of artificially high value.

Listed Personal Property

8-88.   Listed personal property consists of certain specified items of personal use property. The specified items are found in ITA 54 as follows:

(i)   print, etching, drawing, painting, sculpture, or other similar work of art,

(ii)   jewelry,

(iii)   rare folio, rare manuscript, or rare book,

(iv)   stamp, or

(v)   coin.

8-89.   In general, listed personal property is subject to the same capital gains rules as would apply to other personal use property. This would include the applicability of the $1,000 floor rule. However, there is one very important difference. While any losses on personal use property cannot be deducted, allowable capital losses on listed personal property can be deducted subject to a significant restriction.

8-90.   The restriction is that allowable capital losses on listed personal property can only be deducted against taxable capital gains on listed personal property. In the absence of such taxable capital gains, the listed personal property losses cannot be deducted. However, any undeducted losses are subject to the carry over provisions described in Chapter 11.

Exercise Eight - 10

Subject: Personal Use Property

During the current year, Martha Steward disposes of several items. The proceeds of disposition and the adjusted cost base of the various items are as follows:

	Adjusted Cost Base	Proceeds Of Disposition
Sailboat	$43,000	$68,000
Oil Painting	200	25,000
Personal Automobile	33,000	18,000
Diamond Necklace	46,000	23,000

What is the net tax consequence of these dispositions?

End of Exercise.   Solution available in Study Guide.

Gains And Losses On Foreign Currency

Introduction

8-91.   As foreign currency exchange rates are constantly fluctuating, any taxpayer who engages in foreign currency transactions is certain to experience gains and losses that relate to these fluctuations. With respect to dealing with the tax aspects of foreign currency transactions, there are two basic issues:

Income Vs. Capital Transactions   If a foreign exchange gain or loss arises as the result of an income transaction (i.e., buying or selling goods or services with the amounts denominated in foreign currency), the full amount will be taxable or deductible. In contrast, if a foreign exchange gain or loss arises as the result of a capital transaction (i.e., purchase of, sale of, or financing of, a capital asset), only one-half of the amount will be taxable or deductible.

Regular Vs. Foreign Currency Capital Gains   The issue here is whether the gain on a particular capital transaction is a regular capital gain as defined in ITA 39(1) or, alternatively, a "capital gain or loss in respect of foreign currencies" as described in ITA 39(2). While this is not a major issue, for individuals, the first $200 of the foreign currency gains for the year under ITA 39(2) can be excluded from income.

Foreign Currency Income Transactions

8-92.   Foreign currency income transactions usually result in exchange gains and losses. For example, if an enterprise acquires goods in the U.S. for US$5,000 at a point in time when US$1.00 = C$1.00, no gain or loss would arise if the goods were paid for immediately. However, if the goods are paid for at a later point in time when US$1.00 = C$1.02, there would be an exchange loss of C$100 [(US$5,000)(C$1.00 - C$1.02)]. The issue here is whether the loss should be recognized only when the payable is settled or, alternatively, accrued if a Balance Sheet date occurs before the payment.

8-93.   IT-95R indicates that, with respect to income transactions, the taxpayer can use any method that is in accordance with generally accepted accounting principles (GAAP). Under Canadian GAAP, current payables and receivables must be recorded at current rates of exchange as at each Balance Sheet date. No alternative method is acceptable.

8-94.   The resulting changes in value must be recorded as gains or losses at the time they are measured. As this is the only acceptable method under Canadian GAAP, this would appear to require that foreign exchange gains and losses on income transactions be taken into income on an accrual basis, rather than waiting until the foreign exchange balance is settled in Canadian dollars.

Capital Transactions Involving Foreign Currency Financing

8-95.   Purchases or sales of capital assets may be financed with long-term payables or receivables that are denominated in a foreign currency. In such situations, the foreign exchange gains and losses on the payables or receivables are considered to be capital gains or losses.

8-96.   The accounting rules here are consistent with those applicable to income transactions. That is, changes in the value of payables and receivables are recognized and taken into income as of each Balance Sheet date.

8-97.   It is somewhat surprising that the CRA does not permit this approach. While it does not address the issue of gains and losses on long-term receivables, Paragraph 13 of IT-95R states that:

> The Department considers that a taxpayer has "made a gain" or "sustained a loss" in a foreign currency … resulting in the application of subsection 39(2) …
>
> (c) at the time of repayment of part or all of a capital debt obligation.

8-98.   This means that, if a Canadian company has used long-term foreign currency debt to finance capital assets, no exchange gain or loss will be included in the determination of Net Income For Tax Purposes until the debt matures and is paid off in Canadian dollars. This may result in significant differences between accounting Net Income and Net Income For Tax Purposes.

Foreign Currency Purchase And Sale Of Securities

8-99.   Individuals will most commonly encounter foreign exchange gains or losses when they are involved in purchasing or selling securities with settlement amounts denominated in a foreign currency. For purposes of distinguishing between ordinary capital gains and those that can be classified under ITA 39(2) as being in respect of foreign currencies, IT-95R provides the following examples of the time when the Department considers a transaction resulting in the application of ITA 39(2) to have taken place:

(a) At the time of conversion of funds in a foreign currency into another foreign currency or into Canadian dollars.

(b) At the time funds in a foreign currency are used to make a purchase or a payment (in such a case the gain or loss would be the difference between the value of the foreign currency expressed in Canadian dollars when it arose and its value expressed in Canadian dollars when the purchase or payment was made).

8-100.   An example will serve to illustrate this approach:

Example   On August 1, 2009, Mr. Conrad White uses $172,000 to open a British pound (£) account with his broker. Assume that at this time, £1 = $1.72, so that his $172,000 is converted to £100,000.

On December 31, 2009, he uses his entire British pound balance to acquire 10,000 shares in a British company, Underling Ltd. at a cost of £10 per share. At this time, £1 = $1.74. On July 1, 2012, the shares are sold for £21 per share. On this date, £1 = $1.55, and all of the proceeds from the sale are immediately converted into $325,500 [(10,000)(£21)($1.55)] Canadian dollars.

Analysis - Purchase   As a result of his December 31, 2009 purchase, he will have an exchange gain of $2,000 [(£100,000)($1.74 - $1.72)]. As this qualifies as an ITA 39(2) foreign currency capital gain (see Paragraph 8-99), Mr. White will only include $900 [(1/2)($2,000 - $200)] of this in his Net Income For Tax Purposes.

Analysis - Sale   When he sells the shares for £21 per share, his total capital gain is $151,500 [(£210,000)($1.55) - (£100,000)($1.74)]. This entire amount would be treated as an ITA 39(1) (regular) capital gain and would not be eligible for the $200 exclusion that is available to individuals. This result is not influenced by the conversion of the British currency into Canadian dollars. However, if the £210,000 proceeds were not converted and, at a later point in time, were converted into Canadian dollars at a rate other than £1 = $1.55, an ITA 39(2) foreign currency capital gain or loss would arise.

8-101.   Without going into detail, these procedures are not consistent with GAAP or reasonable economic analysis. Under GAAP, no gain would be recognized at the time of the share purchase. Because of this, there would be a gain at the time of sale of $153,500 [(£210,000)($1.55) - (£100,000)($1.72)].

Funds On Deposit

8-102.   IT-95R also notes that foreign currency funds on deposit are not considered to be disposed of until they are converted into another currency, or are used to purchase a negotiable instrument or some other asset. This means that foreign funds on deposit may be moved from one form of deposit to another, as long as such funds can continue to be viewed as "on deposit".

Exercise Eight - 11

Subject: Foreign Currency Gains And Losses

On January 5, 2011, Mr. Michel Pratt purchases 35,000 Trinidad/Tobago dollars (TT$) at a rate of TT$1 = C$0.18. Using TT$30,600 of these funds, on June 5, 2011, he acquires 450 shares of a Trinidadian company, Matim Inc., at a price of TT$68 per share. At this time, TT$1 = C$0.20. During September, 2012, the shares are sold for TT$96 per share. The Trinidad/Tobago dollars are immediately converted into Canadian dollars at a rate of TT$1 = C$0.16. What amounts will be included in Mr. Pratt's 2011 and 2012 Net Income For Tax Purposes as a result of these transactions?

End of Exercise. Solution available in Study Guide.

Options

8-103.   The term "option" would include stock rights, warrants, options to purchase capital assets, as well as stock options granted to executives and other employees (the special rules related to options granted to employees were covered in Chapter 3). From the point of view of the taxpayer acquiring these options, they are treated as capital property. The tax consequences related to such options will vary depending on future events:

- If they are sold before their expiry date, a capital gain or loss will usually arise.

- If they are exercised, the cost of acquiring the options will be added to the adjusted cost base of the assets acquired.

- If the options expire before they are either sold or exercised, a capital loss equal to the cost of the options will be incurred.

8-104.   From the point of view of the issuer of the option, any proceeds from the sale of the option will usually be treated as a capital gain at the time the option is issued. If the holder decides to exercise the option, the sale price of the option becomes part of the proceeds of disposition to the issuer and the original gain on the sale of the option is eliminated. If the sale of the option occurs in a different taxation year than the exercise of the option, the issuer is permitted to file an amended return for the year of sale.

8-105.   An example will serve to illustrate the preceding rules.

> **Example**   John Powers has a capital property with an adjusted cost base of $250,000. During 2012, he sells an option on this property to Sarah Myers for $18,000. This option allows her to acquire the capital property for $300,000 at any time prior to December 31, 2015.

> **Analysis - Option Expires**   Mr. Powers, as a result of selling the option in 2012, will have to record a taxable capital gain of $9,000 [(1/2)($18,000)] in that year. If the option expires, there will be no further tax consequences to Mr. Powers as he has already recognized the $9,000 taxable capital gain in 2012. For Ms. Myers, the expiry of the option will allow her to recognize an allowable capital loss of $9,000.

> **Analysis - Option Is Exercised**   If the option is exercised in 2015, Mr. Powers can file an amended return for 2012, removing the capital gain that was recognized in that year. However, if he does, he will have to include the $18,000 in the proceeds of disposition from the sale of the asset, thereby recording a capital gain of $68,000 ($18,000 + $300,000 - $250,000). Ms. Myers will have acquired the capital property at a cost of $318,000 ($300,000 + $18,000).

8-106.   There are three exceptions to the preceding general rules for vendors of options. The first of these is an exemption from taxation on the proceeds of any options sold on a taxpayer's principal residence.

8-107.   The second involves options sold by a corporation on its capital stock or debt securities. In this situation, the corporation will not be taxed on the proceeds at the time the options are sold. Rather, the proceeds will be treated as part of the consideration for the securities issued if the options are exercised. However, if the options expire without being exercised, the corporation will have a capital gain equal to the amount of the proceeds.

8-108.   The third exception relates to options granted by a trust to acquire units of the trust that are to be issued by the trust.

Deemed Dispositions - Change In Use

General Rules

Deemed Disposition

8-109.   The Glossary to this text (see the Study Guide) defines deeming rules and deemed disposition as follows:

> **Deeming Rules**   Rules that are used to require that an item or event be given a treatment for tax purposes that is not consistent with the actual nature of the item or event.

> **Deemed Disposition**   A requirement to assume that a disposition has taken place when, in fact, a disposition transaction has not occurred.

8-110.   Such rules are fairly common in the *Income Tax Act* and are applied in a wide variety of situations. In this Chapter 8, we will deal with the deemed dispositions that occur when there is a change in use, and the deemed dispositions that occur when a taxpayer departs from Canada. In Chapter 9, we will provide coverage of the deemed dispositions that occur when an individual dies.

8-111.   You should also note that, since no real proceeds of disposition are involved in deemed dispositions, we will also need a deemed proceeds of disposition. The most common situation here is that the proceeds of disposition will be based on fair market values.

Change In Use

8-112.   The basic idea here is that when a property used to produce income is converted to some other purpose or, alternatively, when a property that was acquired for some other purpose becomes an income producing property, ITA 13(7) requires that the change be treated as a deemed disposition combined with a simultaneous deemed reacquisition.

8-113.   Different rules apply, depending on whether the change is from business to personal use or, alternatively, from personal to business use. We will give separate attention to each of these changes. In addition, we will cover some special change in use rules that apply to principal residences and to automobiles that are owned by an individual.

Business To Personal Use

8-114.   This situation is straightforward. If the conversion is from business to personal use, the deemed proceeds will be equal to fair market value, with the transferor recognizing a capital gain, recapture, or terminal loss in the usual manner. The fair market value will also be used as the acquisition cost of the personal use asset.

Personal To Business Use

8-115.   If a personal use asset is converted to an income producing asset, the rules vary depending on the relationship between the fair market value of the asset and its cost.

> **Fair Market Value Less Than Cost**   In this case, the fair market value will serve as both the proceeds of the deemed disposition and as the capital cost of the asset reacquired.

> **Fair Market Value Greater Than Cost**   In this case, the fair market value will serve as the proceeds of the deemed disposition, resulting in the recognition of a capital gain. However, under ITA 13(7)(b), the capital cost of the reacquired asset for CCA purposes will be equal to its cost, plus one-half of the difference between its cost and its fair market value. While this value will be used for determining CCA and recapture amounts, for purposes of determining the capital gain on the deemed disposition, the capital cost will be deemed to be the full fair market value of the asset.

8-116.   There is a reason for this different rule in situations where the fair market value exceeds the cost. It reflects the fact that only one-half of the capital gain that arises on such a deemed disposition will be subject to tax. If the reacquisition was recorded at the full fair market value of the asset, 100 percent of the capital gain amount could be deducted as CCA. A simple example will serve to illustrate this problem.

> **Example**   Shirley Malone owns a pleasure boat which cost $100,000. She is changing its use to a charter boat and, at the time of the change, the fair market value of the boat is $150,000.

> **Analysis**   Shirley's deemed proceeds of disposition will be $150,000, resulting in a capital gain of $50,000. This will increase her Net Income For Tax Purposes by one-half of this amount or $25,000.

For capital gains purposes, the deemed Capital Cost of the boat to the charter operation will also be $150,000. This value will be used in the determination of any capital gain that might arise on a future disposition of the sailboat.

If the $150,000 was also used as the basis for CCA, Shirley would be able to deduct 100 percent of the $50,000 increase in value that occurred while she owned the boat for personal use. This would not be an equitable result as Shirley only paid taxes on $25,000 of this increase. Given this, in situations where there is a gain on the change in use, the capital cost addition for CCA purposes will be limited to the cost of the asset, plus one-half of the gain (the taxable portion of the capital gain). This means that for the purpose of determining CCA or recapture, Shirley's UCC balance will be $125,000 [$100,000 + (1/2)($150,000 - $100,000)].

Example - Change In Use

8-117.   The following example will serve to illustrate the procedures associated with changes in use.

Example On January 1, 2011, Ms. Barker, a professional accountant, acquires a building at a cost of $500,000, with $400,000 allocated to the building and $100,000 allocated to the land. During the entire year, 20 percent of the floor space was used for her accounting practice, while the remainder was used as her principal residence.

On January 1, 2012, an additional 30 percent of the total floor space was converted to business use. On this date, the fair market value of the real property had increased to $620,000, with $480,000 allocated to the building and $140,000 allocated to the land.

On January 1, 2013, the entire building was converted to residential use as Ms. Barker's accounting practice had grown to the point where it had to move to more extensive facilities. On this date, the fair market value had increased to $700,000, with $550,000 allocated to the building and $150,000 allocated to the land.

Analysis   In using this example, we will focus only on the determination of CCA and any tax consequences associated with the changes in use. We will assume that net rental revenues are adequate to claim maximum CCA.

2011 CCA Calculation   The maximum 2011 CCA would be calculated as follows:

January 1, 2011 UCC	Nil
Add: Cost Of Acquiring Business Portion [(20%)($500,000 - $100,000)]	$80,000
Deduct: One-Half Net Additions [(1/2)($80,000)]	(40,000)
Base Amount For CCA Claim	$40,000
Deduct: CCA For The Year [(4%)($40,000)]	(1,600)
Add: One-Half Net Additions	40,000
January 1, 2012 UCC (For 20 Percent Of The Building)	$78,400

2012 Tax Consequences   The change in use would trigger capital gains on the land and building as follows:

	Land	Building
Fair Market Value	$140,000	$480,000
Cost	(100,000)	(400,000)
Change In Value	$ 40,000	$ 80,000
Change In Use Percent	30%	30%
Capital Gain	$ 12,000	$ 24,000
Inclusion Rate	1/2	1/2
Taxable Capital Gain	$ 6,000	$ 12,000

It is likely that this capital gain could be eliminated through the use of the principal residence exemption that was discussed earlier in this Chapter.

The calculation of the 2012 CCA deduction would be as follows:

January 1, 2012 UCC (For 20 Percent Of The Building)		$ 78,400
Add: Deemed Cost Of Increase In Business Usage:		
Cost [(30%)($400,000)]	$120,000	
Bump Up [(1/2)(30%)($480,000 - $400,000)]	12,000	132,000
Deduct: One-Half Net Additions* [(1/2)($132,000)]		(66,000)
Base Amount For CCA Claim		$144,400
Deduct: CCA For The Year [(4%)($144,400)]		(5,776)
Add: One-Half Net Additions		66,000
January 1, 2013 UCC (For 50 Percent Of The Building)		$204,624

*Non-arm's length transfers are exempt from the half-year rule, provided the transferor used the property as a depreciable property prior to the transfer. The portion of the property being transferred was not previously used as a depreciable property and, as a consequence, the half-year rule is applicable.

2013 Tax Consequences As all of the building has been converted to personal use and is no longer being used for business purposes, there would be no CCA for 2013. However, there would be recapture of CCA as follows:

January 1, 2013 UCC	$204,624
Lesser Of:	
• Cost For CCA Purposes ($80,000 + $132,000) = $212,000	
• Deemed Proceeds Of Disposition	
= [(20% + 30%)($550,000) = $275,000	(212,000)
Recapture Of CCA	($ 7,376)

Note that the amount of this recapture of CCA is equal to the sum of the CCA ($1,600 + $5,776) that was taken in the two years during which some of the asset was used for business purposes.

The change in use would trigger capital gains on the land and building as follows:

	Land	Building
Fair Market Value	$150,000	$550,000
Change In Use Percent	50%	50%
Proceeds Of Disposition	$ 75,000	$275,000
Cost Of 2011 Acquisition		
20 Percent Of $100,000 and $400,000	(20,000)	(80,000)
Cost Of 2012 Acquisition		
30 Percent Of $140,000 and $480,000	(42,000)	(144,000)
Capital Gain	$ 13,000	$ 51,000
Inclusion Rate	1/2	1/2
Taxable Capital Gain	$ 6,500	$ 25,500

Exercise Eight - 12

Subject: Change In Use - Personal Property To Rental Property

During July, 2012, Ms. Lynn Larson decides to use her summer cottage as a rental property. It has an original cost of $43,000 (building = $23,000, land = $20,000) and its current fair market value is $231,000 (building = $111,000, land = $120,000). It has never been designated as her principal residence. Describe the 2012 tax consequences of this change in use, including the capital cost and UCC that will be applicable to the rental property. In addition, indicate the maximum amount of CCA that would be available for 2012.

End of Exercise.   Solution available in Study Guide.

Special Rules For Principal Residences

Change In Use - Principal Residence To Rental Property

8-118.   As we have previously noted, when the use of a property is changed from personal to business, the *Income Tax Act* requires that this change be treated as a deemed disposition and reacquisition at fair market value. The conversion of a principal residence to a rental property is a common example of this type of situation and, in the absence of any election, the fair market value at the time of the change will become the capital cost of the rental property. As was previously discussed, if the fair market value exceeds the cost, a different value will be used for the calculation of CCA.

8-119.   An alternative to this treatment is provided under ITA 45(2). Under this Subsection, the taxpayer can make an election under which he will be deemed not to have commenced using the property for producing income. Note that there is no required form for this election. It is made in the taxpayer's income tax return.

8-120.   If this election is made, the taxpayer will still include the rents from the property as rental income and deduct all of the expenses associated with the property other than CCA. However, use of the ITA 45(2) election prevents the taxpayer from deducting any amounts for CCA on this property.

8-121.   While this inability to deduct CCA can be viewed as a disadvantage associated with the election, the election does, in fact, have an offsetting advantage. Based on the ITA 54 definition of a principal residence, the property can continue to be designated as a principal residence for up to four years while the election is in effect. This would appear to be the case even in situations where the individual does not return to live in the property.

8-122.   In practical terms, the preceding means that an individual who moves out of a principal residence can retain principal residence treatment for the property, for up to four years. This allows the individual to enjoy any capital gains that accrue on the property during that period on a tax free basis.

8-123.   This would be of particular importance to an individual who moves to a rental property and does not have an alternative principal residence during this period. Even if the individual purchases an alternative residential property, the election can be helpful as it allows a choice as to which property will be designated as the principal residence during the relevant years. If one of the properties experiences a substantially larger capital gain during this period, the use of this election could produce a significant savings in taxes.

8-124.   Also of interest is the fact that the four year election period can be extended. ITA 54.1 specifies that if the following conditions are met either by the taxpayer or the taxpayer's spouse or common-law partner, the election can be extended without limit:

- you leave the residence because your employer requires you to relocate;

- you return to the original residence while still with the same employer, or before the end of the year following the year you leave that employer, or you die before such employment terminates; and

• the original residence is at least 40 kilometers further from your new place of employment than your temporary residence.

Exercise Eight - 13

Subject: Change In Use - Principal Residence To Rental Property

During 2007, Jan Wheatley acquired a new home at a cost of $220,000. On December 31, 2010, she moves from this home into an apartment. At this time, the home is appraised for $210,000. Because she believes that real estate in her area is temporarily undervalued, she decides to rent the property for a period of time and sell it at a later date. During 2011, she receives rents of $21,600 and has expenses, other than CCA, of $12,600. On January 1, 2012, she sells the home to the current tenant for $345,000. Indicate the 2011 and 2012 tax consequences to Ms. Wheatley assuming that, in 2011, she does not elect under ITA 45(2) and deducts CCA. How would these results differ if she made the ITA 45(2) election? In providing your answers, ignore the cost of the land on which the home is located.

End of Exercise. Solution available in Study Guide.

Change In Use - Rental Property To Principal Residence

8-125.   Here again, unless an election is made, this change in use will be treated as a deemed disposition at fair market value, with possible results including capital gains, recapture, or terminal loss. When this type of change occurs, ITA 45(3) allows an individual to elect out of the deemed disposition for capital gains purposes as long as no CCA has been taken on the property. To make the election, the taxpayer must notify the Minister in writing. The election must be made by the taxpayer's filing deadline for the year following the disposition (April 30 or June 15).

8-126.   When the ITA 45(3) election is used, it is possible to designate the property as a principal residence for up to four years prior to the time it stopped being used as a rental property. This can be beneficial both to individuals who did not own another residential property during this four year period, and to individuals with an alternative residential property that experiences a capital gain at a lower annual rate, or a loss.

Exercise Eight - 14

Subject: Change In Use - Rental Property To Principal Residence

On January 2, 2011, Lance Ho acquires a small condominium in downtown Toronto for $375,000. When his mother threatens to commit suicide if he ever moves out, he rents the unit to a friend until December 31, 2011. Net rental income, before any deduction for CCA, is $9,800. Mr. Ho's mother is hit by a bus and dies on December 26, 2011. The grieving Mr. Ho moves into the unit on January 1, 2012. At this time, the appraised value of the property is $450,000.

After moving in, he finds that the congested traffic in the downtown area is intolerable and, on December 31, 2012, he sells the unit for $510,000. Indicate the 2011 and 2012 tax consequences to Mr. Ho, assuming that he deducts CCA in 2011 and does not elect under ITA 45(3). How would these results differ had he not taken CCA and made the ITA 45(3) election? In providing your answers, ignore the cost of the land on which the condominium is located.

End of Exercise. Solution available in Study Guide.

Special Rules For Automobiles

8-127.   As was illustrated in the Example in Paragraph 8-117, the change in use rules generally apply when there is a change in use involving only a part of an asset. While this is usually not a serious problem with high value assets where changes in use are infrequent, it could be a significant problem in the case of automobiles that are used partially for employment or business, and partially for personal travel.

8-128.   For example, consider an individual who acquires a car for $29,000 and, in the first year of ownership, uses it two-thirds for business and one-third for personal purposes. It is likely that, in each subsequent year, the portions of personal and business use will vary. If the change in use rules were strictly applied to this situation, the fair market value for the vehicle would have to be determined each year, with these values being used in an annual deemed disposition/re-acquisition of a portion of the vehicle.

8-129.   Fortunately, an alternative approach appears to be acceptable to the CRA. A CCA amount is calculated each year on the assumption that the car is used 100 percent for business or employment activities. Using this figure, the deductible amount is determined by multiplying the 100 percent use figure by the portion of the use that was business related during the current year. This procedure avoids the complications associated with determining market values and recording annual deemed dispositions/re-acquisitions.

Example   Joan Stream acquires an automobile for $25,000. It will be used for both business and personal activities. During 2011, business milage is 40 percent of the total driven. In 2012, business usage increases to 60 percent of the total usage.

Analysis   Maximum CCA for 2011, without regard to personal usage, would be $3,750 [(1/2)(30%)($25,000)]. The deductible amount would be $1,500 [(40%)($3,750)].

In calculating CCA for 2012, the 100 percent figure would be $6,375 [(30%)($25,000 - $3,750)] and the deductible amount would be $3,825 [(60%)($6,375)].

Deemed Dispositions - Departures From Canada

Basic Rules

8-130.   When a taxpayer leaves Canada, ITA 128.1(4)(b) calls for a deemed disposition of all property owned at the time of departure. The disposition is deemed to occur at fair market value. If the taxpayer is an individual, certain types of property are exempted from this deemed disposition rule. The major categories of exempted property are as follows:

• Real property situated in Canada, Canadian resource properties, and timber resource properties.

• Property of a business carried on in Canada through a permanent establishment. This would include capital property, eligible capital property, and inventories.

• "Excluded Right or Interest"   This concept is defined in ITA 128.1(10). The definition includes Registered Pension Plan balances, Registered Retirement Savings Plan balances, Deferred Profit Sharing Plan balances, stock options, death benefits, retiring allowances, as well as other rights of individuals in trusts or other similar arrangements.

8-131.   This list of exemptions was once much more broadly based, simply indicating that anything that was classified as Taxable Canadian Property would be considered exempt. Without going into a detailed analysis, the major difference between the current list of exemptions, and assets designated Taxable Canadian Property, is shares of private companies. This means that a departure from Canada now triggers taxation on gains that have accrued on the shares of Canadian controlled private corporations owned by an emigrant. Not surprisingly, this change was not greeted with enthusiasm by the business community.

Additional Complications

8-132.   There are a number of other tax complications associated with both immigration and emigration. These include the ability to elect to have an exempt property taxed at the time of departure and procedures that allow a taxpayer to unwind a deemed disposition. These are given detailed attention in Chapter 20, International Issues In Taxation.

Exercise Eight - 15

Subject: Emigration

John Porker owns publicly traded securities with an adjusted cost base of $920,000 and a fair market value of $1,030,000. On April 21, 2012, he permanently departs from Canada still owning the shares. What would be the tax consequences of his departure, if any, with respect to these securities?

Exercise Eight - 16

Subject: Emigration

Ms. Shari Twain owns a rental property in London, Ontario with a capital cost of $275,000 and a fair market value of $422,000. The land values included in these figures are $75,000 and $122,000, respectively. The UCC of the building is $107,800. On December 31, 2012, Ms. Twain permanently departs from Canada still owning the property. What are the tax consequences of her departure, if any, with respect to this rental property?

End of Exercises. Solutions available in Study Guide.

Deferral Provisions On Small Business Investments

Basic Provision

8-133.   ITA 44.1 was introduced to provide small businesses, especially start-up companies, with greater access to risk capital. It provides for the deferral of capital gains resulting from the disposition of "eligible small business corporation shares" when sold by an individual. The deferral is conditional on reinvestment of some or all of the proceeds of disposition in other eligible small business corporation shares (replacement shares). As you would expect, the adjusted cost base of these replacement shares will be reduced by the capital gain that is eliminated in the current year. In effect, this defers the gain until such time as the new investment is sold and not reinvested in replacement shares.

Definitions

8-134.   ITA 44.1 is a very technical Section of the *Act* and, as such, requires a number of definitions. Some of the more important definitions are as follows:

Eligible Small Business Corporation   To be eligible for the deferral, the corporations must comply with the definition of an eligible small business corporation. This is a Canadian controlled private corporation that has substantially all (meaning more than 90 percent) of the fair market value of its assets devoted principally to an active business carried on primarily (meaning more than 50 percent) in Canada. The corporation's qualifying assets include its holdings of shares or debt in other eligible small business corporations. To be eligible for the ITA 44.1 provisions, the small business corporation and corporations related to it cannot have assets with a carrying value in excess of $50 million. Shares or debt of related corporations are not counted when determining the $50 million limit on assets.

Deferral Provisions On Small Business Investments

Qualifying Disposition   To qualify for the deferral, the gain must result from the sale of common shares in an eligible small business corporation that was owned by the investor throughout the 185 day period that preceded the disposition.

Replacement Shares   These are common shares of an eligible small business corporation that are acquired within 120 days after the end of the year in which the qualifying disposition took place. They must be designated as replacement shares in the individual's tax return. Note that an individual can establish a deferral that is less than the maximum permitted amount by designating a lesser amount of replacement shares.

Permitted Deferral   The deferral is limited to a fraction of the capital gain resulting from the qualifying disposition. The fraction is based on the ratio of the lesser of the cost of the replacement shares and proceeds of disposition, divided by the proceeds of disposition (the value cannot exceed one).

> **Example**   The common shares of an eligible small business corporation with an adjusted cost base of $2,000,000 are sold for $2,500,000. Within 30 days, $1,800,000 of the proceeds are used to purchase replacement shares.
>
> **Analysis**   The total gain is $500,000 ($2,500,000 - $2,000,000). Of this total, the maximum permitted deferral would be $360,000 [($500,000)($1,800,000 ÷ $2,500,000)].

Adjusted Cost Base Reduction   The adjusted cost base of the replacement shares will have to be reduced by the amount of any capital gains deferral. Using the preceding example, the adjusted cost base of the replacement shares would be $1,440,000 ($1,800,000 - $360,000). If there is more than one block of replacement shares, this reduction will be allocated in proportion to their costs.

Example

8-135.   The following example illustrates the application of the ITA 44.1 deferral:

Example   During the current year, an individual makes a qualifying disposition of shares of Corporation A with an adjusted cost base of $3,000,000, for proceeds of disposition of $4,500,000.

Within 120 days after the current year end, the individual purchases replacement shares in Corporation B with a cost of $2,200,000 and in Corporation C with a cost of $2,300,000. Corporations A, B, and C are unrelated.

Analysis   As the $4,500,000 proceeds of disposition is equal to the $4,500,000 ($2,200,000 + $2,300,000) cost of the replacement shares, the permitted deferral is equal to $1,500,000 [($1,500,000)($4,500,000 ÷ $4,500,000)], which is the total capital gain on the disposition.

In calculating the adjusted cost base of the new shares, the $1,500,000 reduction would be allocated as follows:

	B Shares	C Shares
Purchase Price	$2,200,000	$2,300,000
Deferral:		
[($1,500,000)($2,200,000/$4,500,000)]	(733,333)	
[($1,500,000)($2,300,000/$4,500,000)]		(766,667)
Adjusted Cost Base	$1,466,667	$1,533,333

The total adjusted cost base is $3,000,000 ($1,466,667 + $1,533,333), which was the adjusted cost base of the Corporation A shares.

Exercise Eight - 17

Subject: Deferral Of Small Business Gains

On January 15, 2012, Jerri Hamilton sells all of her common shares of Hamilton Ltd., an eligible small business corporation. She had owned the shares for 12 years. The adjusted cost base of these shares is $750,000 and they are sold for $1,350,000. On February 15, 2012, $1,200,000 of these proceeds are invested in the common shares of JH Inc., a new eligible small business corporation. How much of the capital gain arising on the sale of the Hamilton Ltd. shares can be deferred by the investment in JH Inc.? If the maximum deferral is elected, what will be the adjusted cost base of the JH Inc. shares?

End of Exercise. Solution available in Study Guide.

Deferral Provisions On Replacement Property

The Problem
Potential Taxation
8-136. The disposition of a capital property can give rise to capital gains and, in the case of depreciable capital property, recapture of CCA. In certain situations, such dispositions are unavoidable, with the related income inclusions creating significant financial problems for the taxpayer.

> **Example** An enterprise has its only Class 1 building completely destroyed by fire. The building has a capital cost of $1,200,000 and a UCC of $450,000. It is insured for its replacement cost of $4,000,000 and this amount is received during the current year.

> **Analysis** In the absence of any mitigating legislation, these events would result in a taxable capital gain of $1,400,000 [(1/2)($4,000,000 - $1,200,000)] and, if the building is not replaced during the current year, recapture of $750,000. The taxes on this $2,150,000 increase in Taxable Income would be added to the many other problems associated with the fire.

8-137. A similar problem may arise when a business changes its location. The sale of its old facilities may result in significant capital gains. In addition, if these old facilities are not replaced in the same year as their disposition, there may also be recapture of CCA.

Legislative Relief
8-138. Given the problems such situations can generate, it is not surprising that the government has provided relief. The relevant provisions are ITA 13(4) which deals with the recapture problem and ITA 44(1), which deals with the capital gains.

8-139. In somewhat simplified terms, these provisions allow the taxpayer to eliminate or reduce capital gains and recapture that arise on qualifying dispositions. The use of these provisions is conditional on the replacement of the property within a specified period of time. There is a corresponding reduction in the capital cost and UCC of the replacement assets. This, in effect, defers these income inclusions until the replacement assets are sold or used.

8-140. You should note that the application of these provisions is not required. Both ITA 13(4) and ITA 44(1) are elections that are made in filing the taxpayer's return of income (i.e., there is no prescribed form). They do not apply automatically and, if the taxpayer fails to make the required elections, the result can be a significant increase in Tax Payable in the year of disposition.

Voluntary And Involuntary Dispositions

8-141.   There are two types of situations for which the combination of ITA 13(4) and ITA 44(1) provide relief. They can be described as follows:

Involuntary Dispositions   This description is used to describe dispositions of depreciable property resulting from theft, destruction, or expropriation under statutory authority. In the case of this type of disposition, the relieving provisions cover all types of depreciable property. In addition, these provisions are available as long as the replacement occurs within 24 months after the end of the year in which the disposition took place.

Voluntary Dispositions   As the name implies, these are voluntary dispositions, usually involving the relocation of a business. As a relocation may involve a disposition, taxpayers undergoing a move may encounter problems similar to those experienced when there is an involuntary disposition. In these voluntary dispositions, the applicability of ITA 13(4) is more limited.

Specifically, this provision only applies to "former business property", a term that is defined in ITA 248(1) to consist of real property or interests in real property. This means that assets other than those specified in the ITA 248 definition (e.g., equipment, furniture and fixtures) will not benefit from this provision. A further difference here is that the replacement must occur within 12 months after the year in which the disposition took place for the relieving provision to be available.

Timing Considerations

Dispositions

8-142.   Note that, from a technical point of view, a disposition does not take place until the proceeds become receivable. In the case of voluntary dispositions, the proceeds will become receivable at the time of sale. However, in the case of involuntary dispositions, the receipt of insurance or expropriation proceeds may occur in a taxation year subsequent to the theft, destruction, or expropriation of the property. For purposes of determining the 24 month replacement period, the clock will generally start ticking in this later year.

Replacements

8-143.   With respect to capital gains, they will arise when the disposition occurs. They will occur without regard to when the replacement is made. This means that their reduction or elimination will always require the application of ITA 44(1).

8-144.   The situation with recapture is different. You will recall from Chapter 4 that recapture only occurs when there is a negative balance in the class at the end of the period. If the replacement occurs in the same period as the disposition, it is likely that there will be a positive balance in the class at the end of the period. If this is the situation, there is no recapture and the election under ITA 13(4) is not relevant.

8-145.   A further point here is that, if the replacement occurs in a period subsequent to the disposition, the application of ITA 13(4) and ITA 44(1) will have to be implemented via an amended return for the period of disposition. Any capital gain or recapture that occurs at the time of disposition will, in effect, be reversed through the amended return.

Application Of ITA 44(1) To Capital Gains

8-146.   If a qualifying property is disposed of and replaced within the required time frame, ITA 44(1) provides an election that will reduce the capital gain to the lesser of:

• an amount calculated by the usual approach (proceeds of disposition, less adjusted cost base); and

• the excess, if any, of the proceeds of disposition of the old property over the cost of the replacement property.

8-147.   In somewhat simplified terms, if the cost of the replacement property is greater than the proceeds of disposition for the replaced property, no capital gain will be recorded if the appropriate election is made. We would remind you that, in those cases where the replacement occurs in a period subsequent to the disposition, this election will have to be applied as an adjustment to the return for the year of disposition.

> **Example**   A taxpayer has land with an adjusted cost base of $600,000. It is expropriated by the local municipality. Compensation, which is paid immediately, is $1,000,000. It is replaced in the current taxation year with land which costs $1,200,000.
>
> **Analysis**   If no election is made under ITA 44(1), there will be a capital gain of $400,000 ($1,000,000 - $600,000) and the new land will have an adjusted cost base of $1,200,000.
>
> Alternatively, if an election is made under ITA 44(1), the capital gain will be the lesser of:
>
> - $400,000; and
> - Nil (the excess, if any, of the proceeds of disposition of the old land over the cost of the new land).

8-148.   When ITA 44(1) is applied, any amount of capital gain that is eliminated must be removed from the cost of the replacement property. This will leave the adjusted cost base of the new land at $800,000 ($1,200,000 - $400,000).

8-149.   If the replacement cost had been less than the expropriation proceeds, it would not have been possible to eliminate all of the capital gain. For example, if the replacement cost had been $700,000, the minimum capital gain would have been $300,000, the excess of the proceeds of disposition of $1,000,000 over the $700,000 replacement cost of the new property. This alternative would leave the adjusted cost base of the replacement property at $600,000 ($700,000, less the deferred capital gain of $100,000).

Application Of ITA 13(4) To Recapture Of CCA

8-150.   The application of ITA 13(4) is more complex. In order to focus on this application we will use an example in which the fair market value of the building is less than its capital cost, thereby avoiding the need to use ITA 44(1) to eliminate a capital gain.

> **Example** A company's only building is destroyed in a fire in February, 2011. The original cost of the building was $2,500,000, the fair market value is $2,225,000, and it is an older building with a UCC of only $275,000. The insurance proceeds, all of which are received in 2011 prior to the December 31 year end, equal the fair market value of $2,225,000. The replacement building is acquired in July, 2012 at a cost of $3,000,000.
>
> **Analysis** Deducting $2,225,000, the lesser of the proceeds of disposition and the capital cost of the building, from the UCC of $275,000 will leave a negative balance of $1,950,000. As there is no replacement of the asset during 2011, this negative balance will remain at the end of this year, resulting in recapture of CCA. This amount will have to be included in income for the 2011 taxation year and will be added back to the UCC, reducing the class balance to nil.
>
> In 2012, the year in which the replacement occurs, the ITA 13(4) election provides for an alternative calculation of the 2012 recapture:

January 1, 2011 UCC Balance		$275,000
Deduction:		
Lesser Of:		
• Proceeds Of Disposition = $2,225,000		
• Capital Cost = $2,500,000	$2,225,000	
Reduced By The Lesser Of:		
• Normal Recapture = $1,950,000		
• Replacement Cost = $3,000,000	(1,950,000)	(275,000)
Recapture Of 2011 CCA (Amended)		**Nil**

8-151.   IT-259R4 indicates that the election, including the relevant calculations, should be made in the form of a letter attached to the tax return in 2012, the year of replacement. In this example, the election would result in a $1,950,000 reduction in the company's 2011 Net Income For Tax Purposes and would likely provide the basis for a tax refund.

8-152.   The $1,950,000 reduction of Net Income For Tax Purposes in the preceding calculation will have to be treated as deemed proceeds of disposition and subtracted from the UCC of the replacement asset. This will leave a balance of $1,050,000 ($3,000,000 - $1,950,000). This balance correctly reflects the economic substance of the events that have occurred:

Original UCC	$ 275,000
Proceeds Of Disposition	(2,225,000)
Replacement Cost	3,000,000
New UCC Balance	**$1,050,000**

8-153.   Note that the reversal of recapture is limited to the cost of the replacement property. In our example, if the cost of the replacement property had only been $1,800,000, this amount would have been the limit on the recapture reversal and the remaining $150,000 [$275,000 - ($2,225,000 - $1,800,000)] would have remained in 2011 income. In this case, the UCC of the replacement building would be nil ($1,800,000 - $1,800,000).

Exercise Eight - 18

Subject: Involuntary Disposition - ITA 13(4) Election For Recapture

During 2011, the only building owned by Foran Inc. is destroyed by a meteorite. Its original cost was $1,500,000, its fair market value was $1,400,000, and the Class 1 UCC was $650,000. The Company receives $1,400,000 in insurance proceeds during 2011 and replaces the building with a used building at a cost of $2,350,000 in 2012. The Company makes the ITA 13(4) election to defer any recaptured CCA. What is the UCC of the replacement building?

End of Exercise. Solution available in Study Guide.

Combined Application Of ITA 13(4) And 44(1)
Example 1 - Replacement Cost Exceeds Proceeds Of Disposition
8-154.   Our first example of the combined application of ITA 13(4) and ITA 44(1) involves a situation where the replacement cost of the new asset exceeds the proceeds of disposition for the old asset.

Example   During its 2011 taxation year, the Martin Company decides to change the location of its operations. Its current property consists of land with an adjusted cost base of $500,000, as well as a building with a capital cost of $1,500,000 and a UCC of $340,000. These assets are sold for a total price of $2,400,000, of which $600,000 is allocated to the land and $1,800,000 is allocated to the building. During January,

2012, a replacement property is acquired at a new location at a cost of $2,800,000, of which $700,000 is allocated to the land and $2,100,000 is allocated to the building.

Analysis - Capital Gain   As a result of the disposition, the Martin Company will include the following amounts in its 2011 Net Income For Tax Purposes:

	Old Land	Old Building
Proceeds Of Disposition	$600,000	$1,800,000
Adjusted Cost Base	(500,000)	(1,500,000)
Capital Gain	$100,000	$ 300,000
Inclusion Rate	1/2	1/2
Taxable Capital Gain	$ 50,000	$ 150,000
Recapture Of CCA ($340,000 - $1,500,000)	N/A	$1,160,000

When the replacement occurs in 2012, the cost allocated to the land and building exceeds the proceeds of disposition from these assets. As a consequence, the revised capital gain for 2011 will be nil, a fact that would be reflected in an amended 2011 tax return. However, the capital cost of the replacement assets would be reduced as follows:

	New Land	New Building
Cost	$700,000	$2,100,000
Capital Gain Reversal - ITA 44(1) Election	(100,000)	(300,000)
Deemed Adjusted Cost Base/Capital Cost	$600,000	$1,800,000

8-155.   The economic basis for this result can be seen by noting that the combined deemed adjusted cost base of the new land and building is $2,400,000 ($600,000 + $1,800,000). This is equal to the combined adjusted cost base of the old land and building of $2,000,000 ($500,000 + $1,500,000), plus the additional $400,000 in cash ($2,800,000 - $2,400,000) required to finance the acquisition of the new land and building.

8-156.   Using the ITA 13(4) formula, the amended 2011 recapture of CCA would be nil, calculated as follows:

UCC Balance		$340,000
Deduction:		
Lesser Of:		
• Proceeds Of Disposition = $1,800,000		
• Capital Cost = $1,500,000	$1,500,000	
Reduced By The Lesser Of:		
• Normal Recapture = $1,160,000		
• Replacement Cost = $2,100,000	(1,160,000)	(340,000)
Recapture Of CCA (Amended)		Nil

8-157.   As would be expected when the replacement cost of the new building exceeds the normal recapture of CCA, the amended recapture of CCA will be nil. The reversal of the 2011 recapture of CCA will be reflected in the UCC of the new building as follows:

Deemed Capital Cost Of Building	$1,800,000
Recapture Reversal - ITA 13(4) Election	(1,160,000)
UCC	$ 640,000

8-158.   As was the case with the capital cost of the new building, the economic basis for this result can also be explained. The new UCC of $640,000 is equal to the old UCC of $340,000, plus the $300,000 in cash ($2,100,000 - $1,800,000) required to finance the acquisition of the new building.

Example 2 - Proceeds Of Disposition Exceed Replacement Cost

8-159.   In the preceding example, we are able to remove 100 percent of the capital gain through the application of the ITA 44 election. This resulted from the fact that the cost of the replacement property exceeded the proceeds of disposition for the old property. If this is not the case, some of the capital gain will have to remain in income. This point can be illustrated by making a small change in our previous example by decreasing the replacement land cost by $150,000.

> **Example**   During its 2011 taxation year, the Martin Company decides to change the location of its operations. Its current property consists of land with an adjusted cost base of $500,000, as well as a building with a capital cost of $1,500,000 and a UCC of $340,000. These assets are sold for a total price of $2,400,000, of which $600,000 is allocated to the land and $1,800,000 is allocated to the building. During January, 2012, a replacement property is acquired at a new location at a cost of $2,650,000, of which $550,000 is allocated to the land and $2,100,000 is allocated to the building.

8-160.   For the 2011 tax return, the capital gains and recapture on the disposition will be as presented in Paragraph 8-154. In 2012, when ITA 44(1) is applied, the minimum capital gain on the land that can be reversed would be the lesser of:

- $100,000 (the excess of the $600,000 proceeds of disposition over the $500,000 adjusted cost base); and

- $50,000 (the excess of the $600,000 proceeds of disposition over the $550,000 replacement cost).

8-161.   The lesser amount is $50,000. When this amount of the capital gain is reversed, it leaves $50,000 ($100,000 - $50,000) in capital gains in 2011 income. With respect to the replacement values, the relevant tax values are as follows:

	New Land	New Building
Cost	$550,000	$2,100,000
Capital Gain Reversal - ITA 44(1) Election	(50,000)	(300,000)
Deemed Adjusted Cost Base/Capital Cost	$500,000	$1,800,000
Recapture Reversal - ITA 13(4) Election	N/A	(1,160,000)
UCC	N/A	$ 640,000

Election To Reallocate Proceeds Of Disposition

8-162.   In the preceding example, the fact that the replacement cost of the land was less than the proceeds of disposition of the previously owned land, resulted in a situation where a portion of the capital gain on this disposition had to remain in the 2011 tax return. Fortunately, a further election contained in ITA 44 provides, in many cases, a solution to this problem.

8-163.   Under ITA 44(6), the taxpayer is allowed to reallocate the total proceeds of disposition on the sale of a former business property, without regard to the respective market values of the land and building. If, in the example presented in Paragraph 8-159, the total proceeds of $2,400,000 are reallocated on the basis of $550,000 (originally $600,000 in Paragraph 8-154) to the land and $1,850,000 (originally $1,800,000) to the building, the 2011 taxable capital gains will be as follows:

	Old Land	Old Building
Proceeds Of Disposition After Election	$550,000	$1,850,000
Adjusted Cost Base	(500,000)	(1,500,000)
Capital Gain	$ 50,000	$ 350,000
Inclusion Rate	1/2	1/2
Taxable Capital Gain	$ 25,000	$ 175,000

8-164.   While the total taxable capital gain remains the same, this reallocation of the total proceeds of disposition results in a situation where the replacement cost of both the land and building are equal to, or exceed, the proceeds of disposition. This, in turn, means that all of the capital gains on both of these capital assets will be removed from the 2011 amended tax return. Under this scenario, the tax values for the replacement assets would be as follows:

	New Land	New Building
Cost	$550,000	$2,100,000
Capital Gain Reversal - ITA 44(1) Election	(50,000)	(350,000)
Deemed Adjusted Cost Base/Capital Cost	$500,000	$1,750,000
Recapture Reversal - ITA 13(4) Election	N/A	(1,160,000)
UCC	N/A	$ 590,000

8-165.   Note that this election is not made without a cost. Had the $50,000 been left as a capital gain, tax would have applied on only one-half of the total. While we have eliminated this $25,000 in income, we have given up future CCA for the full amount of $50,000. In other words, we have given up $50,000 in future deductions in return for eliminating $25,000 of income in 2011. As explained in our Chapters 12 and 13 on corporate taxation, for some corporations, capital gains are initially taxed at higher rates than business income, which could be a factor in this decision. In addition, anticipated future tax rates could be a consideration.

Exercise Eight - 19

Subject: Involuntary Dispositions - ITA 13(4) and 44(1) Elections

Hadfeld Ltd., a company with a December 31 year end, operates out of a single building that cost $725,000 in 2005. At the beginning of 2011, the UCC for its Class 1 was $623,150. On June 30, 2011, the building was completely destroyed in a fire. The building was insured for its fair market value of $950,000 and this amount was received in September, 2011. The building is replaced in 2012 with a used building that cost $980,000. Hadfeld Ltd. wishes to minimize income taxes. Describe the 2011 and 2012 tax consequences of these events, including the capital cost and UCC for the new building. Ignore any gain or loss related to the land on which the building is located.

End of Exercise. Solution available in Study Guide.

Capital Gains And Tax Planning

8-166.   The capital gains area offers many opportunities for effective tax planning since the realization of capital gains or losses is largely at the discretion of the taxpayer. If the taxpayer desires that gains or losses fall into a particular taxation year, this can often be accomplished by deferring the disposition of the relevant asset until that period. This means that gains can often be deferred until, perhaps retirement, when the taxpayer may be in a lower tax bracket.

8-167. Other examples of tax planning would include selling securities with accrued losses in order to offset gains realized earlier in the taxation year, and deferring until after the end of the year the sale of any asset on which there is a significant capital gain.

8-168. Tax planning for capital gains is more complex if an individual owns small business corporation shares or a farm or fishing property. This is due to the fact that such properties may be eligible for the $750,000 lifetime capital gains deduction. Additional complications result from the application of capital losses, particularly with respect to carry overs of such amounts. These issues are discussed in Chapter 11.

Key Terms Used In This Chapter

8-169. The following is a list of the key terms used in this Chapter. These terms, and their meanings, are compiled in the Glossary Of Key Terms located at the back of the separate paper Study Guide.

Adjusted Cost Base	Listed Personal Property
Allowable Capital Loss	Personal Use Property
Capital Asset	Principal Residence
Capital Cost	Proceeds Of Disposition
Capital Gain	Real Property
Capital Gains Reserve	Recapture Of CCA
Capital Loss	Replacement Property Rules
Deemed Disposition	Reserve
Deeming Rules	Rollover
Disposition	Small Business Corporation
Election	Superficial Loss - ITA 54
Emigration	Taxable Canadian Property
Former Business Property	Taxable Capital Gain
Identical Property Rules	Terminal Loss
Involuntary Disposition	Undepreciated Capital Cost (UCC)

References

8-170. For more detailed study of the material in this Chapter, we would refer you to the following:

ITA 38	Taxable Capital Gain And Allowable Capital Loss
ITA 39	Meaning Of Capital Gain And Capital Loss
ITA 40	General Rules
ITA 41	Taxable Net Gain From Disposition Of Listed Personal Property
ITA 42	Dispositions Subject To Warranties
ITA 43	General Rule For Part Dispositions
ITA 44	Exchanges Of Property
ITA 44.1	Definitions (Eligible Small Business Shares)
ITA 45	Property With More Than One Use
ITA 46	Personal Use Property
ITA 47	Identical Properties
ITA 49	Granting Of Options
ITA 53	Adjustments To Cost Base
ITA 54	Definitions (Capital Gains)

ITA 69	Inadequate Considerations
ITA 70	Death Of A Taxpayer
ITA 73	Inter Vivos Transfer To Individuals (e.g., Transfers To A Spouse)
IC 88-2	General Anti-Avoidance Rule — Section 245 Of The Income Tax Act
IT-95R	Foreign Exchange Gains And Losses
IT-96R6	Options Granted By Corporations To Acquire Shares, Bonds Or Debentures And By Trusts To Acquire Trust Units
IT-102R2	Conversion Of Property, Other Than Real Property, From Or To Inventory
IT-120R6	Principal Residence
IT-159R3	Capital Debts Established To Be Bad Debts
IT-259R4	Exchanges Of Property
IT-262R2	Losses Of Non-Residents And Part-Year Residents
IT-264R	Part Dispositions
IT-268R4	Inter Vivos Transfer Of Farm Property To A Child
IT-381R3	Trusts — Capital Gains And Losses And The Flow Through Of Taxable Capital Gains To Beneficiaries
IT-387R2	Meaning Of Identical Properties (Consolidated)
IT-403R	Options On Real Estate
IT-418	Capital Cost Allowance — Partial Dispositions Of Property
IT-419R2	Meaning Of Arm's Length
IT-437R	Ownership Of Property (Principal Residence)
IT-451R	Deemed Disposition And Acquisition On Ceasing To Be Or Becoming Resident In Canada
IT-456R	Capital Property — Some Adjustments To Cost Base
IT-479R	Transactions In Securities
IT-491	Former Business Property

Problems For Self Study

(The solutions for these problems can be found in the separate Study Guide.)

Self Study Problem Eight - 1 (Identical Properties)

Over the past few years, Mr. Hall has taken an interest in the common shares of Clarkson Industries Ltd., a Canadian public company. As he is approaching retirement age and anticipates moving to Florida, he sold his total holding of Clarkson shares on March 15, 2012, when the shares were trading at $174 per share. Over the years, Mr. Hall has had the following transactions in the shares of Clarkson Industries:

- On October 15, 2006, he purchases 5,500 shares at $40 per share.

- On November 8, 2006, he sells 1,500 shares at $52 per share.

- On December 12, 2008, he purchases 3,200 shares at $79 per share.

- On February 3, 2009, he sells 2,600 shares at $94 per share.

- On January 15, 2010, he receives a 10 percent stock dividend that has been paid by Clarkson Industries. As part of this transaction, the Company transfers retained earnings of $99 per share to contributed capital.

- On June 15, 2010, he acquires 3,800 shares at $104 per share.

- On December 23, 2011, he receives a 10 percent stock dividend that has been paid by Clarkson Industries. As part of this transaction, the Company transfers $125 per share from retained earnings to contributed capital.

Required: Determine the amount of the taxable capital gain or allowable capital loss that would arise from:

- the sale on November 8, 2006,
- the sale on February 3, 2009, and
- the sale on March 15, 2012.

Ignore transaction costs in all of your calculations.

Self Study Problem Eight - 2 (Warranties On Capital Assets)

On May 1, 2011, Mr. Rowe sold a parcel of suburban land to a developer for $2,600,000. The land had cost Mr. Rowe $1,400,000 in 1997, and no additions or improvements had been made to the land. He classifies any gain on the land sale as a capital gain. In order to convince the purchaser that he should pay the full $2,600,000 in cash, Mr. Rowe has agreed to refund a part of the purchase price if less than 100 lots are sold by December 1, 2012.

Specifically, the agreement calls for a refund of $26,000 for each of the 100 lots that is not sold within the specified period. At the time of the sale, Mr. Rowe estimates that he will probably have to pay $104,000 to the purchaser on December 1, 2012.

Over the next two years, a number of plants in the area are closed, substantially reducing the demand for the lots in the development. By December 1, 2012, only 60 lots have been sold and Mr. Rowe is obliged to pay the purchaser $1,040,000 [($26,000)(40 Lots)] as agreed.

Required: Describe the tax effects associated with the sale of the land and the guarantee provided by Mr. Rowe at the time the land is sold and with the payment that he is required to make on December 1, 2012. Include the effects of this payment on the Tax Payable of other years.

Self Study Problem Eight - 3 (Capital Gain Reserves)

On November 1, 2012, Miss Stevens sells a capital property for $500,000. The adjusted cost base of the property is $230,000 and she incurs selling costs in the amount of $20,000. She receives an immediate cash payment of $200,000 on November 1, 2012, with the balance of the $500,000 to be paid on June 1, 2018.

Miss Stevens wishes to use reserves to defer the payment of taxes on capital gains for as long as possible.

Required: Calculate the amount of the minimum taxable capital gain that would be included in Miss Stevens' Net Income For Tax Purposes for each of the years 2012 through 2018.

Self Study Problem Eight - 4 (Bad Debts On Capital Asset Sales)

During July, 2011, Mrs. Simpkins sold a painting to a friend for $25,000. She had purchased the painting in 2000 at a cost of $15,000. As her friend was short of cash, Mrs. Simpkins accepted a down payment of $15,000 and a note that required the friend to make a payment of $10,000 at the end of 2012. No interest payments were required on the note and, because Mrs. Simpkins had no other income during 2011, she did not establish a capital gains reserve.

Shortly before the end of 2012, Mrs. Simpkins tried to locate her friend. She was not successful and it appeared that the friend, along with the painting, had disappeared without a trace. As a reflection of this fact, Mrs. Simpkins wishes to write off the bad debt in 2012.

Required: Determine the 2011 and 2012 tax effects resulting from the preceding transactions.

Self Study Problem Eight - 5 (Principal Residence Designation)

Mr. Stewart Simms has lived most of his life in Vancouver. In 1988, he purchased a three bedroom home near English Bay for $125,000. In 1993, he acquired a cottage in the Whistler ski area at a cost of $40,000. In all subsequent years, he has spent at least a portion of the year living in each of the two locations. When he is not residing in these properties they are left vacant.

On October 1, 2012, Mr. Simms sells the English Bay property for $515,000 and the cottage at Whistler for $320,000.

Mr. Simms wishes to minimize any capital gains resulting from the sale of the two properties.

Required: Describe how the residences should be designated in order to accomplish Mr. Simms' goal. In addition, calculate the amount of the taxable capital gain that would arise under the designation that you have recommended.

Self Study Problem Eight - 6 (Capital Gains On Foreign Securities)

Mr. Brian Levitt is a resident of Canada who owns a large portfolio of investment securities. In order to provide international diversification, he often buys securities that are listed in the U.K. In August, 2008, Brian acquires 5,000 shares of BPL Ltd. at a cost of £25 per share.

In June, 2012, the BPL Ltd. shares are sold for £32 per share, with the cash remaining in British pounds.

In December, 2012, the proceeds from the sale of BPL shares are converted into Canadian dollars and transferred to his Canadian bank account.

Assume relevant exchange rates between the British pound and the Canadian dollar are as follows:

August, 2008	£1.00 = $1.64
June, 2012	£1.00 = $1.57
December, 2012	£1.00 = $1.62

Required: Calculate the minimum amount that will have to be included in Mr. Levitt's Net Income For Tax Purposes for 2012 as a result of these transactions.

Self Study Problem Eight - 7 (Changes In Use - CCA)

Miss Coos purchased a building to be used as her personal residence in 2008 at a cost of $120,000. Of this total, it is estimated that the value of the land is $30,000 and the value of the building is $90,000. On January 1, 2010, a portion of this residence was converted to an office and rented to a local accountant for $400 per month. At the time of the conversion, the fair market value of the building was $120,000. The market value of the land is unchanged. Based on the amount of floor space allocated to the office, Miss Coos indicates that 30 percent of the building was converted into office space at this time.

On January 1, 2012, the office was rented by a new tenant who did not require the same amount of floor space as the previous tenant. As a result, one room was converted back to personal use. This room contained 10 percent of the total floor space, and the fair market value of the building was $140,000 at this time. The market value of the land remains at $30,000.

Required: What is the maximum CCA that can be deducted in 2010, 2011, and 2012? In addition, indicate any capital gains or losses that will result from the changes in use. Ignore land values in calculating your solution.

Self Study Problem Eight - 8 (Changes In Use And Rental Income With CCA)

Mr. Blake purchased a house on June 30, 1993 at a total cost of $176,000. It was estimated that the fair market value of the land at this time was $83,000. Mr. and Mrs. Blake and their two teenage children moved in during the next month.

On January 1, 2011 a portion of this property was converted to an apartment, and rented to a tenant at a rate of $850 per month, for a term of 18 months. At the time of this conversion, the fair market value of the total property was $253,000. At this time, it was estimated that the fair market value of the land was $106,000. The apartment was located in the back of the house, faced a busy parking lot, and occupied 32 percent of the total floor space of the property.

On June 30, 2012, at the end of the lease term, Mr. Blake and the tenant agree to reduce the size of the area rented to 21 percent of the total floor space of the property. A new lease is signed with a reduced rent of $750 per month and a new term of 30 months. On June 30, 2012, the fair market value of the property is $278,000. At this time, it was estimated that the fair market value of the land was $110,000. Two months after the new lease is signed, Mr. Blake makes improvements in the rented area of the property at a cost of $12,350.

During the year ending December 31, 2011, Mr. Blake made payments for insurance, hydro, and property taxes on his property in the amount of $5,600. The corresponding figure for the period January 1, 2012 through June 30, 2012 was $2,900. For the period July 1, 2012 through December 31, 2011, this amount was $3,200. There were no repair costs during either 2011 or 2012. Mr. Blake deducts maximum CCA in each year.

Required: For each of the two taxation years 2011 and 2012, indicate the amounts that would be included in Mr. Blake's Net Income For Tax Purposes as the result of the preceding transactions and events. Assume that Mr. Blake does not designate this property as his principal residence in any of the years under consideration.

Self Study Problem Eight - 9 (Departure From Canada)

Mr. Mark Vargo has been a resident of Canada all of his life. However, after suffering through his third consecutive bad romance, on February 14, 2012 he decides to leave Canada. He is moving to a location near Washington DC where he has been advised that there are at least three single females for every single male.

At the time of his departure, he has the following assets:

	Adjusted Cost Base	Fair Market Value
Antique Sports Car	$ 32,000	$ 46,000
Personal Automobile	32,000	18,000
Shares In Bank Of Nova Scotia (A Public Company)	12,000	16,000
Shares In Vargo Ltd. (A Private Company)	23,000	17,000
Coin Collection	8,000	6,000
Cottage (Not His Principal Residence)	135,000	262,000

Required: Determine the amount of the taxable capital gain or allowable capital loss that Mr. Vargo will report in his Canadian income tax return for 2012 as a result of his departure from Canada. Assume that the usual tax rules apply, with no elections being made by Mr. Vargo.

Self Study Problem Eight - 10 (Deferral On Small Business Investments)

The following two independent Cases involve dispositions of eligible small business corporation shares, with the proceeds being invested in replacement shares. In both Cases, the original shares have been held for more than a year.

Case A   On March 31, 2012, Harold sells his common shares in Corporation A, which is an eligible small business corporation. His proceeds of disposition are $100,000 and his capital gain is $60,000. On July 1, 2012, Harold invests $90,000 in common shares of Corporation B, which is a new eligible small business corporation.

Case B   On November 6, 2011, Kate disposes of common shares in Corporation C, which is an eligible small business corporation. Her proceeds of disposition are $1,000,000 and she realizes a capital gain of $600,000. On February 1, 2012, Kate acquires common shares in Corporation D, which is also an eligible small business corporation, at a cost of $1,000,000.

Required: For both Cases, determine the maximum permitted capital gains deferral, as well as the adjusted cost base of the replacement shares.

Self Study Problem Eight - 11
(Replacement Properties - ITA 13(4) Election On UCC)

Trail Resources Ltd. has a taxation year that ends on December 31. During 2011, its storage building was destroyed in a flash flood. This building was purchased in 1998 at a cost of $500,000 and, on January 1, 2011, its UCC was $368,000. After negotiations with adjustors from the insurance company, a settlement of $490,000 was agreed upon and paid during 2011.

A replacement building was contracted for, and started, in September, 2011. It was completed in January, 2012 for a cost of $650,000. As the building is used exclusively for non-residential purposes, it qualifies for the 6 percent CCA rate.

Trail Resources Ltd. does not own any other buildings and always takes maximum CCA. The appropriate election is made by the Company to defer any recapture under ITA 13(4).

Required: Explain how the preceding transactions will affect the balance in the Company's UCC during the period January 1, 2011 through January 1, 2013.

Self Study Problem Eight - 12 *(Involuntary Dispositions)*

On January 1, 2012, a fire completely destroys Fraser Industries Ltd.'s Edmonton office building and all of its contents. An immediate settlement is negotiated with the Company's fire and casualty insurer. The insurer agrees to pay $4,800,000 for the building and an additional $1,256,000 for the contents of the building. These amounts represent the estimated fair market values of the destroyed assets and a cheque is received for these amounts on May 15, 2012.

As the City has been acquiring adjacent land for the development of a park, the Company is notified on January 15, 2012 that the land on which the building was located will be expropriated in order to expand the park area. The expropriation takes place on April 30, 2012 and Fraser Industries Ltd. receives $723,000, which is the estimated fair market value of the land.

Other information on the Edmonton property is as follows:

Land   The land was acquired in 1993 at a cost of $256,000.

Building   The building was constructed during 1995 at a total cost of $3,700,000. It is the only building owned by Fraser Industries Ltd. and, at the beginning of 2012, the UCC in Class 1 was $1,856,000.

Building Contents   The contents of the building consisted entirely of Class 8 assets. These assets had an original cost in 1994 of $972,000 and the UCC of Class 8 was $72,000 at the beginning of 2012. Fraser Industries Ltd. does not own any other Class 8 assets.

In replacing the destroyed property, the Company decides to relocate to an area that has lower land costs. As a consequence, a replacement property is found in Hinton at a cost of $6,200,000. It is estimated that the fair market value of the land on which the building is located is $500,000. The remaining $5,700,000 is allocated to the building. As the building is not new, it does not qualify for the 6 percent CCA rate that is available on new buildings that are used for non-residential purposes.

The acquisition closes on November 1, 2013 and, during the following month, contents are acquired at a cost of $1,233,000. All of the contents are Class 8 assets.

Fraser Industries has a December 31 year end.

Required:

A. Determine the amounts that would be included in Fraser Industries Ltd.'s 2012 Net Income For Tax Purposes as a result of receiving the insurance and expropriation proceeds.

B. Assume that, in the year ending December 31, 2013, Fraser Industries files an amended 2012 tax return using the elections that are available under ITA 13(4) and ITA 44(1), but not the election under ITA 44(6). Determine the revised amounts that would be included in the Company's 2012 Net Income For Tax Purposes. In addition, indicate the adjusted cost base and, where appropriate, the UCC of the new items of property.

C. Indicate the maximum amount of any reduction in 2012 Net Income For Tax Purposes that could result from the use of the ITA 44(6) election, in addition to the elections under ITA 44(4) and ITA 44(1). Should the Company make the election? Explain your conclusion.

Self Study Problem Eight - 13 (Comprehensive Case Covering Chapters 1 to 8)

Laura Barnes is 37 years of age and lives with her 32 year old common-law partner, Julia Stinson. Julia's 2012 Net Income For Tax Purposes is $4,600.

Also living with the couple are two children that were born to Julia in two previous relationships. The daughter, Allison, is 8 years old and the son, Andrew, is 12 years old. During 2012, Laura formally adopts these two children. Due to stiff opposition from Andrew's father, she incurs legal costs of $14,200 to complete his adoption. The legal fees paid to adopt Allison total $4,000.

Laura's 62 year old mother, Alicia, also lives with her. While she does not qualify for the disability tax credit, she has a physical impairment that makes her totally dependent on Laura. She attends university on a full time basis for four months of the year and Laura pays her tuition fees of $2,400. Alicia has 2012 Net Income For Tax Purposes of $9,400.

Laura pays the following medical expenses in 2012:

Laura	$ 1,800
Julia	2,200
Alicia	4,600
Allison	800
Andrew	6,600
Total Medical Expenses	$16,000

Laura, Julia, Alicia, and the two children use public transit throughout the year. During 2012, the monthly passes are $100 for each adult and $50 per child, with all of these amounts being paid by Laura.

During 2012, Laura makes contributions to registered charities in the amount of $1,600.

During the first 6 months of 2012, Laura operated a successful retail business out of a building which she owned. She keeps her accounting records on a cash basis and, for the 6 month period ending June 30, 2012, her net cash inflow was $53,000. Information on inventories and accruals are as follows:

	January 1, 2012	June 30, 2012
Accounts Receivable	$10,000	$ 8,000
Accounts Payable	14,000	16,000
Inventories	22,000	18,000

Information on the capital assets used in the business is as follows:

	Capital Cost	January 1 2012 UCC	June 30, 2012 Fair Market Value
Building (Acquired In 2004)	$250,000	$211,000	$308,000
Land (Building's Location)	50,000	N/A	125,000
Furniture And Fixtures	35,000	12,900	9,800
Automobile (Used Exclusively In The Business)	29,500	25,075	18,000

On July 1, 2012, the capital assets were sold for their fair market value, with Laura paying $17,320 in sales commissions on the disposition of the land and building. The Accounts Receivable and Inventories were sold for their carrying values, with part of the proceeds being used to pay off the Accounts Payable.

On July 3, 2012, she is employed by a large public company as a sales consultant. Her salary for the period July 3, 2012 through December 31, 2012 is $56,000. In addition, because of her excellent performance she is awarded a $12,000 bonus. The bonus will be paid on April 30, 2013.

During 2012, her employer withholds the following amounts from her income:

RPP Contributions	$2,500
EI	840
CPP	2,307

Because her employer has withheld the maximum amount for 2012, Laura will not have to make CPP contributions on the income from her unincorporated business.

Laura's employer also contributes $2,500 to her RPP. In addition, the employer provides her with an automobile that cost $62,000. The car was used by her for the period July 3, 2012 through December 31, 2012 and, during this period she drives the car 22,000 kilometers, 18,000 of which were employment related.

Information on Laura's investments is as follows:

Dividends Eligible dividends received during 2012 total $5,600.

Interest 2012 interest on Laura's GICs is $4,275.

Income Trusts At the beginning of 2012, Laura had income trust units with an adjusted cost base of $56,000. During the year, she receives distributions of $6,800, of which $2,600 is designated as a return of capital with the remainder designated as business income. On December 15, 2012, she sells all of the trust units for $63,000.

Mutual Funds In January, 2012, Laura acquires 1,000 units of the New World Equity Fund at $9.65 per unit. On June 30, 2012, the fund has a distribution of interest income of $0.50 per unit. At this time the units are trading at $9.40 and Laura chooses to have the distribution re-invested. On December 10, 2012, she sells all of the units for $9,000.

To assist with her investment decisions, during 2012, Laura pays fees to a professional investment counsellor of $875.

Required: Calculate Ms. Barnes' minimum 2012 Net Income For Tax Purposes, her 2012 minimum Taxable Income, and her minimum 2012 federal Tax Payable. Ignore provincial income taxes, any instalments she may have paid during the year, any income tax withholdings that would be made by her employer, and GST/HST/PST considerations.

Self Study Problem Eight - 14 *(Comprehensive Case Covering Chapters 1 to 8)*
Employment Information
Mr. Lorenzo Desoto is 39 years old and is employed by a large public corporation. In addition to his 2012 salary of $136,000, he earns commissions during the year of $43,000. Because of his excellent performance, he has been awarded a bonus of $22,000. One-half of this amount is payable in December, 2012, with the balance being paid on July 15, 2013.

His employer withholds the following amounts from his 2012 income:

RPP Contributions	$4,200
EI	840
CPP	2,307
Professional Association Dues	1,500
United Way Contributions	2,400

Lorenzo's employer makes a matching contribution to his RPP of $2,700.

Lorenzo's employer provides an allowance of $2,500 per month to cover all of his employment related expenses, including the use of his personally owned automobile. This automobile was acquired in 2011 at a cost of $46,500. In that year, he claimed CCA based on the car being used 60 percent for employment related activities. In 2012, his employment related usage increases to 80 percent.

For 2012, Lorenzo's employment related expenses are as follows:

Automobile Operating Expenses	$6,300
Hotels	9,700
Airline And Other Transportation	5,400
Business Meals And Entertainment	9,300

Lorenzo's employer requires him to maintain an office in his home and has provided him with a signed Form T2200. The office occupies 12 percent of the floor space in his home. The 2012 costs of operating this property are as follows:

Mortgage Interest	$7,200
Insurance	1,250
Maintenance And Utilities	1,300
Property Taxes	5,600

In 2009, Lorenzo's employer granted him options to buy 500 shares of the company's stock at a price of $92 per share. This was the market value of the shares at the time the options were granted. In January, 2012, when the shares are trading at $108 per share, Lorenzo exercises all of the options. In December, 2012, the 500 shares are sold for $115 per share.

Family Information

Lorenzo is married to Maria Desoto. She is 37 years old and has 2012 income from inherited investments of $6,300. Now that her children are in their teens, Maria attends university on a full time basis during 8 months of the year. Her tuition for 2012 was $9,300.

The Desotos have two children. Their son Gianni is 16 and has Net Income For Tax Purposes of $6,200, largely from part-time summer jobs. Their daughter Anita is 14 and is sufficiently disabled that she qualifies for the disability tax credit. Anita has no 2012 Net Income For Tax Purposes.

Both children are enrolled in qualifying physical fitness programs. Jeremy's program costs $825 per year, while Anita's program costs $930 per year.

The family's 2012 medical expenses are as follows:

Lorenzo	$ 1,350
Maria	3,425
Gianni	2,600
Anita	10,250
Total	$17,625

Other Information

1. Lorenzo owns a glass sculpture with an adjusted cost base of $800. During 2012, he sells this sculpture for $39,000.

2. Lorenzo owns a cottage on a local lake. It had cost $105,000, including an estimated value for the land of $42,000. While the family has made good use of the property, at the beginning of 2012, he decides to convert the cottage to a rental property. It is estimated that, at this time, the cottage is worth $350,000, with $100,000 of this amount attributable to the land. During 2012, net rental income before the deduction of CCA equals $12,000. Lorenzo does not intend to designate the cottage as his principal residence in any of his years of ownership.

3. Lorenzo owns 500 units of the Real Property Income Trust. The adjusted cost base of these units on January 1, 2012 is $56.00 per unit. During 2012, the trust distributions total $2.40 per unit, with all of this amount being business income. The entire distribution was reinvested in additional units on the basis of $58.50 per unit. During December 2012, all of these Trust units were sold for $60.25 per unit.

4. For several years, Lorenzo has owned a tract of land with an adjusted cost base of $78,000. His intent was to eventually construct a rental property on this site. However, with the conversion of the cottage to a rental property, he decides to reduce his real estate holdings. To this end, the land is sold for $180,000. The buyer provides an immediate payment of $54,000, with the balance payable in annual instalments of $18,000 beginning in 2013.

5. During 2012, Lorenzo received eligible dividends of $4,200.

Required: Calculate Mr. Desoto's minimum 2012 Net Income For Tax Purposes, his 2012 minimum Taxable Income, and his minimum 2012 federal Tax Payable. Ignore provincial income taxes, any instalments he may have paid during the year, any income tax withholdings that would be made by his employer, and GST/HST/PST considerations.

Assignment Problems

(The solutions for these problems are only available in
the solutions manual that has been provided to your instructor.)

Assignment Problem Eight - 1 (Identical Properties)

Miss Wells has purchased the shares of two companies over the years. Purchases and sales of shares in the first of these companies, Memo Inc., are as follows:

February, 2008 purchase	60 @ $24
November, 2009 purchase	90 @ 28
April, 2010 purchase	45 @ 30
October, 2010 sale	(68) @ 36
September, 2012 purchase	22 @ 26
November, 2012 sale	(53) @ 40

Purchases and sales of shares in the second company, Demo Ltd., are as follows:

April, 2011 purchase	200 @ $24
December, 2011 purchase	160 @ 33
July, 2012 sale	(260) @ 36

Required:

A. Determine the cost to Miss Wells of the Memo Inc. shares that are still being held on December 31, 2012.

B. Determine the taxable capital gain resulting from the July, 2012 disposition of the Demo Ltd. shares.

Assignment Problem Eight - 2 (Warranties And Bad Debts On Capital Assets)

Mr. Howard owns a tract of undeveloped land near Ottawa. He has owned the land for several years since he acquired it at a cost of $4,200,000. As he is nearing retirement, on December 31, 2012, he sells the land to local developer for $9,400,000.

As the developer will be developing the land into 200 individual lots over a period of several years, Mr. Howard agrees to the following terms for the sale:

- The purchaser will make an immediate down payment of $1,400,000, followed by annual payments of $2,000,000 on December 31 of each of the years 2013, 2014, 2015, and 2016. The purchaser agrees to pay interest at the rate of 6 percent on the balance that is outstanding on January 1 of each year.

- As there is a considerable amount of risk involved in the project, Mr. Howard agrees to reimburse the purchaser in the amount of $15,000 for each lot that is not sold by December 31, 2015.

Mr. Howard intends to deduct the maximum capital gains reserve in each of the years 2012 through 2016.

In 2013, 2014, and 2015, the developer makes the required interest and principal payments.

By December 31, 2015, only 140 of the lots have been sold, a result which requires Mr. Howard to pay the developer $900,000 [($15,000)(60 Lots)].

While the developer continues his efforts to market the lots through the first part of 2016, he is not successful and, on June 1, 2016, he declares bankruptcy. As the developer appears to have left the country, Mr. Howard does not anticipate being able to collect any of the remaining balance on the loan or the final interest payment.

Required: Calculate the tax effects of the transactions that took place during 2012 through 2016 on Mr. Howard's Net Income For Tax Purposes.

Assignment Problem Eight - 3 (Capital Gain Reserves)
Ms. Fabrice purchased a tract of land in 2006 for $430,000. It was sold during 2012 for consideration of $1,730,000. She receives a down payment of $519,000 and accepts a 14 year, 8 percent mortgage for the balance of $1,211,000. The payments on this mortgage begin in the second year and require the repayment of $86,500 per year in capital.

Ms. Fabrice wishes to use reserves to defer the payment of taxes on capital gains for as long as possible. She classifies any gain on the land sale as a capital gain.

Required: Calculate the capital gains taxation effects of this sale, assuming that Ms. Fabrice deducts the maximum capital gains reserve in 2012 and subsequent years.

Assignment Problem Eight - 4 (Capital Gain Reserves)
In 1989, Ms. Gerhardt purchased a substantial parcel of land in northern Ontario at a cost of $600,000. During May, 2012, she sells it for $1,350,000.

The terms of the sale call for a down payment at the time of closing, with Ms. Gerhardt accepting a 9 percent mortgage for the balance of the $1,350,000. The terms of the mortgage require annual payments beginning in the year subsequent to the sale. The payments are designed to include principal payments of 5 percent of the sales price, or $67,500, per year.

Ms. Gerhardt wishes to use reserves to defer the payment of taxes on capital gains for as long as possible.

Required: Compare the capital gains taxation effects of this sale assuming:

A. The down payment was 15 percent of the sales price.

B. The down payment was 45 percent of the sales price.

Assignment Problem Eight - 5 (Short Cases On Capital Gains)
Each of the following independent Cases describes a situation with a proposed tax treatment.

1. Mr. Acker has owned a small triplex for a number of years and, throughout this period, all three of the units have been rented. In determining his income from this property, he has deducted CCA in each year. During the current year, Mr. Acker has moved into one of the three units and, as a result, will be reporting reduced rental revenues in his tax return. As

Assignment Problems

    he has not sold any property, he will not report any capital gains or losses during the current year.

2.   Mr. Jones has sold a property with an adjusted cost base of $72,000 for total proceeds of $105,000. He is providing a warranty on the property that he estimates will cost him $6,000 to service. As a consequence, he is recognizing a capital gain of $27,000.

3.   Ms. Turner sold her dining room table to her daughter for $400 and a painting to her brother for $900. These prices equalled their estimated fair market values. Several years ago, she purchased the table for $950, and the painting for $667. She does not plan to report any capital gain or loss.

4.   Mrs. Brown purchased corporate bonds for $11,200, of which $800 was accrued interest and $10,400 represented the principal. The bonds were later sold for $11,600 that includes $200 for accrued interest. Mrs. Brown recognizes a taxable capital gain of $500.

5.   Several years ago, Miss Lee transferred three sports cars, with a total value of $182,000, to a corporation in return for all of the shares of the company. The cars are profitably used in her personal escort business. During the current year, all of the cars are destroyed in a fire on her estate. Unfortunately, Miss Lee did not believe that people in her financial position needed insurance and, as a consequence, no compensation was available for the loss. As the corporation had no assets other than the cars, there was no reason for her to continue to hold the shares. In view of this situation, she sells the shares to a friend who requires a corporate shell for some business operations. The sale price is $500 and Miss Lee uses the allowable capital loss of $90,750 [(1/2)($182,000 - $500)] to offset taxable capital gains resulting from real estate transactions.

Required: In each of the preceding Cases, indicate whether or not you believe that the tax treatment being proposed is the correct one. Explain your conclusion.

Assignment Problem Eight - 6 (Principal Residence Designation)

Alice Stewart has owned a large country home near Toronto since 1997. It was acquired at a cost of $850,000.

Because of her growing need to spend time in the city, in 2005 she acquired a Toronto condominium at a cost of $625,000.

At the beginning of 2012, she concludes that she would like to move to the west coast and, to this end, she sells both of her Ontario properties. The country home is sold for $1,200,000 during June, 2012. The Toronto condominium is sold in July, 2012 for $900,000. Real estate commissions of 5 percent of the sales price were charged on both transactions.

As Ms. Stewart has been the only individual to use these properties, either one could be designated as her principal residence for the relevant years. Ms. Stewart wishes to minimize any capital gains resulting from the sale of the two properties.

Required: Describe how the residences should be designated in order to accomplish Ms. Stewart's goal. In addition, calculate the total amount of the gain that would arise under the designation that you have recommended.

Assignment Problem Eight - 7 (Personal Use Property)

Mr. Firenza owns a number of personal assets, all of which were acquired while he was a resident of Canada. As he plans to spend the next 5 years travelling the globe, he will be converting most of his possessions to cash. The assets he will be selling in the current year can be described as follows:

- He owns a vintage automobile which has been restored to like new condition. He acquired the vehicle for $42,000 and has spent $135,000 on the restoration process.

He estimates the current fair market value of the automobile to be $320,000.

- He has an extensive coin collection which has a current fair market value of $23,500. The total cost of all of the coins is $17,600. He believes that the coins can be disposed of without incurring any selling costs.

- At her death, his mother left him a rare 17th century manuscript. His mother had paid $4,000 for the manuscript and, at the time of her death, it was estimated that its fair market value was $42,000. However, since the time of the bequest, several other copies of this manuscript have been found and, as a consequence, its value has decreased to $8,500.

- Mr. Firenza owns a Lawren Harris oil painting which he acquired for $275,000. While he believes it could be sold for $350,000, the auction house will charge a commission of 20 percent of the sales price.

- Mr. Firenza owns a sailboat which cost $162,000. He estimates that its current fair market value, net of selling costs would be $123,000.

- Mr. Firenza has an antique desk that he acquired for $600. He believes that it could be sold for $2,200 and that no selling costs would be incurred.

Required: Mr. Firenza has asked you to determine the amount that would have to be included in his Net Income For Tax Purposes if all of these assets were sold for their estimated values. Indicate any amounts that may be available for carry over to other years.

Assignment Problem Eight - 8 (Capital Gains On Foreign Securities)

Ms. Barbra Laval sometimes make investments on European stock exchanges that must be paid for in Euros (€, hereafter). She is a Canadian resident and makes her purchases through a Canadian brokerage account.

In July, 2010, she acquires 3,500 shares of Euron Ltd. at a cost of €30 per share.

In January, 2012, she sells the Euron Ltd. shares for €33.50 per share. The Euros resulting from this sale are left in her Euro trading account that is maintained with her Canadian broker.

In November, 2012, after becoming concerned about the continued slide in the value of the Euro, she converts her €117,250 [(3,500)(€33.50)] balance into Canadian dollars, with the resulting balance being transferred to her Canadian dollar brokerage account.

Assume relevant exchange rates between the Euro and the Canadian dollar are as follows:

July 2010	€1.00 = $1.40
January, 2012	€1.00 = $1.30
December, 2012	€1.00 = $1.25

Required: Calculate the minimum amount that will have to be included in Ms. Laval's Net Income For Tax Purposes for 2012 as a result of these transactions.

Assignment Problem Eight - 9 (Changes In Use - Depreciable Property)

On January 1, 2010, Mr. Jean Lessard acquires a real property that he will use to operate his appliance repair business. As this is not a new building, it will not qualify for the 6 percent CCA rate on Class 1 assets. The cost of this property is $425,000, with $125,000 of this total being the estimated value of the land. During 2010, his business occupies all of the property.

As during 2010 he did not achieve the volume of business that he anticipated, on January 1, 2011, Mr. Lessard converts 40 percent of the property's floor space into an apartment which he will occupy. At this time, due to the strong possibility that a crematorium would be built next door, the estimated fair market value of the property has fallen to $375,000, with $100,000 of this total attributable to the land.

During 2011, his volume of business increases significantly, resulting in the need to convert his apartment back to business usage. This conversion occurs on January 1, 2012, with the entire building being used for business throughout the following year. On January 1, 2012, the fair market value of the building has increased to $450,000, due to the bankruptcy of the owner of the proposed crematorium, with $135,000 of this total attributable to the land.

Required: Determine the maximum CCA that can be deducted by Mr. Lessard in 2010, 2011, and 2012. In addition, indicate any other tax consequences that will result from the changes in use of this property.

Assignment Problem Eight - 10 *(Departure From Canada)*

Until 2012, Marcie Doan has been a resident of Canada. However, on January 1, 2012, she decides to move to Scottsdale, Arizona. On this date, she owns the following assets:

	Adjusted Cost Base	Fair Market Value
Common Shares In ABC Ltd. (a Canadian controlled private corporation)	$42,000	$86,000
Vacant land	63,000	84,000
Common Shares In Power Corp (a public company)	38,000	72,000
Preferred Shares In TD Bank (a public company)	84,000	72,000
Sailboat	97,000	54,000
Oil Painting	5,000	11,000
Stamp Collection	12,000	3,000

Ms. Doan has come to you for advice just prior to moving to Arizona.

Required: Determine the amount of the taxable capital gain or allowable capital loss that Ms. Doan will report in her Canadian income tax return for 2012 as a result of her departure from Canada. Assume that the usual tax rules apply, with no elections being made by Ms. Doan.

Assignment Problem Eight - 11 *(Involuntary Dispositions)*

Winding Inc. has a Class 1 building with an original cost of $900,000, of which $150,000 can be attributed to the land. It is the only Class 1 asset owned by the Company and, on January 1, 2012, its UCC balance is $425,000.

On July 1, 2012, this building is completely destroyed in a major earthquake. It is estimated that, at the time of this event, the fair market value of the building and land was $1,200,000, with $200,000 of this total applicable to the land. With respect to the building, insurance proceeds of $1,000,000 are received on November 1, 2012. Also on this date, the land is sold for $200,000.

On February 1, 2013, the Company finds a suitable replacement building that is located near the site of the old building. It is acquired on that date at a cost of $1,400,000, including an estimated value for the land of $300,000. As it is not a new building, it does not qualify for the enhanced CCA rate for Class 1 buildings.

Required:

A. Indicate the tax consequences of the involuntary disposition that will be reported in the Company's 2012 tax return.

B. Indicate the changes that will be reported in the amended 2012 return, provided the Company makes elections under ITA 13(4) and ITA 44(1). In addition, determine the capital cost and UCC for the replacement assets, subsequent to the application of these elections.

C. Calculate the maximum CCA that Winding will be able to claim for the building in 2013, assuming the Company makes the elections under ITA 13(4) and ITA 44(1).

Assignment Problem Eight - 12 (Voluntary Dispositions)

The management of Voltec Ltd. has concluded that it would like to relocate to a less urban venue in order to provide for an improved lifestyle for their employees. To this end, on December 1, 2012, they sell their building and all of their depreciable assets. The proceeds for the land, building, and equipment, all of which are located in Vancouver, total $3,240,000. The details of the sale are as follows:

Land The land was acquired in 2002 for $325,000. Of the total proceeds, it is estimated that $1,720,000 represents a payment for the land.

Building The building was constructed in 2003 at a total cost of $1,100,000. Of the total proceeds, it is estimated that $1,200,000 represents a payment for the building. On January 1, 2012, the Class 1 UCC balance was $720,000.

Equipment The equipment was acquired in 2003 at a cost of $620,000. It is estimated that $320,000 of the total sale proceeds represents a payment for this equipment. The UCC for Class 8 on January 1, 2012 was $240,000.

In 2013, the Company acquires replacement property in Vernon at a total cost of $1,500,000. This cost is allocated as follows:

Land	$ 950,000
Building	1,350,000
Equipment	475,000
Total	$2,775,000

The building is used more than 90 percent for non-residential use other than manufacturing. In order to qualify for the enhanced 6 percent CCA rate, it is allocated to a separate Class 1.

The Company would like to minimize any capital gains or recapture resulting from the sale of the Vancouver property. The Company's tax year ends on December 31, 2012, and it does not own any buildings or equipment on this date.

Required:

A. Indicate the tax consequences resulting from the sale of assets on December 1, 2012.

B. Indicate how these tax effects could be altered in an amended 2012 return by using the elections available under ITA 44(1) and 13(4), but without the use of the election under ITA 44(6). Also indicate the adjusted cost base and, where appropriate, the UCC of the replacement properties, subsequent to the application of the ITA 44(1) and ITA 13(4) elections.

C. Indicate the maximum amount of any reduction in the amended 2012 Net Income For Tax Purposes that could result from the use of the ITA 44(6) election. Should the Company make the election? Explain your conclusion.

Assignment Problem Eight - 13 *(Deferral On Small Business Investments)*

The following two independent Cases involve dispositions of eligible small business corporation shares, with the proceeds being invested in replacement shares. In both Cases, the original shares have been held for more than a year.

> **Case A** On May 4, 2012, an individual sells his common shares in an eligible small business corporation for $2,200,000. The adjusted cost base of these shares was $1,400,000. On September 14, 2012, he invests $1,800,000 of these proceeds in common shares of a different eligible small business corporation.

> **Case B** In January, 2012, an individual sells his common shares in an eligible small business corporation for $1,900,000. The shares have an adjusted cost base of $1,200,000. In October, 2012, he invests $500,000 of these proceeds in Corporation A common shares. At the same time, he invests $900,000 of the proceeds in Corporation B common shares. Both Corporation A and Corporation B are eligible small business corporations.

Required: For both Cases, determine the maximum permitted capital gains deferral, as well as the adjusted cost base of the replacement shares.

Assignment Problem Eight - 14 *(Comprehensive Case Covering Chapters 1 to 8)*

Mr. Arnold Bosch is 41 years old and earns most of his income through an unincorporated business, Bosch's Better Boats (BBB). For the taxation year ending December 31, 2012, Mr. Bosch's accountant has determined that BBB had accounting income before taxes, determined in accordance with generally accepted accounting principles, of $196,000. In determining his business income for tax purposes, the following information is relevant:

1. The accounting income figure included a deduction for amortization of $29,000.

2. On January 1, 2012, BBB had the following UCC balances:

    - Class 1 (Building Acquired In 2005) $275,000
    - Class 8   83,000
    - Class 10   28,000

    On March 1, 2012, Class 8 assets with a cost of $46,000 were sold for $28,500. On March 15, 2012, these assets were replaced with other Class 8 assets costing $63,250.

3. During 2012, BBB spent $30,000 landscaping the grounds around its building. This amount was recorded as an asset in the accounting records. It is being amortized over 10 years on a straight line basis and the amortization is included in the $29,000 amortization figure in Part 1 of this problem.

4. BBB's 2012 accounting income included a deduction for meals and entertainment of $27,600.

5. BBB's 2012 accounting income included a deduction for charitable donations of $5,500, as well as a deduction for donations to federal political parties of $700.

6. For accounting purposes, BBB charges estimated warranty costs to expense. On January 1, 2012, the liability for these warranties was $22,000. On December 31, 2012, the liability balance was $17,500.

Because of the income earned by his business, Mr. Bosch is required to make CPP contributions of $4,614 [(2)($2,307)]. He does not choose to make EI contributions.

Mr. Bosch has a common-law partner, Mr. Fritz Mann. Three years ago, Mr. Bosch and his partner adopted two Chinese orphans. Chris, aged 9, has a severe and prolonged disability that qualifies him for the ITA 118.3 disability tax credit. Martin, aged 12, is in good health. Neither Chris nor Martin has any income of their own. Because Mr. Mann provides full time care for the children, he has no income during 2012.

The family's 2012 medical expenses, all paid for by Mr. Bosch, are as follows:

Arnold	$ 2,050
Fritz	1,080
Chris	16,470
Martin	1,645
Total Medical Expenses	**$21,245**

During 2012, Mr. Bosch sold a piece of vacant land for $85,000. Mr. Bosch received a payment of $35,000 during 2012, with the $50,000 balance due in 5 equal instalments in the years 2013 through 2017. The adjusted cost base of this land was $33,000.

Mr. Bosch owns a rural cottage property that he purchased at a property auction in 2004 at a cost of $25,000. As of June 30, 2012, an appraiser indicates that it has a value of $375,000, with $100,000 of that value being associated with the land. The appraiser indicates that, when Mr. Bosch purchased the cottage, the land value was probably about $5,000.

Although Mr. Bosch and Mr. Mann used to spend a great deal of time in the summer at the cottage, since the adoptions, the family has made little use of this property. As a result, he decides to begin renting it as of July 1, 2012.

During the period July 1, 2012 through December 31, 2012, rents on the cottage total $12,000. Expenses other than CCA during this period total $3,200. For 2012, he intends to take maximum CCA on the property.

Mr. Bosch purchased his city home in 2007. Prior to that, he and Mr. Mann lived in a rented apartment. As the city home has experienced a greater increase in value during the last six years, he will designate the city home as his principal residence for the years 2007 through 2012.

Over the years, Mr. Bosch has made several purchases of the common shares of Low Tech Ltd., a widely held public company. In 2010 he bought 150 shares at $55 per share. In 2011, he bought an additional 125 shares at $75 per share. In February, 2012, he bought an additional 300 shares at $95 per share. On November 11, 2012, after the company announced that most of its product claims had been falsified, Mr. Bosch sold 275 shares at $5 per share.

Required: Calculate Mr. Bosch's minimum 2012 Net Income For Tax Purposes, his 2012 minimum Taxable Income, and his minimum 2012 Balance Owing to the CRA, including any CPP contributions payable. Ignore provincial income taxes, any instalment payments he may have made during the year, and GST/HST/PST considerations.

Assignment Problem Eight - 15 (Comprehensive Case Covering Chapters 1 to 8)
Family Information
Mr. Paul Klee is 39 year of age and lives with his spouse, Virginia Klee. They have two children, May who is 9 years old and Max who is 12 years old. May has been blind since birth. During 2012, Max has income of $8,200.

Virginia is 38 years and until recently was employed by a large public company. However, in September, 2011, she commenced full time studies at her local university. During 2012, she was in full time attendance for 9 months. Her tuition fees were $9,350. She had 2012 income from various part time sources of $8,400.

Paul purchases transit passes for himself, Virginia, and Max for all 12 months during 2012. The cost is $200 per month for himself and Virginia and $100 per month for Max. Also during 2012, Max participates in a qualifying arts program that cost $950.

During 2012, the family incurs medical expenses as follows:

Paul	$ 1,100
Virginia	1,750
May	13,300
Max	650
Total	$16,800

Employment Information

Paul is employed as a salesperson by a Canadian public company. His annual salary is $85,000 and, in addition, he earns commissions of $62,500. The following amounts are withheld by his employer during 2012:

RPP Contributions	$4,100
EI	840
CPP	2,307
Professional Association Dues	1,500
United Way Donations	1,200

Paul's employer makes a matching contribution to his RPP of $4,100.

Paul's employer requires that he maintain an office in his home and has provided him with the requisite Form T2200. This office occupies 20 percent of the total floor space in his home. His home operating costs for 2012 are as follows:

Maintenance And Utilities	$3,400
Property Taxes	7,200
Insurance	850
Mortgage Interest	4,200

Paul's employer provides a $2,500 per month allowance to cover all of his employment related expenses, including an automobile that he owns personally. The automobile was acquired in 2011 at a cost of $45,000. In his 2011 tax return he claimed CCA based on the automobile being used 55 percent for employment related activities. For 2012, the usage increased to 80 percent.

Paul's employment related expenses for 2012 are as follows:

Automobile Operating Expenses	$ 6,100
Hotels	11,500
Airline And Other Transportation	9,200
Business Meals And Entertainment	10,400

In 2011, Paul's employer granted him options to buy 1,500 shares of the company stock at $15 per share. At that time, the shares were trading at $12 per share. In February, 2012, when the shares are trading at $19 per share, Paul exercises all of these options. In November, 2012, he sells all of these securities for $22 per share.

Other Information

1. Paul owned two very large oil paintings, each of which cost $10,000. Since he renovated his home and added many more windows, he no longer had the wall space to hang these paintings. During 2012, he sells one painting for $15,000 and the other painting for $4,000.

2. Paul inherited a tract of land from his father. Paul's adjusted cost base for it was $100,000. In July, 2012, he sells the land to help finance his home renovations. The terms of the sale require a 2012 payment of $100,000, with the balance being paid in annual instalments of $50,000 in each of the years 2013 through 2017. Paul would like use a capital gains reserve to defer as much of this gain as possible.

3. During 2012, Paul received non-eligible dividends of $5,400.

4. Since 2008, Paul and his family have owned a cottage on a nearby lake. It had cost $250,000, including an estimated value for the land of $75,000. As their use of this property has declined over the years, they have decided to convert the cottage to a rental property. At the time of the change, the property was appraised at $375,000, including $100,000 for the land. During 2012, net rental income before the deduction of CCA equals $23,000. Since his city home has had a very substantial increase in value, Paul does not intend to designate the cottage as his principal residence for any of the years of ownership.

Required: Calculate Mr. Klee's minimum 2012 Net Income For Tax Purposes, his 2012 minimum Taxable Income, and his minimum 2012 federal Tax Payable. Ignore provincial income taxes, any instalments he may have paid during the year, any income tax withholdings that would be made by his employer, and GST/HST/PST considerations.

Tax Software Assignment Problem For Chapter 8

This Tax Software Assignment Problem was introduced in Chapter 4 and is continued in Chapters 6 through 11. Each Tax Software Assignment Problem must be completed in sequence. While it is not repeated in this problem, all of the information in each of the previous problems (e.g., Mary's T4 content) is applicable to this problem.

If you have not prepared a tax file incorporating the Tax Software Assignment Problem information for the previous Chapters, please do so before continuing with this problem.

When Mary's grandmother died in 2006, she inherited some pieces of jewelry, as well as a dining room set and a chandelier. Since the jewelry is not suited to Mary's relaxed style of dress, she sold some pieces during the year. She replaced the dining room set and chandelier and sold them separately to two colleagues at work.

On December 28, 2011, Mary Career faxes to you information about her sales of securities and other items. Mary has purchased Extreme Wi-Fi Technologies stock over the years. Her transactions in this stock are as follows:

Acquisition Date	Shares Purchased (Sold)	Cost Per Share	Total Cost
April 1, 2009	1,500	$ 2	$ 3,000
October 1, 2009	2,000	12	24,000
April 1, 2010	(1,000)	?	
June 1, 2010	400	25	10,000
January 6, 2011	(800)	?	
February 1, 2011	800	20	16,000
March 14, 2011	(600)	?	

Tax Software Assignment Problem For Chapter 8

Asset Dispositions	Disposition 1	Disposition 2	Disposition 3
(All owned by Mary) Description	Extreme Wi-Fi Technologies	Extreme Wi-Fi Technologies	Fidelity Small Cap Fund
Number of units	800	600	258.92
Year of acquisition	2009	2009	2006
Date of disposition	January 6	March 14	February 17
Proceeds of disposition	11,806	13,465	2,982.31
Adjusted cost base	?	?	5,300.33
Outlays and expenses	29	29	Nil

Asset Dispositions	Disposition 4	Disposition 5	Disposition 6
Description	Diamond Pendant	Gold Ring	Pearl Brooch
Year of acquisition	2006	2006	2006
Date of disposition	July 20	July 20	July 20
Proceeds of disposition	4,000	750	1,300
FMV at grandmother's death	5,800	600	850

Asset Dispositions	Disposition 7	Disposition 8
Description	Dining room set	Crystal Chandelier
Year of acquisition	2006	2006
Date of disposition	July 20	July 20
Proceeds of disposition	200	1,500
FMV at grandmother's death	3,000	800

Required:

A. Open the file that you created for the Chapter 7 version of this Software Problem and save a copy under a different name. This will enable you to check the changes between different versions of this Software Problem.

B. Input the asset disposition information on the form S3Details. Prepare and print the Capital Gains and Losses (Schedule 3) for Mary. As part of your solution, include any calculations and notes that were needed to complete Schedule 3.

C. Access and print Mary's summary (Summary on the Form Explorer, not the T1Summary). This form is a two column summary of the couple's tax information. By opening this form from Mary's return, the order of the columns is the same as the one in the previous chapter. For both returns, list the changes on this Summary form from the previous version of this Software Problem. Exclude totals calculated by the program, but include the final Balance Owing (Refund) amount.

CHAPTER 9

Other Income, Other Deductions, And Other Issues

Introduction

Coverage Of Chapter 9

Subdivisions d and e

9-1. At this point we have provided detailed coverage of all of the major components of Net Income For Tax Purposes. There are, however, certain inclusions and deductions that do not fit into any of the categories that we have described. For example, the receipt of a pension benefit cannot be categorized as employment income, business or property income, or a taxable capital gain. Correspondingly, an RRSP deduction cannot be related to any type of earned income and, as a consequence, cannot be specifically allocated to any of the previously described income categories. These miscellaneous inclusions and deductions will be given detailed attention in this Chapter.

9-2. In terms of the *Income Tax Act*, these miscellaneous sources and deductions are covered in two Subdivisions of Division B. Subdivision d, made up of Sections 56 through 59.1, is titled Other Sources Of Income. Subdivision e, made up of Sections 60 through 66.8, is titled Other Deductions.

9-3. There are a number of items in these two subdivisions that are very closely related. For example, Subdivision d requires the inclusion of spousal support paid, while Subdivision e provides for the deduction of these amounts by the individual making the payments. In contrast, many of the items in the two subdivisions are not related in any manner (e.g., the inclusion of death benefits under subdivision d).

9-4. Given this situation, our coverage of this material will be divided into three sections:

- The first section will deal with those Subdivision d inclusions that do not involve Subdivision e deductions, such as scholarships and workers' compensation.

- A second section will deal with those Subdivision e deductions that do not involve Subdivision d inclusions, such as moving costs and child care expenses.

- A third section will give attention to issues that involve Subdivision d inclusions that are related to Subdivision e deductions such as pension income splitting.

Registered Savings Plans

9-5. As you are likely aware, Canadian taxpayers have access to a number of registered savings plans (e.g., registered retirement savings plans and registered education savings plans). While most of the inclusions and deductions related to these plans are found in subdivisions d and e, the rules related to these plans are complex and involve other components of the *Income Tax Act*.

9-6. Because of this complexity, our coverage of these plans will be divided between this Chapter 9 and a subsequent Chapter 10 which will provide general coverage of retirement savings. More specifically, in this Chapter we will cover the following plans whose contributions are not deductible:

- Registered Education Savings Plans (RESPs)
- Registered Disability Savings Plans (RDSPs)
- Tax Free Savings Accounts (TFSAs)

9-7. In Chapter 10, our coverage of registered savings plans will be extended to:

- Registered Pension Plans (RPPs);
- Registered Retirement Savings Plans (RRSPs);
- Registered Retirement Income Funds (RRIFs);
- Deferred Profit Sharing Plans (DPSPs); and
- Profit Sharing Plans (PSPs).

9-8. We are of the belief that this very extensive coverage of retirement savings vehicles is justified by the fact that these plans are perhaps the most important generally available form of tax planning that can be used by individuals. In addition, their complexity means that they are not well understood by most individuals, including some of the individuals providing professional advice in this area.

Other Issues - Non-arm's Length Transfers, Death, Income Attribution

9-9. This Chapter 9 concludes our coverage of the major components of Net Income For Tax Purposes. The calculation of this value requires the application of a number of special rules, some of which we have covered in previous Chapters. However, there are others which we have not covered to this point. These include:

- Non-arm's length transfers of property;
- Deemed dispositions at the death of a taxpayer; and
- Attribution of income to non-arm's length parties.

9-10. This Chapter will include coverage of these additional rules.

Other Income - Subdivision d Inclusions

Pension Benefits - ITA 56(1)(a)(i)

9-11. ITA 56(1)(a)(i) requires that payments received from certain types of pension plans be included in the income of individuals. For many individuals, the major item here would be amounts received under the provisions of Registered Pension Plans. Also included would be pension amounts received under the *Old Age Security Act* (OAS), as well as any similar payments received from a province. In addition, benefits received under the Canada Pension Plan (CPP) or a provincial pension plan would also become part of the individual's Net Income For Tax Purposes.

9-12. CPP recipients can request that their CPP benefits be split and paid separately to a spouse or common-law partner based on the length of time the individuals have been living together relative to the length of the contributory period. As is discussed later in this Chapter, there is also legislation that allows most other types of pension income to be split between spouses or common-law partners. However, this type of pension split is implemented entirely in the tax returns and does not involve the actual payments being split.

Retiring Allowances - ITA 56(1)(a)(ii)

9-13.   ITA 56(1)(a)(ii) requires that retiring allowances be included in an individual's Net Income For Tax Purposes.   ITA 248(1) defines these payments as follows:

> **"retiring allowance"**   means an amount (other than a superannuation or pension benefit, an amount received as a consequence of the death of an employee or a benefit described in subparagraph 6(1)(a)(iv)) received
>
> (a) on or after retirement of a taxpayer from an office or employment in recognition of the taxpayer's long service, or
>
> (b) in respect of a loss of an office or employment of a taxpayer, whether or not received as, on account or in lieu of payment of, damages or pursuant to an order or judgment of a competent tribunal,
>
> by the taxpayer or, after the taxpayer's death, by a dependant or a relation of the taxpayer or by the legal representative of the taxpayer.

9-14.   The term "retiring allowance" covers most payments on termination of employment. This includes rewards given for good service, payments related to early retirement (e.g., federal government buyout provisions) at either the request of the employee or the employer, as well as damages related to wrongful dismissal actions.

9-15.   Within specified limits, amounts received as a retiring allowance for service prior to 1996 can be deducted if they are transferred to either a Registered Pension Plan (RPP) or a Registered Retirement Savings Plan (RRSP) within 60 days of the end of the year in which they are received. (See Chapter 10.) This serves to defer the taxation on amounts transferred until the funds are withdrawn from the registered plan. For individuals who are retiring, this can be an important component of their tax planning. Note, however, while a deduction is available for the eligible transfer, the entire retiring allowance must be included in income.

Death Benefits - ITA 56(1)(a)(iii)

9-16.   Death benefits are included in the income of the recipient under ITA 56(1)(a)(iii). ITA 248(1) defines these death benefits as follows:

> **"death benefit"**   means the total of all amounts received by a taxpayer in a taxation year on or after the death of an employee in recognition of the employee's service in an office or employment ...

9-17.   When death benefits are received by a surviving spouse or common-law partner, the definition goes on to indicate that only amounts in excess of an exclusion of $10,000 are considered to be a death benefit for purposes of ITA 56(1)(a)(iii). This $10,000 exclusion would be available, even if the benefit was payable over a period of several years. A CPP death benefit is not eligible for the $10,000 exemption as it is not a death benefit paid in recognition of an employee's service.

9-18.   The $10,000 exclusion is also available on payments to individuals other than a spouse or common-law partner, with the amount being reduced to the extent it has been used by the spouse or common-law partner. For example, if Ms. Reid dies and her employer pays a death benefit of $8,000 to her husband and an additional $8,000 to her adult son, the husband could exclude the entire $8,000 from income and the son could use the remaining $2,000 of the exclusion to reduce his income inclusion to $6,000.

9-19.   Although death benefits are normally paid to the family of the deceased, it would appear that the $10,000 exclusion is available without regard to whom the death benefit is paid. This would suggest that an employer could pay any individual, including a related party, a $10,000 tax free death benefit on the death of any employee. Further, it would seem that an employer could repeatedly make such payments on the death of each of his employees.

Income Inclusions From Deferred Income Plans - ITA 56(1)(h), (h.1), (h.2), (i), and (t)

9-20.   Income inclusions from deferred income plans such as Registered Retirement Savings Plans (RRSPs), Registered Retirement Income Funds (RRIFs), and Deferred Profit Sharing Plans (DPSPs) do not fall into any of the major categories of income. Such amounts do not directly relate to employment efforts, business activity, ownership of property, or the disposition of capital assets. However, they clearly constitute income and, as a consequence, the *Income Tax Act* requires that payments from these various deferred income plans be included in the taxpayer's income.

9-21.   The details of these various types of plans are discussed in Chapter 10 where we provide comprehensive coverage of retirement savings arrangements. While you should not expect to understand these plans at this stage, you should note that the various income inclusions that are related to these plans are included in Net Income For Tax Purposes under the provisions of Subdivision d of Division B. Brief descriptions of the various inclusions in this area are as follows:

Payments From RRSPs   All amounts that are removed from a Registered Retirement Savings Plan must be included in income under ITA 56(1)(h).

Income Inclusions From Home Buyers' And Lifelong Learning Plans   If repayments to the RRSP are not made as per the required schedule for these plans (see Chapter 10), the specified amounts must be included in income. These amounts would be included in income under ITA 56(1)(h.1) and (h.2), respectively.

Payments From DPSPs   Under ITA 56(1)(i), all amounts removed from a Deferred Profit Sharing Plan must be included in income.

RRIF Withdrawals   The required minimum withdrawal, plus any additional withdrawals from Registered Retirement Income Funds, must be included in income under ITA 56(1)(h) and (t). Note that ITA 56(1)(t) would require the inclusion of the minimum withdrawal amount in income, even if the amount was not actually withdrawn.

Scholarships And Prizes - ITA 56(1)(n)

9-22.   ITA 56(1)(n) requires that all amounts received as scholarships, bursaries, grants, and prizes be included in income, to the extent that these amounts exceed the student's scholarship exemption under ITA 56(3). Prior to the 2010 federal budget, this exemption included 100 percent of scholarships and prizes that were received in connection with:

- an education program that qualifies for the education tax credit; and
- an elementary or secondary school education program.

9-23.   Reflecting a belief that the scholarship exemption for post-secondary education was too broadly stated, the 2010 budget contained the following to limit this exemption's use:

- At the post-secondary level, the exemption will only be available to the extent it relates to a college or CEGEP diploma, or a bachelor, masters or doctoral degree. This means it will not be available for most post-doctoral fellowships.
- Again, at the post-secondary level, the exemption will only be available in situations where it is reasonable to conclude that the scholarship was received to support the taxpayer's enrolment in a post-secondary program.
- With respect to scholarships received in connection with part-time enrollment, except in cases where the need to enroll on a part time basis is related to a physical or mental impairment, the exemption will be limited to the amount of tuition paid, plus costs of program-related materials.

Note   At the time of this writing (March, 2012), these provisions had not received final reading in Parliament.

Research Grants - ITA 56(1)(o)

9-24.   Research grants are included in income under ITA 56(1)(o). The amount to be included is net of unreimbursed expenses related to carrying on the research work.

Social Assistance And Workers' Compensation Payments - ITA 56(1)(u) And (v)

9-25.   Payments received under various social assistance programs must be included in income under ITA 56(1)(u), while workers' compensation payments are included under ITA 56(1)(v). It is not, however, the intent of the government to tax these amounts. They are sometimes referred to as exempt income, as they have no net effect on Taxable Income. However, they are included in Net Income For Tax Purposes, a figure that is used in a variety of eligibility tests.

9-26.   For example, to get the full tax credit for an infirm dependant over 17, the dependant's income must be less than a threshold amount ($6,420 for 2012). Since the policy is to reduce this credit in proportion to the dependant's income in excess of that amount, it is important that all types of income be included in the Net Income For Tax Purposes calculation. To accomplish this goal, social assistance and workers' compensation payments are included in the calculation of Net Income For Tax Purposes and then deducted in the calculation of Taxable Income.

Universal Child Care Benefit - ITA 56(6)

9-27.   Under the provisions of the *Universal Child Care Benefit Act*, families receive $100 per month for each child under the age of six. To receive this benefit, an individual must live with the child, be the person who is primarily responsible for the care of the child, and be a resident of Canada.

9-28.   For couples, the spouse with the lower Net Income For Tax Purposes must report the amounts received. However, single parents have the option of including the amounts in their own income or, alternatively:

- including the benefit in the income of a dependant who qualifies for the eligible dependant tax credit; or
- if this credit is not claimed, the income of the child for whom the benefit is received.

9-29.   The amounts received under the Universal Child Care Benefit:

- are not taken into account for the purposes of calculating income tested benefits delivered through the *Income Tax Act* (e.g., the GST tax credit),
- do not reduce Old Age Security or Employment Insurance benefits,
- do not reduce the amount of child care expenses that are deductible, and
- are not considered earned income for child care expense purposes.

Other Deductions - Subdivision e Deductions

CPP Contributions On Self-Employed Earnings - ITA 60(e)

9-30.   As was noted in Chapter 3, individuals who are self-employed are required to contribute larger amounts to the CPP than individuals who are employees. The maximum employee CPP contribution for 2012 is $2,307. This payment is eligible for a tax credit equal to 15 percent of the amount paid, an amount of $346 for employees making the maximum contribution.

9-31.   When an individual is an employee, the employer makes a matching contribution, resulting in a maximum total contribution of $4,614 [(2)($2,307)]. This contribution is fully deductible in the determination of the employer's Net Income For Tax Purposes.

9-32.   Self-employed individuals who are earning business income do not have an employer. However, the mechanics of the CPP system are such that an individual must have contributions that are the equivalent to those made by the employee/employer combination in order for that individual to receive the same benefits that would accrue to an employee. This goal is accomplished by having self-employed individuals make contributions that are the equivalent of both the employee and employer shares, a maximum of $4,614.

9-33. In order to put the self-employed individual on the same tax footing as an employee, the CPP contributions made by self-employed individuals are treated as follows:

- One-half of the self-employed individual's contributions, to a maximum of $2,307, are used to generate a 15 percent credit against Tax Payable.

- The remaining one-half, again to a maximum of $2,307, is deducted under Subdivision e in the determination of Net Income For Tax Purposes.

Moving Expenses - ITA 62
General Rules

9-34. ITA 62(1) indicates that a taxpayer can deduct moving expenses incurred as part of an "eligible relocation". Eligible relocation is defined in ITA 248(1) to mean a relocation that occurs to enable the taxpayer:

- to carry on business or to be employed at a new work location (this includes moving from an old work location, moving from a location where the individual was unemployed, and moving from a location where the individual was in full-time attendance at a college, university or other institution offering post-secondary education); or

- to be a student in full-time attendance at a college, university or other institution offering post-secondary education.

9-35. The definition also requires that the taxpayer's residence, both before and after the move, be in Canada. In addition, it specifies that the distance between the old residence and the new work location or institution be not less than 40 kilometers greater than the distance between the new residence and the new work location or institution. This distance is measured using the routes that would normally be traveled by an individual rather than "as the crow flies" (e.g., you can take the bridge, rather than swimming directly across the river).

9-36. Moving expenses can only be deducted against income received in a new work location, or from the educational institution (i.e., scholarships, research grants, etc. that increase Net Income For Tax Purposes). If the moving expenses exceed the income earned at the new location during the year of the move, any undeducted amount can be carried forward and deducted against income at the new location in any subsequent year.

9-37. For employees, to the extent that the moving expenses are directly reimbursed by an employer, they cannot be claimed by the taxpayer. Note, however, if the employer provides a general allowance rather than an item by item reimbursement, the allowance must be included in income, thereby creating a situation in which the employee will be able to deduct the actual amount of expenses incurred.

9-38. As described in ITA 62(3), moving expenses include:

- Traveling costs (including a reasonable amount expended for meals and lodging for the taxpayer and the taxpayer's family), in the course of moving the taxpayer and members of the household from the old residence to the new residence.

- The cost of transporting or storing household effects.

- The cost of meals and lodging for the taxpayer and the taxpayer's family near either the old or new residence for a period not exceeding 15 days. Note that, in measuring the 15 days, days spent while en route to the new location are not included.

- The cost of canceling a lease on the old residence.

- The selling costs of the old residence.

- The legal and other costs associated with the acquisition of the new residence, provided an old residence was sold in conjunction with the move. Note that this does not include any GST/HST/PST paid on the new residence.

- Up to $5,000 of interest, property taxes, insurance, and heating and utilities costs on the old residence, subsequent to the time when the individual has moved out and during which reasonable efforts are being made to sell the property. Deduction of this amount is conditional on the home remaining vacant.

- Costs of revising legal documents to reflect a new address, replacing driver's licenses and non-commercial vehicle permits, and connecting and disconnecting utilities.

9-39.   Any costs associated with decorating or improving the new residence would not be included in the definition of moving expenses, nor would any loss on the sale of the old residence. Also note that, in general, costs associated with trips to find accommodation at the new location are not included in the definition. The exception to this is meals and lodging near the new residence after it has been acquired.

9-40.   As a final point, there doesn't seem to be any time limit on when the move takes place.

Example   In 2008, an individual assumes a new job which is 100 kilometers away from his current residence. For several years he commutes this distance on a daily basis. However, in 2012, he decides to move closer and acquires a residence that is 40 kilometers closer to his job location.

9-41.   With respect to the deductibility of moving expenses in this situation, there have been several court cases supporting the position that he can deduct his moving costs, despite the fact that he has been working at the "new" work location for four years.

Simplified Method Of Calculating Vehicle And Meal Expenses

9-42.   In an effort to simplify claiming vehicle and meal expenses, the CRA permits the optional use of pre-established flat rates. Receipts are not needed to claim these amounts. For 2011 (the 2012 rates do not become available until 2013), the flat rate for meals is $17 per meal, to a daily maximum of $51, per person, per day. The flat rate for vehicle expenses depends on the province from which the move begins and ranges from $0.475 per kilometer for Saskatchewan to $0.635 per kilometer for the Yukon. The vehicle claim is calculated by multiplying the total kilometers driven during the year related to the move by the rate of the originating province.

Employer Reimbursements

9-43.   As noted in Chapter 3, an employer can reimburse an employee's moving expenses without creating a taxable benefit. It would appear that, for this purpose, the definition of moving expenses is broader than that which applies when an employee is deducting such expenses directly.

Example   An employer reimburses costs for an employee to visit a new work location in order to find housing and evaluate local schools.

Analysis   Despite the fact that the employee would not be able to deduct such costs, a reimbursement by the employer does not appear to create a taxable benefit.

9-44.   Another example of this situation involves employer reimbursement for a loss on the sale of a residence at the old work location. An employee would not be able to deduct this type of loss. However, ITA 6(20) indicates that only one-half of any reimbursement in excess of $15,000 will be included in the employee's income as a taxable benefit.

Example   An employer provides a $40,000 reimbursement to an employee for his loss on the sale of his house at the old work location.

Analysis   The employee would be assessed a taxable benefit of $12,500 [(1/2)($40,000 - $15,000)]. Note that, if the loss is not related to an eligible relocation (i.e., 40 kilometers closer to a new work location), the full amount of any loss reimbursement would be considered to be a taxable benefit under ITA 6(19).

9-45.   Employers have also attempted to compensate employees for being required to move to a new work location where housing costs are significantly higher. While there has been a considerable amount of litigation in this area, the issues now seem to be clarified:

Lump Sum Payments   In those situations where an employer provides an employee with a lump sum payment to cover the increased cost of equivalent housing at the new work location, the decision in *The Queen v. Phillips* (94 DTC 6177) has established that such an amount will be treated as a taxable benefit to the employee.

Interest Rate Relief And Other Subsidies   ITA 6(23) makes it clear that an amount paid or assistance provided in respect of an individual's office or employment that is related to the acquisition, financing, or use of a residence, is an employment benefit.

Tax Planning

9-46.   In those cases where the employer does not reimburse 100 percent of an employee's moving expenses, the fact that employers can reimburse certain costs that would not be deductible to the employee can be of some tax planning importance.

9-47.   In such partial reimbursement cases, it is to the advantage of the employee to have the employer's reimbursements specifically directed towards those moving costs that the employee would not be able to deduct from Net Income For Tax Purposes. This procedure costs the employer nothing and, at the same time, it permits the employee to maximize the deduction for moving expenses.

Example   An employee has total moving expenses of $22,000. This includes an $8,000 loss on his old residence as a result of the relocation. Other than this loss, the remaining moving costs totaling $14,000 are deductible to the employee. His employer has agreed to pay 60 percent of all moving costs ($13,200 in this case).

Analysis   Of the $13,200 that will be paid by the employer, $8,000 should be accounted for as a reimbursement for the loss on the old residence, with the remaining $5,200 being treated as an allowance. As the $8,000 reimbursement is less than the $15,000 limit that can be reimbursed, there will be no taxable benefit. Under this approach, the employee will have to include the $5,200 allowance in income, but will be able to deduct the $14,000 in remaining moving costs, a net deduction of $8,800. If the employer had simply paid an allowance of $13,200, the employee would have to include this amount in income, but would only have been only been able to deduct $14,000 of the expenses, a reduction in income of $800.

Exercise Nine - 1

Subject: Moving Expenses

On December 20, 2012, at the request of her employer, Ms. Martinova Chevlak moves from Edmonton to Regina. She has always lived in a rented apartment and will continue to do so in Regina. The total cost of the actual move, including the costs of moving her personal possessions, was $6,400. In addition, she spent $1,300 on a visit to Regina in a search for appropriate accommodation, and $1,200 as a penalty for breaking her lease in Edmonton. During the year, her salary totalled $64,000, of which $2,000 can be allocated to the period after December 20, 2012. Her employer is prepared to pay $6,000 towards the cost of her move. Indicate how Ms. Chevlak can maximize her moving expense deduction. Determine how much of this total can be deducted in 2012 and any carry forward available.

End of Exercise. Solution available in Study Guide.

Child Care Expenses - ITA 63
Basic Definitions
9-48.   The basic idea here is that a taxpayer is permitted to deduct the costs of caring for children if the costs were incurred in order to allow the taxpayer to produce Taxable Income or receive an education.   However, it is the policy of the government to place limits on the amount that can be deducted and, in the process of setting these limits, the rules related to child care costs have become quite complex. In applying these rules, a number of definitions are relevant:

Eligible Child   An eligible child is defined in ITA 63(3) to include a child of the taxpayer, his spouse or common-law partner, or a child who is dependent on the taxpayer or his spouse or common-law partner and whose income does not exceed the basic personal credit amount ($10,822 for 2011). In addition, the child must be under 16 years of age at some time during the year or dependent on the taxpayer or his spouse or common-law partner by reason of physical or mental infirmity.

There are different limits for disabled children who are eligible to claim the disability tax credit and those who are not (see following material). To be defined as an eligible child in the aged 16 or over category requires only that they be dependent solely as the result of some form of mental or physical disability. IT-513R does not provide examples of this level of disability, but states that the degree of the infirmity must be such that it requires the child to be dependent for a considerable period of time.

Annual Child Care Expense Amount   There are three annual limits.   For a dependent child of any age who is eligible for the disability tax credit (e.g., a blind child), the amount is $10,000. For a child under 7 years of age at the end of the year, the amount is $7,000. For a child aged 7 to 16, or a dependent child over 16 who has a mental or physical infirmity, but is not eligible for the disability tax credit, the amount is $4,000.

Periodic Child Care Expense Amount   This weekly amount is defined as being equal to 1/40 of the annual child care expense amount applicable to the particular child. Depending on the child, the value per week will be $250 [(1/40)($10,000)], $175 [(1/40)($7,000)], or $100 [(1/40)($4,000)].

Earned Income   For use in determining deductible child care expenses, earned income is defined as gross employment income (for this purpose, taxable benefits, taxable allowances and stock option benefits are included, but no deductions from employment income are taken into consideration), net business income (for this purpose, business losses are ignored), and amounts of scholarships, training allowances, and research grants that have been included in Net Income For Tax Purposes.

Note that the calculation of earned income for child care expense purposes is different than the earned income calculation used to determine RRSP deduction limits (see Chapter 10). Also note that this calculation does not include payments under the Universal Child Care Benefit Plan.

Supporting Person   A supporting person is usually the child's parent, or the spouse or common-law partner of the child's parent. However, a supporting person is also an individual who can claim the amount for an eligible dependant, an infirm dependant over 17, or the caregiver amount for the child.

9-49.   Using the definitions, we can now give attention to the rules applicable to determining the deductible amount of child care expenses.

Limits For Lower Income Spouse Or Single Parent
9-50.   There is an implicit assumption in the child care cost legislation that two parent families with a single bread winner should not be able to deduct child care costs. This assumption is implemented through the requirement that, in general, only the spouse (or "supporting person") with the lower income can deduct child care costs. This means that, in most

situations, families that have a house parent who is earning no outside income, is not a student, and is capable of taking care of the children, cannot deduct child care costs.

9-51.   The amount that can be deducted by the spouse with the lower Net Income For Tax Purposes in a two parent family, or by the single parent when there is no other supporting person, is the least of three amounts:

1.   The amount actually paid for child care services, plus limited amounts (see Paragraph 9-55) paid for lodging at boarding schools and overnight camps.

2.   The sum of the **Annual Child Care Expense Amounts** for the taxpayer's eligible children ($10,000, $7,000, or $4,000 per child).

3.   2/3 of the taxpayer's **Earned Income**.

9-52.   Note that there is no requirement that these amounts be spent on specific children. For example, a couple with three children under the age of 7 would have an overall amount under limit 2 of $21,000 [(3)($7,000)]. This $21,000 amount would be the applicable limit even if all of it was spent on care for one child and nothing was spent for the other children.

9-53.   Actual costs include amounts incurred for care for an eligible child in order that the taxpayer may earn employment income, carry on a business, or attend a secondary school (e.g. a high school) or a designated educational institution (i.e., an institution that qualifies the individual for the education tax credit). In order to be deductible, amounts paid for child care must be supported by receipts issued by the payee. Where the payee is an individual, the Social Insurance Number of the payee must be provided.

9-54.   Other constraints indicated in IT-495R3, "Child Care Expenses", are that payments are not deductible if they are made to:

• the mother or father of the child;

• a related party under the age of 18 (this does not include nieces, nephews, aunts, or uncles); or

• an individual for whom a supporting person can claim the amount for an eligible dependant, an infirm dependant over 17, or the caregiver amount.

Attendance At Boarding School Or Camp

9-55.   A further limitation on actual costs involves situations where one or more children are attending a boarding school or an overnight camp. The federal government does not wish to provide tax assistance for the cost of facilities that provide services that go beyond child care (e.g., computer lessons). As a consequence, when the actual costs involve overnight camps or boarding school fees, the deductible costs are limited to the Periodic Child Care Expense Amount ($250, $175, or $100 per week, per child). Amounts paid to the camp or boarding school in excess of these amounts would not be deductible.

9-56.   Note that this weekly limit does not apply to fees paid to day camps or sports camps that do not include overnight stays. However, for fees to day camps and day sports schools to be eligible for a child care deduction, the primary goal of the camp must be to care for the children as opposed to providing sports education.

9-57.   You will recall from Chapter 4 that there are tax credits for eligible expenses related to both child fitness and child arts activity. It is likely that, in many cases, costs associated with a boarding school or camp could qualify as both a child care cost and as the base for one of these credits. To avoid providing a credit and a deduction for the same costs, the definition of the expenses that are eligible for the tax credits exclude amounts that have been deducted in computing the taxpayer's Net Income For Tax Purposes. This leaves the question of how a couple or single taxpayer should use receipts for such costs to maximize tax savings. The alternatives would also depend on the willingness of organizations to produce separate receipts for the relevant fitness and/or arts credits. This is a complex issue that goes beyond the scope of this text.

When Deductible By Higher Income Spouse

9-58.   In the preceding material, we noted the general rule that child care costs are to be deducted by the lower income spouse. There are however, a number of exceptions to this general rule. Specifically, the higher income spouse is allowed to make the deduction if:

- the lower income spouse is a student in attendance at a secondary school or a designated educational institution and enrolled in a program of the institution or school that is not less than 3 consecutive weeks duration and provides that each student in the program spend not less than:

  - 10 hours per week on courses or work in the program (i.e., full time attendance); or
  - 12 hours per month on courses or work in the program (i.e., part time attendance);

- the lower income spouse is infirm and incapable of caring for the children for at least 2 weeks because of confinement to a bed, wheelchair, hospital, or asylum (this condition requires a written certificate from a medical doctor supporting the fact that the individual is incapable of caring for children);

- the lower income spouse is likely to be incapable of caring for children for a long and continuous period because of a mental or physical infirmity (this condition requires a written certificate from a medical doctor supporting the fact that the individual is incapable of caring for children);

- the lower income spouse is a person confined to a prison or similar institution throughout a period of not less than 2 weeks in the year; or

- the spouses are separated for more than 90 days beginning in the year.

9-59.   In situations where the higher income spouse is making the deduction, the amount of the deduction would be subject to the same limitations that are applicable when the deduction is being made by the lower income spouse. However, the higher income spouse has a further limitation. This additional limit is calculated by multiplying the sum of the Periodic Child Care Expense Amounts for all eligible children, by the number of weeks that the lower income spouse is infirm, in prison, separated from the higher income spouse, or attending an educational institution on a full-time basis. If the attendance is part-time, the sum of the Periodic Amounts is multiplied by the number of months of part-time attendance, not weeks.

If A Parent Is A Student

9-60.   ITA 63(2.2) allows a taxpayer who is attending a secondary school or a designated educational institution on a full or part time basis to deduct child care costs if there is no other supporting person or, alternatively, if there is another supporting person, if the (student) taxpayer is the higher income supporting person. The amounts involved here are in addition to the normal child care limitations. However, the complications associated with applying this provision go beyond the scope of this text.

Example

9-61.   The following example will serve to clarify some of the general rules for child care costs.

> **Example**   Jack and Joanna Morris have three children, Bruce, Bobby, and Betty. At the end of 2012, Bruce is aged 18 and, while he is physically disabled, his disability is not severe enough that he qualifies for the disability tax credit. With respect to their other children, Bobby is aged 6 and Betty is aged 5 at the end of the year. Jack has 2012 earned income of $45,000, while Joanna has 2012 earned income of $63,000.
>
> The couple has full time help to care for their children during 49 weeks of the year. The cost of this help is $210 per week ($10,290 for the year).
>
> During July, the children are sent to music camp in a provincial park for three weeks. The camp fees total $3,500 for this period for all three children. Assume that these costs do not qualify for either the child fitness credit or the children arts credit.

As the result of a substance abuse conviction, Jack spends seven weeks in November and December in prison.

Analysis   The deductible child care costs would be the least of the following amounts:

	Joanna	Jack
Actual child care costs plus maximum deductible camp fees {$10,290 + [(2)($175)(3 weeks) + (1)($100)(3 weeks)]	$11,640	$11,640
Annual Child Care Expense Amount [(2)($7,000) + (1)($4,000)]	18,000	18,000
2/3 of earned income	42,000	30,000
Periodic Child Care Expense Amounts [(2)($175)(7 weeks) + (1)($100)(7 weeks)]	3,150	N/A

While Joanna is the higher income spouse, she can deduct child care costs for the seven weeks that Jack is in prison. Her maximum deduction is $3,150. Jack's limit is $11,640. This must be reduced by the $3,150 deducted by Joanna to $8,490 ($11,640 - $3,150). Note that, while Bruce, at age 18, is an eligible child because of his disability, the fact that the disability is not severe enough to qualify Bruce for the disability tax credit means that his annual limit is $4,000 rather than $10,000, and that the periodic limit for Joanna and for the camp fees is $100 rather than $250.

Exercise Nine - 2

Subject: Child Care Expenses

Mr. and Mrs. Sampras have three children. The ages of the children are 4, 9, and 14, and they are all in good mental and physical health. During the current year, Mr. Sampras has net employment income of $14,000, after the deduction of employment expenses of $5,500. Mr. Sampras also received $1,200 in universal child care benefits. Mrs. Sampras has net business income during this period of $54,000, after deducting business expenses of $21,000. The child care costs for the current year, all properly documented for tax purposes, are $10,500. Determine the maximum deduction for child care costs and indicate who should claim them.

End of Exercise.   Solution available in Study Guide.

Disability Supports Deduction - ITA 64
Eligibility And Coverage
9-62.   In order to assist disabled individuals who work or go to school, ITA 64 provides a disability supports deduction that is available to disabled individuals who are:

- performing duties of an office or employment,
- carrying on a business, either alone or as a partner actively engaged in the business,
- attending a designated educational institution or a secondary school, or
- carrying on research in respect of which the individual received a grant.

9-63.   The deduction is available for an extensive list of costs that can be associated with a disabled person working or going to school. The costs must be paid for by the disabled individual and include the cost of:

- sign-language interpretation services, a teletypewriter or similar device;
- a Braille printer;
- an optical scanner, an electronic speech synthesizer;
- note-taking services, voice recognition software, tutoring services; and
- talking textbooks.

9-64.   The availability of this deduction is not limited to individuals who qualify for the disability tax credit. As an example, if an individual has a hearing impairment that requires sign language assistance, the costs of such services are deductible, without regard to whether the individual is eligible for the disability tax credit. In most cases, a medical practitioner must provide a prescription, or certify that there is a need for incurring the specific type of cost.

Limits On The Amount Deducted

9-65.   The amount of qualifying costs that can be deducted under ITA 64 is limited to the lesser of:

- An amount determined by the formula:

$$A - B, \text{ where}$$

  A   is equal to the qualifying disability support costs and
  B   is equal to any reimbursement (such as payments from medical insurance) of amounts included in **A** that were not included in income.

- The total of:

  1. Gross employment income, net business income, and scholarships and research grants to the extent they are included in Net Income For Tax Purposes.

  2. Where the individual is in attendance at a designated educational institution or secondary school, the least of:

      - $15,000;
      - $375 times the number of weeks of school attendance at a designated educational institution or secondary school; and
      - the amount by which the individual's Net Income For Tax Purposes exceeds the amounts of income included in item 1.

Disability Supports Deduction Vs. Medical Expenses Tax Credit

9-66.   Since most of the costs that can be deducted under the disability supports deduction could also be claimed for the medical expenses tax credit, it may be difficult for a disabled person to determine the more advantageous way to claim the expenditures. As you would expect, amounts that are deducted under the ITA 64 disability supports deduction cannot be included in the base for the medical expense tax credit.

9-67.   In choosing between the alternative uses of these costs, the following factors should be taken into consideration:

- The base for the medical expense tax credit is reduced by 3 percent of the taxpayer's Net Income For Tax Purposes.

- Tax credits are calculated using the lowest tax bracket. If the taxpayer's income places them in a higher tax bracket, the deduction of costs under the disability supports program will provide a larger reduction in taxes.

- If the taxpayer has only limited amounts of Taxable Income, the ability to use the refundable medical expense tax credit may be more beneficial.

- The deduction is only available to the disabled person on costs that have been paid for personally by the disabled person. If a spouse or supporting person has paid the costs, the spouse or supporting person could claim the medical expense credit with respect to these costs, but could not claim the disability supports deduction.

Complications Related To Attendant Care Costs

9-68.   If an individual qualifies for the ITA 118.3 disability tax credit, he can claim attendant care costs as a medical expense. However, you may recall from Chapter 4 that, if the medical expense claim is for full time attendant care (defined as more than $10,000 per year), the individual loses the ability to claim the disability tax credit. We would note that, if attendant care costs are over $10,000, it may be beneficial to limit the medical expense credit claim to

$10,000 in order to stay within the definition of "part time". This would prevent the taxpayer from losing his claim to the disability tax credit.

9-69. Form T929 indicates that only individuals who qualify for the disability tax credit can claim amounts paid for part time attendant care as a disability supports deduction. However, provided the need for such care is certified by a medical practitioner, full time care can be claimed by individuals who do not qualify for the disability tax credit. This results in a very complex situation with respect to these costs. We have tried to simplify the possibilities in the following general summary:

- If an individual qualifies for the disability tax credit, he can claim attendant care costs as either an addition to the base for the medical expense tax credit, or as a disability supports deduction within the limits of ITA 64. If the disabled individual had sufficient income to move them out of the minimum 15 percent federal tax bracket, the latter choice would provide the larger benefit.

- If an individual qualifies for the disability tax credit and has attendant care costs in excess of $10,000, he is faced with a choice. He can add the full amount of the attendant care costs to the medical expenses tax credit base. However, this claim will result in the loss of the disability tax credit. Alternatively, he can claim these costs as a disability supports deduction, provided a medical practitioner will certify the need for such care. This will usually be preferable as he will continue to qualify for the disability tax credit.

- If an individual is disabled, but does not qualify for the disability tax credit, he can deduct full time attendant care costs under ITA 64, provided a medical practitioner certifies the need for full time attendant care. However, this individual cannot deduct the costs of part time attendant care.

Exercise Nine - 3

Subject: Disability Supports Deduction

Jose Morph has visual, speech, and hearing disabilities. However, they are not severe enough to allow him to qualify for the disability tax credit. During 2012, he worked on a full time basis as a programmer for a large public company and his employment income totaled $78,000.

His need for full time attendant care has been certified by a medical practitioner and, during 2012, such care cost Jose $23,000. Other deductible costs required to support his ability to work as a disabled person totaled $18,000, all of which were certified by a medical practitioner. His medical insurance reimbursed him for $5,000 of these expenses. Jose will not include any of these costs in his base for the medical expenses tax credit. Calculate Jose's disability supports deduction for 2012.

End of Exercise. Solution available in Study Guide.

Related Inclusions And Deductions

Introduction

9-70. At the beginning of this Chapter, we noted that there are several Subdivision e deductions that are directly related to an item that is included in Subdivision d. These items will be dealt with in this Section.

Employment Insurance Benefits - ITA 56(1)(a)(iv) And 60(n)

9-71. ITA 56(1)(a)(iv) requires that Employment Insurance (EI) benefits received be included in income, even if they are subsequently repaid. Repayment of these benefits can be required if an individual has Net Income in excess of a specified level. If EI benefits must be repaid, the repayment can be deducted under ITA 60(n).

Pension Income Splitting - ITA 56(1)(a.2) And 60(c)

General Rules

9-72. When the Harper government announced that it was going to begin taxing the distributions of income trusts, it is likely that the most affected group was senior citizens. They had invested significant portions of their retirement savings in these securities and, as a direct result of the government's change in policy, they saw their investments decline in value by billions of dollars.

9-73. To offset the pain for senior citizens, the Harper government simultaneously announced other measures which would benefit this very vocal group of taxpayers. One of the most important of these measures was a provision which provided for reallocation of up to 50 percent of a taxpayer's pension income.

9-74. While the ability to split CPP amounts has been available to couples for many years, this provision extends this privilege to include most other types of pension income. However, unlike the CPP situation where there is an actual split of the payments being made, this additional split is implemented entirely in the tax returns.

9-75. The basic provision for the split is found in ITA 60.03. This Section allows a pensioner, defined as any resident Canadian who receives eligible pension income, to file a joint election with a spouse or common-law partner to reallocate up to 50 percent of his pension income to a pension transferee (i.e., the spouse or common-law partner). When the election is made, the pension transferee will include the elected amount in income under ITA 56(1)(a.2). The same amount can be deducted by the pensioner under ITA 60(c). The election requires the filing of a prescribed form T1032.

9-76. The types of pension income that are eligible for splitting are the same as those that are eligible for the pension income tax credit. You may recall from Chapter 4 that there are different rules for taxpayers who are under 65 years of age and those 65 and over. In general, most types of pension income other than OAS and CPP can be split for those 65 and over. While the age of the transferor determines the types of pension income that can be split, the age of the transferee has no influence on this matter.

9-77. Another point here relates to withholding. Taxes are withheld at the source from most pension amounts that are paid to an individual. However, ITA 153(2) indicates that, if a portion of this pension income is allocated to a spouse or common-law partner, a proportionate share of the total withholding is deemed to be on behalf of that spouse or common-law partner. This means that this proportionate share of tax withheld will be transferred to the tax return of the spouse or common-law partner to reduce their Tax Payable or increase the amount of their refund.

Complications

9-78. In some cases, the desirability of pension income splitting is fairly obvious. For example, an individual in the highest tax bracket can transfer a significant amount of income to a spouse who has no income, resulting in a large amount of income being taxed at the lowest rate. In addition, the transfer can create a pension income tax credit for the transferee.

9-79. There are, however, many possible offsetting factors, such as the loss of the transferee's age credit or a decrease in the medical expenses credit. In situations where there is less disparity in the two incomes, other factors could come into play. For example, the transfer could create or increase a transferee's OAS clawback.

9-80. Given these complications, it is not possible to have a general rule related to the use of pension income splitting. In cases where one spouse has no pension income, it will generally be desirable to transfer enough pension income to create a pension income tax credit. However, transfer of additional amounts involves a large number of considerations. Fortunately, tax preparation software can assist in determining an optimum solution.

Exercise Nine - 4

Subject: Pension Income Splitting

Joanna Sparks lives with her husband of many years, John Sparks. They are both 67 years of age. During 2012, Joanna received $6,500 in OAS payments. She also receives $85,000 of pension income from a plan that was sponsored by her former employer. She has not, at this point in time, applied for CPP. John's only source of 2012 income is $6,500 in OAS payments. Neither Joanna nor John has any tax credits other than the basic personal credit, age credit, and pension income credit.

Joanna has asked you to indicate the savings in federal tax that would result from making optimum use of pension income splitting for the 2012 taxation year.

End of Exercise. Solution available in Study Guide.

Spousal And Child Support - ITA 56(1)(b) And 60(b)

Definitions

9-81.   ITA 56.1(4) provides definitions for both support and child support:

Support Amount means an amount payable or receivable as an allowance on a periodic basis for the maintenance of the recipient, children of the recipient or both the recipient and children of the recipient, if the recipient has discretion as to the use of the amount, and

(a) the recipient is the spouse or common-law partner or former spouse or common-law partner of the payer, the recipient and payer are living separate and apart because of the breakdown of their marriage or common-law partnership and the amount is receivable under an order of a competent tribunal or under a written agreement; or

(b) the payer is a legal parent of a child of the recipient and the amount is receivable under an order made by a competent tribunal in accordance with the laws of a province.

Child Support Amount means any support amount that is not identified in the agreement or order under which it is receivable as being solely for the support of a recipient who is a spouse or common-law partner or former spouse or common-law partner of the payer or who is a parent of a child of whom the payer is a legal parent.

9-82.   When read together, these two definitions provide, in effect, a definition of spousal support. For an amount to be treated as spousal support, it must be specifically designated as being solely for the support of a recipient who is a spouse or common-law partner, a recipient who is a former spouse or common-law partner, or a recipient who is the parent of a child of whom the payer is a legal parent.

General Tax Treatment

9-83.   Under the currently applicable rules, only those payments that are clearly designated as spousal support are deductible by the payer under ITA 60(b). Such payments would then be taxable to the recipient under ITA 56(1)(b). As noted in the section which follows, there are other conditions that must be met to qualify the payments for deduction and inclusion.

9-84.   Child support, which would include all support amounts that are not clearly designated as spousal support, cannot be deducted by the payer. Consistent with this, the amounts paid are not taxed in the hands of the recipient.

Conditions For Deduction And Inclusion

9-85. As indicated in the preceding material, there are a number of conditions that must be met in order to make spousal support payments deductible to the payer and taxable to the recipient. As described in IT-530R, *Support Payments*, these conditions are as follows:

- the amount is paid as alimony or an allowance for the maintenance of the spouse or common-law partner, or former spouse or common-law partner;

- the spouses or common-law partners, or former spouses or common-law partners, are living apart at the time the payment is made, and were separated pursuant to a divorce, judicial separation, or written separation agreement;

- the amount is paid pursuant to a decree, order, or judgment of a competent tribunal or pursuant to a written agreement;

- the recipient has discretionary use of the amount; and

- the amount is payable on a periodic basis.

9-86. The reasons for most of these conditions are fairly obvious. For example, without the condition that the spouses are living apart, a couple could effectively split income simply by getting a written separation agreement and having the spouse with the higher income make payments to the spouse with the lower income.

9-87. While payments prior to the date of a court decree cannot technically be made pursuant to that decree, ITA 56.1(3) and ITA 60.1(3) deem that payments made in the year of the decree or the preceding year will be considered paid pursuant to the decree, provided that the order or agreement specifies that they are to be so considered.

9-88. Problems often arise with respect to the requirement that payments be made on a periodic basis. Clearly, a single lump sum payment does not qualify, nor does a payment that releases the payer from future obligations. Payments that are in excess of amounts required to maintain the spouse and/or children in the manner to which they were accustomed are also likely to be disallowed. Other factors that should be considered are the interval at which the payments are made and whether the payments are for an indefinite period, or a fixed term.

9-89. Under some circumstances, a person who receives support payments and includes the amount received in income may be required to repay some portion of these amounts. In these circumstances, the person making the repayment is allowed to deduct the amount repaid [ITA 60(c.2)]. As you would expect, the recipient is required to include a corresponding amount in income [ITA 56(1)(c.2)].

Additional Considerations

9-90. There are a number of additional considerations related to the tax treatment of support payments:

- In situations where a required payment includes both child support and spousal support, a problem arises when less than the required amount is remitted. In such cases, the question becomes whether the payments that were made were for child support or, alternatively for spousal support. The required solution in ITA 56(1)(b) and 60(b) is that only payments in excess of the required child support will be deductible/taxable spousal support. For example, consider an individual required to pay $4,000 in child support and $12,000 in spousal support. If a total of $7,000 is paid during the year, only $3,000 of that amount will be deductible/taxable.

- In general, payments to third parties that are clearly for the benefit of the spouse are deductible to the payer and taxable to the spouse.

- Deductible child support payments reduce the payer's earned income for RRSP purposes. Correspondingly, taxable support payments increase the recipient's earned income for RRSP purposes (see Chapter 10).

- The recipient of child support payments will continue to be eligible for the credit for an eligible dependant (see Chapter 4).

- ITA 118(5) prevents an individual from taking a tax credit for a spouse or eligible dependant and, at the same time, deducting support payments to that spouse or child.

- While it is not part of the legislation, the Government of Canada has published an extensive, province by province list of guidelines for child support. These guidelines are dependent on the number of children involved and the income of the payer.

Exercise Nine - 5

Subject: Support Payments

On June 15, 2012, Sandra and Jerry Groom sign a separation agreement that calls for Sandra to pay Jerry $1,500 per month in child support (Jerry will have custody of their five children) and $2,500 per month in spousal support beginning July 1. During 2012, Sandra pays support for only three months. How will the total support paid of $12,000 be dealt with in Sandra and Jerry's 2012 tax returns?

End of Exercise. Solution available in Study Guide.

Annuity Payments Received - ITA 56(1)(d) And 60(a)
Annuities And Their Uses
9-91.   ITA 248(1) defines an annuity as an amount payable on a periodic basis, without regard to whether it is payable at intervals longer or shorter than a year. As the term is usually applied, it refers to the investment contracts that are usually sold by insurance companies. The two basic forms of these contracts involve either payments for a specified period (e.g., annual payments for a period of 10 years), or payments for the life of the annuitant (e.g., annual payments until the recipient of the payment dies).

9-92.   These contracts can also take various types of hybrid forms. For example, a common arrangement would be a life annuity, with payments guaranteed for a minimum of 10 years. In this case, if the annuitant dies prior to the end of 10 years, payments will continue to be made to the deceased's estate until the end of the specified guarantee period.

9-93.   Annuities are widely used in retirement and estate planning because they provide a guaranteed stream of income that is virtually risk free. Also important is the fact that, in the case of life annuities, the annuitant does not have to be concerned with outliving the income stream. As you would expect, these desirable features are offset by low rates of return.

9-94.   The taxation of annuity payments depends on the manner in which the investment contract was acquired:

Acquisition Within A Tax Deferred Plan   Annuities are often purchased by the administrator of such tax deferred plans as Registered Pension Plans (RPPs), Registered Retirement Savings Plans (RRSPs), Registered Retirement Income Funds (RRIFs), and Deferred Profit Sharing Plans (DPSPs). The goal here is to provide the beneficiary of the plan with a fixed and guaranteed stream of income, usually at the time of their retirement. Because contributions to these plans are deductible and earnings on assets held within the plans accumulate on a tax free basis, all payments out of these plans are subject to tax. This means that, the full amount of payments made from annuities that have been purchased within these plans must be included in the recipient's Net Income For Tax Purposes.

Acquisition Outside Tax Deferred Plan   Individuals also purchase annuities outside of tax deferred plans. The potential problem in this case can be illustrated by a simple example:

Example   Pierre Brissette uses funds from his savings account, (i.e., after tax funds), to purchases a 5 year ordinary annuity with payments of $2,309 at the end of each year. The cost of the annuity is $10,000, providing him with an effective yield of 5 percent.

Analysis   The total payments on this annuity would be $11,545. This total is made up of $1,545 of earnings, plus $10,000 which represents a return of Mr. Brissette's capital. It would not be equitable to require Mr. Brissette to include the full amount of the annuity payments in his Net Income For Tax Purposes. Clearly, some type of provision is required to recognize the return of capital components of the annuity payments that he has received.

Capital Element Of An Annuity

9-95.   You will recall from Paragraph 9-20 of this Chapter, that payments from registered plans are included under specific provisions of subdivision d [e.g., payments from RRSPs are included under ITA 56(1)(h)].

9-96.   In order to distinguish these fully taxable annuity payments from payments made by annuities acquired outside of tax deferred plans, ITA 56(1)(d) requires the inclusion in income of annuity payments that are not "otherwise included in income". As payments from RPPs, RRSPs, RRIFs, and DPSPs, are "otherwise included" under other provisions of the *Income Tax Act*, this means that only annuities purchased with after tax funds would be included here.

9-97.   For those annuity payments that are included under ITA 56(1)(d), ITA 60(a) allows a deduction that is designed to reflect the return of capital element that is included in these payments. The capital element that is to be deducted is calculated by multiplying the annuity payment that was included in income for the year by a ratio. As presented in ITR 300, the formula for calculating the capital element of a fixed term annuity payment is as follows:

$$\text{Deduction} = \left[\frac{\text{Capital Outlay To Buy The Annuity}}{\text{Total Payments To Be Received Under The Contract}} \right] [\text{Annuity Payment}]$$

9-98.   To illustrate this procedure, refer to the example in Paragraph 9-94. Since this annuity had been purchased with $10,000 in after tax funds, the entire annual payment of $2,309 would be included in income under ITA 56(1)(d). However, this would be offset by a deduction under ITA 60(a) that is calculated as follows:

$$\left[\frac{\$10,000}{\$11,545} \right] [\$2,309] = \$2,000 \text{ Deduction}$$

9-99.   Note that this treatment would apply to situations where an individual has made a lump-sum withdrawal from a tax deferred plan and used the funds to acquire an annuity. For example, if an individual withdrew $100,000 from his RRSP, this amount would be subject to tax at the time of withdrawal. This means that payments from this annuity would be included in his income under ITA 56(1)(d) and, as a consequence, would be eligible for the ITA 60(a) deduction.

Exercise Nine - 6

Subject: Annuity Payments

On January 1 of the current year, Barry Hollock uses $55,000 of his savings to acquire a fixed term annuity. The term of the annuity is 4 years, the annual payments are $15,873, the payments are received on December 31 of each year, and the rate inherent in the annuity is 6 percent. What is the effect of the $15,873 annual payment on Mr. Hollock's Net Income For Tax Purposes?

End of Exercise. Solution available in Study Guide.

Registered Savings Plans

Introduction

9-100.   Registered savings plans allow individuals to make contributions to a trust that is registered with the CRA. The trustees of the plan are required to provide information returns with respect to contributions to, and withdrawals from, these plans.

9-101.   As indicated in Paragraph 9-6, in this Chapter we will deal with three registered plans. These are Registered Education Savings Plans (RESPs), Registered Disability Savings Plans (RDSPs) and Tax Free Savings Accounts (TFSAs). Other registered plans will be covered in Chapter 10.

9-102.   Contributions to the plans that are being considered in this Chapter are not deductible in determining the taxpayer's Net Income For Tax Purposes. However, they do have significant tax advantages.

> **Tax Deferral**   Once contributions have been made, they will be invested in various types of income producing assets. There will be no taxation of this income, including compounding amounts, as long as the assets remain in the plan. This provides for significant tax deferral.

> **Tax Reduction (RESPs And RDSPs)**   Contributions to these plans will typically be made by a parent or grandparent who has Taxable Income. In some cases, this income will be subject to tax at maximum rates. While earnings distributions from RESPs and RDSPs are subject to tax, they will be paid to either a student or a disabled individual. In many cases, such individuals will not have sufficient income to use their available tax credits, resulting in a situation where some amounts can be distributed without attracting additional taxation. Even if this is not the case, such individuals are likely to be in a lower tax bracket than the individual who made the contributions, resulting in a tax reduction that may be significant.

> **Tax Avoidance (TFSAs Only)**   The fact that both contributions and earnings can be withdrawn from a TFSA on a tax free basis means that amounts earned in these plans is totally exempt from tax.

9-103.   The basic operation of RESPs, RDSPs and TFSAs is depicted in Figure 9-1. As shown in that Figure, the contributions to these plans are non-deductible to the taxpayer. This is in contrast to both RPPs and RRSPs where the contributions can be deducted at the time they are made (see Chapter 10).

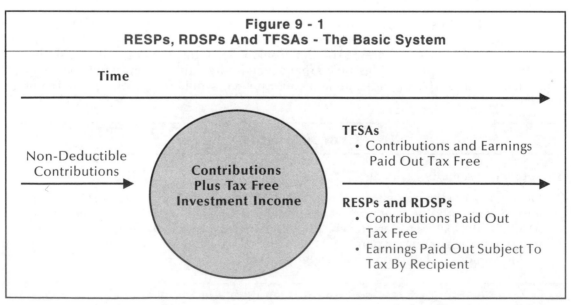

Figure 9 - 1
RESPs, RDSPs And TFSAs - The Basic System

Time

Non-Deductible Contributions

Contributions Plus Tax Free Investment Income

TFSAs
• Contributions and Earnings Paid Out Tax Free

RESPs and RDSPs
• Contributions Paid Out Tax Free
• Earnings Paid Out Subject To Tax By Recipient

Registered Education Savings Plans (RESPs)
Contributions

9-104.   The contribution rules for Registered Education Savings Plans (RESPs) are found in ITA 146.1. As we have noted, unlike contributions to an RRSP, contributions to an RESP do not provide a deduction for the taxpayer. However, they do share the second major tax advantage that is available to contributors to RRSPs. This is the fact that, once contributions to these plans are invested, the earnings accrue on a tax free basis.

9-105.   As is discussed more completely in Chapter 10, over extended periods of time, there is a very large benefit associated with this tax free accumulation of earnings. Note, however, that in the case of RESPs, this tax free accumulation is limited to 35 years after the plan is established (40 years for plans with a single beneficiary who is eligible for the disability tax credit). At the end of that period, the plan is automatically deregistered.

9-106.   An individual, usually a parent or grandparent becomes a subscriber or a joint subscriber of an RESP by signing a contract with an RESP promoter. Total contributions are limited to $50,000 for each beneficiary with no annual limit on contributions. Although there is complete flexibility with respect to the timing, some consideration should be given to the CESG limits (see Paragraph 9-109).

9-107.   There is a penalty for excess contributions. If, at the end of any month, the contributions for a particular beneficiary exceed the total limit of $50,000, the subscribers to the plan are subject to a 1 percent per month tax on the excess. Note that these limits apply for each beneficiary. If several individuals are contributing to different plans with the same beneficiary (e.g., Joan's father and her grandmother are both contributing to a plan on her behalf), the sum of their contributions to Joan's plans cannot exceed the $50,000 limit. Any tax assessed on excess contributions must be shared on a pro rata basis by the subscriber(s).

Canada Education Savings Grants (CESGs)

9-108.   Under the Canada Education Savings Grant (CESG) program, the federal government will make additional contributions to an RESP to supplement those being made by the subscriber(s). The CESG has both a basic and "additional" component.

9-109.   The amount of grant eligible contributions is a balance that accumulates at the rate of $2,500 per year, beginning in the year a child is born. The basic CESG is equal to 20 percent of the current year contributions for a beneficiary up to a maximum of $500 [(20%)($2,500)] per beneficiary. If there is unused contribution room from previous years, up to $1,000 in CESG is available in the current year. The lifetime CESG maximum is $7,200.

9-110.   In order to assist low income families, an additional CESG of 10 or 20 percent of the first $500 of contributions in a year for a beneficiary is available. The amount of the additional CESG depends on the net family income for the second preceding year. This time lag is necessary in order to have the figures from the income tax returns available. On the first $500 in contributions for 2012, the basic and additional CESG is calculated as follows:

- at 40% (20% + 20%) if 2011 family income is $42,707 or less (maximum of $200),
- at 30% (20% + 10%) if 2011 family income is between $42,707 and $85,414 (maximum of $150), and
- at 20% (20% + 0%) if 2011 family income is greater than $85,414 (maximum of $100).

9-111.   For all income brackets, for each beneficiary, contributions between $500 and $2,500 in a year earn a grant equal to 20 percent of the contributions.

> **Example** Tom is born in February, 2011. Tom's father makes an RESP contribution of $1,300 for Tom in 2011 and $1,300 in 2012. In November of 2012, Tom's grandmother makes a $3,000 contribution to another RESP for Tom.
>
> **Analysis** Tom's 2012 contribution room for balances eligible for CESGs is $3,700 [(2)($2,500) - $1,300]. As the combined contributions of the father and grandmother total $4,300, $600 of the total contributions will not be eligible for CESGs. Depending on the net family income of Tom's father, the CESG for 2012 ranges from

$740 [(20%)($3,700)] to $840 [(40%)($500) + (20%)($3,700 - $500)].

It is important to note that the $600 excess contribution does not carry forward and become eligible for CESGs in the following year when more contribution room accrues to Tom. If it is expected that annual contributions to Tom's RESP will be less than $2,500 in the future, this would suggest that Tom's father should limit his 2012 contribution to $700 and defer the extra $600 to the following year. In that year, it would eligible for a grant. Also note that if there is a large carry forward of grant eligible contribution room, the CESG will be limited to a maximum of $1,000 for a year, ($500 current plus $500 carry forward) regardless of the size of the contribution.

For those subscribers who have substantial funds to invest, there is the option of contributing a large initial sum to take advantage of tax free compounding. Whether this would be more advantageous than contributing less, more often, in order to take full advantage of the CESG requires the consideration of a number of factors. That analysis would go beyond the scope of this text.

9-112. CESGs will not be paid for RESP beneficiaries for the year in which they turn 18 years of age, or in any subsequent year. In addition, CESG payments are intended to encourage long-term planning for a child's education. Because of this, in a year in which the beneficiary is between the age of 15 and the age of 17, CESG payments will be made only when:

- a minimum of $2,000 of RESP contributions was made in respect of the beneficiary by December 31 of the calendar year in which the beneficiary attains 15 years of age; or

- a minimum of $100 in annual RESP contributions was made in respect of the beneficiary in any four years before the calendar year in which the beneficiary attains 15 years of age.

Exercise Nine - 7

Subject: Canada Education Savings Grants

Jeanine was born in 2011. During 2011, her father establishes a RESP for her and contributes $500 to the plan, while Jeanine's grandfather contributes an additional $1,200. During 2012, her father contributes $1,500 and her grandfather adds a further $2,400. In all of the years 2009 through 2012, Jeanine's family has family income of less than $30,000. Determine the amount of the CESGs that would be added to Jeanine's RESP in 2011 and 2012.

End of Exercise. Solution available in Study Guide.

Canada Learning Bonds (CLBs)

9-113. A further enhancement to the RESP system, Canada Learning Bonds (CLBs), are like the CESGs in that the government makes contributions to a child's RESP. However, unlike the CESGs, the CLB contributions are not based on contributions made to the RESP by others.

9-114. The CLB provisions apply to children born after 2003 who have an RESP established in their names. Such children are eligible for a CLB contribution to their RESP in each year that their family is eligible for the National Child Benefit supplement. This potential eligibility begins in the year the child is born and ends in the year that the child turns 15 years of age. As noted in Chapter 4, for 2012, this supplement begins to be phased out when 2010 family income reaches $24,863. The family income level at which it disappears varies with the number of children in the family.

9-115. The CLB contributions to individual RESPs are as follows:

- In the first year that the child is eligible for a CLB contribution, an amount of $500 will be provided. In addition, a one-time additional amount of $25 will be added in order to help defray the costs of establishing the RESP.

- In each subsequent year of eligibility, a CLB contribution of $100 will be made. This continues until the year in which the child turns 15 years of age.

9-116.   The child's eligibility will vary with the income of his or her family. In some families, the National Child Benefit supplement will be available every year and, correspondingly, the CLB contributions will be made each year. In situations such as this, the maximum total contribution would be $2,025 {$500 + $25 + [(15)($100)]}. In other cases, eligibility may be present in some years and not present in other years. In such cases, the contributions will total less than $2,025.

9-117.   For families who qualify for the CLB contributions, the establishment of an RESP for each child is clearly a desirable course of action. A potential problem with the CLB program is that families in the income brackets that qualify for this benefit may not be aware of the program or have access to the kind of assistance required to establish an RESP.

Types Of Plans

9-118.   RESP legislation provides for "family plans" in which each of the beneficiaries is related to the subscriber by blood or adoption. Family plans, which are typically established for several siblings under age 18, are subject to the same contribution limits per beneficiary, but provide additional flexibility for the subscriber because educational assistance payments need not be limited to the proportion of each child's "share" of the contributions.

9-119.   This feature is important when an individual has several children and not all of them pursue higher education. Because of the flexibility inherent in family plans, all of the plan distributions could be directed towards the children who are eligible to receive such funds. To ensure that family plans do not provide unintended benefits, no beneficiaries 21 years of age or older can be added to a family plan.

9-120.   In terms of alternatives for investing the funds that have been contributed, there are basically two types of RESPs available. They can be described as follows:

Scholarship Plans are available through "scholarship trust companies" such as the Canadian Scholarship Trust Plan. These plans are distinguished by the fact that all of their funds must be invested in government guaranteed investments. These companies offer group plans (earnings are allocated only to those children who attend college or university), as well as individual plans (subscribers can recover their share of the investment earnings).

Self-Directed Plans allow investors to choose their own investments. The list of qualified investments is similar to that applicable to self-directed RRSPs. For example, publicly traded stocks are eligible, but income producing real estate is not. As is the case with RRSPs, there is no foreign content limit for self-directed RESPs.

Refund Of Contributions

9-121.   Contributions can be paid on a tax free basis to either the subscriber to the plan or to the beneficiary. The only limitations on such payments are those that might be included in the terms and conditions of the plan itself.

Education Assistance Payments

9-122.   Education assistance payments are amounts paid to student beneficiaries from accumulated earnings, CESG amounts, and CLB amounts. These amounts must be included in the income of the recipient.

9-123.   To be eligible for the receipt of such amounts, the individual must be enrolled in a program at the post-secondary level that lasts at least three consecutive weeks. If the student spends not less than 10 hours per week on courses or work it is considered a **qualifying** educational program. If the student spends not less than 12 hours per month on courses or work it is considered a **specified** educational program. In the case of a specified educational program, the student must be at least 16 years old.

9-124.　The limits on the amounts to be paid can be described as follows:

- For studies in a qualifying educational program, the limit is $5,000 for the first 13 consecutive weeks.　Subsequent to that period, there is no limit on payments, provided the student continues to qualify.

- For studies in a specified educational program, the limit is $2,500 for the first 13 week period, whether or not the student is enrolled in the program throughout this period.

9-125.　Note that CESG and CLB amounts can only be paid out as educational assistance payments to beneficiaries.　If the beneficiary does not pursue post-secondary education, these benefits must be returned to the government.

Accumulated Income Payments

9-126.　Payments made to subscribers out of the accumulated income of the plan are referred to as accumulated income payments.　To be eligible to receive such payments, the subscriber must be a resident of Canada.　In addition, one of the following conditions must apply:

- The payment is made after the year that includes the 9th anniversary of the plan and, each beneficiary has reached the age of 21 years and is not currently eligible for educational assistance payments.

- The payments are made after the plan has been de-registered (35 or 40 years, depending on the type of plan).

- All of the beneficiaries are deceased.

9-127.　The accumulated income payments will be included in the subscriber's Net Income For Tax Purposes and Taxable Income.　In calculating the individual's Tax Payable, an additional tax of 20 percent of the accumulated income payments must be added to the total.　This additional tax is designed to offset the fact that the individual has enjoyed tax free earnings compounding inside the RESP.

9-128.　There is a provision which allows a taxpayer to reduce the amount of accumulated income payments that will be subject to the 20 percent additional tax.　Provided the individual has sufficient RRSP contribution room (see Chapter 10 for coverage of this concept), accumulated income payments can be transferred to an RRSP.　Such transfers will provide the individual with a deduction for the amounts of accumulated income payments and provide relief from the additional 20 percent tax.　The limit on such transfers is $50,000 worth of accumulated income payments.

Repayment Of CESG And CLB Contributions

9-129.　As noted in Paragraph 9-125, amounts in the plan that reflect CESG or CLB contributions can only be distributed to a plan beneficiary as an educational assistance payment. They cannot be paid to subscribers.

9-130.　In those situations where it is clear that no beneficiary will qualify for educational assistance payments, the plan will likely contain various types of balances. To the extent that these balances include CESG or CLB contributions, these amounts will have to be returned to the government.　This means that a withdrawal is likely to include amounts that can be retained by the subscriber as well as amounts that must be repaid to the government.

9-131.　Given this situation, a fairly complex set of rules is required to deal with withdrawals from the plan.　Such withdrawals must be segregated into: the return of subscriber contributions, the withdrawals of accumulated earnings amounts, and the CESG and CLB contributions that must be repaid to the government. Coverage of these rules goes beyond the scope of this text.

Comparison Of RESPs And RRSPs

9-132.   For families who manage their resources in a manner that permits taking full advantage of all types of tax deferred investments, there is little question that such plans should be established for children who will likely pursue post-secondary education.

9-133.   However, in the real world, many families expend all of their resources on current consumption and have few funds left for any type of tax deferred investment. For example, only a fraction of the deductible contributions that could be made to RRSPs are, in fact, actually made.

9-134.   In situations where there are sufficient resources to contribute to either an RRSP or an RESP, but not to both, there is the question of which of these two vehicles is more advantageous. A rigorous analysis of this question is dependent on a large number of assumptions and goes beyond the scope of this material. Although detailed coverage of RRSPs is found in Chapter 10, several relevant points can be made here:

- A major advantage of RESPs relative to RRSPs is the fact that RESP contributions can be eligible for a Canada Education Savings Grant.

- A further advantage of RESPs relative to RRSPs is the fact that the establishment of such plans allows contributions to be made under the Canada Learning Bonds program. Note that this program could justify establishing an RESP for children in low income families, even if no contributions were made to the plan.

- A major advantage of RRSPs relative to RESPs is the fact that RRSP contributions are deductible in the calculation of Net Income For Tax Purposes. Given a particular before tax amount available, this allows for larger contributions to be made in the case of RRSPs.

- Offsetting the deductibility of RRSP contributions, all payments out of RRSPs to plan beneficiaries are normally taxed. While some individuals may be in a lower tax bracket in the period of payment, many individuals will be taxed at the same rates as were applicable when their contributions were deductible. In contrast, RESP distributions are tax free to the extent they represent original contributions to the plan. Further, while RESP earnings are included in the student's income, a university or college student could have sufficient tax credits that no tax is paid on the earnings. With personal and education related tax credits available, a student can receive a significant amount of income before having to pay any taxes. Even when taxes must be paid, all amounts are likely to be taxed in the minimum tax bracket.

- Both RRSPs and RESPs offer the advantage of having earnings compound on a tax free basis. As is illustrated in detail in Chapter 10, this is a very powerful mechanism for tax deferral. In this area, an advantage for RRSPs is that the tax free compounding period is potentially longer.

9-135.   Given these offsetting advantages, the choice between contributing to an RRSP and contributing to an RESP can be a very difficult decision.

Registered Disability Savings Plans (RDSPs)

The Problem

9-136.   Parents of children who are severely disabled are usually faced with a life-long commitment for care and support of these children. Further, the needs of these disabled individuals for care and support may extend well beyond the lifetime of the parents. Parents facing this possibility would like to ensure that the needed care and support is, in fact, available as long as it is required.

9-137.   While there are a number of provisions that provide year-to-year tax assistance for disabled individuals and their parents, for many parents there is a need to provide for longer term care that could extend past the life of the parents. To help deal with this problem, the 2007 budget introduced Registered Disability Savings Plans (RDSPs).

The Solution

9-138.   The mechanics of RDSPs are largely the same as those applicable to RESPs. The general features of RDSPs are as follows:

- Non-deductible contributions are made to a registered trust with the disabled person as beneficiary.
- The contributions are invested with earnings accumulating on a tax free basis. There is no annual limit. However, contributions are limited to $200,000 over the beneficiary's lifetime.
- The government will supplement contributions to these plans through Canada Disability Savings Grants and Canada Disability Savings Bonds in a manner similar to Canada Education Savings Grants and Canada Learning Bonds.
- Disability assistance payments are made out of the plan assets to the disabled individual. These payments will be divided between a tax free amount which reflects the contributions made to the plans, and a taxable amount which reflects distributions of accumulated earnings.

9-139.   There are many additional rules related to RDSPs, some of them quite complex. Because of this complexity, as well as the fact that these plans are not as widely used as other registered plans, we will not provide detailed coverage of RDSPs. If you have further interest in RDSPs, we would refer you to the CRA's *Registered Disability Savings Plans* (RC4460).

Tax Free Savings Accounts (TFSAs) - ITA 146.2

General Procedures

9-140.   In 2009, a new type of registered savings vehicle became available to Canadian individuals. The general procedures applicable to these plans, designated as Tax Free Savings Accounts (TFSAs) are as follows:

Eligibility   Any resident individual over 17 years of age can establish a TFSA.

Contribution Room   When TFSAs were introduced in 2009, the maximum contribution to the plan was $5,000. This amount will be indexed when cumulative inflation increases the limit by $500. Given current low inflation rates, this limit has not changed since the introduction of these plans and remains at $5,000 for 2012.

Beginning in 2009, contribution room accumulates each year, without regard to whether the individual has established a TFSA or filed a tax return. Unused amounts of this contribution room can be carried forward indefinitely and any withdrawals (contributions and earnings) will be added back to the total contribution room. It is important to note that this addition does not occur until the year following the withdrawal. Ignoring this timing lag can result in an excess contribution which will be subject to a penalty. To assist taxpayers, the CRA includes unused TFSA contribution room information on the Notice of Assessment.

The contributions are not deductible and contributions in excess of available contribution room will be subject to a tax of 1 percent per month. Interest on money borrowed to make contributions is not deductible. This rule reflects the general principle that interest can only be deducted when the purpose of the borrowing is to produce income from business or property.

Qualified Investments   The contributed funds can be used to invest in the same types of investments that can be acquired in a self-directed RRSP (see Chapter 10). There is, however, a prohibition against holding investments in any entity with which the account holder does not deal at arm's length.

Investment Income   As is the case with other registered savings plans, amounts earned on assets held in the plan are not subject to tax while they remain within the plan. However, unlike other registered savings plans, there is no tax on these earnings when they are withdrawn. As their name implies, TFSAs allow investors to receive investment income on a tax free basis.

Income Attribution Rules   As will be discussed in the final section of this Chapter, when an individual gives assets to a spouse, income on those assets is usually attributed back to that individual. Another attractive feature of TFSAs is that amounts earned in these accounts are not subject to the income attribution rules.

Death Of A Taxpayer   If an individual's spouse or common-law partner is designated as a successor holder, the individual's TFSA can be transferred into the hands of this beneficiary as an ongoing TFSA. It can either be maintained by the individual as a separate TFSA or, alternatively, rolled over into their TFSA without being treated as a contribution. Income on the assets contained in the bequeathed TFSA will continue to accumulate on a tax free basis.

If the decedent's TFSA is transferred to any other beneficiary, that individual can withdraw the funds in the plan at the time of the transferor's death without tax consequences. However, any amounts received in excess of the fair market value of the assets in the plan at the time of the transferor's death will be subject to tax.

Comparison Of TFSA And RRSP

9-141.   For individuals with sufficient resources to maximize contributions to all available types of registered savings plans, making contributions to a TFSA is a no-brainer. However, it appears that, in the real world, such individuals are rare. This means that, for most individuals, a choice must be made among the available alternatives.

9-142.   While the range of available plans can be fairly large for some individuals, the most common choice will be between making contributions to a TFSA and making contributions to a Registered Retirement Savings Plan (RRSP). In comparing these two alternatives, the most significant differences can be described as follows:

- Contributions to an RRSP are tax deductible while contributions made to a TFSA are not deductible.
- Withdrawals from an RRSP are subject to tax, while withdrawals from a TFSA are not subject to tax.

9-143.   Although detailed coverage of RRSPs is found in Chapter 10 and a complete analysis of the impact of these differences goes beyond the scope of this text, a simple example will serve to illustrate their application.

Example   In 2012, Sophia Scarponi has $5,000 in pre tax income that she does not need for current consumption.   She has asked your advice on whether she should contribute to a TFSA or, alternatively to an RRSP. She indicates that her marginal tax rate is 45 percent, a rate that she expects to be the same for the next 10 years. She anticipates that funds invested in either type of plan will enjoy a compounded annual return of 10 percent. She does not anticipate needing the funds for at least 10 years.

Analysis - TFSA   As the $5,000 is a pre tax amount, she will have after tax funds of $2,750 [($5,000)(1 - .45)] to invest in the TFSA. If this amount is left in the TFSA and earnings are compounded for 10 years at 10 percent, she will have a balance of $7,133. None of this amount will be subject to tax when it is withdrawn.

Analysis - RRSP   As contributions to an RRSP are tax deductible, there will be no need to pay taxes on the $5,000 in pre tax income. This means that the full amount can be contributed. If the $5,000 is left in the RRSP and earnings are compounded for 10 years at 10 percent, the balance will be $12,969. If she withdraws this amount, she will have after tax funds of $7,133 [($12,969)(1 - .45)].

9-144.   You will note that, in this very simple example, the results under the two approaches are identical. Whether contributions are made to a TFSA or, alternatively, to an RRSP, Ms. Scarponi will wind up with after tax funds of $7,133. However, this result could be altered by a number of considerations. The most obvious factor would be her current tax rate vs. the tax rate after 10 years. If her current tax rate was lower than the rate expected after 10 years, her year 10 balance using a TFSA would be larger than the after tax funds from an RRSP.

Alternatively, if she expected a lower tax rate after 10 years, this would favour the use of an RRSP.

Non-Arm's Length Transfers Of Property

Introduction
The Problem
9-145.   When a capital asset is transferred between arm's length persons, there is an assumption that the transaction takes place at fair market value. Under the usual rules for capital asset dispositions, this fair market value will be used as both the adjusted cost base or capital cost for the newly acquired asset, as well as for the proceeds of disposition to the person disposing of the asset. These proceeds of disposition will then be used to determine tax consequences to the person disposing of the asset (e.g., capital gain or loss).

9-146.   When a non-arm's length transaction is involved, the fair market value assumption cannot be relied on. While many non-arm's length transactions do, in fact, take place at fair market value, there are many situations where it would be to the advantage of a taxpayer to make the transfer at some value that is above or below fair market value (e.g., an individual selling an asset with an accrued capital gain to his low-income spouse for proceeds below fair market value).

9-147.   This situation is further complicated by the fact that the *Income Tax Act* has special rules for determining the UCC when there has been a non-arm's length transfer of depreciable assets. In addition, there are rollover provisions that apply to certain types of non-arm's length transactions.

9-148.   In this material on non-arm's length transactions, we will deal with the following provisions of the *Income Tax Act*:

ITA 69 - Inadequate Considerations   This Section provides rules for dealing with situations where there has been a non-arm's length transfer at a value that is above or below fair market value (including gifts).

ITA 73(1) And (1.01)   These Subsections provide for a tax free rollover of capital properties to a spouse or common-law partner.

ITA 73(3.1) And (4.1)   These Subsections provide for a tax free rollover of a farming or fishing property to a child.

ITA 13(7)(e)   This Paragraph provides special rules for dealing with non-arm's length transfers of depreciable property.

Non-Arm's Length Defined
9-149.   ITA 251(1), in effect, defines the term, "arm's length", by noting that for purposes of the *Act* "related persons shall be deemed not to deal with each other at arm's length". With respect to individuals, ITA 251(2)(a) points out that they are related if they are connected by blood relationship, marriage, common-law partnership or adoption.

9-150.   With respect to the question of whether corporations are related, ITA 251(2)(b) and (c) have a fairly long list of possibilities. For example, a corporation is related to the person who controls it, and two corporations are related if they are both controlled by the same person. There are, of course, many complications in this area. However, the examples used in this Chapter involve only situations in which the taxpayers are obviously related. More complex situations will be considered in our coverage of corporate taxation.

Inadequate Considerations - ITA 69
The Problem
9-151.   As we have noted, when a transfer of capital property takes place between taxpayers who are dealing with each other at arm's length, there is usually no reason to assume that the transfer took place at a value that was significantly different from the fair market value of the

property transferred. In fact, fair market value is often described as the value that would be used by arm's length parties in an exchange transaction.

9-152. Given this, the consideration given for the property would normally be used as both the proceeds of the disposition for the vendor and the adjusted cost base for the new owner. However, when a transfer takes place between taxpayers who are not dealing at arm's length, there is the possibility that the consideration can be established at a level that will allow one or both taxpayers to reduce or avoid taxes.

> **Example** During 2012, Martin Horst, whose marginal federal tax rate is 29 percent, sells a property with a fair market value of $200,000 to his 25 year old son for its adjusted cost base of $150,000. The son, who has no other source of income in 2012, immediately sells the property for its fair market value of $200,000. The son's only tax credit is the basic personal credit of $1,623.

> **Analysis** If Martin had sold the property for its fair market value of $200,000, he would have paid federal taxes of $7,250 [($200,000 - $150,000)(1/2)(29%)]. In contrast, if the $50,000 capital gain was taxed in the hands of his son, the federal tax would only be $2,127 {[($200,000 - $150,000)(1/2)(15%)] - $1,623}, a savings of $5,123 at the federal level alone.

9-153. There are three possible non-arm's length transfers that may create difficulties here:

- A transfer at an amount greater than fair market value.
- A transfer at a positive amount that is below fair market value.
- A transfer for nil consideration (i.e., a gift).

9-154. Section 69 of the *Income Tax Act*, which is somewhat inappropriately titled "Inadequate Considerations", provides rules for dealing with each of these situations.

General Rules

9-155. When a transfer occurs at fair market value, the general rules for determining capital gains and losses are applicable. However, as listed in Paragraph 9-153, there are three possible situations that create potential problems. The tax rules for fair market value transfers and for the three situations listed in Paragraph 9-153 are outlined in Figure 9-2.

Figure 9 - 2	**Non-Arm's Length Transfers - ITA 69**	
Transfer Price	**Proceeds Of Disposition For Transferor**	**Adjusted Cost Base For Transferee**
Fair Market Value	Fair Market Value	Fair Market Value
Above Fair Market Value	Actual Proceeds	Fair Market Value
Below Fair Market Value	Fair Market Value	Actual Proceeds
Nil (Gift)	Fair Market Value	Fair Market Value

Example

9-156. In order to illustrate the rules presented in Figure 9-2, assume that John Brown has a capital asset with an adjusted cost base of $50,000 and a fair market value of $75,000. If the asset is sold for consideration equal to its fair market value of $75,000, the result will be a capital gain of $25,000 for John Brown and an adjusted cost base for the new owner of $75,000. This would be the result without regard to whether the purchaser was at arm's length with John Brown.

9-157. If the asset is transferred to a non-arm's length party, and the consideration provided is not equal to its fair market value, ITA 69 becomes applicable. The following three Cases illustrate the various possible alternatives. In each Case, we will assume the transfer is to John Brown's adult brother, Sam Brown.

Case A - Transfer At $100,000 (Above Fair Market Value) In this case, there is no special rule for the transferor. Given this, the proceeds to John Brown will be the actual amount of $100,000 and will result in an immediate capital gain to John Brown of $50,000 ($100,000 - $50,000). The adjusted cost base to Sam Brown will be limited by ITA 69(1)(a) to the $75,000 fair market value. This means that $25,000 of the amount that he has paid is not reflected in his adjusted cost base. If, for example, Sam Brown were to sell the asset for $100,000 (the amount he paid), he would have a capital gain of $25,000 ($100,000 - $75,000) and there will have been double taxation of the $25,000 difference between the transfer price of $100,000 and the fair market value of $75,000.

Case B - Transfer At $60,000 (Below Fair Market Value)   If the transfer took place at a price of $60,000, ITA 69(1)(b) would deem John Brown to have received the fair market value of $75,000. As there is no special rule applicable to the purchaser in this case, the adjusted cost base to Sam Brown would be the actual transfer price of $60,000. Here again, double taxation could arise, this time on the difference between the transfer price of $60,000 and the fair market value of $75,000.

Case C - Gift, Bequest, Or Inheritance   In this case, ITA 69(1)(b) would deem the proceeds of disposition to be the fair market value of $75,000, and ITA 69(1)(c) would deem Sam Brown's adjusted cost base to be the same value. Note that this is the same result that would be achieved if the asset was sold to Sam Brown at its fair market value of $75,000. However, there is no double taxation involved in this Case.

9-158.   Given the presence of ITA 69, the general rules for transferring property to related parties are very clear. Either transfer the property at a consideration that is equal to its fair market value or, alternatively, gift the property. A non-arm's length transfer, at a value that is either above or below the fair market value of the property, will result in double taxation on some part of any gain recognized when there is a later sale of the property by the transferee.

Applicability Of ITA 69

9-159.   The inadequate consideration rules in ITA 69 are prefaced by the phrase "except as expressly otherwise provided in this Act". This means that if there is a provision that deals with a particular non-arm's length transfer, that provision takes precedence over the general provisions of ITA 69. Examples of such situations that are discussed later in this Chapter are the transfers to a spouse covered in ITA 73(1) and the transfers of farm property to a child covered in ITA 73(3.1). When these provisions are applicable, ITA 69 can be ignored.

Exercise Nine - 8

Subject: Inadequate Consideration - Non-Depreciable Property

Mr. Carl Lipky owns a piece of land with an adjusted cost base of $100,000 and a fair market value of $75,000. He sells the land to his brother for $95,000 who immediately sells it for $75,000. Determine the amount of any capital gain or loss to be recorded by Mr. Lipky and his brother.

End of Exercise. Solution available in Study Guide.

Using Leases To Avoid ITA 69

9-160.   In the past, it was possible to avoid the provisions of ITA 69 through the use of leasing arrangements. These arrangements involved the rental of a property to a person with whom the owner/lessor was not dealing at arm's length. The required lease payment was set at a sufficiently low level that the fair market value of the property was significantly reduced. This would allow a sale or gift to be made, with the deemed proceeds of disposition being based on this lower value.

9-161. As an example of this type of arrangement, consider a situation where an individual has a property with a fair market value of $100,000. If this property was leased on a long-term basis to a spouse or common-law partner for an unrealistically low value, say $2,000 per year, the fair market value of the property might be reduced to about $20,000. If there were no restrictions, it could then be gifted or sold for $20,000 to a child, and there would be no double taxation under the provisions of ITA 69.

9-162. ITA 69(1.2) is designed to make this an unattractive strategy. Under the provisions of this Subsection, the taxpayer's proceeds of disposition on the gift or sale will be the greater of the actual fair market value at the time of the disposition ($20,000) and the fair market value determined without consideration of the non-arm's length lease ($100,000). This means the transferor will be taxed on the basis of having received the full $100,000 and, under the usual provisions of ITA 69, the transferee will have an adjusted cost base of $20,000. This will result in double taxation of the difference between $100,000 and $20,000 and should serve to discourage this type of avoidance strategy.

Exercise Nine - 9

Subject: Inadequate Consideration - Leased Property

Mr. Ned Bates has land with an adjusted cost base of $33,000 and an unencumbered fair market value of $211,000. He leases this land to his wife for $3,300 per year, for a period of 35 years. Similar leases are based on 10 percent of the value of the property and, as a consequence, the fair market value of the land with the lease in place falls to $33,000. He sells the land to a corporation controlled by his wife for this reduced value. Determine the amount of capital gain or loss to be recorded by Mr. Bates as a result of this sale, as well as the adjusted cost base of the land to the corporation.

End of Exercise. Solution available in Study Guide.

Inter Vivos Transfers To A Spouse - ITA 73(1) And 73(1.01)
General Rules For Capital Property

9-163. An inter vivos transfer is one that occurs while the transferor is still alive, rather than at the time of, or subsequent to, that individual's death. ITA 73(1.01) indicates that the ITA 73(1) rules apply to the following qualifying transfers:

- a transfer to the individual's spouse or common-law partner;

- a transfer to the individual's former spouse or former common-law partner in settlement of rights arising out of their marriage or common-law partnership; and

- a transfer to a trust for which the individual's spouse or common-law partner is the income beneficiary (this type of trust has traditionally been referred to as a spousal trust and the conditions related to this concept are discussed in Chapter 19).

9-164. For the qualifying transfers listed in ITA 73(1.01), ITA 73(1) specifies rules that provide a tax free transfer (such tax free transfers are commonly referred to by tax professionals as rollovers). With respect to the proceeds of disposition for the transferor, the rules are as follows:

Non-Depreciable Capital Property The proceeds will be deemed to be the adjusted cost base of the property transferred.

Depreciable Capital Property The proceeds will be deemed to be the UCC of the class or, if only part of a class is transferred, an appropriate portion of the class.

9-165. From the point of view of the transferee, ITA 73(1) indicates that he will be deemed to have acquired the property at an amount equal to the deemed proceeds to the transferor. Based on this, his values will be as follows:

Non-Depreciable Capital Property   The cost to the transferee will be deemed to be the adjusted cost base to the transferor.

Depreciable Capital Property   The UCC to the transferee will be the old UCC to the transferor. However, under ITA 73(2), the old capital cost will also be retained by the transferee, with the difference between this and his UCC being considered to be deemed CCA. This rule is very important in that it ensures that if the property is subsequently sold for a value in excess of its UCC, the excess will be treated as fully taxable recapture of CCA, not a capital gain, only one-half of which would be taxed.

9-166.   These rules mean that the transfer will have no tax consequences for the transferor and that the transferee will retain the same tax values that were contained in the transferor's records. This is illustrated by the following example:

Example   Marg Cardiff gifts land with an adjusted cost base of $100,000 and a fair market value of $250,000 to her husband, Bernie. At the same time, three-quarters (based on fair market values) of her Class 10 assets are also given to Bernie. The specific Class 10 assets transferred have a capital cost of $225,000 and a fair market value of $310,000. The UCC for Class 10, prior to the gift, is $260,000.

Analysis   Marg would be deemed to have received $100,000 for the disposition of the land and $195,000 [(3/4)($260,000)] for the Class 10 assets. Given these values, the transactions would have no tax consequences for Marg. For Bernie, the land would have an adjusted cost base of $100,000. The transferred Class 10 assets would have a UCC of $195,000, combined with a capital cost of $225,000. This means that, if Bernie sold all the transferred assets immediately for their combined fair market value of $560,000 ($250,000 + $310,000), there would be a capital gain of $150,000 ($250,000 - $100,000) on the land, a capital gain of $85,000 ($310,000 - $225,000) on the Class 10 assets, as well as recapture of CCA of $30,000 ($195,000 - $225,000) on the Class 10 assets.

Electing Out Of The Spousal Rollover

9-167.   The ITA 73(1) rollover automatically applies to spousal rollovers unless the taxpayer takes positive action to remove its applicability. However, the taxpayer can elect out of this approach if he wishes to recognize capital gains or recapture at the time of the transfer. There are a variety of reasons that a taxpayer may wish to make this election. However, the most common probably involves situations where the taxpayer has unused allowable capital losses and wishes to trigger taxable capital gains in order to make use of these losses.

9-168.   With respect to the process of electing to be taxed on an inter vivos spousal transfer, ITA 73(1) uses the phrase "elects in his return of income". The use of this phrase in the *Income Tax Act* means there is no official tax form required in order to make the election. In contrast, in situations where a form is required, the usual *Income Tax Act* terminology is the phrase "elects in the prescribed manner".

9-169.   For a taxpayer wishing to elect out of ITA 73(1), the only requirement is that they include any income resulting from the spousal transfer in their tax return in the year of disposition.

Example Continued   In the example from Paragraph 9-166, Marg could have elected to record the land transaction at the fair market value of $250,000, resulting in a $150,000 capital gain being recorded at the time of transfer. In this case, the adjusted cost base to Bernie would be $250,000. The election would be made by simply including the $75,000 taxable portion of the $150,000 gain in Marg's tax return.

9-170.   You should note that, if the taxpayer elects out of ITA 73(1), ITA 69 becomes applicable. This means that, in such situations, if the transfer is not a gift, or is made in return for consideration that is not equal to the fair market value of the property, the ITA 69 provisions will result in double taxation as was discussed previously. In addition, if a depreciable asset is transferred, special rules apply when calculating the transferee's capital cost. These rules are covered in the next section of this Chapter.

Exercise Nine - 10

Subject:　Inter Vivos Transfer Of Non-Depreciable Asset To A Spouse

Aaron Schwartz owns land with an adjusted cost base of $225,000 and a fair market value of $300,000. He sells this land to his spouse for its fair market value of $300,000. Indicate the tax consequences to Mr. Schwartz and the adjusted cost base of the property to his spouse after the transfer assuming (1) Mr. Schwartz does not elect out of ITA 73(1), and (2) Mr. Schwartz does elect out of ITA 73(1).

End of Exercise. Solution available in Study Guide.

Non-Arm's Length Transfers Of Depreciable Assets - ITA 13(7)(e)
Problem 1 - Fair Market Value Exceeds Transferor's Capital Cost

9-171.　The problem here relates to the fact that, if the transfer is made at a value in excess of the transferor's capital cost, the result will be a capital gain, only one-half of which will be taxed. If we allow this excess amount to be added to the transferee's UCC, it will form the basis for fully deductible CCA.

Example　Jean Tessier has a depreciable asset with a fair market value of $150,000, a capital cost of $110,000, and a UCC of $85,000 (it is the only asset in the Class). He sells this asset to his daughter Francine for its fair market value of $150,000.

Analysis　As a result of this disposition, Jean will have recapture of $25,000 ($110,000 - $85,000) and a capital gain of $40,000 ($150,000 - $110,000). Only $20,000 of this capital gain will be subject to tax, resulting in a total increase in his Taxable Income of $45,000 [$25,000 + (1/2)($40,000)].

If we allow Francine to record the $150,000 as her capital cost for CCA purposes, she will be able to deduct 100 percent of this amount as CCA. This means that, by increasing his Taxable Income by $45,000, the deductions available on this asset would have increased by $65,000 ($150,000 - $85,000). As related parties, Jean and Francine would clearly have an incentive to make this transfer.

Solution To Problem 1

9-172.　Tax legislation acts to prevent such non-arm's length transfers from having this benefit. In those situations where the transfer occurs at a value that exceeds the transferor's capital cost, for the purposes of CCA and recapture calculations only, ITA 13(7)(e) deems the transferee's capital cost to be equal to:

$$A + [(1/2)(B - A)], \text{ where:}$$

A = The Transferor's Old Capital Cost
B = The Transferee's New Capital Cost

Analysis Continued　If we apply this rule to the example in Paragraph 9-171, Francine's capital cost would be $130,000 [$110,000 + (1/2)($150,000 - $110,000)]. Based on this figure, the transfer will generate an additional $45,000 ($130,000 - $85,000) in CCA deductions, an amount equal to the increase in Jean's Taxable Income resulting from the transfer.

It is important to note that the $130,000 is only used for recapture, terminal loss determination, and CCA calculations. The capital cost for capital gains purposes would be based on the actual transfer price of $150,000. For example, if at a later point in time Francine were to sell the asset for $160,000, the taxable capital gain would be $5,000 [(1/2)($160,000 - $150,000)]. Provided she had taken no additional CCA, there would be no recapture on this sale. Specifically, $130,000, which is the lesser of the $160,000 proceeds of disposition and the $130,000 deemed capital cost would be subtracted from the deemed UCC of $130,000 ($130,000 - $130,000 = Nil).

Problem 2 - Fair Market Value Less Than Transferor's Capital Cost
9-173.   A similar problem arises when a non-arm's length transfer occurs at a value that is less than the transferor's capital cost.

Example   Carole Dupre has a depreciable asset with a fair market value of $200,000, a capital cost of $325,000, and a UCC of $150,000 (it is the only asset in the Class). She sells this asset to her son Marcel for the fair market value of $200,000.

Analysis   As a result of this transaction, the only tax consequence for Carole would be recapture of $50,000 ($150,000 - $200,000).

Under the usual rules, the capital cost to Marcel would be the transfer price of $200,000. The problem with this result is that, if Marcel were to later sell this asset for $250,000, the difference between the $250,000 and this $200,000 would be treated as a capital gain, only one-half of which would included in his Taxable Income. In contrast, if Carole had sold the asset for $250,000, the difference would have been fully taxable recapture. As in the problem 1 scenario, this situation provides an incentive for Carole and Marcel to make this transfer.

The Solution To Problem 2
9-174.   When there is a non-arm's length transfer at a value that is less than the transferor's capital cost, ITA 13(7)(e) deems the transferee's new capital cost to be equal to the transferor's old capital cost.

Analysis Continued   If we apply this rule to the example in Paragraph 9-173, the deemed capital cost to Marcel would be $325,000, with the $125,000 difference between this amount and the amount paid considered to be deemed CCA. When this rule is applied, a sale by Marcel at $250,000 would result in fully taxable recapture of $50,000 ($200,000 - $250,000). The $250,000 is the lesser of the proceeds of disposition of $250,000 and the deemed capital cost of $325,000. Unlike the previous case where the transfer is at a value that is greater than the transferor's capital cost, the $325,000 deemed capital cost would be used for determining capital gains as well as for determining recapture.

Application Of ITA 69
9-175.   These rules for non-arm's length transfers of depreciable property apply to all such transactions, including those to which ITA 69 is applicable. In such situations, the ITA 13(7)(e) rules will be applied using the amounts that are required by this section. However, the application of ITA 69 to transfers of depreciable assets is very complex. In addition, there are some who believe that the *Income Tax Act* is not entirely clear on how these provisions interact. Given this, we will not include coverage in this text of non-arm's length transfers of depreciable assets at a positive amount that is not fair market value.

Exercise Nine - 11

Subject: Inter Vivos Transfer Of Depreciable Asset To A Spouse

Aaron Schwartz owns land with an adjusted cost base of $225,000 and a fair market value of $300,000. He sells this land to his spouse for its fair market value of $300,000. Indicate the tax consequences to Mr. Schwartz and the adjusted cost base of the property to his spouse after the transfer assuming (1) Mr. Schwartz does not elect out of ITA 73(1), and (2) Mr. Schwartz does elect out of ITA 73(1).

Exercise Nine - 12

Subject: Inter Vivos Transfer Of Depreciable Property To A Parent

Ms. Jennifer Lee owns a depreciable asset that she has used in her unincorporated business. It has a cost of $53,000 and a fair market value of $40,000. It is the only asset in its CCA class, and the UCC balance in the class is $37,200. Ms. Lee sells the asset to her father for the fair market value of $40,000. During the same year, prior to deducting any CCA, the father resells the asset for $44,000. Determine the amount of income to be recorded by Ms. Lee and her father as a result of these transactions.

End of Exercises. Solutions available in Study Guide.

Inter Vivos Transfer Of Farm Or Fishing Property To A Child

9-176.   ITA 73(3.1) and (4.1) provide for direct inter vivos transfers of farm or fishing property, shares of family farm or fishing corporations, or interests in family farm or fishing partnerships, to children on a tax-free basis. As was the case with ITA 73(1), the provisions of ITA 73(3.1) and (4.1) take precedence over the provisions of ITA 69.

9-177.   For the purposes of this Section, "child" refers to children and their spouses, grandchildren, great grandchildren, and any other person that, prior to their attaining the age of 19, was dependent on the taxpayer and under his custody or control. To qualify, the child must be a resident of Canada at the time of the transfer. In addition, the property must be in use in a farming or fishing business operated by the taxpayer, the taxpayer's spouse, or any of their children.

9-178.   The transfer is deemed to have taken place at the actual proceeds of disposition, restricted by floor and ceiling amounts.

For **Depreciable Property**, the floor is the property's UCC, while the ceiling is its fair market value. The transferee would retain the original capital cost to the transferor with the difference being treated as deemed CCA.

For **Non-Depreciable Property**, which includes shares in a farm or fishing corporation, the floor is the adjusted cost base, while the ceiling is the fair market value.

9-179.   The following example will illustrate these floor and ceiling rules.

Example   Tim Johnson's farm consists of land with an adjusted cost base of $200,000 and a fair market value of $350,000, and depreciable assets with a UCC of $400,000, a capital cost of $550,000, and a fair market value of $675,000. It is transferred to Tim's son.

Analysis - Land   If the transfer is for proceeds of disposition below $200,000 (this includes gifts), the deemed proceeds of disposition and adjusted cost base to the child would be $200,000. If the transfer is for an amount in excess of $350,000, the deemed proceeds of disposition and adjusted cost base to the child would be limited to $350,000. For transfers between $200,000 and $350,000, the actual proceeds of disposition would be used.

Analysis - Depreciable Property   For transfers below the UCC of $400,000, the deemed proceeds of disposition and transfer price to the child would be $400,000. Correspondingly, for transfers above $675,000, the deemed proceeds of disposition and capital cost to the child would be $675,000. For transfers between $400,000 and $675,000, the actual proceeds of disposition would be used.

Exercise Nine - 13

Subject: Inter Vivos Farm Property Transfer To A Child

Thomas Nobel owns farm property consisting of land with an adjusted cost base of $250,000 and a fair market value of $325,000, along with a barn with a UCC of $85,000, a capital cost of $115,000, and a fair market value of $101,000. The property is transferred to his 40 year old daughter in return for a payment of $280,000 for the land. No payment is made for the barn. Describe the tax consequences of this transfer, both for Mr. Nobel and for his daughter.

End of Exercise. Solution available in Study Guide.

Death Of A Taxpayer

General Rules

9-180. There are many special rules that may be applicable when an individual dies. In this Chapter, we cover the rules related to capital property. Other material on final returns can be found in Supplementary Reading No. 6, Final Returns For Deceased Taxpayers.

9-181. ITA 70(5) provides the following general rules for the capital property of a deceased taxpayer:

Capital Property Other Than Depreciable Property The deceased taxpayer is deemed to have disposed of the property at fair market value immediately before his death. The person receiving the property is deemed to have acquired the property at this time, at a value equal to its fair market value.

Depreciable Property The basic rules for this type of property are the same. That is, there is a deemed disposition of the property by the deceased taxpayer at fair market value, combined with an acquisition of the property at the same value by the beneficiary. When the capital cost of the property for the deceased taxpayer exceeds its fair market value, the beneficiary is required to retain the original capital cost, with the difference being treated as deemed CCA.

9-182. A simple example will serve to illustrate the rules for depreciable property:

Example Eric Nadon dies, leaving a depreciable property to his son that has a capital cost of $100,000, a fair market value of $60,000, and a UCC of $50,000.

Analysis Under ITA 70(5), the transfer will take place at the fair market value of $60,000. This means that Mr. Nadon's final tax return will include recaptured CCA of $10,000 ($60,000 - $50,000). While the son's UCC will be the $60,000 transfer price, the capital cost of the asset will remain at Mr. Nadon's original capital cost of $100,000. This means that, if the asset is later sold for a value between $60,000 and $100,000, the resulting gain will be treated as recaptured CCA, rather than as a more favourably taxed capital gain.

9-183. These deemed disposition rules apply to all capital property, including personal use property and listed personal property.

Rollover To A Spouse, A Common-Law Partner, Or A Spousal Trust

9-184. ITA 70(6) provides an exception to the general rules contained in ITA 70(5) in situations where the transfer is to a spouse, a common-law partner, or a testamentary spousal or common-law partner trust. This is a rollover provision that allows the transfer of non-depreciable property at its adjusted cost base and depreciable property at its UCC.

9-185.   This means that the transfer does not generate a capital gain or loss, recapture, or terminal loss, and that the surviving spouse or common-law partner will assume the same property values as those carried by the deceased. This has the effect of deferring any capital gains or recapture until the surviving spouse or common-law partner disposes of the property, or dies.

9-186.   It is possible for the legal representative of the deceased to elect in the taxpayer's final return to have one or all asset transfers take place at fair market value. This election could be used to take advantage of charitable donations, medical expenses, unused loss carry forwards, and, in the case of qualified farm property, qualified fishing property, or the shares of a qualified small business corporation, an unused lifetime capital gains deduction. As was the case with electing out of the ITA 73 inter vivos transfer to a spouse rules, electing out of ITA 70(6) is implemented in the deceased's final tax return and does not require the filing of a form.

9-187.   To qualify as a spousal testamentary trust, ITA 70(6) indicates that the surviving spouse or common-law partner must be entitled to receive all of the income of the trust that arises before the death of the surviving spouse or common-law partner. In addition, no person other than the spouse or common-law partner may receive the use of any of the income or capital of the trust, prior to the death of this spouse or common-law partner.

9-188.   Detailed coverage of spousal testamentary trusts can be found in Chapter 19. As discussed in Chapter 19, there are at least two advantages to using a spousal trust:

- This arrangement allows the deceased to determine the ultimate disposition of any property. For example, if after his death, Mr. Hall wishes his property to go only to his children, this can be specified in the trust arrangement and avoid the possibility that property could be redirected to a new husband, or any additional children that his spouse or common-law partner might have on remarrying.

- Such arrangements can provide for the administration of the assets of the deceased in those situations where the surviving spouse or common-law partner is not experienced in business or financial matters.

Exercise Nine - 14

Subject: Transfers On Death

Ms. Cheryl Lardner, who owns two trucks that were used in her business, dies in July, 2012. Her will transferred truck A to her husband, Michel, and truck B to her daughter, Melinda. Each of the trucks cost $42,000 and had a fair market value at the time of her death of $33,000. The UCC balance for the class that contains the trucks was $51,000. What are the tax consequences resulting from Ms. Lardner's death with respect to these two trucks? Your answer should include the capital cost and the UCC for the trucks in the hands of Michel and Melinda.

End of Exercise. Solution available in Study Guide.

Tax Free Transfers Of Farm And Fishing Property At Death

9-189.   As we have seen, the most common situation in which capital property can be transferred at the time of death on a tax free basis is when the transfer is to a spouse or a spousal testamentary trust. However, ITA 70(9) through ITA 70(9.31) provides for other tax free transfers involving specific types of farm and fishing assets. For each of the following types of transfers, the legal representatives of the deceased can elect to transfer the property at any value between its tax value and its fair market value. These elections can be used to utilize any accumulated losses of the deceased, or any unused lifetime capital gains deduction.

- **Farm Or Fishing Property**   When farm or fishing property has been used by a taxpayer or the taxpayer's family, it can be transferred on a tax free basis to a resident child, grandchild, or great grandchild at the time of the taxpayer's death. These provisions can also be used to transfer farm or fishing property from a child to a parent in situations where the child dies before the parent.

- **Shares Of A Family Farm Or Fishing Corporation**   Shares of a family farm or fishing corporation can be transferred on a tax free basis to a resident child, grandchild, or great grandchild at the time of a taxpayer's death. It is possible to have tax free transfers of farm or fishing corporation shares from a child to a parent and, in addition, the rules provide for the rollover of shares in a family farm or fishing holding company.

- **Interests In Family Farm Or Fishing Partnerships**   Rules similar to those described in the two preceding bullets allow for the tax free transfer of interests in family farm or fishing partnerships to a resident child, grandchild, or great grandchild at the time of the taxpayer's death. Here again, it is possible to have a tax free transfer from a child to a parent in the event of the child's death.

Income Attribution

The Problem
9-190.   In the general discussion of tax planning in Chapter 1, it was noted that income splitting can be the most powerful tool available to individuals wishing to reduce their tax burden. The basic goal is to redistribute income from an individual in a high tax bracket to related individuals, usually a spouse or children, in lower tax brackets. As was illustrated in Chapter 1, when such redistribution can be achieved, it can produce very dramatic reductions in the aggregate tax liability of the family unit.

9-191.   It is obvious that, if there were no restrictions associated with transfers of property to related persons, there would be little standing in the way of a complete equalization of tax rates within a family unit and the achievement of maximum income splitting benefits. For many years, it has been the policy of the government to limit access to the tax benefits of income splitting and, as a consequence, we have a group of legislative provisions that are commonly referred to as the income attribution rules.

9-192.   These attribution rules could be criticized on the basis of fairness. They are very effective in preventing income splitting by low-income Canadians. For example, they prevent income splitting benefits from accruing to an individual who simply gives a term deposit to a spouse or his minor children.

9-193.   However, these rules are less effective in preventing income splitting benefits from accruing to wealthy Canadians. While the imposition of the tax on split income (see Chapter 11) has restricted the ability of high income individuals to distribute certain types of income to their minor children, it is clear that wealthy Canadians, with access to expensive tax counseling and the ability to use complex corporate, partnership, and trust structures, still benefit far more from income splitting than do those in the middle class.

9-194.   If the policy objective was to curtail income splitting, we would have hoped that the government could have dealt with this in a fashion that was more equitable to all Canadians. To a certain extent, this was accomplished with the addition of provisions that allow the splitting of pension income (see Paragraph 9-72) and TFSAs (see Paragraph 9-140).

Basic Rules - ITA 74.1(1) And (2)
Applicable Individuals
9-195.   The income attribution rules are applicable to situations where an individual has transferred property to:

- a spouse or common-law partner [ITA 74.1(1)]; or
- an individual who is under the age of 18 and who does not deal with the individual at arm's length [ITA 74.1(2)].

9-196.   Note that the ITA 74.1(2) rules are applicable, not just to children or grandchildren under the age of 18, but to any non-arm's length individual who is under the age of 18. In addition, this Subsection specifically notes that nieces and nephews are subject to these rules, even though they are not non-arm's length individuals as defined in the *Income Tax Act*.

9-197.   The general idea here is that, unless certain conditions are met, income associated with the transferee holding or disposing of a transferred property may be attributed back to the transferor of the property (i.e., included in the Net Income For Tax Purposes of the transferor).

Applicable To Property Income And Capital Gains

9-198.   There are two types of income that may be attributed under these rules. The first type would be property income, such as interest, dividends, rents, and royalties, which accrues while the transferee is holding the transferred assets. This type of income may be attributed back to the transferor without regard to whether the transferee is a spouse, common-law partner, or a related individual under the age of 18.

9-199.   The second type of income that may be subject to the attribution rules is capital gains resulting from a disposition of the transferred property. Whether or not this type of income is subject to the attribution rules will depend on the relationship of the transferee to the transferor:

Transfers To A Spouse   When property is transferred to a spouse or common-law partner, the application of the ITA 73(1) rollover generally means that the property is transferred at the transferor's tax cost, with no taxation at the time of transfer. This means that the transferred property will be recorded at the adjusted cost base value for non-depreciable assets and at the UCC for depreciable assets. Given this, it seems logical that any capital gain or recaptured CCA from a subsequent sale by the spouse would be measured from that tax cost and attributed back to the transferor. This approach is, in fact, required under ITA 74.1 and 74.2.

Transfers To A Related Minor - General Rule   There is no general rollover provision for related minors that corresponds to ITA 73(1) for a spouse or common-law partner. This means that when property is transferred to a related minor, the transfer will normally take place at the fair market value of the property, resulting in the transferor recognizing any capital gains or recaptured CCA that have accrued to the time of transfer. Reflecting this fact, any gain on a subsequent sale by the related minor would be measured using the fair market value at the time of transfer. Further, such gains are not attributed back to the transferor, but are taxed in the hands of the related minor.

Transfers To A Minor Child - Farming Or Fishing Property   As discussed in this Chapter at Paragraph 9-177, ITA 73(3) and ITA 73(4) provide for a transfer of farm or fishing property to a child at its tax cost. It is not surprising that, when this rollover provision is used, there is attribution of gains arising on a subsequent disposition by the child. More specifically, ITA 75.1 indicates that when a farm or fishing property has been transferred to a child on a rollover basis and the child disposes of that property prior to reaching the age of 18 years, all capital gains and capital losses, both those existing at the time of transfer and those accruing subsequently, are attributed back to the transferor and taxed in the transferor's hands.

Not Applicable To Business Income

9-200.   Note that business income is not subject to the attribution rules. If the assets that are transferred to a spouse, common-law partner, or related minor, are used to produce business income, this type of income will be taxed in the hands of the transferee. The logic of this seems clear. In order to earn business income, an effort is required on the part of the transferee. This means that the resulting business income is not a simple gift, but something that has to be earned. In these circumstances, it would not seem equitable to attribute these amounts to the transferor who provided the property.

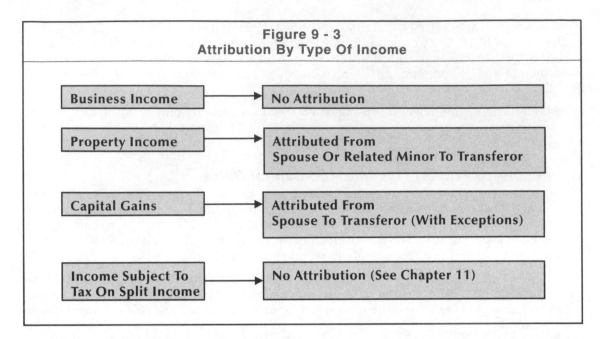

Figure 9 - 3
Attribution By Type Of Income

Business Income → No Attribution

Property Income → Attributed From
Spouse Or Related Minor To Transferor

Capital Gains → Attributed From
Spouse To Transferor (With Exceptions)

Income Subject To
Tax On Split Income → No Attribution (See Chapter 11)

9-201.   Note, however, that if a business is transferred to a spouse or common-law partner, any capital gain on a subsequent sale of the business assets will be attributed back to the transferor, despite the fact that business income earned between the transfer and the sale will not be attributed to the transferor.

Not Applicable If Subject To Tax On Split Income
9-202.   A further exception to the income attribution rules is income that is subject to the tax on split income. While this tax is discussed in detail in Chapter 11, we would note here that this is a special tax on certain types of income that are earned by individuals under the age of 18 on income that is sourced from related parties. This special tax is assessed on the minor individual at the maximum federal rate of 29 percent, beginning with the first dollar of such income received.

9-203.   With income subject to the tax on split income being taxed at the maximum federal rate of 29 percent, any potential income splitting advantage has been eliminated. As a consequence, there is really no point in applying the income attribution rules to income that is subject to this tax. This view is reflected in ITA 74.5(13) which indicates that the income attribution rules in ITA 74.1(2) are not applicable to income that is subject to the tax on split income.

Summary Of Rules
9-204.   The attribution rules, classified by type of income, are summarized in Figure 9-3.

Avoiding Income Attribution
9-205.   The basic idea behind the income attribution rules is to restrict an individual's ability to simply give a source of income to a related individual for income splitting purposes. The procedure for avoiding these rules on a transfer to a related minor is straightforward:

Transfers To A Related Minor   In this case, ITA 74.5(1)(a) indicates that the income attribution rules are not applicable if the related minor provides, from his own resources, consideration equal to the fair market value of the asset transferred. ITA 74.5(1)(b) indicates that, if such consideration includes debt payable by the related minor, it is acceptable only if it requires interest based on at least the prescribed rate at the time of the transfer.

9-206.   The avoidance of the income attribution rules on transfers to a spouse is complicated by the presence of the ITA 73(1) rollover:

Transfers To A Spouse   In the case of transfers to a spouse or common-law partner, avoiding income attribution requires that the transferor elect out of ITA 73(1). Unless this individual elects to record the transfer at fair market value and include any resulting gain or loss in income at the time of transfer, ITA 74.5(1)(c) indicates that the income attribution rules will apply without regard to the consideration provided by the transferee.

In addition to having the transferor elect out of ITA 73(1), avoidance of the income attribution rules requires that the transferee must provide, from his or her own resources, consideration equal to the fair market value of the asset transferred. As noted previously, ITA 74.5(1)(b) indicates that, if such consideration includes debt payable by the related spouse, it is acceptable only if it requires interest based on at least the prescribed rate at the time of the transfer.

Consider a situation in which John Doan has a capital property with an adjusted cost base of $100,000 and a fair market value of $150,000. If he sells this property to his spouse for consideration equal to the fair market value of $150,000, the income attribution rules will apply unless he elects out of ITA 73(1) by recognizing the $50,000 capital gain in his income. Note that, if he fails to elect out of ITA 73(1), the adjusted cost base to his spouse will be John's adjusted cost base of $100,000, not the price she paid of $150,000. This means that any capital gains attribution will be measured from this $100,000 value.

Alternatively, if he gifts the property to his spouse and elects out of ITA 73(1) by recording a $50,000 capital gain, the income attribution rules will apply because she did not give consideration equal to $150,000. Note that, in this case, because ITA 69 applies to spousal transfers when the transferor elects out of ITA 73(1), his spouse's adjusted cost base would be the $150,000 fair market value at the time of the transfer. Any subsequent capital gain attribution would be measured using her adjusted cost base of $150,000.

Example

9-207.   The following example will illustrate the provisions that we have just discussed.

Example   Mrs. Blaine owns a group of equity securities with an adjusted cost base of $200,000. On December 31, 2011, the fair market value of these securities is $300,000. On this date, she gives one-half of the securities to her unemployed husband Mark, and the other one-half to her 5 year old daughter Belinda.

Both Mark and Belinda hold the securities until December 31, 2012, at which point they are sold for a total of $350,000 ($175,000 each). During 2012, the securities paid $37,500 in eligible dividends ($18,750 to both Mark and Belinda).

Transfer To Spouse   Assuming that Mrs. Blaine has not elected out of the ITA 73(1) rules, the transfer to her husband would take place at the adjusted cost base of $100,000 [(1/2)($200,000)] and she would not record a 2011 gain. However, the adjusted cost base of the shares to Mark would be Mrs. Blaine's adjusted cost base of $100,000. This means that when Mark sells the shares, the taxable capital gain will be $37,500 [(1/2)($175,000 - $100,000)], all of which will be attributed to Mrs. Blaine in 2012. In addition, $18,750 in dividends received by Mark in 2012 would also be attributed to Mrs. Blaine.

Transfer To Minor   As indicated previously, the rules for minors are somewhat different. As there is no general rollover provision for minor children in this case, the gift to Belinda would be treated as a disposition at fair market value, resulting in a 2011 taxable capital gain for Mrs. Blaine of $25,000 [(1/2)($150,000 - $100,000)]. Belinda's adjusted cost base for the shares would then be $150,000. When the shares are sold by Belinda, the additional taxable capital gain of $12,500 [(1/2)($175,000 - $150,000)] would be taxed in Belinda's hands and would not be attributed to Mrs.

Blaine. The treatment of the dividends for Belinda is the same as for Mr. Blaine, resulting in an additional $18,750 in dividends being attributed to Mrs. Blaine for 2012.

9-208. If either Mark or Belinda reinvests the proceeds from selling the shares, dividend or interest income resulting from the reinvestment will also be attributed back to Mrs. Blaine. Any capital gains on the new investments that are realized by Mark will also be attributed to Mrs. Blaine. This will not be the case with capital gains realized by Belinda. Note, however, that the compound earnings resulting from the reinvestment of the dividends received from the new investment are not subject to the attribution rules.

Exercise Nine - 15

Subject: Income Attribution From A Spouse

On December 31, 2011, Mrs. Norah Moreau gives shares with an adjusted cost base of $23,000 and a fair market value of $37,000 to her husband, Nick Moreau. On February 24, 2012, the shares pay eligible dividends of $2,500 ($3,450 taxable amount) and, on August 31, 2012, Mr. Moreau sells the shares for $42,000. Assume that Mrs. Moreau does not elect out of ITA 73(1). What are the tax consequences for Mr. and Mrs. Moreau in each of the years 2011 and 2012?

Exercise Nine - 16

Subject: Income Attribution From A Related Minor

On December 31, 2011, Mrs. Norah Moreau gives shares with an adjusted cost base of $23,000 and a fair market value of $37,000 to her 12 year old daughter, Nicki Moreau. On February 24, 2012, the shares pay eligible dividends of $2,500 ($3,450 taxable amount) and, on August 31, 2012, Nicki sells the shares for $42,000. What are the tax consequences for Mrs. Moreau and Nicki in each of the years 2011 and 2012?

Exercise Nine - 17

Subject: Income Attribution - Use Of Loans

On December 31, 2011, Mr. Nadeem Bronski gives corporate bonds to his wife in exchange for a note with a face value of $121,000. The corporate bonds have an adjusted cost base of $115,000 and a fair market value of $121,000. The note from his wife does not pay interest and has no specific maturity date. Mr. Bronski does not report a gain on these bonds in 2011. During 2012, the bonds pay interest to Mrs. Bronski in the amount of $6,100. On October 1, 2012, immediately after an interest payment, Mrs. Bronski sells the bonds for $129,000. She uses $121,000 of the proceeds to pay off the loan owing to her husband. What are the tax consequences for Mr. and Mrs. Bronski in each of the years 2011 and 2012?

End of Exercises. Solutions available in Study Guide.

Income Attribution - Other Related Parties

9-209. The applicability of the income attribution rules that were previously discussed is limited to transfers and loans to spouses and related individuals under the age of 18. There is another income attribution provision that applies to a broader group of individuals. This is found in ITA 56(4.1) and indicates that, if an interest free or low rate loan is made to a related party for the purpose of producing property income, the income can be attributed back to the individual making the loan. A further condition for this attribution is that one of the main reasons for making the loan is to reduce or avoid tax.

9-210. The most important application of this provision is to loans made by parents to their adult children. For children 18 or over, the general income attribution rules do not apply. Although there are no tax consequences associated with cash gifts to adult children, parents interested in providing some financial assistance to their children can be reluctant to completely lose control over the resources involved.

9-211. As an example, a parent might extend an interest free loan to an adult child to assist with the purchase of a property. If the child decides to live in the property, there is no attribution related to the interest free loan used to purchase the principal residence. However, if the child uses the property to produce rental income, this income can be attributed back to the parent making the loan.

9-212. The tax planning conclusion in this situation is obvious. If a parent wishes to provide financial assistance to an adult child to earn property income, the appropriate route is to use an outright gift. While an interest free loan can accomplish the goal of providing financial assistance to the child, ITA 56(4.1) can eliminate the potential tax savings associated with this form of income splitting.

Anti-Avoidance Provisions

9-213. Given the attractiveness of income splitting, it is not surprising that tax planners have shown considerable ingenuity in devising procedures to avoid these attribution rules. It is equally unsurprising that the federal government has continued to come up with new rules to deal with these procedures.

9-214. Current legislation contains a number of provisions directed at preventing the use of indirect transfers, corporations, or trusts to circumvent the attribution rules. Complete coverage of these anti-avoidance rules is beyond the scope of this material. However, some of the more important anti-avoidance rules can be described as follows:

- ITA 74.1(3) prevents the substitution of a new low rate or interest free loan for an existing commercial rate loan.
- ITA 74.5(6) prevents a loan from being made to a person who is not subject to the attribution rules, who then makes a similar loan to a person who would be subject to the attribution rules if the loan had been directly made to that individual. The use of the intermediary would be disregarded and indirect attribution would apply.
- ITA 74.5(7) prevents the use of loan guarantees to avoid the attribution rules. That is, a higher income spouse cannot get around the attribution rules by providing a guarantee on a low rate or interest free loan to a spouse that is made by a third party.
- ITA 74.3 and 74.4 contain a variety of rules designed to prevent the avoidance of the attribution rules through the use of a trust (ITA 74.3) or a corporation (ITA 74.4).

Tax Planning And Income Attribution

9-215. In recent years it has become increasingly difficult to avoid the income attribution rules. Further, many of the plans that are available for this purpose involve corporations and trusts and are too complex to be dealt with in detail in an introductory level text such as this. However, there are a number of relatively simple points that can be helpful:

Split Pension Income As discussed in this Chapter, it is possible to transfer up to 50 percent of qualified pension income to a lower income spouse. This is an important provision which can provide for a significant reduction in family unit taxes.

RESPs Also as discussed in this Chapter, Registered Education Savings Plans can be used for a limited amount of income splitting.

TFSAs Also as discussed in this Chapter, Tax Free Savings Accounts can be used for income splitting as these plans are not subject to the income attribution rules.

Spousal RRSPs   As is discussed in Chapter 10, the spousal Registered Retirement Savings Plan is a readily available device for a limited amount of income splitting.

Assets With Capital Gains Potential   As there is no attribution of capital gains on transfers to related minors, assets with capital gains potential should be given to children, rather than to a spouse.

Loans   The prescribed rate is currently 1 percent (2nd quarter of 2012). With the rate at this level, it is possible to find safe investments that have a higher yield. Given this, it may be useful to loan funds at this prescribed rate to a low income family member who reinvests the funds at a rate higher than 1 percent.

Segregating Gifts To Spouses And Minors   If a spouse or minor child receives a gift or inheritance from a source to which attribution would not apply, the funds should be segregated for investment purposes and, if possible, should not be used for such non-deductible purposes as vacations, reducing the mortgage on the family home, or purchases of personal effects.

Detailed Records   In order to have low income family members acquire investment income, it is necessary for them to have funds to invest. Having the higher income spouse pay for non-deductible expenditures such as household expenses, clothing, vacations, and the lower income spouse's income tax liability can help provide for this. Although tuition fees can be eligible for a tax credit (see Chapter 4), they do not have to be paid by the student to be eligible for the credit. It may be desirable to maintain separate bank accounts and relatively detailed records to ensure that it is clear that the lower income family members' funds are being used for investment purposes.

New Businesses   When a new business is started, low income family members should be allowed to acquire an equity position, particularly if the capital requirements are small. Note, however, if the business experiences losses in its first years of operation, this may not be the best alternative.

Salaries To Family Members   When business income is earned in the family unit, or through a related corporation, the lower income spouse and any children should be paid reasonable salaries for any activity that can be justified as business related. Examples would include bookkeeping, filing, and other administrative work.

Key Terms Used In This Chapter

9-216.   The following is a list of the key terms used in this Chapter. These terms, and their meanings, are compiled in the Glossary Of Key Terms located at the back of the Study Guide.

Alimony	Eligible Child
Annual Child Care Expense Amount	Inadequate Consideration
Annuity	Income Attribution
Anti-Avoidance Provision	Income Splitting
Canada Disability Savings Bonds	Inter Vivos Transfer
Canada Disability Savings Grants	Moving Expenses
Canada Education Savings Grants	Periodic Child Care Expense Amount
Canada Learning Bonds	Registered Disability Savings Plan (RDSP)
Child Care Expenses	Registered Education Savings Plan (RESP)
Child Support	Retiring Allowance
Common-Law Partner	Spousal Support
Death Benefit	Spouse
Deferred Income Plans	Support Amount
Disability Supports Deduction	Tax Free Savings Account (TFSA)
Earned Income (Child Care Expenses)	Universal Child Care Benefit

References

9-217.   For more detailed study of the material in this Chapter, we refer you to the following:

ITA 56	Amounts To Be Included In Income For Year
ITA 56.1	Support
ITA 60	Other Deductions
ITA 60.1	Support
ITA 62	Moving Expenses
ITA 63	Child Care Expenses
ITA 64	Disability Supports Deduction
ITA 74.1(1)	Transfers And Loans To Spouse Or Common-Law Partner
ITA 74.1(2)	Transfers And Loans To Minors
ITA 74.2	Gain Or Loss Deemed That Of Lender Or Transferor
ITA 74.5	Transfers For Fair Market Consideration
ITA 146.1	Registered Education Savings Plans
IIA 146.2	Tax-Free Savings Accounts
ITA 146.4	Registered Disability Savings Plan
ITR 300	Capital Element Of Annuity Payments
IC 93-3R1	Registered Education Savings Plans
IT-75R4	Scholarships, Fellowships, Bursaries, Prizes And Research Grants
IT-178R3	Moving Expenses (Consolidated)
IT-209R	Inter Vivos Gifts Of Capital Property To Individuals Directly or Through Trusts
IT-325R2	Property Transfers After Separation, Divorce And Annulment
IT-337R4	Retiring Allowances (Consolidated)
IT-340R	Scholarships, Fellowships, Bursaries, And Research Grants - Forgivable Loans, Repayable Awards, And Repayable Employment Income
IT-419R2	Meaning Of Arm's Length
IT-495R3	Child Care Expenses
IT-499R	Superannuation Or Pension Benefits
IT-508R	Death Benefits
IT-510	Transfers And Loans Of Property Made After May 22, 1985 To A Related Minor
IT-511R	Interspousal And Certain Other Transfers And Loans Of Property
IT-530R	Support Payments
RC4092	Registered Education Savings Plans
RC4460	Registered Disability Savings Plan
RC4466	Tax Free Savings Account

Problems For Self Study

(The solutions for these problems can be found in the separate Study Guide.)

Self Study Problem Nine - 1 (Moving Expenses)

In May of the current year, following a dispute with her immediate superior, Ms. Elaine Fox resigned from her present job in Halifax and began to look for other employment. She was not able to find suitable work in Halifax. However, she did locate another job in Regina and was expected to report for work on October 1.

After locating the new job, Ms. Fox flew to Regina to find living quarters for herself. After two days of searching, Ms. Fox was able to locate a suitable house. Subsequent to purchasing her new home, Ms. Fox remained in Regina for an additional four days in order to purchase various furnishings for this residence. Her expenses for this trip were as follows:

Air Fare (Halifax - Regina, Return)	$ 689
Car Rental (6 Days At $35)	210
Hotel (6 Days At $110)	660
Food (6 Days At $51)	306
Total Expenses	$1,865

On her return to Halifax, she received the following statements from her attorneys:

Real Estate Commission - Old Home	$ 9,500
Legal Fees - Old Home	1,400
Unpaid Taxes On Old Home To Date Of Sale	800
Legal Fees - New Home	1,850
Transfer Tax On New Home	600
Total	$14,150

On August 31 of the current year, after supervising the final packing of her property and its removal from the old house, Ms. Fox spent three days in a Halifax hotel while she finalized arrangements for her departure. Expenses during this period were as follows:

Hotel (Three Days At $95)	$285
Food (Three Days At $51)	153
Total	$438

On September 3, she leaves Halifax by automobile, arriving in Regina on September 10. As her new residence is not yet available, she is forced to continue living in a Regina hotel until September 26. Her expenses for the period September 3 to September 26 are as follows:

Gasoline	$ 350
Hotel (23 Days At $95)	2,185
Food (23 Days At $51)	1,173
Total	$3,708

On moving into the new residence, she is required to pay the moving company a total of $3,800. This fee includes $675 for the 16 days of storage required because the new home was not available when the furnishings arrived.

Ms. Fox's only income for the current year was employment income and the net amounts to be included in her Net Income For Tax Purposes are as follows:

Old Job (5 Months)	$15,000
New Job (3 Months)	10,500
Net Employment Income	$25,500

Ms. Fox's new employer did not provide any reimbursement for moving expenses.

Required: Calculate the maximum allowable moving expenses that Ms. Fox can deduct from her Net Income For Tax Purposes for the current year and any amount that can be carried forward to a subsequent year. Ms. Fox does not use the simplified method of calculating travel expenses.

Self Study Problem Nine - 2 (Child Care Expenses)

Mr. and Mrs. Pleasant have three children who are 4, 10, and 15 years of age and live at home. All of the children enjoy good physical and mental health. In order to keep up with the costs of a family of this size, both Mr. Pleasant and Mrs. Pleasant are employed.

During 2012, Mr. Pleasant had employment income of $99,000 and deductible employment expenses of $8,500. Mrs. Pleasant had employment income of $18,000 and interest income of $2,200. She also received $1,200 in universal child care benefits.

Payments for child care amounted to $100 per week, for a total of 48 weeks. The payments were made to Mrs. Pleasant's mother, who issued a tax receipt for $4,800.

Also during 2012, there was a period of six weeks during which Mrs. Pleasant was hospitalized for injuries suffered in a fall while rock climbing. This period was part of the 48 weeks for which child care payments were made.

Required: Determine the maximum amount of child care expenses that can be deducted by Mr. Pleasant and by Mrs. Pleasant for the year ending December 31, 2012.

Self Study Problem Nine - 3 (Pension Income Splitting)

John Gupra is 57 years of age. As he began working at an early age for a company with a very generous pension plan, he retired at age 55. During 2012, he receives payments from this plan of $64,000. During 2012 he also has net rental income of $23,000. John has no other sources of income during 2012.

John's wife Fatima is 45 years of age. For 2012, her only income is $8,400 of interest on her savings account.

Neither John nor Fatima have any tax credits other than the basic personal credit, spousal credit, and pension income credit. Further, they have no deductions that will be used in the determination of Taxable Income.

Required: John would like to split his 2012 pension income with Fatima. Calculate the maximum amount of 2012 tax savings that would result from this tax planning strategy.

Self Study Problem Nine - 4 (Other Income And Other Deductions)

Arthur Madison, Jules Madison, and Stanley Madison are brothers and they have asked you to assist them in preparing their tax returns for the 2012 taxation year. They have provided you with the following information:

	Arthur	**Jules**	**Stanley**
Net employment income	$6,000	$18,000	$73,000
Net business income (loss)	Nil	5,000	(12,000)
Net property income (loss)	8,000	(4,000)	11,000
Capital gains	5,626	14,000	Nil
Capital losses	Nil	(17,000)	(10,000)
Employment insurance received	3,000	Nil	Nil
Pension benefits received	Nil	3,000	Nil

	Arthur	Jules	Stanley
Charitable donations	(4,000)	(2,000)	(1,000)
Tuition fees paid	Nil	Nil	(800)
Spousal support payments made	Nil	Nil	(4,800)
Tax Free Savings Account contribution	(500)	Nil	(5,000)
Tax Free Savings Account withdrawal	Nil	Nil	8,200

Required: Determine the 2012 Net Income For Tax Purposes for each of the Madison brothers and indicate any losses that can be carried over to other years.

Self Study Problem Nine - 5 (Non-Arm's Length Transactions)

John Bolton owns 5,000 shares of Marker Manufacturing Ltd., a Canadian public company. These shares were purchased three years ago, at a price of $45 per share. They are currently trading at $105 per share.

John is planning to transfer these shares to his 35 year old brother, Alex Bolton, who will immediately sell them. John is considering four alternatives for the transfer:

   A.   The 5,000 shares are sold to Alex Bolton at a price of $75 per share.

   B.   The 5,000 shares are sold to Alex Bolton at a price of $125 per share.

   C.   The 5,000 shares are sold to Alex Bolton at a price of $105 per share.

   D.   The 5,000 shares are given to Alex Bolton as a gift.

Required: For each of these four alternatives, determine the effect on Net Income For Tax Purposes of John Bolton and Alex Bolton for the current year. Include in your solution the adjusted cost base that will apply for Alex Bolton.

Self Study Problem Nine - 6 (Deemed Dispositions On Death And Emigration)

Mr. Howard Caswell is 67 years of age and his spouse, Charlene, is 58. They have one son, John, who is 36 years of age. Mr. Caswell has used all of his lifetime capital gains deduction on dispositions that occurred prior to the current year.

On September 1 of the current year, Mr. Howard Caswell owns the following properties:

Rental Property   Mr. Caswell owns a rental building that was acquired at a cost of $120,000. This includes an estimated value for the land on which the building is situation of $25,000. As at September 1 of the current year, the UCC of the building is $67,000. As of this date, the fair market value of the property has increased to $158,000, including an unchanged value for the land of $25,000.

General Industries Ltd.   Mr. Caswell owns 5,000 shares of General Industries Ltd., a Canadian public company. These shares have a cost of $200,000 and a current fair market value of $350,000. Mr. Caswell has never owned more than 3 percent of the outstanding shares of this Company.

Farm Land   Mr. Caswell owns farm land with a cost of $325,000 and a current fair market value of $550,000. The land is farmed on a full time basis by Mr. Caswell's son, John.

Caswell Enterprises   Mr. Caswell owns 100 percent of the voting shares of Caswell Enterprises, a Canadian controlled private corporation. The Company was established with an investment of $275,000 and it is estimated that the current fair market value of the shares is $426,000.

Required: Explain the tax consequences that would result in each of the following Cases for Mr. Caswell for the current year. In your solutions for Cases A and B, include the tax base of the assets to the transferee.

A. Mr. Caswell dies on September 1 of the current year, leaving all of his property to his spouse, Charlene.
B. Mr. Caswell dies on September 1 of the current year, leaving all of his property to his son, John.
C. Mr. Caswell departs from Canada and ceases to be a resident on September 1 of the current year.

Assume that no elections are made and that normal deemed disposition values apply.

Self Study Problem Nine - 7 (Income Attribution)

During the current year, Mr. Langdon makes a non-interest bearing loan of $100,000 to his wife, who acquires a $100,000 bond with the proceeds. He also makes a non-interest bearing loan of $100,000 to both of his children:

- Pat, aged 15, who uses the funds to acquire a $100,000 bond, and

- Heather, aged 23, who uses the funds as a down payment on her principal residence. Without this loan she would have paid mortgage interest of $6,000 during the year.

During the year, the bonds acquired by Mr. Langdon's spouse pay interest of $5,000. The bonds acquired by Pat pay interest of $5,500.

Required: Determine the amount of income that will be attributed to Mr. Langdon for the current taxation year as the result of the non-interest bearing loans.

Self Study Problem Nine - 8 (Gifts And Income Attribution)

Mrs. Sarah Long, a management consultant, is married with two children. Her son, Barry, is 27 years old and her daughter, Mary, is 13. Mrs. Long has not previously gifted or sold property to her husband or either of her children.

On April 1 of the current year, Mrs. Long owns the following properties:

Long Consulting Ltd.   Mrs. Long owns 100 percent of the voting shares of Long Consulting Ltd., a Canadian controlled private corporation. These shares have a cost of $210,000 and a current fair market value of $475,000.

Rental Property   Mrs. Long owns a rental building. The building was acquired at a cost of $190,000. On April 1 of the current year, its UCC is $125,000 and its fair market value is estimated to be $275,000. The fair market value of the land has remained at $100,000 since the building's acquisition.

Dynamics Inc.   Mrs. Long owns 4,000 shares of Dynamics Inc., a Canadian public company. These shares have a cost of $212,000 and a current fair market value of $384,000.

Farm Land   Mrs. Long owns farm land with a cost of $80,000 and a current fair market value of $175,000. Mrs. Long's son, Barry, uses the farm land on a full time basis to grow various crops.

Mrs. Long is considering giving all or part of the properties to her spouse and/or her two children.

Required: You have been hired as a tax consultant to Mrs. Long. She would like a report that would detail, for each of the four properties, the tax consequences to her of making a gift of the item to her husband, to her son Barry, or her daughter Mary.

Your report should include:

- the tax consequences to Mrs. Long at the time of the gift;
- the tax cost of the properties to the recipient of the gift;
- the tax treatment of any income on the property subsequent to the gift; and
- the tax consequences that would result from a subsequent sale of the gifted property at

$50,000 more than its fair market value at the time of the gift.

The tax consequences to Mrs. Long should include the effects if she chooses to have ITA 73(1) apply and if she chooses to elect out of ITA 73(1). Assume that the recipient of the rental property does not take CCA prior to the subsequent sale of the property. In addition, ignore the possibility that either the lifetime capital gains deduction or the tax on split income is applicable to any of these transactions. These provisions are not covered until Chapter 11 of the text.

Self Study Problem Nine - 9 (Income Attribution)

Dr. Sandra Bolt is 49 years of age and an extremely successful physician in Halifax, Nova Scotia. She is married to Tod Bolt and has two children. On December 31, 2011, her son, Dirk, is 20 years old and her daughter, Dolly, is 15 years old. Each of the children earns about $10,000 per year in income from part time acting jobs. While her husband Tod qualified as a professional accountant, he did not enjoy the work and, for the last ten years, he has assumed the role of house parent. As a consequence, his only current source of income is the interest on $335,000 that he has in his personal savings account. This interest amounts to about $20,000 per year and all of the savings were accumulated from amounts that he earned while working as a professional accountant.

On December 28, 2011, Dr. Bolt is holding shares in a Canadian public company that have an adjusted cost base of $185,000 and a fair market value of $225,000. She is considering transferring these shares to either her husband or to one of her two children. She seeks your advice as to the tax consequences, both to herself and to the transferee, that would result from such a transfer.

During your discussions, Dr. Bolt has indicated the following:

- The transfer will take place on December 31, 2011.
- Any proceeds she receives from her family on the share transfer will not be invested in income producing assets.
- She wishes you to assume that the securities would pay eligible dividends during 2012 of $18,500 ($25,530 taxable amount) and that the transferee would sell the securities on January 1, 2013 for $260,000.

Required: Each of the following independent Cases involves a transfer by Dr. Bolt to a member of her family. Indicate, with respect to the Net Income For Tax Purposes of both Dr. Bolt and the transferee, the 2011, 2012, and 2013 tax effects of:

- the transfer on December 31, 2011,
- the assumed 2012 receipt of the dividends, and
- the assumed 2013 disposition by the transferee.

Note that some of the Cases have been included to illustrate specific provisions of the relevant legislation and do not necessarily represent a reasonable course of action on the part of Dr. Bolt.

Case A   Dr. Bolt gives the securities to her husband and does not elect out of the provisions of ITA 73(1).

Case B   Dr. Bolt's husband uses money from his savings account to purchase the securities for their fair market value of $225,000. Dr. Bolt does not elect out of the provisions of ITA 73(1).

Case C   Dr. Bolt's husband uses money from his savings account to purchase the securities for their fair market value of $225,000. Dr. Bolt elects out of the provisions of ITA 73(1).

Case D   Dr. Bolt's husband uses money from his savings account to purchase the securities for $140,000. Dr. Bolt does not elect out of the provisions of ITA 73(1).

Case E   Dr. Bolt's husband uses money from his savings account to purchase the securities for $140,000. Dr. Bolt elects out of the provisions of ITA 73(1).

Case F   Dr. Bolt gives the securities to her daughter, Dolly.

Case G   Dr. Bolt gives her daughter, Dolly, a $225,000 loan. The loan requires interest to be paid at commercial rates and Dolly uses the proceeds of the loan to purchase her mother's securities at fair market value. Dr. Bolt believes that the combination of dividends on the securities and Dolly's income from part time jobs will be sufficient to pay the interest on the loan.

Case H   Dr. Bolt gives her son, Dirk, a $225,000 interest free loan. Dirk uses the proceeds to purchase his mother's securities at their fair market value of $225,000.

Self Study Problem Nine - 10 (Comprehensive Case Covering Chapters 1 to 9)

Chantale Bergeron is 33 years old and has two children. Her son Marc is 5 years old and her daughter Michelle is 12 years old. Neither child has any income of their own. During 2012, she receives universal child care benefit payments of $1,200.

Chantale is employed as a technician by Pomme, a Canadian public company specializing in the creation of Apple accessories and applications. Her salary is $90,000 per year and, during 2012, Pomme withheld the following amounts from her earnings:

RPP Contributions	$4,500
EI	840
CPP	2,307
Professional Dues	1,200

Pomme makes a matching contribution to her RPP of $4,500.

Pomme provides her with an automobile that the company acquired in 2011 at a cost of $28,000. During 2012 she drove the automobile a total of 52,000 kilometers, of which 34,000 were employment related. Operating costs totaled $7,400 during the year, all of which were paid for by the company. The automobile was used by Chantale throughout 2012.

Pomme provides Chantale with an allowance for food and lodging while traveling on company business of $400 per month. Chantale's actual travel costs during 2012 totalled $4,500.

Until 2009, the family owned a home in Peterborough. Because of her husband's work, the Peterborough home was sold and, in January, 2010, they moved into rented premises in Carleton Place. At this time, Chantale began her employment with Pomme in their Carleton Place office.

Near the end of 2011, Chantale and her husband were divorced. The terms of their settlement require that her former husband pay $600 per month in child support and $200 per month in spousal support. During 2012, he made 10 monthly payments totaling $8,000.

Prior to their divorce, Chantale's husband had transferred to her securities with an adjusted cost base of $26,000. This was also the fair market value of the securities at that time. During 2012, these securities pay eligible dividends to Chantale of $1,500. In October 2012, Chantale sells these securities for $34,400.

After their divorce, Chantale continued to live in the rented premises in Carleton Place for the remainder of 2011. However, as Chantale did not enjoy the rural atmosphere of Carleton Place, she asked to be transferred to her employer's Ottawa office. This request was granted and, in early 2012, Chantale begin looking for a home in Ottawa.

Chantale made several house hunting trips into Ottawa, incurring travel costs of $260. In May she made an offer on a home near Pomme's Ottawa office that was accepted (this home was 65 kilometres closer to the new work location). The closing date on the new home was September 3, 2012. In order to give her children time to adjust to their new neighbourhood before school started, on August 15th she moved her belongings out of the Carleton Place apartment. As the lease on this property had several months remaining, she was required to pay a penalty of $1,200.

As she was not able to move into her new Ottawa home until September 3rd, it was necessary for her and her children to stay in a nearby Ottawa hotel from August 15th to September 3rd. The various costs associated with the move are as follows:

Cost Of Storing Belongings Prior To September 3rd	$1,500
Cost Of Moving Belongings	6,400
Legal Fees On Purchase Of New Home	850
Food And Hotel In Ottawa (19 Days At $250)	4,750

Pomme provided her with a $6,000 allowance to assist with her moving costs.

After moving to Ottawa, Chantale acquired transit passes for the months of September through December. Her pass cost $100 per month, while the pass for Michelle cost $75 per month.

The family's 2012 medical and dental expenses were as follows:

Chantale	$ 1,400
Marc	950
Michelle	11,200
Total	$13,550

While living in Carleton Place, Chantale incurred child care costs of $300 per week for 32 weeks. After moving to Ottawa, these costs increased to $350 per week and were incurred for 16 weeks. The children spent four weeks during the summer at a camp near Montreal. The camp cost $400 per week for each child. The camp fees do not qualify for the child fitness credit or the children's arts credit.

In November, 2012, Chantale was overjoyed to find that she had won $1,500,000 in an Ontario provincial lottery. Because she had been praying for this result and felt that her prayers had been answered, she immediately donated $200,000 of this amount to her church. The balance was invested in GICs which pay no interest until 2013.

Required: Calculate the following for Chantale:

- her minimum 2012 Net Income For Tax Purposes,
- her minimum 2012 Taxable Income,
- her minimum 2012 Tax Payable,
- any carry over that is available to Chantale, indicating any rules that are applicable to claiming the carry over.

Ignore GST and HST considerations, as well as any amounts of income tax that would have been withheld by Chantale's employer.

Assignment Problems

(The solutions for these problems are only available in
the solutions manual that has been provided to your instructor.)

Assignment Problem Nine - 1 (Death Benefits)

On January 2, 2012, Mrs. Long died in an automobile crash. Mrs. Long was 55 years old and, at the time of her death, was a full time employee of Apex Distribution Systems. During 2011, Mrs. Long earned $47,000 in employment income.

Because of her years of faithful service, Apex decides to pay a death benefit to Mrs. Long's surviving spouse in the amount of $24,000. The amount is to be paid in annual instalments of $6,000 per year, with the first instalment being paid in 2012.

Required: What effect will this death benefit have on the Net Income For Tax Purposes of Mrs. Long's spouse in 2012 and in subsequent years?

Assignment Problem Nine - 2 (Moving Expenses)

Mr. Leonard Ho has worked for Quality Construction Ltd. (QCL) for over 15 years. During this entire period he has been located in the employer's Regina office. However, in 2012, he requests a transfer to the firm's Kelowna office. QCL agrees to this transfer.

For 2012, Leonard's salary is $12,000 per month. Because he is a highly valued employee, QCL agrees to pay a moving allowance of $15,000 to cover his general moving costs. In addition, QCL agrees to negotiate additional payments for any housing loss that arises in Regina, as well as any additional costs associated with acquiring a new home in Kelowna.

In August, Leonard flies to Kelowna to look for alternative housing. He spends three days in the city and, after two days, he locates and purchases a residence similar to his Regina property at a cost of $427,000. His costs for this trip are as follows:

Airfare	$ 872
Rental Car Costs	326
Food And Lodging (3 Days At $190 Per Day)	570
Total	$1,768

On his return to Regina, he lists his residence at that location for sale. His original cost for this residence is $395,000. However, he is anxious to sell and, in early September, he accepts an offer of $360,000. The closing date is November 1. The new residence in Kelowna will not be available until December 1.

After some discussion, the employer agrees to fully compensate him for the $35,000 loss on the sale of his Regina property and, in addition, provide him with an additional allowance of $15,000 to compensate him for the additional cost of the Kelowna property. While the Regina office will pay the general moving allowance of $15,000, the Kelowna office will provide the additional $50,000 in housing related payments. All of these amounts will be paid during December, 2012.

The costs associated with the housing transactions are as follows:

Real Estate Commissions	$14,400
Legal Fees - Regina Property	625
Unpaid Property Taxes To Date Of Sale	1,200
Cost Of Cleaning And Minor Repairs Prior To Sale	2,650
Legal Fees Kelowna Property	895
Land Transfer Tax - Kelowna Property	4,600
Total	$24,370

Leonard continues to work in Regina until November 10th. As his old residence closes on November 1, he and his family live in a hotel until their departure for Kelowna on November 11. Costs for food and lodging during this period are $2,500 ($250 per day for 10 days).

The drive from Regina to Kelowna requires two days. The costs for this trip are as follows:

Gas	$125
Food And Lodging	460
Total	$585

Leonard and his family arrive in Kelowna on November 13th. As their new home will not be available until December 1, they live in a hotel until that date. The food and lodging costs total $4,275 ($225 per day for 19 days). Because of accumulated vacation time, Leonard does not begin working in Kelowna until December 1.

Leonard receives a bill from his moving company for $8,500. Of this total, $1,500 is for storage during the period November 1, 2012, through December 1, 2012.

Leonard would like to take the maximum moving expense deduction for 2012.

Required: Determine the amount that Leonard's Net Income For Tax Purposes will be increased or decreased by the transactions related to the move. Leonard makes no use of the simplified method of calculating vehicle and meal expenses.

Assignment Problem Nine - 3 *(Child Care Expenses)*

Maureen Hadley and her common-law partner Sue Brendal have three adopted children. At the end of 2012, their ages are as follows:

- Their daughter Lori is 4 years old.
- Their son Jack is 8 years old and qualifies for the disability tax credit.
- Their son Bob is 14 years old.

None of the children have any income of their own.

Maureen is a very successful accountant with net business income in 2012 of $216,000. Her partner, Sue Brendal, works on a part time basis in retail. Her 2012 gross employment income is $24,000. In addition, because she was previously married, she receives child support payments of $1,200 per month from the father of Lori.

Both Maureen and Sue spend a considerable amount of time at their work and, because of this, they employ a full time person to care for the children. The cost for this care is $12,480 ($260 per week for 48 weeks).

During the four week period in the summer when they do not employ the child care worker, the children attend a live-in camp. The cost for this camp is $2,000 per week, per child. None of the camp fees are eligible for the fitness credit or the arts credit.

In January, 2012, Maureen slipped on an icy sidewalk and broke both of her ankles. As a consequence of this accident, she spent three weeks in the hospital.

Sue has always been concerned about her lack of formal education. To make progress in this area, she enrolls in an intensive 5 week accounting course at a designated educational institution. Class attendance and work in this course require nearly 60 hours per week of Sue's time.

Required: Determine the maximum amount that can be deducted by Maureen and Sue for child care costs for the year ending December 31, 2012.

Assignment Problem Nine - 4 *(Pension Income Splitting)*

Both Jean Belanger and his wife Carole are 66 years of age. During 2012, they each received OAS payments of $6,500.

As a long-term employee of a Canadian public company, Jean receives an annual pension benefit. For 2012, the amount is $168,000. This payment, along with the OAS payment, are his only sources of income.

Because she was blinded in work related accident, Carole qualifies for the disability tax credit. As the accident involved negligence on the part of her employer, Carole receives a monthly annuity payment of $3,500. This payment will continue as long as she lives. This is her only source of income other than the OAS payment.

Neither Jean nor Carole are eligible for any tax credits other than the basic personal credit, the spousal credit, the age credit, the pension income credit, and the disability tax credit. Further, they have no deductions that will be used in the determination of Taxable Income.

On the advice of his grandson, Jean plans to split his 2012 pension income with Carole.

Required: Compare the 2012 Amount Owing to the CRA by Jean and Carole assuming:

A.   Jean does not split his pension income.

B.   Jean splits his pension income with Carole on a 50:50 basis.

Assignment Problem Nine - 5 (Other Income And Deductions Including RESP)

Katrina Watts is 42 years old and has custody of her two children from a previous marriage. The son is 11 years old and the daughter is 9 years old. They are both in good health. She is currently married to very successful electrician who earns an income in excess of $300,000 per year.

As her children are now in school most of the year, she has decided to pursue a career in environmental design. To this end, she has enrolled, on a full time basis, at the University of Calgary. Her studies began on January 1, 2012.

As she was very successful in her first term of studies, she was able to obtain summer employment as an assistant in an environment study in Cold Lake, Alberta. As this location was over 600 kilometres from Calgary, she and her children moved to a rented cottage in Cold Lake for the period June 1, 2012 through September 1, 2012. As this was a temporary move, it was accomplished using a rented van at a total cost of $685.

During her summer in Cold Lake, Ms. Watts required someone to take care of her two children while she was at work. For this service, she paid a local retired teacher $125 per week for a period of 12 weeks. She has the appropriate documentation to support these costs.

She returned to Calgary on September 1, 2012 in order to resume her studies at the University of Calgary. Once again, the move was accomplished using a rented van. The total cost was $826. During the fall term, she found a part time job working in a Calgary architecture firm.

On January 1, 2012, Ms. Watts did not have a Tax Free Savings Account (TFSA). In October, 2012, she opened a TFSA and deposited a total of $4,500. Her husband also made a contribution in the amount of $5,000.

During 2012, Ms. Watts received the following amounts:

Wages From Cold Lake Employment	$9,600
Wages From Part Time Employment In Calgary	600
Scholarship Granted By University for September 2012 semester	4,000
Eligible Dividends Received	3,500
Child Support Received	10,500
Inheritance From Aunt	30,000
TFSA Withdrawal	8,000

During November, 2012 Ms. Watts establishes RESPs for both of her children. She contributes $1,000 to each of these plans.

Required:

A.   Determine the minimum Net Income For Tax Purposes that Ms. Watts will have to report for her 2012 taxation year. Provide reasons for omitting items that you have not included in your calculations. Also, indicate any amounts that can be carried forward to future years.

B.   Provide any advice you feel would assist her in planning future actions concerning the RESPs that have been established for her children.

Assignment Problem Nine - 6 (Non-Arm's Length Transactions)

Mr. Bryant Shaw owns a tract of land which he acquired several years ago at a cost of $275,000. An appraiser has indicated that it has a current fair market value of $400,000.

As he is planning on moving to a warmer climate, Mr. Bryant would like to dispose of this property. His preference would be to have it transferred to a family member and, to this end, he is considering the following four alternatives:

A. Gifting the property to his sister Sally. As she is currently living on welfare, it is likely that she would sell the property immediately to have access to the additional funds.

B. Selling the property to his mother Sarah for its fair market value. She is not likely to sell the property in the foreseeable future.

C. Selling the property to his younger brother Bob for $275,000. Bob is attending university on a full time basis and has no other source of income. Bob would likely sell the property immediately for its fair market value in order to take advantage of his current low tax bracket.

D. Selling the property to his older brother Norman for $500,000. Norman would likely sell the property immediately for its fair market value. Norman plans to use the resulting loss to offset capital gains that he has realized in the current year.

Required: For each of the alternatives under consideration, advise Bryant of the tax consequences that will result from the disposition. In addition, in those cases where the property is resold by the transferee, indicate the tax consequences of the sale to that individual.

Assignment Problem Nine - 7 (Non-Arm's Length Transfer of Depreciable Asset)

The following two independent case involve a non-arm's length transfer of a depreciable asset.

Case One   Jason Lasarge owns a depreciable asset with a fair market value of $255,000. It has a capital cost of $187,000 and a UCC of $145,000. It is the only asset in its class. He sells this asset to his brother for cash of $255,000.

Case Two   Christine Drummond owns a depreciable asset with a fair market value $320,000. It has a capital cost of $520,000 and a UCC of $240,000. It is the only asset in its class. She sells the asset to her sister for cash of $320,000.

Required: For each of the two cases, indicate the tax consequences for the transferor that result from the sale. In addition, indicate the tax values that will be used by the transferee subsequent to the transfer.

Assignment Problem Nine - 8
(Deemed Dispositions At Death Including Disposition Of Land And Building)

Ms. Samantha Kneebone lives with her common-law partner, Alice. She has a 36 year old son, Chester. Chester has annual employment income of over $65,000 a year, and has had taxable capital gains of at least $30,000 for the last three years.

For a number of years, Ms. Kneebone has owned a small apartment building in Regina. The property was acquired for $452,000, with $122,000 of this amount being attributable to the land. The building's cost of $330,000 ($452,000 - $122,000) was allocated to a separate Class 1. From its date of acquisition through 2012, the building was normally fully occupied. As of January 1, 2011, the UCC balance for this Class 1 was $234,000.

On July 1, 2012, Ms. Kneebone died as the result of pancreatic cancer. It was estimated that, on this date, the rental property had a fair market value of $876,000. The estimate allocations were $425,000 for the land and $451,000 for the building.

In March, 2013, the building is sold for a total price of $784,000, of which $376,000 is allocated to the land and $408,000 to the building.

Required:

A. For each of the following cases, indicate the tax effects to be included in Ms. Kneebone's tax return as a result of the 2012 deemed disposition at her death, as well as the tax effects associated with the 2013 sale of the property.

Case 1 Her will leaves the apartment building to Alice. During 2012, Alice continues to operate the building and takes maximum CCA for that year.

Case 2 Her will leaves the apartment building to Chester. During 2012, he continues to operate the building and takes maximum CCA for that year.

B. Assume that in Case 2, the proceeds of the 2013 sale of the property by Chester were allocated $435,000 to the land and $349,000 to the building. Calculate the tax effects associated with the sale of the property for Chester.

Assignment Problem Nine - 9 (Transfers To A Spouse - Income Attribution)

For a number of years, Mr. James Hadley has owned several rental properties. On January 1, 2012, he marries Ms. Gwyneth Rowe and, on the following day, as part of their pre-nuptial agreement, he gifts one of these properties to her. At the time of the gift, the relevant information on the property is as follows:

	Land	Building
Original Cost	$ 52,000	$170,000
Market Value - Date Of Transfer	102,000	214,000
UCC - Date Of Transfer	N/A	97,000

During 2012, there was a net rental loss on the property of $7,400 and no CCA was deducted on the building.

On January 1, 2013, after concluding that other investments would provide a better return, Gwyneth sells the rental property for $346,000. At this time, an appraisal indicates that the market value of the land is unchanged at $102,000.

Required: Determine the tax effects associated with the transfer and subsequent sale of the property for both Mr. and Mrs. Hadley assuming:

A. The facts are as stated in the problem and that Mr. Hadley does not elect out of ITA 73(1).

B. Instead of receiving the rental property as a gift, Gwyneth purchases the property for its fair market value, using funds that were accumulated prior to the marriage. Mr. Hadley elects out of ITA 73(1) on this sale.

Assignment Problem Nine - 10 (Income Attribution)

For a number of years, Mr. Alonso Robelo has owned 15,000 shares of Lisgar Inc., a Canadian public company. These shares were acquired at a cost of $12.50 per share.

On March 2, 2012, Alonso gives 5,000 shares of these shares to his spouse Alice. The remaining 10,000 shares are given to his 12 year old son Alonso Jr. On this date the shares are trading at $17.00 per share.

On July 1, 2012, the Lisgar Inc. shares pay an eligible dividend of $0.80 per share.

On November 1, 2012, Alice and Alonso Jr. sell all of their Lisgar Inc. shares for $16.00 per share.

Required: Determine the total Net Income For Tax Purposes to be recorded for the 2012 taxation year by Alonso, his spouse Alice, and his son Alonso Jr., on the preceding transactions. Assume that Alonso did not elect out of the ITA 73(1) spousal rollover provision.

Assignment Problem Nine - 11 (Gifts And Income Attribution)

Ms. Vaughn is a very successful attorney with an income of over $500,000 per year. She is married to Jonathan Flex, a former Mr. Canada. Jonathan has no income of his own.

She and Jonathan have two children. Their daughter Sheila is 27, while their son Biff is 15. To date, Vicky has not gifted or sold property to either her spouse or to her children.

At the end of the current year, Ms. Vaughn owns the following assets:

Shares Of TD Bank   Ms. Vaughn owns 10,000 shares with a current fair market value of $700,000. The adjusted cost base for these shares is $550,000.

Vaughn Enterprises Ltd.   Ms. Vaughn owns all of the shares of this Canadian controlled private company. Her adjusted cost base for these shares is $475,000. A business valuator has concluded that the shares are currently worth $1,200,000.

Rental Property   Ms. Vaughn owns a 22 unit apartment building with a current fair market value of $2,400,000. It is estimated that $400,000 of this value is associated with the land. Ms. Vaughn purchased the unit several years ago at a total cost of $1,500,000, with $300,000 of this value associated with the land. As of January 1 of the current year, the UCC of the Class 1 building is $960,000.

Farm Land   Ms. Vaughn owns farm land that cost $800,000 and has a current fair market value of $1,200,000. Sheila uses the farm land on a full time basis to grow certified organic vegetables.

As Ms. Vaughn's income is more than sufficient for her needs, she is considering giving all or part of the properties to her spouse and/or her two children. She has fully utilized her lifetime capital gains deduction.

Required: You have been hired as a tax consultant to Ms. Vaughn. She would like a report that would detail, for each of the four properties, the tax consequences to her of making a gift of the item to her husband or to either one of her children. Your report should include:

- the tax consequences to Ms. Vaughn at the time of the gift;
- the tax cost of the properties to the recipient of the gift;
- the tax treatment of any income on the property subsequent to the gift; and
- the tax consequences that would result from a subsequent sale of the gifted property at $100,000 more than its fair market value at the time of the gift. In the case of the rental property, assume that all of this extra $100,000 can be allocated to the building.

In preparing your answer, assume that Ms. Vaughn does not elect out of ITA 73(1) if the gifts are made to Jonathan Flex. In addition, assume that the recipient of the rental property does not take CCA prior to the subsequent sale of the property.

Assignment Problem Nine - 12 (Comprehensive Case Covering Chapters 1 to 9)

Carolyn Hadley is 29 years old and recently divorced. The terms of the 2011 divorce settlement require that her former spouse pay $1,000 per month in child support, as well as $500 per month in spousal support. Because he lost his job in 2012, payments during this year have totaled only $12,500.

Carolyn has two children. Her younger child, Deborah, is 4 years old. Her older child Mark is 7 years old. Neither child has any income of their own. During 2012, she receives universal child care benefit payments of $100 per month.

Prior to the divorce, the family had lived in property that Carolyn owned in Lethbridge, Alberta. Prior to 2012, Carolyn had been a stay at home mom with no source of income of her own. Because she did not feel her support payments would provide an adequate amount of income for herself and her children, she accepted a job in Edmonton, Alberta. Her employment contract calls for her to begin work on March 1, 2012.

During January, 2012, Carolyn made several house hunting trips to Edmonton. The cost of these trips was $785. In February, she made an offer on an Edmonton home and it was accepted. The closing date for the sale is March 10, 2012. Her Lethbridge house was sold, with a closing date of February 15, 2012.

After the closing on her Lethbridge home, she and her children spent 14 days in a Lethbridge hotel. The trip to Edmonton took 2 days and required driving 506 kilometers. On arriving in Edmonton, she spent an additional 9 days in hotels prior to her new home becoming available.

Carolyn will use the simplified method of calculating meal and vehicle costs for the trip to Edmonton. Assume that the 2012 vehicle rate for Alberta is $.53 per kilometer. The 2012 rate for meals is $51 per day per person.

The various other costs associated with the real estate transactions and the move to Edmonton are as follows:

Selling Costs Of Lethbridge Property	$12,500
Legal Fees - Sale Of Lethbridge Property	600
Legal Fees - Purchase Of Edmonton Property	450
Storage Costs - February 15th Through March 10th	1,400
Cost Of Moving Belongings	7,250
Food And Lodging In Lethbridge After Closing [(14 Days)($250)]	3,500
Food And Lodging In Edmonton Prior To Closing [(9 Days)($250)]	2,250
Total	$27,950

After moving to Edmonton, Carolyn incurred child care costs of $175 per week for 38 weeks. Both children spent two weeks during the summer at a camp near Red Deer. The camp cost $500 per week for each child. The camp fees do not qualify for the child fitness credit or the children's arts credit.

During the regular school year, Carolyn's older child Mark was enrolled in a qualifying fitness program at a cost of $50 per week for a total of 28 weeks.

The family's 2012 medical and dental expenses were as follows:

Carolyn	$1,200
Deborah	4,200
Mark	2,200
Total	$7,600

Carolyn's new employer is a large Canadian public company. Her basic salary is $5,000 per month and, during 2012, her employer withheld the following amount from her earnings.

RPP Contributions	$2,600
EI	840
CPP	2,307
United Way Contributions	600

Her employer makes a matching contribution to her RPP of $2,600.

Her employer provides her with an automobile that the company acquired on April 1, 2012 at a cost of $42,000. During 2012, she drove the car a total of 46,000 kilometers, of which 38,000 were employment related. The company paid all of the operating costs of the vehicle, a total of $7,200 during 2012. The car was used by Carolyn from April 1, 2012, through December 31, 2012.

Her employer provides an allowance for food and lodging while traveling on company business. The allowance is $600 per month, a total of $5,400 for the 9 months that Carolyn was traveling for her employer during 2012. Her actual cost for employment related food and lodging in 2012 totaled $5,700.

Her employer also provides a moving cost allowance of $10,000. In addition, the employer is reimbursing Carolyn for the $4,000 loss on the sale of her Lethbridge home, as well as providing a $7,500 payment to assist with the higher housing costs she has encountered in Edmonton.

During 2011, Carolyn is given a group of securities by her father. The adjusted cost base of these securities was $45,000 in the hands of her father. At the time of the gift, their fair market value was $62,000. During 2012, these securities pay eligible dividends of $5,800. In December, 2012, Carolyn sells these securities for $74,000.

In June, 2012, Carolyn's mother dies, leaving her with a rental property that has a fair market value of $320,000, of which $50,000 represents the value of the land. At the time of her mother's death, the UCC of the building was $240,000 and it was not occupied by a tenant. Her mother had purchased the property several years ago for $400,000.

At the time her mother acquired the property it was estimated that the value of the land was $100,000. Carolyn was not able to find a tenant and, in December, 2012, she sells the property for $340,000. An appraiser indicates that the value of the land at this time is unchanged at $50,000.

Required: Calculate the following for Carolyn:

- her minimum 2012 Net Income For Tax Purposes,
- her minimum 2012 Taxable Income,
- her minimum 2012 Tax Payable,

Ignore GST and HST considerations, as well as any amounts of income tax that would have been withheld by Carolyn's employer.

Assignment Problem Nine - 13 (Comprehensive Case Covering Chapters 1 to 9)

John Winded celebrated his 65th birthday on February 14, 2012. On February 28, 2012, John retired from Celebrate Ltd., a public corporation, after 35 years of service. John's annual remuneration was $84,000. A review of his last pay stub reveals the following deductions:

CPP contributions	$700
EI premiums	200
RPP contributions	500
Employee premiums to the company dental and health plan	150

John had the use of a company car for January and February. The car was leased at a monthly rate of $360. During these two months, Celebrate Ltd. paid the $800 in automobile operating expenses. John drove a total of 3,000 kilometers, 90 percent of which were personal.

As a token of their appreciation for John's dedicated service, the company gave him a watch that cost $700.

Since John wanted to live in the Vancouver area once retired, he asked his employer to transfer him from their Winnipeg to their Vancouver office, effective January 1, 2012. He incurred the following expenses related to his move:

October, 2011

Air fare for John and his spouse for trip to Vancouver to find a home	$	900
Hotel for four days in Vancouver for purposes of finding a new home		800
Meals while in Vancouver for purposes of finding a new home		320
Car rental while in Vancouver for purposes of finding a new home		325

December, 2011

Legal fees and land transfer taxes on purchase of new home	$ 4,800

January, 2012

Air fare for John and his spouse to Vancouver	$ 1,200
Legal fees and commissions on sale of old home (sold in January, 2012)	13,000
Cost of transporting furniture and other household goods from Winnipeg to Vancouver	4,000

Mr. Winded has kept all of his receipts with respect to his moving costs.

Mr. Winded made sure he acquired the maximum allowable number of shares under the company stock option plan prior to his retirement date. On February 1, 2012, when the shares were trading for $11 per share, he acquired 1,500 shares at $8 per share. When the option was granted, the shares were trading for $7 per share. Mr. Winded sold 1,000 of the 1,500 shares in June, 2012 for $17 per share. Mr. Winded did not own any other shares of Celebrate Ltd., other than the ones he acquired in February.

Mr. Winded received the following "pension" income for the period March 1 through December 31:

Old Age Security	$ 5,350
Canada Pension Plan	9,600
Pension Income from his company pension plan	44,000
Registered Retirement Income Fund	8,000

Mr. Winded also has a number of investments. During 2012, he received interest income of $3,478 and eligible dividends from Canadian public corporations of $1,700. He owns shares of Sail Ltd., a private investment corporation that is controlled by his brother-in-law. During 2012, he received non-eligible dividends from Sail Ltd. of $800.

Mr. Winded owns two rental properties. The information for 2012 is as follows:

	Property A	Property B
Rental Revenues	$ 98,000	$ 62,000
Operating Expenses	(104,000)	(54,000)
Net Rental Income (Loss)	($ 6,000)	$ 8,000
Class 1 UCC Balance	$180,000	$210,000
Class 8 UCC Balance	12,000	16,000

Mr. Winded divested himself of a number of capital assets during 2012:

Description	Cost	Gross Proceeds
Stamp collection	$ 8,000	$ 5,000
Rare book	700	4,200
Furniture	4,800	900
Painting	300	800
Shares of Sail Ltd. (Note 1)	12,000	48,000
Shares of CNR Company	Note 2	20,100
Shares of BCE Ltd.	Note 2	36,000
Sale of Winnipeg home (Note 3)	140,000	300,000
Sale of Lake Winnipeg cottage (Note 3)	80,000	290,000

Note 1   Sail Ltd. is a private company whose shares do not qualify for the lifetime capital gains deduction.

Note 2   Mr. Winded's history of purchases and sales in the shares of Canadian National Railway (CNR) Company and BCE Ltd. are as follows:

May 1, 2008 purchase	200 CNR shares @ $52 per share
May 1, 2009 purchase	300 CNR shares @ $46 per share
May 1, 2010 sale	400 CNR shares @ $55 per share
May 1, 2011 purchase	200 CNR shares @ $64 per share
May 1, 2012 sale	300 CNR shares @ $67 per share
July 11, 2012 purchase	1,000 BCE shares @ $38 per share
August 1, 2012 sale	1,000 BCE shares @ $36 per share
August 29, 2012 purchase	600 BCE shares @ $39 per share

Note 3 The cottage was acquired in 1997. It was sold for gross proceeds of $290,000. Mr. Winded incurred $10,000 of selling costs on this property.

The Winnipeg home which was acquired in 2003 was sold for gross proceeds of $300,000. Mr. Winded incurred selling costs of $13,000 on the sale of his Winnipeg home.

Mr. Winded plans to deduct the selling costs on the house as moving expenses and account for the selling costs on the cottage as selling costs.

In 1993, Mr. Winded started a sideline woodworking business, which he has continued in Vancouver. For 2012, the details are as follows:

Revenues	$38,000
Supplies	16,000
Advertising	1,000
Purchase of a new computer	3,800
Sale of old computer (Class 45)	200
Purchase of woodworking equipment	1,600
Purchase of two hand tools	450

Mr. Winded converted his large Vancouver garage to a woodworking shop in December, 2011. The shop occupies 20 percent of the total area of his Vancouver home. His 2012 home expenses are as follows:

Mortgage interest	$4,000
Utilities	3,600
Property taxes	4,500
Home telephone line	700
Insurance	1,400
Maintenance	1,800

UCC balances related to his woodworking business at January 1, 2012 are as follows:

| Class 8 | $2,400 |
| Class 45 | 800 |

As he does not wish to have to report any capital gain or recapture upon its eventual disposition, Mr. Winded does not claim CCA on the portion of his home that is used in his woodworking business.

Mr. Winded's spouse, Rachel, is 67 years old. Her 2012 income consists of $6,500 in Old Age Security, $3,100 from the Canada Pension Plan and $1,400 of eligible dividends that she received from preferred shares that were given to her as a birthday present in 2011 by her husband. The shares, which have an adjusted cost base of $27,000, were sold for $31,000 in 2012.

Mrs. Winded is disabled and qualifies for the disability tax credit. In 2012, she incurred $4,600 in medical expenses, $1,200 of which was reimbursed by Mr. Winded's dental and health plan when he was an employee of Celebrate Ltd.

In 2012, Mr. Winded made $3,700 in charitable donations to registered charities.

Mr. Winded would like to use all possible elections in order to minimize their tax liability.

Required: In determining these amounts, ignore GST, PST and HST considerations.

A. For the 2012 taxation year, calculate Mr. Winded's minimum:

1. Net Income For Tax Purposes,
2. Taxable Income,
3. Federal Balance Owing Or Refund (tax plus any social benefits repayment).

B. For the 2012 taxation year, calculate Mrs. Winded's minimum:

1. Net Income For Tax Purposes,
2. Taxable Income,
3. Federal Tax Payable.

Tax Software Assignment Problem For Chapter 9

This Tax Software Assignment Problem was introduced in Chapter 4 and is continued in Chapters 6 through 11. Each Tax Software Assignment Problem must be completed in sequence. While it is not repeated in this problem, all of the information in each of the previous problems (e.g., Mary's T4 content) is applicable to this problem.

If you have not prepared a tax file incorporating the Tax Software Assignment Problem information for the previous Chapters, please do so before continuing with this problem.

During a phone call from Mary Career on December 28, 2011, she tells you that Seymour made all of the required payments to his ex-wife Monica Career (SIN 527-000-186) in 2011. In your files, you have noted that his 2007 divorce agreement requires Seymour to pay spousal support to his ex-wife of $200 per month. He also pays her child support of $250 per month for his 19 year old daughter, Faith.

Mary tells you that her parents have established an RESP for William in 2011, and are the sole contributors. They have contributed $300 in lieu of Christmas and birthday presents.

Mary has learned that Seymour's mother purchased Canada Savings Bonds in William's name in 2011. The bonds paid interest of $120 in 2011 which Seymour had spent without advising her. She expects a T5 to be issued in William's name.

In an effort to wean William from his passion for violent computer games, Mary registered him for art classes at the Da Vinci Institute on Saturdays. Mary faxes you the following receipts:

Child	Child Related Expenses (Organization or Name and SIN)	No. of weeks	Amount
William	Gaye Normandin SIN 527-000-392		3,100
	(after school and summer)		
William	Da Vinci Institute - Saturday art classes	16	1,000

On December 30, 2011, you receive a call from Mary Career with the terrible news that Seymour has just suffered a massive heart attack and died. Mary, his executor, inherits all of his assets except for the rental property and appliances in Moncton (see Chapter 7 version of this Software Problem). He has left that house to his daughter, Faith. Assume the transfer of the property and appliances takes place in 2011.

As Seymour was thinking of selling the property, he had it appraised in early December. The appraisal valued the land at $60,000, the building at $180,000, and the appliances at $700. Seymour had purchased the property on May 1, 1998 for $195,000 (land of $45,000 and building of $150,000) and lived in it until his marriage to Mary in 2009.

Required:

A. What advice would you give Mary on the RESP for William?

B. Open the file that you created for the Chapter 8 version of this Software Problem and save a copy under a different name. This will enable you to check the changes between different versions of this Software Problem.

C. Input the information needed on Seymour's "Support Payments" form and print the form.

D. With the objective of optimizing the deduction for the family, prepare and print the T778 Child Care Expenses Deduction forms.

E. Complete and print the T2091, Designation Of Property As A Principal Residence for Seymour's Moncton property. Print his Schedule 3 which shows the capital gain from the disposition of his house.

F. Revise Seymour's Statement of Real Estate Rentals for any changes necessary. Print the statement and the related CCA worksheet.

G. With the objective of minimizing Seymour's Tax Payable, prepare, but do not print, his final income tax return. List any assumptions you have made and provide any explanatory notes and tax planning issues you feel should be placed in the files. Ignore GST/HST implications. **Hint:** On his "Info" page, input his date of death. Answer No to the question "Is this an Early Filed ...?". On Mary's return, change her marital status to widowed and include the date of change.

H. Review both returns with the objective of minimizing the tax liability for the family and make any changes required.

I. Access and print Mary's summary (Summary on the Form Explorer, not the T1Summary). This form is a two column summary of the couple's tax information. By opening this form from Mary's return, the order of the columns is the same as the one in the previous chapter. For both returns, list the changes on this Summary form from the previous version of this Software Problem. Exclude totals calculated by the program, but include the final Balance Owing (Refund) amount.

CHAPTER 10

Retirement Savings And Other Special Income Arrangements

Planning For Retirement

Introduction

10-1.   Increasing life expectancies and lower birth rates are creating a situation in which the portion of the Canadian population that is of retirement age has been increasing, and will continue to do so. This, in turn, leads to the need to allocate a growing proportion of our society's resources to caring for this older segment of the population. There are enormous social and economic considerations resulting from this trend and, given the growing political clout of Canadian senior citizens, it is not a situation that the government can ignore.

Providing Consistency

10-2.   Minimal financial requirements for the retirement years are provided by Old Age Security (OAS) payments and the Canada Pension Plan (CPP) system. However, the maximum payment under the Canada Pension Plan is about $12,000 per year for a person with no disability. When this is combined with the current OAS payments of about $6,500 per year, the total does not provide for the lifestyle most individuals would like to enjoy during their retirement years. In response to this situation, the Canadian income tax system contains a number of provisions that encourage the development of various private retirement savings arrangements to supplement benefits provided under the government provided plans. These include:

- Registered Retirement Savings Plans (RRSPs)
- Registered Pension Plans (RPPs), including Individual Pension Plans
- Pooled Registered Pension Plans (Proposed)
- Registered Retirement Income Funds (RRIFs)
- Deferred Profit Sharing Plans (DPSPs)

10-3.   The current retirement savings system was initiated in 1990. At the heart of this system is the concept that retirement savings should have an annual limit that is consistently applied. In general, this limit is defined in terms of an annual amount of contributions to a money purchase (a.k.a., defined contribution) Registered Pension Plan. This limit was phased in over the period 1990 through 2010. Since 2011, it has been indexed to reflect inflation.

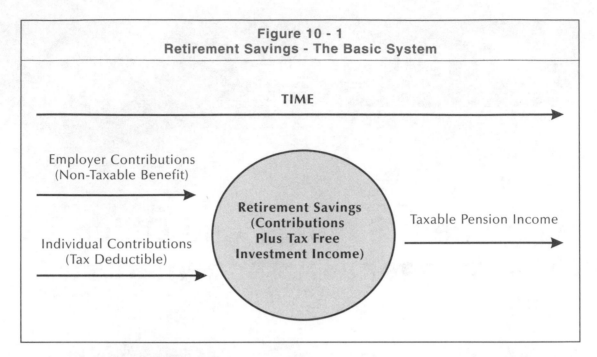

Figure 10 - 1
Retirement Savings - The Basic System

10-4.   The major problem faced by the government in designing the current system was to ensure that, despite the variety of retirement savings vehicles available, the annual contribution limit was applied in a consistent manner, without regard to the variety of retirement savings vehicles used by an individual, or the manner in which the ultimate retirement benefit was determined. In our view, an outstanding job was done in accomplishing this goal.

10-5.   The detailed provisions related to the different types of tax assisted retirement savings plans show considerable variation. For example, Registered Pension Plans and Deferred Profit Sharing Plans require employer sponsorship. In contrast, any Canadian resident can establish a Registered Retirement Savings Plan or a Registered Retirement Income Fund.

10-6.   Despite such variations, the basic idea underlying all of these plans is the same. They allow individuals to invest a considerable amount of funds into a trusteed arrangement. The amounts invested are either deductible to the taxpayer (RRSP contributions and employee RPP contributions) or can be paid by an employer without creating a taxable benefit (employer RPP and DPSP contributions). Inside the trusteed arrangement, the invested funds can earn income on a tax free basis for long periods of time. While all amounts will ultimately be subject to taxation, there is a substantial amount of tax deferral. This arrangement can be seen graphically in Figure 10-1.

10-7.   You will recall that we also discussed registered savings plans in Chapter 9. The discussion in that Chapter focused on Registered Education Savings Plans (RESPs) and Tax Free Savings Accounts (TFSAs). We would remind you of a major difference between those plans and the ones that are under consideration here. The contributions made to RESPs, and TFSAs are not deductible. In contrast, the retirement savings plans under consideration here provide tax advantaged contribution arrangements. As noted in Paragraph 10-6, contributions made by beneficiaries are tax deductible and contributions made by employers are not treated as taxable benefits.

Tax Deferred Savings
Sources Of Deferral
10-8.   As shown in Figure 10-1, there are two basic sources for the investment funds going into retirement savings plans. First, for employed individuals, employers may make contributions to RPPs and DPSPs. As these contributions do not create a taxable benefit until they are withdrawn as retirement income, the employee has received a benefit on which the payment

of tax has been deferred.

10-9.   The second source of investment funds is the contributions made by employed individuals to RPPs, and by all individuals to RRSPs. As the individual can deduct these contributions against all types of income, they are the equivalent of receiving income on which the tax has been deferred.

10-10.   This means that, whether an employer has made contributions on behalf of the individual, or the individual has personally made the contributions, the taxes on the amounts involved have been deferred from the year of contribution to the year of withdrawal from the plan. This period may exceed 45 years for contributions made at the beginning of an individual's working life.

Tax Free Compounding

10-11.   Also of great importance is the fact that the income earned by investments contained in these plans is not taxed until it is withdrawn. This allows earnings to accumulate at before tax rates, rather than after tax rates. Given that such plans may be in place over long periods of time, this provides for a significantly larger accumulation of assets.   As illustrated in the following example, the importance of tax free accumulation should not be underestimated.

> **Example** Mr. Kerr is a 35 year old taxpayer who pays taxes at a marginal rate of 45 percent. For the next 30 years, he has $5,000 per year of pre-tax income that he wishes to put aside for his anticipated retirement at age 65.
>
> **Analysis**   If Mr. Kerr contributes this amount to an RRSP, it can be deducted and no taxes will be paid on the $5,000 per year of pre-tax income. If this $5,000 per year is invested in an RRSP at a 10 percent per annum rate of return, it will accumulate to $822,470 at the end of 30 years. If the full amount is withdrawn when he reaches age 65, and he is still paying taxes at a marginal rate of 45 percent, he will be left with after tax funds of $452,359.
>
> If Mr. Kerr had not invested in an RRSP, taxes at 45 percent would have been paid on the $5,000, leaving only $2,750 per year to invest. Further, if he invests these funds at 10 percent outside of an RRSP, his after tax return will only be 5.5 percent [(10%)(1-.45)]. At this after tax rate, the investment of $2,750 per year for 30 years would result in an accumulation of only $199,198 by the time Mr. Kerr is 65 years old, less than half of the after tax accumulation resulting from using the RRSP approach.

10-12.   In effect, the deferral of taxes on the deductible contributions, as well as the deferral of tax on the income from fund investments, has allowed for an additional accumulation of income resulting from the investment of the amounts deferred. As this fairly realistic example illustrates, the amounts involved can be very substantial.

Early Contributions

10-13.   The availability of tax free compounding in an RRSP makes it advantageous to contribute as early as possible. RRSP contributions for 2012 can be made as early as January 1, 2012, or as late as 60 days after the end of 2012. It can be demonstrated that, over a contribution period of 35 years, making contributions at the earliest date as opposed to the latest date can result in a 10 percent increase in the balance in the plan.

Advantages At Retirement

10-14.   The use of these tax deferred retirement savings plans may have additional advantages. If either federal or provincial tax rates have been lowered, the effective tax rate at the time of withdrawal may be lower than the rate when the contributions are made. Note, however, the opposite effect may arise if federal or provincial rates are increased.

10-15.   In addition, for some individuals, retirement may result in a sufficient reduction in income that they find themselves in a lower tax bracket. Someone who spends their working life subject to a 45 percent tax rate could find that, subsequent to retirement, they are subject to taxes at 25 percent. As this lower rate would apply to amounts withdrawn from a retirement savings plan, the deferral of taxation on contributions and investment earnings will result in an absolute reduction in taxes paid (tax avoidance).

10-16.   Even if the individual is not paying taxes at a lower rate after retirement, there are additional advantages associated with the funds taken out of these plans. The first $2,000 of eligible pension income entitles the recipient to a credit against federal Tax Payable each year equal to 15 percent of amounts received. This is worth $300 at the federal level alone, and can be increased to $600 per couple through the pension income splitting provisions. (See Chapter 9.)

Defined Benefit Vs. Money Purchase Plans

10-17.   A major problem in the design of Canada's retirement savings system is the fact that, unlike RRSPs, DPSPs, and RRIFs, RPPs may be designed to provide a specified benefit after retirement. Such plans are normally referred to as defined benefit plans, while other types of RPPs are referred to as money purchase (a.k.a., defined contribution) plans. A basic under-standing of the difference between these two types of plans is essential to the comprehension of the material in this Chapter. In view of this, the following brief descriptions are provided:

Defined Benefit Plans   In defined benefit plans, the plan sponsor undertakes to provide a specified benefit, usually expressed as a percentage of earnings, for each year of qualifying service. For example, such a plan might require an employer to provide a retirement benefit equal to 2 percent of an employee's average lifetime earnings for each year of service. Thus, if an employee worked for 20 years and earned an average salary of $50,000 per year, the retirement benefit would be $20,000 per year [(2%)(20)($50,000)].

In promising this benefit, the employer has effectively agreed to make whatever amount of contributions is required to provide these benefits. The required amount of contributions will vary depending on a number of factors, including earnings rates on fund assets, employee turnover, and employee life expectancy at retirement. In this type of plan, the employer is assuming all of the risks associated with these factors.

Money Purchase Plans (a.k.a. Defined Contribution Plans)   These plans are distin-guished by the fact that the employer agrees to make specified contributions for each plan participant. A typical plan might find an employer agreeing to contribute 3 percent of each employee's annual wages to a fund that would be established to provide retirement benefits. The employer would have no obligations beyond making the specified contributions and the employee would have no guarantee as to the amount of the retirement benefit that is to be received.

The actual benefit that will be received will be based on the amounts contributed and the rates of return earned on the investment of these contributions. In money purchase plans, it is the employee who is assuming the risks associated with invest-ment of the contributed funds.

10-18.   Before leaving these descriptions we would note that, while the term is not usually applied to them, RRSPs, DPSPs, and RRIFs are essentially money purchase plans. That is, the benefits to be received from such plans are based on the amounts transferred into the plan and the earnings resulting from the investment of these amounts. Such plans do not guarantee that the individual will receive a specified benefit after retirement. Currently, the only widely used retirement savings arrangement that uses the defined benefit approach is the employer spon-sored RPP. However, RPPs can take either form and, in recent years, there has been a growing trend towards the use of money purchase plans.

10-19.   It is perhaps because of this trend that the government is introducing Pooled Registered Pension Plans (PRPPs). These plans, which will be described later in this Chapter 10, allow employers with a small number of employees to provide a defined benefit plan on a pooled basis with other employers.

Registered Retirement Savings Plans (RRSPs)

Basic Operations

Establishment

10-20.   The general rules for Registered Retirement Savings Plans (RRSPs) are contained in ITA 146. Under these rules, an RRSP is a trust with the individual as the beneficiary and a financial institution acting as the administrator. Financial institutions offering such plans include Canadian chartered banks, Canadian mutual funds, Canadian trust companies, Canadian credit unions, Canadian brokerage firms, and Canadian insurance companies.

10-21.   Registration of the plan results in the investor being able to deduct a limited amount of contributions to the plan for income tax purposes. Further, the individual is not subject to tax on the income earned by the assets in the plan until it is withdrawn.

Withdrawals

10-22.   Amounts that an individual withdraws from an RRSP must be included in income unless received under the Home Buyers' Plan or the Lifelong Learning Plan (these programs are discussed in Paragraphs 10-106 and 10-117, respectively). Depending on the amount withdrawn, the trustee will be required to withhold a percentage of the amount withdrawn as a partial payment towards the tax that will be assessed on the withdrawal.

10-23.   Withdrawals are treated as an ordinary income inclusion under ITA 56(1)(h), even if they were earned as dividends or capital gains within the plan. This latter point is important in that dividends and capital gains are normally taxed at more favourable rates than other types of income. This favourable treatment is lost when the amounts are earned inside an RRSP.

Investment Options For An RRSP

10-24.   There are two basic types of RRSPs. The managed RRSP is managed by the financial institution that holds the fund assets. The self-administered (a.k.a. self-directed) RRSP is managed by the taxpayer. For individuals who prefer to make their own investment decisions with respect to the fund assets, the self-administered type of plan is the obvious choice.

10-25.   An additional advantage of the self-administered type of plan is that the taxpayer can transfer securities that he already owns into the plan. However, with the availability of discount brokers charging minimal commissions, the importance of this advantage for many taxpayers has declined over time. As the RRSP is a separate taxable entity, such transfers are dispositions and any gains arising on the transfer will be subject to tax. Note, however, that ITA 40(2)(g)(iv) prevents the recognition of losses on such transfers.

> **Example**   An individual transfers securities to his RRSP. The shares of Company A have an adjusted cost base of $5,000 and a fair market value of $7,000. The shares of Company B have an adjusted cost base of $5,000 and a fair market value of $4,000.

> **Analysis**   While the individual would have to record a capital gain on the Company A shares of $2,000, the $1,000 loss on the shares of Company B cannot be deducted.

10-26.   If the taxpayer's preference is to have a financial institution manage the plan, he will be confronted with a wide variety of choices. Managed funds include those that invest entirely in equity securities, funds that hold only long-term bonds, funds with mixed portfolios, and funds that specialize in one type of asset such as Canada Savings Bonds or mortgages.

10-27.   Choosing between the alternatives involves an assessment of many factors, including the investment goals of the individual taxpayer, as well as the fees charged by the various plans. With literally hundreds of choices available, the decision can be a very difficult one to make. However, considering the amount of financial resources that may eventually be invested in RRSP assets, it is not a decision that should be made without a thorough investigation of the alternatives.

10-28.   Since an individual can own any number of separate RRSPs, it is possible to have both a self-administered and a managed plan. Further diversification could be achieved by having two or more types of managed plans. However, the extra effort and costs required to keep track of the multiple plans should be considered.

10-29.   The *Act* is flexible with respect to the types of investments that can be included in either a self-administered or a managed RRSP. ITR Part XLIX provides a detailed listing of the specific investment categories and includes publicly traded shares, mutual fund units, bonds, mortgages, warrants, and rights. The only significant restrictions relate to investments in the shares of private companies and direct investments in real estate. There is no limit on foreign content (e.g., shares of U.S. public companies).

10-30.   While it is not likely that this is a common problem, new rules are applicable to publicly traded securities where the RRSP registrant holds more than a 10 percent interest (number of shares or fair market value). These holdings are referred to as "prohibited investments" and, significant penalties apply if they are contained in either an RRSP or a RRIF.

10-31.   It is interesting to note that an RRSP can provide a mortgage on Canadian real property to the registrant of the plan, provided that the mortgage is insured under the National Housing Act, or by some other company providing mortgage insurance. The extra costs associated with this insurance have served to limit the use of this option.

The Capital Gains Problem

10-32.   As noted previously, capital gains that are earned within an RRSP are treated as ordinary income when they are withdrawn from the plan. As the favourable tax treatment that this type of income normally receives is lost when earned in an RRSP, it would appear that it is better to earn capital gains outside an RRSP. This would suggest that, if an individual has investments both inside and outside an RRSP, it would be preferable to hold those investments that earn capital gains outside the plan.

10-33.   There has been some discussion of whether it makes sense to hold investments with potential capital gains inside an RRSP. The discussion is based on two considerations. First, with the inclusion rate at one-half, the tax on capital gains earned inside an RRSP is essentially double the tax that would apply to capital gains earned outside of an RRSP.

10-34.   The other factor is that, in situations where investors hold securities for long periods of time, tax free earnings accumulation effectively occurs even when investments are held outside of an RRSP. The fact that capital gains are not taxed until there is a disposition of the investment significantly reduces the importance of the tax free deferral feature of RRSP investing.

10-35.   Offsetting these factors which favour keeping capital gains outside of RRSPs is the fact that amounts invested in these retirement savings accounts are deductible. For an individual in a marginal tax bracket of 48 percent, this means that the government is, in effect, putting up nearly half of the investment funds.

Example   Rachel Morgan, an individual with a marginal tax rate of 45 percent, has $10,000 of before tax income that she does not need for current consumption. She is trying to decide whether it would be better to invest the after tax amount of these funds outside of her RRSP or, alternatively, contribute $10,000 into her RRSP and deduct the full amount. She has an investment opportunity which she is confident will result in her investment increasing in value by 50 percent over the next two years. At that point she will use the available funds for a two week vacation.

Analysis - Investment Inside RRSP   As contributions are fully deductible, the full amount of $10,000 can be contributed to her RRSP. If the investment increases to $15,000 and she withdraws the full amount for her two week vacation, she will be taxed at her marginal rate of 45 percent on both the original contribution and the capital gain that accrued while the investment was in the RRSP. The tax cost will be $6,750 [(45%)($15,000)], leaving her with $8,250 in after tax funds for her vacation. Note that 100 percent of the capital gain was subject to tax, a much less favourable treatment than is normally received by this type of income.

Analysis - Investment Outside RRSP After paying taxes on the $10,000, Ms. Morgan will have $5,500 left to invest outside of the RRSP [($10,000)(1 - .45)]. If this investment increases in value by 50 percent, she will be able to sell it for $8,250 and will be subject to taxes on a taxable capital gain of $1,375 [(1/2)($8,250 - $5,500)]. The taxes will be $619 [(45%)($1,375)], leaving her with after tax funds of $7,631 ($8,250 - $619).

10-36. This simple example indicates that the benefits of being able to deduct contributions to an RRSP can more than offset the unfavourable tax treatment that is given to capital gains that are withdrawn from such plans. Using the RRSP results in an additional $619 ($8,250 - $7,631) in funds being available for Ms. Morgan's vacation.

The Dividends Problem

10-37. As was the case with capital gains, dividend income loses its favourable tax treatment when it is earned within an RRSP. When such income is withdrawn from the plan, it is taxed as ordinary income and does not qualify for the dividend tax credit procedures.

10-38. This problem is applicable to both eligible and non-eligible dividends. For an individual in the 29 percent federal tax bracket, the federal rate on non-eligible dividends is 19.6 percent. For eligible dividends, this rate falls slightly to 19.3 percent. This clearly makes it less attractive to earn dividends inside an RRSP.

10-39. As was the case in our discussion of capital gains and RRSPs, if you start with a given amount of pre tax income, the deductibility of contributions to an RRSP provides for a larger investment amount. Unlike the situation with capital gains, there would be no deferral of taxation outside the RRSP. While capital gains taxation can be deferred until there is a disposition of the investment, dividends earned outside an RRSP will be taxed as they are received.

Exercise Ten - 1

Subject: Dividends Earned In An RRSP

Brian Forthright has $20,000 in pre tax income that he does not need for current consumption. He is trying to decide whether it would be better to invest the after tax amount of these funds outside of his RRSP or, alternatively, contribute the $20,000 to his RRSP and deduct the full amount. He will invest the available funds in preferred shares that pay an annual eligible dividend of 5 percent. At the end of five years, he will use all of the available funds for an extended vacation. Brian's combined marginal tax rate on ordinary income is 40 percent and his combined tax rate on eligible dividends is 22 percent. Ignoring the effect of any reinvestment of the dividend income, determine which alternative will provide more funds for Brian's trip.

End of Exercise. Solution available in Study Guide.

Non-Deductible Financing Costs

10-40. As a final point, it is important to note that interest paid on funds borrowed to finance RRSP contributions is not deductible. This suggests that it may not be desirable for an individual to borrow in order to make RRSP contributions. A complete analysis of this issue requires an estimate of how long the loan will be outstanding and a comparison of the individual's borrowing rate with his expected return on funds invested in the plan.

RRSP Deduction Limit

The Basic Formula

10-41. At the heart of this retirement savings system is the RRSP Deduction Limit. It is this amount that determines the maximum contribution to an RRSP that can be deducted in a year. While this amount is sometimes referred to as the contribution limit, this is not an accurate

---

Figure 10 - 2
RRSP Deduction Limit Formula - ITA 146(1)

"RRSP deduction limit" of a taxpayer for a taxation year means the amount determined by the formula

$$A + B + R - C, \text{ where}$$

A   is the taxpayer's **unused RRSP deduction room** at the end of the preceding taxation year,

B   is the amount, if any, by which

    (a) the lesser of the **RRSP dollar limit** for the year and 18% of the taxpayer's **earned income** for the preceding taxation year,

    exceeds the total of all amounts each of which is

    (b) the taxpayer's **pension adjustment** for the preceding taxation year in respect of an employer, or

    (c) a **prescribed amount** in respect of the taxpayer for the year,

C   is the taxpayer's net **past service pension adjustment** for the year, and

R   is the taxpayer's total **pension adjustment reversal** for the year.

Example of relevant years   Contributions made during the first 60 days of 2013 and undeducted contributions made in years prior to 2012 can be deducted against the RRSP Deduction Limit for 2012. Adding to the confusion is the fact that the RRSP Deduction Limit for 2012 is based on Earned Income for 2011, as well as a Pension Adjustment that is calculated using 2011 figures.

---

description. The definition of RRSP Deduction Limit is found in ITA 146(1) and is reproduced in Figure 10-2. There are several technical terms included in this definition and they are highlighted in Figure 10-2 with bold, italic type. Explanations for each term will be provided in the material which follows.

10-42.   The RRSP Deduction Limit is neither a limit on contributions that can be made during the current year, nor a requirement that the contributions deducted in the current year be made in that year. A limited amount of non-deductible contributions can be made that are in excess of the RRSP Deduction Limit. Further, contributions made in earlier years that were not deducted in those years, or contributions made in the first 60 days of the following year, can be deducted under the RRSP Deduction Limit for the current year.

10-43.   The reason for using an Earned Income figure from a previous year is to allow an individual to determine his maximum contribution for the current year during the early part of that year. If the limit had been based on the current year's Earned Income, an individual would have to make contributions during the year based only on an estimate of his Earned Income, a situation that would commonly result in contributions that are either over or under the limit.

10-44.   To assist taxpayers in dealing with this deduction limit calculation, the CRA issues an RRSP Deduction Limit Statement to individuals who have filed income tax returns. It is included with the Notice of Assessment and, assuming the return is filed on time, calculates the taxpayer's maximum RRSP deduction for the year after the assessed year.

    Example   The RRSP Statement included with the Notice of Assessment for the 2012 return will normally be received during April or May, 2013. This statement indicates the maximum RRSP contribution that can be deducted for 2013.

Unused RRSP Deduction Room

10-45.   As it is used in the Figure 10-2 formula, a taxpayer's Unused RRSP Deduction Room at the end of the preceding year is simply the cumulative total of all of the amounts determined under the formula for years prior to the current year, less any amounts that have been deducted in those years.

10-46.   This approach provides for a carry forward of deduction room that is not time limited. As a result, a taxpayer who lacks the funds to make a deductible contribution in a particular year does not lose the deduction room applicable to that year. The deduction room is carried forward and provides the basis for a deductible contribution in any future year.

RRSP Dollar Limit

10-47.   The RRSP Dollar Limit is defined in terms of the Money Purchase Limit that is specified in quantitative terms in ITA 147.1(1). The Money Purchase Limit is the annual ceiling applicable to contributions made to RPPs. Because of the one year lag in the data used for the RRSP Deduction Limit, the RRSP Dollar Limit is generally defined as the Money Purchase Limit for the preceding year.

10-48.   Money Purchase Limits and the RRSP Dollar Limits for years 2010 through 2013 are as follows:

Year	Money Purchase Limit	RRSP Dollar Limit
2010	22,450	22,000
2011	22,970	22,450
2012	23,820	22,970
2013	Indexed	23,820

Earned Income

10-49.   Earned Income for RRSP purposes is defined in ITA 146(1). Note that Earned Income for child care expense purposes (see Chapter 9) is different than Earned Income for RRSP purposes. The basic idea underlying this definition of Earned Income for RRSP purposes is that the income to be included in this designation is earned by the individual, rather than received as the result of owning property. This means that interest, dividends, and capital gains are excluded from the definition.

10-50.   Surprisingly, however, net rental income is included, despite the fact that, for individuals, rental income is usually a form of property income. Another unusual feature of the definition is that it does not include either net or gross employment income in unaltered form. Rather, the net employment income component of Earned Income is a hybrid concept that excludes RPP contributions and is not used anywhere else in the determination of Net Income For Tax Purposes.

10-51.   As found in ITA 146(1), the basic components of Earned Income are as follows:

Additions

- Net employment income, computed without the deduction for RPP contributions
- Income from carrying on a business
- Net rental income from real property
- Income earned as an active partner
- Royalties, provided the recipient is the author, composer, or inventor of the work
- Taxable support payments received by a spouse (This does not include non-taxable child support payments. See Chapter 9 for a discussion of child support payments.)
- Research grants, net of certain related expenses
- Canada and Quebec Pension Plan disability benefits received
- Supplementary unemployment benefit plan payments (This does not include the regular Employment Insurance benefit payments)

Deductions

- Deductible support payments (This does not include non-deductible child support payments)
- Losses from carrying on a business
- Losses allocated to an active partner
- Losses from the rental of real property

Exercise Ten - 2

Subject: Earned Income

Mr. Jarwhol Nacari has net employment income of $56,000 (he is not a member of an RPP), interest income of $22,000, net rental income of $2,500, and receives taxable support payments from his former spouse of $12,000 during the current year. What is Mr. Nacari's Earned Income for RRSP purposes for the current year?

Exercise Ten - 3

Subject: Earned Income

Ms. Shelly Devine has net employment income of $82,000 (after the deduction of $3,000 in RPP contributions), a business loss of $12,500, taxable dividends of $4,200, and pays deductible support to her former spouse of $18,000 during the current year. What is Ms. Devine's Earned Income for RRSP purposes for the current year?

End of Exercises. Solutions available in Study Guide.

Pension Adjustments (PAs) - Overview

10-52.   If an individual participates in an RPP or a DPSP, his RRSP Deduction Limit must be reduced to reflect retirement savings that are taking place in these plans. If this did not happen, individuals belonging to RPPs and DPSPs could have access to larger amounts of tax deferred retirement savings than would be the case for other individuals.

10-53.   Pension Adjustments (PAs) are designed to reflect the benefits earned by an individual through defined benefit RPPs or contributions made to money purchase RPPs and DPSPs by an individual or his employer during a particular year. As RPPs and DPSPs are always sponsored by an employer, the CRA requires the employer to calculate an annual PA for each employee who is a member of that employer's RPP or DPSP. This amount is reported on the employee's T4.

10-54.   Employers do not issue T4s until January or February of the year following the calendar year in which contributions are made or benefits granted. Because of this, the PA that is deducted in the calculation of the taxpayer's RRSP Deduction Limit for the current year, is based on the employer's contributions or benefits granted during the preceding year. More specifically, the 2012 RRSP Deduction Limit is reduced by PAs calculated with reference to 2011 RPP benefits earned and RPP and DPSP contributions made. These PAs are reported to the CRA and the taxpayer in the T4s that are issued in January or February of 2012. These PAs are also incorporated into the 2012 RRSP Deduction Limit Statement that the CRA includes with the Notice of Assessment for the 2011 taxation year.

Exercise Ten - 4

Subject: Retirement Savings

How does the Canadian retirement savings system prevent individuals who are a member of their employer's RPP or DPSP from being treated more favourably than individuals who can only use an RRSP for retirement savings?

End of Exercise. Solution available in Study Guide.

Pension Adjustments - Money Purchase RPPs And DPSPs

10-55.   The calculation of PAs for money purchase plans is relatively straightforward. As RRSPs operate in the same general format as money purchase plans (i.e., they do not promise a specific benefit), contributions to money purchase plans are directly comparable, on a dollar for dollar basis, with contributions to an RRSP.

10-56.   As a consequence, the PA for a money purchase RPP is simply the sum of all employee and employer contributions for the year. Following the same reasoning, an employee's PA for a DPSP is simply the employer's contributions for the year that are allocated to the individual (employees cannot contribute to a DPSP). A simple example will illustrate these calculations:

> **Example**   Ms. Jones' employer sponsors a money purchase RPP and a DPSP. Ms. Jones is a member of both. During 2011, she has Earned Income of $70,000 and contributes $2,000 to the RPP. Her employer contributes $2,000 to the RPP and $1,500 to the DPSP on her behalf. She has no Unused RRSP Deduction Room at the end of 2011. Calculate Ms. Jones' maximum deductible RRSP contribution for 2012.

> **Analysis**   Ms. Jones' 2011 PA is $5,500 ($2,000 + $2,000 + $1,500), an amount that will be reported on the 2011 T4 that she will receive in early 2012. After filing her 2011 tax return, Ms. Jones will receive her RRSP Deduction Limit Statement for 2012 from the CRA that will contain the following calculation.

> As she has no Unused RRSP Deduction Room at the end of 2011, her RRSP Deduction Limit will be calculated by taking the lesser of the $22,970 RRSP Dollar Limit for 2012 and $12,600, 18 percent of Ms. Jones' 2011 Earned Income of $70,000. The 2011 PA of $5,500 will be subtracted from the lesser figure of $12,600, to arrive at her maximum deductible RRSP contribution for 2012 of $7,100.

Pension Adjustments - Defined Benefit RPPs

10-57.   As defined benefit plans guarantee the benefit to be provided, rather than specify the amount of contributions required, contributions made to these plans cannot be compared directly to contributions made to RRSPs, DPSPs, or money purchase RPPs. However, if retirement savings limits are to be applied equitably to all individuals, without regard to the type of arrangements available to them, it is necessary to find a basis for equating the benefits earned under these plans with the contributions made to the other types of plans.

10-58.   It is unfortunate that there is no simple way to convert a benefit earned into an equivalent amount of contributions. While there are a number of problems in dealing with this conversion, the most significant is the age of the employee. Because of the difference in years during which earnings will accumulate, it costs an employer much less in terms of current contributions to provide a $1 per year retirement benefit to an employee who is 25 years old and 40 years away from receiving that benefit, than it does to provide the same retirement benefit to an employee who is 60 years old and only 5 years away from receiving the benefit.

10-59.   To have a completely equitable system for dealing with this problem, different values would have to be assigned to benefits that are earned by employees of different ages. Benefits earned by older employees would have to be assigned a higher value than those earned by younger employees. Unfortunately, it appears that the government believes that the benefits of such an equitable system do not warrant the costs of associating different levels of benefits with individuals of differing ages.

10-60.   Rather than a system that takes into account the different ages of participants in defined benefit RPPs, the current solution is to equate $1 of benefits earned with $9 of contributions. If, during the current year, an individual earns $1 of future benefits under the provisions of a defined benefit RPP, in the calculation of his PA for the year, this will be viewed as the equivalent of $9 in contributions to a money purchase RPP or DPSP.

10-61.   The use of the multiple nine is an arbitrary solution that fails to give any consideration to the age of the employee. (There is an unconfirmed rumour that this number was selected because it was the shoe size of the Minister of Finance at the time the legislation was passed.) It is systematically unfair to younger individuals as it overstates the cost of providing their pension benefits, thereby generating an excessive PA which, in turn, creates a corresponding reduction in their ability to contribute to their RRSP.

> **Example** Bryan is 25 years of age. In 2012, he earns a pension benefit in his employer's defined benefit RPP of $1,000 per year to be received beginning in 2052 when Bryan reaches 65 years of age. His PA for 2012 is $9,000 which decreases his RRSP deduction room by $9,000.
>
> **Analysis** If, alternatively, he had deposited this same $9,000 per year in his RRSP and made investments that earned 10 percent per annum, the balance in 2052 would be over $400,000. Even at a low investment return of 5 percent, this would purchase an annuity of over $32,000 per year for 20 years. This is far in excess of the value of a $1,000 per year benefit that would be received at age 65 under the defined benefit plan.

10-62.   While it was probably essential to the implementation of this system that some type of averaging process be used, it is unfortunate that the selected alternative has such a systematic bias against younger individuals. It is unlikely that the government could have arrived at any administratively convenient solution that would not appear inequitable to some individuals. However, it would have been more equitable to have used some type of age dependent sliding scale, as opposed to the inflexible application of the factor of nine.

Exercise Ten - 5

Subject: Pension Adjustments

Mr. Arnett's employer sponsors both a money purchase RPP and a DPSP. During the current year, his employer contributes $2,300 to the RPP and $1,800 to the DPSP on behalf of Mr. Arnett. Mr. Arnett contributes $2,300 to the RPP. Calculate the amount of the Pension Adjustment that will be included on Mr. Arnett's T4 for the current year.

End of Exercise. Solution available in Study Guide.

Prescribed Amount - ITA 146(1)
10-63.   The Prescribed Amount (see Figure 10-2) is a deduction that may arise as the result of an individual transferring accumulated benefits from one RPP to a different RPP.

Past Service Pension Adjustments (PSPAs)
10-64.   Past Service Pension Adjustments (PSPAs) are designed to deal with benefits under defined benefit RPPs related to credit for past service. They are far less common than PAs. Some of the events giving rise to PSPAs are as follows:

- A new RPP is implemented by an employer and benefits are extended retroactively for years of service prior to the plan initiation.

- The benefit formula is changed, increasing the percentage that is applied to pensionable earnings to determine benefits earned. Again, a PSPA is created only if the increased benefits are extended retroactively to years of service prior to the plan amendment.

- An individual, either voluntarily or because of terms contained in the plan, works for a number of years without being a member of the plan. On joining the plan, the employee is credited for years of service prior to entry into the plan.

10-65. If an individual were to receive such past service benefits without experiencing any reduction in his RRSP Deduction Limit, he would have effectively beaten the system. That is, he would be receiving additional pension benefits over and above the limits that are normally applicable to individual taxpayers. The role of PSPAs is to prevent this from happening.

10-66. PSPAs are calculated on the basis of all of the PAs that would have applied in the years prior to the year of change if the plan or improvement had been in effect, or if the individual had been a member in those years. From these "as if" PAs, the actual PAs reported would be deducted. The resulting difference is then reported as a PSPA for the current year.

10-67. As with PAs, the employer is responsible for calculating and reporting PSPAs, normally within 60 days of the past service event. The amount is reported on a PSPA information form (not on a T4) that is sent to both the employee and the CRA. Since the current year's PA will reflect the new benefits, only years prior to the year of change are used to calculate the PSPA. As a result, unlike the one year lag in deducting PAs, PSPAs are deducted from the RRSP deduction room formula in the year in which they occur.

10-68. A simplified example will serve to illustrate the basic procedures involved in PSPA calculations:

Example Wally Oats has been a member of his employer's defined benefit RPP since 2006. Until 2012, the benefit formula provided a retirement benefit equal to 1.5 percent of pensionable earnings for each year of service. During 2012, the benefit formula was increased to 1.75 percent of pensionable earnings for each year of service, a change that is to be applied to all prior years of service. Mr. Oats has had $48,000 in pensionable earnings in each prior year.

Analysis The calculation of the PSPA for 2012 would be based on the six years of service prior to the current year (2006 to 2011) as follows:

New Formula PAs [(1.75%)($48,000)(9)(6 Years)]	$45,360
Previously Reported PAs [(1.50%)($48,000)(9)(6 Years)]	(38,880)
2012 PSPA	$ 6,480

10-69. Note that PSPAs only occur in the context of defined benefit plans. If additional contributions for past service are made to a money purchase plan, these amounts will be included in the regular Pension Adjustment for the year in which the contributions are made. This eliminates the need for any sort of catch up adjustment.

Pension Adjustment Reversals (PARs)

10-70. A vested pension benefit is one in which the employee has an irrevocable property right. That is, he is entitled to receive the value of the benefit, without regard to whether he remains an employee of the employer providing the benefit.

10-71. In order to give their employees an incentive to remain with them, many employers grant pension benefits that do not become vested unless the employee remains for a specified period of time. A common arrangement would be for an employer to grant benefits that do not vest until the employee has completed five years of service. If an employee leaves before the end of this five year period, he loses the benefits that he has earned to that point in time.

10-72. This creates a problem in that employers are required to report PAs for all benefits or contributions earned by an employee during the year, regardless of when the pension benefits become vested. This means that an employer may report PAs for benefits that will not, in fact, be received by the employee. This, in turn, means that the RRSP deduction room that was eliminated by these PAs would also be lost.

10-73.   To deal with this problem, Pension Adjustment Reversals (PARs) were added to the pension legislation. Note that this is only a problem with the employer's share of benefits or contributions earned. Provincial legislation requires that employees have a vested right to all of their own contributions.

10-74.   A PAR is calculated by the employer whenever an employee terminates membership in an RPP or DPSP and receives less from the plan than the total of the PAs and PSPAs reported for the employee. The PAR is reported to the CRA and to the employee, and will be added to the individual's RRSP deduction room in the year of termination. The following simple example illustrates the use of a PAR:

> **Example**   Stan Kapitany is a member of an RPP in which benefits are not vested until the fourth year of service. He leaves after three years when he is offered an opportunity to develop high performance race cars. His employer was required to report PAs for the first three years of his employment and this, in turn, reduced Mr. Kapitany's ability to make deductible contributions to an RRSP.

> **Analysis**   Since he ceases to work for his employer prior to the benefits becoming vested, the benefits for which PAs were previously reported will not be transferred to him. This means that there will be no retirement benefits corresponding to the previously reported PAs and, as a consequence, Mr. Kapitany might have lost a portion of his entitlement to tax deferred retirement savings. This problem is solved with the addition of a PAR to Mr. Kapitany's RRSP deduction room.

Examples Of RRSP Deduction Calculations

10-75.   The following three examples illustrate the calculation of the RRSP Deduction Limit, Unused RRSP Deduction Room, and the carry forward of undeducted RRSP contributions.

Example A

Miss Brown has 2011 net employment income of $15,000, 2011 net rental income of $10,000, and 2011 interest income of $5,000. She is not a member of an RPP or a DPSP. During 2012, she contributes $5,000 to her RRSP and makes an RRSP deduction of $4,000 in her 2012 tax return. Her Unused RRSP Deduction Room carried forward from 2011 was nil and there were no undeducted contributions in her RRSP account.

Unused Deduction Room Carried Forward From 2011	Nil
Lesser Of:	
• 2012 RRSP Dollar Limit = $22,970	
• 18% Of 2011 Earned Income Of $25,000 = $4,500	$4,500
2012 RRSP Deduction Limit	$4,500
RRSP Deduction ($5,000 Contributed)	(4,000)
Unused Deduction Room - End Of 2012	$ 500

Although Miss Brown could have deducted $4,500, she chose not to deduct her maximum. She has an undeducted RRSP contribution of $1,000 ($5,000 - $4,000) that can be carried forward and deducted in a subsequent year. The interest income is not included in Earned Income as defined in ITA 146(1).

Example B

After deducting an RPP contribution of $2,000, Mrs. Blue has 2011 net employment income of $34,000. In February, 2012, her employer reports a PA of $4,500 on her 2011 T4. Her 2012 RRSP contributions total $5,000 and she deducts $3,200 of this amount in her 2012 tax return. At the end of 2011, her Unused RRSP Deduction Room was $2,500 and there were no undeducted contributions in her RRSP account.

Unused Deduction Room Carried Forward From 2011	$2,500
Lesser Of:	
• 2012 RRSP Dollar Limit = $22,970	
• 18% Of 2011 Earned Income Of $36,000 = $6,480	6,480
Less 2011 PA	(4,500)
2012 RRSP Deduction Limit	$4,480
RRSP Deduction ($5,000 Contributed)	(3,200)
Unused Deduction Room - End Of 2012	$1,280

Mrs. Blue has 2011 Earned Income of $36,000 (net employment income of $34,000, plus her $2,000 RPP contribution that was deducted). She has an undeducted RRSP contribution of $1,800 ($5,000 - $3,200) that can be carried forward and deducted in a subsequent year.

Example C

Mr. Green receives taxable 2011 spousal support of $150,000 and has no other source of income during 2011. He is not a member of an RPP or DPSP. In January, 2012, he contributes $11,500 to his RRSP. This full amount is deducted in his 2012 tax return. His Unused RRSP Deduction Room carried forward from 2011 was $1,200 and there were no undeducted contributions in his RRSP account.

Unused Deduction Room Carried Forward From 2011	$ 1,200
Lesser Of:	
• 2012 RRSP Dollar Limit = $22,970	
• 18% Of 2011 Earned Income Of $150,000 = $27,000	22,970
2012 RRSP Deduction Limit	$24,170
RRSP Deduction ($11,500 Contributed)	(11,500)
Unused Deduction Room - End Of 2012	$12,670

Exercise Ten - 6

Subject: Unused RRSP Deduction Room

Mr. Victor Haslich has 2011 Earned Income for RRSP purposes of $38,000. He is not a member of an RPP or a DPSP. His Unused RRSP Deduction Room carried forward from 2011 was $4,800. During 2012, he contributes $6,000 to his RRSP and makes an RRSP deduction of $4,500. What is the amount of Mr. Haslich's Unused RRSP Deduction Room and undeducted RRSP contributions at the end of 2012? If instead of deducting only $4,500, Mr. Haslich wanted to deduct his maximum RRSP deduction, how much more would he have to contribute to do so?

End of Exercise. Solution available in Study Guide.

Exercise Ten - 7

Subject: Maximum RRSP Deduction

During 2011, Mr. Black has taxable capital gains of $23,650, net rental income of $6,530, pays spousal support of $18,000, and has net employment income of $75,600. Based on his RPP contributions of $2,400 and the matching contributions made by his employer, his employer reports a 2011 PA of $4,800. Mr. Black has Unused RRSP Deduction Room carried forward from 2011 of $10,750. Also at this time, his RRSP contains undeducted contributions of $6,560. During 2012, he makes contributions to his RRSP of $13,200.

Determine Mr. Black's maximum RRSP deduction for 2012. Assuming he deducts his maximum, determine the amount of any Unused RRSP Deduction Room that he will have available at the end of 2012, and indicate whether he has any undeducted contributions remaining at the end of 2012.

End of Exercise. Solution available in Study Guide.

Undeducted RRSP Contributions

General Rules

10-76.   As we have previously noted, there is no requirement that contributions made to an RRSP be deducted immediately. If an individual has available funds to invest, it may be desirable to transfer these funds into an RRSP in order to enjoy the tax deferral on investment earnings that these arrangements provide. However, in some situations, it may be desirable to defer the deduction of all or part of these contributions.

10-77.   An example of this type of situation would be a taxpayer who is currently in a low tax bracket and expects to be in a higher bracket in the future. Provided an amount was contributed after 1990, it can be deducted in any subsequent taxation year in which there is sufficient RRSP deduction room. There is no time limit applicable to this deduction and, in the event of death, it can be deducted in the taxpayer's final tax return.

Excess RRSP Contributions

10-78.   As long as an individual has a corresponding amount of available deduction room, the CRA is not concerned about undeducted contributions. However, because of the desirability of having earnings accumulate on a tax free basis inside an RRSP, it is not surprising that rules have been developed to limit the amount of contributions that are in excess of an individual's deduction room.

10-79.   The basic limiting provision is found in ITA 204.1(2.1) which imposes a tax of 1 percent per month on the "cumulative excess amount in respect of registered retirement savings plans". The "cumulative excess" is defined in ITA 204.2(1.1), as undeducted contributions in excess of the sum of the RRSP Deduction Limit, plus a $2,000 cushion. This, in effect, means that the penalty applies to undeducted contributions that are more than $2,000 greater than the individual's RRSP Deduction Limit.

10-80.   This $2,000 cushion provides for a margin of error when a taxpayer makes contributions early in the taxation year on the basis of estimates of the amount that will be deductible. Note, however, the $2,000 cushion is only available to individuals who are 18 years of age or older throughout the year. This is to prevent parents from making undeducted contributions to an RRSP in the name of their minor children.

10-81.   The following simple example illustrates the application of this rule.

Example   At the beginning of 2011, Mr. Woods has an RRSP Deduction Limit of nil and no undeducted contributions in his plan. During 2011, his RRSP Deduction Limit increases by $9,000. On April 1, 2011, Mr. Woods makes a contribution of $10,000 to his RRSP. No RRSP deduction is taken for 2011.

During 2012, his RRSP Deduction Limit increases by $10,000. On July 1, 2012, $15,000 is contributed to the plan. No RRSP deduction is taken for 2012.

Analysis   There would be no penalty for 2011 as his $10,000 in undeducted contributions is only $1,000 more than his $9,000 unused deduction room for 2011. There would, however, be a penalty in 2012. It would be calculated as follows:

	January To June	July To December
Undeducted RRSP Contributions	$10,000	$25,000
RRSP Deduction Limit ($9,000 + $10,000)	(19,000)	(19,000)
Cushion	(2,000)	(2,000)
Monthly Cumulative Excess Amount	$ Nil	$ 4,000
Penalty Rate	1%	1%
Monthly Penalty	$ Nil	$ 40
Number Of Months	N/A	6
Total Penalty	$ Nil	$ 240

Exercise Ten - 8

Subject: Excess RRSP Contributions

Ms. Lucie Brownell is not a member of an RPP or a DPSP. At the beginning of 2011, Ms. Brownell has no Unused RRSP Deduction Room. During 2010 and 2011 she has Earned Income of $160,000 each year. On July 1, 2011, she makes a $22,950 RRSP contribution, but does not make any deduction for the year. In 2012, she has Earned Income of $50,000, makes a $26,000 contribution on May 1, but still does not make a deduction for the year. Determine any penalty that will be assessed to Ms. Brownell for excess contributions during either 2011 or 2012.

End of Exercise. Solution available in Study Guide.

Tax Planning - Excess RRSP Contributions

10-82.   It would be very difficult to find an investment for which the elimination of tax effects would offset a non-deductible penalty of 1 percent per month. Clearly, excess contributions that subject the taxpayer to this penalty should be avoided.

10-83.   If excess contributions are withdrawn from the RRSP prior to the end of the year following the year in which an assessment is received for the year in which the contribution is made, an offsetting deduction is available. If, however, any excess is not withdrawn within this specified time frame, it will be included in income and taxed on withdrawal, even though it was never deducted from income.

10-84.   This still leaves the question of whether it is worthwhile to make use of the $2,000 penalty free cushion. If an individual has no contribution room left in his TFSA and still has an additional $2,000 in available funds, the ability to have earnings compound on a tax free basis within the RRSP would usually make this a desirable strategy.

10-85.   Alternatively, if an individual has not contributed the maximum allowable to his TFSA and only has limited funds available for investment, the TFSA would be the preferable alternative. This reflects the fact that, while both the TFSA and the non-deductible contributions to an RRSP enjoy tax-free compounding of earnings, withdrawals from a TFSA are not subject to tax. In contrast, any withdrawal from an RRSP, even amounts that have not been deducted, will be subject to tax.

RRSP And RRIF Administration Fees

10-86.   Administration fees for these plans, as well as investment counseling fees related to investments in these plans, cannot be deducted by an individual. As a consequence, such fees should be paid with funds that are in the plan. While there was some controversy associated with this issue, it has been concluded that such payments are not a withdrawal from the plan, nor do they create a taxable benefit for the taxpayer.

RRSP Withdrawals And Voluntary Conversions

Lump Sum Withdrawals

10-87.   A lump sum withdrawal from an RRSP is possible at any point in time. The tax conse-quences of partial or complete withdrawals are very straightforward. In general, the amount withdrawn must be added to income in the year of withdrawal. Further, as a withdrawal does not result in an increase in the ability to make future contributions, such transactions result in a permanent reduction in the balances that will enjoy tax free earnings accumulation.

10-88.   Even when the individual is at or approaching retirement, a lump-sum withdrawal of all funds would not usually be a reasonable alternative. This course of action could subject a large portion of the withdrawal to maximum tax rates at that time and, in the absence of other retirement income, would result in lost tax credits in subsequent years.

10-89.   We would also call your attention to the fact that lump sum withdrawals are subject to withholding. The trustee of the plan is required to withhold a portion of the funds with-drawn and remit them to the government. The taxpayer will, of course, be able to use these withholdings to offset the taxes that will be assessed on the amounts withdrawn. Withholding is based on the following schedule:

Amount	Rate
Less Than $5,001	10%
$5,001 To $15,000	20%
More Than $15,000	30%

10-90.   An additional point with respect to lump sum withdrawals is that such amounts are not eligible for the ITA 118(3) pension income tax credit. In addition, they are not eligible for the pension income splitting provisions that are available (see Chapter 9).

Conversion To Income Stream

10-91.   Besides lump sum withdrawals, the following options are available for converting an RRSP into an income stream:

Life Annuity   Funds from within an RRSP can be used to purchase a single life annuity or, alternatively, a joint life annuity with a spouse or common-law partner. Taxation occurs only as the annuity payments are received.

Note that a life annuity can guarantee that it is paid for a minimum number of periods. For example, a life annuity with a ten year guaranteed term would make payments for a minimum of ten years, even if the annuitant died prior to the end of the period.

A further point here is that the term "annuitant" is correctly used only with respect to an individual who is receiving an annuity. Unless the individual has chosen to convert his RRSP to an annuity, the appropriate description of the individual is registrant. Unfortunately, tax publications often use the term annuitant to describe someone who is, in fact, a registrant.

Fixed Term Annuity   In a similar fashion, a fixed term annuity can be purchased. As with the life annuity, taxation would occur as the annuity payments are received.

10-92.   Note that these conversions can be made at any age, and without regard to whether the taxpayer has retired. Further, there are no tax consequences resulting from the conver-sion. However, the income stream from the annuity will be fully taxable as it is received (see the discussion in Chapter 9 with respect to the taxation of annuity payments).

10-93.   Unlike lump sum withdrawals, annuity payments resulting from RRSP conversions are eligible for both the pension income tax credit and the pension income splitting provisions.

Conversion To RRIF
10-94.   A final alternative for winding up an RRSP is as follows:

> **Registered Retirement Income Fund (RRIF)** The funds can be transferred on a tax free basis to one or more Registered Retirement Income Funds (RRIFs). This arrangement will be described beginning in Paragraph 10-163.

Involuntary Termination Due To Age Limitation
Objective
10-95.   The options for termination of an RRSP that were discussed in the preceding section are available at any age and without regard to whether the individual actually retires. However, government policy in this area takes the view that the tax sheltering features of RRSPs should not continue to be available to taxpayers in periods that are substantially beyond normal retirement age. Because of this view, RRSPs must be terminated in the year an individual turns 71.

Post Termination
10-96.   While individuals cannot have their own RRSP after reaching the age of 71, it is still possible for such individuals to make deductible RRSP contributions. If their spouse or common-law partner has not reached the age of 71, and if the individual continues to have income that qualifies as Earned Income for RRSP purposes (pension income does not), contributions can still be made to an RRSP in the name of the spouse or common-law partner.

Spousal RRSP
Benefits
10-97.   Under ITA 146(5.1), a taxpayer can deduct payments that are made to a plan that is registered in the name of a spouse or common-law partner. Any RRSP that is registered with the taxpayer's spouse or common-law partner as the registrant, and to which the taxpayer has made a contribution, is considered to be a spousal RRSP. Note that this term is still the most commonly used, despite the fact that the legislation covers both spouses and common-law partners.   This means that, if an individual makes any contribution to his spouse or common-law partner's existing RRSP, that plan becomes a spousal RRSP, even if the great majority of the contributions were made by the individual's spouse or common-law partner.

10-98.   Unlike the pension income splitting provision which is only available to couples who have eligible pension income, a spousal RRSP is an income splitting plan that is available to all couples. In situations where one spouse or common-law partner is likely to have either no retirement income or a significantly lower amount, having the spouse or common-law partner with the higher expected retirement income make contributions to a plan in which the spouse or common-law partner is the registrant will generally result in the withdrawals from the plan being taxed at lower rates.

10-99.   In addition, if one spouse or common-law partner has no other source of qualifying pension income, a spousal RRSP allows that individual to make use of the $300 [(15%)($2,000)] annual pension income credit against Tax Payable. Note, however, that in most circumstances, the provision for splitting pension income could accomplish this same goal.

10-100.   When an individual makes contributions to an RRSP in the name of his spouse or common-law partner, the contributions will be deductible in the contributor's tax return. However, the contributor must have available deduction room and, as you would expect, contributions to a spousal plan erode this room in exactly the same manner as would contributions to an RRSP in the contributor's name.

10-101.   We have noted previously that an individual can continue making contributions to a spousal RRSP, even if his own plan has been collapsed because he is over 71 years of age. In addition, a deceased taxpayer's representative can make contributions to a spousal RRSP for up to 60 days after the end of the year in which the taxpayer dies.

Attribution Rules

10-102.   The objective of all of the RRSP legislation is to encourage retirement savings. In the case of spousal RRSPs, the legislation also provides for an element of income splitting. However, as the federal government does not want this element of income splitting to over-ride the basic objective of retirement savings, there is an income attribution provision that discourages the use of spousal RRSPs in a manner that provides for an immediate transfer of income to a lower income spouse.

10-103.   ITA 146(8.3) contains an income attribution provision that requires certain with-drawals from a spousal RRSP to be attributed to the spouse or common-law partner who made the contribution. Withdrawals from non-spousal RRSPs are normally taxed in the hands of the registrant. However, if a withdrawal is made from a spousal RRSP and the registrant's spouse or common-law partner has made a contribution to the plan, either in the current year or in the two preceding calendar years, the lesser of the withdrawal or the total of the spousal contributions in the 3 years will be attributed to the contributing spouse or common-law partner. The registrant of the plan will not be taxed on this amount.

10-104.   Other considerations related to the application of this rule are as follows:

• This attribution rule applies to withdrawals up to the amount of the relevant contributions, but does not apply to withdrawals in excess of this amount.

• This attribution rule applies without regard to whether the contributing spouse or common-law partner has deducted the contributions.

• This attribution rule is applicable even when there are funds that were contributed by the registrant of the plan prior to the spouse or common-law partner making additional contributions.

• This attribution rule does not apply when the taxpayer and spouse or common-law partner are living apart due to a marital breakdown at the time of the withdrawal.

• It is the calendar year in which the spousal contributions are made that is relevant, as a February 1, 2013 contribution is counted in 2013, even if it is deducted in 2012.

10-105.   When the taxpayer's spouse or common-law partner is eligible to make his or her own contributions to an RRSP, it can be useful to have these contributions made to a separate, non-spousal RRSP. If there is a need to withdraw funds, this precaution allows the withdrawal to be made from a plan that has not received spousal contributions. As a result, there would be no attribution and the withdrawal would be taxed in the hands of the individual making the withdrawal. However, if no withdrawals are anticipated in the foreseeable future, there is no tax related need to have a separate, non-spousal plan.

Exercise Ten - 9

Subject: Spousal RRSP

During 2010, Mr. Garveau makes a $5,000 contribution to a new RRSP in which he is the registrant. His wife, Mrs. Charron Garveau also makes a $5,000 contribution to his RRSP in 2010. In 2011, Mrs. Garveau does not make any further contribution to her husband's RRSP. However, Mr. Garveau makes a $6,500 contribution. During 2012, Mr. Garveau withdraws $9,000 from his RRSP. How will this withdrawal be taxed?

End of Exercise. Solution available in Study Guide.

Home Buyers' Plan (HBP)

Qualifying HBP Withdrawals

10-106.   The Home Buyers' Plan (HBP) permits a non-taxable withdrawal of "eligible amounts" from one or more of an individual's RRSPs. The current limit on non-taxable withdrawals is $25,000. In order to receive this withdrawal without tax consequences, the individual must meet several conditions:

- On January 1 of the year of withdrawal, all amounts related to previous HBP withdrawals must have been repaid.

- All amounts, up to the limit of $25,000 per individual, must have been received in a single year or by the end of January of the following year.

- The individual must have bought or built a "qualifying home" before October 1 of the year following the year of withdrawal(s). Extensions of the deadline are available where there is a written agreement to purchase a home, or payments have been made towards the construction of a home, by the October 1 deadline. A "qualifying home" is defined as a housing unit located in Canada, including a share of the capital stock of a cooperative housing corporation that provides an equity interest in the housing unit.

- Within one year of the acquisition of this "qualifying home", the taxpayer must begin, or intend to begin, using it as a principal place of residence. Note, however, there is no minimum holding period for the home, provided that at some point it becomes a principal residence.

- Neither the individual nor his spouse or common-law partner can have owned a home that he or she has occupied during the four calendar years preceding the withdrawal. However, there is an exception to this constraint for disabled individuals. More specifically, if the home purchase is being made by, or for the benefit of, an individual who qualifies for the disability tax credit (see Chapter 4), and the home is more accessible for the individual, or is better suited for the care of the individual, the HBP can be used even if the individual owned a home that was occupied during the specified four year period.

- The individual must complete Form T1036, Home Buyers' Plan Request To Withdraw Funds From An RRSP.

10-107.   There is nothing in these rules to prevent withdrawals by both an individual and his or her spouse or common-law partner, provided all of the withdrawn funds are used to acquire a single property. This would allow couples to make withdrawals totaling $50,000 towards the purchase of a home.

Restrictions On The Deduction Of New RRSP Contributions

10-108.   The intent of this legislation is to allow individuals, who have not recently owned a home, to use accumulated RRSP contributions to acquire a residence. The government does not want to allow individuals to abuse the HBP by making contributions that are immediately withdrawn. To prevent this from happening, a special rule denies a tax deduction for contributions to an RRSP or a spousal RRSP that are withdrawn within 90 days under the Home Buyers' Plan.

10-109.   For this purpose, contributions to an RRSP within the 90 day period will not be considered to be part of the funds withdrawn, except to the extent that the RRSP balance after the withdrawal is less than the amount of the new contributions. This means that an individual can make the maximum $25,000 withdrawal and still make deductible contributions in the preceding 90 days, provided they had at least $25,000 in the RRSP prior to making the additional contributions.

> **Example**   At the beginning of 2012, Mr. Garth has an accumulated RRSP balance of $20,000. In order to make the maximum $25,000 HBP withdrawal, he makes a $5,000 contribution to the RRSP on June 1, 2012. If he then withdraws the $25,000 within 90 days of making the $5,000 contribution, the resulting nil balance will be less than the amount of the contribution and no deduction will be allowed for the $5,000

contribution. If Mr. Garth withdrew only $12,000, the resulting $8,000 balance will be greater than the $5,000 contribution and the contribution will be deductible.

10-110.   As a final point you should note that this rule is applied on a plan by plan basis. If a withdrawal under the HBP serves to reduce the balance of a particular plan below the level of contributions made in the preceding 90 days, the contributions will not be deductible to the extent of this deficiency. This would be the case even if the taxpayer has balances in excess of $25,000 in other RRSPs.

Repayment Of HBP

10-111.   Eligible amounts are not taxed when they are withdrawn from the RRSP and, if there was not a requirement for these funds to be returned to the plan at some point in time, they would constitute a significant tax free leakage from the retirement savings system. As a consequence, repayment of amounts withdrawn must begin as per a specified schedule in the second calendar year following the year of withdrawal.

10-112.   Any RRSP contribution made during the year, or in the first 60 days of the following year, can be designated an HBP repayment (on Schedule 7 of the tax return). Undeducted contributions from previous years can also be so designated. These designated repayments are not deductible in the determination of Taxable Income. Repayment begins in the second year following the withdrawal.

10-113.   Any amounts that are not returned to the plan as per the required schedule must be included in the taxpayer's income in the year in which they were scheduled to be returned. There is no upper limit on the amounts that can be repaid in any year subsequent to withdrawal. However, repayment must be made within 16 years. This is accomplished by requiring a minimum repayment based on the following calculation:

Eligible Amounts Withdrawn	$xx,xxx
Repayments In Previous Years	(xxx)
Amounts Included In Income In Previous Years	(xxx)
Balance	**$ x,xxx**

10-114.   A fraction is then applied to this balance, beginning at 1/15 for the second year following the withdrawal. In each subsequent year, the denominator of the fraction is then reduced by one, resulting in 1/14 for the third year after withdrawal, 1/13 for the fourth year after withdrawal, and so on, until the fraction reaches 1/1 in the sixteenth year following the withdrawal. These are minimum payments and, if they are made as per this schedule, there will be a 15 year, straight line repayment of the eligible amounts.

10-115.   If the payments are less than these minimum amounts, any deficiency must be included in that year's Taxable Income. As any income inclusions will be deducted from the balance to which the fraction is applied in the same manner as if they were repayments, this will not alter the schedule for the remaining payments.

10-116.   However, if payments are accelerated in any year, the schedule is changed. While the multiplier fractions remain the same, the excess payments will reduce the balance to which the fractions are applied. A simple example will help clarify these points:

Example   Ms. Ritchie withdraws an eligible amount of $15,000 from her RRSP in July, 2010, and uses the funds for a down payment on a qualifying home. In 2012, a repayment of $2,400 is made and, in 2013, a repayment of $600 is made.

Analysis   The minimum payment for 2012 is $1,000 [(1/15)($15,000)] and, since this is less than the actual payment, no income inclusion is required. The required payment for 2013 is $900 [(1/14)($15,000 - $2,400)]. As the actual payment is $600, an income inclusion of $300 will be required. This is the case, despite the fact that the $3,000 in cumulative payments for the two years exceeds the $2,000 minimum that would have been required for the two years. This illustrates the fact that making payments in excess of the required level in one year does not provide an equivalent reduction in the payment for the following year. Note that the required payment for 2014 is also $900 [(1/13)($15,000 - $2,400 - $600 - $300)].

Exercise Ten - 10

Subject: Home Buyers' Plan

During 2010, Ms. Farah DeBoo withdraws $18,000 from her RRSP under the provisions of the Home Buyers' Plan. Due to some unexpected income received during 2011, she repays $5,000 in that year. What is the amount of her minimum repayment during 2012?

End of Exercise. Solution available in Study Guide.

Lifelong Learning Plan (LLP)

General Format

10-117.   ITA 146.02 contains provisions that allow an individual to make tax free withdrawals from their RRSPs in order to finance the education of themselves or their spouse or common-law partner. Withdrawals under this Lifelong Learning Plan (LLP) must be repaid over a period of ten years. The repayment amounts are not deductible and, if they are not made as per the required schedule, deficiencies will be included in the individual's income.

Withdrawals

10-118.   To qualify for the tax free withdrawals, the individual or his spouse or common-law partner must be enrolled as a full-time student in a qualifying educational program at a designated educational institution. In general, a qualifying educational program is a post-secondary program that requires students to spend ten hours or more per week on courses that last three consecutive months or more. A designated educational institution is a university, college, or other educational institution that qualifies the individual for the education tax credit (see Chapter 4).

10-119.   The maximum withdrawal is $10,000 in any one calendar year, to a maximum of $20,000 over a period of up to four calendar years. While the designated person for these withdrawals can be either the individual or his spouse or common-law partner, an individual cannot have a positive LLP balance (withdrawals, less repayments) for more than one person at any point in time. However, both an individual and his spouse or common-law partner can participate at the same time, provided they use funds from their own RRSPs.

10-120.   As is the case with HBPs (see Paragraph 10-108), if an RRSP contribution is withdrawn within 90 days as a non-taxable amount under the LLP provisions, it is not deductible in the calculation of the individual's Net Income For Tax Purposes.

Repayment Of LLP

10-121.   Minimum repayments must be made on a straight line basis over a period of ten years. In a manner similar to that used for HBPs, this is accomplished by using a formula in which 1/10 is repaid the first year of repayment, 1/9 the second year, 1/8 the third year, etc. Also in a manner similar to HBPs, deficient repayments will be included in the taxpayer's income. Repayments in excess of the required minimum reduce the balance to which the fractions will be applied.

10-122.   Any RRSP contribution made during the year, or in the first 60 days of the following year, can be designated a LLP repayment. Undeducted contributions from previous years can also be designated. Repayments must begin no later than the fifth year after the year of the first LLP withdrawal (actually the sixth year if payments are made within 60 days of the end of the fifth year).

Example Sarah makes LLP withdrawals from 2012 to 2015. She continues her education from 2012 to 2017, and is entitled to claim the education tax credit as a full time student for at least three months on her return every year. Since 2017 is the fifth year after the year of her first LLP withdrawal, Sarah's repayment period is from 2017 to 2026. The due date for her first repayment is no later than March 1, 2018, which is 60 days after the end of 2017, her first repayment year.

10-123. Repayments must begin earlier if the beneficiary of the program does not qualify for the full time education tax credit (see Chapter 4) for at least three months in each of two consecutive years. Specifically, repayment must begin in the second of the two non-qualifying years (or the first 60 days of the following year).

Example Joseph makes an LLP withdrawal in 2012 for a qualifying educational program he is enrolled in during 2012. He is entitled to the education tax credit as a full time student for five months of 2012. Joseph completes the educational program in 2013, and he is entitled to the education tax credit as a full time student for five months of 2013. He is not entitled to the education tax credit for 2014 or 2015. As a result, Joseph's repayment period begins in 2015.

Other Considerations

10-124. There is no limit on the number of times an individual can participate in the LLP. However, an individual may not participate in a new plan before the end of the year in which all repayments from any previous participation have been made.

10-125. For a withdrawal to be eligible for tax free status, the designated person must complete the qualified educational program before April of the year following the withdrawal or, alternatively, be enrolled in a qualified educational program at the end of March of the year following the withdrawal. If this is not the case, the withdrawal will still be eligible for tax free treatment, provided less than 75 percent of the tuition paid for the program is refunded.

Exercise Ten - 11

Subject: Lifelong Learning Plan

Jean Paul Riopelle makes a Lifelong Learning Plan (LPP) withdrawal of $5,000 during July, 2012. This is subsequent to his acceptance in a community college art program that runs from September to November, 2012. He completes the course.

On February 28 of each year from 2015 through 2024, he makes payments of $500 per year to his RRSP. These amounts are designated as LLP repayments in his tax returns for the years 2014 through 2023. Indicate the tax consequences to Jean Paul of these transactions.

End of Exercise. Solution available in Study Guide.

Departure From Canada

RRSP Balances

10-126. ITA 128.1(4)(b) requires a deemed disposition of most capital property when an individual departs from Canada (see coverage of this subject in Chapter 8). However, most pension benefits are exempt from these rules and, as a consequence, a departure from Canada will not automatically result in the collapse of an RRSP.

10-127. Once the taxpayer has ceased to be a resident of Canada, he may find it desirable to collapse the plan. The collapse and subsequent payment to a non-resident will result in taxation under ITA Part XIII. The Part XIII tax is a 25 percent tax on payments to a non-resident and, for those countries with which Canada has a tax treaty, the rate can be as low as 10 percent. Unlike the withholding tax that is assessed on withdrawals by Canadian residents, this is a final tax, and the withdrawn balances will not be subject to further taxation in Canada.

10-128.   Whether or not the proceeds resulting from the collapse of the plan will be taxed in the new country of residence will depend on a number of factors, including which country is involved and the manner in which the RRSP income was reported prior to the individual leaving Canada. While there are significant tax planning opportunities in this area, detailed coverage of this subject goes beyond the scope of this text.

10-129.   If the plan is not collapsed and payments are made to a non-resident, such payments are also subject to Part XIII tax at a 10 percent, or greater, rate. As was the case with the proceeds resulting from collapsing the plan, how this will be taxed in the individual's new country of residence is determined by a number of factors.

Home Buyers' Plan Balances
10-130.   If an individual ceases to be a resident of Canada, any unpaid balance under the HBP must be repaid before the date the tax return for the year of departure should be filed, or 60 days after becoming a non-resident, whichever date is earlier. If this deadline is not met, the unpaid balance must be included in income.

Lifelong Learning Plan Balances
10-131.   Similar to the provisions under the HBP, if an individual ceases to be a resident of Canada, any unpaid balance under the LLP must be repaid before the date the tax return for the year of departure should be filed, or 60 days after becoming a non-resident, whichever date is earlier. If this deadline is not met, the unpaid balance must be included in income.

Death Of The Registrant
General Rules
10-132.   When an individual dies, there can be many tax implications. In this Chapter 10, we will cover the complications associated with RRSPs owned by an individual at the time of death. Supplementary Reading No. 6 on the Student CD-ROM, "Final Returns For Deceased Taxpayers" describes some of the other special rules that are applicable.

10-133.   The general rules for RRSPs depend on whether the plan is an unmatured plan (i.e., the registrant has not converted the plan to an annuity) or a matured plan (i.e., the plan has been converted to an annuity which is producing a regular stream of income). As described in RC4177, "Death Of An RRSP Annuitant", the general rules are as follows:

> **Unmatured RRSPs** When the registrant of an unmatured RRSP dies, he or she is considered to have received, immediately before death, an amount equal to the fair market value of all the property held in the RRSP at the time of death. This amount, and all other amounts the registrant received in the year from the RRSP, have to be reported on the registrant's return for the year of death.

> **Matured RRSPs** When the annuitant of a matured RRSP dies, the annuitant is considered to have received, immediately before death, an amount equal to the fair market value of all remaining annuity payments under the RRSP at the time of death. This amount, and all other amounts the annuitant received in the year from the RRSP, have to be reported on the annuitant's return for the year of death. Note that, if a straight life annuity was involved, there would be no further payments after death.

10-134.   If these general rules are applied, with the lump-sum or annuity amounts included in the decedent's final tax return, the assets will pass to the specified beneficiaries at fair market value, with no immediate tax consequences for the beneficiaries. However, when the RRSP assets or annuity are transferred to certain qualified beneficiaries, there are important exceptions to this general rule. (See material which follows.)

10-135.   An additional point here is that there are two different ways in which RRSP assets can be transferred at death. The preferable approach is for the registrant to specify the beneficiary, or beneficiaries, in the RRSP contract. This will result in the assets being passed immediately at death. Perhaps more importantly, probate fees will be avoided.

10-136.   If this approach is not used, the RRSP assets will pass into the deceased's estate. If this happens, their distribution will be subject to probate fees. In Ontario, these fees are 1.5 percent of the value of the estate with no upper limit.

Exception - Transfers To A Spouse Or Common-Law Partner

10-137.   The various possibilities that could arise when the disposition of an RRSP after death is to a spouse or common-law partner can be described as follows:

Unmatured RRSP - Spouse Is Beneficiary If the spouse is the sole beneficiary and there is a transfer to an RRSP with the spouse as the registrant, there will be no tax consequences for either the decedent or the spouse. The assets in the decedent's RRSP simply become assets in the spouse's RRSP. This is usually the most tax advantageous arrangement for dealing with an unmatured RRSP.

Matured RRSP - Spouse Is Beneficiary If the RRSP is in the form of an annuity with the spouse as the sole beneficiary, the RRSP will continue with the spouse receiving the payments. There will be no tax consequences for the decedent and the spouse will be taxed as the annuity payments are received. For matured RRSPs, this is clearly the most tax advantageous arrangement.

Estate Is Beneficiary Whether the RRSP has or has not matured, the general rules will be applicable here. If the spouse is the beneficiary of the estate, the same rollover results can be achieved here through the use of elections. However, probate fees will be applicable and the procedures will be more complex.

Exception - Transfers To A Financially Dependent Child Or Grandchild

10-138.   Without becoming involved in the details, there are provisions that allow both matured and unmatured RRSPs to be transferred to a financially dependent child or grandchild on a basis that shifts the tax burden from the decedent to the transferee.

10-139.   While the relevant amounts could be taxed in the hands of the dependant, there are other options. If the child has a physical or mental infirmity, the dependant can avoid current taxation by transferring the amounts to an RRSP, RRIF, Registered Disability Savings Plan (RDSP as described in Chapter 9) or an annuity. If there is no physical or mental infirmity, the only option that avoids current taxation is to purchase an annuity. In this case, the life of the annuity cannot exceed 18 years, minus the age of the child or grandchild when the annuity is purchased. As a result, if the child is over 17 years of age, this option cannot be used.

Home Buyers' Plan Balances

10-140.   If a participant in the HBP dies prior to repaying all amounts to the RRSP, any unpaid balance will be included in income in the final tax return. However, a surviving spouse may elect with the legal representatives of the deceased to avoid the income inclusion. If this election is made, the surviving spouse assumes the position of the deceased by being treated as having received an eligible amount equal to the unpaid balance outstanding at the time of the deceased's death. This amount is added to any balance of eligible amounts received by the surviving spouse that have not been previously repaid to the RRSPs.

Lifelong Learning Plan Balances

10-141.   If an individual dies and has a positive LLP balance, this balance must be included in the individual's income for the year of death. As is the case with HBPs, there is an election that allows a spouse to make the repayments under the deceased's LLP terms.

Registered Pension Plans (RPPs)

Establishing An RPP

Types Of Plans

10-142.   The most important type of Canadian pension arrangement is the Registered Pension Plan (RPP) provided by some employers for their employees. These plans have assets that are larger than those of all other types of plans combined. Such plans are established by a contract between the employer and the employees and provide either for a pension benefit that is determined under a prescribed formula (a defined benefit or benefit based plan), or for a specified annual contribution by the employer that will provide a benefit that will be based on the funds available at the time of retirement (a money purchase or contribution based plan).

10-143.   An additional variable is the question of whether, in addition to the contributions made by the employer, the employees make contributions to the plan. If they do, it is referred to as a contributory plan.   Both employer and employee contributions to the RPPs are normally deposited with a trustee who is responsible for safeguarding and managing the funds deposited.

Registration Of The Plan

10-144.   It would be possible for an employer to have a pension plan that is not registered. However, such an arrangement would make very little sense. In order to deduct contributions for tax purposes, an employer sponsored pension plan must be registered with the CRA.

10-145.   In most situations, the basic requirements for registration are not difficult to meet. The plan must provide a definite arrangement, established as a continuing policy by an employer, under which benefits are provided to employees after their retirement. The terms and conditions must be set out in writing and the amounts of benefits to be provided must be reasonable in the circumstances.

Employer Contributions To The RPP

General Rules

10-146.   As is noted in Chapter 6 on business income, ITA 20(1)(q) allows an employer to deduct contributions to an RPP in the determination of Net Income For Tax Purposes. It indicates that such amounts can be deducted to the extent that they are provided for by ITA 147.2(1) or 147.5(10).

10-147.   Turning to these subsections, we find that contributions to money purchase plans are deductible as long as they are made in accordance with the plan as registered. For defined benefit plans there is a similar requirement. Contributions made during the year, or within 120 days after the year end, are deductible as long as they have not been deducted previously.

10-148.   Note that the reference is to contributions made, establishing the fact that the availability of deductions for pension costs is on a cash basis. As deductions under GAAP must be determined on an accrual basis, there are likely to be differences between the accounting expense for the period and the tax deduction for the period.

Restrictions

10-149.   The preceding general rules appear to provide for any level of deductions, as long as the amount is consistent with the plan as registered. As we have noted, however, the restrictions on contributions are implemented through the registration process. More specifically, ITA 147.1(8) indicates that RPPs become revocable if the PA of a member of the plan exceeds the lesser of:

- the money purchase limit for the year, and
- 18 percent of the member's compensation from the employer for the year.

10-150.   Given the fact that the RRSP Deduction Limit is also based on these same factors (with a one year lag), this restriction means that, in general, an RPP cannot provide for more retirement savings than would be available to an individual whose only retirement savings vehicle is an RRSP. To illustrate this, consider a member of a money purchase RPP who has 2012 compensation of $110,000. The RPP must be designed in such a fashion that it does not produce a combined employer/employee contribution that is in excess of the lesser of $23,820 (the money purchase limit for 2012) and $19,800 (18 percent of the compensation of $110,000).

10-151.   An individual with Earned Income equal to the same $110,000 compensation, who is not a member of an RPP or DPSP, would be subject to the same limit, with a one year lag. That is, in 2013, the maximum RRSP deduction for this individual would be the lesser of 18 percent of 2012 Earned Income of $110,000, and the 2013 RRSP Dollar Limit of $23,820 (See Paragraph 10-48).

10-152.   An RPP that provides benefits to an employee that creates a PA in excess of the money purchase limit for the year or 18 percent of the employee's compensation will have its registration revoked. Given that registration is required for RPP contributions to be deductible, this requirement should ensure that benefits are limited to the specified levels.

10-153.   Before leaving this discussion of employer contributions, you should note that this restriction on PAs would effectively restrict both employer and employee contributions to an RPP. Both types of contributions go into the PA calculation and, as a consequence, placing the limit on this measure of pension benefits ensures that the combined employee/employer contributions will be restricted to the desired maximum level.

Employee Contributions To The RPP

10-154.   As is noted in Chapter 3, the basic provision here is ITA 8(1)(m) which indicates that, in the determination of employment income, individuals can deduct contributions to an employer's RPP as specified in ITA 147.2(4). Taking the same approach that was used for employer contributions, this Subsection indicates that amounts contributed for current service are deductible if they are made in accordance with the terms of the plan. This places employee contributions under the same overall limit as employer contributions. That is, they must be made under the terms of a plan that does not produce a PA that exceeds the lesser of the money purchase limit for the year and 18 percent of the employee's compensation for the year.

Options At Retirement

10-155.   Individual RPPs generally involve rules that are applicable to the employee group in its entirety. As a consequence, the employee's options are usually limited to the receipt of the specified pension benefit. If the plan permits a lump sum payment of benefits, it would become taxable on receipt by the employee. The plan might also permit transfers to other types of plans at, or before, retirement age. Such transfers are discussed beginning in Paragraph 10-192.

Phased Retirement

The Problem

10-156.   Until 2008, an employee could not accrue benefits under a defined benefit RPP if he was currently receiving benefits from that plan. This prohibition also applied if the employee was receiving benefits from another defined benefit RPP sponsored by the same employer or an employer related to that employer. This meant that:

- If an individual had wanted to phase in retirement by working on a part time basis after he had started to receive his basic pension benefits, he could not receive any further pension benefits for this part time work.

- If an individual continued on a full time basis after beginning to receive his basic pension benefit, he could not be rewarded with a partial pension benefit for this additional work.

The Solution

10-157.   The problem has been dealt with in ITR 8503(16) through (25). Starting in 2008, an employer can offer employees up to 60 percent of their accrued defined benefit pension entitlement, while accruing additional pension benefits on a current service basis with respect to their post-pension commencement employment. This program is limited to employees who are at least 55 years of age and who are otherwise eligible to receive a pension without being subject to an early retirement reduction.

Pooled Registered Pension Plans (PRPPs)

The Problem

10-158.   It is very clear that a large majority of Canadian individuals are not making adequate financial arrangements for their retirement years. While this is not a problem for those fortunate individuals who are members of a generous RPP sponsored by a government organization, a large public company or a large union, there are many other individuals who may be facing a bleak future once their working years have ended.

10-159.   To some extent, RRSPs provide a solution to this problem. However, it appears that the majority of Canadian individuals do not have sufficient self discipline to consistently make adequate contributions to these plans. For example, in 2010 a total of $33.9 billion in contributions were made to RRSPs. However, this was only 5.1% of the total room available to eligible taxpayers. This was down from 5.4% in 2009.

10-160.   An obvious solution to these problems is to have a larger percentage of Canadians enrolled in plans that require regular contributions. However, the maintenance of a registered pension plan is very expensive, making it difficult for small organizations to sponsor such plans, and impossible for self-employed individuals to participate in such plans.

The Solution

10-161.   As one solution to these problems, the government has proposed the introduction of Pooled Registered Pension Plans (PRPPs). The basic features of these plans can be described as follows:

- Regulated financial institutions that are capable of taking on a fiduciary role (trusts and insurance companies) would establish and manage defined benefit plans independently of any specific employer. These administrators would be responsible for ensuring compliance with the relevant tax rules.

- There would be two classes of members. One class would be employees of an employer that offers participation in a PRPP. For this class of member, the employer would be responsible for selecting a particular plan, enrolling their employees in that plan and establishing the level of both employer and employee contributions. They would also be responsible for remitting their contributions to the plan administrator, and for collecting and remitting their employees' contributions.

- The second class of members would include employees of an employer that does not offer participation in a PRPP, as well as self-employed individuals. These "individual" members would assume the responsibilities associated with selecting a plan, establishing contribution rates, and making the required remittances to the plan.

- For the members who belong to a plan selected by their employer, the plans will generally be portable.

- The PRPP legislation will have a vehicle which will allow interested jurisdictions to require mandatory participation for employers.

- Modifications to the tax rules will be made to ensure that these plans operate within the limits established for all types of retirement savings.

10-162.   It is expected that the introduction of PRPPs will result in a large increase in the number of individuals that participate in a registered plan that requires regular contributions.

Registered Retirement Income Funds (RRIFs)

Establishment

Only Transfers From Other Plans

10-163   A RRIF is a trusteed arrangement, administered in much the same manner as an RRSP. A basic difference, however, is the fact that deductible contributions cannot be made to a RRIF. ITA 146.3(2)(f) makes it clear that the only types of property that can be accepted by the RRIF trustee are transfers from other types of retirement savings arrangements. The most common type of transfer would be the tax free rollover that can be made from an RRSP. As was indicated previously, this commonly occurs when an individual reaches age 71 and can no longer maintain an RRSP.

10-164.   There is no limit on the number of RRIFs that can be owned by a taxpayer and, in addition, the taxpayer has complete flexibility as to the number of RRSPs that can be transferred to a RRIF on a tax free basis. Further, the taxpayer is free to divide any RRSP and only transfer a portion of the funds to a RRIF. This in no way limits the options available for any remaining balance from the RRSP.

10-165.   A RRIF can be established by an individual of any age and without regard to whether the individual is retiring. However, the individual must have an eligible savings plan, such as an RRSP, from which funds can be transferred. As explained in Paragraphs 10-168 and 10-169, there can be advantages to establishing a RRIF once age 65 is reached.

Other Considerations

10-166.   Any amount transferred from an RRSP to a RRIF is not subject to taxation until such time as it is withdrawn by the taxpayer from the RRIF. As was the case with RRSPs, withdrawals are taxed as ordinary income, without regard to how they were earned inside the RRIF (e.g., capital gains realized within the RRIF are taxed in full on withdrawal from the plan).

10-167.   Once inside the RRIF, the assets can be managed by the trustee of the plan according to the directions of the taxpayer. The list of qualified investments for RRIFs is similar to that for RRSPs and allows for considerable latitude in investment policies. As is the case with RRSPs, fees paid by an individual for the administration of a RRIF are not deductible.

RRIF Withdrawals

Pension Income Tax Credit And Pension Income Splitting

10-168.   In our discussion of RRSP withdrawals, we noted that lump sum withdrawals from RRSPs are not eligible for the pension income tax credit or the pension income splitting provision. Fortunately, this is not the case with lump sum withdrawals from a RRIF. If the taxpayer is aged 65 or over, all taxable withdrawals from a RRIF qualify for the pension income tax credit and can be split with a spouse or common-law partner.

Withdrawals Greater Than The Minimum Withdrawal

10-169.   While legislation establishes the minimum withdrawal from a RRIF (see the following paragraph), there is no maximum withdrawal. The entire balance in the RRIF can be withdrawn at any time. However, as was noted, any amounts removed from the RRIF must be included in Net Income For Tax Purposes in the year of withdrawal. In contrast to RRSPs where tax is withheld on any regular withdrawals, tax is only withheld on RRIF withdrawals in excess of the minimum withdrawal.

Calculating The Amount Of The Minimum Withdrawal

10-170.   We noted previously that, unlike the situation with RRSPs, an individual cannot make deductible contributions to a RRIF. Another difference between an RRSP and a RRIF is that a minimum annual withdrawal must be made from a RRIF beginning in the year following the year it is established.

10-171.   For an individual who is under 79 at the beginning of the year, the minimum withdrawal is determined by dividing the fair market value of the RRIF assets at the beginning of the year, by 90 minus the age of the individual at the beginning of the year.

> **Example**   A 65 year old individual, who had established a RRIF in a previous year, had $1,000,000 in RRIF assets at the beginning of the year.
>
> **Analysis**   This individual would have to withdraw a minimum of $40,000 [$1,000,000 ÷ (90 - 65)] during the current year.

10-172.   Once an individual is 79 or over at the beginning of the year, the rules require a different calculation. A specified percentage [ITR 7308(3)] is applied to the fair market value of the RRIF assets at the beginning of the year. The percentage increases each year, starting at 8.53 percent at age 79, rising to 8.75 percent at age 80, and 13.62 percent at age 90. However, when it hits 20 percent at age 94, it remains at that level until the registrant dies. This, of course, means that the RRIF balance will never reach zero if minimum withdrawals are made.

Use Of Spouse's Age For Minimum Withdrawal

10-173.   It is possible to irrevocably elect to use a spouse's age to calculate the minimum RRIF withdrawal. If the spouse is younger, the minimum amount is lower and offers an opportunity to defer the tax effect of the withdrawals.

Exercise Ten - 12

Subject: Minimum RRIF Withdrawal

On January 1, 2012, Mr. Larry Harold transfers all of his RRSP funds into a RRIF. Mr. Harold is 65 years old on that date. The fair market value of these assets on January 1, 2012 is $625,000. The corresponding figure on January 1, 2013 is $660,000. What is the minimum withdrawal that Mr. Harold must make from the RRIF during 2012 and during 2013?

End of Exercise. Solution available in Study Guide.

Death Of The Registrant

General Rules

10-174.   As was the case with an RRSP, the general rule is that, when a taxpayer dies, the fair market value of the assets in his RRIF will be included as income in his final tax return. Also following this pattern, there are exceptions when the RRIF is transferred to either a spouse or common-law partner, or a financially dependent child or grandchild of the taxpayer.

Rollovers

10-175.   If an individual has a spouse or common-law partner, the most tax advantageous approach to estate planning is usually to name that person as the successor registrant of the RRIF. In this situation, the RRIF will simply continue with the surviving spouse receiving the payments. There will be no tax consequences for the decedent and future withdrawals from the RRIF will be taxed in the hands of the spouse.

10-176.   If a RRIF is left to the decedent's estate, the alternatives for transfers to a spouse or common-law partner, or to a financially dependent child or grandchild, are the same as those for an RRSP (see Paragraphs 10-137 to 10-139).

10-177.   As was the case with RRSPs, a tax free rollover to a spouse or common-law partner is available by making appropriate elections. Also as with RRSPs, if a financially dependent child or grandchild is physically or mentally infirm, current taxation can be avoided if the assets are transferred to an RRSP, a RRIF, a RDSP, or an annuity. In the absence of a physical or mental infirmity, the only option is the purchase of a limited term annuity.

Evaluation Of RRIFs

10-178.   For individuals required by age to terminate their RRSP, lump sum withdrawals are usually not a good solution. This reflects the fact that such withdrawals can often result in a large portion of the income being taxed at high rates. In addition, the pension income splitting provisions cannot be utilized. A possible exception to this view would be situations in which the taxpayer plans to give up Canadian residency.

10-179.   This leaves individuals with a choice between using a RRIF and purchasing an annuity. The fact that life annuities are only available through life insurance companies means that the rates of return implicit in these financial instruments are often not competitive with other investments.

10-180.   Further, annuities lack flexibility. Once an individual has entered into an annuity contract, there is usually no possibility of acquiring larger payments if they are required by some unforeseen event. In contrast, RRIFs offer some degree of flexibility with respect to amounts available to the taxpayer.

10-181.   As a final point, the wide range of qualifying investments that can be acquired in RRIFs provide individuals with the opportunity to achieve better rates of return than those available through the purchase of annuities. It would appear that, for most individuals, the use of a RRIF is the most desirable option when the individual's age forces the collapse of an RRSP.

Deferred Profit Sharing Plans

General Rules

10-182.   ITA 147 provides for an arrangement where an employer can deduct contributions made to a trustee of a Deferred Profit Sharing Plan (DPSP, hereafter) for the benefit of the employees. Employees cannot make contributions to an employer sponsored DPSP. However, certain direct transfers of balances from other plans belonging to the employee can be made (see Paragraph 10-192).

10-183.   Amounts placed in the plan will be invested, with investment earnings accruing on a tax fee basis. As with the other retirement savings vehicles, the beneficiary of the plan is taxed only when assets are distributed from the plan.

10-184.   As was the case with RPPs, the employer's contributions to these plans are limited by a maximum PA that must be complied with to avoid having the DPSP revoked. This is found in ITA 147(5.1) and is more restrictive than the corresponding limit for RPPs. Like the situation with RPPs, contributions to DPSPs cannot result in a PA that exceeds 18 percent of a beneficiary's employment income for the year. However, contributions to these plans are limited to only one-half of the money purchase limit for the year.

Tax Planning

10-185.   From the point of view of the employer, DPSPs are similar to RPPs. However, they have the advantage of providing greater flexibility in the scheduling of payments. Such plans are tied to the profits of the business and, if the business has a bad year, it will normally result in a reduction of payments into the DPSP. Further, no specific benefits are promised to the employees. This relieves the employer from any responsibility for bad investment decisions by the fund trustee or estimation errors in the actuarial valuation process, factors that can cause significant uncertainty for the sponsors of defined benefit RPPs.

10-186.   From the point of view of the employee, a DPSP operates in a manner similar to an RPP. The major difference is that employees are not permitted to contribute to DPSPs. A further difference is that DPSPs do not provide a defined benefit at the time of retirement.

10-187.   DPSPs must invest in certain qualified investments and there are penalties for purchases of non-qualified investments. A final important consideration is that DPSPs cannot be registered if the employer or a member of the employer's family is a beneficiary under the plan. This would include major shareholders if the employer is a corporation, individual owners if the employer is a proprietorship or partnership, and beneficiaries when the employer is a trust.

Profit Sharing Plans

General Rules

10-188.   ITA 144 provides for Profit Sharing Plans. These plans are similar to DPSPs in that the employer can deduct contributions made on behalf of employees. Unlike the DPSPs, there are no specified limits on the employer's contributions as long as they are reasonable and are paid out of profits.

Tax Planning

10-189.   However, these plans have not achieved the popularity of DPSPs for a very simple reason. The employer's contributions to Profit Sharing Plans are taxable income to the employee in the year in which they are made. In addition, any income that accrues on the assets in the fund is allocated to the employee as it accrues. Although payments to the employees out of the fund are received on a tax free basis, this form of compensation offers no deferral of tax and requires the payment of taxes on amounts that have not been realized by the employee. Given these facts, it is not surprising that such Profit Sharing Plans have not been a popular compensation mechanism.

Profit Sharing Plans - 2012 Budget Changes

10-190.   The preceding suggests that there are not really any tax advantages associated with the use of profit sharing plans. However, the CRA has found that such plans are being used:

- to direct business profits to family members in order to reduce taxes; and
- to avoid employee withholding requirements, as well as CPP and EI payments.

10-191.   To curtail these practices, the 2012 budget proposes a new tax on "excess employee profit sharing plan payments". The tax will be on the employer for payments to employees who do not deal at arm's length with the employer, on amounts that exceed 20 percent of the employee's salary for the year. The rate for the tax will be the maximum federal/provincial rate on individuals in the province of residence of the employee.

Transfers Between Plans

Accumulated Benefits

10-192.   As individuals may belong to several different retirement savings plans over their working lives, it is important that tax free transfers between different types of retirement savings plans can be made. For example, an individual who goes from a position where the employer provides RPP benefits, to a different position where no such benefits are provided, may wish to have his accumulated RPP benefits transferred to his RRSP. In the absence of a special provision to deal with this transfer, the benefits coming out of the RPP would have to be included in the individual's Taxable Income in the year of withdrawal. This, of course, would make such a transfer very unattractive.

10-193.   Fortunately, the *Act* allows for great flexibility in this area. Provided the transfer is made directly between the plans, the following transfers can be made on a tax free basis:

Registered Pension Plans   ITA 147.3 provides for the direct transfer of a lump sum amount from an RPP to a different RPP, to an RRSP, and to a RRIF. The Section also permits a transfer from a taxpayer's RPP to an RPP, RRSP, or RRIF of his or her spouse, former spouse, common-law partner or former common-law partner under a court order or written separation agreement in the event of a marriage or common-law partnership breakdown.

Registered Retirement Savings Plans   ITA 146(16) provides for the transfer of lump sum amounts from an RRSP to a RRIF, an RPP, or to another RRSP. The Subsection also permits a transfer from a taxpayer's RRSP to an RRSP or RRIF of his or her spouse, former spouse, common-law partner or former common-law partner under a court order or written separation agreement in the event of a marriage or common-law partnership breakdown.

Deferred Profit Sharing Plans   ITA 147(19) provides for the direct transfer of a lump sum amount from a DPSP to an RPP, an RRSP, or to a different DPSP. There are additional tax free transfers to the taxpayer's RRIF and to an RPP, RRSP, DPSP or RRIF of his or her spouse, former spouse, common-law partner or former common-law partner under a court order or written separation agreement in the event of a marriage or common-law partnership breakdown.

Retiring Allowances

10-194.   The full amount of any retiring allowance, which includes amounts received for loss of office or employment and unused sick leave, must be included in the taxpayer's income in the year received. However, a deduction is available under ITA 60(j.1) for certain amounts transferred to either an RPP or an RRSP. This, in effect, creates a tax free transfer of all, or part, of a retiring allowance into an RRSP, without affecting the available RRSP deduction room. The limit on this tax free transfer is as follows:

- $2,000 for each year, or part year, the taxpayer was employed by the employer prior to 1996. This includes non-continuous service with the same employer.

- An additional $1,500 for each year, or part year, the taxpayer was employed by the employer prior to 1989 for which the employer's contributions to an RPP or DPSP had not vested by the time the retiring allowance was paid.

10-195.   This transfer does not have to be directly from the employer to the RRSP. The deduction is available if the taxpayer receives the funds and deposits the eligible amount into his RRSP within 60 days of the end of the year it is received. The eligible amount must be contributed to the employee's RRSP (not a spousal RRSP) to be deducted. However, if a direct transfer is used, the taxpayer will avoid having income tax withheld on the retiring allowance. It should also be noted that, for the individual to deduct the amount transferred to his RRSP, the trustee must issue the usual RRSP contribution receipt.

Example   Joan Marx retires at the end of 2012, receiving from her employer a retiring allowance of $150,000. She began working for this employer in 1982. The employer has never sponsored an RPP or a DPSP.

Analysis   The entire $150,000 must be included in Ms. Marx's 2012 Net Income For Tax Purposes. Provided she makes a $38,500 [($2,000)(the 14 years 1982 through 1995) + ($1,500)(the 7 years 1982 through 1988)] contribution to her RRSP, she will be able to deduct the $38,500 RRSP contribution, without eroding her RRSP deduction room.

Exercise Ten - 13

Subject: Retiring Allowance

On December, 31, 2012, Mr. Giovanni Bartoli retires after 37 years of service with his present employer. In recognition of his outstanding service during these years, his employer pays him a retiring allowance of $100,000. His employer has never sponsored an RPP or a DPSP. What is the maximum deductible contribution that Mr. Bartoli can make to his RRSP as a result of receiving this retiring allowance?

End of Exercise. Solution available in Study Guide.

Retirement Compensation Arrangements

The Problem

10-196.   As we have seen throughout this Chapter, the rules related to maximum contributions by employers to RPPs and DPSPs are very specific. While these maximum limits are sufficient to provide a reasonable level of retirement income to the majority of employees, they fall short of this goal for highly paid senior executives. Such individuals are often accustomed to a lifestyle that cannot be sustained by the maximum amounts that can be produced by RPPs and DPSPs. A similar analysis can be made for owner/managers of successful private corporations.

10-197.   Given this situation, both public and private corporations use plans other than RPPs and DPSPs to provide benefits that are not limited by the rules applicable to the more conventional plans. In general, such arrangements can be classified as Retirement Compensation Arrangements (RCAs).

Arrangements Defined

10-198.   RCAs are defined in the *Income Tax Act* as follows:

> **ITA 248(1)   Retirement compensation arrangement** means a plan or arrangement under which contributions are made by an employer or former employer of a taxpayer, or by a person with whom the employer or former employer does not deal at arm's length, to another person or partnership in connection with benefits that are to be received or may be received or enjoyed by any person on, after, or in contemplation of any substantial change in the services rendered by the taxpayer, the retirement of the taxpayer or the loss of an office or employment of the taxpayer.

10-199.   The definition goes on to indicate that the term retirement compensation arrangement does not include RPPs, PRPPs, DPSPs, RRSPs, profit sharing plans, supplementary unemployment benefit plans, or plans established for the purpose of deferring the salary or wages of a professional athlete.

10-200.   Provided the arrangement involves a contractual obligation to ultimately make payments to the covered employees, a corporation's contributions to a RCA are fully deductible when made. However, as we shall see in the following material, both contributions and subsequent earnings on the invested contributions are subject to a special refundable tax.

Part XI.3 Refundable Tax

10-201.   Contributions made to a RCA are subject to a 50 percent refundable tax under ITA Part XI.3. In addition, earnings on the assets contained in the plan are subject to this same 50 percent refundable tax. The tax amounts are refunded at a 50 percent rate when distributions are made to the beneficiaries of the plan.

> **Example** During 2012, Borscan Ltd. contributes $50,000 to a plan established for several of its senior executives. The funds are used to purchase investments that earn interest of $4,500, and no payments are made to the executives during the year. On January 1, 2013, $20,000 is distributed to the beneficiaries of the plan.

> **Analysis** Borscan Ltd. would be able to deduct the $50,000 payment into the plan in determining its 2012 Net Income For Tax Purposes. However, the Company would be required to pay Part XI.3 tax of $27,250 [(50%)($50,000 + $4,500)]. In 2013, when the $20,000 distribution is made to the beneficiaries, the Company would receive a refund of $10,000 [(50%)($20,000)].

10-202.   In legislating this tax provision, it was clearly the intent of the government to discourage the use of RCAs. The 50 percent tax that is required at the corporate level is higher, in some provinces significantly so, than the rate that would be paid by an individual if the equivalent funds were simply distributed as salary.

10-203.   As a result, this means that more taxes will be paid initially, in situations where a RCA is used to compensate employees. Although the Part XI.3 tax is totally refundable, the corporation will not receive any refund of the tax until distributions from the RCA are made.

10-204.   Despite this analysis, the use of RCAs appears to be on the rise, particularly with respect to providing retirement benefits to the owner/managers of private corporations. The explanation for this phenomenon probably lies in the not always rational preference that such owner/managers have for having taxation occur at the corporate, rather than the personal level.

RCAs - 2012 Budget Changes

10-205.   It appears that the CRA has discovered the use of "tax motivated arrangements" that are perceived to be an abuse of the retirement compensation arrangement rules. These arrangements are very technical and covering them goes beyond the scope of this text. However, we would note that the 2012 Budget has added new rules which will assess penalties in some situations where retirement compensation arrangements are established between non-arm's length parties.

Salary Deferral Arrangements

The Problem

10-206.   The fact that business income is on an accrual basis while employment income is on a cash basis has made it advantageous for employers to accrue bonuses prior to the actual payment of the amount to the employee. As was discussed in Chapter 3, if payment to the employee is made within 180 days of the employer's year end, the employer can deduct the amount when accrued, while the employee will not be taxed until the bonus is paid.

10-207.   If, however, the actual payment occurs more than 180 days after the employer's year end, ITA 78(4) defers the deductibility of the bonus until the point in time when it is actually paid. However, even if the employer cannot deduct the amounts until they are paid, it may still be attractive to make an arrangement that will defer compensation and postpone the payment of taxes by the employee. The concept of a salary deferral arrangement serves to place a time limit on the ability of employers and employees to make such arrangements.

The Solution

10-208.   The *Act* defines a salary deferral arrangement as follows:

ITA 248(1)   Salary deferral arrangement   A plan or arrangement, whether funded or not, under which any person has a right in a taxation year to receive an amount after the year where it is reasonable to consider that one of the main purposes for the creation or existence of the right is to postpone tax payable under this Act by the taxpayer in respect of an amount that is, or is on account or in lieu of, salary or wages of the taxpayer for services rendered by the taxpayer in the year or a preceding taxation year (including such a right that is subject to one or more conditions unless there is a substantial risk that any one of those conditions will not be satisfied).

10-209.   Converting this to everyday terms, a salary deferral arrangement involves an amount of salary that has been earned by an individual during the taxation year. However, the employee has made an arrangement with his employer to defer the actual receipt of the amount with the intent of postponing the payment of taxes.

10-210.   The definition of a salary deferral arrangement also contains a number of exclusions from its scope. These include RPPs, DPSPs, profit sharing plans, supplementary unemployment benefit plans, plans for providing education or training (sabbaticals), or plans established for the purpose of deferring the salary of a professional athlete.

10-211.   A further important exception is that the definition of a salary deferral arrangement excludes bonus arrangements where the amount is paid within three years of the employer's year end. This means that the ITA 78(4) rules deferring deductibility will apply to amounts that are paid more than 180 days after the employer's year end, but within three years of that date. If the payment is beyond three years, it is subject to the salary deferral arrangement rules.

10-212. Under the salary deferral arrangement rules, employers can deduct amounts that fall within this definition, but employees cannot defer taxation on these amounts. They are required to include such amounts in their Net Income For Tax Purposes on an accrual basis, rather than on the cash basis that is the normal basis for employment income. In many cases, this will serve to remove any tax incentive from this type of arrangement and will discourage their continued use.

10-213. Despite these restrictions, certain deferral arrangements can be effective in that they do not fall within the ITA 248(1) definition. These include:

- self funded leave of absence arrangements (sabbaticals);
- bonus arrangements with payment deferred not more than three years, provided the employer accepts the loss of deductibility that occurs after 180 days;
- deferred compensation for professional athletes; and
- retiring allowances. (These escape the salary deferral arrangement rules and, within limits, can be transferred on a tax free basis to an RRSP as discussed in Paragraph 10-194.)

Individual Pension Plans (IPPs)

10-214. It is possible to establish a defined benefit plan for a single individual. Such plans are usually marketed in conjunction with insurance products and their establishment requires the use of an actuarial valuation for the specific individual covered by the plan.

10-215. Such plans have grown in popularity in recent years, particularly for successful owner/managers of private companies. However, the actuarial concepts involved in these plans go beyond the scope of this text. As a consequence, we will not provide detailed coverage of these specialized arrangements.

Key Terms Used In This Chapter

10-216. The following is a list of the key terms used in this Chapter. These terms, and their meanings, are compiled in the Glossary Of Key Terms located at the back of the separate paper Study Guide.

Annuitant	Individual Pension Plan
Annuity	Life Annuity
Beneficiary	Lifelong Learning Plan (LLP)
Business Income	Money Purchase Limit
Canada Pension Plan (CPP)	Money Purchase Plan
Capital Gain	Net Income For Tax Purposes
Deferred Income Plans	Past Service Cost
Deferred Profit Sharing Plan	Past Service Pension Adjustment (PSPA)
Defined Benefit Plan	Pension Adjustment (PA)
Defined Contribution Plan	Pension Adjustment Reversal (PAR)
Earned Income (RRSP Limit)	Pension Income Tax Credit
Employment Income	Phased Retirement
Fixed Term Annuity	Pooled Registered Pension Plan
Home Buyer's Plan (HBP)	Profit Sharing Plan
Income Attribution	Property Income
Income Splitting	Refundable Part XI.3 Tax

Continued On Following Page

Registered Pension Plan (RPP)   RRSP Dollar Limit
Registered Retirement Income Fund (RRIF)   Salary Deferral Arrangement
Registered Retirement Savings Plan (RRSP) Spousal RRSP
Retirement Compensation Arrangement   Spouse
Retiring Allowance   Tax Deferral
Rollover   Unused RRSP Deduction Room
RRSP Deduction Limit   Vested Benefit
RRSP Deduction Room   Vested Contribution

References

10-217.   For more detailed study of the material in this Chapter, we would refer you to the following:

ITA 144	Employees Profit Sharing Plans
ITA 146	Registered Retirement Savings Plans
ITA 146.01	Home Buyers' Plan
ITA 146.02	Lifelong Learning Plan
ITA 146.3	Registered Retirement Income Funds
ITA 147	Deferred Profit Sharing Plans
ITA 147.1	Definitions, Registration And Other Rules (Registered Pension Plans)
ITA 147.2	Pension Contributions Deductible – Employer Contributions
ITA 147.3	Transfer – Money Purchase To Money Purchase, RRSP Or RRIF
ITA 147.4	RPP Annuity Contract

ITR 8503	
(16) to (25)	Defined Benefit Provisions - Phased Retirement

IC 72-13R8	Employees' Pension Plans
IC 72-22R9	Registered Retirement Savings Plans
IC 78-18R6	Registered Retirement Income Funds

IT-124R6	Contributions To Registered Retirement Savings Plans
IT-167R6	Registered Pension Plans — Employees' Contributions
IT-280R	Employees Profit Sharing Plans - Payments Computed By Reference To Profits
IT-307R4	Spousal Or Common-Law Partner Registered Retirement Savings Plans
IT-320R3	Qualified Investments - Trusts Governed by Registered Retirement Savings Plans, Registered Education Savings Plans and Registered Retirement Income Funds
IT-337R4	Retiring Allowances (Consolidated)
IT-379R	Employees Profit Sharing Plans — Allocations To Beneficiaries
IT-500R	Registered Retirement Savings Plans — Death of An Annuitant
IT-528	Transfer Of Funds Between Registered Plans

RC4112	Lifelong Learning Plan (Guide)
RC4135	Home Buyers' Plan (Guide)
RC4177	Death Of An RRSP Annuitant (Pamphlet)

T4040	RRSPs And Other Registered Plans For Retirement (Guide)
T4041	Retirement Compensation Arrangements (Guide)

Problems For Self Study

(The solutions for these problems can be found in the separate Study Guide.)

Self Study Problem Ten - 1 (RRSP Contributions)

During 2011 and 2012, Mr. Donald Barnes has the following income, loss and withholdings data:

	2012	2011
Gross Salary	$57,000	$55,000
Taxable Benefits	1,250	1,150
CPP Contributions	(2,307)	(2,218)
EI Premiums	(840)	(787)
Union Dues	(175)	(175)
Profit From Tax Advisory Service	12,220	4,150
Net Loss From Rental Property	(6,480)	(11,875)
Spousal Support Received From Former Wife	2,400	2,400
Taxable Dividends (Grossed Up Amount)	2,900	3,210
Interest On Government Bonds	2,110	3,640

At the end of 2011, Mr. Barnes had Unused RRSP Deduction Room of $700.

Required: For 2012, determine Mr. Barnes' maximum allowable deduction for contributions to a Registered Retirement Savings Plan under the following assumptions:

A. During 2011 and 2012, Mr. Barnes is not a member of a Registered Pension Plan or a Deferred Profit Sharing Plan.

B. Mr. Barnes is a member of a Registered Pension Plan, but not a member of a Deferred Profit Sharing Plan. His employer reports that his Pension Adjustment is $4,200 for 2011 and $4,300 for 2012, all of which reflects contributions made by his employer.

Self Study Problem Ten - 2 (RRSPs, TFSAs And Tax Planning)

Mr. Jonathan Beasley graduated from university in May, 2011. He immediately began work as an industrial designer, earning gross employment income of $24,000 during the calendar year ending December 31, 2011. Prior to 2011, Mr. Beasley had no Earned Income and had made no contributions to any type of retirement savings plan.

Up until May, 2011, Mr. Beasley had been supported by his spouse, Samantha. However, they were separated on June 1, 2011. On July 1, 2011, Samantha was convicted of spouse abuse and was ordered by the court to pay spousal support to Jonathan in the amount of $1,500 per month (a total of $9,000 was received during 2011). In addition, she was required to pay damages to Jonathan in the amount of $100,000. Jonathan deposited this entire amount in his savings account, resulting in 2011 interest income of $1,500.

Jonathan did not contribute to an RRSP during 2011. However, his employer sponsored an RPP to which Jonathan contributed $1,300 during 2011. This contribution was matched by a $1,300 contribution by Jonathan's employer, resulting in a 2011 Pension Adjustment of $2,600.

During 2011, Jonathan received royalties of $500 on a song written by his mother, eligible dividends from Canadian public corporations totaling $700, and a $50,000 separation gift from his parents. His parents also gave him a rental property in early 2011. This property experienced a net rental loss of $5,000 for the year ending December 31, 2011.

For 2011, Mr. Beasley's income places him in the lowest federal income tax bracket. Further, he anticipates that most of his 2012 income will also be taxed at this rate. However, he expects to receive a significant promotion at the end of 2012 and, as a consequence, he is likely to be in the maximum federal income tax bracket in 2013 and subsequent years.

Required:

A. Calculate Mr. Beasley's net employment income for 2011.

B. Determine Mr. Beasley's maximum deductible RRSP contribution for 2012.

C. As Mr. Beasley's personal financial consultant, what advice would you give him regarding his TFSA and RRSP contribution and deduction for 2012?

Self Study Problem Ten - 3 (Employment Income With RRSP)

Ms. Stratton has been the controller for a large publicly traded corporation for the last five years. The following information relates to the year ending December 31, 2012:

1. Ms. Stratton had a gross salary of $130,000, from which her employer made the following deductions:

Income taxes	$33,342
Registered Pension Plan contributions	2,390
Employment Insurance premiums	840
Canada Pension Plan contributions	2,307
Contributions to registered charities	1,600
Employee's portion of benefit plans (See Point 2 below)	1,436

2. It is the policy of the company to pay one-half of the cost of certain benefit plans. The following amounts were paid by the company for Ms. Stratton:

Group term life insurance	$ 96
Provincial health insurance plan	482
Dental plan	173
Major medical care (Private insurer)	396
Group income protection	289
Total	$1,436

3. Ms. Stratton's employer paid $2,300 for her annual membership in the Hot Rocks Curling Club. Ms. Stratton uses the club largely for employment related entertaining.

4. Ms. Stratton was awarded a one week trip to Bermuda by her employer for being with the company for fifteen long years. The fair market value of this trip was $5,000.

5. Ms. Stratton is required to travel to the offices of her employer's clients on a regular and continuing basis. As a result, her employer reimburses her for actual expenses. These payments totaled $8,462 for the year.

6. During the year, Ms. Stratton paid professional dues of $225.

7. During the year, Ms. Stratton made contributions to a Registered Retirement Savings Plan (RRSP) in the amount of $19,000 and to a Tax Free Savings Account (TFSA) in the amount of $5,000 (her maximum contribution room). At the end of 2011, Ms. Stratton's Unused RRSP Deduction Room was nil and she had no undeducted RRSP contributions. Her employer reported that she had a 2011 Pension Adjustment of $5,560. Her Earned Income for 2011 is equal to her 2012 Earned Income.

Required:

A. Calculate Ms. Stratton's net employment income for the year ending December 31, 2012 and indicate the reasons that you have not included items in your calculations. Ignore GST/HST/PST implications.

B. Calculate Ms. Stratton's maximum RRSP deduction for 2012.

C. Comment on the advisability of her $19,000 contribution to her RRSP.

Self Study Problem Ten - 4
(Comprehensive Employment Income With RRSP - Plus Death Of Registrant)

Mr. Frank Sabatini has been a salesman for a large, publicly traded Canadian corporation for the last fifteen years. During the year ending December 31, 2012, he earned a base salary of $58,000 and commissions of $74,000. In addition, the corporation reimbursed him for invoiced travel costs of $12,300. Included in these travel costs were $5,600 in expenditures for business meals and entertainment.

Other Information:

1. The corporation made a number of deductions from Mr. Sabatini's salary. The amounts were as follows:

Canada Pension Plan contributions	$ 2,307
Employment Insurance premiums	840
Income taxes	39,000
Registered Pension Plan contributions	3,500
Contributions to a registered charity	600
Parking fees - company garage	240
Employee share of life insurance premium (See point #2)	1,500
Employee share of sickness and accident insurance premium (See point #3)	550

2. Mr. Sabatini is covered by a group life insurance policy that pays $150,000 in the event of his death. The total annual premium on this policy is $3,000, with one-half of this amount paid by the employer.

3. Mr. Sabatini is covered by a group sickness and accident insurance plan that he joined on January 1, 2012. The premium on this plan is $100 per month, one-half of which is paid by Mr. Sabatini's employer. The plan provides periodic benefits that compensate for lost employment income. During 2012, Mr. Sabatini was hospitalized during all of June and received a benefit from the sickness and accident insurance plan in the amount of $4,500. Payment of the monthly premium was waived during the one month period of disability.

4. Mr. Sabatini's employer provides him with an automobile that was purchased in 2011 for $68,000. During 2012 Mr. Sabatini drives this automobile 99,000 kilometers, 92,000 of which are employment related. All operating costs, amounting to $16,200 for 2012, are paid by the employer. During the period of his hospitalization, his employer required that the vehicle be returned to the company garage. Mr. Sabatini pays the company $1,000 for his personal use of the automobile during 2012.

5. As a result of his extensive employment related travel, Mr. Sabatini has accumulated over 300,000 points in a frequent flier program. All of Mr. Sabatini's travel costs have been charged to his personal credit card and his employer has reimbursed him for all of these charges.

    On December 30, 2012, he uses 150,000 of these points for two first class tickets to Cancun. Mr. Sabatini is accompanied on this one week trip by his secretary and, while there is some discussion of business matters, the trip is primarily for pleasure. At the same time, Mr. Sabatini uses another 30,000 of the points to provide his wife with an airline ticket to visit her mother in Leamington, Ontario. The normal cost of the Cancun tickets is $11,000, while the normal cost of the Leamington ticket is $600.

6. In 2009, Mr. Sabatini received options to purchase 1,000 shares of his employer's stock at a price of $12.50 per share. At the time the options were granted, the shares were trading at $10.00 per share. During December, 2012, Mr. Sabatini exercises these options. At the time of exercise, the stock is trading at $23.50 per share.

7. Mr. Sabatini's employer allows him to purchase merchandise at a discount of 30 percent off the normal retail prices. During 2012, Mr. Sabatini acquires such merchandise at a cost (after the applicable discount) of $6,790.

Problems For Self Study

8. In addition to reimbursing him for invoiced travel costs, Mr. Sabatini's employer pays a $5,000 annual fee for his membership in a local golf and country club. During 2012, Mr. Sabatini spends $6,800 entertaining clients at this club. None of these costs are reimbursed by Mr. Sabatini's employer.

9. Mr. Sabatini's employer contributes $2,400 to the company's Registered Pension Plan on his behalf and, in addition, contributes $2,000 in his name to the company's Deferred Profit Sharing Plan.

10. Mr. Sabatini has correctly calculated his 2011 Earned Income for RRSP purposes from his employment to be $116,000. This Earned Income figure has not taken into consideration the following items:

	2012	2011
Business Loss	($ 3,300)	($12,500)
Taxable Dividends (After Gross Up)	600	800
Interest Income	1,100	660
Rental Income	2,000	7,500
Taxable Capital Gains	7,900	3,800
Child Support Received (For 8 Year Old Son)	6,000	6,000

11. Mr. Sabatini's Unused RRSP Deduction Room carried forward from 2011 was nil and he had no undeducted RRSP contributions. His employer reports that his Pension Adjustment for 2011 was $6,800.

12. On May 18, 2012, Mr. Sabatini contributes $2,600 to his wife's RRSP. His only contribution to his own RRSP in 2012 and 2013 was $10,000 in February, 2012. This contribution was deducted in full on his 2011 tax return.

13. In July, 2013, Mr. Sabatini drowns in his swimming pool.

Required:

A. Determine Mr. Sabatini's minimum net employment income for the year ending December 31, 2012, and indicate the reasons that you have not included items in your calculations. Ignore GST implications.

B. Calculate Mr. Sabatini's RRSP Deduction Limit for 2012 and determine his RRSP deduction in the calculation of his Net Income For Tax Purposes for 2012.

C. Assume that Mr. Sabatini's RRSP does not specify a beneficiary if he dies. Describe the tax consequences of his death on his RRSP.

D. Assume Mr. Sabatini's wife is the sole beneficiary of his RRSP. Describe the tax consequences of his death on his RRSP.

Self Study Problem Ten - 5 (Retiring Allowance With RRSP)

Mr. Colt, an employee of Jeffco Ltd., has agreed to accept early retirement in 2012, in return for a retiring allowance of $125,000. Mr. Colt began working for Jeffco Ltd. in 1977. He has been a member of the Company's Registered Pension Plan for only the last 10 years.

At the beginning of 2012, Mr. Colt had Unused RRSP Deduction Room of $32,000. His 2011 Earned Income was $46,000 and his T4 for 2011 included a Pension Adjustment of $8,000. Mr. Colt plans to contribute $50,000 of the retiring allowance into a Registered Retirement Savings Plan (RRSP) in his name, and the remaining $75,000 into a spousal RRSP.

Required:

A. Determine the maximum RRSP contribution that Mr. Colt can deduct in 2012.

B. What are the tax implications for Mr. Colt in 2012 if he makes his planned contributions

($50,000 payment to his RRSP and the remainder to a spousal RRSP)? As Mr. Colt's financial consultant, what advice would you give him regarding his RRSP contributions and deductions?

Self Study Problem Ten - 6 (Employment Compensation Tax Planning)

Mr. Jones is 62 years old and his wife, Mabel, is 58 years old. Mabel has no income of her own as she spends most of her waking hours maintaining her supernatural phenomena blog.

In January, 2012, he agreed to undertake a special project for the Martin Manufacturing Company, a company that produces large industrial use motors. The project is expected to take three years to complete. Mr. Jones was previously employed by the Martin Manufacturing Company for 11 years from 1985 to 1995. However, since then, he has operated his own consulting organization in Vancouver.

Accepting the special project for the Martin Manufacturing Company will require that Mr. Jones discontinue his consulting operation and move to Hamilton, where the head offices of the Company are located. This does not concern Mr. Jones as he plans to retire in three years under any circumstances. It will, however, require that he sell his home in Vancouver and acquire a new residence in Hamilton. Mr. Jones anticipates that he will require a mortgage of approximately $100,000 in order to purchase a residence.

Mr. Jones and the Company have agreed to a salary of $100,000 per year for the three year period, with no additional benefits other than the required payments for Employment Insurance and the Canada Pension Plan. However, the Company has indicated that it is prepared to be flexible with respect to the type of compensation that is given to Mr. Jones, subject to the condition that the total cost of providing the compensation does not exceed $300,000 over the three year period.

The Martin Manufacturing Company is a Canadian controlled public company and is subject to a combined federal and provincial tax rate of 40 percent. It currently has a Registered Pension Plan for its employees. However, this plan was not in place during the earlier 11 year period in which Mr. Jones was employed by the Company.

Mr. Jones has other income and is concerned about the fact that his $100,000 per year salary will attract high levels of taxation. He is seeking your advice with respect to how his compensation arrangement with the Martin Manufacturing Company might be altered to provide some reduction or deferral of taxes. He indicates that, subsequent to retirement, his income is likely to be less than $60,000 per year.

Required: Advise Mr. Jones with respect to alternative forms of compensation that could reduce or defer taxes on the $300,000 that he is to receive from the Martin Manufacturing Company.

Self Study Problem Ten - 7 (Comprehensive Case Covering Chapters 1 to 10)

Ms. Kerri Sosteric is 33 years of age. She is divorced from her former husband and has custody of the two children from that marriage. Her son Barry is 5 years old and her daughter Kim is 8 years old. Neither of her children have any income during 2012.

During 2012, she receives $1,200 in universal child care benefit payments.

The terms of Kerri's 2010 divorce decree require that her former husband pay $1,500 per month in child support and an additional $500 per month in spousal support. During 2011 and 2012, all amounts were paid in a timely fashion.

Because she works on a full time basis, Kerri sends her children to a commercially operated day care centre. During 2012, the cost of this care was $8,600. The day care centre provides receipts for this amount.

During 2012, medical expenses for Kerri and her family are as follows:

Kerri	$ 560
Barry	240
Kim	1,820
Total	$2,620

Kerri is employed by a large public company. Employment related information for the years 2011 and 2012 is as follows:

	2011	**2012**
Gross Salary	$47,000	$53,000
Commissions	6,200	7,800
Canada Pension Plan Contributions	2,218	2,307
Employment Insurance Premiums	787	840
RPP Contributions (Note)	1,800	1,950

Note   Kerri's employer makes a matching contribution to the money purchase RPP in each of the two years.

Other than the RPP contributions, Kerri's employer provides no other benefits. In addition, she is required to maintain an office in her home with no reimbursement provided. Her employer provides the required T2200 form. Kerri's home had cost $420,000 on January 1, 2011, with $120,000 of this amount being the estimated value of the land. For 2011 and 2012, the total costs of owning and operating this home are as follows:

	2011	**2012**
Utilities And Maintenance	$ 1,850	$ 2,040
Insurance	625	715
Property Taxes	4,200	4,400
Mortgage Interest	12,000	11,800

Kerri's home office occupies 15 percent of the total floor space in the home.

In January 1, 2011, Kerri acquires a residential duplex that she uses as a rental property. The cost of the property is $340,000, with $80,000 of this amount being the estimated value for the land. For the two years 2011 and 2012 rents and expenses other than CCA are as follows:

	2011	**2012**
Rents	$ 8,400	$13,800
Expenses Other Than CCA	10,300	11,100

In January, 2011, Kerri acquired 5,000 shares of her employer's stock at its fair market value of $12.00 per share. During 2011, these shares paid eligible dividends of $0.75 per share. During 2012, she receives eligible dividends of $0.60 per share. During December, 2012, Kerri sells all of her shares at their fair market value of $14.75 per share.

Kerri has unused RRSP deduction room carried forward from 2011 of $6,200. In addition, her plan contains $5,800 in undeducted contributions. Based on the undeducted contributions in the plan, along with any additional contributions required to meet this goal, Kerri would like to deduct an amount in 2012 that would reduce her unused RRSP deduction room to nil at the end of the year.

Required: Ignore GST/HST/PST considerations.

A. Calculate the additional contribution Ms. Sosteric must make to her RRSP.

B. Assume that Ms. Sosteric contributes the amount calculated in Part A to her RRSP. Calculate Ms. Sosteric's 2012 minimum:

- Net Income For Tax Purposes,
- Taxable Income, and
- federal Tax Payable before consideration of any income tax that would have been withheld or paid in instalments.

Self Study Problem Ten - 8 (Comprehensive Case Covering Chapters 1 to 10)

Mr. Ahmed Sidi is 72 years old and has been retired for 5 years. Prior to his retirement, he had been a long-term employee of a large public company. During 2012, he receives payments from the employer's RPP of $86,000. Both the employee and employer contributions to this RPP ended when Mr. Sidi retired.

In addition to the pension income from his employer's RPP, in 2012, Ahmed is entitled to $11,000 in Canada Pension Plan benefits. When Ahmed first began to receive CPP benefits, he elected to split these benefits with his wife, Adrianna. Because his income is consistently in excess of $100,000 per year, he has not applied for and does not receive OAS payments.

Ahmed has a 45 year old son who has been blind since birth. The son lives with Ahmed and has no income of his own.

Adrianna has provided all of the care required for their son. She is 66 years old and, during 2012, she received OAS payments of $6,500 in addition to the $5,500 in CPP benefits that Ahmed has elected to split with her. She has no other personal source of income. However, for 2012, Ahmed will split all of his qualifying pension income with Adrianna.

The family's medical expenses are as follows:

Ahmed	$ 2,500
Adrianna	3,100
Son	9,800
Total	$15,400

Ahmed makes an annual donation to the Canadian National Institute For The Blind of $4,000.

While he was still employed, he was granted options to acquire 5,000 shares of his employer's stock. The option price was $15 per share and, at the time the options were granted, this was also the fair market value of his employer's shares. All of these options were exercised in February, 2012. At this time, the shares were trading at $21 per share. In November, 2012, all of the shares are sold for $23 per share.

Ahmed had other investment income during 2012 as follows:

Interest From Canadian Sources	$18,000
Eligible Dividends Received	2,200
Foreign Source Interest (Net Of 10 Percent Withholding)	2,700
Total	$22,900

On January 1, 2012, Ahmed owns three rental properties. They are all Class 1 properties. Relevant information on these properties is as follows:

	Property A	Property B	Property C
Capital Cost - Building	$560,000	$685,000	$426,000
UCC On January 1	422,000	571,000	$385,000
Rental Revenues	34,000	42,000	26,000
Expenses (Other Than CCA)	29,000	37,000	23,000

On December 31, 2012, property A is sold for $960,000. The value of the land for this property was $100,000 at the time of purchase and had increased to $340,000 at the time of sale. The vendor pays $96,000 in cash, with Ahmed taking back a mortgage for the $864,000 balance. The mortgage requires annual payments of $86,400 on the principal, beginning in 2013.

When he turned 71 in 2011, Ahmed transferred his RRSP assets into a RRIF. On January 1, 2012, the fair market value of these assets is $1,250,000. As he has little need for current income, Ahmed would like to minimize his withdrawals from the plan.

At the beginning of 2012, Ahmed opens an RRSP with his wife as the registrant. He has no unused RRSP deduction room carried forward from 2011. He would like to make the maximum deductible contribution to his wife's RRSP during 2012. In calculating this amount, assume that his 2011 earned income is equal to his 2012 earned income.

Required: Ignore GST/HST/PST considerations.

A. Calculate Mr. Sidi's maximum deductible spousal RRSP contribution for 2012.

B. Assume that Mr. Sidi contributes the amount calculated in Part A to his wife's RRSP. Calculate Mr. Sidi's 2012 minimum:

- Net Income For Tax Purposes,
- Taxable Income, and
- federal Tax Payable before consideration of any income tax that would have been withheld or paid in instalments.

C. In general terms, without doing calculations, describe the factors that Mr. Sidi should consider when deciding how much pension income he should split with his spouse.

Assignment Problems

(The solutions for these problems are only available in
the solutions manual that has been provided to your instructor.)

Assignment Problem Ten - 1 (Net Income With RRSP)

At the end of 2011, Mr. Jonathan Detwiller had Unused RRSP Deduction Room of $10,000. In addition, he had undeducted contributions of $4,500.

For the year ending December 31, 2011, Mr. Detwiller had the following amounts of income and deductions under the various subdivisions of Division B of the *Income Tax Act*:

Net employment income	$56,000
Eligible dividends received	7,800
Gross up [(38%)($7,800)]	2,964
Subdivision e deductions (child care costs)	(2,500)
Taxable capital gains	5,400
Allowable capital losses	(8,200)
Net rental loss	(9,000)

Required:

A. Calculate Mr. Detwiller's 2011 Net Income For Tax Purposes. In addition, indicate any carry overs available to him at the end of the year.

B. For each of the following **independent** cases, calculate:

- the maximum RRSP contribution that Mr. Detwiller can make for 2012 without incurring a penalty;
- Mr. Detwiller's maximum RRSP deduction for 2012, assuming that he makes the maximum contribution that you have calculated.

Case 1   During 2011, he is a member of a money purchase Registered Pension Plan (RPP) in which he has contributed $1,500 and his employer has contributed $3,000. He is also a member of a Deferred Profit Sharing Plan (DPSP) to which his employer has contributed $1,000.

Case 2   During 2011, he is a member of a DPSP in which his employer contributed $4,500 per employee. His employer does not sponsor a RPP.

Case 3   During 2011, he is not a member of a RPP or DPSP. Assume that in addition to the preceding information, he also has net business income of $220,000.

Assignment Problem Ten - 2 (RRSPs, TFSAs And Tax Planning)

Ms. Janine Wheeler found a position in retail sales in September, 2011. During the remainder of that year, she had gross employment income of $22,000. Prior to 2011, Ms. Wheeler had no Earned Income and made no contributions to any type of retirement savings plan.

Prior to July, 2011, Ms. Wheeler had been supported by and living with her common-law partner. On June 30, they formally separate and sign a document which provides Ms. Wheeler with a lump-sum payment of $80,000, plus $1,200 per month in spousal support.

The lump-sum payment was deposited in a savings account which earned interest of $550 during the remainder of 2011. She receives six months of support payments in 2011.

Janine did not contribute to an RRSP during 2011. However, her employer sponsored an RPP to which Janine contributed $1,200 during 2011. This contribution was matched by a $1,200 contribution by Janine's employer.

In addition to her employment income and interest income, Janine had the following other sources of income during 2011:

• Dividends from Canadian public companies of $900.
• A net business loss of $2,500 from her new web-based photos on canvas service.
• An inheritance from an uncle of $50,000.

For 2011, Ms. Wheeler's income places her in the lowest federal income tax bracket. Further, she anticipates that most of her 2012 income will also be taxed at this rate. However, she has been promised a management position beginning in January, 2013.

This position involves a significant increase in salary and this, combined with her increasingly profitable web-based business, will result in her being in the 26 percent federal income tax bracket.

Required:

A. Calculate Ms. Wheeler's net employment income for 2011.

B. Determine Ms. Wheeler's maximum deductible RRSP contribution for 2012.

C. As Ms. Wheeler's personal financial consultant, what advice would you give her regarding her TFSA and RRSP contribution and deduction for 2012?

Assignment Problem Ten - 3 (RRSP Contributions)

During 2011, Ms. Storm is employed in Vernon by a large public company. The employer sponsors a defined contribution pension plan and, during 2011, the company made contributions on Ms. Storm's behalf of $2,500. Ms. Storm made a matching contribution of $2,500.

At the end of 2011, Ms. Storm had unused deduction room of $17,000 and undeducted contributions of $8,000.

During 2011, Ms. Storm has the following income and loss data:

Salary	$86,200
Taxable Benefits From Employer	5,600
Union Dues	(450)
Net Loss From Mail Order Business	(4,500)
Net Rental Income	6,700
Common-Law Partner Support Paid	(12,000)
Eligible Dividends Received	2,850
Interest On Savings Account	850

Required: Calculate the maximum deductible RRSP contribution that can be made by Ms. Storm for 2012.

Assignment Problem Ten - 4 (RRSP Contributions)

Carla Goodman has been employed by Army Brake Products (ABP), a Canadian controlled private corporation, since 2010. The following information pertains to her income over the past two years:

	2012	2011
Salary Before Benefits	$120,000	$120,000
Employee Stock Option Benefit	8,000	5,000
Benefit On Interest Free Loan	6,000	5,000
Registered Pension Plan Contributions	(4,000)	(3,000)
Deductible Employment Expenses	(4,500)	(4,000)
Interest Income	1,800	1,600
Taxable Capital Gains	15,000	10,000
Business Income	34,000	35,000
Royalty Income	7,000	5,000
Rental Loss	(5,000)	(10,000)
Spousal Support Payments	(15,000)	(12,000)
Non-Eligible Dividends On ABP Stock	900	1,000
Totals	$164,200	$153,600

The royalty income listed above is 2 percent of the sales of the "Handy Shopper," a gadget Ms. Goodman invented three years ago. The business income listed above is earned from selling leather goods.

Ms. Goodman had no Earned Income for RRSP purposes prior to 2009. While in 2009 and 2010, she had sufficient Earned Income to enable her to deduct the maximum allowable RRSP contribution for 2010 and 2011, she made no RRSP contributions in either of these years.

Beginning in 2011, Ms. Goodman participates in ABP's employee money purchase Registered Pension Plan. ABP contributes twice the amount contributed by an employee to the plan. Her Pension Adjustment for 2011 is $9,000.

Required   Ignore all GST considerations.

A. Calculate Ms. Goodman's Earned Income for the purpose of determining her maximum 2012 RRSP contribution by listing the items and amounts that would be included in her Earned Income. List separately the items that are not included in the Earned Income calculation.

B. Calculate Ms. Goodman's maximum deductible RRSP contribution for 2012.

Assignment Problem Ten - 5 (Excess RRSP Contributions)

On December 1, 2011, Mary Jo Bush, on the advice of her hairdresser, deposited her inheritance of $54,000 in her RRSP. She had made no RRSP contributions prior to this. Because she had very little Taxable Income in 2011, she did not deduct any portion of her RRSP contribution in that year.

She has provided you with the following information:

• Her Unused RRSP Deduction Room is $10,000 at the end of 2011.
• She made an additional RRSP contribution of $5,000 on February 1, 2012.
• Mary Jo withdraws $35,000 from the RRSP on December 1, 2012.
• For 2012, the annual increase in Mary Jo's RRSP Deduction Limit is $9,000 (18 percent of her 2011 Earned Income of $50,000).

Required: Determine the ITA 204.1 penalty (excess RRSP contributions), if any, that would be assessed to Mary Jo for the year ending December 31, 2012.

Assignment Problem Ten - 6 (Retiring Allowance)

Jerry White is married and his wife has not worked since she gave birth to triplets 8 years ago. Mr. White began working for Dynamics Inc. in 1984. The Company does not have a Registered Pension Plan or a Deferred Profit Sharing Plan.

Due to competitive pressures, Dynamics Inc. is attempting to reduce its overall work force. With this goal in mind, they have offered Mr. White a cash payment of $68,000 if he will immediately resign his position with the Company.

Required: Describe the tax consequences to Mr. White if he accepts this offer in 2012. Explain any alternatives that he might have in this regard and advise Mr. White as to an appropriate course of action.

Assignment Problem Ten - 7 (Calculation Of PAs And PSPAs)

In each of the following **independent** Cases, calculate the Pension Adjustment (PA) or Past Service Pension Adjustment (PSPA) that would be reported by the employer:

Case A   John Brokow's employer sponsors both a defined contribution RPP and a DPSP. He is a member of both. During 2012, his employer contributes, on his behalf, $3,200 to the RPP and $1,100 to the DPSP. In addition, Mr. Brokow contributes $1,500 to the RPP. His employment earnings for 2012 are $120,000. Calculate his 2012 PA.

Case B   Sarah Halfhill's employer sponsors a defined benefit RPP and, during 2012, contributes $3,100 on her behalf. Sarah also contributes $3,100 to the plan in 2012. The plan provides a benefit equal to 1.65 percent of pensionable earnings for each year of service. Sarah's pensionable earnings for 2012 are $52,000. Calculate her 2012 PA.

Case C   Bob Carver has worked for his current employer since 2010. In January, 2012, this employer institutes a defined benefit RPP, with benefits extended for all years of service prior to the inception of the plan. The benefit formula calls for a retirement benefit equal to 1.10 percent of pensionable earnings for each year of service. In the current year and both previous years, Bob's pensionable earnings were $48,000. Calculate his 2012 PSPA.

Case D   Marianne Underwood has worked for her current employer since 2010. She has been a member of her employer's defined benefit RPP during all of this period. In January, 2012, her employer agrees to retroactively increase the benefit formula from 1.4 percent of pensionable earnings for each year of service, to 1.7 percent of pensionable earnings for each year of service. In the current year and both previous years, Marianne's pensionable earnings were $52,000. Calculate her 2012 PSPA.

Assignment Problem Ten - 8 (Comprehensive Case Covering Chapters 1 to 10)

Mrs. Rhonda Sorenson is 44 years old and lives in Waterloo Ontario. She is married to Martin Sorenson and they have one child. Martin is currently unemployed and his only 2012 income is $8,400 in Employment Insurance Benefits.

Their 19 year old daughter Cissy is in full time attendance at the University Of Waterloo for 8 months during 2012. Ms. Sorenson pays Cissy's 2012 tuition of $7,800 and, because Cissy's 2012 income is only $6,500, she agrees to her mother using all of the available tax credits that result from her attendance at University.

Other Information:

1.   Mrs. Sorenson is employed by a large publicly traded company, earning a gross salary of $67,000 in 2012. In addition, she received commissions of $3,150. During 2012, her

employer withheld the following amounts from her salary.

Canada Pension Plan Contributions	$2,307
Employment Insurance Premiums	840
Registered Pension Plan Contributions	2,750
Donations To United Way	600
Professional Dues	350
Contribution To Disability Insurance Plan	1,000

Rhonda's employer makes a matching contribution of $2,750 to her RPP, as well as a matching contribution of $1,000 to her disability insurance plan. The plan provides periodic benefits that compensate for lost employment income. Mrs. Sorenson began contributing to the disability insurance plan in 2011. Her contribution in that year was $900.

2. Mrs. Sorenson's employer provides her with a car that was purchased in 2011 for $45,200. The car was used by Mrs. Sorenson throughout the year, except for a period of one month during which she was hospitalized for a nervous disorder. During this one month period, she was required to return the car to the company garage.

   During 2012, the car was driven a total of 62,000 kilometers, of which 51,000 were employment related. Her employer paid all of the operating costs which totaled $9,300 for 2012.

3. Her employer reimburses 100 percent of her airline tickets and meals, but only a portion of her lodging costs. As a result, she has unreimbursed employment related travel costs. For 2012, these totalled $4,200.

   She is required to maintain an office in her home without reimbursement from her employer. Her employer provides the required T2200 form. Based on the portion of her house that is used for this office, the related costs are as follows:

Utilities And Maintenance	$ 850
Insurance	725
Property Taxes	1,340
Mortgage Interest	960

4. During her one month hospitalization, Mrs. Sorenson received disability insurance benefits of $4,800.

5. During 2012 Mrs. Sorenson earned interest on term deposits of $3,200. In addition, she received eligible dividends of $1,500.

6. On May 1, 2012, Mrs. Sorenson sold a piece of land for $143,000, receiving a down payment of $43,000 in cash. The remaining balance will be paid in 5 annual instalments in the years 2013 through 2017. The adjusted cost base of the land was $87,000.

7. The family medical expenses were as follows:

Rhonda	$ 1,200
Martin	2,750
Cissy	8,395
Total	$12,345

8. In 2011, Mrs. Sorenson's had Net Income For Tax Purposes of $57,525. This was made up of net employment income of $55,000 (after the deduction of $2,400 of RPP contributions), a net business loss of $8,600, interest income of $2,000, grossed up dividends of $3,525, and royalties on a song she wrote eight years ago of $5,600.

9. At the end of 2011, Mrs. Sorenson's Unused RRSP Deduction Room was $7,400 and she had no undeducted RRSP contributions. Her employer reported that she had a 2011 Pension Adjustment of $5,200.

Required: Ignore GST considerations.

A. Calculate Mrs. Sorenson's maximum deductible RRSP contribution for 2012.

B. Assume that Mrs. Sorenson contributes the amount calculated in Part A to her RRSP. Calculate Mrs. Sorenson's 2012 minimum

- Net Income For Tax Purposes,
- Taxable Income, and
- federal Tax Payable before consideration of any income tax that would have been withheld or paid in instalments.

Assignment Problem Ten - 9
(Comprehensive Case Covering Chapters 1 to 10 - Three Individuals)

Zhi and Meng Liu are both 45 years old. They are married and support Zhi's 19 year old son from his former marriage, Sheng. In January, 2012, the family moved from Edmonton, Alberta to London, Ontario, so that Zhi could accept a new position. Meng continued her party planning business in London. What follows is information about the income of each of the three family members.

1. Information About Zhi's Income

a. In 2012, Zhi earned $170,000 from employment, all of it after the move from Edmonton to London. CPP of $2,417 and EI of $840 were deducted from Zhi's employment income during 2012.

b. The following expenses were incurred as a result of the move from Edmonton to London:

Air Fare - House Hunting Trip To London	$ 550
Hotel And Meals (3 Days) - London Trip	500
Airfare For Moving Family (1 Day Of Travel)	2,000
Costs - Waiting For New Home (20 Days)	
Hotel (All Receipts Available)	3,000
Meals (No Receipts Available)	unknown
Cost Of Repairing Old Home For Sale	1,000
Legal Fees And Commission - Old Home	3,700
Actual Loss On Sale Of Old Home	27,000
Transportation Of Household Goods	4,900
Legal Fees - New Home	2,900
Decorations For New Home	9,500

c. Zhi received a moving allowance of $8,000 from his new employer.

d. Zhi and his former spouse divorced in 2001. As per their divorce settlement, Zhi's former spouse has paid him an annual amount of $6,000 in spousal support payments since then.

e. Zhi and Meng share a joint personal chequing and savings account. The interest earned on the account for 2012 was $350. Both Zhi and Meng contribute equally to this account.

f. Zhi had invested in Matel Industries Inc. (a public company) over the years, and on January 30, 2012 he sold 250 shares for $20 each. His history of trading in these shares was as follows:

    May 24, 2000 - Purchased 130 Shares @ $26 Per Share
    June 30, 2001 - Purchased 170 Shares @ $31 Per Share
    October 31, 2003 - Purchased 300 Shares @ $29 Per Share
    June 9, 2004 - Sold 400 Shares @ $15 Per Share
    July 5, 2004 - Purchased 400 Shares @ $12 Per Share
    June 3, 2007 - Purchased 385 Shares @ $18 Per Share

g. Zhi borrowed $10,000 to make an RRSP contribution in 2011. Interest on this loan paid in 2012 was $500. The RRSP contribution was properly deducted in 2011. Zhi had a Notice of Assessment from 2011 that indicated his 2012 deduction limit was $4,000, and also indicated that there were no undeducted contributions. In 2000, Zhi withdrew RRSP funds under the Home Buyers' Plan. His Notice of Assessment indicated that a repayment of $1,500 was required under the Home Buyers' Plan for 2012. Zhi did not make the necessary contribution in 2012 or the first 60 days of 2013. A payment of the same amount will be required on the Home Buyers' Plan loan in the 2013 year or the first 60 days of 2014.

h. Zhi inherited a rental property from his mother, Mrs. Liu, who passed away in 2012. The relevant details are provided in Appendix A.

2. **Information About Meng's Income**

a. Meng's income is business income from her business, Meng's Party Services. Financial information related to this business is provided in Appendix B.

b. Meng made an RRSP contribution on October 31, 2012 in the amount of $12,000. According to her 2011 Notice of Assessment, her deduction limit for 2012 was $8,000. She had no undeducted contributions after filing her 2011 tax return.

c. See Zhi's information for interest on the joint chequing account.

3. **Information About Sheng**

a. Sheng is a full time university student. He paid $6,000 in tuition in 2012. Of this total, $3,000 was for the 4 months he attended in 2012, and the balance was for 2013. He was enrolled in University full time for 4 months in 2012. Sheng is willing to transfer any unused education tax credits to his mother.

b. Zhi's wealthy ailing father, a Canadian resident and Sheng's grandfather, has given Sheng $100,000 to make him more marriageable in the hopes he will marry soon and have a son to carry on the lineage. The grandfather has promised more funds at the wedding if he is still alive. Sheng was uncertain as to how to deal with this situation, so on February 15, 2012, he invested the $100,000 in an interest bearing term deposit at 4 percent. Interest is paid every 6 months.

c. Sheng was the successful applicant for a scholarship and was awarded $1,000 to assist him with his tuition costs.

d. Sheng had the following income in 2012 from his RESP:

Accumulated Earnings	$1,000
Canada Education Savings Grant Payment	2,500
Payment Of Contributions By Zhi And Meng	7,500

e. Sheng had employment income of $10,000 which he earned working as a server for his mother's business. As Sheng is related to his employer, these earnings are not insurable and no EI was deducted from his pay. CPP premiums of $322 were correctly calculated and deducted by his employer.

Required: In determining the following amounts, ignore GST, PST and HST considerations.

A. For the 2012 taxation year, calculate Zhi Liu's minimum:

1. Net Income For Tax Purposes,
2. Taxable Income,
3. Federal Balance Owing Or Refund (Tax Plus Any CPP Contributions).

B. For the 2012 taxation year, calculate Sheng Liu's minimum:

1. Net Income For Tax Purposes,

2.   Taxable Income,
3.   Federal Tax Payable.

C.   For the 2012 taxation year, calculate Meng Liu's minimum:

1.   Net Income For Tax Purposes,
2.   Taxable Income,
3.   Federal Balance Owing Or Refund (Tax Plus Any CPP Contributions).

D.   Determine the amounts of any carry forwards available to Zhi or Meng.   In addition, indicate the ending UCC balances for Meng's business assets.

E.   Determine the maximum deductible RRSP contribution for Zhi and Meng for 2013.   What advice would you give them regarding their RRSP contributions and other tax planning considerations?

Appendix A - Inherited Rental Property

In 2001, Ms. Liu (Zhi's mother) purchased a small apartment building at a cost of $350,000. Of the total cost, $100,000 was allocated to the land with the $250,000 balance going to the building.   For CCA purposes, the building was included in Class 1.

During the years 2001 through 2011, the building was usually fully occupied.   At the beginning of 2012, the UCC of the building was $170,000.

On October 10, 2012, Ms. Liu passed away.   At the time of her death, the fair market value of the land was $212,000 and the fair market value of the building was $325,000.   The property was transferred to Zhi on October 11, 2012.   Rental income received by Zhi for his period of ownership from October 11 until December 31, 2012 was $26,000.   Rental expenses before CCA totalled $22,000.

Appendix B - Meng's Business Income

The business provides complete party planning services for all occasions.   A summarized Income Statement is as follows:

Meng's Party Services
Statement Of Income
For the year ended December 31, 2012

Sales		$561,000
Expenses:		
General And Administrative	$ 485,120	
Amortization Of Fixed Assets	28,170	513,290
Operating Profit		$ 47,710
Gain On Disposal Of Fixed Assets (See Details Below)		99,290
Net Income		$147,000

General and administrative expenses includes a payment of $50,000 in drawings to Meng.

Additional information related to Meng's business is as follows:

1.   The UCC balances as at January 1, 2012 were:

Class 3	$30,000
Class 6	2,100
Class 8	2,000
Class 10	11,000

2. During the year, the business purchased the following new depreciable assets, all of which were capitalized for accounting purposes:

Office Furniture	$15,000
Delivery Van	30,000
Computer Equipment And Systems Software	10,000
Photocopier (No Separate Class Election Was Filed)	2,600
Landscaping Around New Leased Office Space	12,000

In January, 2012, as a result of the move to London, Meng sold the owned business premises (consisting of Land and a Class 3 building). Meng found leased premises in London that meet her needs, so she has not replaced this property, however, she was not happy with the external appearance of the leased premises, so she did have some landscaping work completed.

The details of the sale of the land and building are described in the table that follows. The Class 6 asset listed is the fence that was erected around these former business premises. On the sale of these premises, no proceeds were allocated to the fence. This was the only asset in Class 6.

To facilitate the sale, Meng agreed to take 10 percent of the total purchase price as a down payment, with the balance due in 2013.

The details of the sale of the former land and building and some other assets sold at the time of the move are as follows:

	Proceeds	Original Cost	Net book value
Land	$ 20,000	$ 5,000	$ 5,000
Class 3 building	125,000	45,000	40,000
Class 8 chairs and tables	6,000	8,000	5,120
Delivery van	4,500	18,000	6,175
Office equipment	5,000	15,000	4,915
Class 6 fence	Nil	3,000	Nil

Tax Software Assignment Problem For Chapter 10

This Tax Software Assignment Problem was introduced in Chapter 4 and is continued in Chapters 6 through 11. Each Tax Software Assignment Problem must be completed in sequence. While it is not repeated in this problem, all of the information in each of the previous problems (e.g., Mary's T4 content) is applicable to this problem.

If you have not prepared a tax file incorporating the Tax Software Assignment Problem information for the previous Chapters, please do so before continuing with this problem.

On January 10, 2012, you receive a phone call from Mary Career. She has just received a T4RSP in the mail which shows that Seymour had withdrawn virtually all the funds from his RRSP without her knowledge. She knows this could substantially increase Seymour's tax liability and is very concerned. At the moment, she cannot find any trace of the funds that were withdrawn.

Her stockbroker has told her that a spousal contribution can be made to her RRSP to utilize Seymour's unused contribution room. She would like you to calculate the maximum RRSP contribution that can be deducted on Seymour's return. Mary will contribute that amount to her RRSP and have the RRSP receipt issued with Seymour's name as the contributor.

She faxes you the following T4RSP as well as information related to her and Seymour's RRSP limits.

T4RSP - Seymour	Box	Amount
Issuer of receipt - Royal Bank		
Withdrawal payments	22	126,000
Income tax deducted	30	12,600

RRSP information - Seymour	(Y/M/D)	Amount
Issuer of receipt - TD Asset Management		Maximum ?
Contributions made prior to 2012/03/02 and not deducted		Nil
Unused deduction room at the end of 2010		19,762
Earned income for 2010		45,000

RRSP information - Mary	(Y/M/D)	Amount
Issuer of receipt - TD Asset Management	2011-12-10	5,400
Issuer of receipt - TD Asset Management	2012-01-05	16,800
Contributions made prior to 2012/03/02 and not deducted		Nil
Unused deduction room at the end of 2010		14,091
Earned income for 2010		125,000

As Mary expects to receive a substantial life insurance benefit shortly, she hopes to have funds to contribute to her RRSP in her own name before the end of February, 2012.

Required:

A. Open the file that you created for the Chapter 9 version of this Software Problem and save a copy under a different name. This will enable you to check the changes between different versions of this Software Problem.

B. Calculate Seymour's maximum RRSP deduction for 2011 and assume that Mary contributes the amount you have calculated. Print the RRSP form for Seymour.

C. Revise Seymour's 2011 final income tax return to incorporate the T4RSP and RRSP contribution, but do not print the return.

D. Complete and print Mary's RRSP form. Assume she does not contribute further to her RRSP in her name in 2011. Print the RRSPLimit form for Mary which calculates her maximum RRSP deduction for 2012.

E. What advice would you give Mary regarding her RRSP contributions?

F. Access and print Mary's summary (Summary on the Form Explorer, not the T1Summary). This form is a two column summary of the couple's tax information. By opening this form from Mary's return, the order of the columns is the same as the one in the previous chapter. For both returns, list the changes on this Summary form from the previous version of this Software Problem. Exclude totals calculated by the program, but include the final Balance Owing (Refund) amount.

INDEX

Index entries related to the Supplementary Readings are labelled CD-Supp #.
The 9 Supplementary Readings are available on the Student CD-ROM.

This index includes the entries for both Volume I and II. Volume II begins on page 519.

This index includes the entries for both Volume I and II. Volume II begins on page 519.

This index includes the entries for both Volume I and II. Volume II begins on page 519.

This index includes the entries for both Volume I and II. Volume II begins on page 519.

This index includes the entries for both Volume I and II. Volume II begins on page 519.

This index includes the entries for both Volume I and II. Volume II begins on page 519.

This index includes the entries for both Volume I and II. Volume II begins on page 519.

This index includes the entries for both Volume I and II. Volume II begins on page 519.

This index includes the entries for both Volume I and II. Volume II begins on page 519.

About FITAC/CTP Infobase on the Student CD-ROM

Available on the Student CD-ROM that accompanies *Byrd & Chen's Canadian Tax Principles 2012-2013 Edition,* the Canadian Institute of Chartered Accountants (CICA) has included the Federal Income Tax Collection (FITAC) Infobase, which includes the following:

- the electronic text of *Canadian Tax Principles 2012-2013 Edition*
- the complete *Income Tax Act*
- Interpretation Bulletins, Information Circulars, and additional primary and secondary information.

To install the FITAC/CTP Infobase, insert the Student CD-ROM into your computer, and click on the button "Install FITAC Folio Views/CTP Infobase." Or browse the CICA folder on the CD, and double-click "setup.exe." The Folio software and FITAC/CTP Infobase require approximately 500 MB. This software is Windows compatible only.

The setup routine will automatically install the Folio software and FITAC/CTP Infobase on your hard drive and place an icon on your desktop. Double-click this icon to launch the application.

For tips on how this can help you maximize your use of *Canadian Tax Principles*, open and review the Getting Started file. You can find it by clicking on the Start menu, selecting "Programs," then "FITACCTP," and finally "Getting Started."

Guidance on how to use the Folio software can be found under the Folio Help menu.

Please see the next page for Pearson Canada's license agreement. Do not open the CD-ROM package until you have read this license.